Robert Inhnput
Ph. Benardion Benson
1945

THE MAN WHO WAS

CHESTERTON

THE MAN WHO WAS
CHESTERTON

THE BEST ESSAYS, STORIES, POEMS AND OTHER WRITINGS OF G. K. CHESTERTON

Compiled and Edited by
RAYMOND T. BOND

DODD, MEAD & COMPANY
PUBLISHERS · NEW YORK
MCMXLV

PRINTED IN THE UNITED STATES OF AMERICA
BY THE VAIL-BALLOU PRESS, INC., BINGHAMTON, N. Y.

FOREWORD

THE true Chestertonian will maintain that there is something presumptuous, if not preposterous, in the title of this book. In this he will be right, for it is impossible to confine the ranging genius of G. K. C. within the pinfold of a single volume. Indeed, this collection of Chesterton's writings in diverse fields might well be the forerunner of a half-dozen such assemblies. A smacking anthology might be made of his passages on food and drink; another of his relentless orthodoxy on marriage and divorce; still another of his love for things mediaeval.

There is, however, a particular significance, it is hoped, in the title of this present volume, as it applies to the material included. It holds, as far as possible, the best of Chesterton's work appearing between 1902 and 1937. Eighty of his rare essays are here, evenly divided between the informal, familiar type and the more serious discussions. Five Father Brown stories are included; also sections on American travel; on philosophy and religion; several discussions of his economic theories of Distributism; and a selection of his poetry. A large part of the contents of the volume is otherwise out of print and unavailable, except on the shelves of old and rare bookshops. This is especially true of many of the bubbling essays of his earlier days, before the controversial tendency intensified his writings. Dodd, Mead and Company were the publishers of most of Chesterton's books in America, from "The Defendant" in 1902 to "The Paradoxes of Mr. Pond" in 1937, and it has been pleasant to find that there has been no diminution of the charm and force of his writings between those dates, and to realize that something from each volume is, of necessity, here.

There is a French proverb which says that every choice implies a contempt for the thing refused. This has not been true in compiling the present volume. The difficulty was not what to include but what to omit. It is regretted that many brilliant but brief excerpts—on religion, for instance—could not be considered for a book that was planned for general reading. Many longer pieces of paramount interest to some readers may also be missing; in such cases, the editor pleads a difference of opinion rather than unintentional oversight and advises the disappointed reader to run to his nearest bookseller and there gather to his heart the volume in which the desired piece first appeared. He is advised to hurry, for original Chestertons, in this country, are growing scarce.

No recent author has so richly deserved an anthology—and for the average reader no author needs one more. It is hoped that "The Man Who Was Chesterton" may supply this need. If so, no more delightful volume will be found in the field of contemporary writing than this reflection of the many-sided genius and personality of G. K. C.

R. T. B.

CONTENTS

WHAT I SAW IN AMERICA

FATHER BROWN STORIES

CONTENTS ix

THE MAN WHO WAS

CHESTERTON

Essays

"There are normal things that a normal man ought to do, as he sleeps or wakes or walks. One of them is to sing, to a plain tune with a common chorus, as our fathers did round their supper tables. Another is to dance, however clumsily, at least some of the dances of his native land. Another is to speak with clearness and moderate cogency in any council of his equals or on any not disreputable public occasion. Another is to recite poetry if he likes it; another is to be at ease and tolerably intimate with domestic animals; another is to know, even slightly, the uses of some weapon; another is to know quite common remedies for quite common maladies. And another is to be able to write down in pen and ink what he really thinks about public questions, and why he thinks it: which is all that I have done here."

ON GARGOYLES

Alone at some distance from the wasting walls of a disused abbey I found half sunken in the grass the grey and goggle-eyed visage of one of those graven monsters that made the ornamental water-spouts in the cathedrals of the Middle Ages. It lay there, scoured by ancient rains or striped by recent fungus, but still looking like the head of some huge dragon slain by a primeval hero. And as I looked at it, I thought of the meaning of the grotesque, and passed into some symbolic reverie of the three great stages of art.

I

Once upon a time there lived upon an island a merry and inno-cent people, mostly shepherds and tillers of the earth. They were republicans, like all primitive and simple souls; they talked over their affairs under a tree, and the nearest approach they had to a personal ruler was a sort of priest or white witch who said their prayers for them. They worshipped the sun, not idolatrously, but as the golden crown of the god whom all such infants see almost as plainly as the sun.

Now this priest was told by his people to build a great tower, pointing to the sky in salutation of the Sun-god; and he pondered long and heavily before he picked his materials. For he was re-solved to use nothing that was not almost as clear and exquisite as sunshine itself; he would use nothing that was not washed as white as the rain can wash the heavens, nothing that did not sparkle as spotlessly as that crown of God. He would have nothing grotesque or obscure; he would not have even anything emphatic or even anything mysterious. He would have all the arches as light as laughter and as candid as logic. He built the temple in three con-centric courts, which were cooler and more exquisite in substance

3

each than the other. For the outer wall was a hedge of white lilies, ranked so thick that a green stalk was hardly to be seen; and the wall within that was of crystal, which smashed the sun into a million stars. And the wall within that, which was the tower itself, was a tower of pure water, forced up in an everlasting fountain; and upon the very tip and crest of that foaming spire was one big and blazing diamond, which the water tossed up eternally and caught again as a child catches a bill.

"Now," said the priest, "I have made a tower which is a little worthy of the sun."

II

But about this time the island was caught in a swarm of pirates; and the shepherds had to turn themselves into rude warriors and seamen; and at first they were utterly broken down in blood and shame; and the pirates might have taken the jewel flung up for ever from their sacred fount. And then, after years of horror and humiliation, they gained a little and began to conquer because they did not mind defeat. And the pride of the pirates went sick within them after a few unexpected foils; and at last the invasion rolled back into the empty seas and the island was delivered. And for some reason after this men began to talk quite differently about the temple and the sun. Some, indeed, said, "You must not touch the temple; it is classical; it is perfect, since it admits no imperfections." But the others answered, "In that it differs from the sun, that shines on the evil and the good and on mud and monsters everywhere. The temple is of the noon; it is made of white marble clouds and sapphire sky. But the sun is not always of the noon. The sun dies daily; every night he is crucified in blood and fire."

Now the priest had taught and fought through all the war, and his hair had grown white, but his eyes had grown young. And he said, "I was wrong and they are right. The sun, the symbol of our father, gives life to all those earthly things that are full of ugliness and energy. All the exaggerations are right, if they exaggerate the right thing. Let us point to heaven with tusks and horns and fins and trunks and tails so long as they all point to heaven. The ugly animals praise God as much as the beautiful. The frog's eyes stand out of his head because he is staring at heaven. The giraffe's neck is long because he is stretching towards heaven. The donkey has ears to hear—let him hear."

And under the new inspiration they planned a gorgeous cathedral in the Gothic manner, with all the animals of the earth crawling over it, and all the possible ugly things making up one common beauty, because they all appealed to the god. The columns of the temple were carved like the necks of giraffes; the dome was like an ugly tortoise; and the highest pinnacle was a monkey standing on his head with his tail pointing at the sun. And yet the whole was beautiful, because it was lifted up in one living and religious gesture as a man lifts his hands in prayer.

But this great plan was never properly completed. The people had brought up on great wagons the heavy tortoise roof and the huge necks of stone, and all the thousand and one oddities that made up that unity, the owls and the efts and the crocodiles and the kangaroos, which hideous by themselves might have been magnificent if reared in one definite proportion and dedicated to the sun. For this was Gothic, this was romantic, this was Christian art; this was the whole advance of Shakespeare upon Sophocles. And that symbol which was to crown it all, the ape upside down, was really Christian; for man is the ape upside down.

But the rich, who had grown riotous in the long peace, obstructed the thing, and in some squabble a stone struck the priest on the head and he lost his memory. He saw piled in front of him frogs and elephants, monkeys and giraffes, toadstools and sharks, all the ugly things of the universe which he had collected to do honour to God. But he forgot why he had collected them. He could not remember the design or the object. He piled them all wildly into one heap fifty feet high; and when he had done it all the rich and influential went into a passion of applause and cried, "This is real art! This is Realism! This is things as they really are!"

·   ·   ·   ·   ·

That, I fancy, is the only true origin of Realism. Realism is simply Romanticism that has lost its reason. This is so not merely in the sense of insanity but of suicide. It has lost its reason; that is its reason for existing. The old Greeks summoned godlike things to worship their god. The mediæval Christians summoned all things to worship theirs, dwarfs and pelicans, monkeys and madmen. The modern realists summon all these million creatures to worship their god; and then have no god for them to worship. Paganism was in art a pure beauty; that was the dawn. Christianity was a beauty created by controlling a million monsters of ugliness; and that in my belief was the zenith and the noon. Modern art and science practically mean having the million monsters and being unable to control them; and I will venture to call that the disruption and the decay. The finest lengths of the Elgin marbles consist of splendid horses going to the temple of a virgin. Christianity, with its gargoyles and grotesques, really amounted to saying this: that a donkey could go before all the horses of the world when it was really going to the temple. Romance means a holy donkey going to the temple. Realism means a lost donkey going nowhere.

The fragments of futile journalism or fleeting impression which are here collected are very like the wrecks and riven blocks that were piled in a heap round my imaginary priest of the sun. They are very like that grey and gaping head of stone that I found overgrown with the grass. Yet I will venture to make even of these trivial fragments the high boast that I am a mediævalist and not a modern. That is, I really have a notion of why I have collected all the nonsensical things there are. I have not the patience nor perhaps the constructive intelligence to state the connecting link between all these chaotic papers. But it could be stated. This row of shapeless and ungainly monsters which I now set before the reader does not consist of separate idols cut out capriciously in lonely valleys or various islands. These monsters are meant for the gargoyles of a definite cathedral. I have to carve the gargoyles, because I can carve nothing else; I leave to others the angels and the arches and the spires. But I am very sure of the style of the architecture and of the consecration of the church.

ON LYING IN BED

LYING in bed would be an altogether perfect and supreme experience if only one had a coloured pencil long enough to draw on the ceiling. This, however, is not generally a part of the domestic apparatus on the premises. I think myself that the thing might be managed with several pails of Aspinall and a broom. Only if one worked in a really sweeping and masterly way, and laid on the colour in great washes, it might drip down again on one's face in floods of rich and mingled colour like some strange fairy rain; and that would have its disadvantages. I am afraid it would be necessary to stick to black and white in this form of artistic composition. To that purpose, indeed, the white ceiling would be of the greatest possible use; in fact it is the only use I think of a white ceiling being put to.

But for the beautiful experiment of lying in bed I might never have discovered it. For years I have been looking for blank spaces in a modern house to draw on. Paper is much too small for any really allegorical design; as Cyrano de Bergerac says: "Il me faut des géants." But when I tried to find these fine clear spaces in the modern rooms such as we all live in I was continually disappointed. I found an endless pattern and complication of small objects hung like a curtain of fine links between me and my desire. I examined the walls; I found them to my surprise to be already covered with wall-paper, and I found the wall-paper to be already covered with very uninteresting images, all bearing a ridiculous resemblance to each other. I could not understand why one arbitrary symbol (a symbol apparently entirely devoid of any religious or philosophical significance) should thus be sprinkled all over my nice walls like a sort of small-pox. The Bible must be referring to wall-papers, I think, when it says "Use not vain repetitions, as the Gentiles do." I found the Turkey carpet a mass of unmeaning colours, rather like the Turkish Empire, or like the sweetmeat called Turkish delight. I do not exactly know what Turkish delight really is; but I suppose it is Macedonian Massacres. Everywhere that I went forlornly, with my pencil or my paint brush, I found that others had unaccountably been before me, spoiling the walls, the curtains, and the furniture with their childish and barbaric designs.

Nowhere did I find a really clear place for sketching until this occasion when I prolonged beyond the proper limit the process of lying on my back in bed. Then the light of that white heaven broke upon my vision, that breadth of mere white which is indeed almost the definition of Paradise, since it means purity and also means freedom. But alas! like all heavens, now that it is seen it is found to be unattainable; it looks more austere and more distant than the blue sky outside the window. For my proposal to paint on it with the bristly end of a broom has been discouraged—never mind by whom; by a person debarred from all political rights—and even my minor proposal to put the other end of the broom into the kitchen fire and turn it into charcoal has not been conceded. Yet I am certain that it was from persons in my position that all the original inspiration came for covering the ceilings of palaces and cathedrals with a riot of fallen angels or victorious gods. I am sure that it was only because Michael Angelo was engaged in the ancient and honourable occupation of lying in bed that he ever realised how the roof of the Sistine Chapel might be made into an awful imitation of a divine drama that could only be acted in the heavens.

The tone now commonly taken towards the practice of lying in bed is hypocritical and unhealthy. Of all the marks of modernity that seem to mean a kind of decadence, there is none more menacing and dangerous than the exultation of very small and secondary matters of conduct at the expense of very great and primary ones, at the expense of eternal public and tragic human morality. If there is one thing worse than the modern weakening of major morals it is the modern strengthening of minor morals. Thus it is considered more withering to accuse a man of bad taste than of bad ethics. Cleanliness is not next to godliness nowadays, for cleanliness is made an essential and godliness is regarded as an offence. A playwright can attack the institution of marriage so long as he does not misrepresent the manners of society, and I have met Ibsenite pessimists who thought it wrong to take beer but right to take prussic acid. Especially this is so in matters of hygiene; notably such matters as lying in bed. Instead of being regarded, as it ought to be, as a matter of personal convenience and adjustment, it has come to be regarded by many as if it were a part of essential morals to get up early in the morning. It is upon the whole part of practical wisdom; but there is nothing good about it or bad about its opposite.

. . . . .

Misers get up early in the morning; and burglars, I am informed, get up the night before. It is the great peril of our society that all its mechanism may grow more fixed while its spirit grows more fickle. A man's minor actions and arrangements ought to be free, flexible, creative; the things that should be unchangeable are his principles, his ideals. But with us the reverse is true; our views change constantly; but our lunch does not change. Now, I should like men to have strong and rooted conceptions, but as for their lunch, let them have it sometimes in the garden, sometimes in bed, sometimes on the roof, sometimes in the top of a tree. Let them argue from the same first principles, but let them do it in a bed, or a boat, or a balloon. This alarming growth of good habits really means a too great emphasis on those virtues which mere custom can misuse, it means too little emphasis on those virtues which custom can never quite ensure, sudden and splendid virtues of inspired pity or of inspired candour. If ever that abrupt appeal is made to us we may fail. A man can get used to getting up at five o'clock in the morning. A man cannot very well get used to being burnt for his opinions; the first experiment is commonly fatal. Let us pay a little more attention to these possibilities of the heroic and the unexpected. I daresay that when I get out of this bed I shall do some deed of an almost terrible virtue.

For those who study the great art of lying in bed there is one emphatic caution to be added. Even for those who can do their work in bed (like journalists), still more for those whose work cannot be done in bed (as, for example, the professional harpooner of whales), it is obvious that the indulgence must be very occasional. But that is not the caution I mean. The caution is this: if you do lie in bed, be sure you do it without any reason or justification at all. I do not speak, of course, of the seriously sick. But if a healthy man lies in bed, let him do it without a rag of excuse; then he will get up a healthy man. If he does it for some secondary hygienic reason, if he has some scientific explanation, he may get up a hypochondriac.

CHEESE

My forthcoming work in five volumes, "The Neglect of Cheese in European Literature," is a work of such unprecedented and laborious detail that it is doubtful if I shall live to finish it. Some overflowings from such a fountain of information may therefore be permitted to sprinkle these pages. I cannot yet wholly explain the neglect to which I refer. Poets have been mysteriously silent on the subject of cheese. Virgil, if I remember right, refers to it several times, but with too much Roman restraint. He does not let himself go on cheese. The only other poet I can think of just now who seems to have had some sensibility on the point was the nameless author of the nursery rhyme which says: "If all the trees were bread and cheese"—which is, indeed, a rich and gigantic vision of the higher gluttony. If all the trees were bread and cheese there would be considerable deforestation in any part of England where

I was living. Wild and wide woodlands would reel and fade before me as rapidly as they ran after Orpheus. Except Virgil and this anonymous rhymer, I can recall no verse about cheese. Yet it has every quality which we require in exalted poetry. It is a short, strong word; it rhymes to "breeze" and "seas" (an essential point); that it is emphatic in sound is admitted even by the civilisation of the modern cities. For their citizens, with no apparent intention except emphasis, will often say, "Cheese it!" or even "Quite the cheese." The substance itself is imaginative. It is ancient—sometimes in the individual case, always in the type and custom. It is simple, being directly derived from milk, which is one of the ancestral drinks, not lightly to be corrupted with soda-water. You know, I hope (though I myself have only just thought of it), that the four rivers of Eden were milk, water, wine, and ale. Aerated waters only appeared after the Fall.

But cheese has another quality, which is also the very soul of song. Once in endeavouring to lecture in several places at once, I made an eccentric journey across England, a journey of so irregular and even illogical shape that it necessitated my having lunch on four successive days in four roadside inns in four different counties. In each inn they had nothing but bread and cheese; nor can I imagine why a man should want more than bread and cheese, if he can get enough of it. In each inn the cheese was good; and in each inn it was different. There was a noble Wensleydale cheese in Yorkshire, a Cheshire cheese in Cheshire, and so on. Now, it is just here that true poetic civilisation differs from that paltry and mechanical civilisation which holds us all in bondage. Bad customs are universal and rigid, like modern militarism. Good customs are universal and varied, like native chivalry and self-defence. Both the good and bad civilisation cover us as with a canopy, and protect us from all that is outside. But a good civilisation spreads over us freely like a tree, varying and yielding because it is alive. A bad civilisation stands up and sticks out above us like an umbrella—artificial, mathematical in shape; not merely universal, but uniform. So it is with the contrast between the substances that vary and the substances that are the same wherever they penetrate. By a wise doom of heaven men were commanded to eat cheese, but not the same cheese. Being really universal it varies from valley to valley. But if, let us say, we compare cheese with soap (that vastly inferior substance), we shall see that soap tends more and more to be merely Smith's Soap or Brown's Soap, sent automatically all over the world. If the Red Indians have soap it is Smith's Soap. If the Grand Lama has soap it is Brown's Soap. There is nothing subtly and strangely Buddhist, nothing tenderly Tibetan, about his soap. I fancy the Grand Lama does not eat cheese (he is not worthy), but if he does it is probably a local cheese, having some real relation to his life and outlook. Safety matches, tinned foods, patent medicines are sent all over the world; but they are not produced all over the world. Therefore there is in them a mere dead identity, never that soft play of slight variation which exists in things produced everywhere out of the soil, in the milk of the kine, or the fruits of the orchard. You can get a whisky and soda at every outpost of the Empire: that is why so many Empire-builders go mad. But you are not tasting or touching any environment, as in the cider of Devonshire or the grapes of the Rhine. You are not approaching Nature in one of her myriad tints of mood, as in the holy act of eating cheese.

When I had done my pilgrimage in the four wayside public-houses I reached one of the great northern cities, and there I proceeded, with great rapidity and complete inconsistency, to a large and elaborate restaurant, where I knew I could get many other things besides bread and cheese. I could get that also, however; or at least I expected to get it; but I was sharply reminded that I had entered Babylon, and left England behind. The waiter brought me cheese, indeed, but cheese cut up into contemptibly small pieces; and it is the awful fact that, instead of Christian bread, he brought me biscuits. Biscuits—to one who had eaten the cheese of four great countrysides! Biscuits—to one who had proved anew for himself the sanctity of the ancient wedding between cheese and bread! I addressed the waiter in warm and moving terms. I asked him who he was that he should put asunder those whom Humanity had joined. I asked him if he did not feel, as an artist, that a solid but yielding substance like cheese went naturally with a solid, yielding substance like bread; to eat it off biscuits is like eating it off slates. I asked him if, when he said his prayers, he was so supercilious as to pray for his daily biscuits. He gave me generally to understand that he was only obeying a custom of Modern Society. I have therefore resolved to raise my voice, not against the waiter, but against Modern Society, for this huge and unparalleled modern wrong.

ON THE PRISON OF JAZZ

I HAVE already remarked, with all the restraint that I could command, that of all modern phenomena, the most monstrous and ominous, the most manifestly rotting with disease, the most grimly prophetic of destruction, the most clearly and unmistakably inspired by evil spirits, the most instantly and awfully overshadowed by the wrath of heaven, the most near to madness and moral chaos, the most vivid with devilry and despair, is the practice of having to listen to loud music while eating a meal in a restaurant. It has in it that sort of distraction that is worse than dissipation. For, though we talk lightly of doing this or that to distract the mind, it remains really as well as verbally true that to be distracted is to be distraught. The original Latin word does not mean relaxation; it means being torn asunder as by wild horses. The original Greek word, which corresponds to it, is used in the text which says that Judas burst asunder in the midst. To think of one thing at a time is the best sort of thinking; but it is possible, in a sense, to think of two things at a time, if one of them is really subconscious and therefore really subordinate. But to deal with a second thing which by its very nature trusts itself more and more aggressively in front of the first thing is to find the very crux of psychological crucifixion. I have generally found that the refined English persons who think it idolatrous to contemplate a religious image, turn up next time full of delighted admiration of some Yogi or Esoteric Hindu who only contemplates his big toe. But at least he contemplates something, and does not have to have ten thousand brazen drums to encourage him to do it. He is so far a real philosopher, in spite of his philosophy. He does not try to do two incompatible things at once.

Some social gestures have been found compatible with social intercourse by that very practical psychology which is as old as the world. Drinking is a help to talking; eating may be indulged in with due moderation and proportion; smoking is also a subconscious and therefore soothing pleasure. But talking to people who are listening to something else which is not the talk is a sort of complex or nexus of futility. To listen to a loud noise which is noisy enough to make speech inaudible, and not noisy enough to make silence conventional, is a strangling cross-purposes of contradiction. Also, as I have often pointed out, it is rude to everybody concerned. It is as if I went to hear Paderewski or Kreisler, at a concert, and started to spread out an elegant supper in front of me, with oysters and pigeon-pie and champagne, coffee and liqueurs. One is an insult to the cook and the other to the musician; but both would be an insult to a companion who had come under the impression that he was to enjoy himself under normal and traditional conditions; of attention during the performance of a concert, or conversation during the progress of a dinner. Sometimes a guest is actually described as being invited to "a quiet dinner." It is rather a quaint phrase when one considers it; as implying that the dinner itself could be noisy; that the soup would roar like the sea, or the asparagus become talkative, or the mutton-chop shriek aloud like the mandrake. But it does bear witness to the normal conception of comfort; that a quiet dinner means a quiet talk. Why, then, should two people walk into the middle of an enormous noise in order to have a quiet talk?

Nevertheless, in contradiction of all my present remarks, in violation of all my principles, I did actually the other day pay some attention to the band that was playing in a restaurant. For one thing, the nightmare of noise, recalling the horns of hell rather than the horns of elfland, is generally accompanied by that undercurrent of battering monotony which I believe is supposed to be one of the charms of jazz. And, without professing to know much about music, I have formed a very strong impression about jazz. It does express something; and what it expresses is Slavery. That is why the same sort of thrill can be obtained by the throb of savage tom-toms, in music or drama connected with the great slave-land of Africa. Jazz is the very reverse of an expression of liberty, or even an excessive expression of liberty, or even an expression of licence. It is the expression of the pessimist idea that nature never gets beyond nature, that life never rises above life, that man always finds himself back where he was at the beginning, that there is no revolt, no redemption, no escape for the slaves of the earth and of the desires of the earth. There is any amount of pessimistic poetry on that theme that is thrilling enough in its own way; and doubtless the music on that theme can be thrilling also. But it cannot be liberating, or even loosening; it does not escape as a common or vulgar melody can escape. It is the Song of the Treadmill. I had grown sufficiently used to the dull roar of it, in such places, that it did not prevent me from thinking, even if it did prevent me from talking. And then, of a sudden, the musicians began to play the tunes of a particular pre-war period, which was more or less the period of my own early youth. Most of them were quite cheap tunes attached to quite silly songs. But they were tunes and they were songs. And therefore they expressed something which has hitherto been the secret of man, and the whole meaning of his position in nature: they expressed Liberty.

For that is exactly the paradox of the transformation that has taken place. The old popular tune was banal, but it was free. Its rhythm was not only repetition. It ran only in order to jump;

and its last lap was a great leap that was called a chorus. The swing in it was not the swing of a pendulum, but the swing of a hammer when it is flung finally hurtling from the hand in the old Highland sport. In other words, it escaped; somewhere in the course of it, however crude, however obvious, there was a movement of escape; and the only meaning of jazz is that there is no escape. As it was with the music (save the mark!), so it was with the literature (God help it!). The silly old song was sentimental, but it was also romantic. That is, it believed in itself and its own chances of individual happiness; and happiness has to be taken seriously. But the modern world can only believe in unhappiness, and therefore refuses to take it seriously. But the result is a great loss of the purely lyrical quality and instinct. I do not demand a high place in English letters, or a prominent position in the *Golden Treasury*, for the chorus of my youth which ran "Beer, beer, glorious beer, fill yourself right up to here." But I do say that nobody, after consuming any number of cocktails, has yet been inspired to cry aloud anything so spirited and spontaneous and direct. The poetry inspired by cocktails is timid and tortuous and self-conscious and indirect. I do not say that the song beginning "Daisy, Daisy," is one of the supreme achievements of the English muse, but I do say that it is a song that can be sung. And in the age of jazz and cocktails, men either write songs that could not possibly be sung, or leave off writing songs and write fragments of a demented diary instead.

It is the loss of this great Gusto that seems to me the most curious result of the relaxation of Victorian conventions. For we are always told that we were always restricted; that conventions crushed our fathers and mothers and chilled our childhood with respectability. And yet it is certainly true that, if those old songs were bad or banal, they were much more bold and boisterous than anything that has succeeded them. Sometimes I think that our fathers were hard workers and really had holidays. Their holidays were often an orgy of bathos, but they were free. But the modern poet must always be on his best behaviour; I mean, of course, that he must always be on his worst behaviour. He must never be seen except in uniform; that is, in the funeral motley of the cynic. He can never become part of a crowd, even for the singing of a chorus. I looked round sadly in my restaurant, full of fashionably dressed people; but none of them attempted to join in the chorus of "Beer, beer, glorious beer." So, as they say in the short stories, I paid my bill and sadly went out into the night.

MARRIAGE AND THE MODERN MIND

I HAVE been requested to write something about Marriage and the Modern Mind. It would perhaps be more appropriate to write about Marriage and the Modern Absence of Mind. In much of their current conduct, those who call themselves "modern" seem to have abandoned the use of reason; they have sunk back into their own subconsciousness, perhaps under the influence of the psychology now most fashionable in the drawing-room; and it is an understatement to say that they act more automatically than the animals. Wives and husbands seem to leave home more in the manner of somnambulists.

If anybody thinks I exaggerate the mindlessness of modern comment on this matter, I am content to refer him to the inscription under a large photograph of a languishing lady, in the newspaper now before me. It states that the lady has covered herself with glory as the inventor of "Companionate Divorce." It goes on to state, in her own words, that she will marry her husband again if he asks her again; and that she has been living with him ever since she was divorced from him. If mortal muddle-headedness can go deeper than that, in this vale of tears, I should like to see it. The newspaper picture and paragraph I can actually see; and stupidity so stupendous as that has never been known in human history before. The first thing to say about marriage and the modern mind, therefore, is that it is natural enough that people with no mind should want to have no marriage.

But there is another simple yet curious illustration of modern stupidity in the matter. And that is that, while I have known thousands of people arguing about marriage, sometimes furiously against it, sometimes rather feebly in favour of it, I have never known any one of the disputants begin by asking what marriage is. They nibble at it with negative criticism; they chip pieces off it and exhibit them as specimens, called "hard cases"; they treat every example of the rule as an exception to the rule; but they never look at the rule. They never ask, even in the name of history or human curiosity, what the thing is, or why it is, or why the overwhelming mass of mankind believes that it must be. Let us begin with the alphabet, as one does with infants.

Marriage, humanly considered, rests upon a fact of human nature, which we may call a fact of natural history. All the higher animals require much longer parental protection than do the lower; the baby elephant is a baby much longer than the baby jellyfish. But even beyond this natural tutelage, man needs something quite unique in nature. Man alone needs education. I know that animals train their young in particular tricks; as cats teach kittens to catch mice. But this is a very limited and rudimentary education. It is what the hustling millionaires call Business Education; that is, it is not education at all. Even at that, I doubt whether any pupil presenting himself for Matriculation or entrance into Standard VI, would now be accepted if flaunting the stubborn boast of a capacity to catch mice. Education is a complex and many-sided culture to meet a complex and many-sided world; and the animals, especially the lower animals, do not require it. It is said that the herring lays thousands of eggs in a day. But, though evidently untouched by the stunt of Birth-Control, in other ways the herring is highly modern. The mother herring has no need to remember her own children, and certainly therefore, no need to remember her own mate. But then the duties of a young herring, just entering upon life, are very simple and largely instinctive; they come, like a modern religion, from within. A herring does not have to be taught to take a bath; for he never takes anything else. He does not have to be trained to take off a hat to a lady herring, for he never puts on a hat, or any other Puritanical disguise to hamper the Greek grace of his movements. Consequently his father and mother have no common task or responsibility; and they can safely model their union upon the boldest and most advanced of the new novels and plays. Doubtless the female herring does say to the male herring, "True marriage must be free from the dogmas of priests; it must be a thing of one exquisite moment." Doubtless the male herring does say to the female herring, "When Love has died in the heart, Marriage is a mockery in the home."

This philosophy, common among the lower forms of life, is obviously of no use among the higher. This way of talking, however suitable for herrings, or even for rats and rabbits, who are said to be so prolific, does not meet the case of the creature endowed with reason. The young of the human species, if they are to reach the full possibilities of the human culture, so various, so laborious, so elaborate, must be under the protection of responsible persons through very long periods of mental and moral growth. I know there are some who grow merely impatient and irrational at this point; and say they could do just as well without education. But they lie; for they could not even express that opinion, if they had not laboriously learnt one particular language in which to talk nonsense. The moment we have realized this, we understand why the relations of the sexes normally remain static; and in most cases, permanent. For though, taking this argument alone, there would be a case for the father and mother parting when the children were mature, the number of people who at the age of fifty really wish to bolt with the typist or be abducted by the chauffeur is less than is now frequently supposed.

Well, even if the family held together as long as that, it would be better than nothing; but in fact even such belated divorce is based on bad psychology. All the modern licence is based on bad psychology; because it is based on the latest psychology. And that is like knowing the last proposition in Euclid without knowing the first. It is the first elements of psychology that the people called "modern" do not know. One of the things they cannot comprehend is the thing called "atmosphere"; as they show by shrieking with derision when anybody demands "a religious atmosphere" in the schools. The atmosphere of something safe and settled can only exist where people see it in the future as well as in the past. Children know exactly what is meant by having really come home; and the happier of them keep something of the feeling as they grow up. But they cannot keep the feeling for ten minutes, if there is an assumption that Papa is only waiting for Tommy's twenty-first birthday to carry the typist off to Trouville; or that the chauffeur actually has the car at the door, that Mrs. Brown may go off the moment Miss Brown has "come out."

That is, in practical experience, the basic idea of marriage; that the founding of a family must be on a firm foundation; that the rearing of the immature must be protected by something patient and enduring. It is the common conclusion of all mankind; and all common sense is on its side. A small minority of what may be called the idle Intelligentsia, have, just recently and in our corner of the world, criticized this idea of Marriage in the name of what they call the Modern Mind. The first obvious or apparent question is how they deal with the practical problem of children. The first apparent answer is that they do not deal with it at all.

At best, they propose to get rid of babies, or the problem of babies, in one of three typically modern ways. One is to say that there shall be no babies. This suggestion may be addressed to the individual; but it is addressed to every individual. Another is that the father should instantly send the babies, especially if they are boys, to a distant and inaccessible school, with bounds like a prison, that the babies may become men, in a manner that is considered impossible in the society of their own father. But this is rapidly ceasing to be a Modern method; and even the Moderns have found that it is rather behind the times. The third way, which is unimpeachably Modern, is to imitate Rousseau, who left his baby on the door-step of the Foundling Hospital. It is true that, among the Moderns, it is generally nothing so human or traditional as the Foundling Hospital. The baby is to be left on the door-step of the State Department for Education and Universal Social Adjustment. In short, these people mean, with various degrees of vagueness, that the place of the Family can now be taken by the State.

The difficulty of the first method, and so far, of the second and third, is that they may be carried out. The suggestion is made to everybody in the hope that it will not be accepted by everybody; it is offered to all in the hope that it may not be accepted by all. If *nobody* has any children, everybody can still be satisfied by Birth-Control methods and justified by Birth-Control arguments. Even the reformers do not want this; but they cannot offer any objection to any individual—or every individual. In somewhat the same way, Rousseau may act as an individual and not as a social philosopher; but he could not prevent all the other individuals acting as individuals. And if all the babies born in the world were left on the door-step of the Foundling Hospital, the Hospital, and the door-step, would have to be considerably enlarged. Now something like this is what has really happened, in the vague and drifting centralization of our time. The Hospital has been enlarged into the School and then into the State; not the guardian of some abnormal children, but the guardian of all normal children. Modern mothers and fathers, of the emancipated sort, could not do their quick-change acts of bewildering divorce and scattered polygamy, if they did not believe in a big benevolent Grandmother, who could ultimately take over ten million children by very grandmotherly legislation.

This modern notion about the State is a delusion. It is not founded on the history of real States, but entirely on reading about unreal or ideal States, like the Utopias of Mr. Wells. The real State, though a necessary human combination, always has been and always will be, far too large, loose, clumsy, indirect and even insecure, to be the "home" of the human young who are to be trained in the human tradition. If mankind had not been organized into families, it would never have had the organic power to be organized into commonwealths. Human culture is handed down in the customs of countless households; it is the only way in which human culture can remain human. The households are right to confess a common loyalty or federation under some king or republic. But the king cannot be the nurse in every nursery; or even the government become the governess in every schoolroom. Look at the real story of States, modern as well as ancient, and you will see a dissolving view of distant and uncontrollable things, making up most of the politics of the earth. Take the most populous centre. China is now called a Republic. In consequence it is ruled by five contending armies and is much less settled than when it was an Empire. What has preserved China has been its domestic religion. South America, like all Latin lands, is full of domestic graces and gaieties; but it is governed by a series of revolutions. We ourselves may be governed by a Dictator; or by a General Strike; or by a banker living in New York. Government grows more elusive every day. But the traditions of humanity support humanity; and the central one is this tradition of Marriage. And the essential of it is that a free man and a free woman choose to found on earth the only voluntary state; the only state which creates and which loves its citizens. So long as these real responsible beings stand together, they can survive all the vast changes, deadlocks and disappointments which make up mere political history. But if they fail each other, it is as certain as death that "the State" will fail them.

WHAT I FOUND IN MY POCKET

ONCE when I was very young I met one of those men who have made the Empire what it is—a man in an astracan coat, with an astracan moustache—a tight, black, curly moustache. Whether he put on the moustache with the coat or whether his Napoleonic will enabled him not only to grow a moustache in the usual place, but also to grow little moustaches all over his clothes, I do not know. I only remember that he said to me the following words: "A man can't get on nowadays by hanging about with his hands in his pockets." I made reply with the quite obvious flippancy that perhaps a man got on by having his hands in other people's pockets; whereupon he began to argue about Moral Evolution, so I suppose what I said had some truth in it. But the incident now comes back to me, and connects itself with another incident—if you can call it an incident—which happened to me only the other day.

I have only once in my life picked a pocket, and then (perhaps through some absent-mindedness) I picked my own. My act can really with some reason be so described. For in taking things out of my own pocket I had at least one of the more tense and quivering emotions of the thief; I had a complete ignorance and a profound curiosity as to what I should find there. Perhaps it would be the exaggeration of eulogy to call me a tidy person. But I can always pretty satisfactorily account for all my possessions. I can always tell where they are, and what I have done with them, so long as I can keep them out of my pockets. If once anything slips into those unknown abysses, I wave it a sad Virgilian farewell. I suppose that the things that I have dropped into my pockets are still there; the same presumption applies to the

things that I have dropped into the sea. But I regard the riches
stored in both these bottomless chasms with the same reverent
ignorance. They tell us that on the last day the sea will give up
its dead; and I suppose that on the same occasion long strings of
extraordinary things will come running out of my pockets. But
I have quite forgotten what any of them are; and there is really
nothing (excepting the money) that I shall be at all surprised at
finding among them.

Such at least has hitherto been my state of innocence. I here
only wish briefly to recall the special, extraordinary, and hitherto
unprecedented circumstances which led me in cold blood, and
being of sound mind, to turn out my pockets. I was locked up
in a third-class carriage for a rather long journey. The time was
towards evening, but it might have been anything, for everything resembling earth or sky or light or shade was painted out
as if with a great wet brush by an unshifting sheet of quite colourless rain. I had no books or newspapers. I had not even a
pencil and a scrap of paper with which to write a religious epic.
There were no advertisements on the walls of the carriage, otherwise I could have plunged into the study of them, for any collection of printed words is quite enough to suggest infinite
complexities of mental ingenuity. When I find myself opposite
the words "Sunlight Soap" I can exhaust all the aspects of Sun
Worship, Apollo, and Summer poetry before I go on to the less
congenial subject of soap. But there was no printed word or
picture anywhere; there was nothing but blank wood inside the
carriage and blank wet without. Now I deny most energetically
that anything is, or can be, uninteresting. So I stared at the
joints of the walls and seats, and began thinking hard on the
fascinating subject of wood. Just as I had begun to realise why,
perhaps, it was that Christ was a carpenter, rather than a bricklayer, or a baker, or anything else, I suddenly started upright,
and remembered my pockets. I was carrying about with me an
unknown treasury. I had a British Museum and a South Kensing-

ton collection of unknown curios hung all over me in different places. I began to take the things out.

The first thing I came upon consisted of piles and heaps of Battersea tram tickets. There were enough to equip a paper chase. They shook down in showers like confetti. Primarily, of course, they touched my patriotic emotions, and brought tears to my eyes; also they provided me with the printed matter I required, for I found on the back of them some short but striking little scientific essays about some kind of pill. Comparatively speaking, in my then destitution, those tickets might be regarded as a small but well-chosen scientific library. Should my railway journey continue (which seemed likely at the time) for a few months longer, I could imagine myself throwing myself into the controversial aspects of the pill, composing replies and rejoinders pro and con upon the data furnished to me. But after all it was the symbolic quality of the tickets that moved me most. For as certainly as the cross of St. George means English patriotism, those scraps of paper meant all that municipal patriotism which is now, perhaps, the greatest hope of England.

The next thing that I took out was a pocket-knife. A pocket-knife, I need hardly say, would require a thick book full of moral meditations all to itself. A knife typifies one of the most primary of those practical origins upon which as upon low, thick pillows all our human civilisation reposes. Metals, the mystery of the thing called iron and of the thing called steel, led me off half-dazed into a kind of dream. I saw into the intrails of dim, damp wood, where the first man among all the common stones found the strange stone. I saw a vague and violent battle, in which stone axes broke and stone knives were splintered against something shining and new in the hand of one desperate man. I heard all the hammers on all the anvils of the earth. I saw all the swords of Feudal and all the weals of Industrial War. For the knife is only a short sword; and the pocket-knife is a secret sword. I opened it and looked at that brilliant and terrible tongue which we call a blade; and I thought that perhaps it was the symbol of the oldest of the needs of man. The next moment I knew that I was wrong; for the thing that came next out of my pocket was a box of matches. Then I saw fire, which is stronger even than steel, the old, fierce female thing, the thing we all love, but dare not touch.

The next thing I found was a piece of chalk; and I saw in it all the art and all the frescoes of the world. The next was a coin of a very modest value; and I saw in it not only the image and superscription of our own Cæsar, but all government and order since the world began. But I have not space to say what were the items in the long and splendid procession of poetical symbols that came pouring out. I cannot tell you all the things that were in my pocket. I can tell you one thing, however, that I could not find in my pocket. I allude to my railway ticket.

ON MR. THOMAS GRAY

A NEWSPAPER appeared with the news, which it seemed to regard as exciting and even alarming news, that Gray did not write the "Elegy in a Country Churchyard" in the churchyard of Stoke Poges, but in some other country churchyard of the same sort in the same country. What effect the news will have on the particular type of American tourist who has chipped pieces off trees and tombstones, when he finds that the chips come from the wrong trees, or the wrong tombstones, I do not feel impelled to inquire. Nor, indeed, do I know whether the new theory is proved or not. Nor do I care whether the new theory is proved or not. What is most certainly proved, if it needed any proving, is the complete lack of imagination, in many journalists and archæologists, about how any poet writes any poem.

In such a controversy it is implied, generally on both sides, that what happens is something like this. The poet comes and sits on a tombstone, or wherever he was supposed to sit, in the one and only churchyard of Stoke Poges, or whatever place be the rival of Stoke Poges. He hears the Curfew; and there is a dreadful doubt and dispute about whether anybody sitting among the tombs of Stoke Poges can hear the Curfew, which does really ring from Windsor, though I imagine it sounds pretty much like any other bell at evening. Then the poet produces a portable pen and ink, preferably a large quill and a scroll (the poet in question lived before the time of fountain-pens), and writes down the first line: "The curfew tolls the knell of parting day." Then he looks round to make quite sure that there are some lowing herds winding over that particular lea, that the ploughman is present and doing his duty in plodding homeward his weary way, and that all the other fittings are in the offing. Later, he will have to insist peremptorily on an ivy-mantled tower being in the immediate neighbourhood, inhabited by an (if possible) moping owl. It will not be the only owl involved in the business. If there are not all these correct conditions provided on the spot, he will not be able to write the Elegy. If, on the other hand, they are all there and everything has been properly provided, he will then write the whole of the Elegy, steadily, right through, and not roll up his scroll or rise from his tombstone until he has left the unfortunate young man in the poem finally safe in the bosom of his Father and his God. Then he will go home to tea; and I should imagine he would need it, after so prolonged and sustained a literary effort achieved in such damp and clammy conditions. That, with very little exaggeration, is what is really suggested by those who talk about Gray writing the poem in this place or that place, and under this or that condition of local colour.

Now, I should have thought that anybody would know that poetry is not written like that. But perhaps, in this case, even a bad poet is better than a good critic. Anybody who has ever written any verse, good, bad, or indifferent, will know that calculations of this sort are calculations about the incalculable. Gray might have written the poem, or any part of the poem, in any place on the map; he might have visited the New Stoke Poges or the Old Stoke Poges, or quite probably both, or possibly neither. But, if I may be allowed to pick out one thread of speculation from a thousand threads of possibility, I would suggest that the "Elegy in a Country Churchyard," even if it did refer to one particular churchyard, is very likely to have been begun, continued, and ended rather like this:

Mr. Thomas Gray was sitting one evening in a coffee-house; let us hope a coffee-house that did not confine itself to coffee. Something or other, a fiddle or a few glasses of wine, or a good dinner, had thrown him into a mood of musing, of pleasant musing, though touched with a manly and generous melancholy. His thoughts turned round and round, as they do at such times, the tantalizing old riddle of what we really feel about life and death; about the toy God gave us which is beautiful and brittle, yet certainly not trivial. He said to himself: "After all, who doesn't really feel that it really matters, with all its botherations? . . . A queer business . . . pleasing . . . anxious. . . ." Then something stirred quicker within him, and he said to himself, in warm poetic emotion—

> For who tytumpty tumpty tumpty tum,
> This pleasing anxious being e'er resigned.

Then his impulse gathered speed and power; and he struck the table and said the next line straight off—

> Left the warm precincts of the cheerful day.

He said that line several times. He liked it very much. Then it was almost a matter of form, certainly a matter of facility, to put the tail on the verse—

> Nor cast one longing, lingering look behind.

Then he got up and put on his hat. He left the warm precincts of the cheerful coffee-house, and went home and forgot all about it.

Some time afterwards, perhaps quite a long time afterwards, he was walking in the countryside at dusk. It is quite possible that he was walking in Stoke Poges, or through Stoke Poges, or through any number of other places in the neighbourhood. Perhaps he did hear the Curfew, or what he thought was the Curfew, or what he pretended was the Curfew. He made up another verse or two about the twilight landscape, full of the same spirit of stoical thankfulness and genial resignation. Then he noticed, with great joy, that they would work into the same metre as the lines he had made up in the coffee-house. They were very much in the same mood. But he did not write many of the verses in the churchyard. Possibly he did not write any of the verses in the churchyard. It is more likely that the third act has for its scene Mr. Gray's private study, lined with the classics in old leather bindings, and adorned with the celebrated cat and the bowl of goldfish. There he jotted down disjointed verses, and began to put them together; until it looked as if they might some day make a poem. But, subject to any information that may exist on the subject, it would not in the ordinary way surprise me to learn that it was a devil of a long time before they did make a poem. It is most likely, in the abstract, that he got sick of it half-way through, and chucked it away, and found it again years afterwards. It is extremely likely that there was another very long interval, when he was just finishing it, but could not finish finishing it. Many a man writing such a poem has held it up for a year for want of one verse. Nor would the newspaper assist him, in such a difficulty, by pointing out that there was another churchyard much more suitable than that of Stoke Poges.

Now, it is possible—nay, it is probable—that there is not one word of truth in this particular description of the proceedings of Mr. Gray. I have not read any of the literary and biographical records of Mr. Gray, at least for a long time; and there are plenty of records to read. It is quite likely that there are details of his daily life that destroy altogether the details I have here suggested. It is even possible that, by some amazing eccentricity, he did write the whole thing in a churchyard; or, by some unscrupulous exaggeration, pretended that he had done so. But my story is a great deal nearer to the normal story of the production of a poem than any story that supposes particular places and conditions to be *necessary* to the poem. Even if Gray did write with all the stage properties stuck up around him, the lowing cow, the plodding ploughman, the moping owl, they were not the materials of the poem; and he would probably have written pretty much the same sort of poem without them. All this business of clues and tests is not criticism. It is a very good thing that people are applying literature to detective stories and detectives. But it is not a good thing to apply detectives to literature. Gray's unmistakable foot-mark or favourite tobacco-ash may be found in Stoke Poges or anywhere else. But it is not in those ashes that there lived his wonted fires.

The real relation of Gray's great poem to the present stage of our history will probably not be understood until a later stage. Yet the poem is a monument, a trophy, and, at the same time, a beacon or signal, standing up as solid and significant as the monument stands up in the Stoke Poges fields. Many poems have been written since, and grown more fashionable, if not more famous, which have not the particular meaning for the modern world stored up in this very storied urn. For Gray wrote at the very beginning of a certain literary epoch of which we, perhaps, stand at the very end. He represented that softening of the Classic which slowly turned it into the Romantic. We represent that ultimate hardening of the Romantic which has turned it into the Realistic. Both changes have, of course, been criticized in their time by the more conservative critics. Dr. Johnson said, probably with a partly humorous impatience, that Gray had only proved that he "could be dull in a new way." And most of us will agree that the modern realistic writers, who have in their turn replaced the romantic writers, have indubitably discovered a marvellous and amazing number of new ways of being dull.

But the change, as it hung uncompleted in Gray, strangely

resembled the twilight changes of that landscape which the poem describes. Indeed, the whole episode has a curious, almost uncanny, harmony that even includes coincidence. Concerned as he was with a fine shade of twilight, it is even odd that his name was Gray. The whole legend is like that of something colourless and classical fading into mere shadow. For something was, indeed, fading before the eyes of Thomas Gray, the poet, and it was something that he did not wish to see fade. It may be noted that the first impression, especially in the first verses, is one of things moving away from the poet and leaving him alone. We see only the back of the ploughman, so to speak, as he plods away into the darkness; the herds of cattle have the perspective of vanishing things; for a whole world was indeed passing out of the sight and reach of that learned and sensitive and secluded gentleman, who represented the culture of eighteenth-century England, and could only watch a twilight transformation which he could not understand. For when the ploughman comes back out of that twilight, he will come back different. He will be either a scientific works-manager or an entirely new kind of agrarian citizen, great as in the first days of Rome; a free peasant or a servant of alien machinery; but never the same again.

I am not very fond of committees and societies of specialists or amateurs who sit upon this or that sort of problem; but in the particular problem of the preservation of the rural and cultural traditions of our own countryside, I cannot see at the moment that any other machinery is possible. And it seems to me that the Penn-Gray Society is a good example of a machine suited to its work and doing work that is wanted. The trouble is that the typical cultured Englishman, like Gray or the traditional admirer of Gray, was generally a certain kind of gentleman, of the sort that had some kind of country seat. Since then, to continue the figure, the gentleman with the country seat has rather fallen between two stools. He is no longer so rich and powerful as a landlord. He generally has not become rich and powerful as a local politician. There were any number of men, of course, who appreciated the country without owning a country seat. But if they were not the sort of men to own a country seat, still less were they the sort of men to stand for a county council. And, as the old organization of England went, the organization that has been gradually dying since the days of Gray, men of this artistic sort were mostly attached in some more or less indirect way to the gentry. That is the point; that, for good or ill, it was the system peculiar to a gentry. It was never, for instance, the system peculiar to a peasantry. When there is anything like a peasantry, even as there is in Scotland, it was possible to produce a peasant poet like Burns. And the memory of a peasant like Burns would be preserved by other peasants, even if there were nobody else to preserve it. But nobody could expect the agricultural labourers to preserve the memory of a scholar like Gray. It is amusing to remember that Burns put a verse from the Elegy as a motto to his own homely and pungent picture of peasant life; as some have thought, consciously stressing the contrast between his own realism and the scholar's classicism:

> Let not ambition mock their useful toil,
> Their humble joys, and destiny obscure;
> Nor grandeur hear, with a disdainful smile,
> The short and simple annals of the poor.

Indeed, I rather fancy that, in citing those rather patronizing lines, it was the poor poet who had the disdainful smile.

But we must take the rough with the smooth in that noble aristocratic story that has made South England like a garden among the nations. And with it weakened the only organization for protecting the art and antiquities of rural life. Gray could not be a popular poet like Burns; at least, not in that sort of rural life. Perhaps there is a hint of it in his own phrase; that the Village Milton would have remained mute and inglorious. Perhaps he deliberately did not finish the tale of the Village Hampden, who was possibly a poacher, but could not possibly be a peasant. Anyhow, the old organization of culture has weakened; and the new organization of local politics is not an organization of culture. There can be a culture of peasants, but not a culture of petty politicians. In this dilemma there is nothing to be done except to work through groups of sympathetic individuals, students or artists or lovers of landscape, who take the trouble to support each other in defending the tradition of the national history and poetry. Otherwise the whole country will be swept bare for the sort of motorist to whom every object is an obstacle to rushing from nowhere to nowhere. Roads will not be roads, for there will be no places for them to go to; there will be only those ominously called arterial, and resembling, indeed, those open and spouting arteries that are an inevitable sign of death. I should say the ultimate moral is that we ought to have made up our minds between real aristocracy and real democracy, and should have either preserved a gentry or created a peasantry. But the immediate moral is that we must preserve what we can of all that reminds us that rural life was a civilization and not a savagery, and especially support such groups as the society here in question, which is defending the great tradition of Gray.

ON RUNNING AFTER ONE'S HAT

I FEEL an almost savage envy on hearing that London has been flooded in my absence, while I am in the mere country. My own Battersea has been, I understand, particularly favoured as a meeting of the waters. Battersea was already, as I need hardly say, the most beautiful of human localities. Now that it has the additional splendour of great sheets of water, there must be something quite incomparable in the landscape (or waterscape) of my own romantic town. Battersea must be a vision of Venice. The boat that brought the meat from the butcher's must have shot along those lanes of rippling silver with the strange smoothness of the gondola. The greengrocer who brought cabbages to the corner of the Latchmere Road must have leant upon the oar with the unearthly grace of the gondolier. There is nothing so perfectly poetical as an island; and when a district is flooded it becomes an archipelago.

Some consider such romantic views of flood or fire slightly lacking in reality. But really this romantic view of such inconveniences is quite as practical as the other. The true optimist who sees in such things an opportunity for enjoyment is quite as logical and much more sensible than the ordinary "Indignant Ratepayer" who sees in them an opportunity for grumbling. Real pain, as in the case of being burnt at Smithfield or having a toothache, is a positive thing; it can be supported, but scarcely enjoyed. But, after all, our toothaches are the exception, and as for being burnt at Smithfield, it only happens to us at the very longest intervals. And most of the inconveniences that make men swear or women cry are really sentimental or imaginative inconveniences—things altogether of the mind. For instance, we often hear grown-up people complaining of having to hang about a railway station and wait for a train. Did you ever hear a small boy complain of having to hang about a railway station and wait for a train? No; for to him to be inside a railway station is to be inside a cavern of wonder and a palace of poetical pleasures. Because to him the red light and the green light on the signal are like a new sun and a new moon. Because to him when the wooden arm of the signal falls down suddenly, it is as if a great king had thrown down his staff as a signal and started a shrieking tournament of trains. I myself am of little boys' habit in this matter. They also serve who only stand and wait for the two fifteen. Their meditations may be full of rich and fruitful things. Many of the most purple hours of my life have been passed at Clapham Junction, which is now, I suppose, under water. I have been there in many moods so fixed and mystical that the water might well have come up to my waist before I noticed it particularly. But in the case of all such annoyances, as

I have said, everything depends upon the emotional point of view. You can safely apply the test to almost every one of the things that are currently talked of as the typical nuisance of daily life.

For instance, there is a current impression that it is unpleasant to have to run after one's hat. Why should it be unpleasant to the well-ordered and pious mind? Not merely because it is running, and running exhausts one. The same people run much faster in games and sports. The same people run much more eagerly after an uninteresting little leather ball than they will after a nice silk hat. There is an idea that it is humiliating to run after one's hat; and when people say it is humiliating they mean that it is comic. It certainly is comic; but man is a very comic creature, and most of the things he does are comic—eating, for instance. And the most comic things of all are exactly the things that are most worth doing—such as making love. A man running after a hat is not half so ridiculous as a man running after a wife.

Now a man could, if he felt rightly in the matter, run after his hat with the manliest ardour and the most sacred joy. He might regard himself as a jolly huntsman pursuing a wild animal, for certainly no animal could be wilder. In fact, I am inclined to believe that hat-hunting on windy days will be the sport of the upper classes in the future. There will be a meet of ladies and gentlemen on some high ground on a gusty morning. They will be told that the professional attendants have started a hat in such-and-such a thicket, or whatever be the technical term. Notice that this employment will in the fullest degree combine sport with humanitarianism. The hunters would feel that they were not inflicting pain. Nay, they would feel that they were inflicting pleasure, rich, almost riotous pleasure, upon the people who were looking on. When last I saw an old gentleman running after his hat in Hyde Park, I told him that a heart so benevolent as his ought to be filled with peace and thanks at the thought of how much unaffected pleasure his every gesture and bodily attitude were at that moment giving to the crowd.

The same principle can be applied to every other typical domestic worry. A gentleman trying to get a fly out of the milk or a piece of cork out of his glass of wine often imagines himself to be irritated. Let him think for a moment of the patience of anglers sitting by dark pools, and let his soul be immediately irradiated with gratification and repose. Again, I have known some people of very modern views driven by their distress to the use of theological terms to which they attached no doctrinal significance, merely because a drawer was jammed tight and they could not pull it out. A friend of mine was particularly afflicted in this way. Every day his drawer was jammed, and every day in consequence it was something else that rhymes to it. But I pointed out to him that this sense of wrong was really subjective and relative; it rested entirely upon the assumption that the drawer could, should, and would come out easily. "But if," I said, "you picture to yourself that you are pulling against some powerful and oppressive enemy, the struggle will become merely exciting and not exasperating. Imagine that you are tugging up a lifeboat out of the sea. Imagine that you are roping up a fellow-creature out of an Alpine crevassé. Imagine even that you are a boy again and engaged in a tug-of-war between French and English." Shortly after saying this I left him; but I have no doubt at all that my words bore the best possible fruit. I have no doubt that every day of his life he hangs on to the handle of that drawer with a flushed face and eyes bright with battle, uttering encouraging shouts to himself, and seeming to hear all round him the roar of an applauding ring.

So I do not think that it is altogether fanciful or incredible to suppose that even the floods in London may be accepted and enjoyed poetically. Nothing beyond inconvenience seems really to have been caused by them; and inconvenience, as I have said, is only one aspect, and that the most unimaginative and accidental aspect of a really romantic situation. An adventure is only an inconvenience rightly considered. An inconvenience is only an adventure wrongly considered. The water that girdled the houses and shops of London must, if anything, have only in-

creased their previous witchery and wonder. For as the Roman
Catholic priest in the story said: "Wine is good with everything
except water," and on a similar principle, water is good with
everything except wine.

ON THE ENGLISHMAN ABROAD

IT was an old objection to the Englishman abroad that he made
himself too much at home. He was accused of treating a first-
class foreign hotel as if it were only a fourth-class English hotel;
and of brawling in it as if it were a bad variety of public-house.
If there was a truth in the charge, it has since been transferred
to a more vigorous type of vulgarian; and compared with a certain sort of American traveller, the English tripper might be
mistaken for a civilized man. He has even taken on the colour
of his Continental surroundings; and is indistinguishable from
what he himself would once have described as "the natives." It
might almost be regarded as a form of going *fantee*. But there
is one particular aspect of the old accusation, which seems to me
much more curious and puzzling than any other. It is that when
the Englishman did blunder or bully, in demanding certain
things merely because they were familiar, they were not really
the things that had long been familiar to him; or to his fathers.
I can understand the Englishman asking for English things; the
odd thing is that it was not for the most English things that he
asked. Some of the most English things he had already lost in
England, and could hardly hope to find in Europe. Most of the
things he did hope to find in Europe, he had only recently found
even in England. When he asked for a drink, he asked for a
Scotch drink; he even submitted to the intolerable national
humiliation of calling it Scotch. When he asked for a game, he
asked for a Scotch game; he looked to see whole landscapes
transformed by the game of golf; which he himself had hardly

played for ten years. He did not go about looking for cricket, which he had played for six hundred years. And just as he asked for Scotch links instead of cricket-fields and Scotch whisky instead of ale, so he expected a number of appliances and conveniences which were often much less English than American; and sometimes much less English than German. It would perhaps be pressing the argument fantastically far to say that even tea is originally a thing as oriental as hashish. But certainly an Englishman demanding tea in all the cafés of the Continent was as unreasonable as a Chinaman demanding opium in all the public-houses of the Old Kent Road. He was at least comparable to a Frenchman roaring to have red wine included in his bill in a series of tea-shops in Tooting. But I am not so much complaining of the old-fashioned Englishman who asked for something like the "five o'clock" which was recognized as English. I am rather complaining of a new-fashioned Englishman who would insist on American ice-cream sodas in the plains of Russia, while refusing tea because it was taken with lemon or served in a samovar. This bizarre contradiction and combination of the blind acceptance of some foreign things and the blind refusal of others, does seem to me a mystery to be added to what is perhaps the most mysterious national character in Christendom. That a man from Market Harborough should miss the oldest things in Old England, when travelling in Lithuania, may be intelligible and pardonable enough. That a man from Market Harborough should miss the newest things in New York, and be seriously surprised not to find them among Lithuanian peasants, is even more extraordinary than that he should want them himself.

But there goes along with this English eccentricity an even more serious English error. The things of which England has most reason to be proud are the things which England has preserved out of the ancient culture of the Christian world, when all the rest of that world has neglected them. They are at once unique and universal triumphs and trophies of the national life.

They are things that are English in the sense that the English have kept them; but human in the sense that all humanity ought to have kept them. They are European in the sense of really belonging to the whole white civilization; they are English in the sense of having been largely lost in Europe. And I have heard Englishmen boasting of all sorts of absurd things, from the possession of German blood to the possession of Jewish politicians; and I have never heard a single Englishman say a single word about a single one of these really English things.

One obvious case, for example, is that of having a fire in the old Latin sense of a focus. The idea of the hearth is one to be found in ancient Roman culture, and therefore in all the European cultures that have come from it. The idea of the hearth is to be found everywhere; but the hearth is not to be found everywhere. It is now most easily and universally to be found in England. And it is a strange irony that the French poet or the Italian orator, full of the splendours of the great pagan past, naturally speaks of a man fighting for his hearth and his altar; when he himself in practice has as much neglected hearths as we have neglected altars. And the only man in Christendom who really retains a hearth is one who has unfortunately rather dropped out of the habit of fighting for it. I do not mean, of course, that there are not really firesides scattered everywhere throughout Europe, especially among the poor, who always retain the highest and proudest traditions of the past. I am talking of a matter of proportion; of the preponderating presence of the custom in one place rather than another; and in this sense it is certain that it preponderates in England more than in any other country. Almost everywhere else the much more artificial and prosaic institution called the stove has become solidly established. In every eternal and essential sense, there is simply no comparison between that open domestic altar, on which the visible flame dances and illuminates, and the mere material habit of shutting up heat in a big box. The comparison is as sharp as that between the wild but splendid pagan custom of burning a dead man on a tower of timber, so that he went up to the sky in a column of fire and cloud, and the paltry paganism of our own time, which is content with the thing called cremation. Similarly there is about the stove all the essential utilitarian ugliness of the oven. There must always be something more magnificent about an open furnace, even from the standpoint of Shadrek, Meshach, and Abednego. Theirs was perhaps a rather heroic form of affection for the fireside. But, in comparison, we can all feel that there is something cold and desolate about the condition of the unhappy foreigner, who cannot really hope to sit in the glow of a fireside except by the extreme experiment of setting his house on fire.

Now I appeal to all those who have sung a hundred English songs, heard a hundred English speeches, read a hundred English books of more or less breezy or bombastic patriotism, to say whether they have ever seen the continuity of this Christian custom properly praised as a matter of pride among the English. And this strange gap in our glory seems to me another example of something that I noted recently in this place; the dangerous lack of an intensive national feeling in this country; and above all a much too supine surrender to other influences; from Germany; from Scotland; and above all from America.

I have taken only one domestic detail here, for the sake of clearness; but of course the principle could be extended to any number of larger examples of the same truth. The English inn, although a most Christian institution, was something more than an institution of Christendom. It was in its day a thing very specially English. I say it was; for I very much fear that capitalist monopoly and prohibitionist madness have between them turned it into something historical. It may be that the public-house will soon be dead enough to become a glorious historical monument. But the point to be noted here is the comparison with other countries, which had similar institutions, yet never had exactly the same institution. Sometimes, as in the case of the open hearth or fireside, they really had the same institution; and yet never had it so long. But anyone travelling in foreign countries can note that the new things are not erected on the basis of this particular old thing. We have spoilt the English inn; but at least we had it to spoil; and many national traditions, admirable in other ways, have had something much less admirable to spoil. In Europe, especially in outlying parts of Europe, we may see the latest modern machinery introduced without any of that intermediate type of comfort and convenience. The new American barbarism is applied direct to the oldest European barbarism. That interlude of moderate and mellow civilization has never been known. Men of many countries, both new and old, could only see it by coming to England; and even then they might come too late. The English might have already destroyed the last glories of England. When I think of these things, I still stand astounded at the strange quality of my countrymen; at their arrogance and especially at their modesty.

THE ROMANTIC IN THE RAIN

THE middle classes of modern England are quite fanatically fond of washing; and are often enthusiastic for teetotalism. I cannot therefore comprehend why it is that they exhibit a mysterious dislike of rain. Rain, that inspiring and delightful thing, surely combines the qualities of these two ideals with quite a curious perfection. Our philanthropists are eager to establish public baths everywhere. Rain surely is a public bath; it might almost be called mixed bathing. The appearance of persons coming fresh from this great natural lustration is not perhaps polished or dignified; but for the matter of that, few people are dignified when coming out of a bath. But the scheme of rain in itself is one of an enormous purification. It realises the dream of some insane hygienist: it scrubs the sky. Its giant brooms and mops seem to reach the starry rafters and starless corners of the cosmos; it is a cosmic spring-cleaning.

If the Englishman is really fond of cold baths, he ought not to grumble at the English climate for being a cold bath. In these days we are constantly told that we should leave our little special possessions and join in the enjoyment of common social institutions and a common social machinery. I offer the rain as a thoroughly Socialistic institution. It disregards that degraded delicacy which has hitherto led each gentleman to take his shower-bath in private. It is a better shower-bath, because it is public and communal; and, best of all, because somebody else pulls the string.

. . . . .

As for the fascination of rain for the water drinker, it is a fact the neglect of which I simply cannot comprehend. The enthusiastic water drinker must regard a rainstorm as a sort of universal banquet and debauch of his own favourite beverage. Think of the imaginative intoxication of the wine drinker if the crimson clouds sent down claret or the golden clouds hock. Paint upon primitive darkness some such scenes of apocalypse, towering and gorgeous skyscapes in which champagne falls like fire from heaven or the dark skies grow purple and tawny with the terrible colours of port. All this must the wild abstainer feel, as he rolls in the long soaking grass, kicks his ecstatic heels to heaven, and listens to the roaring rain. It is he, the water drinker, who ought to be the true bacchanal of the forests; for all the forests are drinking water. Moreover, the forests are apparently enjoying it: the trees rave and reel to and fro like drunken giants; they clash boughs as revellers clash cups; they roar undying thirst and howl the health of the world.

All around me as I write is a noise of Nature drinking: and Nature makes a noise when she is drinking, being by no means refined. If I count it Christian mercy to give a cup of cold water to a sufferer, shall I complain of these multitudinous cups of cold water handed round to all living things; a cup of water for every shrub; a cup of water for every weed? I would be ashamed to grumble at it. As Sir Philip Sidney said, their need is greater than mine—especially for water.

.   .   .   .   .   .

There is a wild garment that still carries nobly the name of a wild Highland clan: a clan come from those hills where rain is not so much an incident as an atmosphere. Surely every man of imagination must feel a tempestuous flame of Celtic romance spring up within him whenever he puts on a mackintosh. I could never reconcile myself to carrying an umbrella; it is a pompous Eastern business, carried over the heads of despots in the dry, hot lands. Shut up, an umbrella is an unmanageable walking-stick; open, it is an inadequate tent. For my part, I have no taste for pretending to be a walking pavilion; I think nothing of my hat, and precious little of my head. If I am to be protected against wet, it must be by some closer and more careless protection, something that I can forget altogether. It might be a Highland plaid. It might be that yet more Highland thing, a mackintosh.

And there is really something in the mackintosh of the military qualities of the Highlander. The proper cheap mackintosh has a blue and white sheen as of steel or iron; it gleams like armour. I like to think of it as the uniform of that ancient clan in some of its old and misty raids. I like to think of all the Macintoshes, in their mackintoshes, descending on some doomed Lowland village, their wet waterproofs flashing in the sun or moon. For indeed this is one of the real beauties of rainy weather, that while the amount of original and direct light is commonly lessened, the number of things that reflect light is unquestionably increased. There is less sunshine; but there are more shiny things; such beautifully shiny things as pools and puddles and mackintoshes. It is like moving in a world of mirrors.

.   .   .   .   .   .

And indeed this is the last and not the least gracious of the casual works of magic wrought by rain: that while it decreases light, yet it doubles it. If it dims the sky, it brightens the earth. It gives the roads (to the sympathetic eye) something of the beauty of Venice. Shallow lakes of water reiterate every detail of earth and sky; we dwell in a double universe. Sometimes walking upon bare and lustrous pavements, wet under numerous lamps, a man seems a black blot on all that golden looking-glass, and could fancy he was flying in a yellow sky. But wherever trees and towns hang head downwards in a pigmy puddle, the sense of Celestial topsy-turvydom is the same. This bright, wet, dazzling confusion of shape and shadow, of reality and reflection, will appeal strongly to any one with the transcendental instinct about this dreamy and dual life of ours. It will always give a man the strange sense of looking down at the skies.

PHONETIC SPELLING

A CORRESPONDENT asks me to make more lucid my remarks about phonetic spelling. I have no detailed objection to items of spelling reform: my objection is to a general principle; and it is this. It seems to me that what is really wrong with all modern and highly civilised language is that it does so largely consist of dead words. Half our speech consists of similes that remind us of no similarity; of pictorial phrases that call up no picture; of historical allusions the origin of which we have forgotten. Take any instance on which the eye happens to alight. I saw in the paper some days ago that the well-known leader of a certain religious party wrote to a supporter of his the following curious words: "I have not forgotten the talented way in which you held up the banner at Birkenhead." Taking the ordinary vague meaning of the word "talented," there is no coherency in the picture. The trumpets blow, the spears shake and glitter, and in the thick of the purple battle there stands a gentleman holding up a banner in a talented way. And when we come to the original force of the word "talent" the matter is worse: a talent is a Greek coin used in the New Testament as a symbol of the mental capital committed to an individual at birth. If the religious leader in question had really meant anything by his phrases, he would have been puzzled to know how a man could use a Greek coin to hold up a banner. But really he meant nothing by his phrases. "Holding up the banner" was to him a colourless term for doing the proper thing, and "talented" was a colourless term for doing it successfully.

Now my own fear touching anything in the way of phonetic spelling is that it would simply increase this tendency to use words as counters and not as coins. The original life in a word (as in the word "talent") burns low as it is: sensible spelling might extinguish it altogether. Suppose any sentence you like: suppose a man says, "Republics generally encourage holidays." It looks like the top line of a copy-book. Now, it is perfectly true that if you wrote that sentence exactly as it is pronounced, even by highly educated people, the sentence would run: "Ripubliks jenrally inkurrij hollidies." It looks ugly: but I have not the smallest objection to ugliness. My objection is that these four words have each a history and hidden treasures in them: that this history and hidden treasure (which we tend to forget too much as it is) phonetic spelling tends to make us forget altogether. Republic does not mean merely a mode of political choice. Republic (as we see when we look at the structure of the word) means the Public Thing: the abstraction which is us all.

A Republican is not a man who wants a Constitution with a President. A Republican is a man who prefers to think of Government as impersonal; he is opposed to the Royalist, who prefers to think of Government as personal. Take the second word, "generally." This is always used as meaning "in the majority of cases." But, again, if we look at the shape and spelling of the word, we shall see that "generally" means something more like "generically," and is akin to such words as "generation" or "regenerate." "Pigs are generally dirty" does not mean that pigs are, in the majority of cases, dirty, but that pigs as a race or genus are dirty, that pigs as pigs are dirty—an important philosophical distinction. Take the third word, "encourage." The word "encourage" is used in such modern sentences in the merely automatic sense of promote; to encourage poetry means merely to advance or assist poetry. But to encourage poetry means properly to put courage into poetry—a fine idea. Take the fourth word, "holidays." As long as that word remains, it will always answer the ignorant slander which asserts that religion was opposed to human cheerfulness; that word will always assert that when a day is holy it should also be happy. Properly spelt, these words all tell a sublime story, like Westminster Abbey. Phonetically spelt, they might lose the last traces of any such story. "Generally" is an exalted metaphysical term; "jenrally" is not. If you "encourage" a man, you pour into him the chivalry of a hundred princes; this does not happen if you merely "inkurrij" him. "Republics," if spelt phonetically, might actually forget to be public. "Holidays," if spelt phonetically, might actually forget to be holy.

Here is a case that has just occurred. A certain magistrate told somebody whom he was examining in court that he or she "should always be polite to the police." I do not know whether the magistrate noticed the circumstance, but the word "polite" and the word "police" have the same origin and meaning. Politeness means the atmosphere and ritual of the city, the symbol of human civilisation. The policeman means the representative and guardian of the city, the symbol of human civilisation. Yet it may be doubted whether the two ideas are commonly connected in the mind. It is probable that we often hear of politeness without thinking of a policeman; it is even possible that our eyes often alight upon a policeman without our thoughts instantly flying to the subject of politeness. Yet the idea of the sacred city is not only the link of them both, it is the only serious justification and the only serious corrective of them both. If politeness means too often a mere frippery, it is because it has not enough to do with serious patriotism and public dignity; if policemen are coarse or casual, it is because they are not sufficiently convinced that they are the servants of the beautiful city and the agents of sweetness and light. Politeness is not really a frippery. Politeness is not really even a thing merely suave and deprecating. Politeness is an armed guard, stern and splendid and vigilant, watching over all the ways of men; in other words, politeness is a policeman. A policeman is not merely a heavy man with a truncheon: a policeman is a machine for the smoothing and sweetening of the accidents of everyday existence. In other words, a policeman is politeness: a veiled image of politeness—sometimes impenetrably veiled. But my point is here that by losing the original idea of the city, which is the force and youth of both the words, both the things actually degenerate. Our politeness loses all manliness because we forget that politeness is only the Greek for patriotism. Our policemen lose all delicacy because we forget that a policeman is only the Greek for something civilised. A policeman should often have the functions of a knight-errant. A policeman should always have the elegance of a knight-errant. But I am not sure that he would succeed any the better in remembering this obligation of romantic grace if his name were spelt phonetically, supposing that it could be spelt phonetically. Some spelling-reformers, I am told, in the poorer parts of London do spell his name phonetically, very phonetically. They call him a "pleeceman." Thus the whole romance of the ancient city disappears from the word; and the policeman's reverent courtesy of demeanour deserts him quite suddenly. This does seem to me the case against any extreme revolution in spelling. If you spell a word wrong you have some temptation to think it wrong.

THE MAN AND HIS NEWSPAPER

At a little station, which I decline to specify, somewhere between Oxford and Guildford, I missed a connection or miscalculated a route in such manner that I was left stranded for rather more than an hour. I adore waiting at railway stations, but this was not a very sumptuous specimen. There was nothing on the platform except a chocolate automatic machine, which eagerly absorbed pennies but produced no corresponding chocolate, and a small paper-stall with a few remaining copies of a cheap imperial organ which we will call the *Daily Wire*. It does not matter which imperial organ it was, as they all say the same thing.

Though I knew it quite well already, I read it with gravity as I strolled out of the station and up the country road. It opened with the striking phrase that the Radicals were setting class against class. It went on to remark that nothing had contributed more to make our Empire happy and enviable, to create that obvious list of glories which you can supply for yourself, the prosperity of all classes in our great cities, our populous and growing villages, the success of our rule in Ireland, etc., etc., than the sound Anglo-Saxon readiness of all classes in the State "to work heartily hand-in-hand." It was this alone, the paper assured me, that had saved us from the horrors of the French Revolution. "It is easy for the Radicals," it went on very solemnly, "to make jokes about the dukes. Very few of these revolutionary gentlemen have given to the poor one half of the earnest thought, tireless unselfishness, and truly Christian patience that are given to them by the great landlords of this country. We are very sure that the English people, with their sturdy common sense, will prefer to be in the hands of English gentlemen rather than in the miry claws of Socialistic buccaneers."

.   .   .   .   .

Just when I had reached this point I nearly ran into a man. Despite the populousness and growth of our villages, he appeared to be the only man for miles, but the road up which I had wandered turned and narrowed with equal abruptness, and I nearly knocked him off the gate on which he was leaning. I pulled up to apologise, and since he seemed ready for society, and even pathetically pleased with it, I tossed the *Daily Wire* over a hedge and fell into speech with him. He wore a wreck of respectable clothes, and his face had that plebeian refinement which one sees in small tailors and watchmakers, in poor men of sedentary trades. Behind him a twisted group of winter trees stood up as gaunt and tattered as himself, but I do not think that the tragedy that he symbolised was a mere fancy from the spectral wood. There was a fixed look in his face which told that he was one of those who in keeping body and soul together have difficulties not only with the body, but also with the soul.

He was a Cockney by birth, and retained the touching accent of those streets from which I am an exile; but he had lived nearly all his life in this countryside; and he began to tell me the affairs of it in that formless, tail-foremost way in which the poor gossip about their great neighbours. Names kept coming and going in the narrative like charms or spells, unaccompanied by any biographical explanation. In particular the name of somebody called Sir Joseph multiplied itself with the omnipresence of a deity. I took Sir Joseph to be the principal landowner of the district; and as the confused picture unfolded itself, I began to form a definite and by no means pleasing picture of Sir Joseph. He was spoken of in a strange way, frigid and yet familiar, as a child might speak of a stepmother or an unavoidable nurse; something intimate, but by no means tender; something that was waiting for you by your own bed and board; that told you to do this and forbade you to do that, with a caprice that was cold and yet somehow personal. It did not appear that Sir Joseph was popular, but he was "a household word." He was not so much a public man as a sort of private god or omnipotence. The particular man to whom I spoke said he had "been in trouble," and that Sir Joseph had been "pretty hard on him."

And under the grey and silver cloudland, with a background of those frost-bitten and wind-tortured trees, the little Londoner told me a tale which, true or false, was as heartrending as Romeo and Juliet.

He had slowly built up in the village a small business as a photographer, and he was engaged to a girl at one of the lodges, whom he loved with passion. "I'm the sort that 'ad better marry," he said; and for all his frail figure I knew what he meant. But Sir Joseph, and especially Sir Joseph's wife, did not want a photographer in the village; it made the girls vain, or perhaps they disliked this particular photographer. He worked and worked until he had just enough to marry on honestly; and almost on the eve of his wedding the lease expired, and Sir Joseph appeared in all his glory. He refused to renew the lease; and the man went wildly elsewhere. But Sir Joseph was ubiquitous; and the whole of that place was barred against him. In all that country he could not find a shed to which to bring home his bride. The man appealed and explained; but he was disliked as a demagogue, as well as a photographer. Then it was as if a black cloud came across the winter sky; for I knew what was coming. I forget even in what words he told of Nature maddened and set free. But I still see, as in a photograph, the grey muscles of the winter trees standing out like tight ropes, as if all Nature were on the rack.

"She 'ad to go away," he said.

"Wouldn't her parents," I began, and hesitated on the word "forgive."

"Oh, her people forgave her," he said. "But Her Ladyship—"

"Her Ladyship made the sun and moon and stars," I said, impatiently. "So of course she can come between a mother and the child of her body."

"Well, it does seem a bit 'ard . . ." he began with a break in his voice.

"But, good Lord, man," I cried, "it isn't a matter of hardness! It's a matter of impious and indecent wickedness. If your Sir Joseph knew the passions he was playing with, he did you a wrong for which in many Christian countries he would have a knife in him."

The man continued to look across the frozen fields with a frown. He certainly told his tale with real resentment, whether it was true or false, or only exaggerated. He was certainly sullen and injured; but he did not seem to think of any avenue of escape. At last he said:

"Well, it's a bad world; let's 'ope there's a better one."

"Amen," I said. "But when I think of Sir Joseph, I understand how men have hoped there was a worse one."

Then we were silent for a long time and felt the cold of the day crawling up, and at last I said, abruptly:

"The other day at a Budget meeting, I heard—"

He took his elbows off the stile and seemed to change from head to foot like a man coming out of sleep with a yawn. He said in a totally new voice, louder but much more careless, "Ah, yes, sir, . . . this 'ere Budget . . . the Radicals are doing a lot of 'arm."

I listened intently, and he went on. He said with a sort of careful precision, "Settin' class against class; that's what I call it. Why, what's made our Empire except the readiness of all classes to work 'eartily 'and-in-'and?"

He walked a little up and down the lane and stamped with the cold. Then he said, "What I say is, what else kept us from the 'orrors of the French Revolution?"

My memory is good, and I waited in tense eagerness for the phrase that came next. "They may laugh at dukes; I'd like to see them 'alf as kind and Christian and patient as lots of the landlords are. Let me tell you, sir," he said, facing round at me with the final air of one launching a paradox. "The English people 'ave some common sense, and they'd rather be in the 'ands of gentlemen than in the claws of a lot of Socialist thieves."

I had an indescribable sense that I ought to applaud, as if I were at a public meeting. The insane separation in the man's soul between his experience and his ready-made theory was but a type of what covers a quarter of England. As he turned away, I saw the *Daily Wire* sticking out of his shabby pocket. He bade me farewell in quite a blaze of catchwords, and went stumping up the road. I saw his figure grow smaller and smaller in the great green landscape; even as the Free Man has grown smaller and smaller in the English countryside.

ON AMERICAN MORALS

AMERICA is sometimes offered to us, even by Americans (who ought to know better), as a moral example. There are indeed very real American virtues; but this virtuous attitude is hardly one of them. And if anyone wants to know what a welter of weakness and inconsequence the moral mind of America can sometimes be, he may be advised to look, not so much to the Crime Wage or the Charleston, as to the serious idealistic essays by highbrows and cultured critics, such as one by Miss Avis D. Carlson on "Wanted: a Substitute for Righteousness." By righteousness she means, of course, the narrow New England taboos; but she does not know it. For the inference she draws is that we should recognize frankly that "the standard of abstract right and wrong is moribund." This statement will seem less insane if we consider, somewhat curiously, what the standard of abstract right and wrong seems to mean—at least in her section of the States. It is a glimpse of an incredible world.

She takes the case of a young man brought up "in a home where there was an attempt to make the dogmatic cleavage of right and wrong." And what was the dogmatic cleavage? Ah, what indeed! His elders told him that some things were right and some wrong; and for some time he accepted this strange assertion. But when he leaves the home he finds that "apparently perfectly nice people do the things he has been taught to think evil." Then follows the revelation. "The flowerlike girl he envelops in a mist of romantic idealization smokes like an imp from the lower regions and pets like a movie vamp. The chum his heart yearns towards cultivates a hip-flask, etc." And this is what the writer calls a dogmatic cleavage between right and wrong!

The standard of abstract right and wrong apparently is this. That a girl by smoking a cigarette makes herself one of the company of the fiends in hell. That such an action is much the same as that of a sexual vampire. That a young man who continues to drink fermented liquor must necessarily be entirely "evil" and must deny the very existence of any difference between right and wrong. That is the "standard of abstract right and wrong" that is apparently taught in the American home. And it is perfectly obvious, on the face of it, that it is not a standard of abstract right and wrong at all. That is exactly what it is not. That is the very last thing that any clear-headed person would call it. It is not a standard; it is not abstract; it has not the vaguest notion of what is meant by right and wrong. It is a chaos of social and sentimental accidents and associations, some of them snobbish, all of them provincial, but, above all, nearly all of them concrete and connected with a materialistic prejudice against particular materials. To have a horror of tobacco is not to have an abstract standard of right; but exactly the opposite. It is to have no standard of right whatever; and to take certain local likes or dislikes as a substitute. We need not be very much surprised if the young man repudiates these meaningless vetoes as soon as he can; but if he thinks he is repudiating morality, he must be almost as muddle-headed as his father. And yet the writer in question calmly proposes that we should abolish all ideas of right and wrong, and abandon the whole human conception of a standard of abstract justice, because a boy in Boston cannot be induced to think that a nice girl is a devil when she smokes a cigarette.

If the rising generation were faced with no worse doubts and difficulties than this, it would not be very difficult to reconcile them to the traditions of truth and justice. But I think the episode worth mentioning, merely because it throws a ray of light on the moral condition of American culture, in the decay of Puritanism. And when next we are told that the idealism of America is to set a "standard" by which England must transform herself, it will be well to remember what is apparently meant by a standard and an ideal; and that the fire of that idealism seems both to begin and end in smoke.

Incidentally, I may say I can bear witness to this queer taboo about tobacco. Of course numberless Americans smoke numberless cigars; a great many others eat cigars, which seems to me a more occult pleasure. But there does exist an extraordinary idea that ethics are involved in some way; and many who smoke really disapprove of smoking. I remember once receiving two American interviewers on the same afternoon; there was a box of cigars in front of me and I offered one to each in turn. Their reaction (as they would probably call it) was very curious to watch. The first journalist stiffened suddenly and silently and declined in a very cold voice. He could not have conveyed more plainly that I had attempted to corrupt an honourable man with a foul and infamous indulgence; as if I were the Old Man of the Mountain offering him the hashish that would turn him into an assassin. The second reaction was even more remarkable. The second journalist first looked doubtful; then looked sly; then seemed to glance about him nervously, as if wondering whether we were alone, and then said with a sort of crestfallen and covert smile: "Well, Mr. Chesterton, I'm afraid I have the habit."

As I also have the habit, and have never been able to imagine how it could be connected with morality or immorality, I confess that I plunged with him deeply into an immoral life. In the course of our conversation, I found he was otherwise perfectly sane. He was quite intelligent about economics or architecture; but his moral sense seemed to have entirely disappeared. He really thought it was rather wicked to smoke. He had no "standard of abstract right and wrong"; in him it was not merely moribund; it was apparently dead. But anyhow, that is the point and that is the test. Nobody who has an abstract standard of right and wrong can possibly think it wrong to smoke a cigar. But he had a concrete standard of particular cut and dried customs of a particular tribe. Those who say that the Americans are largely descended from the American Indians might certainly make a case out of the suggestion that this mystical horror of material things is largely a barbaric sentiment. The Red Indian is said to have tried and condemned a tomahawk for committing a murder. In this he was certainly the prototype of the white man who curses a bottle because too much of it goes into a man. Prohibition is sometimes praised for its simplicity; on these lines it may be equally condemned for its savagery. But I myself do not say anything so absurd as that Americans are savages; nor do I think that it would matter much even if they were descended from savages. It is culture that counts and not ethnology; and the culture that is concerned here derives indirectly rather from New England than from Old America. Wherever it derives form, however, this is the thing to be noted about it: that it really does not seem to understand what is meant by a standard of right and wrong. It has a vague sentimental notion that certain habits were not suitable to the old log cabin or the old hometown. It has a vague utilitarian notion that certain habits are not directly useful in the new amalgamated stores or the new financial gambling-hell. If his aged mother or his economic master dislikes to see a young man hanging about with a pipe in his mouth, the action becomes a sin; or the nearest that such a moral philosophy can come to the idea of a sin. A man does not chop wood for the log hut by smoking; and a man does not make dividends for the Big Boss by smoking; and therefore a smoke has a smell as of something sinful. Of what the great theologians and moral philosophers have meant by a sin, these people have no more idea than a child drinking milk has of a great toxicologist analysing poisons. It may be to the credit of their virtue to be thus vague about vice. The man who is silly enough to say, when offered a cigarette, "I have no vices," may not always deserve the rapier-thrust of the reply given by the Italian Cardinal, "It is not a vice, or doubtless you would have it." But at least a Cardinal knows it is not a vice; which assists the clarity of his mind. But the lack of clear standards among those who vaguely think of it as a vice may yet be the beginning of much peril and oppression. My two American journalists, between them, may yet succeed in adding the sinfulness of cigars to the other curious things now part of the American Constitution.

I would therefore venture to say to Miss Avis Carlson (whose article in other respects contains much that is very thoughtful and valuable) that the quarrel in question does not arise from the Yankee Puritans having too much morality, but from their having too little. It does not arise from their drawing too hard and fast a line of distinction between right and wrong, but from their line being much too loose and indistinct. They go by associations and not by abstractions. Therefore they class smoking with vamping or a flask in the pocket with a sin in the soul. I hope at least that some of the Fundamentalists will succeed in being a little more fundamental than this. The men of Tennessee are supposed to be very anxious to draw the line between men and monkeys. They are also supposed by some to be rather too anxious to draw the line between black men and white men. May I be allowed to hope that they will succeed in drawing a rather more logical line between bad men and good men? Something of the difference and the difficulty may be seen by comparing the old Ku Klux Klan with the new Ku Klux Klan. The old secret society may have been justified or not; but it had a definite object: it was directed against somebody. The new secret society seems to have been directed against anybody; often against anybody who drank; in time, for all I know, against anybody who smoked. It is this sort of formless fanaticism that is the great danger of the American temperament; and it is well to insist that if men must persecute, they will be more clear-headed if they persecute for a creed.

ON TURNPIKES AND MEDIÆVALISM

OPENING my newspaper the other day, I saw a short but emphatic leaderette entitled "A Relic of Mediævalism." It expressed a profound indignation upon the fact that somewhere or other, in some fairly remote corner of this country, there is a turnpike-gate, with a toll. It insisted that this antiquated tyranny is insupportable, because it is supremely important that our road traffic should go very fast; presumably a little faster than it does. So it described the momentary delay in this place as a relic of mediævalism. I fear the future will look at that sentence, somewhat sadly and a little contemptuously, as a very typical relic of modernism. I mean it will be a melancholy relic of the only period in all human history when people were proud of being modern. For though today is always today and the moment is always modern, we are the only men in all history who fell back upon bragging about the mere fact that today is not yesterday. I fear that some in the future will explain it by saying that we had precious little else to brag about. For, whatever the mediæval faults, they went with one merit. Mediæval people never worried about being mediæval; and modern people do worry horribly about being modern.

To begin with, note the queer, automatic assumption that it must always mean throwing mud at a thing to call it a relic of mediævalism. The modern world contains a good many relics of mediævalism, and most of us would be surprised if the argument were logically enforced even against the things that are commonly called mediæval. We should express some regret if somebody blew up Westminster Abbey, because it is a relic of mediævalism. Doubts would trouble us if the Government burned all existing copies of Dante's *Divine Comedy* and Chaucer's *Canterbury Tales*, because they are quite certainly relics of mediævalism. We could not throw ourselves into unreserved and enthusiastic rejoicing even if the Tower of Giotto were destroyed as a relic of mediævalism. And only just lately, in Oxford and Paris (themselves, alas! relics of mediævalism), there has been a perverse and pedantic revival of the Thomist Philosophy and the logical method of the mediæval Schoolmen. Similarly, curious and restless minds, among the very youngest artists and art critics, have unaccountably gone back even further into the barbaric period than the limit of the Tower of Giotto, and are even now telling us to look back to the austerity of Cimabue and the Byzantine diagrams of the Dark Ages. These relics must be more mediæval even than mediævalism.

But, in fact, this queer phase would not cover only what is commonly called mediævalism. If a relic of mediævalism only means something that has come down to us from mediæval times, such writers would probably be surprised at the size and solidity of the relics. If I told these honest pressmen that the Press is a relic of mediævalism, they would probably prove their love of a cliché by accusing me of a paradox. But it is at least certain that the Printing Press is a relic of mediævalism. It was discovered and established by entirely mediæval men, steeped in mediæval ideas, stuffed with the religion and social spirit of the Middle Ages. There are no more typically mediæval words than those noble words of the eulogy that was pronounced by the great English printer on the great English poet; the words of Caxton upon Chaucer. If I were to say that Parliament is a relic of mediævalism, I should be on even stronger ground; for, while the Press did at least come at the end of the Middle Ages, the Parliaments came much more nearly at the beginning of the Middle Ages. They began, I think, in Spain and the provinces of the Pyrenees; but our own traditional date, connecting them with the revolt of Simon de Montfort, if not strictly accurate, does roughly represent the time. I need not say that half the great educational foundations, not only Oxford and Cambridge, but Glasgow and Paris, are relics of mediævalism. It would seem rather hard on the poor journalistic reformer if he is not allowed to pull down a little turnpike-gate till he has proved his right to pull down all these relics of mediævalism.

Next we have, of course, the very considerable historic doubt about whether the turnpike-gate is a relic of mediævalism. I do not know what was the date of this particular turnpike; but turnpikes and tolls of that description were perhaps most widely present, most practically enforced, or, at least, most generally noted, in the eighteenth century. When Pitt and Dundas, both of them roaring drunk, jumped over a turnpike-gate and were fired at with a blunderbuss, I hope nobody will suggest that those two great politicians were relics of mediævalism. Nobody surely could be more modern than Pitt and Dundas, for one of them was a great financial statesman, depending entirely on the bankers, and the other was a swindler. It is possible, of course, that some such local toll was really mediæval, but I rather doubt whether the journalist even inquired whether it was mediæval. He probably regards everything that happened before the time of Jazz and the Yellow Press as mediæval. For him mediæval only means old, and old only means bad; so that we come to the last question, which ought to have been the first question, of whether a turnpike really is necessarily bad.

If we were really relics of mediævalism—that is, if we had really been taught to think—we should have put that question first, and discussed whether a thing is bad or good before discussing whether it is modern or mediæval. There is no space to discuss it here at length, but a very simple test in the matter may be made. The aim and effect of tolls is simply this: that those who use the roads shall pay for the roads. As it is, the poor people of a district, including those who never stir from their villages, and hardly from their firesides, pay to maintain roads which are ploughed up and torn to pieces by the cars and lorries of rich men and big businesses, coming from London and the distant cities. It is not self-evident that this is a more just arrangement than that by which wayfarers pay to keep up the way, even if that arrangement were a relic of mediævalism.

Lastly, we might well ask, is it indeed so certain that our roads suffer from the slowness of petrol traffic; and that, if we can only make every sort of motor go faster and faster, we shall all be saved at last? That motors are more important than men is doubt-less an admitted principle of a truly modern philosophy; never-theless, it might be well to keep some sort of reasonable ratio be-tween them, and decide exactly how many human beings should be killed by each car in the course of each year. And I fear that a mere policy of the acceleration of traffic may take us beyond the normal modern recognition of murder into something re-sembling a recognition of massacre. And about this, I for one still have a scruple; which is probably a relic of mediævalism.

A CAB RIDE ACROSS COUNTRY

Sown somewhere far off in the shallow dales of Hertfordshire there lies a village of great beauty, and I doubt not of admirable virtue, but of eccentric and unbalanced literary taste, which asked the present writer to come down to it on Sunday after-noon and give an address.

Now it was very difficult to get down to it at all on Sunday afternoon, owing to the indescribable state into which our na-tional laws and customs have fallen in connection with the seventh day. It is not Puritanism; it is simply anarchy. I should have some sympathy with the Jewish Sabbath, if it were a Jew-ish Sabbath, and that for three reasons; first, that religion is an intrinsically sympathetic thing; second, that I cannot conceive any religion worth calling a religion without a fixed and mate-rial observance; and third, that the particular observance of sit-ting still and doing no work is one that suits my temperament down to the ground.

But the absurdity of the modern English convention is that it does not let a man sit still; it only perpetually trips him up when it has forced him to walk about. Our Sabbatarianism does not forbid us to ask a man in Battersea to come and talk in Hert-fordshire; it only prevents his getting there. I can understand that a deity might be worshipped with joys, with flowers, and fire-works in the old European style. I can understand that a deity might be worshipped with sorrows. But I cannot imagine any deity being worshipped with inconveniences. Let the good Mos-lem go to Mecca, or let him abide in his tent, according to his feelings for religious symbols. But surely Allah cannot see any-thing particularly dignified in his servant being misled by the time-table, finding that the old Mecca express is not running, missing his connection at Bagdad, or having to wait three hours in a small side station outside Damascus.

So it was with me on this occasion. I found there was no tele-graph service at all to this place; I found there was only one weak thread of train-service. Now if this had been the authority of real English religion, I should have submitted to it at once. If I believed that the telegraph clerk could not send the telegram because he was at that moment rigid in an ecstasy of prayer, I should think all telegrams unimportant in comparison. If I could believe that railway porters when relieved from their duties rushed with passion to the nearest place of worship, I should say that all lectures and everything else ought to give way to such a consideration. I should not complain if the national faith forbade me to make any appointments of labour or self-expression on the Sabbath. But, as it is, it only tells me that I may very probably keep the Sabbath by not keeping the appointment.

But I must resume the real details of my tale. I found that there was only one train in the whole of that Sunday by which I could even get within several hours or several miles of the time or place. I therefore went to the telephone, which is one of my favourite toys, and down which I have shouted many valuable, but prematurely arrested, monologues upon art and morals. I re-member a mild shock of surprise when I discovered that one could use the telephone on Sunday; I did not expect it to be cut off, but I expected it to buzz more than on ordinary days, to the advancement of our national religion. Through this instrument, in fewer words than usual, and with a comparative economy of epigram, I ordered a taxi-cab to take me to the railway station. I have not a word to say in general either against telephones or taxi-cabs; they seem to me two of the purest and most poetic of the creations of modern scientific civilisation. Unfortunately, when the taxi-cab started, it did exactly what modern scientific civilisation has done—it broke down. The result of this was that when I arrived at King's Cross my only train was gone; there was a Sabbath calm in the station, a calm in the eyes of the porters, and in my breast, if calm at all, if any calm, a calm despair.

There was not, however, very much calm of any sort in my breast on first making the discovery; and it was turned to blinding horror when I learnt that I could not even send a telegram to the organisers of the meeting. To leave my entertainers in the lurch was sufficiently exasperating; to leave them without any intimation was simply low. I reasoned with the official. I said: "Do you really mean to say that if my brother were dying and my mother in this place, I could not communicate with her?" He was a man of literal and laborious mind; he asked me if my brother was dying. I answered that he was in excellent and even offensive health, but that I was inquiring upon a question of principle. What would happen if England were invaded, or if I alone knew how to turn aside a comet or an earthquake. He waved away these hypotheses in the most irresponsible spirit, but he was quite certain that telegrams could not reach this particular village. Then something exploded in me; that element of the outrageous which is the mother of all adventures sprang up ungovernable, and I decided that I would not be a cad merely because some of my remote ancestors had been Calvinists. I would keep my appointment if I lost all my money and all my wits. I went out into the quiet London street, where my quiet London cab was still waiting for its fare in the cold and misty morning. I placed myself comfortably in the London cab and told the

London driver to drive me to the other end of Hertfordshire. And he did.

. . . . .

I shall not forget that drive. It was doubtful whether, even in a motor-cab, the thing was possible with any consideration for the driver, not to speak of some slight consideration for the people in the road. I urged the driver to eat and drink something before he started, but he said (with I know not what pride of profession or delicate sense of adventure) that he would rather do it when we arrived—if we ever did. I was by no means so delicate; I bought a varied selection of pork-pies at a little shop that was open (why was that shop open?—it is all a mystery), and ate them as we went along. The beginning was sombre and irritating. I was annoyed, not with people, but with things, like a baby; with the motor for breaking down and with Sunday for being Sunday. And the sight of the northern slums expanded and ennobled, but did not decrease, my gloom: Whitechapel has an Oriental gaudiness in its squalour; Battersea and Camberwell have an indescribable bustle of democracy; but the poor parts of North London . . . well, perhaps I saw them wrongly under that ashen morning and on that foolish errand.

It was one of those days which more than once this year broke the retreat of winter; a winter day that began too late to be spring. We were already clear of the obstructing crowds and quickening our pace through a borderland of market and gardens and isolated public-houses, when the grey showed golden patches and a good light began to glitter on everything. The cab went quicker and quicker. The open land whirled wider and wider; but I did not lose my sense of being battled with and thwarted that I had felt in the thronged slums. Rather the feeling increased, because of the great difficulty of space and time. The faster went the car, the fiercer and thicker I felt the fight.

The whole landscape seemed charging at me—and just missing me. The tall, shining grass went by like showers of arrows; the very trees seemed like lances hurled at my heart, and shaving

it by a hair's breadth. Across some vast, smooth valley I saw a
beech-tree by the white road stand up little and defiant. It grew
bigger and bigger with blinding rapidity. It charged me like a
tilting knight, seemed to hack at my head, and pass by. Sometimes when we went round a curve of road, the effect was yet
more awful. It seemed as if some tree or windmill swung round
to smite like a boomerang. The sun by this time was a blazing
fact; and I saw that all Nature is chivalrous and militant. We do
wrong to seek peace in Nature; we should rather seek the nobler
sort of war; and see all the trees as green banners.

I gave my address, arriving just when everybody was decid-
ing to leave. When my cab came reeling into the market-place
they decided, with evident disappointment, to remain. Over the
lecture I draw a veil. When I came back home I was called to
the telephone, and a meek voice expressed regret for the failure
of the motor-cab, and even said something about any reasonable
payment. "Payment!" I cried down the telephone. "Whom can
I pay for my own superb experience? What is the usual charge
for seeing the clouds shattered by the sun? What is the market
price of a tree blue on the sky-line and then blinding white in
the sun? Mention your price for that windmill that stood behind the hollyhocks in the garden. Let me pay you for . . ."
Here it was, I think, that we were cut off.

THE ARCHITECT OF SPEARS

THE other day, in the town of Lincoln, I suffered an optical illusion which accidentally revealed to me the strange greatness of
the Gothic architecture. Its secret is not, I think, satisfactorily
explained in most of the discussions on the subject. It is said that
the Gothic eclipses the classical by a certain richness and complexity, at once lively and mysterious. This is true; but Oriental

decoration is equally rich and complex, yet it awakens a widely different sentiment. No man ever got out of a Turkey carpet the emotions that he got from a cathedral tower. Over all the exquisite ornament of Arabia and India there is the presence of something stiff and heartless, of something tortured and silent. Dwarfed trees and crooked serpents, heavy flowers and hunchbacked birds accentuate by the very splendour and contrast of their colour the servility and monotony of their shapes. It is like the vision of a sneering sage, who sees the whole universe as a pattern. Certainly no one ever felt like this about Gothic, even if he happens to dislike it. Or, again, some will say that it is the liberty of the Middle Ages in the use of the comic or even the coarse that makes the Gothic more interesting than the Greek. There is more truth in this; indeed, there is real truth in it. Few of the old Christian cathedrals would have passed the Censor of Plays. We talk of the inimitable grandeur of the old cathedrals; but indeed it is rather their gaiety that we do not dare to imitate. We should be rather surprised if a chorister suddenly began singing "Bill Bailey" in church. Yet that would be only doing in music what the mediævals did in sculpture. They put into a Miserere seat the very scenes that we put into a music-hall song: comic domestic scenes similar to the spilling of the beer and the hanging out of the washing. But though the gaiety of Gothic is one of its features, it also is not the secret of its unique effect. We see a domestic topsy-turvydom in many Japanese sketches. But delightful as these are, with their fairy tree-tops, paper houses, and toddling, infantile inhabitants, the pleasure they give is of a kind quite different from the joy and energy of the gargoyles. Some have even been so shallow and illiterate as to maintain that our pleasure in mediæval building is a mere pleasure in what is barbaric, in what is rough, shapeless, or crumbling like the rocks. This can be dismissed after the same fashion; South Sea idols, with painted eyes and radiating bristles, are a delight to the eye; but they do not affect it in at all the same way as Westminster Abbey. Some again (going to another and almost equally foolish extreme) ignore the coarse and comic in mediævalism; and praise the pointed arch only for its utter purity and simplicity, as of a saint with his hands joined in prayer. Here, again, the uniqueness is missed. There are Renaissance things (such as the ethereal silvery drawings of Raphael), there are even pagan things (such as the Praying Boy) which express as fresh and austere a piety. None of these explanations explain. And I never saw what was the real point about Gothic till I came into the town of Lincoln, and saw it behind a row of furniture-vans.

I did not know they were furniture-vans; at the first glance and in the smoky distance I thought they were a row of cottages. A low stone wall cut off the wheels, and the vans were somewhat of the same colour as the yellowish clay or stone of the buildings around them. I had come across that interminable Eastern plain which is like the open sea, and all the more so because the one small hill and tower of Lincoln stands up in it like a light-house. I had climbed the sharp, crooked streets up to this ecclesiastical citadel; just in front of me was a flourishing and richly coloured kitchen garden; beyond that was the low stone wall; beyond that the row of vans that looked like houses; and beyond and above that, straight and swift and dark, light as a flight of birds, and terrible as the Tower of Babel, Lincoln Cathedral seemed to rise out of human sight.

As I looked at it I asked myself the questions that I have asked here; what was the soul in all those stones? They were varied, but it was not variety; they were solemn, but it was not solemnity; they were farcical, but it was not farce. What is it in them that thrills and soothes a man of our blood and history, that is not there in an Egyptian pyramid or an Indian temple or a Chinese pagoda? All of a sudden the vans I had mistaken for cottages began to move away to the left. In the start this gave to my eye and mind I really fancied that the Cathedral was moving towards the right. The two huge towers seemed to start striding across the plain like the two legs of some giant whose body was covered with the clouds. Then I saw what it was.

The truth about Gothic is, first, that it is alive, and second, that it is on the march. It is the Church Militant; it is the only fighting architecture. All its spires are spears at rest; and all its stones are stones asleep in a catapult. In that instant of illusion, I could hear the arches clash like swords as they crossed each other. The mighty and numberless columns seemed to go swinging by like the huge feet of imperial elephants. The graven foliage wreathed and blew like banners going into battle; the silence was deafening with all the mingled noises of a military march; the great bell shook down, as the organ shook up its thunder. The thirsty-throated gargoyles shouted like trumpets from all the roofs and pinnacles as they passed; and from the lectern in the core of the cathedral the eagle of the awful evangelist clashed his wings of brass.

And amid all the noises I seemed to hear the voice of a man shouting in the midst like one ordering regiments hither and thither in the fight; the voice of the great half-military master-builder; the architect of spears. I could almost fancy he wore armour while he made that church; and I knew indeed that, under a scriptural figure, he had borne in either hand the trowel and the sword.

I could imagine for the moment that the whole of that house of life had marched out of the sacred East, alive and interlocked, like an army. Some Eastern nomad had found it solid and silent in the red circle of the desert. He had slept by it as by a world-forgotten pyramid; and been woke at midnight by the wings of stone and brass, the tramping of the tall pillars, the trumpets of the waterspouts. On such a night every snake or sea-beast must have turned and twisted in every crypt or corner of the architecture. And the fiercely coloured saints marching eternally in the flamboyant windows would have carried their glorioles like torches across dark lands and distant seas; till the whole mountain of music and darkness and lights descended roaring on the lonely Lincoln hill. So for some hundred and sixty seconds I saw the battle-beauty of the Gothic; then the last furniture-van shifted itself away; and I saw only a church tower in a quiet English town, round which the English birds were floating.

THE BROKEN RAINBOW

I WILL take one case that will serve both as symbol and example: the case of color. We hear the realists (those sentimental fellows) talking about the gray streets and the gray lives of the poor. But whatever the poor streets are they are not gray; but motley, striped, spotted, piebald and patched like a quilt. Hoxton is not æsthetic enough to be monochrome; and there is nothing of the Celtic twilight about it. As a matter of fact, a London gutter-boy walks unscathed among furnaces of color. Watch him walk along a line of hoardings, and you will see him now against glowing green, like a traveler in a tropic forest; now black like a bird against the burning blue of the Midi; now *passant* across a field gules, like the golden leopards of England. He ought to understand the irrational rapture of that cry of Mr. Stephen Phillips about "that bluer blue, that greener green." There is no blue much bluer than Reckitt's Blue and no blacking blacker than Day and Martin's; no more emphatic yellow than that of Colman's Mustard. If, despite this chaos of color, like a shattered rainbow, the spirit of the small boy is not exactly intoxicated with art and culture, the cause certainly does not lie in universal grayness or the mere starving of his senses. It lies in the fact that the colors are presented in the wrong connection, on the wrong scale, and, above all, from the wrong motive. It is not colors he lacks, but a philosophy of colors. In short, there is nothing wrong with Reckitt's Blue except that it is not Reckitt's. Blue does not belong to Reckitt, but to the sky; black does not belong to Day and Martin, but to the abyss. Even the finest posters are only very little things on a very large scale. There is something specially irritant in this way about the iteration of advertisements of mustard: a condiment, a small luxury; a thing in its nature not to be taken in quantity. There is a special irony in these starving streets to see such a great deal of mustard to such very little meat. Yellow is a bright pigment; mustard is a pungent pleasure. But to look at these seas of yellow is to be' like a man who should swallow gallons of mustard. He would either die, or lose the taste of mustard altogether.

Now suppose we compare these gigantic trivialities on the hoardings with those tiny and tremendous pictures in which the mediævals recorded their dreams; little pictures where the blue sky is hardly longer than a single sapphire, and the fires of judgment only a pigmy patch of gold. The difference here is not merely that poster art is in its nature more hasty than illumination art; it is not even merely that the ancient artist was serving the Lord while the modern artist is serving the lords. It is that the old artist contrived to convey an impression that colors really were significant and precious things, like jewels and talismanic stones. The color was often arbitrary; but it was always authoritative. If a bird was blue, if a tree was golden, if a fish was silver, if a cloud was scarlet, the artist managed to convey that these colors were important and almost painfully intense; all the red red-hot and all the gold tried in the fire. Now that is the spirit touching color which the schools must recover and protect if they are really to give the children any imaginative appetite or pleasure in the thing. It is not so much an indulgence in color; it is rather, if anything, a sort of fiery thrift. It fenced in a green field in heraldry as straitly as a green field in peasant proprietorship. It would not fling away gold leaf any more than gold coin; it would not heedlessly pour out purple or crimson, any more than it would spill good wine or shed blameless blood. That is the hard task before educationists in this special matter; they have to teach people to relish colors like liquors. They have the heavy business of turning drunkards into wine tasters. If even the twentieth century succeeds in doing these things, it will almost catch up with the twelfth.

The principle covers, however, the whole of modern life. Morris and the merely æsthetic mediævalists always indicated that a crowd in the time of Chaucer would have been brightly clad and glittering, compared with a crowd in the time of Queen Victoria. I am not so sure that the real distinction is here. There would be brown frocks of friars in the first scene as well as brown bowlers of clerks in the second. There would be purple plumes of factory girls in the second scene as well as purple lenten vestments in the first. There would be white waistcoats against white ermine; gold watch chains against gold lions. The real difference is this: that the brown earth-color of the monk's coat was instinctively chosen to express labor and humility, whereas the brown color of the clerk's hat was not chosen to express anything. The monk did mean to say that he robed himself in dust. I am sure the clerk does not mean to say that he crowned himself with clay. He is not putting dust on his head, as the only diadem of man. Purple, at once rich and somber, does suggest a triumph temporarily eclipsed by a tragedy. But the factory girl does not intend her hat to express a triumph temporarily eclipsed by a tragedy; far from it. White ermine was meant to express moral purity; white waistcoats were not. Gold lions do suggest a flaming magnanimity; gold watch chains do not. The point is not that we have lost the material hues, but that we have lost the trick of turning them to the best advantage. We are not like children who have lost their paint-box and are left alone with a gray lead-pencil. We are like children who have mixed all the colors in the paint-box together and lost the paper of instructions. Even then (I do not deny) one has some fun.

Now this abundance of colors and loss of a color scheme is a pretty perfect parable of all that is wrong with our modern ideals and especially with our modern education. It is the same with ethical education, economic education, every sort of education. The growing London child will find no lack of highly controversial teachers who will teach him that geography means painting the map red; that economics means taxing the foreigner;

that patriotism means the peculiarly un-English habit of flying a flag on Empire Day. In mentioning these examples specially I do not mean to imply that there are no similar crudities and popular fallacies upon the other political side. I mention them because they constitute a very special and arresting feature of the situation. I mean this, that there were always Radical revolutionists; but now there are Tory revolutionists also. The modern Conservative no longer conserves. He is avowedly an innovator. Thus all the current defenses of the House of Lords which describe it as a bulwark against the mob, are intellectually done for; the bottom has fallen out of them; because on five or six of the most turbulent topics of the day, the House of Lords is a mob itself; and exceedingly likely to behave like one.

THE MEANING OF MOCK TURKEY

HAVING lately taken part in a pageant of Nursery Rhymes, in the character of Old King Cole, I meditated not so much on the glorious past of the great kingdom of Colchester, as on the more doubtful future of Nursery Rhymes. The Modern Movements cannot produce a nursery rhyme; it is one of the many such things they cannot even be conceived as doing. But if they cannot create the nursery rhyme, will they destroy it? The new poets have already abolished rhyme; and presumably the new educationalists will soon abolish nurseries. Or if they do not destroy, will they reform; which is worse? Nursery rhymes are a positive network of notions and allusions of which the enlightened disapprove. To take only my own allotted rhyme as an example, some might think the very mention of a king a piece of reactionary royalism, inconsistent with that democratic self-determination we all enjoy under some five Controllers and a committee of the Cabinet. Perhaps in the amended version he will be called President Cole. Probably he will be confused with

Mr. G. D. H. Cole, the first President of the Guild Socialistic Republic. With the greatest admiration for Mr. Cole, I cannot quite picture him as so festive a figure; and I incline to think that the same influences will probably eliminate the festivity. It is said that America, having already tried to abolish the bowl, is now attempting to abolish the pipe. After that it might very reasonably go on to abolish the fiddlers; for music can be far more maddening than wine. Tolstoy, the only consistent prophet of the Simple Life, did really go on to denounce music as a mere drug. Anyhow, it is quite intolerable that the innocent minds of children should be poisoned with the idea of anybody calling for his pipe and his bowl. There will have to be some other version, such as: "He called for his milk and he called for his lozenge," or whatever form of bodily pleasure is still permitted to mankind. This particular verse will evidently have to be altered a great deal; it is founded on so antiquated a philosophy, that I fear even the alteration will not be easy or complete. I am not sure, for instance, that there is not a memory of animism and spiritism in the very word "soul," used in calling the monarch a merry old soul. It would seem that some other simple phrase, such as "a merry old organism," might be used with advantage. Indeed it would save more advantages than one; for if the reader will say the amended line in a flowing and lyrical manner, he cannot but observe that the experiment has burst the fetters of formal metre, and achieved one of these larger and lovelier melodies that we associate with *vers libre*.

It is needless to note the numberless other examples of nursery rhymes to which the same criticism applies. Some of the other cases are even more shocking to the true scientific spirit. For instance, in the typically old-world rhyme of "Girls and boys come out to play," there appear the truly appalling words: "Leave your supper and leave your sleep." As the great medical reformer of our day observed, in a striking and immortal phrase, "All Eugenists are agreed upon the importance of sleep." The case of supper may be more complex and controversial. If the supper were a really hygienic and wholesome supper, it might not be so difficult to leave it. But it is obvious that the whole vision which the rhyme calls up is utterly incompatible with a wise educational supervision. It is a wild vision of children playing in the streets by moonlight, for all the world as if they were fairies. Moonlight, like music, is credited with a power of upsetting the reason; and it is at least obvious that the indulgence is both unseasonable and unreasonable. No scientific reformer desires hasty and destructive action; for his reform is founded on that evolution which has produced the anthropoid from the amœba, a process which none have ever stigmatized as hasty. But when the eugenist recalls the reckless and romantic love affairs encouraged by such moonlight, he will have to consider seriously the problem of abolishing the moon.

But indeed I have much more sympathy with the simplicity of the baby who cries for the moon than with the sort of simplicity that dismisses the moon as all moonshine. And indeed I think that these two antagonistic types of simplicity are perhaps the pivotal terms of the present transition. It is a new thing called the Simple Life against an older thing which may be called the Simple Soul; possibly exemplified, so far as nursery rhymes are concerned, by the incident of Simple Simon. I prefer the old Simple Simon, who, though ignorant of the economic theory of exchange, had at least a positive and poetic enthusiasm for pies. I think him far wiser than the new Simple Simon, who simplifies his existence by means of a perverse and pedantic antipathy to pies. It is unnecessary to add that this philosophy of pies is applicable with peculiar force to mince-pies; and thus to the whole of the Christmas tradition which descended from the first carols to the imaginative world of Dickens. The morality of that tradition is much too simple and obvious to be understood to-day. Awful as it may seem to many modern people, it means no less than that Simple Simon should have his pies, even in the absence of his pennies.

But the philosophy of the two Simple Simons is plain enough.

The former is an expansion of simplicity towards complexity; Simon, conscious that he cannot himself make pies, approaches them with an ardour not unmixed with awe. But the latter is a reaction of complexity towards simplicity; in other words the other Simon refuses pies for various reasons, often including the fact that he has eaten too many of them. Most of the Simple Life as we see it to-day is, of course, a thing having this character of the surfeit or satiety of Simon, when he has become less simple and certainly less greedy. This reaction may take two diverse forms; it may send Simon searching for more and more expensive and extravagant confectionery, or it may reduce him to nibbling at some new kind of nut biscuit. For it may be noted, in passing, that it probably will not reduce him to eating dry bread. The Simple Life never accepts anything that is simple in the sense of self-evident and familiar. The thing must be uncommonly simple; it must not be simply common. Its philosophy must be something higher than the ordinary breakfast table, and something drier than dry bread. The usual process, as I have observed it in vegetarian and other summaries, seems in one sense indeed to be simple enough. The pie-man produces what looks like the same sort of pie, or is supposed to look like it; only it has thinner crust outside and nothing at all inside. Then instead of asking Simple Simon for a penny he asks him for a pound, or possibly a guinea or a five-pound note. And what is strangest of all, the customer is often so singularly Simple a Simon that he pays for it. For that is perhaps the final and most marked difference between Simon of the Simple Spirit and Simon of the Simple Life. It is the fact that the ardent and appreciative Simon was not in possession of a penny. The more refined and exalted Simon is generally in possession of far too many pennies. He is often very rich and needs to be; for the drier and thinner and emptier are the pies, the more he is charged for them. But this alone will reveal another side of the same paradox; and if it be possible to spend a lot of money on the Simple Life, it is also possible to make a great deal of money out of it. There are several self-advertisers doing very well out of the new self-denial. But wealth is always at one end of it or the other; and that is the great difference between the two Simons. Perhaps it is the difference between Simon Peter and Simon Magus.

I have before me a little pamphlet in which the most precise directions are given for a Mock Turkey, for a vegetarian mince-pie, and for a cautious and hygienic Christmas pudding. I have never quite understood why it should be a part of the Simple Life to have anything so deceptive and almost conspiratorial as an imitation turkey. The coarse and comic alderman may be expected, in his festive ribaldry, to mock a turtle; but surely a lean and earnest humanitarian ought not to mock a turkey. Nor do I understand the theory of the imitation in its relation to the ideal. Surely one who thinks meat eating mere cannibalism ought not to arrange vegetables so as to look like an animal. It is as if a converted cannibal in the Sandwich Islands were to arrange joints of meat in the shape of a missionary. The missionaries would surely regard the proceedings of their convert with something less than approval, and perhaps with something akin to alarm. But the consistency of these concessions I will leave on one side, because I am not here concerned with the concessions but with the creed itself. And I am concerned with the creed not merely as affecting its practice in diet or cookery but its general theory. For the compilers of the little book before me are great on philosophy and ethics. There are whole pages about brotherhood and fellowship and happiness and healing. In short, as the writer observes, we have "also some Mental Helps, as set forth in the flood of Psychology Literature to-day—but raised to a higher plane." It may be a little risky to set a thing forth in a flood, or a little difficult to raise a flood to a higher plane; but there is behind these rather vague expressions a very real modern intelligence and point of view, common to considerable numbers of cultivated people, and well worthy of some further study.

Under the title of "How to Think" there are twenty-four rules of which the first few are: "Empty Your Mind," "Think

of the Best Things," "Appreciate," "Analyze," "Prepare Physically," "Prepare Mentally," and so on. I have met some earnest
students of this school, who had apparently entered on this
course, but at the time of our meeting had only graduated so far
as the fulfilment of the first rule. It was more obvious, on the
whole, that they had succeeded in the preliminary process of
emptying the mind than that they had as yet thought of the best
things, or analyzed or appreciated anything in particular. But
there were others, I willingly admit, who had really thought of
certain things in a genuinely thoughtful fashion, though whether
they were really the best things might involve a difference of
opinion between us. Still, so far as they are concerned, it is a
school of thought, and therefore worth thinking about. Having
been able to this extent to appreciate, I will now attempt to
analyze. I have attempted to discover in my own mind where
the difference between us really lies, apart from all these superficial jests and journalistic points; to ask myself why it is exactly
that their ideal vegetarian differs so much from my ideal Christian. And the result of the concentrated contemplation of their
ideal is, I confess, a somewhat impatient forward plunge in the
progress of their initiations. I am strongly disposed to "Prepare
Physically" for a conflict with the ideal vegetarian, with the only
hope of hitting him on the nose. In one of Mr. P. G. Wode-
house's stories the vegetarian rebukes his enemy for threatening
to skin him, by reminding him that man should only think beautiful thoughts; to which the enemy gives the unanswerable answer: "Skinning you is a beautiful thought." In the same way I
am quite prepared to think of the best things; but I think hitting
the ideal vegetarian on the nose would be one of the best things
in the world. This may be an extreme example; but it involves
a much more serious principle. What such philosophers often
forget is that among the best things in the world are the very
things which their placid universalism forbids; and that there
is nothing better or more beautiful than a noble hatred. I do not
profess to feel it for them; but they themselves do not seem to

feel it for anything.

But as my new idealistic instructor tells me to analyze, I will attempt to analyze. In the ordinary way it would perhaps be enough to say that I do not like his ideals, and that I prefer my own, as I should say I did not like the taste of nut cutlet so much as the taste of veal cutlet. But just as it is possible to resolve the food into formulas about proteids, so it is partly possible to resolve the religious preference into formulas about principles. The most we can hope to do is to find out which of these principles are the first principles. And in this connexion I should like to speak a little more seriously, and even a little more respectfully, of the formulas about emptying the mind. I do not deny that it is sometimes a good thing to empty the mind of the mere accumulation of secondary and tertiary impressions. If what is meant is something which a friend of mine once called "a mental spring clean," then I can see what it means. But the most drastic spring clean in a house does not generally wash away the house. It does not tear down the roof like a cobweb, or pluck up the walls like weeds. And the true formula is not so much to empty the mind as to discover that we cannot empty the mind, by emptying it as much as we can. In other words we always came back to certain fundamentals which are convictions, because we can hardly even conceive their contraries. But it is the paradox of human language that though these truths are in a manner past all parallel, hard and clear, yet any attempt to talk about them always has the appearance of being hazy and elusive.

Now this antagonism, when thus analyzed, seems to me to arise from one ultimate thing at the back of the minds of these men; that they believe in taking the body seriously. The body is a sort of pagan god, though the pagans are more often stoics than epicureans. To begin with, it is itself a beginning. The body, if not the creator of the soul in Heaven, is regarded as the practical producer of it on earth. In this their materialism is the very foundation of their asceticism. They wish us to consume clean fruit and clear water that our minds may be clear or our lives clean. The body is a sort of magical factory where these things go in as vegetables and come out as virtues. Thus digestion has the first sign of a deity; that of being an origin. It has the next sign of a deity; that if it is satisfied other things do not matter, or at any rate other things follow in their place. And so, they would say, the services of the body should be serious and not grotesque; and its smallest hints should be taken as terrible warnings. Art has a place in it because the body must be draped like an altar; and science is paraded in it because the service must be in Latin or Greek or some hieratic tongue. I quite understand these things surrounding a god or an altar; but I do not happen to worship at that altar or to believe in that god. I do not think the body ought to be taken seriously; I think it is far safer and saner when it is taken comically and even coarsely. And I think that when the body is given a holiday, as it is in a great feast, I think it should be set free not merely for wisdom but for folly, not merely to dance but to turn head over heels. In short, when it is really allowed to exaggerate its own pleasures, it ought also to exaggerate its own absurdity. The body has its own rank, and its own rights, and its own place under government; but the body is not the king but rather the Court Jester. And the human and historical importance of the old jests and buffooneries of Christmas, however vulgar or stale or trivial they appear, is that in them the popular instinct always resisted this pagan solemnity about sensual things. A man was meant to feel rather a goose when he was eating goose; and to realize that he is such stuff as stuffing is made of. That is why anyone who has in these things the touch of the comic will also have the taste for the conservative; he will be unwilling to alter what that popular instinct has made in its own absurd image. He will be doubtful about a Christmas pudding moulded in the shape of the Pyramid or the Parthenon, or anything that is not as round and ridiculous as the world. And when Mr. Pickwick, as round and ridiculous as any Christmas pudding or any world worth living in, stood straddling and smiling under the mistletoe he disinfected that vegetable of its ancient and almost vegetarian sadness and heathenism, of the blood of Baldur and the human sacrifice of the Druids.

ON DETECTIVE NOVELS

It is now some years since an American lady who has produced many of our most charming stories of murder and mystification, wrote to a magazine to complain of the unsatisfactory sort of review accorded to that sort of book; but not yet has the abuse been corrected. She said it is only too obvious that the task of reviewing detective stories is given to people who do not like detective stories. She says, and I think not unreasonably, that this is very unreasonable: a book of poems is not sent to a man who hates poetry; an ordinary novel is not reviewed by a rigid moralist who regards all novels as immoral. If mystery stories have any right to be reviewed at all, they have a right to be reviewed by the sort of person who understands why they were written. And the lady proceeds to say that, by this neglect, the nature of the technique really required in such a tale is never adequately discussed. I, for one, agree with her that it is a matter well worthy of discussion. There is no better reading, and in the true sense no more serious reading, than the few critical passages which great critics have devoted to this literary question; such as Edgar Allan Poe's disquisition on analysis at the beginning of the beautiful idyll about the murderous ape; or the studies of Andrew Lang on the problem of Edwin Drood; or the remarks of Stevenson on the police novel at the end of *The Wrecker*. Any such discussion, clearly conducted, will soon show that the rules of art are as much involved in this artistic form as in any other; and it is not any objection to such a form that people can enjoy it who cannot criticize it. The same is true of any good song or any sound romance. By a curious confusion, many modern critics have passed from the proposition that a masterpiece

may be unpopular to the other proposition that unless it is unpopular it cannot be a masterpiece. It is as if one were to say
that because a clever man may have an impediment in his speech,
therefore a man cannot be clever unless he stammers. For all unpopularity is a sort of obscurity; and all obscurity is a defect
of expression like a stammer. Anyhow, I am in this matter on
the popular side; I am interested in all sorts of sensational fiction,
good, bad and indifferent, and would willingly discuss it with a
much less capable exponent of it than the author of *Vicky Van*.
And if anyone likes to say that my tastes are vulgar and inartistic
and illiterate, I can only say I am quite content to be as vulgar as
Poe and as inartistic and illiterate as Andrew Lang.

Now, it is all the more curious that the technique of such tales
is not discussed, because they are exactly the sort in which technique is nearly the whole of the trick. It is all the more odd that
such writers have no critical guidance, because it is one of the
few forms of art in which they could to some extent be guided.
And it is all the more strange that nobody discusses the rules, because it is one of the rare cases in which some rules could be
laid down. The very fact that the work is not of the highest
order of creation makes it possible to treat it as a question of
construction. But while people are willing to teach poets imagination, they seem to think it hopeless to help plotters in a matter
of mere ingenuity. There are text-books instructing people in the
manufacture of sonnets, as if the visions of bare ruined quires
where late sweet birds sang, or of the ground-whirl of the perished leaves of hope, the wind of death's imperishable wing, were
things to be explained like a conjuring trick. We have mono-
graphs expounding the art of the Short Story, as if the dripping
horror of the *House of Usher* or the sunny irony of the *Treasure
of Franchard* were recipes out of a cookery book. But in the
case of the only kind of story to which the strict laws of logic
are in some sense applicable, nobody seems to bother to apply
them, or even to ask whether in this or in that case they are
applied. Nobody writes the simple book which I expect every

day to see on the bookstalls, called *How to Write a Detective Story*.

I myself have got no further than discovering how not to write one. But even from my own failures I have gained stray glimpses of what such a scheme of warnings might be. Of one preliminary principle I am pretty certain. The whole point of a sensational story is that the secret should be simple. The whole story exists for the moment of surprise; and it should be a moment. It should not be something that it takes twenty minutes to explain, and twenty-four hours to learn by heart, for fear of forgetting it. The best way of testing it is to make an imaginative picture in the mind of some such dramatic moment. Imagine a dark garden at twilight, and a terrible voice crying out in the distance, and coming nearer and nearer along the serpentine garden paths until the words become dreadfully distinct; a cry coming from some sinister yet familiar figure in the story, a stranger or a servant from whom we subconsciously expect some such rending revelation. Now, it is clear that the cry which breaks from him must be something short and simple in itself, as, "The butler is his father," or "The Archdeacon is Bloody Bill," or "The Emperor has cut his throat," or what not. But too many otherwise ingenious romancers seem to think it their duty to discover what is the most complicated and improbable series of events that could be combined to produce a certain result. The result may be logical, but it is not sensational. The servant cannot rend the silence of the twilight garden by shrieking aloud: "The throat of the Emperor was cut under the following circumstances: his Imperial Majesty was attempting to shave himself and went to sleep in the middle of it, fatigued with the cares of state; the Archdeacon was attempting at first in a Christian spirit to complete the shaving operation on the sleeping monarch, when he was suddenly tempted to a murderous act by the memory of the Disestablishment Bill, but repented after making a mere scratch and flung the razor on the floor; the faithful butler, hearing the commotion, rushed in and snatched up the weapon, but in the confusion of the moment cut the Emperor's throat instead of the Archdeacon's; so everything is satisfactory, and the young man and the girl can leave off suspecting each other of assassination and get married." Now, this explanation, however reasonable and complete, is not one that can be conveniently uttered as an exclamation or can sound suddenly in the twilight garden like the trump of doom. Anyone who will try the experiment of crying aloud the above paragraph in his own twilight garden will realize the difficulty here referred to. It is exactly one of those little technical experiments, illustrated with diagrams, with which our little text-book would abound.

Another truth to which our little text-book would at least tentatively incline is that the *roman policier* should be on the model of the short story rather than the novel. There are splendid exceptions: *The Moonstone* and one or two Gaborius are great works in this style; as are, in our own time, Mr. Bentley's *Trent's Last Case*, and Mr. Milne's *Red House Mystery*. But I think that the difficulties of a long detective novel are real difficulties, though very clever men can by various expedients get over them. The chief difficulty is that the detective story is, after all, a drama of masks and not of faces. It depends on men's false characters rather than their real characters. The author cannot tell us until the last chapter any of the most interesting things about the most interesting people. It is a masquerade ball in which everybody is disguised as somebody else, and there is no true personal interest until the clock strikes twelve. That is, as I have said, we cannot really get at the psychology and philosophy, the morals and the religion, of the thing until we have read the last chapter. Therefore, I think it is best of all when the first chapter is also the last chapter. The length of a short story is about the legitimate length for this particular drama of the mere misunderstanding of fact. When all is said and done, there have never been better detective stories than the old series of Sherlock Holmes; and though the name of that magnificent magician has been spread over the whole world, and is perhaps the one great popular legend made in the modern world, I do not think that Sir Arthur Conan Doyle has ever been thanked enough for them. As one of many millions, I offer my own mite of homage.

THE ADVANTAGES OF HAVING ONE LEG

A FRIEND of mine who was visiting a poor woman in bereavement and casting about for some phrase of consolation that should not be either insolent or weak, said at last, "I think one can live through these great sorrows and even be the better. What wears one is the little worries." "That's quite right, mum," answered the old woman with emphasis, "and I ought to know, seeing I've had ten of 'em." It is, perhaps, in this sense that it is most true that little worries are most wearing. In its vaguer significance the phrase, though it contains a truth, contains also some possibilities of self-deception and error. People who have both small troubles and big ones have the right to say that they find the small ones the most bitter; and it is undoubtedly true that the back which is bowed under loads incredible can feel a faint addition to those loads; a giant holding up the earth and all its animal creation might still find the grasshopper a burden. But I am afraid that the maxim that the smallest worries are the worst is sometimes used or abused by people, because they have nothing but the very smallest worries. The lady may excuse herself for reviling the crumpled rose-leaf by reflecting with what extraordinary dignity she would wear the crown of thorns—if she had to. The gentleman may permit himself to curse the dinner and tell himself that he would behave much better if it were a mere matter of starvation. We need not deny that the grasshopper on man's shoulder is a burden; but we need not pay much respect to a gentleman who is always calling out that he would rather have an elephant when he knows there are no elephants in the country. We may concede that a straw may break the camel's back, but we like to know that it really is the last straw and not the first.

I grant that those who have serious wrongs have a real right to grumble, so long as they grumble about something else. It is a singular fact that if they are sane they almost always do grumble about something else. To talk quite reasonably about your own quite real wrongs is the quickest way to go off your head. But people with great troubles talk about little ones, and the man who complains of the crumpled rose leaf very often has his flesh full of the thorns. But if a man has commonly a very clear and happy daily life then I think we are justified in asking that he shall not make mountains out of molehills. I do not deny that molehills can sometimes be important. Small annoyances have this evil about them, that they can be more abrupt because they are more invisible; they cast no shadow before, they have no atmosphere. No one ever had a mystical premonition that he was going to tumble over a hassock. William III. died by falling over a molehill; I do not suppose that with all his varied abilities he could have managed to fall over a mountain. But when all this is allowed for, I repeat that we may ask a happy man (not William III.) to put up with pure inconveniences, and even make them part of his happiness. Of positive pain or positive poverty I do not here speak. I speak of those innumerable accidental limitations that are always falling across our path—bad weather, confinement to this or that house or room, failure of appointments or arrangements, waiting at railway stations, missing posts, finding unpunctuality when we want punctuality, or, what is worse, finding punctuality when we don't. It is of the poetic pleasures to be drawn from all these that I sing—I sing with confidence because I have recently been experimenting in the poetic pleasures which arise from having to sit in one chair with a sprained foot, with the only alternative course of standing on one leg like a stork—a stork is a poetic simile; therefore I eagerly adopted it.

To appreciate anything we must always isolate it, even if the thing itself symbolise something other than isolation. If we wish to see what a house is it must be a house in some uninhabited landscape. If we wish to depict what a man really is we must depict a man alone in a desert or on a dark sea sand. So long as he is a single figure he means all that humanity means; so long as he is solitary he means human society; so long as he is solitary he means sociability and comradeship. Add another figure and the picture is less human—not more so. One is company, two is none. If you wish to symbolise human building draw one dark tower on the horizon; if you wish to symbolise light let there be no star in the sky. Indeed, all through that strangely lit season which we call our day there is but one star in the sky—a large, fierce star which we call the sun. One sun is splendid; six suns would be only vulgar. One Tower of Giotto is sublime; a row of Towers of Giotto would be only like a row of white posts. The poetry of art is in beholding the single tower; the poetry of nature in seeing the single tree; the poetry of love in following the single woman; the poetry of religion in worshipping the single star. And so, in the same pensive lucidity, I find the poetry of all human anatomy in standing on a single leg. To express complete and perfect leggishness the leg must stand in sublime isolation, like the tower in the wilderness. As Ibsen so finely says, the strongest leg is that which stands most alone. This lonely leg on which I rest has all the simplicity of some Doric column. The students of architecture tell us that the only legitimate use of a column is to support weight. This column of mine fulfils its legitimate function. It supports weight. Being of an animal and organic consistency, it may even improve by the process, and during these few days that I am thus unequally balanced, the helplessness or dislocation of the one leg may find compensation in the astonishing strength and classic beauty of the other leg. Mrs. Mountstuart Jenkinson in Mr. George Meredith's novel might pass by at any moment, and seeing me in the stork-like attitude would exclaim, with equal admiration and a more literal exactitude, "He has a leg." Notice how this famous literary phrase supports my contention touching this isolation of any admirable thing. Mrs. Mountstuart Jenkinson, wishing to make a clear and perfect picture of human grace, said that Sir Willoughby Patterne had a leg. She delicately glossed over and concealed the clumsy and offensive fact that he had really two legs. Two legs were superfluous and irrelevant, a reflection, and a confusion. Two legs would have confused Mrs. Mountstuart Jenkinson like two Monuments in London. That having had one good leg he should have another—this would be to use vain repetitions as the Gentiles do. She would have been as much bewildered by him as if he had been a centipede.

All pessimism has a secret optimism for its object. All surrender of life, all denial of pleasure, all darkness, all austerity, all desolation has for its real aim this separation of something so that it may be poignantly and perfectly enjoyed. I feel grateful for the slight sprain which has introduced this mysterious and fascinating division between one of my feet and the other. The way to love anything is to realise that it might be lost. In one of my feet I can feel how strong and splendid a foot is; in the other I can realise how very much otherwise it might have been. The moral of the thing is wholly exhilarating. This world and all our powers in it are far more awful and beautiful than even we know until some accident reminds us. If you wish to perceive that limitless felicity, limit yourself if only for a moment. If you wish to realise how fearfully and wonderfully God's image is made, stand on one leg. If you want to realise the splendid vision of all visible things—wink the other eye.

THE APPETITE OF EARTH

I was walking the other day in a kitchen garden, which I find has somehow got attached to my premises, and I was wondering why I liked it. After a prolonged spiritual self-analysis I came to the conclusion that I like a kitchen garden because it contains things to eat. I do not mean that a kitchen garden is ugly; a kitchen garden is often very beautiful. The mixture of green and purple on some monstrous cabbage is much subtler and grander than the mere freakish and theatrical splashing of yellow and violet on a pansy. Few of the flowers merely meant for ornament are so ethereal as a potato. A kitchen garden is as beautiful as an orchard; but why is it that the word "orchard" sounds as beautiful as the word "flower-garden," and yet also sounds more satisfactory? I suggest again my extraordinarily dark and delicate discovery: that it contains things to eat.

The cabbage is a solid; it can be approached from all sides at once; it can be realised by all senses at once. Compared with that the sunflower, which can only be seen, is a mere pattern, a thing painted on a flat wall. Now, it is this sense of the solidity of things that can only be uttered by the metaphor of eating. To express the cubic content of a turnip, you must be all round it at once. The only way to get all round a turnip at once is to eat the turnip. I think any poetic mind that has loved solidity, the thickness of trees, the squareness of stones, the firmness of clay, must have sometimes wished that they were things to eat. If only brown peat tasted as good as it looks; if only white fir-wood were digestible! We talk rightly of giving stones for bread: but there are in the Geological Museum certain rich crimson marbles, certain split stones of blue and green, that make me wish my teeth were stronger.

Somebody staring into the sky with the same ethereal appetite declared that the moon was made of green cheese. I never could conscientiously accept the full doctrine. I am Modernist in this matter. That the moon is made of cheese I have believed from childhood; and in the course of every month a giant (of my acquaintance) bites a big round piece out of it. This seems to me a doctrine that is above reason, but not contrary to it. But that the cheese is green seems to be in some degree actually contradicted by the senses and the reason; first because if the moon were made of green cheese it would be inhabited; and second because if it were made of green cheese it would be green. A blue moon is said to be an unusual sight; but I cannot think that a green one is much more common. In fact, I think I have seen the moon looking like every other sort of cheese except a green cheese. I have seen it look exactly like a cream cheese: a circle of warm white upon a warm faint violet sky above a cornfield in Kent. I have seen it look very like a Dutch cheese, rising a dull red copper disk amid masts and dark waters at Honfleur. I have seen it look like an ordinary sensible Cheddar cheese in an or- dinary sensible Prussian blue sky; and I have once seen it so naked and ruinous-looking, so strangely lit up, that it looked like a Gruyère cheese, that awful volcanic cheese that has horrible holes in it, as if it had come in boiling unnatural milk from mys- terious and unearthly cattle. But I have never yet seen the lunar cheese green; and I incline to the opinion that the moon is not old enough. The moon, like everything else, will ripen by the end of the world; and in the last days we shall see it taking on those volcanic sunset colours, and leaping with that enormous and fantastic life.

But this is a parenthesis; and one perhaps slightly lacking in prosaic actuality. Whatever may be the value of the above speculations, the phrase about the moon and green cheese remains a good example of this imagery of eating and drinking on a large scale. The same huge fancy is in the phrase "if all the trees were bread and cheese" which I have cited elsewhere in this connec- tion; and in that noble nightmare of a Scandinavian legend, in which Thor drinks the deep sea nearly dry out of a horn. In an essay like the present (first intended as a paper to be read before the Royal Society) one cannot be too exact; and I will concede that my theory of the gradual virescence of our satellite is to be regarded rather as an alternative theory than as a law finally demonstrated and universally accepted by the scientific world. It is a hypothesis that holds the field, as the scientists say of a theory when there is no evidence for it so far.

But the reader need be under no apprehension that I have suddenly gone mad, and shall start biting large pieces out of the trunks of trees; or seriously altering (by large semicircular mouthfuls) the exquisite outline of the mountains. This feeling for expressing a fresh solidity by the image of eating is really a very old one. So far from being a paradox of perversity, it is one of the oldest commonplaces of religion. If any one wandering about wants to have a good trick or test for separating the wrong idealism from the right, I will give him one on the spot. It is a mark of false religion that it is always trying to express concrete facts as abstract; it calls sex affinity; it calls wine alcohol; it calls brute starvation the economic problem. The test of true religion is that its energy drives exactly the other way; it is always trying to make men feel truths as facts; always trying to make abstract things as plain and solid as concrete things; always trying to make men, not merely admit the truth, but see, smell, handle, hear, and devour the truth. All great spiritual scriptures are full of the invitation not to test, but to taste; not to examine, but to eat. Their phrases are full of living water and heavenly bread, mysterious manna and dreadful wine. Worldliness, and the polite society of the world, has despised this instinct of eating; but religion has never despised it. When we look at a firm, fat, white cliff of chalk at Dover, I do not suggest that we should desire to eat it; that would be highly abnormal. But I really mean that we should think it good to eat; good for some one else to eat. For, indeed, some one else is eating it; the grass that grows upon its top is devouring it silently, but, doubtless, with an uproarious appetite.

THE FEAR OF THE PAST

THE last few decades have been marked by a special cultivation of the romance of the future. We seem to have made up our minds to misunderstand what has happened; and we turn, with a sort of relief, to stating what will happen—which is (apparently) much easier. The modern man no longer preserves the memoirs of his great-grandfather; but he is engaged in writing a detailed and authoritative biography of his great-grandson. Instead of trembling before the specters of the dead, we shudder abjectly under the shadow of the babe unborn. This spirit is apparent everywhere, even to the creation of a form of futurist romance. Sir Walter Scott stands at the dawn of the nineteenth century for the novel of the past; Mr. H. G. Wells stands at the dawn of the twentieth century for the novel of the future. The old story, we know, was supposed to begin: "Late on a winter's evening two horsemen might have been seen—." The new story has to begin: "Late on a winter's evening two aviators will be seen—." The movement is not without its elements of charm; there is something spirited, if eccentric, in the sight of so many people fighting over again the fights that have not yet happened; of people still glowing with the memory of to-morrow morning. A man in advance of the age is a familiar phrase enough. An age in advance of the age is really rather odd.

But when full allowance has been made for this harmless element of poetry and pretty human perversity in the thing, I shall not hesitate to maintain here that this cult of the future is not only a weakness but a cowardice of the age. It is the peculiar evil of this epoch that even its pugnacity is fundamentally frightened; and the Jingo is contemptible not because he is impudent, but because he is timid. The reason why modern armaments do not inflame the imagination like the arms and emblazonments of the Crusades is a reason quite apart from optical ugliness or beauty. Some battleships are as beautiful as the sea; and many Norman nosepieces were as ugly as Norman noses. The atmospheric ugliness that surrounds our scientific war is an emanation from that evil panic which is at the heart of it. The charge of the Crusades was a charge; it was charging towards God, the wild consolation of the braver. The charge of the modern arma-

ments is not a charge at all. It is a rout, a retreat, a flight from the
devil, who will catch the hindmost. It is impossible to imagine
a mediæval knight talking of longer and longer French lances,
with precisely the quivering employed about larger and larger
German ships. The man who called the Blue Water School the
"Blue Funk School" uttered a psychological truth which that
school itself would scarcely essentially deny. Even the two-
power standard, if it be a necessity, is in a sense a degrading necessity. Nothing has more alienated many magnanimous minds
from Imperial enterprises than the fact that they are always exhibited as stealthy or sudden defenses against a world of cold
rapacity and fear. The Boer War, for instance, was colored not
so much by the creed that we were doing something right, as by
the creed that Boers and Germans were probably doing something wrong; driving us (as it was said) to the sea. Mr. Chamberlain, I think, said that the war was a feather in his cap; and
so it was: a white feather.

Now this same primary panic that I feel in our rush towards
patriotic armaments I feel also in our rush towards future visions
of society. The modern mind is forced towards the future by a
certain sense of fatigue, not unmixed with terror, with which it
regards the past. It is propelled towards the coming time; it is,
in the exact words of the popular phrase, knocked into the middle of next week. And the goad which drives it on thus eagerly
is not an affectation for futurity. Futurity does not exist, because
it is still future. Rather it is a fear of the past; a fear not merely
of the evil in the past, but of the good in the past also. The brain
breaks down under the unbearable virtue of mankind. There
have been so many flaming faiths that we cannot hold; so many
harsh heroisms that we cannot imitate; so many great efforts of
monumental building or of military glory which seem to us at
once sublime and pathetic. The future is a refuge from the fierce
competition of our forefathers. The older generation, not the
younger, is knocking at our door. It is agreeable to escape, as
Henley said, into the Street of By-and-Bye, where stands the

Hostelry of Never. It is pleasant play with children, especially unborn children. The future is a blank wall on which every man can write his own name as large as he likes; the past I find already covered with illegible scribbles, such as Plato, Isaiah, Shakespeare, Michael Angelo, Napoleon. I can make the future as narrow as myself; the past is obliged to be as broad and turbulent as humanity. And the upshot of this modern attitude is really this: that men invent new ideals because they dare not attempt old ideals. They look forward with enthusiasm, because they are afraid to look back.

Now in history there is no Revolution that is not a Restoration. Among the many things that leave me doubtful about the modern habit of fixing eyes on the future, none is stronger than this: that all the men in history who have really done anything with the future have had their eyes fixed upon the past. I need not mention the Renaissance, the very word proves my case. The originality of Michael Angelo and Shakespeare began with the digging up of old vases and manuscripts. The mildness of poets absolutely arose out of the mildness of antiquaries. So the great mediæval revival was a memory of the Roman Empire. So the Reformation looked back to the Bible and Bible times. So the modern Catholic movement has looked back to patristic times. But that modern movement which many would count the most anarchic of all is in this sense the most conservative of all. Never was the past more venerated by men than it was by the French Revolutionists. They invoked the little republics of antiquity with the complete confidence of one who invokes the gods. The Sansculottes believed (as their name might imply) in a return to simplicity. They believed most piously in a remote past; some might call it a mythical past. For some strange reason man must always thus plant his fruit trees in a graveyard. Man can only find life among the dead. Man is a misshappen monster, with his feet set forward and his face turned back. He can make the future luxuriant and gigantic, so long as he is thinking about the past. When he tries to think about the future itself, his mind diminishes to a pin point with imbecility, which some call Nirvana. To-morrow is the Gorgon; a man must only see it mirrored in the shining shield of yesterday. If he sees it directly he is turned to stone. This has been the fate of all those who have really seen fate and futurity as clear and inevitable. The Calvinists, with their perfect creed of predestination, were turned to stone. The modern sociological scientists (with their excruciating Eugenics) are turned to stone. The only difference is that the Puritans make dignified, and the Eugenists somewhat amusing, statues.

But there is one feature in the past which more than all the rest defies and depresses the moderns and drives them towards this featureless future. I mean the presence in the past of huge ideals, unfulfilled and sometimes abandoned. The sight of these splendid failures is melancholy to a restless and rather morbid generation; and they maintain a strange silence about them—sometimes amounting to an unscrupulous silence. They keep them entirely out of their newspapers and almost entirely out of their history books. For example, they will often tell you (in their praises of the coming age) that we are moving on towards a United States of Europe. But they carefully omit to tell you that we are moving away from a United States of Europe; that such a thing existed literally in Roman and essentially in mediæval times. They never admit that the international hatreds (which they call barbaric) are really very recent, the mere breakdown of the ideal of the Holy Roman Empire. Or again, they will tell you that there is going to be a social revolution, a great rising of the poor against the rich; but they never rub it in that France made that magnificent attempt, unaided, and that we and all the world allowed it to be trampled out and forgotten. I say decisively that nothing is so marked in modern writing as the prediction of such ideals in the future combined with the ignoring of them in the past. Anyone can test this for himself. Read any thirty or forty pages of pamphlets advocating peace in Europe and see how many of them praise the old Popes or

Emperors for keeping the peace in Europe. Read any armful of essays and poems in praise of social democracy, and see how many of them praise the old Jacobins who created democracy and died for it. These colossal ruins are to the modern only enormous eyesores. He looks back along the valley of the past and sees a perspective of splendid but unfinished cities. They are unfinished, not always through enmity or accident, but often through fickleness, mental fatigue, and the lust for alien philosophies. We have not only left undone those things that we ought to have done, but we have even left undone those things that we wanted to do.

It is very currently suggested that the modern man is the heir of all the ages, that he has got the good out of these successive human experiments. I know not what to say in answer to this, except to ask the reader to look at the modern man, as I have just looked at the modern man—in the looking-glass. Is it really true that you and I are two starry towers built up of all the most towering visions of the past? Have we really fulfilled all the great historic ideals one after the other, from our naked ancestor who was brave enough to kill a mammoth with a stone knife, through the Greek citizen and the Christian saint to our own grandfather or great-grandfather, who may have been sabred by the Manchester Yeomanry or shot in the '48? Are you still strong enough to spear mammoths, but now tender enough to spare them? Does the cosmos contain any mammoth that we have either speared or spared? When we decline (in a marked manner) to fly the red flag and fire across a barricade like our grandfathers, are we really declining in deference to sociologists—or to soldiers? Have we indeed outstripped the warrior and passed the ascetical saint? I fear we only outstrip the warrior in the sense that we should probably run away from him. And if we have passed the saint, I fear we have passed him without bowing.

This is, first and foremost, what I mean by the narrowness of the new ideas, the limiting effect of the future. Our modern prophetic idealism is narrow because it has undergone a per-sistent process of elimination. We must ask for new things because we are not allowed to ask for old things. The whole position is based on this idea that we have got all the good that can be got out of the ideas of the past. But we have not got all the good out of them, perhaps at this moment not any of the good out of them. And the need here is a need of complete freedom for restoration as well as revolution.

We often read nowadays of the valor or audacity with which some rebel attacks a hoary tyranny or an antiquated superstition. There is not really any courage at all in attacking hoary or antiquated things, any more than in offering to fight one's grandmother. The really courageous man is he who defies tyrannies young as the morning and superstitions fresh as the first flowers. The only true free-thinker is he whose intellect is as much free from the future as from the past. He cares as little for what will be as for what has been; he cares only for what ought to be. And for my present purpose I specially insist on this abstract independence. If I am to discuss what is wrong, one of the first things that are wrong is this: the deep and silent modern assumption that past things have become impossible. There is one metaphor of which the moderns are very fond; they are always saying, "You can't put the clock back." The simple and obvious answer is "You can." A clock, being a piece of human construction, can be restored by the human finger to any figure or hour. In the same way society, being a piece of human construction, can be reconstructed upon any plan that has ever existed.

There is another proverb, "As you have made your bed, so you must lie on it"; which again is simply a lie. If I have made my bed uncomfortable, please God I will make it again. We could restore the Heptarchy or the stage coaches if we chose. It might take some time to do, and it might be very inadvisable to do it; but certainly it is not impossible as bringing back last Friday is impossible. This is, as I say, the first freedom that I claim: the freedom to restore. I claim a right to propose as a solution the

old patriarchal system of a Highland clan, if that should seem
to eliminate the largest number of evils. It certainly would eliminate some evils; for instance, the unnatural sense of obeying cold
and harsh strangers, mere bureaucrats and policemen. I claim
the right to propose the complete independence of the small
Greek or Italian towns, a sovereign city of Brixton or Bromp-
ton, if that seems the best way out of our troubles. It would be
a way out of some of our troubles; we could not have in a small
state, for instance, those enormous illusions about men or meas-
ures which are nourished by the great national or international
newspapers. You could not persuade a city state that Mr. Beit
was an Englishman, or Mr. Dillon a desperado, any more than
you could persuade a Hampshire village that the village drunkard
was a teetotaler or the village idiot a statesman. Nevertheless, I
do not as a fact propose that the Browns and the Smiths should
be collected under separate tartans. Nor do I even propose that
Clapham should declare its independence. I merely declare my
independence. I merely claim my choice of all the tools in the
universe; and I shall not admit that any of them are blunted
merely because they have been used.

PATRIOTISM AND SPORT

I NOTICE that some papers, especially papers that call themselves
patriotic, have fallen into quite a panic over the fact that we have
been twice beaten in the world of sport, that a Frenchman has
beaten us at golf, and that Belgians have beaten us at rowing. I
suppose that the incidents are important to any people who ever
believed in the self-satisfied English legend on this subject. I suppose that there are men who vaguely believe that we could never
be beaten by a Frenchman, despite the fact that we have often
been beaten by Frenchmen, and once by a Frenchwoman. In the
old pictures in *Punch* you will find a recurring piece of satire.

The English caricaturists always assumed that a Frenchman could not ride to hounds or enjoy English hunting. It did not seem to occur to them that all the people who founded English hunting were Frenchmen. All the Kings and nobles who originally rode to hounds spoke French. Large numbers of those Englishmen who still ride to hounds have French names. I suppose that the thing is important to any one who is ignorant of such evident matters as these. I suppose that if a man has ever believed that we English have some sacred and separate right to be athletic, such reverses do appear quite enormous and shocking. They feel as if, while the proper sun was rising in the east, some other and unexpected sun had begun to rise in the north-north-west by north. For the benefit, the moral and intellectual benefit of such people, it may be worth while to point out that the Anglo-Saxon has in these cases been defeated precisely by those competitors whom he has always regarded as being out of the running; by Latins, and by Latins of the most easy and unstrenuous type; not only by Frenchmen, but by Belgians. All this, I say, is worth telling to any intelligent person who believes in the haughty theory of Anglo-Saxon superiority. But, then, no intelligent person does believe in the haughty theory of Anglo-Saxon superiority. No quite genuine Englishman ever did believe in it. And the genuine Englishman these defeats will in no respect dismay.

The genuine English patriot will know that the strength of England has never depended upon any of these things; that the glory of England has never had anything to do with them, except in the opinion of a large section of the rich and a loose section of the poor which copies the idleness of the rich. These people will, of course, think too much of our failure, just as they thought too much of our success. The typical Jingoes who have admired their countrymen too much for being conquerors will, doubtless, despise their countrymen too much for being conquered. But the Englishman with any feeling for England will know that athletic failures do not prove that England is weak, any more than athletic successes proved that England was strong. The truth is that athletics, like all other things, especially modern, are insanely individualistic. The Englishmen who win sporting prizes are exceptional among Englishmen, for the simple reason that they are exceptional even among men. English athletes represent England just about as much as Mr. Barnum's freaks represent America. There are so few of such people in the whole world that it is almost a toss-up whether they are found in this or that country.

If any one wants a simple proof of this, it is easy to find. When the great English athletes are not exceptional Englishmen they are generally not Englishmen at all. Nay, they are often representative of races of which the average tone is specially incompatible with athletics. For instance, the English are supposed to rule the natives of India in virtue of their superior hardiness, superior activity, superior health of body and mind. The Hindus are supposed to be our subjects because they are less fond of action, less fond of openness and the open air. In a word, less fond of cricket. And, substantially, this is probably true, that the Indians are less fond of cricket. All the same, if you ask among Englishmen for the very best cricket-player, you will find that he is an Indian. Or, to take another case: it is, broadly speaking, true that the Jews are, as a race, pacific, intellectual, indifferent to war, like the Indians, or, perhaps, contemptuous of war, like the Chinese: nevertheless, of the very good prize-fighters, one or two have been Jews.

This is one of the strongest instances of the particular kind of evil that arises from our English form of the worship of athletics. It concentrates too much upon the success of individuals. It began, quite naturally and rightly, with wanting England to win. The second stage was that it wanted some Englishmen to win. The third stage was (in the ecstasy and agony of some special competition) that it wanted one particular Englishman to win. And the fourth stage was that when he had won, it discovered that he was not even an Englishman.

This is one of the points, I think, on which something might really be said for Lord Roberts and his rather vague ideas which vary between rifle clubs and conscription. Whatever may be the advantages or disadvantages otherwise of the idea, it is at least an idea of procuring equality and a sort of average in the athletic capacity of the people; it might conceivably act as a corrective to our mere tendency to see ourselves in certain exceptional athletes. As it is, there are millions of Englishmen who really think that they are a muscular race because C. B. Fry is an Englishman. And there are many of them who think vaguely that athletics must belong to England because Ranjitsinhji is an Indian.

But the real historic strength of England, physical and moral, has never had anything to do with this athletic specialism; it has been rather hindered by it. Somebody said that the Battle of Waterloo was won on Eton playing-fields. It was a particularly unfortunate remark, for the English contribution to the victory of Waterloo depended very much more than is common in victories upon the steadiness of the rank and file in an almost desperate situation. The Battle of Waterloo was won by the stubbornness of the common soldier—that is to say, it was won by the man who had never been to Eton. It was absurd to say that Waterloo was won on Eton cricket-fields. But it might have been fairly said that Waterloo was won on the village green, where clumsy boys played a very clumsy cricket. In a word, it was the average of the nation that was strong, and athletic glories do not indicate much about the average of a nation. Waterloo was not won by good cricket-players. But Waterloo was won by bad cricket-players, by a mass of men who had some minimum of athletic instincts and habits. It is a good sign in a nation when such things are done badly. It shows that all the people are doing them. And it is a bad sign in a nation when such things are done very well, for it shows that only a few experts and eccentrics are doing them, and that the nation is merely looking on. Suppose that whenever we heard of walking in England it always meant walking forty-five miles a day without fatigue. We should be perfectly certain that only a few men were walking at all, and that all the other British subjects were being wheeled about in Bath-chairs. But if when we hear of walking it means slow walking, painful walking, and frequent fatigue, then we know that the mass of the nation still is walking. We know that England is still literally on its feet.

The difficulty is therefore that the actual raising of the standard of athletics has probably been bad for national athleticism. Instead of the tournament being a healthy *mêlée* into which any ordinary man would rush and take his chance, it has become a fenced and guarded tilting-yard for the collision of particular champions against whom no ordinary man would pit himself or even be permitted to pit himself. If Waterloo was won on Eton cricket-fields it was because Eton cricket was probably much more careless then than it is now. As long as the game was a game, everybody wanted to join in it. When it becomes an art, every one wants to look at it. When it was frivolous it may have won Waterloo: when it was serious and efficient it lost Magersfontein.

In the Waterloo period there was a general rough-and-tumble athleticism among average Englishmen. It cannot be re-created by cricket, or by conscription, or by any artificial means. It was a thing of the soul. It came out of laughter, religion, and the spirit of the place. But it was like the modern French duel in this—that it might happen to anybody. If I were a French journalist it might really happen that Monsieur Clemenceau might challenge me to meet him with pistols. But I do not think that it is at all likely that Mr. C. B. Fry will ever challenge me to meet him with cricket-bats.

THE METHUSELAHITE

I saw in a newspaper paragraph the other day the following entertaining and deeply philosophical incident. A man was enlisting as a soldier at Portsmouth, and some form was put before him to be filled up, common, I suppose, to all such cases, in which was, among other things, an inquiry about what was his religion. With an equal and ceremonial gravity the man wrote down the word "Methuselahite." Whoever looks over such papers must, I should imagine, have seen some rum religions in his time; unless the Army is going to the dogs. But with all his specialist knowledge he could not "place" Methuselahism among what Bossuet called the variations of Protestantism. He felt a fervid curiosity about the tenets and tendencies of the sect; and he asked the soldier what it meant. The soldier replied that it was his religion "to live as long as he could."

Now, considered as an incident in the religious history of Europe, that answer of that soldier was worth more than a hundred cartloads of quarterly and monthly and weekly and daily papers discussing religious problems and religious books. Every day the daily paper reviews some new philosopher who has some new religion; and there is not in the whole two thousand words of the whole two columns one word as witty or as wise as that word "Methuselahite." The whole meaning of literature is simply to cut a long story short; that is why our modern books of philosophy are never literature. That soldier had in him the very soul of literature; he was one of the great phrase-makers of modern thought, like Victor Hugo or Disraeli. He found one word that defines the paganism of to-day.

Henceforward, when the modern philosophers come to me with their new religions (and there is always a kind of queue of them waiting all the way down the street) I shall anticipate their circumlocutions and be able to cut them short with a single inspired word. One of them will begin, "The New Religion, which is based upon that Primordial Energy in Nature . . ." "Methu-selahite," I shall say sharply; "good morning." "Human Life," another will say, "Human Life, the only ultimate sanctity, freed from creed and dogma . . ." "Methuselahite!" I shall yell. "Out you go!" "My religion is the Religion of Joy," a third will ex-plain (a bald old man with a cough and tinted glasses), "the Religion of Physical Pride and Rapture, and my . . ." "Methu-selahite!" I shall cry again, and I shall slap him boisterously on the back, and he will fall down. Then a pale young poet with serpentine hair will come and say to me (as one did only the other day): "Moods and impressions are the only realities, and these are constantly and wholly changing. I could hardly there-fore define my religion. . . ." "I can," I should say, somewhat sternly. "Your religion is to live a long time; and if you stop here a moment longer you won't fulfil it."

A new philosophy generally means in practice the praise of some old vice. We have had the sophist who defends cruelty, and calls it masculinity. We have had the sophist who defends prof-ligacy, and calls it the liberty of the emotions. We have had the sophist who defends idleness, and calls it art. It will almost cer-tainly happen—it can almost certainly be prophesied—that in this saturnalia of sophistry there will at some time or other arise a sophist who desires to idealise cowardice. And when we are once in this unhealthy world of mere wild words, what a vast deal there would be to say for cowardice! "Is not life a lovely thing and worth saving?" the soldier would say as he ran away. "Should I not prolong the exquisite miracle of consciousness?" the householder would say as he hid under the table. "As long as there are roses and lilies on the earth shall I not remain there?" would come the voice of the citizen from under the bed. It would be quite as easy to defend the coward as a kind of poet and mystic as it has been, in many recent books, to defend the emotionalist as a kind of poet and mystic, or the tyrant as a kind of poet and mystic. When that last grand sophistry and morbidity is preached in a book or on a platform, you may depend upon it there will be a great stir in its favour, that is, a great stir among the little people who live among books and platforms. There will be a new great Religion, the Religion of Methuselahism: with pomps and priests and altars. Its devout crusaders will vow themselves in thousands with a great vow to live long. But there is one comfort: they won't.

For, indeed, the weakness of this worship of mere natural life (which is a common enough creed to-day) is that it ignores the paradox of courage and fails in its own aim. As a matter of fact, no men would be killed quicker than the Methuselahites. The paradox of courage is that a man must be a little careless of his life even in order to keep it. And in the very case I have quoted we may see an example of how little the theory of Methuselahism really inspires our best life. For there is one riddle in that case which cannot easily be cleared up. If it was the man's religion to live as long as he could, why on earth was he enlisting as a soldier?

THE RIDDLE OF THE IVY

More than a month ago, when I was leaving London for a holiday, a friend walked into my flat in Battersea and found me surrounded with half-packed luggage.

"You seem to be off on your travels," he said. "Where are you going?"

With a strap between my teeth I replied, "To Battersea."

"The wit of your remark," he said, "wholly escapes me."

"I am going to Battersea," I repeated, "to Battersea viâ Paris, Belfort, Heidelberg, and Frankfort. My remark contained no wit. It contained simply the truth. I am going to wander over the whole world until once more I find Battersea. Somewhere in the seas of sunset or of sunrise, somewhere in the ultimate archipelago of the earth, there is one little island which I wish to find: an island with low green hills and great white cliffs. Travellers tell me that it is called England (Scotch travellers tell me that it is called Britain), and there is a rumour that somewhere in the heart of it there is a beautiful place called Battersea."

"I suppose it is unnecessary to tell you," said my friend, with an air of intellectual comparison, "that this is Battersea?"

"It is quite unnecessary," I said, "and it is spiritually untrue. I cannot see any Battersea here; I cannot see any London or any England. I cannot see that door. I cannot see that chair: because a cloud of sleep and custom has come across my eyes. The only way to get back to them is to go somewhere else; and that is the real object of travel and the real pleasure of holidays. Do you suppose that I go to France in order to see France? Do you suppose that I go to Germany in order to see Germany? I shall enjoy them both; but it is not them that I am seeking. I am seeking Battersea. The whole object of travel is not to set foot on foreign land; it is at last to set foot on one's own country as a foreign land. Now I warn you that this Gladstone bag is compact and heavy, and that if you utter that word 'paradox' I shall hurl it at your head. I did not make the world, and I did not make it paradoxical. It is not my fault, it is the truth, that the only way to go to England is to go away from it."

But when, after only a month's travelling, I did come back to England, I was startled to find that I had told the exact truth. England did break on me at once beautifully new and beautifully old. To land at Dover is the right way to approach England (most things that are hackneyed are right), for then you see first the full, soft gardens of Kent, which are, perhaps, an exaggeration, but still a typical exaggeration, of the rich rusticity of England. As it happened, also, a fellow-traveller with whom I had fallen into conversation felt the same freshness, though for another cause. She was an American lady who had seen Europe, and had never yet seen England, and she expressed her enthusiasm in that simple and splendid way which is natural to Americans, who are the most idealistic people in the whole world. Their only danger is that the idealist can easily become the idolator. And the American has become so idealistic that he even idealises money. But (to quote a very able writer of American short stories) that is another story.

"I have never been in England before," said the American lady, "yet it is so pretty that I feel as if I have been away from it for a long time."

"So you have," I said; "you have been away for three hundred years."

"What a lot of ivy you have," she said. "It covers the churches and it buries the houses. We have ivy; but I have never seen it grow like that."

"I am interested to hear it," I replied, "for I am making a little list of all the things that are really better in England. Even a month on the Continent, combined with intelligence, will teach you that there are many things that are better abroad. All the things that the *Daily Mail* calls English are better abroad. But there are things entirely English and entirely good. Kippers, for instance, and Free Trade, and front gardens, and individual liberty, and the Elizabethan drama, and hansom cabs, and cricket, and Mr. Will Crooks. Above all, there is the happy and holy custom of eating a heavy breakfast. I cannot imagine that Shakespeare began the day with rolls and coffee, like a Frenchman or a German. Surely he began with bacon or bloaters. In fact, a light bursts upon me; for the first time I see the real meaning of Mrs. Gallup and the Great Cipher. It is merely a mistake in the matter of a capital letter. I withdraw my objections; I accept everything; bacon did write Shakespeare."

"I cannot look at anything but the ivy," she said, "it looks so comfortable."

While she looked at the ivy I opened for the first time for many weeks an English newspaper, and I read a speech of Mr. Balfour in which he said that the House of Lords ought to be preserved because it represented something in the nature of permanent public opinion of England, above the ebb and flow of the parties. Now Mr. Balfour is a perfectly sincere patriot, a man who, from his own point of view, thinks long and seriously about the public needs, and he is, moreover, a man of entirely exceptionable intellectual power. But alas, in spite of all this, when I had read that speech I thought with a heavy heart that there was one more thing that I had to add to the list of the specially English things, such as kippers and cricket; I had to add the specially English kind of humbug. In France things are attacked and defended for what they are. The Catholic Church is attacked because it is Catholic, and defended because it is Catholic. The Republic is defended because it is Republican, and attacked because it is Republican. But here is the ablest of English politicians consoling everybody by telling them that the House of Lords is not really the House of Lords, but something quite different, that the foolish, accidental peers whom he meets every night are in some mysterious way experts upon the psychology of the democracy; that if you want to know what the very poor want you must ask the very rich, and that if you want the truth about Hoxton you must ask for it at Hatfield. If the Conservative defender of the House of Lords were a logical French politician he would simply be a liar. But being an English politician he is simply a poet. The English love of believing that all is as it should be, the English optimism combined with the strong English imagination, is too much even for the obvious facts. In a cold, scientific sense, of course, Mr. Balfour knows that nearly all the Lords who are not Lords by accident are Lords by bribery. He knows, and (as Mr. Belloc excellently said) everybody in Parliament knows the very names of the peers who have purchased their peerages. But the glamour of comfort, the pleasure of reassuring himself and reassuring others, is too strong for this original knowledge; at last it fades from him, and he sincerely and earnestly calls on Englishmen to join with him in admiring an august and public-spirited Senate, having wholly forgotten that the Senate really consists of idiots whom he has himself despised; and adventurers whom he has himself ennobled.

"Your ivy is so beautifully soft and thick," said the American lady, "it seems to cover almost everything. It must be the most poetical thing in England."

"It is very beautiful," I said, "and, as you say, it is very English. Charles Dickens, who was almost more English than England, wrote one of his rare poems about the beauty of ivy. Yes, by all means let us admire the ivy, so deep, so warm, so full of a genial gloom and a grotesque tenderness. Let us admire the ivy; and let us pray to God in His mercy that it may not kill the tree."

ON DOGS WITH BAD NAMES

A NEGATIVE disadvantage attaches to almost any man who has a positive character or, what commonly goes with it and is even more important, positive convictions. A literary man, for instance, who has strong likes and dislikes, in the style of Dr. Johnson or Cobbett or Coventry Patmore, becomes so much of a proverb or a joke that nobody can believe there is anything new to be learnt about him. Anything new that he does say is coloured, or rather discoloured, either by what people know he has said or by what people think he would say. Even what they know they very often know wrong; and when they come to guess, they almost invariably guess wrong. But the still more curious fact is that even when they know they still go on guessing. When the new statement is actually written, it is not actually read. Something else is read into it, which is the recognized rumour about what the eccentric in question is likely to state. For, in truth, most of the critics have not realized anything about the writer except that he is an eccentric, and even in that they are wrong. He has generally earned that reputation by being concentrated on certain fundamental or cosmic convictions. If he is very religious or very irreligious, for instance, he will probably be called eccentric. Obviously he ought to be called centric, since the centre of his mind is rightly fixed on the central problems of existence. But these people called eccentrics, like Johnson or Patmore in one way, or Shelley or Shaw in another way, always suffer from this curious disadvantage— that while people nearly always admit that they are great talkers, people hardly ever listen to what they actually say. People *never* listen to anything they say in correction or re- consideration of anything they have said, or are supposed to have said. What they have said they have said, or what we have said they have said they have said, and there is an end of it. Their position is fixed in the popular mind; and, curiously enough, they generally begin by being very unpopular and end by being very popular. But they are not popular enough to be allowed to point out the meaning of their own words.

Thus I have seen critic after critic throwing out general sug- gestions and summaries of what Mr. Bernard Shaw would "char- acteristically" say, which I knew for a fact to be flatly contrary to everything that he was saying. Thus, because he was an Irish- man and presumed to be a comic Irishman, and because he often made fun of some aspects of the Englishman, numbers of people have believed he was a sort of Fenian and fierce Irish National- ist in revolt against the British Empire. Whereas Bernard Shaw not only never pretended for a moment to believe in any sort of Nationalism, but at the political crisis he was rather especially cold towards the nationalism of Ireland. Nay, he definitely pre- ferred, if anything, the Imperialism of England. For instance, he was on the side of the British Empire against the Boers, when all the national Irish were on the side of the Boers against the Brit- ish Empire. But I suppose that the English people will always cling to the lovely legend of Shaw scorning them and deriding them, though he actually defended them when all Europe de- nounced them. You could not add that last fact to the popular legend of Bernard Shaw by any possible hook or crook, not if you printed his actual words in letters eight feet high. The pub- lic had got its picture of Shaw long before that particular in- cident, and would continue to believe the legend against the fact; the picture against the face.

I remember being involved in a comic little tangle in which two or three eminent men were treated in this way; I might almost say that they treated each other in this way. Mr. H. G. Wells, in one of his phases, wrote a chapter denouncing the invocation of a Superman as a sort of separate type of giant or god, like the colossal kings of Egyptian Art. I should have thought there was a touch of this in Mr. Wells himself, in another of his phases, when he described the case for the Giants in *The Food of the Gods*. But I may be wrong; I may myself be falling into this error, which nearly everybody else fell into on this occasion. Anyhow, Mr. Wells not only repudiated the Superman as a solitary king, but accused Mr. Bernard Shaw of having assisted to crown that monstrous monarch. Mr. Shaw had doubtless talked of the Superman sometimes, but he had no difficulty in showing that he had never believed in one Superman ruling all men; but only, like Mr. Wells, in the hope of raising all men to a sort of Supermanhood. But, curiously enough, in the course of this Mr. Shaw had occasion to refer to Mr. Belloc, and said that the theory of the Servile State was only Herbert Spencer's old attack on Socialism. From which it was obvious that Mr. Shaw had never read Mr. Belloc's book on the Servile State, or he would have known that it is not an attack on Socialism, and that it has not the remotest resemblance to Herbert Spencer. But, just as Mr. Wells took it for granted that Mr. Shaw *would* write certain things about the Superman, so Mr. Shaw took it for granted that Mr. Belloc *would* write certain things about the Servile State. And in revenge, as I have said, everybody takes it for granted that Mr. Shaw *would* write certain things about anything or everything. What he did write, or does write, seems to make no difference.

This curious crooked doom, on strong characters with strong convictions, has pursued Mr. Belloc also in later times, in connexion with his historical biographies. I notice some reviews of his book on Napoleon which read to me as if the reviewers had never read his book on Napoleon, but only made a bold guess at what a book on Napoleon by Belloc would be like. Mr. Belloc does not in the least turn Napoleon into a Superman; he even argues that some acknowledged victories were essentially defeats. A still more curious case was that of his book on Cranmer. Everybody knows Mr. Belloc's beliefs on the religion of Cranmer, but they do not appear very much in his book on Cranmer. It is a very swift and simple personal story, that can be read by Protestants or Catholics. What is still more quaint, it is a much more favourable personal story than has generally been written by Protestants. I do not suppose anybody will believe me when I state this fact, because of this interesting preference for a fixed fancy over a fact. But it is fact that the Protestant Macaulay was much more hostile to Cranmer than the Papistical Belloc. In Macaulay's version we feel stark contempt for a dirty little scoundrel; in Belloc's we feel considerable compassion for a timid scholar partly trapped into tricks that were not wholly his own. Yet I have seen scores of reviews which answered the book on Cranmer as if it were a pamphlet challenging all the reformed churches. The truth is simply as I have stated it: when a man has become a public figure famed for certain opinions, any number of critics refuse to criticize anything except those opinions. It is no use for him to have other opinions, or new opinions, even upon new topics. Bernard Shaw must be guying John Bull, though *John Bull's Other Island* is really rather favourable to him; and Belloc must be slandering Cranmer, even when he is almost excusing him.

THE REAL JOURNALIST

OUR age which has boasted of realism will fail chiefly through lack of reality. Never, I fancy, has there been so grave and startling a divorce between the real way a thing is done and the

look of it when it is done. I take the nearest and most topical instance to hand—a newspaper. Nothing looks more neat and
regular than a newspaper, with its parallel columns, its mechanical printing, its detailed facts and figures, its responsible, poly-
syllabic leading articles. Nothing, as a matter of fact, goes every
night through more agonies of adventure, more hairbreadth escapes, desperate expedients, crucial councils, random compromises, or barely averted catastrophes. Seen from the outside, it
seems to come round as automatically as the clock and as silently as the dawn. Seen from the inside, it gives all its organisers
a gasp of relief every morning to see that it has come out at all;
that it has come out without the leading article upside down or
the Pope congratulated on discovering the North Pole.

I will give an instance (merely to illustrate my thesis of unreality) from the paper that I know best. Here is a simple story,
a little episode in the life of a journalist, which may be amusing
and instructive: the tale of how I made a great mistake in quotation. There are really two stories: the story as seen from the
outside, by a man reading the paper; and the story seen from the
inside, by the journalists shouting and telephoning and taking
notes in shorthand through the night.

This is the outside story; and it reads like a dreadful quarrel.
The notorious G. K. Chesterton, a reactionary Torquemada
whose one gloomy pleasure was in the defence of orthodoxy and
the pursuit of heretics, long calculated and at last launched a
denunciation of a brilliant leader of the New Theology which he
hated with all the furnace of his fanatic soul. In this document
Chesterton darkly, deliberately, and not having the fear of God
before his eyes, asserted that Shakespeare wrote the line "that
wreaths its old fantastic roots so high." This he said because he
had been kept in ignorance by Priests; or, perhaps, because he
thought craftily that none of his dupes could discover a curious
and forgotten rhyme called *Elegy in a Country Churchyard*.
Anyhow, that orthodox gentleman made a howling error; and

received some twenty-five letters and post-cards from kind correspondents who pointed out the mistake.

But the odd thing is that scarcely any of them could conceive that it was a mistake. The first wrote in the tone of one wearied of epigrams, and cried, "What is the joke *now?*" Another professed (and practised, for all I know, God help him) that he had read through all Shakespeare and failed to find the line. A third wrote in a sort of moral distress, asking, as in confidence, if Gray was really a plagiarist. They were a noble collection; but they all subtly assumed an element of leisure and exactitude in the recipient's profession and character which is far from the truth. Let us pass on to the next act of the external tragedy.

In Monday's issue of the same paper appeared a letter from the same culprit. He ingenuously confessed that the line did not belong to Shakespeare, but to a poet whom he called Grey. Which was another cropper—or whopper. This stranger and illiterate outbreak was printed by the editor with the justly scornful title, "Mr. Chesterton 'Explains'?" Any man reading the paper at breakfast saw at once the meaning of the sarcastic quotation marks. They meant, of course, "Here is a man who doesn't know Gray from Shakespeare; he tries to patch it up and he can't even spell Gray. And that is what he calls an Explanation." That is the perfectly natural inference of the reader from the letter, the mistake, and the headline—as seen from the outside. The falsehood was serious; the editorial rebuke was serious. The stern editor and the sombre, baffled contributor confront each other as the curtain falls.

And now I will tell you exactly what really happened. It is honestly rather amusing; it is a story of what journals and journalists really are. A monstrously lazy man lives in South Bucks partly by writing a column in the Saturday *Daily News*. At the time he usually writes it (which is always at the last moment) his house is unexpectedly invaded by infants of all shapes and sizes. His secretary is called away; and he has to cope with the invading pigmies. Playing with children is a glorious thing; but the journalist in question has never understood why it was considered a soothing or idyllic one. It reminds him, not of watering little budding flowers, but of wrestling for hours with gigantic angels and devils. Moral problems of the most monstrous complexity besiege him incessantly. He has to decide before the awful eyes of innocence, whether, when a sister has knocked down a brother's bricks, in revenge for the brother having taken two sweets out of his turn, it is endurable that the brother should retaliate by scribbling on the sister's picture-book, and whether such conduct does not justify the sister in blowing out the brother's unlawfully lighted match.

Just as he is solving this problem upon principles of the highest morality, it occurs to him suddenly that he has not written his Saturday article; and that there is only about an hour to do it in. He wildly calls to somebody (probably the gardener) to telephone to somewhere for a messenger; he barricades himself in another room and tears his hair, wondering what on earth he shall write about. A drumming of fists on the door outside and a cheerful bellowing encourage and clarify his thoughts; and he is able to observe some newspapers and circulars in wrappers lying on the table. One is a dingy book catalogue; the second is a shiny pamphlet about petrol; the third is a paper called *The Christian Commonwealth*. He opens it anyhow, and sees in the middle of a page a sentence with which he honestly disagrees. It says that the sense of beauty in Nature is a new thing, hardly felt before Wordsworth. A stream of images and pictures pour through his head, like skies chasing each other or forests running by. "Not felt before Wordsworth!" he thinks. "Oh, but this won't do . . . . bare ruined choirs where late the sweet birds sang . . . night's candles are burnt out . . . glowed with living sapphires . . . leaving their moon-loved maze . . . antique roots fantastic . . . antique roots wreathed high . . . what is it in *As You Like It?*"

He sits down desperately; the messenger rings at the bell; the children drum on the door; the servants run up from time to time to say the messenger is getting bored; and the pencil staggers along, making the world a present of fifteen hundred unimportant words, and making Shakespeare a present of a portion of Gray's Elegy; putting "fantastic roots wreathed high" instead of "antique roots peep out." Then the journalist sends off his copy and turns his attention to the enigma of whether a brother should commandeer a sister's necklace because the sister pinched him at Littlehampton. That is the first scene; that is how an article is really written.

The scene now changes to the newspaper office. The writer of the article has discovered his mistake and wants to correct it by the next day: but the next day is Sunday. He cannot post a letter, so he rings up the paper and dictates a letter by telephone. He leaves the title to his friends at the other end; he knows that they can spell "Gray," as no doubt they can: but the letter is put down by journalistic custom in a pencil scribble and the vowel may well be doubtful. The friend writes at the top of the letter " 'G. K. C.' Explains," putting the initials in quotation marks. The next man passing it for press is bored with these initials (I am with him there) and crosses them out, substituting with austere civility, "Mr. Chesterton Explains." But—and now he hears the iron laughter of the Fates, for the blind bolt is about to fall—but he neglects to cross out the second "quote" (as we call it) and it goes up to press with a "quote" between the last words. Another quotation mark at the end of "explains" was the work of one merry moment for the printers upstairs. So the inverted commas were lifted entirely off one word on to the other and a totally innocent title suddenly turned into a blasting sneer. But that would have mattered nothing so far, for there was nothing to sneer at. In the same dark hour, however, there was a printer who was (I suppose) so devoted to this Government that he could think of no Gray but Sir Edward Grey. He spelt it

"Grey" by a mere misprint, and the whole tale was complete: first blunder, second blunder, and final condemnation.

That is a little tale of journalism as it is; if you call it egotistic and ask what is the use of it I think I could tell you. You might remember it when next some ordinary young workman is going to be hanged by the neck on circumstantial evidence.

ON ARCHITECTURE

WE have all of us been hearing for some time about the proposal to pull down the City churches. Some of us have a certain sympathy with the view that it would be much better to pull down the City. In the long reaches of history the irony of the contrast disappears. There must be a good many Greek or Egyptian temples still standing when the towns or villages that clustered about them have dissolved into dust. In looking at those temples we still have, if we are at all imaginative, a sort of mystical sympathy. We have a sense that, after all, the temple did not really exist to serve the city, but to serve the god. But it is a sort of sympathy we seem only able to feel in the case of a heathen god. Any number of neo-pagan poems have been written describing such gods as still hovering like ghosts over such temples. Any number of modern poets have written about ancient ruins still haunted by dog-headed Anubis or great green-eyed Pasht. They seldom expressed much sympathy for the human inhabitants of those vanished cities. But, in the case of the vanished cities, at least the inhabitants did inhabit. They worked, wedded, dined, and slept in their own town, and were often attached to it by a high religion of patriotism. So did the inhabitants of our City, in the days when people built churches there. Now that the City has become a vast warehouse, there is much

less cause for a poetic lament over its destruction. The reader
will be relieved to hear, however, that I have no immediate intention of setting fire to London, or of attempting to repeat the
great conflagration which was recorded (entirely wrong) on
the Monument. I merely say, in a general historical sense, that
the mysterious description of a man as being Something in the
City might have been extended in ancient times even to so humble a calling as being a Priest in the City. And I do say that,
when we see humanity in retrospect and perspective, we generally find their religion more interesting than their commerce.
Even the most commercial cities of antiquity, like Tyre and
Carthage, were not so lively and entertaining when they were
making out bills-of-lading or recording the fluctuation of the
shekel as compared with the drachma, as when the more poetic
side of their nature led them to throw babies into the furnace of
Moloch.

But the comparison of commercial and religious centres is connected with another question that is perhaps more immediately
modern than the worship of Moloch. We have not got quite so
far as reviving that sort of Eastern mysticism as yet, though there
is no saying what we may come to eventually, with a judicious
combination of neo-pagan nature-worship and our efforts to
restrict the population. But, anyhow, it is more and more plain
that commerce is cosmopolitan, while religion is generally to
some extent national, even if it is also international. Being an expression of the whole life of a people, it gives some expression to
the local and traditional life; whereas mere commercialism of its
nature becomes more and more a shuffling and interchange of
different products. The London churches do preserve a certain
historic character of London; they do remind us of a typical
passage in the history of England. But the merely commercial
life of England becomes less and less English; and the material
machinery of London is looking more and more like New York.
It seems likely that, as has so often happened, things native and
domestic will have to retire into sanctuary. It will be a long time

at least before the last monument of Wren vanishes with the fall of St. Paul's Cathedral, as the last monument of the Regent has vanished with the fall of Regent Street.

In that sense it is not so much a question of the preservation of London churches as of the preservation of London. London has a soul of its own; it therefore has a soul to be saved; but nobody seems to bother very much about saving it. And it seems possible that the quaint old Wren churches might still do something towards saving the soul of London, even if we have given up all hope of any churches saving the souls of Londoners. For those seventeenth-century buildings had a character and expressed a spirit, even if it be not what I myself should regard as the highest spirit. I am (as my enemies have discovered with diabolical, but slightly monotonous, glee) a mediævalist; and it is my instinct to seek the highest spirit in what was once the highest spire. For the old Gothic St. Paul's, that stood on Ludgate Hill before the Great Fire, was said to be the loftiest building in Christendom. It must have looked very magnificent, rising to such a height upon such a hill. Old St. Paul's might even have been spared by the American invader as being quite a respectable sky-scraper.

Nevertheless, I do not desire the present Renaissance dome of St. Paul's to be immediately replaced by a Woolworth tower. However it may stand in relation to Christendom, it stands in a very important position in relation to Europe. It does to that extent represent the spirit of Europe; and in this particular conflict I sympathize with the spirit of Europe as against the spirit of America. Something of the same part is played in a smaller way by the other Renaissance churches; in so far as they do testify to the idea that culture is a thing rather of quality than quantity. They do suggest that quaint things in quiet places may reveal the secret of our deep human past often better than buildings that take up much more room in the streets, and also much more room in the newspapers. They do stand, in some fashion, for the moment, for the fact that it is not the sky-scraper that is nearest to the sky. A man must have some little sense of craftsmanship and history to know how good is some of the seventeenth-century carving, even of the florid and lightly classical sort. He does not need anything but a neck to crane and eyes to goggle with in order to appreciate a sky-scraper. The taste for mere size is not merely more vulgar; it is also more backward and barbaric. It is all the difference between Rembrandt or Velas-quez studying the subtleties of an ordinary face and the yokels in a village staring at the giant in a show. And, in so far as it is a war between barbarism and civilization, I hope I am on the side of civilization not for the first time.

But even where the larger thing is all right in its place, it is here out of place. Even when it is good as a sky-scraper, it is not suited to the sky. The first rule of all good scene-painting is to remember the back-scene. It is an error to paint even Aladdin's Palace without knowing whether its domes and minarets are to be outlined against the back-scene of the Blasted Heath or of the Nile with the barge of Cleopatra. The more inappropriate is the background, the more it will fall forward into the foreground. And our scenery, in several senses, has rather a way of falling down on the actors. Our scenery is of the sort that keeps the scene-shifter very busy shifting. Our back-scene is always a transformation scene. To some it may seem a rather dismal sort of dissolving view. To others (including myself) its cold clouds and gradations of grey seem to be the very vision of real ro-mance. But, anyhow, English weather is emphatically weather; as is implied when we talk of having to weather it. There is no such thing as the English climate. Now the best American architecture is very fine architecture, as, for example, the Penn-sylvania Railway Station in New York. But the best American architecture is classical architecture, of the same kind as the best Greek and Roman architecture. At least, it is partly of the same kind, and partly for the same reason. It was built for a climate; it was built to stand up clear and clean-cut against a sky that looks as solid and steady as the stone; a pure pattern of white upon blue. It is suitable to the hard light and the cloudless spaces about the towers of Manhattan; and there, like anything else that is in its place, it is a splendid thing to see. But even the invaders who have brought over American buildings have not yet imported any large blue fragments of American sky.

THE TELEGRAPH POLES

My friend and I were walking in one of those wastes of pinewood which make inland seas of solitude in every part of Western Europe; which have the true terror of a desert, since they are uniform, and so one may lose one's way in them. Stiff, straight, and similar, stood up all around us the pines of the wood, like the pikes of a silent mutiny. There is a truth in talking of the variety of Nature; but I think that Nature often shows her chief strangeness in her sameness. There is a weird rhythm in this very repetition; it is as if the earth were resolved to repeat a single shape until the shape shall turn terrible.

Have you ever tried the experiment of saying some plain word, such as "dog," thirty times? By the thirtieth time it has become a word like "snark" or "pobble." It does not become tame, it becomes wild, by repetition. In the end a dog walks about as startling and undecipherable as Leviathan or Croquemitaine.

It may be that this explains the repetitions in Nature; it may be for this reason that there are so many million leaves and pebbles. Perhaps they are not repeated so that they may grow familiar. Perhaps they are repeated only in the hope that they may at last grow unfamiliar. Perhaps a man is not startled at the first cat he sees, but jumps into the air with surprise at the seventy-ninth cat. Perhaps he has to pass through thousands of pine trees before he finds the one that is really a pine tree. However this may be, there is something singularly thrilling, even something urgent and intolerant, about the endless forest repetitions; there is the hint of something like madness in that musical monotony of the pines.

I said something like this to my friend; and he answered with sardonic truth, "Ah, you wait till we come to a telegraph post."

.   .   .   .   .

My friend was right, as he occasionally is in our discussions, especially upon points of fact. We had crossed the pine forest by one of its paths which happened to follow the wires of the provincial telegraphy; and though the poles occurred at long intervals they made a difference when they came. The instant we came to the straight pole we could see that the pines were not really straight. It was like a hundred straight lines drawn with schoolboy pencils all brought to judgment suddenly by one straight line drawn with a ruler. All the amateur lines seemed to reel to right and left. A moment before I could have sworn they stood as straight as lances; now I could see them curve and waver everywhere, like scimitars and yataghans. Compared with the telegraph post the pines were crooked—and alive. That lonely vertical rod at once deformed and enfranchised the forest. It tangled it all together and yet made it free, like any grotesque undergrowth of oak or holly.

"Yes," said my gloomy friend, answering my thoughts. "You don't know what a wicked shameful thing straightness is if you think these trees are straight. You never will know till your precious intellectual civilisation builds a forty-mile forest of telegraph poles."

We had started walking from our temporary home later in the day than we intended; and the long afternoon was already lengthening itself out into a yellow evening when we came out of the forest on to the hills above a strange town or village, of which the lights had already begun to glitter in the darkening valley. The change had already happened which is the test and definition of evening. I mean that while the sky seemed still as bright, the earth was growing blacker against it, especially at the edges, the hills and the pine-tops. This brought out yet more clearly the owlish secrecy of pine-woods; and my friend cast a regretful glance at them as he came out under the sky. Then he turned to the view in front; and, as it happened, one of the tele-graph posts stood up in front of him in the last sunlight. It was no longer crossed and softened by the more delicate lines of pine wood; it stood up ugly, arbitrary, and angular as any crude fig-ure in geometry. My friend stopped, pointing his stick at it, and all his anarchic philosophy rushed to his lips.

"Demon," he said to me briefly, "behold your work. That palace of proud trees behind us is what the world was before you civilised men, Christians or democrats or the rest, came to make it dull with your dreary rules of morals and equality. In the silent fight of that forest, tree fights speechless against tree, branch against branch. And the upshot of that dumb battle is in-equality—and beauty. Now lift up your eyes and look at equality and ugliness. See how regularly the white buttons are arranged on that black stick, and defend your dogmas if you dare."

"Is that telegraph post so much a symbol of democracy?" I asked. "I fancy that while three men have made the telegraph to get dividends, about a thousand men have preserved the forest to cut wood. But if the telegraph pole is hideous (as I admit) it is not due to doctrine but rather to commercial anarchy. If any one had a doctrine about a telegraph pole it might be carved in ivory and decked with gold. Modern things are ugly, because modern men are careless, not because they are careful."

"No," answered my friend with his eye on the end of a splen-did and sprawling sunset, "there is something intrinsically dead-ening about the very idea of a doctrine. A straight line is always ugly. Beauty is always crooked. These rigid posts at regular in-tervals are ugly because they are carrying across the world the real message of democracy."

"At this moment," I answered, "they are probably carrying across the world the message, 'Buy Bulgarian Rails.' They are probably the prompt communication between some two of the wealthiest and wickedest of His children with whom God has ever had patience. No; these telegraph poles are ugly and detestable, they are inhuman and indecent. But their baseness lies in their privacy, not in their publicity. That black stick with white buttons is not the creation of the soul of a multitude. It is the mad creation of the souls of two millionaires."

"At least you have to explain," answered my friend gravely, "how it is that the hard democratic doctrine and the hard telegraphic outline have appeared together; you have . . . But bless my soul, we must be getting home. I had no idea it was so late. Let me see, I think this is our way through the wood. Come, let us both curse the telegraph post for entirely different reasons and get home before it is dark."

We did not get home before it was dark. For one reason or another we had underestimated the swiftness of twilight and the suddenness of night, especially in the threading of thick woods. When my friend, after the first five minutes' march, had fallen over a log, and I, ten minutes after, had stuck nearly to the knees in mire, we began to have some suspicion of our direction. At last my friend said, in a low, husky voice:

"I'm afraid we're on the wrong path. It's pitch dark."

"I thought we went the right way," I said, tentatively.

"Well," he said; and then, after a long pause, "I can't see any telegraph poles. I've been looking for them."

"So have I," I said. "They're so straight."

We groped away for about two hours of darkness in the thick of the fringe of trees which seemed to dance round us in derision. Here and there, however, it was possible to trace the outline of something just too erect and rigid to be a pine tree. By these we finally felt our way home, arriving in a cold green twilight before dawn.

THE FURROWS

As I see the corn grow green all about my neighbourhood, there rushes on me for no reason in particular a memory of the winter. I say "rushes," for that is the very word for the old sweeping lines of the ploughed fields. From some accidental turn of a train-journey or a walking tour, I saw suddenly the fierce rush of the furrows. The furrows are like arrows; they fly along an arc of sky. They are like leaping animals; they vault an inviolable hill and roll down the other side. They are like battering battalions; they rush over a hill with flying squadrons and carry it with a cavalry charge. They have all the air of Arabs sweeping a desert, of rockets sweeping the sky, of torrents sweeping a watercourse. Nothing ever seemed so living as those brown lines as they shot sheer from the height of a ridge down to their still whirl of the valley. They were swifter than arrows, fiercer than Arabs, more riotous and rejoicing than rockets. And yet they were only thin straight lines drawn with difficulty, like a diagram, by painful and patient men. The men that ploughed tried to plough straight; they had no notion of giving great sweeps and swirls to the eye. Those cataracts of cloven earth; they were done by the grace of God. I had always rejoiced in them; but I had never found any reason for my joy. There are some very clever people who cannot enjoy the joy unless they understand it. There are other and even cleverer people who say that they lose the joy the moment they do understand it. Thank God I was never clever, and could always enjoy things when I understood them and when I didn't. I can enjoy the orthodox Tory, though I could never understand him. I can also enjoy the orthodox Liberal, though I understand him only too well.

But the splendour of furrowed fields is this: that like all brave things they are made straight, and therefore they bend. In everything that bows gracefully there must be an effort at stiffness. Bows are beautiful when they bend only because they try to remain rigid; and sword-blades can curl like silver ribbons only because they are certain to spring straight again. But the same is true of every tough curve of the tree trunk, of every strong-backed bend of the bough; there is hardly any such thing in Nature as a mere droop of weakness. Rigidity yielding a little, like justice swayed by mercy, is the whole beauty of the earth. The cosmos is a diagram just bent beautifully out of shape. Everything tries to be straight; and everything just fortunately fails.

The foil may curve in the lunge; but there is nothing beautiful about beginning the battle with a crooked foil. So the strict aim, the strong doctrine, may give a little in the actual fight with facts; but that is no reason for beginning with a weak doctrine or a twisted aim. Do not be an opportunist; try to be theoretic at all the opportunities; fate can be trusted to do all the opportunist part of it. Do not try to bend, any more than the trees try to bend. Try to grow straight, and life will bend you.

Alas! I am giving the moral before the fable; and yet I hardly think that otherwise you could see all that I mean in that enormous vision of the ploughed hills. These great furrowed slopes are the oldest architecture of man: the oldest astronomy was his guide, the oldest botany his object. And for geometry, the mere word proves my case.

But when I looked at those torrents of ploughed parallels, that great rush of rigid lines, I seemed to see the whole huge achievement of democracy. Here was mere equality: but equality seen in bulk is more superb than any supremacy. Equality free and flying, equality rushing over hill and dale, equality charging the world—that was the meaning of those military furrows, military in their identity, military in their energy. They sculptured hill and dale with strong curves merely because they did not mean to curve at all. They made the strong lines of landscape with their stiffly driven swords of the soil. It is not only nonsense, but blasphemy, to say that man has spoilt the country. Man has created the country; it was his business, as the image of God. No hill, covered with common scrub or patches of purple heath, could have been so sublimely hilly as that ridge up to which the ranked furrows rose like aspiring angels. No valley, confused with needless cottages and towns, can have been so utterly valleyish as that abyss into which the down-rushing furrows raged like demons into the swirling pit.

It is the hard lines of discipline and equality that mark out a landscape and give it all its mould and meaning. It is just because the lines of the furrow are ugly and even that the landscape is living and superb. As I think I have remarked before, the Republic is founded on the plough.

THE WHITE HORSES

It is within my experience, which is very brief and occasional in this matter, that it is not really at all easy to talk in a motor-car. This is fortunate; first, because, as a whole, it prevents me from motoring; and second because, at any given moment, it prevents me from talking. The difficulty is not wholly due to the physical conditions, though these are distinctly unconversational. FitzGerald's Omar, being a pessimist, was probably rich, and being a lazy fellow, was almost certainly a motorist. If any doubt could exist on the point, it is enough to say that, in speaking of the foolish profits, Omar has defined the difficulties of colloquial motoring with a precision which cannot be accidental. "Their words to wind are scattered; and their mouths are stopped with dust." From this follows not (as many of the cut-and-dried philosophers would say) a savage silence and mutual hostility, but rather one of those rich silences that make the mass and bulk of all friendship; the silence of men rowing the same boat or fighting in the same battle line.

It happened that the other day I hired a motor-car, because I wanted to visit in very rapid succession the battle-places and hiding-places of Alfred the Great; and for a thing of this sort a motor is really appropriate. It is not by any means the best way of seeing the beauty of the country; you see beauty better by walking, and best of all by sitting still. But it is a good method in any enterprise that involves a parody of the military or governmental quality—anything which needs to know quickly the whole contour of a country or the rough, relative position of men and towns. On such a journey, like jagged lightning, I sat from morning till night by the side of the chauffeur; and we scarcely exchanged a word to the hour. But by the time the yellow stars came out in the villages and the white stars in the skies, I think I understood his character; and I fear he understood mine.

He was a Cheshire man with a sour, patient, and humorous face; he was modest, though a north countryman, and genial, though an expert. He spoke (when he spoke at all) with a strong northland accent; and he evidently was new to the beautiful south country, as was clear both from his approval and his complaints. But though he came from the north he was agricultural and not commercial in origin; he looked at the land rather than the towns, even if he looked at it with a somewhat more sharp and utilitarian eye. His first remark for some hours was uttered when we were crossing the more coarse and desolate heights of Salisbury Plain. He remarked that he had always thought that Salisbury Plain was a plain. This alone showed that he was new to the vicinity. But he also said, with a critical frown, "A lot of this land ought to be good land enough. Why don't they use it?" He was then silent for some more hours.

At an abrupt angle of the slopes that lead down from what is called (with no little humour) Salisbury Plain, I saw suddenly, as by accident, something I was looking for—that is, something I did not expect to see. We are all supposed to be trying to walk into heaven; but we should be uncommonly astonished if we suddenly walked into it. As I was leaving Salisbury Plain (to put it roughly) I lifted up my eyes and saw the White Horse of Britain.

One or two truly fine poets of the Tory and Protestant type, such as Swinburne and Mr. Rudyard Kipling, have eulogised England under the image of white horses, meaning the white-maned breakers of the Channel. This is right and natural enough. The true philosophical Tory goes back to ancient things because he thinks they will be anarchic things. It would startle him very much to be told that there are white horses of artifice in England that may be older than those wild white horses of the elements. Yet it is truly so. Nobody knows how old are those strange green and white hieroglyphics, those straggling quadrupeds of chalk, that stand out on the sides of so many of the Southern Downs. They are possibly older than Saxon and older than Roman times. They may well be older than British, older than any recorded times. They may go back, for all we know, to the first faint seeds of human life on this planet. Men may have picked a horse out of the grass long before they scratched a horse on a vase or pot, or messed and massed any horse out of clay. This may be the oldest human art—before building or graving. And if so, it may have first happened in another geological age; before the sea burst through the narrow Straits of Dover. The White Horse may have begun in Berkshire when there were no white horses at Folkestone or Newhaven. That rude but evident white outline that I saw across the valley may have been begun when Britain was not an island. We forget that there are many places where art is older than nature.

We took a long detour through somewhat easier roads, till we came to a breach or chasm in the valley, from which we saw our friend the White Horse once more. At least, we thought it was our friend the White Horse; but after a little inquiry we discovered to our astonishment that it was another friend and another horse. Along the leaning flanks of the same fair valley there was (it seemed) another white horse, as rude and as clean, as ancient and as modern, as the first. This, at least, I thought must be the aboriginal White Horse of Alfred, which I had always heard associated with his name. And yet before we had driven into Wantage and seen King Alfred's quaint grey statue in the sun, we had seen yet a third white horse. And the third white horse was so hopelessly unlike a horse that we were sure that it was genuine. The final and original white horse, the white horse of the White Horse Vale, has that big, babyish quality that truly belongs to our remotest ancestors. It really has the prehistoric, preposterous quality of Zulu or New Zealand native drawings. This at least was surely made by our fathers when they were barely men; long before they were civilised men.

But why was it made? Why did barbarians take so much trouble to make a horse nearly as big as a hamlet; a horse who could bear no hunter, who could drag no load? What was this titanic, sub-conscious instinct for spoiling a beautiful green slope with a very ugly white quadruped? What (for the matter of that) is this whole hazardous fancy of humanity ruling the earth, which may have begun with white horses, which may by no means end with twenty horse-power cars? As I rolled away out of that country, I was still cloudily considering how ordinary men ever came to want to make such strange chalk horses, when my chauffeur startled me by speaking for the first time for nearly two hours. He suddenly let go one of the handles and pointed at a gross green bulk of down that happened to swell above us.

"That would be a good place," he said.

Naturally I referred to his last speech of some hours before; and supposed he meant that it would be promising for agriculture. As a fact, it was quite unpromising; and this made me suddenly understand the quiet ardour in his eye. All of a sudden I saw what he really meant. He really meant that this would be a splendid place to pick out another white horse. He knew no more than I did why it was done; but he was in some unthinkable prehistoric tradition, because he wanted to do it. He became so acute in sensibility that he could not bear to pass any broad breezy hill of grass on which there was *not* a white horse. He could hardly keep his hands off the hills. He could hardly leave any of the living grass alone.

Then I left off wondering why the primitive man made so many white horses. I left off troubling in what sense the ordinary eternal man had sought to scar or deface the hills. I was content to know that he did want it; for I had seen him wanting it.

COCKNEYS AND THEIR JOKES

A WRITER in the *Yorkshire Evening Post* is very angry indeed with my performances in this column. His precise terms of reproach are, "Mr. G. K. Chesterton is not a humourist: not even a Cockney humourist." I do not mind his saying that I am not a humourist—in which (to tell the truth) I think he is quite right. But I do resent his saying that I am not a Cockney. That envenomed arrow, I admit, went home. If a French writer said of me, "He is no metaphysician: not even an English metaphysician," I could swallow the insult to my metaphysics, but I should feel angry about the insult to my country. So I do not urge that I am a humourist; but I do insist that I am a Cockney. If I were a humourist, I should certainly be a Cockney humourist; if I were a saint, I should certainly be a Cockney saint. I need not recite the splendid catalogue of Cockney saints who have written their names on our noble old City churches. I need not trouble you with the long list of the Cockney humourists who have discharged their bills (or failed to discharge them) in our noble old City taverns. We can weep together over the pathos of the poor Yorkshireman, whose county has never produced some humour not intelligible to the rest of the world. And we can smile together when he says that somebody or other is "not even" a Cockney humourist like Samuel Johnson or Charles Lamb. It is surely sufficiently obvious that all the best humour that exists in our language is Cockney humour. Chaucer was a Cockney; he had his house close to the Abbey. Dickens was a Cockney; he said he could not think without the London streets. The London taverns heard always the quaintest conversation, whether it was Ben Jonson's at the Mermaid or Sam Johnson's at the Cock. Even in our own time it may be noted that the most vital and genuine humour is still written about London. Of this type is the mild and humane irony which marks Mr. Pett Ridge's studies of the small grey streets. Of this type is the simple but smashing laughter of the best tales of Mr. W. W. Jacobs, telling of the smoke and sparkle of the Thames. No; I concede that I am not a Cockney humourist. No; I am not worthy to be. Some time, after sad and strenuous after-lives; some time, after fierce and apocalyptic incarnations; in some strange world beyond the stars, I may become at last a Cockney humourist. In that potential paradise I may walk among the Cockney humourists, if not an equal, at least a companion. I may feel for a moment on my shoulder the hearty hand of Dryden and thread the labyrinths of the sweet insanity of Lamb. But that could only be if I were not only much cleverer, but much better than I am. Before I reach that sphere I shall have left behind, perhaps, the sphere that is inhabited by angels, and even passed that which is appropriated exclusively to the use of Yorkshiremen.

No; London is in this matter attacked upon its strongest ground. London is the largest of the bloated modern cities; London is the smokiest; London is the dirtiest; London is, if you will, the most sombre; London is, if you will, the most miserable. But London is certainly the most amusing and the most amused. You may prove that we have the most tragedy; the fact remains that we have the most comedy, that we have the most farce. We have at the very worst a splendid hypocrisy of humour. We conceal our sorrow behind a screaming derision. You speak of people who laugh through their tears; it is our boast that we only weep through our laughter. There remains always this great boast, perhaps the greatest boast that is possible to human nature. I mean the great boast that the most unhappy part of our population is also the most hilarious part. The poor can forget that social problem which we (the moderately rich) ought never to forget. Blessed are the poor; for they alone have not the poor always with them. The honest poor can sometimes forget poverty. The honest rich can never forget it.

I believe firmly in the value of all vulgar notions, especially of vulgar jokes. When once you have got hold of a vulgar joke, you may be certain that you have got hold of a subtle and spiritual idea. The men who made the joke saw something deep which they could not express except by something silly and emphatic. They saw something delicate which they could only express by something indelicate. I remember that Mr. Max Beerbohm (who has every merit except democracy) attempted to analyse the jokes at which the mob laughs. He divided them into three sections: jokes about bodily humiliation, jokes about things alien, such as foreigners, and jokes about bad cheese. Mr. Max Beerbohm thought he understood the first two forms; but I am not sure that he did. In order to understand vulgar humour it is not enough to be humourous. One must also be vulgar, as I am. And in the first case it is surely obvious that it is not merely at the fact of something being hurt that we laugh (as I trust we do) when a Prime Minister sits down on his hat. If that were so we should laugh whenever we saw a funeral. We do not laugh at the mere fact of something falling down; there is nothing humorous about leaves falling or the sun going down. When our house falls down we do not laugh. All the birds of the air might drop around us in a perpetual shower like a hailstorm without arousing a smile. If you really ask yourself why we laugh at a man sitting down suddenly in the street you will discover that the reason is not only recondite, but ultimately religious. All the jokes about men sitting down on their hats are really theological jokes; they are concerned with the Dual Nature of Man. They refer to the primary paradox that man is superior to all the things around him and yet is at their mercy.

Quite equally subtle and spiritual is the idea at the back of laughing at foreigners. It concerns the almost torturing truth of a thing being like oneself and yet not like oneself. Nobody laughs at what is entirely foreign; nobody laughs at a palm tree. But it is funny to see the familiar image of God disguised behind the black beard of a Frenchman or the black face of a Negro. There is nothing funny in the sounds that are wholly inhuman, the howling of wild beasts or of the wind. But if a man begins to talk like oneself, but all the syllables come out different, then if one is a man one feels inclined to laugh, though if one is a gentleman one resists the inclination.

Mr. Max Beerbohm, I remember, professed to understand the first two forms of popular wit, but said that the third quite stumped him. He could not see why there should be anything funny about bad cheese. I can tell him at once. He has missed the idea because it is subtle and philosophical, and he was looking for something ignorant and foolish. Bad cheese is funny because it is (like the foreigner or the man fallen on the pavement) the type of the transition or transgression across a great mystical boundary. Bad cheese symbolises the change from the inorganic to the organic. Bad cheese symbolises the startling prodigy of matter taking on vitality. It symbolises the origin of life itself. And it is only about such solemn matters as the origin of life that the democracy condescends to joke. Thus, for instance, the democracy jokes about marriage, because marriage is a part of mankind. But the democracy would never deign to joke about Free Love, because Free Love is a piece of priggishness.

As a matter of fact, it will be generally found that the popular joke is not true to the letter, but is true to the spirit. The vulgar joke is generally in the oddest way the truth and yet not the fact. For instance, it is not in the least true that mothers-in-law are as a class oppressive and intolerable; most of them are both devoted and useful. All the mothers-in-law I have ever had were admirable. Yet the legend of the comic papers is profoundly true. It draws attention to the fact that it is much harder to be a nice mother-in-law than to be nice in any other conceivable relation of life. The caricatures have drawn the worst mother-in-law a monster, by way of expressing the fact that the best mother-in-law is a problem. The same is true of the perpetual jokes in comic papers about shrewish wives and henpecked husbands. It is all a frantic exaggeration, but it is an exaggeration of a truth; whereas all the modern mouthings about oppressed women are the exaggerations of a falsehood. If you read even the best of the intellectuals of to-day you will find them saying that in the mass of the democracy the woman is the chattel of her lord, like his bath or his bed. But if you read the comic literature of the democracy you will find that the lord hides under the bed to escape from the wrath of his chattel. This is not the fact, but it is much nearer the truth. Every man who is married knows quite well, not only that he does not regard his wife as a chattel, but that no man can conceivably ever have done so. The joke stands for an ultimate truth, and that is a subtle truth. It is one not very easy to state correctly. It can, perhaps, be most correctly stated by saying that, even if the man is the head of the house, he knows he is the figure-head.

But the vulgar comic papers are so subtle and true that they are even prophetic. If you really want to know what is going to happen to the future of our democracy, do not read the modern sociological prophecies, do not read even Mr. Wells's Utopias for this purpose, though you should certainly read them if you are fond of good honesty and good English. If you want to know what will happen, study the pages of *Snaps* or *Patchy Bits* as if they were the dark tablets graven with the oracles of the gods. For, mean and gross as they are, in all seriousness, they contain what is entirely absent from all Utopias and all the sociological conjectures of our time: they contain some hint of the actual habits and manifest desires of the English people. If we are really to find out what the democracy will ultimately do with itself, we shall surely find it, not in the literature which studies the people, but in the literature which the people studies.

I can give two chance cases in which the common or Cockney joke was a much better prophecy than the careful observations of the most cultured observer. When England was agitated, previous to the last General Election, about the existence of Chinese labour, there was a distinct difference between the tone of the politicians and the tone of the populace. The politicians who disapproved of Chinese labour were most careful to explain that they did not in any sense disapprove of Chinese. According to them, it was a pure question of legal propriety, of whether certain clauses in the contract of indenture were not inconsistent with our constitutional traditions: according to them, the case would have been the same if the people had been Kaffirs or Englishmen. It all sounded wonderfully enlightened and lucid; and in comparison the popular joke looked, of course, very poor. For the popular joke against the Chinese labourers was simply that they were Chinese; it was an objection to an alien type; the popular papers were full of gibes about pigtails and yellow faces. It seemed that the Liberal politicians were raising an intellectual objection to a doubtful document of State; while it seemed that the Radical populace were merely roaring with idiotic laughter at the sight of a Chinaman's clothes. But the popular instinct was justified, for the vices revealed were Chinese vices.

But there is another case more pleasant and more up to date. The popular papers always persisted in representing the New Woman or the Suffragette as an ugly woman, fat, in spectacles, with bulging clothes, and generally falling off a bicycle. As a matter of plain external fact, there was not a word of truth in this. The leaders of the movement of female emancipation are not at all ugly; most of them are extraordinarily good-looking. Nor are they at all indifferent to art or decorative costume; many of them are alarmingly attached to these things. Yet the popular instinct was right. For the popular instinct was that in this movement, rightly or wrongly, there was an element of indifference to female dignity, of a quite new willingness of women to be grotesque. These women did truly despise the pontifical quality of woman. And in our streets and around our Parliament we have seen the stately woman of art and culture turn into the comic woman of *Comic Bits*. And whether we think the exhibition justifiable or not, the prophecy of the comic papers is justified: the healthy and vulgar masses were conscious of a hidden enemy to their traditions who has now come out into the daylight, that the scriptures might be fulfilled. For the two things that a healthy person hates most between heaven and hell are a woman who is not dignified and a man who is.

THE FALLACY OF SUCCESS

THERE has appeared in our time a particular class of books and articles which I sincerely and solemnly think may be called the silliest ever known among men. They are much more wild than the wildest romances of chivalry and much more dull than the dullest religious tract. Moreover, the romances of chivalry were at least about chivalry; the religious tracts are about religion. But these things are about nothing; they are about what is called Success. On every bookstall, in every magazine, you may find works telling people how to succeed. They are books showing men how to succeed in everything; they are written by men who cannot even succeed in writing books. To begin with, of course, there is no such thing as Success. Or, if you like to put it so, there is nothing that is not successful. That a thing is successful merely means that it is; a millionaire is successful in being a millionaire and a donkey in being a donkey. Any live man has succeeded in living; any dead man may have succeeded in committing suicide. But, passing over the bad logic and bad philosophy in the phrase, we may take it, as these writers do, in the ordinary sense of success in obtaining money or worldly position. These writers profess to tell the ordinary man how he may succeed in his trade or speculation—how, if he is a builder, he may succeed as a builder; how, if he is a stockbroker, he may succeed as a stockbroker. They profess to show him how, if he is a grocer, he may become a sporting yachtsman; how, if he is a tenth-rate journalist, he may become a peer; and how, if he is a German Jew, he may become an Anglo-Saxon. This is a definite and business-like proposal, and I really think that the people who buy these books (if any people do buy them) have a moral, if not a legal, right to ask for their money back. Nobody would dare to publish a book about electricity which literally told one nothing about electricity; no one would dare to publish an article on botany which showed that the writer did not know which end of a plant grew in the earth. Yet our modern world is full of books about Success and successful people which literally contain no kind of idea, and scarcely any kind of verbal sense.

It is perfectly obvious that in any decent occupation (such as bricklaying or writing books) there are only two ways (in any special sense) of succeeding. One is by doing very good work, the other is by cheating. Both are much too simple to require any literary explanation. If you are in for the high jump, either jump higher than any one else, or manage somehow to pretend that you have done so. If you want to succeed at whist, either be a good whist-player, or play with marked cards. You may want a book about jumping; you may want a book about whist; you may want a book about cheating at whist. But you cannot want a book about Success. Especially you cannot want a book about Success such as those which you can now find scattered by the hundred about the book-market. You may want to jump or to play cards; but you do not want to read wandering statements to the effect that jumping is jumping, or that games are won by winners. If these writers, for instance, said anything about success in jumping it would be something like this: "The jumper must have a clear aim before him. He must desire definitely to jump higher than the other men who are in for the same competition. He must let no feeble feelings of mercy (sneaked from the sickening Little Englanders and Pro-Boers) prevent him from trying to *do his best*. He must remember that a competition in jumping is distinctly competitive, and that, as Darwin has gloriously demonstrated, THE WEAKEST GO TO THE WALL." That is the kind of thing the book would say, and very useful it would be, no doubt, if read out in a low and tense voice to a young man just about to take the high jump. Or suppose that in the course of his intellectual rambles the philosopher of Success dropped upon our other case, that of playing cards, his bracing advice would run—"In playing cards it is very necessary to avoid the mistake (commonly made by maudlin humanitarians and Free Traders) of permitting your opponent to win the game. You must have grit and snap and *go in to win*. The days of idealism and superstition are over. We live in a time of science and hard common sense, and it has now been definitely proved that in any game where two are playing IF ONE DOES NOT WIN THE OTHER WILL." It is all very stirring, of course; but I confess that if I were playing cards I would rather have some decent little book which told me the rules of the game. Beyond the rules of the game it is all a question either of talent or dishonesty; and I will undertake to provide either one or the other—which, it is not for me to say.

Turning over a popular magazine, I find a queer and amusing example. There is an article called "The Instinct that Makes People Rich." It is decorated in front with a formidable portrait of Lord Rothschild. There are many definite methods, honest and dishonest, which make people rich; the only "instinct" I know of which does it is that instinct which theological Christianity crudely describes as "the sin of avarice." That, however, is beside the present point. I wish to quote the following exquisite paragraphs as a piece of typical advice as to how to succeed. It is so practical; it leaves so little doubt about what should be our next step—

"The name of Vanderbilt is synonymous with wealth gained by modern enterprise. 'Cornelius,' the founder of the family, was the first of the great American magnates of commerce. He started as the son of a poor farmer; he ended as a millionaire twenty times over.

"He had the money-making instinct. He seized his opportunities, the opportunities that were given by the application of the steam-engine to ocean traffic, and by the birth of railway locomotion in the wealthy but undeveloped United States of America, and consequently he amassed an immense fortune.

"Now it is, of course, obvious that we cannot all follow exactly in the footsteps of this great railway monarch. The precise opportunities that fell to him do not occur to us. Circumstances have changed. But, although this is so, still, in our own sphere and in our own circumstances, we *can* follow his general methods; we can seize those opportunities that are given us, and give ourselves a very fair chance of attaining riches."

In such strange utterances we see quite clearly what is really at the bottom of all these articles and books. It is not mere business; it is not even mere cynicism. It is mysticism; the horrible mysticism of money. The writer of that passage did not really have the remotest notion of how Vanderbilt made his money, or of how anybody else is to make his. He does, indeed, conclude his remarks by advocating some scheme; but it has nothing in the world to do with Vanderbilt. He merely wished to prostrate himself before the mystery of a millionaire. For when we really worship anything, we love not only its clearness but its obscurity. We exult in its very invisibility. Thus, for instance, when a man is in love with a woman he takes special pleasure in the fact that a woman is unreasonable. Thus, again, the very pious poet, celebrating his Creator, takes pleasure in saying that God moves in a mysterious way. Now, the writer of the paragraph which I have quoted does not seem to have had anything to do with a god, and I should not think (judging by his extreme unpracticality) that he had ever been really in love with a woman. But the thing he does worship—Vanderbilt—he treats in exactly this mystical manner. He really revels in the fact his deity Vanderbilt is keeping a secret from him. And it fills his soul with a sort of transport of cunning, an ecstasy of priestcraft, that he should pretend to be telling to the multitude that terrible secret which he does not know.

Speaking about the instinct that makes people rich, the same writer remarks—

"In olden days its existence was fully understood. The Greeks enshrined it in the story of Midas, of the 'Golden Touch.' Here was a man who turned everything he laid his hands upon into gold. His life was a progress amidst riches. Out of everything that came in his way he created the precious metal. 'A foolish legend,' said the wiseacres of the Victorian age. 'A truth,' say we of to-day. We all know of such men. We are ever meeting or reading about such persons who turn everything they touch into gold. Success dogs their very footsteps. Their life's pathway leads unerringly upwards. They cannot fail."

Unfortunately, however, Midas could fail; he did. His path did not lead unerringly upward. He starved because whenever he touched a biscuit or a ham sandwich it turned to gold. That was the whole point of the story, though the writer has to suppress it delicately, writing so near to a portrait of Lord Rothschild. The old fables of mankind are, indeed, unfathomably wise; but we must not have them expurgated in the interests of Mr. Vanderbilt. We must not have King Midas represented as an example of success; he was a failure of an unusually painful kind. Also, he had the ears of an ass. Also (like most other prominent and wealthy persons) he endeavoured to conceal the fact. It was his barber (if I remember right) who had to be treated on a confidential footing with regard to this peculiarity; and his barber, instead of behaving like a go-ahead person of the Succeed-at-all-costs school and trying to blackmail King Midas, went away and whispered this splendid piece of society scandal to the reeds, who enjoyed it enormously. It is said that they also whispered it as the winds swayed them to and fro. I look reverently at the portrait of Lord Rothschild; I read reverently about the exploits of Mr. Vanderbilt. I know that I cannot turn everything I touch to gold; but then I also know that I have never tried, having a preference for other substances, such as grass, and good wine. I know that these people have certainly succeeded in something; that they have certainly overcome somebody; I know that they are kings in a sense that no men were ever kings before; that they create markets and bestride continents. Yet it always seems to me that there is some small domestic fact that they are hiding, and I have sometimes thought I heard upon the wind the laughter and whisper of the reeds.

At least, let us hope that we shall all live to see these absurd books about Success covered with a proper derision and neglect. They do not teach people to be successful, but they do teach people to be snobbish; they do spread a sort of evil poetry of worldliness. The Puritans are always denouncing books that inflame lust; what shall we say of books that inflame the viler passions of avarice and pride? A hundred years ago we had the ideal of the Industrious Apprentice; boys were told that by thrift and work they would all become Lord Mayors. This was fallacious, but it was manly, and had a minimum of mortal truth. In our society, temperance will not help a poor man to enrich himself, but it may help him to respect himself. Good work will not make him a rich man, but good work may make him a good workman. The Industrious Apprentice rose by virtues few and narrow indeed, but still virtues. But what shall we say of the gospel preached to the new Industrious Apprentice; the Apprentice who rises not by his virtues, but avowedly by his vices?

WISDOM AND THE WEATHER

It is admitted, one may hope, that common things are never commonplace. Birth is covered with curtains precisely because it is a staggering and monstrous prodigy. Death and first love, though they happen to everybody, can stop one's heart with the very thought of them. But while this is granted, something further may be claimed. It is not merely true that these universal things are strange; it is moreover true that they are subtle. In the last analysis most common things will be found to be highly complicated. Some men of science do indeed get over the difficulty by dealing only with the easy part of it: thus, they will call first love the instinct of sex, and the awe of death the instinct of self-preservation. But this is only getting over the difficulty of describing peacock green by calling it blue. There is blue in it. That there is a strong physical element in both romance and the *Memento Mori* makes them if possible more baffling than if they had been wholly intellectual. No man could say exactly how much his sexuality was colored by a clean love of beauty, or by the mere boyish itch for irrevocable adventures, like running away to sea. No man could say how far his animal dread of the end was mixed up with mystical traditions touching morals and religion. It is exactly because these things are animal, but not quite animal, that the dance of all the difficulties begins. The materialists analyze the easy part, deny the hard part and go home to their tea.

It is complete error to suppose that because a thing is vulgar therefore it is not refined; that is, subtle and hard to define. A drawing-room song of my youth which began "In the gloaming, O, my darling," was vulgar enough as a song; but the connection between human passion and the twilight is none the less an exquisite and even inscrutable thing. Or to take another obvious instance: the jokes about a mother-in-law are scarcely delicate, but the problem of a mother-in-law is extremely delicate. A mother-in-law is subtle because she is a thing like the twilight. She is a mystical blend of two inconsistent things—law and a mother. The caricatures misrepresent her; but they arise out of a real human enigma. "Comic Cuts" deals with the difficulty wrongly, but it would need George Meredith at his best to deal with the difficulty rightly. The nearest statement of the problem perhaps is this: it is not that a mother-in-law must be nasty, but that she must be very nice.

But it is best perhaps to take in illustration some daily custom we have all heard despised as vulgar or trite. Take, for the sake of argument, the custom of talking about the weather. Stevenson calls it "the very nadir and scoff of good conversationalists." Now there are very deep reasons for talking about the weather, reasons that are delicate as well as deep; they lie in layer upon layer of stratified sagacity. First of all it is a gesture of primeval worship. The sky must be invoked; and to begin everything with the weather is a sort of pagan way of beginning everything with prayer. Jones and Brown talk about the weather: but so do Milton and Shelley. Then it is an expression of that elementary idea in politeness—equality. For the very word politeness is only the Greek for citizenship. The word politeness is akin to the word policeman; a charming thought. Properly understood, the citizen should be more polite than the gentleman; perhaps the policeman should be the most courtly and elegant of the three. But all good manners must obviously begin with the sharing of something in a simple style. Two men should share an umbrella; if they have not got an umbrella, they should at least share the rain, with all its rich potentialities of wit and philosophy. "For He maketh His sun to shine . . ." This is the second element in the weather; its recognition of human equality in that we all have our hats under the dark blue spangled umbrella of the universe. Arising out of this is the third wholesome strain in the custom; I mean that it begins with the body and with our inevitable bodily brotherhood. All true friendliness begins with fire and food and drink and the recognition of rain or frost. Those who will not *begin* at the bodily end of things are already prigs and may soon be Christian Scientists. Each human soul has in a sense to enact for itself the gigantic humility of the Incarnation. Every man must descend into the flesh to meet mankind.

Briefly, in the mere observation "a fine day" there is the whole

great human idea of comradeship. Now, pure comradeship is
another of those broad and yet bewildering things. We all enjoy
it; yet when we come to talk about it we almost always talk
nonsense, chiefly because we suppose it to be a simpler affair
than it is. It is simple to conduct; but it is by no means simple to
analyze. Comradeship is at the most only one half of human life;
the other half is Love, a thing so different that one might fancy
it had been made for another universe. And I do not mean mere
sex love; any kind of concentrated passion, maternal love, or
even the fiercer kinds of friendship are in their nature alien to
pure comradeship. Both sides are essential to life; and both are
known in differing degrees to everybody of every age or sex.
But very broadly speaking it may still be said that women stand
for the dignity of love and men for the dignity of comradeship.
I mean that the institution would hardly be expected if the males
of the tribe did not mount guard over it. The affections in which
women excel have so much more authority and intensity that
pure comradeship would be washed away if it were not rallied
and guarded in clubs, corps, colleges, banquets and regiments.
Most of us have heard the voice in which the hostess tells her
husband not to sit too long over the cigars. It is the dreadful voice
of Love, seeking to destroy Comradeship.

All true comradeship has in it those three elements which I
have remarked in the ordinary exclamation about the weather.
First, it has a sort of broad philosophy like the common sky, em-
phasizing that we are all under the same cosmic conditions. We
are all in the same boat, the "winged rock" of Mr. Herbert
Trench. Secondly, it recognizes this bond as the essential one;
for comradeship is simply humanity seen in that one aspect in
which men are really equal. The old writers were entirely wise
when they talked of the equality of men; but they were also very
wise in not mentioning women. Women are always authoritar-
ian; they are always above or below; that is why marriage is a
sort of poetical see-saw. There are only three things in the world
that women do not understand; and they are Liberty, Equality,

and Fraternity. But men (a class little understood in the modern world) find these things the breath of their nostrils; and our most learned ladies will not even begin to understand them until they make allowance for this kind of cool camaraderie. Lastly, it contains the third quality of the weather, the insistence upon the body and its indispensable satisfaction. No one has even begun to understand comradeship who does not accept with it a certain hearty eagerness in eating, drinking, or smoking, an uproarious materialism which to many women appears only hoggish. You may call the thing an orgy or a sacrament; it is certainly an essential. It is at root a resistance to the superciliousness of the individual. Nay, its very swaggering and howling are humble. In the heart of its rowdiness there is a sort of mad modesty; a desire to melt the separate soul into the mass of unpretentious masculinity. It is a clamorous confession of the weakness of all flesh. No man must be superior to the things that are common to men. This sort of equality must be bodily and gross and comic. Not only are we all in the same boat, but we are all seasick.

The word comradeship just now promises to become as fatuous as the word "affinity." There are clubs of a Socialist sort where all the members, men and women, call each other "Comrade." I have no serious emotions, hostile or otherwise, about this particular habit: at the worst it is conventionality, and at the best flirtation. I am convinced here only to point out a rational principle. If you choose to lump all flowers together, lilies and dahlias and tulips and chrysanthemums and call them all daisies, you will find that you have spoiled the very fine word daisy. If you choose to call every human attachment comradeship, if you include under that name the respect of a youth for a venerable prophetess, the interest of a man in a beautiful woman who baffles him, the pleasure of a philosophical old fogy in a girl who is impudent and innocent, the end of the meanest quarrel or the beginning of the most mountainous love; if you are going to call all these comradeship, you will gain nothing; you will only lose a word. Daisies are obvious and universal and open; but they are only one kind of flower. Comradeship is obvious and universal and open; but it is only one kind of affection; it has characteristics that would destroy any other kind. Anyone who has known true comradeship in a club or in a regiment, knows that it is impersonal. There is a pedantic phrase used in debating clubs which is strictly true to the masculine emotion; they call it "speaking to the question." Women speak to each other; men speak to the subject they are speaking about. Many an honest man has sat in a ring of his five best friends under heaven and forgotten who was in the room while he explained some system. This is not peculiar to intellectual men; men are all theoretical, whether they are talking about God or about golf. Men are all impersonal; that is to say, republican. No one remembers after a really good talk who has said the good things. Every man speaks to a visionary multitude; a mystical cloud, that is called the club.

It is obvious that this cool and careless quality which is essential to the collective affection of males involves disadvantages and dangers. It leads to spitting; it leads to coarse speech; it must lead to these things so long as it is honorable; comradeship must be in some degree ugly. The moment beauty is mentioned in male friendship, the nostrils are stopped with the smell of abominable things. Friendship must be physically dirty if it is to be morally clean. It must be in its shirt sleeves. The chaos of habits that always goes with males when left entirely to themselves has only one honorable cure; and that is the strict discipline of a monastery. Anyone who has seen our unhappy young idealists in East End Settlements losing their collars in the wash and living on tinned salmon will fully understand why it was decided by the wisdom of St. Bernard or St. Benedict, that if men were to live without women, they must not live without rules. Something of the same sort of artificial exactitude, of course, is obtained in an army; and an army also has to be in many ways monastic; only that it has celibacy without chastity. But these things do not apply to normal married men. These have a quite sufficient restraint on their instinctive anarchy in the savage common-sense of the other sex. There is only one very timid sort of man that is not afraid of women.

THE ROMANCE OF THRIFT

THE larger part of womankind, however, have had to fight for things slightly more intoxicating to the eye than the desk or the typewriter; and it cannot be denied that in defending these, women have developed the quality called prejudice to a powerful and even menacing degree. But these prejudices will always be found to fortify the main position of the woman, that she is to remain a general overseer, an autocrat within small compass but on all sides. On the one or two points on which she really misunderstands the man's position, it is almost entirely in order to preserve her own. The two points on which woman, actually and of herself, is most tenacious may be roughly summarized as the ideal of thrift and the ideal of dignity.

Unfortunately for this book it is written by a male, and these two qualities, if not hateful to a man, are at least hateful in a man. But if we are to settle the sex question at all fairly, all males must make an imaginative attempt to enter into the attitude of all good women toward these two things. The difficulty exists especially, perhaps, in the thing called thrift; we men have so much encouraged each other in throwing money right and left, that there has come at last to be a sort of chivalrous and poetical air about losing sixpence. But on a broader and more candid consideration the case scarcely stands so.

Thrift is the really romantic thing; economy is more romantic than extravagance. Heaven knows I for one speak disinterestedly in the matter; for I cannot clearly remember saving a half-penny ever since I was born. But the thing is true; economy, properly understood, is the more poetic. Thrift is poetic because it is creative; waste is unpoetic because it is waste. It is prosaic to

throw money away, because it is prosaic to throw anything
away; it is negative; it is a confession of indifference, that is, it
is a confession of failure. The most prosaic thing about the house
is the dustbin, and the one great objection to the new fastidious
and æsthetic homestead is simply that in such a moral *ménage* the
dustbin must be bigger than the house. If a man could undertake
to make use of all things in his dustbin he would be a broader
genius than Shakespeare. When science began to use by-
products; when science found that colors could be made out of
coal-tar, she made her greatest and perhaps her only claim on the
real respect of the human soul. Now the aim of the good woman
is to use the by-products, or, in other words, to rummage in the
dustbin.

A man can only fully comprehend it if he thinks of some
sudden joke or expedient got up with such materials as may be
found in a private house on a rainy day. A man's definite daily
work is generally run with such rigid convenience of modern science that thrift, the picking up of potential helps here and there,
has almost become unmeaning to him. He comes across it most
(as I say) when he is playing some game within four walls; when
in charades, a hearthrug will just do for a fur coat, or a tea-cozy
just do for a cocked hat; when a toy theater needs timber and
cardboard, and the house has just enough firewood and just
enough bandboxes. This is the man's occasional glimpse and
pleasing parody of thrift. But many a good housekeeper plays
the same game every day with ends of cheese and scraps of silk,
not because she is mean, but on the contrary, because she is
magnanimous; because she wishes her creative mercy to be over
all her works, that not one sardine should be destroyed, or cast
as rubbish to the void, when she has made the pile complete.

The modern world must somehow be made to understand (in
theology and other things) that a view may be vast, broad, universal, liberal and yet come into conflict with another view that
is vast, broad, universal and liberal also. There is never a war
between two sects, but only between two universal Catholic

Churches. The only possible collision is the collision of one cosmos with another. So in a smaller way it must be first made clear that this female economic ideal is a part of that female variety of outlook and all-round art of life which we have already attributed to the sex: thrift is not a small or timid or provincial thing; it is part of that great idea of the woman watching on all sides out of all the windows of the soul and being answerable for everything. For in the average human house there is one hole by which money comes in and a hundred by which it goes out; man has to do with the one hole, woman with the hundred. But though the very stinginess of a woman is a part of her spiritual breadth, it is none the less true that it brings her into conflict with the special kind of spiritual breadth that belongs to the males of the tribe. It brings her into conflict with that shapeless cataract of Comradeship, of chaotic feasting and deafening debate, which we noted in the last section. The very touch of the eternal in the two sexual tastes brings them the more into antagonism; for one stands for a universal vigilance and the other for an almost infinite output. Partly through the nature of his moral weakness, and partly through the nature of his physical strength, the male is normally prone to expand things into a sort of eternity; he always thinks of a dinner party as lasting all night; and he always thinks of a night as lasting forever. When the working women in the poor districts come to the doors of the public houses and try to get their husbands home, simple-minded "social workers" always imagine that every husband is a tragic drunkard and every wife a broken-hearted saint. It never occurs to them that the poor woman is only doing under coarser conventions exactly what every fashionable hostess does when she tries to get the men from arguing over the cigars to come and gossip over the teacups. These women are not exasperated merely at the amount of money that is wasted in beer; they are exasperated also at the amount of time that is wasted in talk. It is not merely what goeth into the mouth but what cometh out of the mouth that, in their opinion, defileth a man.

They will raise against an argument (like their sisters of all ranks) the ridiculous objection that nobody is convinced by it; as if a man wanted to make a body-slave of anybody with whom he had played single-stick. But the real female prejudice on this point is not without a basis; the real feeling is this, that the most masculine pleasures have a quality of the ephemeral. A duchess may ruin a duke for a diamond necklace; but there is the necklace. A coster may ruin his wife for a pot of beer; and where is the beer? The duchess quarrels with another duchess in order to crush her, to produce a result; the coster does not argue with another coster in order to convince him, but in order to enjoy at once the sound of his own voice, the clearness of his own opinions and the sense of masculine society. There is this element of a fine fruitlessness about the male enjoyments; wine is poured into a bottomless bucket; thought plunges into a bottomless abyss. All this has set woman against the Public House—that is, against the Parliament House. She is there to prevent waste; and the "pub" and the parliament are the very palaces of waste. In the upper classes the "pub" is called the club, but that makes no more difference to the reason than it does to the rhyme. High and low, the woman's objection to the Public House is perfectly definite and rational; it is that the Public House wastes the energies that could be used on the private house.

As it is about feminine thrift against masculine waste, so it is about feminine dignity against masculine rowdiness. The woman has a fixed and very well-founded idea that if she does not insist on good manners nobody else will. Babies are not always strong on the point of dignity, and grown-up men are quite unpresentable. It is true that there are many very polite men, but none that I ever heard of who were not either fascinating women or obeying them. But indeed the female ideal of dignity, like the female ideal of thrift, lies deeper and may easily be misunderstood. It rests ultimately on a strong idea of spiritual isolation; the same that makes women religious. They do not like being melted down; they dislike and avoid the mob. That anony-

mous quality we have remarked in the club conversation would
be common impertinence in a case of ladies. I remember an
artistic and eager lady asking me in her grand green drawing-
room whether I believed in comradeship between the sexes, and
why not. I was driven back on offering the obvious and sincere answer "Because if I were to treat you for two minutes like
a comrade you would turn me out of the house." The only certain rule on the subject is always to deal with woman and never
with women. "Women" is a profligate word; I have used it repeatedly in this chapter; but it always has a blackguard sound.
It smells of oriental cynicism and hedonism. Every woman is a
captive queen. But every crowd of women is only a harem
broken loose.

I am not expressing my own views here, but those of nearly all
the women I have known. It is quite unfair to say that a woman
hates other women individually; but I think it would be quite
true to say that she detests them in a confused heap. And this is
not because she despises her own sex, but because she respects
it; and respects especially that sanctity and separation of each
item which is represented in manners by the idea of dignity and
in morals by the idea of chastity.

ON THE YOUNG IDEA

THERE are two modern malcontents who are very often confused together. There is the man who grumbles because the poor
are educated and the man who grumbles because they are not.
A doubt about education is identified with a denial of education,
in the sense of a refusal or repudiation of it in the abstract; a thing
that does exist, but exists in a totally different type of man. He
is, in my opinion, a highly offensive and foolish sort of man.
Years ago he used to go about bursting with indignation because
somebody wanted poor children taught the piano. Why they

should not be taught the letter F on the piano as much as in the spelling-book I never could understand. But we might lawfully conduct an inquiry into exactly how much good is actually done by their learning either one or the other. Suppose that literally the only result of teaching a child the piano were that he went on hammering one note with one finger for hours at a time, not only without any notion of a tune, but without any notion that one note is supposed to follow another. We should not complain of his having learnt to play, but of his not having learnt to play. We should recognize that a piano is in itself an ingenious and harmonious structure; but we should still think that a piano without a piano-player was something of a white elephant; and none the less for having, like any other white elephant, a magnificent display of ivory. Now that sort of result, in relation to the piano, would be something like the ultimate result in relation to the spelling-book. A spelling-book is not really intended to teach people to spell, but rather ultimately to read, and even to write. That is, we do not want to dwell on one word, any more than one note; we want people to string words together in a sequence like notes in a tune. And we want them ultimately to string sentences together, not exactly as they are in a sentence in an exercise, but as they ought to be in a serious sequence of ideas. As we want a person to play for pleasure, we want him to think for pleasure. And it is hard to believe that anyone can go on tapping one note or repeating one catchword for pleasure.

What is the matter with the curious cultural atmosphere around us is that it abounds, not in trains of thought, but in tags of language. Vast numbers know that a certain phrase should be used about a certain subject; but it never occurs to them even to wonder how it would apply to some other subject. There is such and such a set piece of argument against Pianos for the People, and such and such a set piece for Pianos for the People; or whatever the question may be. But it is rare to find any individual, on any side, guilty of the intellectual restlessness of asking himself whether the argument about Pianos for the Peo-

ple would also apply to Pianolas for the People, or wherein lies
the difference of principle between pianos and bagpipes and
guitars. To ask what an argument depends on; to consider where
it leads; to speculate on whether there are other cases to which
it applies; all this seems to be an unknown world to many who
use the words of the debate glibly enough. The point is that
they only use those words in connexion with that debate. They
deal in formulas like those provided by the old debating club
text-books; with A Hundred Points For and Against Home Rule.

Here is a phrase, for instance, which I heard the other day
from a very agreeable and intelligent person, and which we have
all heard hundreds of times from hundreds of such persons. A
young mother remarked to me, "I don't want to teach my child
any religion. I don't want to influence him; I want him to choose
for himself when he grows up." That is a very ordinary example
of a current argument; which is frequently repeated and yet
never really applied. Of course the mother was always influencing the child. Of course the mother might just as well have said,
"I hope he will choose his own friends when he grows up; so I
won't introduce him to any aunts or uncles." The grown-up
person cannot in any case escape from the responsibility of influencing the child; not even if she accepts the enormous responsibility of not influencing the child. The mother can bring
up the child without choosing a religion for him; but not without choosing an environment for him. If she chooses to leave out
the religion, she is choosing the environment; and an infernally
dismal, unnatural environment too. The mother can bring up the
child alone on a solitary island in the middle of a large lake, lest
the child should be influenced by superstitions and social traditions. But the mother is choosing the island and the lake and
the loneliness; and is just as responsible for doing so as if she had
chosen the sect of the Mennonites or the theology of the Mor-
mons. It is entirely obvious, to anybody who will think for two
minutes, that this responsibility for determining childhood belongs inevitably to the relation of child and adult, quite apart

from the relations of religion and irreligion. But the people who
repeat these fragments of phraseology do not think for two
minutes. They do not make any attempt to connect such a
phraseology with a philosophy. They have heard that argument
applied to religion; and they never think of applying it to anything else except religion. They never think of taking those ten
or twelve words out of their conventional context; and seeing
whether they apply to any other context. They have heard that
there are people who refuse to train children even in their own
religion. There might just as well be people who refuse to train
children in their own civilization. If the child, when he has
grown up, may prefer another creed, it is equally true that he
may prefer another culture. He may be annoyed at having been
brought up as a Swedenborgian; he may passionately regret that
he was not brought up as a Sandemanian. But so he may regret
that he was brought up as an English gentleman and not as a
wild Arab of the desert. He may, as (with the assistance of a
sound geographical education) he surveys the world from China
to Peru, feel envious of the dignity of the code of Confucius or
weep over the ruins of the great Aztec civilization. But somebody has obviously got to bring him up as something; and it is
perhaps the heaviest responsibility of all to bring him up as nothing.

I could give many other examples of this fragmentary sort of
argument, which everybody quotes and nobody develops. It is
making, for instance, the wildest confusion in the discussions
about decorum and the dignity of the body. Any number of people are content to say that the human body is beautiful; though
that argument would lead to a conclusion which they themselves
would regard as rank lunacy. The true answer of philosophy and
theology is that there is nothing the matter with the human
body; the trouble is with the human soul. But I am not so much
talking about the true answer as about the absence of any answer. The point is that these people ask a question which they
themselves are not prepared to answer, even along the lines which

they themselves suggest. They only see the question as applied to some particular silly discussion about a French novel or an American ballet; and they never make any attempt to deal with the question as a whole. They only repeat the tame, controversial comment that is attached to that little local controversy. That is the thing which bears the same relation to thinking that hitting the same note on the piano a hundred and fifty times bears to playing in the style of Paderewski. We cannot all play like Paderewski or think like Plato; but we should be a great deal nearer to it if we could forget these little tags of talk from the daily papers and the debating clubs, and start afresh, thinking for ourselves.

ON CALLING NAMES—CHRISTIAN AND OTHERWISE

IT is said that there has been a moral breakdown; but let us be comforted; it is only a mental breakdown. Indeed I only call it a breakdown, because that was the name of a nigger dance. But it is not so much like the breakdown as it is like the cake-walk. And the case against the cake-walk is that it claims to be one in which you can eat your cake and have it. In other words, the real objection to much of modern fashion is an objection based on reason, and not specially on morality. In certain respects (not all or even perhaps most), current culture seems to me to have simply fallen to a lower level of civilization and to be now a little nearer to niggers or even to monkeys.

I will take one example of what I mean, precisely because it has nothing directly to do with morality at all. It is now the custom of most young people to shout at each other by their Christian names, or the abbreviations of their Christian names, or the most intimate substitutes for their Christian names, as soon as they know each other, or before they know each other. If (as you and I and all smart people are aware) the dashing and distinguished Miss Vernon-Vavasour was known in baptism as Gloria but among her most devoted friends as Gurgles, there is now no difference between those who call her Gurgles and those who call her Glory and those who would normally prefer, when suddenly presented to somebody they do not know from Eve, to call her Miss Vernon-Vavasour. As soon as she is seen as a distant dot on the other side of the tennis court, a total stranger will yell at her as Gurgles, because he hears a crowd of other total strangers doing the same. He will use her nickname, because he has never known enough about her to have heard her name. Or he will use the first name, because he has not been in her company for a sufficient number of seconds to get as far as the last one.

Now all this has nothing directly to do with right and wrong. I suppose there are savage tribes in which a person only possesses one name, and so has to be addressed by it. It might be maintained that the first name is always the noblest and most sacred in a religious and moral sense. Perhaps the Bright Young Things only use Christian names to express their holy zeal for anything that is Christian. Perhaps they talk of Tom only to remind him of his solemn dedication to St. Thomas of Canterbury or St. Thomas Aquinas. Perhaps they shriek at Peter to thrill him with the thought that he is the rock on which the Church is built. Perhaps they compress into the loud and sometimes peremptory cry of "Jack!" all the mingled mysteries of St. John the Baptist and St. John the Evangelist. Perhaps, on the other hand, they don't. But anyhow, it is quite true that Tom, Dick and Harry are the names of saints; while Jones, Brown and Robinson are often only the names of snobs. Therefore the practice of talking about Tom, Dick and Harry instead of about Mr. Jones, Mr. Brown and Mr. Robinson, might be adopted for many reasons, noble and ignoble, worldly and unworldly. I complain of it here, not because it is worldly, but on the contrary, because it shows a lack of appreciation of the world. It especially shows a lack of appreciation of the civilized world. It shows a dullness in distinguishing and tasting the arts of civilization.

Anyhow, the matter of Christian names does not itself involve Christian morals. To take another alternative possibility; some of those happy Utopias described by Mr. Wells might possibly abolish all Christian names, or even abolish all names. It might entirely deprive us of names and only provide us with numbers. We might have labels, alphabetical and numerical, as if we were motor-cars; or be known by such figures as are convicts and policemen. And all this would not involve any direct question of misconduct. We might hear Gurgles shrieking across the tennis court, "Play up, K.P. 7983501, old thing; we've got to go on to M.M. 9018972's to tea." Or one of her young friends would be heard saying languidly, "Chuck us a cig., Q.B. 9973588; I've left my filthy case in X.Y. 318220's car." And in all this there could arise no particular criticism of morals, whatever the crabbed and cantakerous might offer in the way of a criticism of manners. There is nothing erotic or even too emotional in those alphabetical forms of address. There is nothing calculated to inflame the passions in the figure 7983501. Our criticism of it would be that it dulled the edge of fine cultural intercourse; that it let us down to a lower level of artistic interest and invention; or, as Gurgles would prefer to say, that it is a bloody bore. It takes away certain fine shades of personal interest, of appropriateness or inappropriateness, which help the coloured comedy of life. For though one Gloria differs from another Gloria in glory and even every Gurgles does not gurgle alike, there is always some artistic interest, serious or humorous, in the association of an individual person with an individual name, perhaps carrying memories of legend or history. But our chief objection would still remain the same; that it is barbaric and reactionary to destroy these cultural distinctions between one thing and another; because it is like rubbing out all the lines of a fine drawing.

Now there were many things in which the Victorians were quite wrong. But in their punctiliousness about etiquette in things like this, they were quite right. In insisting that the young lady should be called at one stage Miss Vavasour, and only at another stage Gloria, and only in extreme and almost desperate cases of confidence Gurgles, they were a thousand times right. They were maintaining a wholly superior social system, by which social actions were significant, and not (as they are now) all of them equally insignificant. There is a meaning in each of those names, as there is a meaning in a name given in baptism or a name given in religion; there is no meaning in the name that is merely a number. When first we are presented to Mr. Robinson, he ought to be presented as Mr. Robinson. The formal title and the family name mean that he is what he is, whatever else he is. He is a man and a free man and a fellow citizen and a person living under the protection of a certain social order. In short, it means that he is worthy of a certain kind of respect and consideration, *before* we know anything else whatever about his worth. If we afterwards reach such a degree of spontaneous friendship as to wish to call him Belisarius, or whatever his first name may happen to be, we shall have done so because we have formed certain independent opinions of our own, about qualities in him which we did not know of at the beginning; and the change will there-fore have an intelligent and intelligible meaning. It will be a record of something real in our minds and in his mind. The auto-matic adoption of his first name by everybody creates an at-mosphere of utter unreality. When I was a boy there was a real symbolism, a real poetry, and in the sane sense a real romance, in the transition from being supposed to call a lady Miss Brown to being allowed to call her Mabel. I do not discuss, of course, the dark infernal underworld where she was sometimes called Miss Mabel. The transition did not mean (as the silly senti-mentalists who write against the sentimentalism of their grand-mothers probably imagine) that you were in love with Mabel; it did not necessarily mean that you were even flirting with Mabel; but it did mean something. It meant that she felt a certain confidence in you and did not object to counting you among her particular personal companions. Today it means nothing at all.

And intelligent people have a strong objection to things that mean nothing at all.

There is also this further point. The old stages of intimacy were individual, and in that sense even unconventional. The new comradeship is entirely conventional. It is in the exact and solid sense a convention. The old admission to special friendship occurred at different stages with different people; it was an adventure. The new familiarity is really a formality. It is a thing made common like the rules of a game; it is a thing dictated by what the instinct of the people themselves calls "the crowd." But the essential point about it is that this sort of simplification merely impoverishes life. Life is much more rich and interesting when there are individual initiations, special favours and different titles for different relations of life. This is a real and serious social criticism; and you do not get rid of it by ranting or sentimentalizing; either by saying that Mabel by being called Mabel is well on the road to being called Jezebel; or by saying that in allowing half a hundred men to call her whatever they choose, she is heroically emancipating herself from the tyranny of Man.

I fancy that a real advance in progress and civilization would do exactly the opposite. If I were constructing a Utopia, which God forbid, I should describe a higher civilization in which every human being had a hundred names; in which each had a particular name known only to a particular friend; in which there were more and not less ceremonies differentiating the various kinds of love and friendship and in which the suitor had to go through ten names before he got to Glory. That would be a Utopia really worth constructing; for it would really be a question of construction. Most of the Utopias represent only a dull sort of destruction; the sort of destruction that we call simplification. It would really be something like fun to invent a ritual; but since the neglect of religion, no man has really had the courage to invent a ritual. It would be a great lark to draw up a code of law, decorating Tom, Dick and Harry with their Seven Secret Names. But these things will not come until the modern world

has realized that its cure lies in distribution and even in differentiation; and not in mixing up everything together in one great
mess. Comradeship has become a sort of Combine; bearing the
same relation to true friendship that a Trust does to true trade.
Nobody seems to have any notion of improving anything except
by pouring it into something else; as if a man were to pour the
tea into the coffee or the sherry into the port. The one idea in
all human things, from friendship to finance, is to pool everything. It is a very stagnant pool.

I have taken only this one type of a general tendency, because
it does not mix the matter up with gushing morality or more
gushing immorality. It gives some sort of chance for a little
dry light of social criticism. And on a critical consideration, I
repeat that these things seem to me a mere decline in civilization;
like the beginning of the Dark Ages.

THE COWARDICE OF COCKTAILS AND OTHER THINGS

MOST of the modernizers are so much concerned to boast that
their art is a Jazz pattern that they tend to forget that it is a
pattern. Most of its social results are as much cut to a pattern
as any Victorian fashion-plate. This is up to a point quite consistent with common sense; but it is not consistent with the extreme claims to liberty and originality that are actually made for
it. A dance can be danced to ragtime; but it cannot be wholly
and solely a rag. The fullness of freedom could only be found
if all the couples were dancing to different tunes. Perhaps it
would be even more in the liberal spirit of the age, if even the
partners were divided upon the point and the lady danced the
Can-Can or the Carmagnole, while the gentleman gravely trotted
round the room to the tune of "The Bluebells of Scotland." But
the ultimate moral would be the same which a thoughtful mind
will discover in so much of current fashions and fictions. On that

showing, the perfect relation of the sexes would consist in their not being related at all. So that the last orgy of divorce and independence would end in the separation of monks and nuns. But it would be amusing if they were jumping monks and skipping nuns; if the ballroom were dotted with isolated dancers, each shouting his own accompaniment to guide his own footsteps. Certainly, under these conditions, it would be easier for one individual to go swinging down the room, roaring the air of the Wagnerian Wedding March, while the corresponding bride or bridegroom whirled far away in frantic gyrations to the tune of "I'm off to Callao," or a Czechoslovakian movement expressive of being divorced for the fourth time. Then only could we say that we had Free Dancing, after the manner of Free Verse. Otherwise it is obvious enough that any social action has an element of convention. But these social actions have a very large element of convention. What is called "a daring costume" only means a costume which dares to be a little more conventional than the rest. For in this particular phase of fashion, that sort of daring is itself the convention. If any lady ventured to appear in the conventional costume of exactly twenty-five years ago, she indeed might claim to be unconventional.

Now it may be natural to follow the fashions because, in one sense, it is natural to be artificial. It may be that fashions are the expression of both sides of the human paradox: that desire for a perfect system which creates Utopias, and that failure of every system which creates revolutions. And, in the case of the fashions, we know at least that they have the virtue of vanishing very quickly; whereas, in the case of the Utopias, there is always just the horrid hint of possibility that one of them might remain. But when we make every allowance for fashion as a human habit, we may make two demands of it on behalf of human reason. One is that we should be allowed to call a fashion a fashion, and not be called upon to worship it as an evolution pointing to the end and perfection of man. The other is that we should be allowed to compare one fashion with another, in a calm and level-headed manner, as if we were comparing two Chinese or Egyptian dynasties almost equally remote from us; and that we should not be embroiled in silly political squabbles about progress and reaction when we do so. We are not accused of holding up the whole march of mankind, because we happen to like the Doric column better than the Corinthian column or the pointed Gothic better than the flattened Tudor arch. We can use our common sense about things that are too old to be old-fashioned.

Now I have endeavoured to point out that there are some of these changes of fashion which are changes for the worse, intrinsically and intelligently considered. It is not a question of comparing the new fashion with the old fashion, or the old fashion with the new; but of comparing them both with right reason and all the things that survive every fashion in turn. We are not judging the new convention in the light of the old convention it has destroyed, any more than in the light of the newer convention that will soon destroy it. We are prepared to consider all three as if they existed side by side or had passed through history in the reverse order.

Thus there are some quite recent developments, especially in America, which we may truly call intrinsically idiotic. Their silliness is a thing of simple logic; they would have been made game of by Aristophanes or Erasmus or Voltaire, as much as any Victorian or Post-Victorian could make game of them. The upholders of Prohibition, strangely enough, seem to be quite proud of the fact that many are buying motor-cars instead of wine or beer. For my part, I think it rather more foolish merely to rush from one place to another and back again, and pay money for wind (not to mention dust) than to pay money for wine, with its not quite extinct accompaniment of wit. But at least we may admit that motor-cars were meant to move, and that young people may naturally like them to move fast. But that young people should go and sit in motor-cars that do not move at all, in order that they may drink the wine (or rather the spirits) which they are not allowed to drink decently in the

dining-room—that is simply a half-witted and humiliating manner of playing the goat, or some much more degraded animal.
Its imbecility is in its essence; it has nothing to do with any
customs or conventions to which we are or were attached; and
no customs or conventions should be able to reconcile us to it.
If Aristophanes were called on to consider a hero and heroine
who hid in a chariot without any horses, in order to worship
Dionysus with such secret rites, he would think the hero and
heroine were not very heroic. If Voltaire had put into a satiric
romance a lady and gentleman who could only pledge each other
when they were inside the coach that was inside the stable, we
should recognize that the satiric romance was more satirical than
romantic. Yet this custom is now quite common in the great
Dry Democracy; and sitting in the motionless motor seems to be
regarded by some as quite a wild adventure of youth.

It is sometimes complained that the ultra-modern youth is
critical. It does not seem to me that those thus employed shine
in the function of criticism; and certainly not of self-criticism.
And there are a good many milder forms of folly, even in England, which one would expect to see criticized by a very critical
generation. I fear that in most cases these things do not represent
any real criticism at all; that whatever element there may be of
impudence is not really intellectual independence, but is much
more like that very ancient thing that has been complained of
in all ages as the "thoughtlessness of youth." Personally, I think
it a very agreeable quality. But it is rather too much to ask us
to take anything seriously, merely because it takes everything
lightly. I may add here, in parenthesis, that of course all this is
equally true of the many modern manifestations which are really
modern improvements. These also seem to me to be mostly instinctive and artistic, rather than intellectual and philosophical.
And these also can only be properly appreciated in relation to
the rest of history and the normal standard of humanity. Much
of the popularity of sports and games is really classic as well as
human; we all know that an ordinary game of tennis can be in

the fullest sense a graceful and beautiful thing. But here again we do not test the new life merely by its novelty. An ancient Greek like Aristophanes would instantly appreciate the real beauty of athletics, and of garments or habits suited to athletics. But the ancient Greek would like them because they were ancient quite as much as because they were modern. In fact he would not care about their being either; but only about their being completely human and therefore humane.

But as we are concerned here with criticism, I may return to the case that I have taken for convenience on this occasion; the case of the new customs that have arisen round what is called the Drink Question. Now there is a human and eternal philosophy of the Drink Question; and three-quarters of the present trouble arises from not facing what it really is. It could not be better illustrated than in the way in which people quarrel over what is called the Cocktail Habit. The quarrel is as much a habit as the cocktail; and neither is referred back to any independent reason. Here perhaps the old buffers have a slight advantage over the young boozers; for being drunk is a matter of fact, while being Victorian is only a matter of fashion. But the old buffers do not know how to defend their own fine shade of drunkenness; nor could they give any particular reason for thinking a Dry Martini as deadly as a Martini rifle, while regarding a Benedictine as a Benediction.

Now I have watched the cock-fight about cocktails with all its crowings and scratchings, with some interest; I have heard snobbish praises and priggish reproofs. But I have hardly heard anybody remark on the most interesting thing; the real reason for cocktails. Perhaps it would be fairer to say, one of the two or three real reasons for it. The reason is Prohibition; or the morality that was the making of Prohibition. In other words, the reason was Hypocrisy. It is worth remarking, when the cocktail has become the pledge and symbol of a social life boasting of frankness and freedom. The Bright Young Thing is the better for brazening it out; but she is the worse for having selected, of all things, as a thing to be brandished, a thing that was really invented in order to be concealed.

Cocktails are perhaps the only practical product of Prohibition. They are certainly, I should imagine, the only part of Prohibition in which America will really succeed in setting a Great Example to the world. But the way in which the Prohibitionist morality operated is obvious enough. The reason why the American millionaire does not drink wine or beer with his meals, like all poorer and better Christians, is simple if not dignified. It was summed up admirably by an American in an excellent cartoon in *Life;* a cartoon entitled "Henpecked." He prefers to be a Prohibitionist on public occasions; especially those highly important public occasions when he meets his wife. Hence arose, originally, the habit of the males of the party consuming hurried, secret and very potent drinks before they assembled at the table. It was necessary that the sort of drink should be one that could be gulped down quickly; it was necessary that it should be very strong for its size; and it was natural that it should be made a sort of separate science of luxury in itself. Later, of course, the case was complicated by other modern movements, and some sections of feminine society becoming fast society. But that was what determined the novelty and the nature of this remarkable sort of refreshment. It was, quite simply, a tippling husband hiding from a nagging wife. It is not a very noble origin even for a modern mode.

Now this fashion of accepting fashions from anywhere or anybody, and merely as such, has, as in the present case, produced fashions that are really inferior, even as such. America happens to be teetotal (in theory) and America happens to be very rich; and for these two rather undignified reasons we are bound to accept the dregs of its secret drinking. We are to swill the rinsings of its ridiculous cocktail glasses, like sneakish servants or schoolboys after a dinner-party; instead of drinking decently at our own dinner-table after our own dinner. These historical origins of the thing explain but do not excuse. The Cocktail Habit is to be condemned, not because it is American or alcoholic, not because it is fast or fashionable, but because it is, on a common-sense consideration, a worse way of drinking; more hasty, less healthy, even less desirable to anybody left to the honest expression of his own desires. It is not Victorian or Edwardian; it is not peculiar to Victoria any more than Vespasian; it is rudimentary human nature that it is more natural to sit still and talk, and even drink, after dinner, than to stand up and gulp before dinner.

I know it is possible to hear a feeble voice pleading, in the defence of these things, that they give a man an appetite for his meals. Perhaps the last touch is given to their degradation and destruction, by this being said in their defence. The cocktail is the coward's drink; in the light of its actual origins in America. The cocktail is the weakling's drink; even in the light of the excuses made for it in England. In the first aspect, it is unworthy of a generation that is always claiming to be candid and courageous. In the second aspect, it is utterly unworthy of a generation that claims to keep itself fit by tennis and golf and all sorts of athletics. What are these athletes worth if, after all their athletics, they cannot scratch up such a thing as a natural appetite? Most of my own work is, I will not venture to say, literary, but at least sedentary. I never do anything except walk about and throw clubs and javelins in the garden. But I never require anything to give me an appetite for a meal, I never yet needed a tot of rum to help me to go over the top and face the mortal perils of luncheon.

Quite rationally considered, there has been a decline and degradation in these things. First came the old drinking days which are always described as much more horrible, and which were obviously much more healthy. In those days men worked or played, hunted or herded or ploughed or fished, or even, in their rude way, wrote or spoke, if only expressing the simple minds of Socrates or Shakespeare, and *then* got reasonably drunk in the evening when their work was done. We find the first step of the degradation, when men do not drink when their work is done, but drink in order to do their work. Workmen used to wait in queues outside the factories of forty years ago, to drink nips of neat whisky to enable them to face life in the progressive and scientific factory. But at least it may be admitted that life in the factory was something that it took some courage to face. These men felt they had to take an anæsthetic before they could face pain. What are we to say of those who have to take an anæsthetic before they can face pleasure? What of those, who when faced with the terrors of mayonnaise, eggs or sardines, can only utter a faint cry for brandy? What of those who have to be drugged, maddened, inspired and intoxicated to the point of partaking of meals, like the Assassins to the point of committing murders? If, as they say, the use of the drug means the increase of the dose, where will it stop, and at what precise point of frenzy and delusion will a healthy grown-up man be ready to rush headlong upon a cutlet or make a dash for death or glory at a ham-sandwich? This is obviously the most abject stage of all; worse than that of the man who drinks for the sake of work, and much worse than that of the man who drinks for the sake of play. And this judgment has nothing to do with prejudice or period or age or youth; but is such as any rational sort of rationalist, however young, ought to be able to see for himself. I am well aware that any number of nice people drink cocktails; that they do not always do it basely and morbidly for this reason; that they often do it more nobly and honourably, for no reason. But that does not make such rationalists very much more rational.

THE AMERICAN IDEAL

THERE is nothing the matter with Americans except their ideals. The real American is all right; it is the ideal American who is all wrong. It is the code and conception of life imposed from above, much more than the merely human faults and weaknesses working up from below.

In so far as the citizens of the Western democracy have really gone wrong, they have not inherently or quite naturally gone wrong. They have been taught wrong; instructed wrong; educated wrong; exalted and uplifted wrong. A huge heresy, rather peculiar to modern times, yet singularly uncriticized by modern critics, has actually perverted them in a way which is not really very consonant to their personalities. The real, natural Americans are candid, generous, capable of a beautiful wonder and gratitude; enthusiastic about things external to themselves; easily contented and not particularly conceited. They have been deliberately and dogmatically taught to be conceited. They have been systematically educated in a theory of enthusiasm, which degrades it into mere egotism. The American has received as a sort of religion the notion that blowing his own trumpet is as important as the trump of doom.

It is, I am almost certain, in the main an example of the hardening effect of a heresy, and even of a hostile heresy. There are more examples of it than those admit who ignore the peril of heresy. The Scots are an example; they were never naturally Calvinists; and when they break free, it is to become very romantic figures like Stevenson or Cunninghame Graham. The Americans were never naturally boomsters or business bullies. They would have been much happier and more themselves as a race of simple and warm-hearted country people eager for country sports or gazing at the wonders in country fairs. An egotistic heresy, produced by the modern heathenry, has taught them against all their Christian instincts that boasting is better than courtesy and pride better than humility.

It is queer to note how raw and recent is the heresy; and how little it has been spotted by any heresy-hunt. We have heard much of modern polygamy or promiscuity reversing the Christian idea of purity. We have heard something, and we ought to hear more, of modern capitalism and commercialism reversing the Christian idea of charity to the poor. But we have not heard much about Advertisement, with its push, publicity and self-assertion, reversing the idea of Christian humility. Yet we can at once test the ethics of publicity by removing it from public life; by merely applying it to private life. What should we think, in a private party, if an old gentleman had written on his shirt-front in large fine flowing hand: "I am the only well-bred person in this company." What should we think of any person of taste and humour who went about wearing a placard inscribed "Please note quiet charm of my personality." What should we say if people gravely engraved on their visiting card the claim to be the handsomest or the wittiest or the most subtly, strangely attractive people about town. We should not only think, with great accuracy, that they were behaving like asses, and certainly destroying beforehand any social advantages they might really have. We should also think they were wantonly reversing and destroying a principle of social amenity and moral delicacy, recognized in all civilized states and ages, but especially emphasized in the ethics of Christianity. Yet modern business, especially in America, does really enforce this sort of publicity in public life; and has begun to press it even in private life. But the point to be emphasized here is that it is really pressed upon most of the Americans; they are goaded and driven into this sort of public life; large numbers of them would have been perfectly contented with private life. They would have endured it, even if it had retained all the old decency and dignity of private life. For this is where the critic must deal most delicately with the subtlety of their simplicity.

The Americans are always excused as a new nation; though it is no longer exactly a new excuse. But in truth these terms are very misleading; and in some ways they have rather the atmosphere of an old nation. Over whole tracts of that vast country, they are certainly what we should call an old-fashioned nation. In no nation in the world are so many people attached to a certain sort of old texts, familiar quotations, or the pieces of sentiment that were written on the pink pages of Victorian albums. A popular book was published, while I was in America, bearing the somewhat alarming name of *Heart Throbs*, from which compilation one might learn that some great and grim judge of the High Court had for his favourite poem "Grandmother's Blessing," or that some colossus of commerce, a Steel-King or an Oil-King, preferred the simple lines entitled, "Daddy's Hat." It is only fair to say that some of these hard-headed and ruthless rulers had never forgotten the real classical claims of "Love's Young Dream," or "The Seven Ages of Man." Some may sneer at these extracts, but surely not at their novelty or crudity. I do not mention them for the purpose of sneering at them, but, on the contrary, for the purpose of showing that there must be a great block of solid and normal sentiment, even of traditional sentiment. And people having that sentiment, people inheriting that tradition, would not necessarily, on their own account, have become believers in selfish, sensational self-advertisement. I suspect, as a matter of fact, that there is rather less of such callous and contemptuous egoism in America than anywhere else. The older civilizations, some of which I will venture to call the more civilized civilizations, have a great many advantages in variety of culture and a conspectus of criticism; but I should guess that their wickedness is more wicked. A Frenchman can be much more cynical and sceptical than an American; a German much more morbid and perverted than an American; an Englishman much more frozen and sophisticated with pride. What has happened to America is that a number of people who were meant to be heroic and fighting farmers, at once peasants and pioneers, have been swept by the pestilence of a particular fad or false doctrine; the ideal which has and deserves the detestable title of Making Good. The very words are a hypocrisy, that would have been utterly unintelligible to any man of any other age or creed; as meaningless to a Greek sophist as to a Buddhist monk. For they manage, by one mean twist of words, to combine the notion of making money with the entirely opposite notion of being good. But the abnormality of this notion can best be seen, as I have said, in its heathen and barbaric appeal to a brazen self-praise. Selling the goods meant incidentally, of course, lying about the goods; but it was almost worse that it meant bragging about the goods.

There is a very real sense in which certain crudities in the Americans are not so much a part of American crudity as actually a part of American culture. They are not mere outbreaks of human nature; they are something systematically impressed upon human nature. It is not for nothing that some of the most prominent features of their actual academic training are things like schools of commerce or schools of journalism. There is a vital distinction between these things and all that the world has generally meant by a school; especially the most scholastic sort of school. Even those who think little of learning Greek and Latin will agree that it carried with it a vague suggestion of admiring Greeks and Latins. The schoolboy was supposed in some sense to feel inferior. But even in a commercial academy the boy is not occupied in gazing at some great millionaire doing a straddle in wheat, with the feelings of the simplest pagan of antiquity gazing at the Colossus of Rhodes. It would not do him much good if he did; but in general practice he does not. If he learns anything, he learns to do a straddle in wheat himself, or to hope that he will do it as acrobatically as any other acrobat. He does not even learn to venerate Mr. Rockefeller, but only to imitate Mr. Rockefeller.

Nor does the practical study of journalism lead to any particular veneration for literature. The qualities inculcated and encouraged are the same as those which commerce inculcates and encourages. I say it with no particular hostility or bitterness, but it is a fact that the school of commerce or the school of journalism might almost as well be called a school of impudence or a school of swagger or a school of grab and greed.

But the point is that people are taught to be impudent or greedy, not that they are naturally impudent and greedy. As a matter of fact, they are not. And that is the whole paradox of the position, which I have already suggested and should like here to expand. I have seen in the United States young people, coming out of this course of culture, who actually pulled themselves together to be rude, as normal young people have always pulled themselves together to be polite. They were shy in fact and shameless on principle. They would ask rude questions, but they were as timid about asking a rude question as an ordinary youth about paying a compliment. They would use the most brazen methods to induce somebody to see them, and anybody who did see them would pity them for their bashfulness. They were always storming the stage in a state of stage fright..

The very simple explanation of this puzzling contradiction is that they were perfectly nice and normal people in themselves, but they had never been left to themselves by those who were always telling them to assert themselves. They had been bounced into bouncing and bullied into being bullies. And the explanation is the existence of this modern heresy, or false ideal, that has been preached to everybody by every organ of publicity and plutocracy: the theory that self-praise is the only real recommendation.

I have suggested that the American character might have developed in an infinitely more healthy and human fashion if it had not been for this heresy. Of course the American character would in any case have been very much more alert and lively and impetuous than the English character. But that has nothing to do with the particular features and fashions of commercial advertisement and ambition. There are many other races that are more vivacious or vehement than the English and who yet live the normal life of contented country folk, and practice the traditional ideas of modesty and courtesy.

The trouble with the false commercial ideal is that it has made these men struggle against modesty as if it were morbidity; and actually try to coarsen their natural courtesy, as other men stifle a natural crudity. I do not think that bragging and go-getting are American faults. I hate them as American virtues; I think the quarrel is not so much with the men as with the gods: the false gods they have been taught to worship and still only worship

with half their hearts. And these gods of the heathen are stone
and brass, but especially brass; and there is an eternal struggle
in that half-hearted idolatry; for often, while the gods are of
brass, the hearts are of gold.

STREET CRIES AND STRETCHING THE LAW

ABOUT a hundred years ago some enemy sowed among our people the heresy that it is more practical to use a corkscrew to open
a sardine-tin, or to employ a door-scraper as a paper-weight.
Practical politics came to mean the habit of using everything for
some other purpose than its own; of snatching up anything as
a substitute for something else. A law that had been meant to do
one thing, and had conspicuously failed to do it, was always excused because it might do something totally different and perhaps
directly contrary. A custom that was supposed to keep everything white was allowed to survive on condition that it made
everything black. In reality this is so far from being practical
that it does not even rise to the dignity of being lazy. At the best
it can only claim to save trouble, and it does not even do that.
What it really means is that some people will take every other
kind of trouble in the world, if they are saved the trouble of
thinking. They will sit for hours trying to open the tin with a
corkscrew, rather than make the mental effort of pursuing the
abstract, academic, logical connexion between a corkscrew and
a cork.

Here is an example of the sort of thing I mean, which I came
across in a daily paper to-day. A headline announces in staring
letters, and with startled notes of exclamation, that some abominable judicial authority has made the monstrous decision that
musicians playing in the street are not beggars. The journalist
bitterly remarks that they may shove their hats under our very
noses for money, but yet we must not call them beggars. He fol-

lows this remark with several notes of exclamation, and I feel inclined to add a few of my own. The most astonishing thing about the matter, to my mind, is that the journalist is quite innocent in his own indignation. It never so much as crosses his mind that organ-grinders are not classed as beggars because they are not beggars. They may be as much of a nuisance as beggars; they may demand special legislation like beggars; it may be right and proper for every philanthropist to stop them, starve them, harry them, and hound them to death just as if they were beggars. But they are not beggars, by any possible definition of begging. Nobody can be said to be a mere mendicant who is offering something in exchange for money, especially if it is something which some people like and are willing to pay for. A street singer is no more of a mendicant than Madame Clara Butt, though the method (and the scale) of remuneration differs more or less. Anybody who sells anything, in the streets or in the shops, is begging in the sense of begging people to buy. Mr. Selfridge is begging people to buy; the Imperial International Universal Cosmic Stores is begging people to buy. The only possible definition of the actual beggar is not that he is begging people to buy, but that he has nothing to sell.

Now, it is interesting to ask ourselves what the newspaper really meant, when it was so wildly illogical in what it said. Superficially, and as a matter of mood or feeling, we can all guess what was meant. The writer meant that street musicians looked very much like beggars, because they wore thinner and dirtier clothes than his own; and that he had grown quite used to people who looked like that being treated anyhow and arrested for everything. That is a state of mind not uncommon among those whom economic security has kept as superficial as a varnish. But what was intellectually involved in his vague argument was more interesting. What he meant was, in that deeper sense, that it would be a great convenience if the law that punishes beggars could be *stretched* to cover people who are certainly not beggars, but who may be as much of a botheration as beggars. In other words, he wanted to use the mendicity laws in a matter quite unconnected with mendicity; but he wanted to use the old laws because it would save the trouble of making new laws—as the corkscrew would save the trouble of going to look for the tin-opener. And for this notion of the crooked and anomalous use of laws, for ends logically different from their own, he could, of course, find much support in the various sophists who have attacked reason in recent times. But, as I have said, it does not really save trouble; and it is becoming increasingly doubtful whether it will even save disaster. It used to be said that this rough-and-ready method made the country richer; but it will be found less and less consoling to explain why the country is richer when the country is steadily growing poorer. It will not comfort us in the hour of failure to listen to long and ingenious explanations of our success. The truth is that this sort of practical compromise has not led to practical success. The success of England came as the culmination of the highly logical and theoretical eighteenth century. The method was already beginning to fail by the time we came to the end of the compromising and constitutional nineteenth century. Modern scientific civilization was launched by logicians. It was only wrecked by practical men. Anyhow, by this time everybody in England has given up pretending to be particularly rich. It is, therefore, no appropriate moment for proving that a course of being consistently unreasonable will always lead to riches.

In truth, it would be much more practical to be more logical. If street musicians are a nuisance, let them be legislated against for being a nuisance. If begging is really wrong, a logical law should be imposed on all beggars, and not merely on those whom particular persons happen to regard as being also nuisances. What this sort of opportunism does is simply to prevent any question being considered as a whole. I happen to think the whole modern attitude towards beggars is entirely heathen and inhuman. I should be prepared to maintain, as a matter of general morality, that it is intrinsically indefensible to punish human beings for asking for human assistance. I should say that it is intrinsically insane to urge people to give charity and forbid people to accept charity. Nobody is penalized for crying for help when he is drowning; why should he be penalized for crying for help when he is starving? Every one would expect to have to help a man to save his life in a shipwreck; why not a man who has suffered a shipwreck of his life? A man may be in such a position by no conceivable fault of his own; but in any case his fault is never urged against him in the parallel cases. A man is saved from shipwreck without inquiry about whether he has blundered in the steering of his ship; and we fish him out of a pond before asking whose fault it was that he fell into it. A striking social satire might be written about a man who was rescued again and again out of mere motives of humanity in all the wildest places of the world; who was heroically rescued from a lion and skilfully saved out of a sinking ship; who was sought out on a desert island and scientifically recovered from a deadly swoon; and who only found himself suddenly deserted by all humanity when he reached the city that was his home.

In the ultimate sense, therefore, I do not myself disapprove of mendicants. Nor do I disapprove of musicians. It may not unfairly be retorted that this is because I am not a musician. I allow full weight to the fairness of the retort, but I cannot think it a good thing that even musicians should lose all their feelings except the feeling for music. And it may surely be said that a man must have lost most of his feelings if he does not feel the pathos of a barrel organ in a poor street. But there are other feelings besides pathos covered by any comprehensive veto upon street music and minstrelsy. There are feelings of history, and even of patriotism. I have seen in certain rich and respectable quarters of London a notice saying that all street cries are forbidden. If there were a notice up to say that all old tombstones should be carted away like lumber, it would be rather less of an act of vandalism. Some of the old street cries of London are among the last links that we have with the London of Shakespeare and the

London of Chaucer. When I meet a man who utters one I am so far from regarding him as a beggar; it is I who should be a beggar, and beg him to say it again.

But in any case it should be made clear that we cannot make one law do the work of another. If we have real reasons for forbidding something like a street cry, we should give the reasons that are real; we should forbid it because it is a cry, because it is a noise, because it is a nuisance, or perhaps, according to our tastes, because it is old, because it is popular, because it is historic and a memory of Merry England. I suspect that the subconscious prejudice against it is rooted in the fact that the pedlar or hawker is one of the few free men left in the modern city; that he often sells his own wares directly to the consumer, and does not pay rent for a shop. But if the modern spirit wishes to veto him, to harry him, or to hang, draw, and quarter him for being free, at least let it so far recognize his dignity as to define him; and let the law deal with him in principle as well as in practice.

THE PRUDERY OF THE FEMINISTS

In the ultimate and universal sense I am astonished at the lack of astonishment. Starting from scratch, so to speak, we are all in the position of the first frog, whose pious and compact prayer was "Lord, how you made me jump!" Matthew Arnold told us to see life steadily and see it whole. But the flaw in his whole philosophy is that when we do see life whole we do not see it steadily, in Arnold's sense, but as a staggering prodigy of creation. There is a primeval light in which all stones are precious stones; a primeval darkness against which all flowers are as vivid as fireworks. Nevertheless, there is one kind of surprise that does surprise me, the more, perhaps, because it is not true surprise but supercilious fuss. There is a kind of man who not only

claims that his stone is the only pebble on the beach, but declares it must be the one and only philosopher's stone, because
he is the one and only philosopher. He does not discover suddenly the sensational fact that grass is green. He discovers it very
slowly, and proves it still more slowly, bringing us one blade of
grass at a time. He is made haughty instead of humble by hitting
on the obvious. The flowers do not make him open his eyes,
but, rather, cover them with spectacles; and this is even more true
of the weeds and thorns. Even his bad news is banal. A young
man told me he had abandoned his Bible religion and vicarage
environment at the withering touch of the one line of Fitzgerald:
"The flower that once has blown, for ever dies." I vainly pointed
out that the Bible or the English burial service could have told
him that man cometh up as a flower and is cut down. If that were
self-evidently final, there would never have been any Bibles or
any vicarages. I do not see how the flower can be any more
dead, when a mower can cut it down, merely because a botanist
can cut it up. It should further be remembered that the belief in
the soul, right or wrong, arose and flourished among men who
knew all there is to know about cutting down, not unfrequently
cutting each other down, with considerable vivacity. The physical fact of death, in a hundred horrid shapes, was more naked
and less veiled in times of faith or superstition than in times of
science or scepticism. Often it was not merely those who had
seen a man die, but those who had seen him rot, who were most
certain that he was everlastingly alive.

There is another case somewhat analogous to this discovery
of the new disease of death. I am puzzled in somewhat the same
way when I hear, as we often hear just now, somebody saying
that he was formerly opposed to Female Suffrage but was converted to it by the courage and patriotism shown by women in
nursing and similar war work. Really, I do not wish to be superior in my turn, when I can only express my wonder in a
question. But from what benighted dens can these people have
crawled, that they did not know that women are brave? What

horrible sort of women have they known all their lives? Where
do they come from? Or, what is a still more apposite question,
where do they think they come from? Do they think they fell
from the moon, or were really found under cabbage-leaves, or
brought over the sea by storks? Do they (as seems more likely)
believe they were produced chemically by Mr. Schefer on principles of abiogenesis? Should we any of us be here at all if
women were not brave? Are we not all trophies of that
war and triumph? Does not every man stand on the earth like
a graven statue as the monument of the valour of a woman?

As a matter of fact, it is men much more than women who
needed a war to redeem their reputation, and who have redeemed
it. There was much more plausibility in the suspicion that the
old torture of blood and iron would prove too much for a somewhat drugged and materialistic male population long estranged
from it. I have always suspected that this doubt about manhood
was the real sting in the strange sex quarrel, and the meaning of
the new and nervous tattoo about the unhappiness of women.
Man, like the Master Builder, was suspected by the female intelligence of having lost his nerve for climbing that dizzy battle-
tower he had built in times gone by. In this the war did certainly
straighten out the sex tangle; but it did also make clear on how
terrible a thread of tenure we hold our privileges—and even our
pleasures. For even bridge parties and champagne suppers take
place on the top of that toppling war-tower; an hour can come
when even a man who cared for nothing but bridge would have
to defend it like Horatius; or when the man who only lives for
champagne would have to die for champagne, as certainly as
thousands of French soldiers have died for that flat land of vines;
when he would have to fight as hard for the wine as Jeanne
D'Arc for the oil of Rheims.

Just as civilization is guarded by potential war, so it is guarded
by potential revolution. We ought never to indulge in either
without extreme provocation; but we ought to be cured for ever
of the fancy that extreme provocation is impossible. Against the

tyrant within, as against the barbarian without, every voter should be a potential volunteer. "Thou goest with women, forget not thy whip," said the Prussian philosopher; and some such echo probably infected those who wanted a war to make them respect their wives and mothers. But there would really be a symbolic sense in saying, "Thou goest with men, forget not thy sword." Men coming to the council of the tribe should sheathe their swords, but not surrender them. Now I am not going to talk about Female Suffrage at this time of day; but these were the elements upon which a fair and sane opposition to it were founded. These are the risks of real politics; and the woman was not called upon to run such a risk, for the very simple reason that she was already running another risk. It was not laws that fixed her in the family; it was the very nature of the family. If the family was a fact in any very full sense, and if popular rule was also a fact in any very full sense, it was simply physically impossible for the woman to play the same part in such politics as the man. The difficulty was only evaded because the democracy was not a free democracy or the family not a free family. But whether this view was right or wrong, it is at least clear that the only honourable basis for any limitations of womanhood is the same as the basis of the respect for womanhood. It consisted in certain realities, which it may be undesirable to discuss, but is certainly even more undesirable to ignore. And my complaint against the more fussy Feminists (so called from their detestation of everything feminine) is that they do ignore these realities. I do not even propose the alternative of discussing them; on that point I am myself content to be what some call conventional, and others, civilized. I do not in the least demand that anyone should accept my own deduction from them; and I do not care a brass farthing what deduction anybody accepts about such a rag as modern ballot paper. But I do suggest that the peril with which one half of humanity is perpetually at war should be at least present in the minds of those who are perpetually bragging about breaking conventions, rending veils, and violating antiquated taboos. And, in nine cases out of ten, it seems to be quite absent from their minds. The mere fact of using the argument before mentioned, of women's strength vindicated by war work, shows that it is absent from their minds.

If this oddity of the new obscurantism means, rather, that women have shown the moral courage and mental capacity needed for important concerns, I am equally unable to summon up any surprise at the revelation. Nothing can well be more important than our own souls and bodies; and they, at their most delicate and determining period, are almost always and almost entirely confided to women. Those who have been appointed as educational experts in every age are not surely a new order of priestesses? If it means that in a historic crisis all kinds of people must do all kinds of work, and that women are the more to be admired for doing work to which they are unaccustomed, or even unsuited, it is a point which I should quite as easily concede. But if it means that in planning the foundations of a future society we should ignore the one eternal and incurable contrast in humanity; if it means that we may now go ahead gaily as if there were really no difference at all; if it means, as I read in a magazine to-day, and as almost anyone may now read almost anywhere, that if such and such work is bad for women it must be bad for men; if it means that patriotic women in munition factories prove that any women can be happy in any factories; if, in short, it means that the huge and primeval facts of the family no longer block the way to a mere social assimilation and regimentation—then I say that the prospect is not one of liberty but of perpetuation of the dreariest sort of humbug. It is not emancipation, it is not even anarchy; it is simply prudery in the thoughts. It means that we have Bowdlerized our brains as well as our books. It is every bit as senseless a surrender to a superstitious decorum as it would be to force every woman to cut herself with a razor, because it was not etiquette to admit that she cannot grow a beard.

⌒ *What I Saw in America* ⌒

"I am a bad traveller, or at least a bad
tourist. My weakness as a traveller is that
the world seems to me so amusing everywhere that it is hardly worth while to
travel. When I start out for the ends of
the earth, I am stopped on the road by
an entertaining lamp-post or a wildly
signalling window-blind; and have not
even sufficient sense of the scale of difference between these passing questions
and the Quest."

WHAT I SAW IN AMERICA

WHAT IS AMERICA?

I HAVE never managed to lose my old conviction that travel narrows the mind. At least a man must make a double effort of moral humility and imaginative energy to prevent it from narrowing his mind. Indeed there is something touching and even tragic about the thought of the thoughtless tourist, who might have stayed at home loving Laplanders, embracing Chinamen, and clasping Patagonians to his heart in Hampstead or Surbiton, but for his blind and suicidal impulse to go and see what they looked like. This is not meant for nonsense; still less is it meant for the silliest sort of nonsense, which is cynicism. The human bond that he feels at home is not an illusion. On the contrary, it is rather an inner reality. Man is inside all men. In a real sense any man may be inside any men. But to travel is to leave the inside and draw dangerously near the outside. So long as he thought of men in the abstract, like naked toiling figures in some classic frieze, merely as those who labour and love their children and die, he was thinking the fundamental truth about them. By going to look at their unfamiliar manners and customs he is inviting them to disguise themselves in fantastic masks and costumes. Many modern internationalists talk as if men of different nationalities had only to meet and mix and understand each other. In reality that is the moment of supreme danger—the moment when they meet. We might shiver, as at the old euphemism by which a meeting meant a duel.

Travel ought to combine amusement with instruction; but most travellers are so much amused that they refuse to be instructed. I do not blame them for being amused; it is perfectly natural to be amused at a Dutchman for being Dutch or a Chinaman for being Chinese. Where they are wrong is that they take their own amusement seriously. They base on it their serious ideas of international instruction. It was said that the Englishman takes his pleasures sadly; and the pleasure of despising foreigners is one which he takes most sadly of all. He comes to scoff and does not remain to pray, but rather to excommunicate. Hence in international relations there is far too little laughing, and far too much sneering. But I believe that there is a better way which largely consists of laughter; a form of friendship between nations which is actually founded on differences.

Let me begin my American impressions with two impressions I had before I went to America. One was an incident and the other an idea; and when taken together they illustrate the attitude I mean. The first principle is that nobody should be ashamed of thinking a thing funny because it is foreign; the second is that he should be ashamed of thinking it wrong because it is funny. The reaction of his senses and superficial habits of mind against something new, and to him abnormal, is a perfectly healthy reaction. But the mind which imagines that mere unfamiliarity can possibly prove anything about inferiority is a very inadequate mind. It is inadequate even in criticising things that may really be inferior to the things involved here. It is far better to laugh at a negro for having a black face than to sneer at him for having a sloping skull. It is proportionally even more preferable to laugh rather than judge in dealing with highly civilised peoples. Therefore I put at the beginning two working examples of what I felt about America before I saw it; the sort of thing that a man has a right to enjoy as a joke, and the sort of thing he has a duty to understand and respect, because it is the explanation of the joke.

When I went to the American consulate to regularise my passports, I was capable of expecting the American consulate to be American. Embassies and consulates are by tradition like islands of the soil for which they stand; and I have often found the tradition corresponding to a truth. I have seen the unmistakable French official living on omelettes and a little wine and serving his sacred abstractions under the last palm-trees fringing a desert. In the heat and noise of quarrelling Turks and Egyptians, I have come suddenly, as with the cool shock of his own shower-bath, on the listless amiability of the English gentleman. The officials I interviewed were very American, especially in being very polite; for whatever may have been the mood or meaning of Martin Chuzzlewit, I have always found Americans by far the politest people in the world. They put in my hands a form to be filled up, to all appearances like other forms I had filled up in other passport offices. But in reality it was very different from any form I had ever filled up in my life. At least it was a little like a freer form of the game called "Confessions" which my friends and I invented in our youth; an examination paper containing questions like, "If you saw a rhinoceros in the front garden, what would you do?" One of my friends, I remember, wrote, "Take the pledge." But that is another story, and might bring Mr. Pussyfoot Johnson on the scene before his time.

One of the questions on the paper was, "Are you an anarchist?" To which a detached philosopher would naturally feel inclined to answer, "What the devil has that to do with you? Are you an atheist?" along with some playful efforts to cross-examine the official about what constitutes an ἀρχή. Then there was the question, "Are you in favour of subverting the government of the United States by force?" Against this I should write, "I prefer to answer that question at the end of my tour and not the beginning." The inquisitor, in his more than morbid curiosity, had then written down, "Are you a polygamist?" The answer to this is, "No such luck" or "Not such a fool," according to our experience of the other sex. But perhaps a better answer would be that given to W. T. Stead when he circulated the rhetorical question, "Shall I slay my brother Boer?"—the answer that ran, "Never interfere in family matters." But among many things that amused me almost to the point of treating the form thus disrespectfully, the most amusing was the thought of the ruthless outlaw who should feel compelled to treat it respectfully. I like to think of the foreign desperado, seeking to slip into America with official papers under official protection, and sitting down to write with a beautiful gravity, "I am an anarchist. I hate you all and wish to destroy you." Or, "I intend to subvert by force the government of the United States as soon as possible, sticking the long sheath-knife in my left trouser-pocket into your President at the earliest opportunity." Or again, "Yes, I am a polygamist all right, and my forty-seven wives are accompanying me on the voyage disguised as secretaries." There seems to be a certain simplicity of mind about these answers; and it is reassuring to know that anarchists and polygamists are so pure and good that the police have only to ask them questions and they are certain to tell no lies.

Now that is the model of the sort of foreign practice, founded on foreign problems, at which a man's first impulse is naturally to laugh. Nor have I any intention of apologising for my laughter. A man is perfectly entitled to laugh at a thing because he happens to find it incomprehensible. What he has no right to do is to laugh at it as incomprehensible, and then criticise it as if he comprehended it. The very fact of its unfamiliarity and mystery ought to set him thinking about the deeper causes that make people so different from himself, and that without merely assuming that they must be inferior to himself.

Superficially this is rather a queer business. It would be easy enough to suggest that in this America has introduced a quite abnormal spirit of inquisition; an interference with liberty unknown among all the ancient despotisms and aristocracies. About that there will be something to be said later; but superficially it is true that this degree of officialism is comparatively unique. In a journey which I took only the year before I had occasion to have my papers passed by governments which many worthy people in the West would vaguely identify with corsairs and assassins; I have stood on the other side of Jordan, in the land ruled by a rude Arab chief, where the police looked so like brigands that one wondered what the brigands looked like. But they did

not ask me whether I had come to subvert the power of the
Shereef; and they did not exhibit the faintest curiosity about my
personal views on the ethical basis of civil authority. These ministers of ancient Moslem despotism did not care about whether I
was an anarchist; and naturally would not have minded if I had
been a polygamist. The Arab chief was probably a polygamist
himself. These slaves of Asiatic autocracy were content, in the
old liberal fashion, to judge me by my actions; they did not inquire into my thoughts. They held their power as limited to the
limitation of practice; they did not forbid me to hold a theory.
It would be easy to argue here that Western democracy perse-
cutes where even Eastern despotism tolerates or emancipates. It
would be easy to develop the fancy that, as compared with the
sultans of Turkey or Egypt, the American Constitution is a thing
like the Spanish Inquisition.

Only the traveller who stops at that point is totally wrong;
and the traveller only too often does stop at that point. He has
found something to make him laugh, and he will not suffer it to
make him think. And the remedy is not to unsay what he has
said, not even, so to speak, to unlaugh what he has laughed, not
to deny that there is something unique and curious about this
American inquisition into our abstract opinions, but rather to
continue the train of thought, and follow the admirable advice of
Mr. H. G. Wells, who said, "It is not much good thinking of a
thing unless you think it out." It is not to deny that American
officialism is rather peculiar on this point, but to inquire what it
really is which makes America peculiar, or which is peculiar to
America. In short, it is to get some ultimate idea of what America is; and the answer to that question will reveal something much
deeper and grander and more worthy of our intelligent interest.

It may have seemed something less than a compliment to compare the American Constitution to the Spanish Inquisition. But
oddly enough, it does involve a truth, and still more oddly perhaps, it does involve a compliment. The American Constitution
does resemble the Spanish Inquisition in this: that it is founded

on a creed. America is the only nation in the world that is founded on a creed. That creed is set forth with dogmatic and even theological lucidity in the Declaration of Independence; perhaps the only piece of practical politics that is also theoretical politics and also great literature. It enunciates that all men are equal in their claim to justice, that governments exist to give them that justice, and that their authority is for that reason just. It certainly does condemn anarchism, and it does also by inference condemn atheism, since it clearly names the Creator as the ultimate authority from whom these equal rights are derived. Nobody expects a modern political system to proceed logically in the application of such dogmas, and in the matter of God and Government it is naturally God whose claim is taken more lightly. The point is that there is a creed, if not about divine, at least about human things.

Now a creed is at once the broadest and the narrowest thing in the world. In its nature it is as broad as its scheme for a brotherhood of all men. In its nature it is limited by its definition of the nature of all men. This was true of the Christian Church, which was truly said to exclude neither Jew nor Greek, but which did definitely substitute something else for Jewish religion or Greek philosophy. It was truly said to be a net drawing in of all kinds; but a net of a certain pattern, the pattern of Peter the Fisherman. And this is true even of the most disastrous distortions or degradations of that creed; and true among others of the Spanish Inquisition. It may have been narrow about theology, it could not confess to being narrow about nationality or ethnology. The Spanish Inquisition might be admittedly Inquisitorial; but the Spanish Inquisition could not be merely Spanish. Such a Spaniard, even when he was narrower than his own creed, had to be broader than his own empire. He might burn a philosopher because he was heterodox; but he must accept a barbarian because he was orthodox. And we see, even in modern times, that the same Church which is blamed for making sages heretics is also blamed for making savages priests. Now in a much vaguer and

more evolutionary fashion, there is something of the same idea
at the back of the great American experiment; the experiment of
a democracy of diverse races which has been compared to a
melting-pot. But even that metaphor implies that the pot itself is
of a certain shape and a certain substance; a pretty solid substance. The melting-pot must not melt. The original shape was
traced on the lines of Jeffersonian democracy; and it will remain
in that shape until it becomes shapeless. America invites all men
to become citizens; but it implies the dogma that there is such a
thing as citizenship. Only, so far as its primary ideal is concerned,
its exclusiveness is religious because it is not racial. The missionary can condemn a cannibal, precisely because he cannot condemn a Sandwich Islander. And in something of the same spirit
the American may exclude a polygamist, precisely because he
cannot exclude a Turk.

Now for America this is no idle theory. It may have been
theoretical, though it was thoroughly sincere, when that great
Virginian gentleman declared it in surroundings that still had
something of the character of an English countryside. It is not
merely theoretical now. There is nothing to prevent America
being literally invaded by Turks, as she is invaded by Jews or
Bulgars. In the most exquisitely inconsequent of the *Bab Ballads*,
we are told concerning Pasha Bailey Ben:—

> One morning knocked at half-past eight
> A tall Red Indian at his gate.
> In Turkey, as you'r' p'raps aware,
> Red Indians are extremely rare.

But the converse need by no means be true. There is nothing in
the nature of things to prevent an emigration of Turks increasing and multiplying on the plains where the Red Indians wandered; there is nothing to necessitate the Turks being extremely
rare. The Red Indians, alas, are likely to be rarer. And as I much
prefer Red Indians to Turks, I speak without prejudice; but the
point here is that America, partly by original theory and partly

by historical accident, does lie open to racial admixtures which most countries would think incongruous or comic. That is why it is only fair to read any American definitions or rules in a certain light, and relatively to a rather unique position. It is not fair to compare the position of those who may meet Turks in the back street with that of those who have never met Turks except in the *Bab Ballads*. It is not fair simply to compare America with England in its regulations about the Turk. In short, it is not fair to do what almost every Englishman probably does; to look at the American international examination paper, and laugh and be satisfied with saying, "We don't have any of that nonsense in England."

We do not have any of that nonsense in England because we have never attempted to have any of that philosophy in England. And, above all, because we have the enormous advantage of feeling it natural to be national, because there is nothing else to be. England in these days is not well governed; England is not well educated; England suffers from wealth and poverty that are not well distributed. But England is English; *esto perpetua*. England is English as France is French or Ireland is Irish; the great mass of men taking certain national traditions for granted. Now this gives us a totally different and a very much easier task. We have not got an inquisition, because we have not got a creed; but it is arguable that we do not need a creed, because we have got a character. In any of the old nations the national unity is preserved by the national type. Because we have a type we do not need to have a test.

Take that innocent question, "Are you an anarchist?" which is intrinsically quite as impudent as "Are you an optimist?" or "Are you a philanthropist?" I am not discussing here whether these things are right, but whether most of us are in a position to know them rightly. Now it is quite true that most Englishmen do not find it necessary to go about all day asking each other whether they are anarchists. It is quite true that the phrase occurs on no British forms that I have seen. But this is not only because most of the Englishmen are not anarchists. It is even more because even the anarchists are Englishmen. For instance, it would be easy to make fun of the American formula by noting that the cap would fit all sorts of bald academic heads. It might well be maintained that Herbert Spencer was an anarchist. It is practically certain that Auberon Herbert was an anarchist. But Herbert Spencer was an extraordinary typical Englishman of the Nonconformist middle class. And Auberon Herbert was an extraordinarily typical English aristocrat of the old and genuine aristocracy. Every one knew in his head that the squire would not throw a bomb at the Queen, and the Nonconformist would not throw a bomb at anybody. Every one knew that there was something subconscious in a man like Auberon Herbert, which would have come out only in throwing bombs at the enemies of England; as it did come out in his son and namesake, the generous and unforgotten, who fell flinging bombs from the sky far beyond the German line. Every one knows that normally, in the last resort, the English gentleman is patriotic. Every one knows that the English Nonconformist is national even when he denies that he is patriotic. Nothing is more notable indeed than the fact that nobody is more stamped with the mark of his own nation than the man who says that there ought to be no nations. Somebody called Cobden the International Man; but no man could be more English than Cobden. Everybody recognises Tolstoy as the iconoclast of all patriotism; but nobody could be more Russian than Tolstoy. In the old countries where there are these national types, the types may be allowed to hold any theories. Even if they hold certain theories they are unlikely to do certain things. So the conscientious objector, in the English sense, may be and is one of the peculiar by-products of England. But the conscientious objector will probably have a conscientious objection to throwing bombs.

Now I am very far from intending to imply that these American tests are good tests or that there is no danger of tyranny becoming the temptation of America. I shall have something to say later on about that temptation or tendency. Nor do I say that they apply consistently this conception of a nation with the soul of a church, protected by religious and not racial selection. If they did apply that principle consistently, they would have to exclude pessimists and rich cynics who deny the democratic ideal; an excellent thing but a rather improbable one. What I say is that when we realize that this principle exists at all, we see the whole position in a totally different perspective. We say that the Americans are doing something heroic or doing something insane, or doing it in an unworkable or unworthy fashion, instead of simply wondering what the devil they are doing.

When we realise the democratic design of such a cosmopolitan commonwealth, and compare it with our insular reliance or instincts, we see at once why such a thing has to be not only democratic but dogmatic. We see why in some points it tends to be inquisitive or intolerant. Any one can see the practical point by merely transferring into private life a problem like that of the two academic anarchists, who might by a coincidence be called the two Herberts. Suppose a man said, "Buffle, my old Oxford tutor, wants to meet you; I wish you'd ask him down for a day or two. He has the oddest opinions, but he's very stimulating." It would not occur to us that the oddity of the Oxford don's opinions would lead him to blow up the house; because the Oxford don is an English type. Suppose somebody said, "Do let me bring old Colonel Robinson down for the week-end; he's a bit of crank but quite interesting." We should not anticipate the colonel running amuck with a carving-knife and offering up human sacrifice in the garden; for these are not among the daily habits of an old English colonel; and because we know his habits, we do not care about his opinions. But suppose somebody offered to bring a person from the interior of Kamskatka to stay with us for a week or two, and added that his religion was a very extraordinary religion, we should feel a little more inquisitive about what kind of religion it was. If somebody wished to add a Hairy Ainu to the family party at Christmas, explaining that his point of view was so individual and interesting, we should want to know a little more about it and him. We should be tempted to draw up as fantastic an examination paper as that presented to the emigrant going to America. We should ask what a Hairy Ainu was, and how hairy he was, and above all what sort of Ainu he was. Would etiquette require us to ask him to bring his wife? And if we did ask him to bring his wife, how many wives would he bring? In short, as in the American formula, is he a polygamist? Merely as a point of housekeeping and accommodation the question is not irrelevant. Is the Hairy Ainu content with hair, or does he wear any clothes? If the police insist on his wearing clothes, will he recognise the authority of the police? In short, as in the American formula, is he an anarchist?

Of course this generalisation about America, like other historical things, is subject to all sorts of cross divisions and exceptions, to be considered in their place. The negroes are a special problem, because of what white men in the past did to them. The Japanese are a special problem, because of what men fear that they in the future may do to white men. The Jews are a special problem, because of what they and the Gentiles, in the past, present and future, seem to have the habit of doing to each other. But the point is not that nothing exists in America except this idea; it is that nothing like this idea exists anywhere except in America. This idea is not internationalism; on the contrary it is decidedly nationalism. The Americans are very patriotic, and wish to make their new citizens patriotic Americans. But it is the idea of making a new nation literally out of any old nation that comes along. In a word, what is unique is not America but what is called Americanisation. We understand nothing till we understand the amazing ambition to Americanise the Kamskatkan and the Hairy Ainu. We are not trying to Anglicise thousands of French cooks or Italian organ grinders. France is not trying to Gallicise thousands of English trippers or German prisoners of war. America is the one place in the world where this process, healthy or unhealthy, possible or impossible, is going on. And the process, as I have pointed out, is *not* internationalisation. It

would be truer to say it is the nationalisation of the internationalised. It is making a home out of vagabonds and a nation out of
exiles. This is what at once illuminates and softens the moral regulations which we may really think faddist or fanatical. They are
abnormal; but in one sense this experiment of a home for the
homeless is abnormal. In short, it has long been recognised that
America was an asylum. It was only during Prohibition that it
looked a little like a lunatic asylum.

It was before sailing for America, as I have said, that I stood
with the official paper in my hand and these thoughts in my head.
It was while I stood on English soil that I passed through the two
stages of smiling and then sympathising; of realising that my
momentary amusement, at being asked if I were not an Anarchist, was partly due to the fact that I was not an American. And
in truth I think there are some things a man ought to know about
America before he sees it. What we know of a country beforehand may not affect what we see that it is; but it will vitally
affect what we appreciate it for being, because it will vitally affect what we expected it to be. I can honestly say that I had
never expected America to be what nine-tenths of the newspaper
critics invariably assume it to be. I never thought it was a sort
of Anglo-Saxon colony, knowing that it was more and more
thronged with crowds of very different colonists. During the
war I felt that the very worst propaganda for the Allies was the
propaganda for the Anglo-Saxons. I tried to point out that in one
way America is nearer to Europe than England is. If she is not
nearer to Bohemia, she is nearer to Bohemians. In my New York
hotel the head waiter in the dining-room was a Bohemian; the
head waiter in the grill-room was a Bulgar. Americans have nationalities at the end of the street which for us are at the ends of
the earth. I did my best to persuade my countrymen not to appeal to the American as if he were a rather dowdy Englishman,
who had been rusticating in the provinces and had not heard the
latest news about the town. I shall record later some of those arresting realities which the traveller does not expect; and which,

in some cases I fear, he actually does not see because he does not
expect. I shall try to do justice to the psychology of what Mr.
Belloc has called "Eye-Openers in Travel." But there are some
things about America that a man ought to see even with his eyes
shut. One is that a state that came into existence solely through
its repudiation and abhorrence of the British Crown is not likely
to be a respectful copy of the British Constitution. Another is
that the chief mark of the Declaration of Independence is something that is not only absent from the British Constitution,
but something which all our constitutionalists have invariably
thanked God, with the jolliest boasting and bragging, that they
had kept out of the British Constitution. It is the thing called abstraction or academic logic. It is the thing which such jolly people call theory; and which those who can practice it call thought.
And the theory or thought is the very last to which English people are accustomed, either by their social structure or their traditional teaching. It is the theory of equality. It is the pure classic
conception that no man must aspire to be anything more than a
citizen, and that no man shall endure to be anything less. It is by
no means especially intelligible to an Englishman, who tends at
his best to the virtues of the gentleman and at his worst to the
vices of the snob. The idealism of England, or if you will the
romance of England, has not been primarily the romance of the
citizen. But the idealism of America, we may safely say, still re-
volves entirely round the citizen and his romance. The realities
are quite another matter, and we shall consider in its place the
question of whether the ideal will be able to shape the realities or
will merely be beaten shapeless by them. The ideal is besieged by
inequalities of the most towering and insane description in the
industrial and economic field. It may be devoured by modern
capitalism, perhaps the worst inequality that ever existed among
men. Of all that we shall speak later. But citizenship is still the
American ideal; there is an army of actualities opposed to that
ideal; but there is no ideal opposed to that ideal. American plutocracy has never got itself respected like English aristocracy.

Citizenship is the American ideal, and it has never been the English ideal. But it is surely an ideal that may stir some imaginative generosity and respect in an Englishman, if he will condescend to be also a man. In this vision of moulding many peoples into the visible image of the citizen, he may see a spiritual adventure which he can admire from the outside at least as much as he admires the valour of the Moslems and much more than he admires the virtue of the Middle Ages. He need not set himself to develop equality, but he need not set himself to misunderstand it. He may at least understand what Jefferson and Lincoln meant, and he may possibly find some assistance in this task by reading what they said. He may realise that equality is not some crude fairy tale about all men being equally tall or equally tricky; which we not only cannot believe but cannot believe in anybody believing. It is an absolute of morals by which all men have a value invariable and indestructible and a dignity as intangible as death. He may at least be a philosopher and see that equality is an idea; and not merely one of these soft-headed sceptics who, having risen by low tricks to high places, drink bad champagne in tawdry hotel lounges, and tell each other twenty times over, with unwearied iteration, that equality is an illusion.

In truth it is inequality that is the illusion. The extreme disproportion between men, that we seem to see in life, is a thing of changing lights and lengthening shadows, a twilight full of fancies and distortions. We find a man famous and cannot live long enough to find him forgotten; we see a race dominant and cannot linger to see it decay. It is the experience of men that always returns to the equality of men; it is the average that ultimately justifies the average man. It is when men have seen and suffered much and come at the end of more elaborate experiments, that they see men under an equal light of death and daily laughter; and none the less mysterious for being many. Nor is it in vain that these Western democrats have sought the blazonry of their flag in that great multitude of immortal lights that endure behind the fires we see, and gathered them into the corner of Old

Glory whose ground is like the glittering night. For veritably, in the spirit as well as in the symbol, suns and moons and meteors pass and fill our skies with a fleeting and almost theatrical conflagration; and wherever the old shadow stoops upon the earth, the stars return.

A MEDITATION IN A NEW YORK HOTEL

ALL this must begin with an apology and not an apologia. When I went wandering about the States disguised as a lecturer, I was well aware that I was not sufficiently well disguised to be a spy. I was even in the worst possible position to be a sight-seer. A lecturer to American audiences can hardly be in the holiday mood of a sight-seer. It is rather the audience that is sight-seeing; even if it is seeing a rather melancholy sight. Some say that people come to see the lecturer and not to hear him; in which case it seems rather a pity that he should disturb and distress their minds with a lecture. He might merely exhibit himself on a stand or platform for a stipulated sum; or be exhibited like a monster in a menagerie. The circus elephant is not expected to make a speech. But it is equally true that the circus elephant is not allowed to write a book. His impressions of travel would be somewhat sketchy and perhaps a little over-specialised. In merely travelling from circus to circus he would, so to speak, move in rather narrow circles. Jumbo, the great elephant (with whom I am hardly so ambitious as to compare myself), before he eventually went to the Barnum show, passed a considerable and I trust happy part of his life in the Regent's Park. But if he had written a book on England, founded on his impressions of the Zoo, it might have been a little disproportionate and even misleading in its version of the flora and fauna of that country. He might imagine that lions and leopards were commoner than they are in our hedgerows and country lanes, or that the head and neck of a giraffe was as native to our landscapes as a village spire. And that is why I apologise in anticipation for a probable lack of proportion in this work. Like the elephant, I may have seen too much of a special enclosure where a special sort of lions are gathered together. I may exaggerate the territorial, as distinct from the vertical space occupied by the spiritual giraffe; for the giraffe may

198

surely be regarded as an example of Uplift, and is even, in a manner of speaking, a high-brow. Above all, I shall probably make generalisations that are much too general; and are insufficient through being exaggerative. To this sort of doubt all my impressions are subject; and among them the negative generalisation with which I shall begin this rambling meditation on American hotels.

In all my American wanderings I never saw such a thing as an inn. They may exist; but they do not arrest the traveller upon every road as they do in England and in Europe. The saloons no longer existed when I was there, owing to the recent reform which restricted intoxicants to the wealthier classes. But we feel that the saloons have been there; if one may so express it, their absence is still present. They remain in the structure of the streets and the idiom of the language. But the saloons were not inns. If they had been inns, it would have been far harder even for the power of modern plutocracy to root them out. There will be a very different chase when the White Hart is hunted to the forests or when the Red Lion turns to bay. But people could not feel about the American saloon as they will feel about the English inns. They could not feel that the Prohibitionist, that vulgar chucker-out, was chucking Chaucer out of the Tabard and Shakespeare out of the Mermaid. In justice to the American Prohibitionists it must be realised that they were not doing quite such desecration; and that many of them felt the saloon a specially poisonous sort of place. They did feel that drinking-places were used only as drug-shops. So they have effected the great reconstruction, by which it will be necessary to use only drug-shops as drinking-places. But I am not dealing here with the problem of Prohibition except in so far as it is involved in the statement that the saloons were in no sense inns. Secondly, of course, there are the hotels. There are indeed. There are hotels toppling to the stars, hotels covering the acreage of villages, hotels in multitudinous number like a mob of Babylonian or Assyrian monuments; but the hotels also are not inns.

Broadly speaking, there is only one hotel in America. The pattern of it, which is a very rational pattern, is repeated in cities as remote from each other as the capitals of European empires. You may find that hotel rising among the red blooms of the warm spring woods of Nebraska, or whitened with Canadian snows near the eternal noise of Niagara. And before touching on this solid and simple pattern itself, I may remark that the same system of symmetry runs through all the details of the interior. As one hotel is like another hotel, so one hotel floor is like another hotel floor. If the passage outside your bedroom door, or hallway as it is called, contains, let us say, a small table with a green vase and a stuffed flamingo, or some trifle of the sort, you may be perfectly certain that there is exactly the same table, vase, and flamingo on every one of the thirty-two landings of that towering habitation. This is where it differs most perhaps from the crooking landings and unexpected levels of the old English inns, even when they call themselves hotels. To me there was something weird, like a magic multiplication, in the exquisite sameness of these suites. It seemed to suggest the still atmosphere of some eerie psychological story. I once myself entertained the notion of a story, in which a man was to be prevented from entering his house (the scene of some crime or calamity) by people who painted and furnished the next house to look exactly like it; the assimilation going to the most fantastic lengths, such as altering the numbering of houses in the street. I came to America and found an hotel fitted and upholstered throughout for the enactment of my phantasmal fraud. I offer the skeleton of my story with all humility to some of the admirable lady writers of detective stories in America. Surely it might be possible for the unsophisticated Nimrod K. Moose, of Yellow Dog Flat, to come to New York and be entangled somehow in this net of repetitions or recurrences. Surely something tells me that his beautiful daughter, the Rose of Red Murder Gulch, might seek for him in vain amid the apparently unmistakable surroundings of the thirty-second floor, while he was being quietly butchered by

WHAT I SAW IN AMERICA   201

the floor-clerk on the thirty-third floor, an agent of the Green
Claw (that formidable organisation); and all because the two
floors looked exactly alike to the virginal Western eye. The
original point of my own story was that the man to be en-
trapped walked into his own house after all, in spite of its being
differently painted and numbered, simply because he was absent-
minded and used to taking a certain number of mechanical steps.
This would not work in a hotel; because a lift has no habits. It
is typical of the real tameness of machinery, that even when we
talk of a man turning mechanically we only talk metaphorically;
for it is something that a mechanism cannot do. But I think there
is only one real objection to my story of Mr. Moose in the New
York hotel. And that is unfortunately a rather fatal one. It is that
far away in the remote desolation of Yellow Dog, among those
outlying and outlandish rocks that almost seem to rise beyond
the sunset, there is undoubtedly an hotel of exactly the same sort,
with all its floors exactly the same.

Anyhow the general plan of the American hotel is commonly the same, and, as I have said, it is a very sound one so far
as it goes. When I first went into one of the big New York
hotels, the first impression was certainly its bigness. It was called
the Biltmore; and I wondered how many national humorists had
made the obvious comment of wishing they had built less. But it
was not merely the Babylonian size and scale of such things, it
was the way in which they are used. They are used almost as
public streets, or rather as public squares. My first impression
was that I was in some sort of high street or market-place during
a carnival or a revolution. True, the people looked rather rich
for a revolution and rather grave for a carnival; but they were
congested in great crowds that moved slowly like people passing
through an overcrowded railway station. Even in the dizzy
heights of such a sky-scraper there could not possibly be room
for all those people to sleep in the hotel, or even to dine in it.
And, as a matter of fact, they did nothing whatever except drift
into it and drift out again. Most of them had no more to do with

the hotel than I have with Buckingham Palace. I have never been
in Buckingham Palace, and I have very seldom, thank God, been
in the big hotels of this type that exist in London or Paris. But I
cannot believe that mobs are perpetually pouring through the
Hotel Cecil or the Savoy in this fashion, calmly coming in at one
door and going out of the other. But this fact is part of the fundamental structure of the American hotel; it is built upon a compromise that makes it possible. The whole of the lower floor is
thrown open to the public streets and treated as a public square.
But above it and all round it runs another floor in the form of a
sort of deep gallery, furnished more luxuriously and looking
down on the moving mobs beneath. No one is allowed on this
floor except the guests or clients of the hotel. As I have been one
of them myself, I trust it is not unsympathetic to compare them
to active anthropoids who can climb trees, and so look down in
safety on the herds or packs of wilder animals wandering and
prowling below. Of course there are modifications of architectural plan, but they are generally approximations to it; it is
the plan that seems to suit the social life of the American cities.
There is generally something like a ground floor that is more
public, a half-floor or gallery above that is more private, and
above that the bulk of the block of bedrooms, the huge hive with
its innumerable and identical cells.

The ladder of ascent in this tower is of course the lift, or, as it
is called, the elevator. With all that we hear of American hustle
and hurry, it is rather strange that Americans seem to like more
than we do to linger upon long words. And indeed there is an
element of delay in their diction and spirit, very little understood,
which I may discuss elsewhere. Anyhow they say elevator when
we say lift, just as they say automobile when we say motor and
stenographer when we say typist, or sometimes (by a slight confusion) typewriter. The Americans may have another reason for
giving long and ceremonious titles to the lift. When first I came
among them I had a suspicion that they possessed and practised a
new and secret religion, which was the cult of the elevator. I

fancied they worshipped the lift, or at any rate worshipped in the lift. The details or data of this suspicion it were now vain to collect, as I have regretfully abandoned it, except in so far as they illustrate the social principles underlying the structural plan of the building. Now an American gentleman invariably takes off his hat in the lift. He does not take off his hat in the hotel, even if it is crowded with ladies. But he always so salutes a lady in the elevator; and this marks the difference of atmosphere. The lift is a room, but the hotel is a street. But during my first delusion, of course, I assumed that he uncovered in this tiny temple merely because he was in church. There is something about the very word elevator that expresses a great deal of his vague but idealistic religion. Perhaps that flying chapel will eventually be ritualistically decorated like a chapel; possibly with a symbolic scheme of wings. Perhaps a brief religious service will be held in the elevator as it ascends; in a few well-chosen words touching the Utmost for the Highest. Possibly he would consent even to call the elevator a lift, if he could call it an uplift. There would be no difficulty, except what I cannot but regard as the chief moral problem of all optimistic modernism. I mean the difficulty of imagining a lift which is free to go up, if it is not also free to go down.

I think I know my American friends and acquaintances too well to apologise for any levity in these illustrations. Americans make fun of their own institutions; and their own journalism is full of such fanciful conjectures. The tall building is itself artistically akin to the tall story. The very word skyscraper is an admirable example of an American lie. But I can testify quite as eagerly to the solid and sensible advantages of the symmetrical hotel. It is not only a pattern of vases and stuffed flamingoes; it is also an equally accurate pattern of cupboards and baths. It is a dignified and humane custom to have a bathroom attached to every bedroom; and my impulse to sing the praises of it brought me once at least into a rather quaint complication. I think it was in the city of Dayton; anyhow I remember there was a Laundry Con-

204 THE MAN WHO WAS CHESTERTON

vention going on in the same hotel, in a room very patriotically
and properly festooned with the stars and stripes, and doubtless
full of promise for the future of laundering. I was interviewed on
the roof, within earshot of this debate, and may have been the
victim of some association or confusion; anyhow, after answering
the usual questions about Labour, the League of Nations, the
length of ladies' dresses, and other great matters, I took refuge
in a rhapsody of warm and well-deserved praise of American
bathrooms. The editor, I understand, running a gloomy eye
down the column of his contributor's "story," and seeing nothing but metaphysical terms such as justice, freedom, the abstract
disapproval of sweating, swindling, and the like, paused at last
upon the ablutionary allusion, and his eye brightened. "That's
the only copy in the whole thing," he said, "A Bath-Tub in
Every Home." So these words appeared in enormous letters
above my portrait in the paper. It will be noted that, like many
things that practical men make a great point of, they miss the
point. What I had commended as new and national was a bathroom in every bedroom. Even feudal and moss-grown England
is not entirely ignorant of an occasional bath-tub in the home.
But what gave me great joy was what followed. I discovered
with delight that many people, glancing rapidly at my portrait
with its prodigious legend, imagined that it was a commercial
advertisement, and that I was a very self-advertising commercial
traveller. When I walked about the streets, I was supposed to be
travelling in bath-tubs. Consider the caption of the portrait, and
you will see how similar it is to the true commercial slogan: "We
offer a Bath-Tub in Every Home." And this charming error was
doubtless clinched by the fact that I had been found haunting
the outer courts of the temple of the ancient guild of Lavenders.
I never knew how many shared the impression; I regret to say
that I only traced it with certainty in two individuals. But I understand that it included the idea that I had come to the town to
attend the Laundry Convention, and had made an eloquent

speech to that senate, no doubt exhibiting my tubs.

Such was the penalty of too passionate and unrestrained an admiration for American bathrooms; yet the connection of ideas, however inconsequent, does cover the part of social practice for which these American institutions can really be praised. About everything like laundry or hot and cold water there is not only organisation, but what does not always or perhaps often go with it, efficiency. Americans are particular about these things of dress and decorum; and it is a virtue which I very seriously recognise, though I find it very hard to emulate. But with them it is a virtue; it is not a mere convention, still less a mere fashion. It is really related to human dignity rather than to social superiority. The really glorious thing about the American is that he does not dress like a gentleman; he dresses like a citizen or a civilised man. Puritan particularity on certain points is really detachable from any definite social ambitions; these things are not a part of getting into society but merely of keeping out of savagery. Those millions and millions of middling people, that huge middle class especially of the Middle West, are not near enough to any aristocracy even to be sham aristocrats, or to be real snobs. But their standards are secure; and though I do not really travel in a bath-tub, or believe in the bath-tub philosophy and religion, I will not on this matter recoil misanthropically from them: I prefer the tub of Dayton to the tub of Diogenes. On these points there is really something a million times better than efficiency, and that is something like equality.

In short, the American hotel is not America; but it is American. In some respects it is as American as the English inn is English. And it is symbolic of that society in this among other things: that it does tend too much to uniformity; but that that very uniformity disguises not a little natural dignity. The old Romans boasted that their republic was a nation of kings. If we really walked abroad in such a kingdom, we might very well grow tired of the sight of a crowd of kings, of every man with a gold crown on his head or an ivory sceptre in his hand. But it is arguable that we ought not to grow tired of the repetition of crowns and sceptres, any more than of the repetition of flowers and stars. The whole imaginative effort of Walt Whitman was really an effort to absorb and animate these multitudinous modern repetitions; and Walt Whitman would be quite capable of including in his lyric litany of optimism a list of the nine hundred and ninety-nine identical bathrooms. I do not sneer at the generous effort of the giant; though I think, when all is said, that it is criticism of modern machinery that the effort should be gigantic as well as generous.

While there is so much repetition there is little repose. It is the pattern of a kaleidoscope rather than a wall-paper; a pattern of figures running and even leaping like the figures in a zoetrope. But even in the groups where there was no hustle there was often something of homelessness. I do not mean merely that they were not dining at home; but rather that they were not at home even when dining, and dining at their favourite hotel. They would frequently start up and dart from the room at a summons from the telephone. It may have been fanciful, but I could not help feeling a breath of home, as from a flap or flutter of St. George's cross, when I first sat down in a Canadian hostelry, and read the announcement that no such telephonic or other summonses were allowed in the dining-room. It may have been a coincidence, and there may be American hotels with this merciful proviso and Canadian hotels without it; but the thing was symbolic even if it was not evidential. I felt as if I stood indeed upon English soil, in a place where people liked to have their meals in peace.

The process of the summons is called "paging," and consists of sending a little boy with a large voice through all the halls and corridors of the building, making them resound with a name. The custom is common, of course, in clubs and hotels even in England; but in England it is a mere whisper compared with the wail with which the American page repeats the formula of "Calling Mr. So and So." I remember a particularly crowded *parterre* in the somewhat smoky and oppressive atmosphere of Pittsburg, through which wandered a youth with a voice the like of which I have never heard in the land of the living, a voice like the cry of a lost spirit, saying again and again for ever, "Carling Mr. Anderson." One felt that he never would find Mr. Anderson. Perhaps there never had been any Mr. Anderson to be found. Perhaps he and every one else wandered in an abyss of bottomless scepticism; and he was but the victim of one out of numberless nightmares of eternity, as he wandered a shadow with shadows and wailed by impassable streams. This is not exactly my philosophy, but I feel sure it was his. And it is a mood that may frequently visit the mind in the centres of highly active and successful industrial civilisation.

Such are the first idle impressions of the great American hotel, gained by sitting for the first time in its gallery and gazing on its drifting crowds with thoughts equally drifting. The first impression is of something enormous and rather unnatural, an impression that is gradually tempered by experience of the kindliness and even the tameness of so much of that social order. But I should not be recording the sensations with sincerity, if I did not touch in passing the note of something unearthly about that vast system to an insular traveller who sees it for the first time. It is as if he were wandering in another world among the fixed stars; or worse still, in an ideal Utopia of the future.

Yet I am not certain; and perhaps the best of all news is that nothing is really new. I sometimes have a fancy that many of these new things in new countries are but the resurrections of old things which have been wickedly killed or stupidly stunted in old countries. I have looked over the sea of little tables in some light and airy open-air café; and my thoughts have gone back to the plain wooden bench and wooden table that stands solitary and weather-stained outside so many neglected English inns. We talk of experimenting in the French café, as of some fresh and almost impudent innovation. But our fathers had the French café, in the sense of the free-and-easy table in the sun and air. The only difference was that French democracy was allowed to develop its café, or multiply its tables, while English plutocracy prevented any such popular growth. Perhaps there are other examples of old types and patterns, lost in the old oligarchy and saved in the new democracies. I am haunted with a hint that the new structures are not so very new: and that they remind me of something very old. As I look from the balcony floors the crowds seem to float away and the colours to soften and grow pale, and I know I am in one of the simplest and most ancestral of human habitations. I am looking down from the old wooden gallery upon the courtyard of an inn. This new architectural model, which I have described, is after all one of the oldest European models, now neglected in Europe and especially in England. It was the theatre in which were enchanted innumerable picaresque comedies and romantic plays, with figures ranging from Sancho Panza to Sam Weller. It served as the apparatus, like some gigantic toy set up in bricks and timber, for the ancient and perhaps eternal game of tennis. The very terms of the original game were taken from the inn courtyard, and the players scored accordingly as they hit the buttery-hatch or the roof. Singular speculations hover in my mind as the scene darkens and the quadrangle below begins to empty in the last hours of night. Some day perhaps this huge structure will be found standing in a solitude like a skeleton; and it will be the skeleton of the Spotted Dog or the Blue Boar. It will wither and decay until it is worthy at last to be a tavern. I do not know whether men will play tennis on its ground floor, with various scores and prizes for hitting the electric fan, or the lift, or the head waiter. Perhaps the very words will only remain as part of some such rustic game. Perhaps the electric fan will no longer be electric and the elevator will no longer elevate, and the waiter will only wait to be hit. But at least it is only by the decay of modern plutocracy, which seems already to have begun, that the secret of the structure even of this plutocratic palace can stand revealed. And after long years, when its lights are extinguished and only the long shadows inhabit its halls and vestibules, there may come a new noise like thunder; of D'Artagnan knocking at the door.

A MEDITATION IN BROADWAY

WHEN I had looked at the lights of Broadway by night, I made to my American friends an innocent remark that seemed for some reason to amuse them. I had looked, not without joy, at that long kaleidoscope of coloured lights arranged in large letters and sprawling trade-marks, advertising everything, from pork to pianos, through the agency of the two most vivid and most mystical of the gifts of God; colour and fire. I said to them, in my simplicity, "What a glorious garden of wonders this would be, to any one who was lucky enough to be unable to read."

Here it is but a text for a further suggestion. But let us suppose that there does walk down this flaming avenue a peasant, of the sort called scornfully an illiterate peasant; by those who think that insisting on people reading and writing is the best way to keep out the spies who read in all languages and the forgers who write in all hands. On this principle indeed, a peasant merely acquainted with things of little practical use to mankind, such as ploughing, cutting wood, or growing vegetables, would very probably be excluded; and it is not for us to criticise from the outside the philosophy of those who would keep out the farmer and let in the forger. But let us suppose, if only for the sake of argument, that the peasant is walking under the artificial suns and stars of this tremendous thoroughfare; that he has escaped to the land of liberty upon some general rumour and romance of the story of its liberation, but without being yet able to understand the arbitrary signs of its alphabet. The soul of such a man would surely soar higher than the sky-scrapers, and embrace a brotherhood broader than Broadway. Realising that he had arrived on an evening of exceptional festivity, worthy to be blazoned with all this burning heraldry, he would please himself by guessing what great proclamation or principle of the Republic hung in the sky like a constellation or rippled across the street like a comet. He would be shrewd enough to guess that the three festoons fringed with fiery words of somewhat similar pattern stood for "Government of the People, For the People, By the People"; for it must obviously be that, unless it were "Liberty, Equality, Fraternity." His shrewdness would perhaps be a little shaken if he knew that the triad stood for "Tang Tonic To-day; Tang Tonic To-morrow; Tang Tonic All the Time." He will soon identify a restless ribbon of red lettering, red hot and rebellious, as the saying, "Give me liberty or give me death." He will fail to identify it as the equally famous saying, "Skyoline Has Gout Beaten to a Frazzle." Therefore it was that I desired the peasant to walk down that grove of fiery trees, under all that golden foliage and fruits like monstrous jewels, as innocent as Adam before the Fall. He would see sights almost as fine as the flaming sword or the purple and peacock plumage of the seraphim; so long as he did not go near the Tree of Knowledge.

In other words, if once he went to school it would be all up; and indeed I fear in any case he would soon discover his error. If he stood wildly waving his hat for liberty in the middle of the road as Chunk Chutney picked itself out in ruby stars upon the sky, he would impede the excellent but extremely rigid traffic system of New York. If he fell on his knees before a sapphire splendour, and began saying an Ave Maria under a mistaken association, he would be conducted kindly but firmly by an Irish policeman to a more authentic shrine. But though the foreign simplicity might not long survive in New York, it is quite a mistake to suppose that such foreign simplicity cannot enter New York. He may be excluded for being illiterate, but he cannot be excluded for being ignorant, nor for being innocent. Least of all can he be excluded for being wiser in his innocence than the world in its knowledge. There is here indeed more than one distinction to be made. New York is a cosmopolitan city; but it is not a city of cosmopolitans. Most of the masses in New York have a nation, whether or no it be the nation to which New York belongs. Those who are Americanised are American, and very patriotically American. Those who are not thus nationalised are not in the least internationalised. They simply continue to be themselves; the Irish are Irish; the Jews are Jewish; and all sorts of other tribes carry on the traditions of remote European valleys almost untouched. In short, there is a sort of slender bridge between their old country and their new, which they either cross or do not cross, but which they seldom simply occupy. They are exiles or they are citizens; there is no moment when they are cosmopolitans. But very often the exiles bring with them not only rooted traditions, but rooted truths.

Indeed it is to a great extent the thought of these strange souls in crude American garb that gives a meaning to the masquerade of New York. In the hotel where I stayed the head waiter in one room was a Bohemian; and I am glad to say that he called himself a Bohemian. I have already protested sufficiently, before American audiences, against the pedantry of perpetually talking about Czecho-Slovakia. I suggested to my American friends that the abandonment of the word Bohemian in its historical sense might well extend to its literary and figurative sense. We might be expected to say, "I'm afraid Henry has got into very Czecho-Slovakian habits lately," or "Don't bother to dress; it's quite a Czecho-Slovakian affair." Anyhow my Bohemian would have nothing to do with such nonsense; he called himself a son of Bohemia, and spoke as such in his criticisms of America, which were both favourable and unfavourable. He was a squat man, with a sturdy figure and a steady smile; and his eyes were like dark pools in the depth of a darker forest; but I do not think he had ever been deceived by the lights of Broadway.

But I found something like my real innocent abroad, my real peasant among the sky-signs, in another part of the same establishment. He was a much leaner man, equally dark, with a hook nose, hungry face, and fierce black moustaches. He also was a waiter, and was in the costume of a waiter, which is a smarter edition of the costume of a lecturer. As he was serving me with clam chowder or some such thing, I fell into speech with him and he told me he was a Bulgar. I said something like, "I'm afraid I don't know as much as I ought to about Bulgaria. I suppose most of your people are agricultural, aren't they?" He did not stir an inch from his regular attitude, but he slightly lowered his low voice and said, "Yes. From the earth we come and to the earth we return; when people get away from that they are lost."

To hear such a thing said by the waiter was alone an epoch in the life of an unfortunate writer of fantastic novels. To see him clear away the clam chowder like an automaton, and bring me more iced water like an automaton or like nothing on earth except an American waiter (for piling up ice is the cold passion of their lives), and all this after having uttered something so dark and deep, so starkly incongruous and so startlingly true, was an indescribable thing, but very like the picture of the peasant admiring Broadway. So he passed, with his artificial clothes and manners, lit up with all the ghastly artificial light of the hotel, and all the ghastly artificial life of the city; and his heart was like his own remote and rocky valley, where those unchanging words were carved as on a rock.

I do not profess to discuss here at all adequately the question this raises about the Americanisation of the Bulgar. It has many aspects, of some of which most Englishmen and even some Americans are rather unconscious. For one thing, a man with so rugged a loyalty to land could not be Americanised in New York; but it is not so certain that he could not be Americanised in America. We might almost say that a peasantry is hidden in the heart of America. So far as our impressions go, it is a secret. It is rather an open secret; covering only some thousand square miles of open prairie. But for most of our countrymen it is something invisible, unimagined, and unvisited; the simple truth that where all those acres are there is agriculture, and where all that agriculture is there is considerable tendency towards distributive or decently equalised property, as in a peasantry. On the other hand, there are those who say that the Bulgar will never be Americanised, that he only comes to be a waiter in America that he may afford to return to be a peasant in Bulgaria. I cannot decide this issue, and indeed I did not introduce it to this end. I was led to it by a certain line of reflection that runs along the Great White Way, and I will continue to follow it. The criticism, if we could put it rightly, not only covers more than New York but more than the whole New World. Any argument against it is quite as valid against the largest and richest cities of the Old World, against London or Liverpool or Frankfort or Belfast. But it is in New York that we see the argument most clearly, because we see the thing thus towering into its own turrets and breaking into its own fireworks.

I disagree with the aesthetic condemnation of the modern city with its sky-scrapers and sky-signs. I mean that which laments the loss of beauty and its sacrifice to utility. It seems to me the very reverse of the truth. Years ago, when people used to say the Salvation Army doubtless had good intentions, but we must all deplore its methods, I pointed out that the very contrary is the case. Its method, the method of drums and democratic appeal, is that of the Franciscans or any other march of the Church Militant. It was precisely its aims that were dubious, with their dissenting morality and despotic finance. It is somewhat the same with things like the sky-signs in Broadway. The aesthete must not ask me to mingle my tears with his, because these things are merely useful and ugly. For I am not specially inclined to think them ugly; but I am strongly inclined to think them useless. As a matter of art for art's sake, they seem to me rather artistic. As a form of practical social work they seem to me stark stupid waste. If Mr. Bilge is rich enough to build a tower four hundred feet high and give it a crown of golden crescents and crimson stars, in order to draw attention to his manufacture of the Paradise Tooth Paste or the Seventh Heaven Cigar, I do not feel the least disposition to thank him for any serious form of social service. I have never tried the Seventh Heaven Cigar; indeed a premonition moves me towards the belief that I shall go down to the dust without trying it. I have every reason to doubt whether it does any particular good to those who smoke it, or any good to any-body except those who sell it. In short Mr. Bilge's usefulness con-sists in being useful to Mr. Bilge, and all the rest is illusion and sentimentalism. But because I know that Bilge is only Bilge, shall I stoop to the profanity of saying that fire is only fire? Shall I blaspheme crimson stars any more than crimson sunsets, or deny that those moons are golden any more than that this grass is green? If a child saw these coloured lights, he would dance with as much delight as at any other coloured toys; and it is the duty of every poet, and even of every critic, to dance in respectful imitation of the child. Indeed I am in a mood of so much sym-pathy with the fairy lights of this pantomime city, that I should be almost sorry to see social sanity and a sense of proportion re-turn to extinguish them. I fear the day is breaking, and the broad daylight of tradition and ancient truth is coming to end all this delightful nightmare of New York at night. Peasants and priests and all sorts of practical and sensible people are coming back into power, and their stern realism may wither all these beauti-ful, unsubstantial, useless things. They will not believe in the Seventh Heaven Cigar, even when they see it shining as with stars in the seventh heaven. They will not be affected by adver-tisements, any more than the priests and peasants of the Middle Ages would have been affected by advertisements. Only a very soft-headed, sentimental and rather servile generation of men could possibly be affected by advertisements at all. People who are a little more hard-headed, humorous, and intellectually in-dependent, see the rather simple joke; and are not impressed by this or any other form of self-praise. Almost any other men in almost any other age would have seen the joke. If you had said to a man in the Stone Age, "Ugg says Ugg makes the best stone hatchets," he would have perceived a lack of detachment and disinterestedness about the testimonial. If you had said to a medi-eval peasant, "Robert the Bowyer proclaims, with three blasts of a horn, that he makes good bows," the peasant would have said, "Well, of course he does," and thought about something more important. It is only among people whose minds have been weakened by a sort of mesmerism that so transparent a trick as that of advertisement could ever have been tried at all. And if ever we have again, as for other reasons I cannot but hope we shall, a more democratic distribution of property and a more agricultural basis of national life, it would seem at first sight only too likely that all this beautiful superstition will perish, and the fairy-land of Broadway with all its varied rainbows fade away. For such people the Seventh Heaven Cigar, like the nineteenth-century city, will have ended in smoke. And even the smoke of it will have vanished.

But the next stage of reflection brings us back to the peasant looking at the lights of Broadway. It is not true to say in the strict sense that the peasant has never seen such things before. The truth is that he has seen them on a much smaller scale, but for a much larger purpose. Peasants also have their ritual and ornament, but it is to adorn more real things. Apart from our first fancy about the peasant who could not read, there is no doubt about what would be apparent to a peasant who could read, and who could understand. For him also fire is sacred, for him also colour is symbolic. But where he sets up a candle to light the little shrine of St. Joseph, he finds it takes twelve hundred candles to light the Seventh Heaven Cigar. He is used to the colours in church windows showing red for martyrs or blue for madonnas; but here he can only conclude that all the colours of the rainbow belong to Mr. Bilge. Now upon the aesthetic side he might well be impressed; but it is exactly on the social and even scientific side that he has a right to criticise. If he were a Chinese peasant, for instance, and came from a land of fireworks, he would naturally suppose that he had happened to arrive at a great fireworks display in celebration of something; perhaps the Sacred Emperor's birthday, or rather birthnight. It would gradually dawn on the Chinese philosopher that the Emperor could hardly be born every night. And when he learnt the truth the philosopher, if he was a philosopher, would be a little disappointed . . .

possibly a little disdainful.

Compare, for instance, these everlasting fireworks with the damp squibs and dying bonfires of Guy Fawkes Day. That quaint and even queer national festival has been fading for some time out of English life. Still, it was a national festival, in the double sense that it represented some sort of public spirit pursued by some sort of popular impulse. People spent money on the display of fireworks; they did not get money by it. And the people who spent money were often those who had very little money to spend. It had something of the glorious and fanatical character of making the poor poorer. It did not, like the advertisements, have only the mean and materialistic character of making the rich richer. In short, it came from the people and it appealed to the nation. The historical and religious cause in which it originated is not mine; and I think it has perished partly through being tied to a historical theory for which there is no future. I think this is illustrated in the very fact that the ceremonial is merely negative and destructive. Negation and destruction are very noble things as far as they go, and when they go in the right direction; and the popular expression of them has always something hearty and human about it. I shall not therefore bring any fine or fastidious criticism, whether literary or musical, to bear upon the little boys who drag about a bolster and a paper mask, calling out

Guy Fawkes Guy
Hit him in the eye.

But I admit it is a disadvantage that they have not a saint or hero to crown in effigy as well as a traitor to burn in effigy. I admit that popular Protestantism has become too purely negative for people to wreathe in flowers the statue of Mr. Kensit or even of Dr. Clifford. I do not disguise my preference for popular Catholicism; which still has statues that can be wreathed in flowers. I wish our national feast of fireworks revolved round something positive and popular. I wish the beauty of a Catherine Wheel

were displayed to the glory of St. Catherine. I should not especially complain if Roman candles were really Roman candles.
But this negative character does not destroy the national character; which began at least in disinterested faith and has ended at
least in disinterested fun. There is nothing disinterested at all
about the new commercial fireworks. There is nothing so dignified as a dingy guy among the lights of Broadway. In that
thoroughfare, indeed, the very word guy has another and milder
significance. An American friend congratulated me on the impression I had produced on a lady interviewer, observing, "She says
you're a regular guy." This puzzled me a little at the time. "Her
description is no doubt correct," I said, "but I confess that it
would never have struck me as specially complimentary." But it
appears that it is one of the most graceful of compliments, in the
original American. A guy in America is a colourless term for a
human being. All men are guys, being endowed by their Creator
with certain . . . but I am misled by another association. And a
regular guy means, I presume, a reliable or respectable guy. The
point here, however, is that the guy in the grotesque English
sense does represent the dilapidated remnant of a real human
tradition of symbolising real historic ideals by the sacramental
mystery of fire. It is a great fall from the lowest of these lowly
bonfires to the highest of the modern sky-signs. The new illumination does not stand for any national ideal at all; and what is
yet more to the point, it does not come from any popular enthusiasm at all. That is where it differs from the narrowest national Protestantism of the English institution. Mobs have risen
in support of No Popery; no mobs are likely to rise in defence of
the New Puffery. Many a poor, crazy Orangeman has died saying, "To Hell with the Pope"; it is doubtful whether any man
will ever, with his last breath, frame the ecstatic words, "Try
Hugby's Chewing Gum." These modern and mercantile legends
are imposed upon us by a mercantile minority, and we are merely
passive to the suggestion. The hypnotist of high finance or big
business merely writes his commands in heaven with a finger of

fire. All men really are guys, in the sense of dummies. We are only the victims of his pyrotechnic violence; and it is he who hits us in the eye.

This is the real case against that modern society that is symbolised by such art and architecture. It is not that it is toppling, but that it is top-heavy. It is not that it is vulgar, but rather that it is not popular. In other words, the democratic ideal of countries like America, while it is still generally sincere and sometimes intense, is at issue with another tendency, an industrial progress which is of all things on earth the most undemocratic. America is not alone in possessing the industrialism, but she is alone in emphasising the ideal that strives with industrialism. Industrial capitalism and ideal democracy are everywhere in controversy; but perhaps only here are they in conflict. France has a democratic ideal; but France is not industrial. England and Germany are industrial; but England and Germany are not really democratic. Of course when I speak here of industrialism I speak of great industrial areas; there is, as will be noted later, another side to all these countries; there is in America itself not only a great deal of agricultural society, but a great deal of agricultural equality, just as there are still peasants in Germany and may some day again be peasants in England. But the point is that the ideal and its enemy the reality are here crushed very close to each other in the high, narrow city; and that the sky-scraper is truly named because its top, towering in such insolence, is scraping the stars off the American sky, the very heaven of the American spirit.

That seems to me the main outline of the whole problem. Earlier I have emphasised the fact that equality is still the ideal though no longer the reality of America. I should like to conclude by emphasising the fact that the reality of modern capitalism is menacing that ideal with terrors and even splendours that might well stagger the wavering and impressionable modern spirit. Upon the issue of that struggle depends the question of whether this new great civilisation continues to exist, and even whether any one cares if it exists or not. I have already used the parable of the American flag, and the stars that stand for a multitudinous equality; I might here take the opposite symbol of these artificial and terrestrial stars flaming on the forehead of the commercial city; and note the peril of the last illusion, which is that the artificial stars may seem to fill the heavens, and the real stars to have faded from sight. But I am content for the moment to reaffirm the merely imaginative pleasure of those dizzy turrets and dancing fires. If those nightmare buildings were really all built for nothing, how noble they would be! The fact that they were really built for something need not unduly depress us for a moment, or drag down our soaring fancies. There is something about these vertical lines that suggests a sort of rush upwards, as of great cataracts topsy-turvy. I have spoken of fireworks, but here I should rather speak of rockets. There is only something underneath the mind murmuring that nothing remains at last of a flaming rocket except a falling stick. I have spoken of Babylonian perspectives, and of words written with a fiery finger, like that huge unhuman finger that wrote on Belshazzar's wall. . . . But what did it write on Belshazzar's wall? . . . I am content once more to end on a note of doubt and a rather dark sympathy with those many-coloured solar systems turning so dizzily, far up in the divine vacuum of the night.

"From the earth we come and to the earth we return; when people get away from that they are lost."

IN THE AMERICAN COUNTRY

THE sharpest pleasure of a traveller is in finding the things which he did not expect, but which he might have expected to expect. I mean the things that are at once so strange and so obvious that they must have been noticed, yet somehow they have not been noted. Thus I had heard a thousand things about Jerusalem before I ever saw it; I had heard rhapsodies and disparagements of every description. Modern rationalistic critics, with characteristic consistency, had blamed it for its accumulated rubbish and its modern restoration, for its antiquated superstition and its up-to-date vulgarity. But somehow the one impression that had never pierced through their description was the simple and single impression of a city on a hill, with walls coming to the very edge of slopes that were almost as steep as walls; the turreted city which crowns a cone-shaped hill in so many mediaeval landscapes. One would suppose that this was at once the plainest and most picturesque of all the facts; yet somehow, in my reading, I had always lost it amid a mass of minor facts that were merely details. We know that a city that is set upon a hill cannot be hid; and yet it would seem that it is exactly the hill that is hid; though perhaps it is only hid from the wise and the understanding. I had a similar and simple impression when I discovered America. I cannot avoid the phrase; for it would really seem that each man discovers it for himself.

Thus I had heard a great deal, before I saw them, about the tall and dominant buildings of New York. I agree that they have an instant effect on the imagination; which I think is increased by the situation in which they stand, and out of which they arose. They are all the more impressive because the building, while it is vertically so vast, is horizontally almost narrow. New York is an island, and has all the intensive romance of an island. It is a thing of almost infinite height upon very finite foundations. It is almost like a lofty lighthouse upon a lonely rock. But this story of the sky-scrapers, which I had often heard, would by itself give a curiously false impression of the freshest and most curious characteristic of American architecture. Told only in terms of these great towers of stone and brick in the big industrial cities, the story would tend too much to an impression of something cold and colossal like the monuments of Asia. It would suggest a modern Babylon altogether too Babylonian. It would imply that a man of the new world was a sort of new Pharaoh, who built not so much a pyramid as a pagoda of pyramids. It would suggest houses built by mammoths out of mountains; the cities reared by elephants in their own elephantine school of architecture. And New York does recall the most famous of all sky-scrapers—the tower of Babel. She recalls it none the less because there is no doubt about the confusion of tongues. But in truth the very reverse is true of most of the buildings in America. I had no sooner passed out into the suburbs of New York on the way to Boston than I began to see something else quite contrary and far more curious. I saw forests upon forests of small houses stretching away to the horizon as literal forests do; villages and towns and cities. And they were, in another sense, literally like forests. They were all made of wood. It was almost as fantastic to an English eye as if they had been all made of cardboard. I had long outlived the silly old joke that referred to Americans as if they all lived in the backwoods. But, in a sense, if they do not live in the woods they are not yet out of the wood.

I do not say this in any sense as a censure. As it happens, I am particularly fond of wood. Of all the superstitions which our fathers took lightly enough to love, the most natural seems to me the notion it is lucky to touch wood. Some of them affect me the less as superstitions, because I feel them as symbols. If humanity had really thought Friday unlucky it would have talked about bad Friday instead of good Friday. And while I feel the thrill of thirteen at a table, I am not so sure that it is the most miserable of all human fates to fill the places of the Twelve Apostles. But the idea that there was something cleansing or wholesome about the touching of wood seems to me one of those ideas which are truly popular, because they are truly poetic. It is probable enough that the conception came originally from the healing of the wood of the Cross; but that only clinches the divine coincidence. It is like that other divine coincidence that the Victim was a carpenter, who might almost have made His own cross. Whether we take the mystical or the mythical explanation, there is obviously a very deep connection between the human working in wood and such plain and pathetic mysticism. It gives something like a touch of the holy childishness to the tale, as if that terrible engine could be a toy. In the same fashion a child fancies that mysterious and sinister horse, which was the downfall of Troy, as something plain and staring, and perhaps spotted, like his own rocking-horse in the nursery.

It might be said symbolically that Americans have a taste for rocking-horses, as they certainly have a taste for rocking-chairs. A flippant critic might suggest that they select rocking-chairs so that, even when they are sitting down, they need not be sitting still. Something of this restlessness in the race may really be involved in the matter; but I think the deeper significance of the rocking-chair may still be found in the deeper symbolism of the rocking-horse. I think there is behind all this fresh and facile use of wood a certain spirit that is childish in the good sense of the word; something that is innocent, and easily pleased. It is not altogether untrue, still less is it unamiable, to say that the landscape seems to be dotted with dolls' houses. It is the true tragedy of every fallen son of Adam that he has grown too big to live in a dolls' house. These things seem somehow to escape the irony of time by not even challenging it; they are too temporary even to be merely temporal. These people are not building tombs; they are not, as in the fine image of Mrs. Meynell's poem, merely building ruins. It is not easy to imagine the ruins of a dolls' house; and that is why a dolls' house is an everlasting habitation. How far it promises a political permanence is a matter for further discussion; I am only describing the mood of discovery, in which all these cottages built of lath, like the palaces of a pantomime, really seemed coloured like the clouds of morning, which are both fugitive and eternal.

There is also in all this an atmosphere that comes in another sense from the nursery. We hear much of Americans being educated on English literature; but I think few Americans realise how much English children have been educated on American literature. It is true, and it is inevitable, that they can only be educated on rather old-fashioned American literature. Mr. Bernard Shaw, in one of his plays, noted truly the limitations of the young American millionaire, and especially the staleness of his English culture; but there is necessarily another side to it. If the American talked more of Macaulay than of Nietzsche, we should probably talk more of Emerson than of Ezra Pound. Whether this staleness is necessarily a disadvantage is, of course, a different question. But, in any case, it is true that the old American books were often the books of our childhood, even in the literal sense of the books of our nursery. I know few men in England who have not left their boyhood to some extent lost and entangled in the forests of *Huckleberry Finn*. I know few women in England, from the most revolutionary Suffragette to the most carefully preserved Early Victorian, who will not confess to having passed a happy childhood with the *Little Women* of Miss Alcott. *Helen's Babies* was the first and by far the best book in the modern scriptures of baby-worship. And about all this old-fashioned American literature there was an undefinable savour that satisfied, and even pleased, our growing minds. Perhaps it was the smell of growing things; but I am far from certain that it was not simply the smell of wood. Now that all the memory comes back to me, it seems to come back heavy in a hundred forms with the fragrance and the touch of timber. There was the perpetual reference to the wood-pile, the perpetual background of the woods. There was something crude and clean about everything; something fresh and strange about those far-off houses, to which I could not then have put a name. Indeed, many things become clear in this wilderness of wood, which could only be expressed in symbol and even in fantasy. I will not go so far as to say that it shortened the transition from Log Cabin to White House; as if the White House were itself made of white wood (as Oliver Wendell Holmes said), "that cuts like cheese, but lasts like iron for things like these." But I will say that the experience illuminates some other lines by Holmes himself:—

> Little I ask, my wants are few,
> I only ask a hut of stone.

I should not have known, in England, that he was already asking for a good deal even in asking for that. In the presence of this wooden world the very combination of words seems almost a contradiction, like a hut of marble, or a hovel of gold.

It was therefore with an almost infantile pleasure that I looked at all this promising expansion of fresh-cut timber and thought of the housing shortage at home. I know not by what incongruous movement of the mind there swept across me, at the same moment, the thought of things ancestral and hoary with the light of ancient dawns. The last war brought back body-armour; the next war may bring back bows and arrows. And I suddenly had a memory of old wooden houses in London, and a model of Shakespeare's town.

It is possible indeed that such Elizabethan memories may receive a check or a chill when the traveller comes, as he sometimes does, to the outskirts of one of these strange hamlets of new frame-houses, and is confronted with a placard inscribed in enormous letters, "Watch Us Grow." He can always imagine that he sees the timbers swelling before his eyes like pumpkins in some super-tropical summer. But he may have formed the conviction that no such proclamation could be found outside Shakespeare's town. And indeed there is a serious criticism here, to any one who knows history; since the things that grow are not always the things that remain; and pumpkins of that ex-pansiveness have a tendency to burst. I was always told that Americans were harsh, hustling, rather rude and perhaps vulgar; but they were very practical and the future belonged to them. I confess I felt a fine shade of difference; I liked the Americans; I thought they were sympathetic, imaginative, and full of fine enthusiasm; the one thing I could not always feel clear about was their future. I believe they were happier in their frame-houses than most people in most houses; having democracy, good ed-ucation, and a hobby of work; the one doubt that did float across me was something like, "Will all this be here at all in two hun-dred years?" That was the first impression produced by the wooden houses that seemed like the waggons of gipsies; it is a serious impression, but there is an answer to it. It is an answer that opens on the traveller more and more as he goes westward, and finds the little towns dotted about the vast central prairies. And the answer is agriculture. Wooden houses may or may not last; but farms will last; and farming will always last.

The houses may look like gipsy caravans on a heath or com-mon; but they are not on a heath or common. They are on the most productive and prosperous land, perhaps, in the modern world. The houses might fall down like shanties, but the fields would remain; and whoever tills those fields will count for a great deal in the affairs of humanity. They are already counting for a great deal, and possibly for too much, in the affairs of America. The real criticism of the Middle West is concerned with two facts, neither of which has been yet adequately ap-preciated by the educated class in England. The first is that the turn of the world has come, and the turn of the agricultural countries with it. That is the meaning of the resurrection of Ireland; that is the meaning of the practical surrender of the Bolshevist Jews to the Russian peasants. The other is that in most places these peasant societies carry on what may be called the Catholic tradition. The Middle West is perhaps the one consid-erable place where they still carry on the Puritan tradition. But the Puritan tradition was originally a tradition of the town; and the second truth about the Middle West turns largely on its moral relation to the town. As I shall suggest presently, there is much in common between this agricultural society of America and the great agricultural societies of Europe. It tends, as the agricultural society nearly always does, to some decent degree of democracy. The agricultural society tends to the agrarian law. But in Puritan America there is an additional problem, which I can hardly explain without a periphrasis.

There was a time when the progress of the cities seemed to mock the decay of the country. It is more and more true, I think, to-day that it is rather the decay of the cities that seems to poison the progress and promise of the countryside. The cinema boasts of being a substitute for the tavern, but I think it a very bad substitute. I think so quite apart from the question about fermented liquor. Nobody enjoys cinemas more than I, but to enjoy them a man has only to look and not even to listen, and in a tavern he has to talk. Occasionally, I admit, he has to fight; but he need never move at the movies. Thus in the real village inn are the real village politics, while in the other are only the remote and unreal metropolitan politics. And those central city politics are not only cosmopolitan politics but corrupt politics. They corrupt everything that they reach, and this is the real point about many perplexing questions.

For instance, so far as I am concerned, it is the whole point about feminism and the factory. It is very largely the point about feminism and many other callings, apparently more cultured than the factory, such as the law court and the political platform. When I see women so wildly anxious to tie themselves to all this machinery of the modern city my first feeling is not indignation, but that dark and ominous sort of pity with which we should see a crowd rushing to embark in a leaking ship under a lowering storm. When I see wives and mothers going in for business government I not only regard it as a bad business but as a bankrupt business. It seems to me very much as if the peasant

women, just before the French revolution, had insisted on being
made duchesses or (as is quite as logical and likely) on being
made dukes.

It is as if those ragged women, instead of crying out for bread,
had cried out for powder and patches. By the time they were
wearing them they would be the only people wearing them. For
powder and patches soon went out of fashion, but bread does
not go out of fashion. In the same way, if women desert the
family for the factory, they may find they have only done it
for a deserted factory. It would have been very unwise of the
lower orders to claim all the privileges of the higher orders in
the last days of the French monarchy. It would have been very
laborious to learn the science of heraldry or the tables of precedence when all such things were at once most complicated and
most moribund. It would be tiresome to be taught all those tricks
just when the whole bag of tricks was coming to an end. A
French satirist might have written a fine apologue about Jacques
Bonhomme coming up to Paris in his wooden shoes and demanding to be made Gold Stick in Waiting in the name of Liberty,
Equality, and Fraternity; but I fear the stick in waiting would be
waiting still.

One of the first topics on which I heard a conversation turning
in America was that of a very interesting book called *Main
Street*, which involves many of these questions of the modern
industrial and eternal feminine. It is simply the story, or perhaps
rather the study than the story, of a young married woman in
one of the multitudinous little towns on the great central plains
of America; and of a sort of struggle her own more restless culture and the provincial prosperity of her neighbours. There are a
number of true and telling suggestions in the book, but the one
touch which I found tingling in the memory of many readers
was the last sentence, in which the master of the house, with
unshaken simplicity, merely asks for the whereabouts of some
domestic implement; I think it was a screw-driver. It seems to
me a harmless request, but from the way people talked about it

one might suppose he had asked for a screw-driver to screw down the wife in her coffin. And a great many advanced persons would tell us that the wooden house in which she lived really was like a wooden coffin. But this appears to me to be taking a somewhat funereal view of the life of humanity.

For, after all, on the face of it at any rate, this is merely the life of humanity, and even the life which all humanitarians have striven to give to humanity. Revolutionists have treated it not only as the normal but even as the ideal. Revolutionary wars have been waged to establish this; revolutionary heroes have fought, and revolutionary martyrs have died, only to build such a wooden house for such a worthy family. Men have taken the sword and perished by the sword in order that the poor gentleman might have liberty to look for his screw-driver. For there is here a fact about America that is almost entirely unknown in England. The English have not in the least realised the real strength of America. We in England hear a great deal, we hear far too much, about the economic energy of industrial America, about the money of Mr. Morgan, or the machinery of Mr. Edison. We never realise that while we in England suffer from the same sort of successes in capitalism and clockwork, we have not got what the Americans have got; something at least to balance it in the way of a free agriculture, a vast field of free farms dotted with small freeholders. For the reason I shall mention in a moment, they are not perhaps in the fullest and finest sense a peasantry. But they are in the practical and political sense a pure peasantry, in that their comparative equality is a true counterweight to the toppling injustice to the towns.

And, even in places like that described as Main Street, that comparative equality can immediately be felt. The men may be provincials, but they are certainly citizens; they consult on a common basis. And I repeat that in this, after all, they do achieve what many prophets and righteous men have died to achieve. This plain village, fairly prosperous, fairly equal, untaxed by tyrants and untroubled by wars, is after all the place which reformers have regarded as their aim; whenever reformers have used their wits sufficiently to have any aim. The march to Utopia, the march to the Earthly Paradise, the march to the New Jerusalem, has been very largely the march to Main Street. And the latest modern sensation is a book written to show how wretched it is to live there.

All this is true, and I think the lady might be more contented in her coffin, which is more comfortably furnished than most of the coffins where her fellow creatures live. Nevertheless, there is an answer to this, or at least a modification of it. There is a case for the lady and a case against the gentleman and the screwdriver. And when we have noted what it really is we have noted the real disadvantage in a situation like that of modern America, and especially the Middle West. And with that we come back to the truth with which I started this speculation; the truth that few have yet realised, but of which I, for one, am more and more convinced—that industrialism is spreading because it is decaying; that only the dust and ashes of its dissolution are choking up the growth of natural things everywhere and turning the green world grey.

In this relative agricultural equality the Americans of the Middle West are far in advance of the English of the twentieth century. It is not their fault if they are still some centuries behind the English of the twelfth century. But the defect by which they fall short of being a true peasantry is that they do not produce their own spiritual food, in the same sense as their own material food. They do not, like some peasantries, create other kinds of culture besides the kind called agriculture. Their culture comes from the great cities; and that is where all the evil comes from.

If a man had gone across England in the Middle Ages, or even across Europe in more recent times, he would have found a culture which showed its vitality by its variety. We know the adventures of the three brothers in the old fairy tales who passed across the endless plain from city to city, and found one kingdom ruled by a wizard and another wasted by a dragon, one people living in castles of crystal and another sitting by fountains of wine. These are but legendary enlargements of the real adventures of a traveller passing from one patch of peasantry to another and finding women wearing strange head-dresses and men singing new songs.

A traveller in America would be somewhat surprised if he found the people in the city of St. Louis all wearing crowns and crusading armour in honour of their patron saint. He might even feel some faint surprise if he found all the citizens of Philadelphia clad in a composite costume, combining that of a Quaker with that of a Red Indian, in honour of the noble treaty of William Penn. Yet these are the sort of local and traditional things that would really be found giving variety to the valleys of mediaeval Europe. I myself felt a perfectly genuine and generous exhilaration of freedom and fresh enterprise in new places like Oklahoma. But you would hardly find in Oklahoma what was found in Oberammergau. What goes to Oklahoma is not the peasant play, but the cinema. And the objection to the cinema is not so much that it goes to Oklahoma as that it does not come from Oklahoma. In other words, these people have on the economic side a much closer approach than we have to economic freedom. It is not for us, who have allowed our land to be stolen by squires and then vulgarized by sham squires, to sneer at such colonists as merely crude and prosaic. They at least have really kept something of the simplicity and, therefore, the dignity of democracy; and that democracy may yet save their country even from the calamities of wealth and science.

But, while these farmers do not need to become industrial in order to become industrious, they do tend to become industrial in so far as they become intellectual. Their culture, and to some great extent their creed, do come along the railroads from the great modern urban centres, and bring with them a blast of death and a reek of rotting things. It is that influence that alone prevents the Middle West from progressing towards the Middle Ages.

For, after all, linked up in a hundred legends of the Middle Ages, may be found a symbolic pattern of hammers and nails and saws; and there is no reason why they should not have also sanctified screw-drivers. There is no reason why the screw-driver that seemed such a trifle to the author should not have been borne in triumph down Main Street like a sword of state, in some pageant of the Guild of St. Joseph of the Carpenters or St. Dunstan of the Smiths. It was the Catholic poetry and piety that filled common life with something that is lacking in the worthy and virile democracy of the West. Nor are Americans of intelligence so ignorant of this as some may suppose. There is an admirable society called the Mediaevalists in Chicago, whose name and address will strike many as suggesting a certain struggle of the soul against the environment. With the national heartiness they blazon their note-paper with heraldry and the hues of Gothic windows; with the national high spirits they assume the fancy dress of friars; but any one who should essay to laugh at them instead of with them would find out his mistake. For many of them do really know a great deal about mediaevalism; much more than I do, or most other men brought up on an island that is crowded with its cathedrals. Something of the same spirit may be seen in the beautiful new plans and buildings of Yale, deliberately modelled not on classical harmony but on Gothic irregularity and surprise. The grace and energy of the mediaeval architecture resurrected by a man like Professor Cram of Boston has behind it not merely artistic but historical and ethical enthusiasm; an enthusiasm for the Catholic creed which made mediaeval civilisation. Even on the huge Puritan plains of Middle West the influence strays in the strangest fashion. And it is notable that among the pessimistic epitaphs of the Spoon River Anthology, in that churchyard compared with which most churchyards are cheery, among the suicides and secret drinkers and monomaniacs and hideous hypocrites of that happy village, almost the only record of respect and a recognition of wider hopes is dedicated to the Catholic priest.

But Main Street is Main Street in the main. Main Street is Modern Street in its multiplicity of mildly half-educated people; and all these historic things are a thousand miles from them. They have not heard the ancient noise either of arts or arms, the building of the cathedral or the marching of the crusade. But at least they have not deliberately slandered the crusade and defaced the cathedral. And if they have not produced the peasant arts, they can still produce the peasant crafts. They can sow and plough and reap and live by these everlasting things; nor shall the foundations of their state be moved. And the memory of those colossal fields, of those fruitful deserts, came back the more readily into my mind because I finished these reflections in the very heart of a modern industrial city, if it can be said to have a heart. It was in fact an English industrial city, but it struck me that it might very well be an American one. And it also struck me that we yield rather too easily to America the dusty palm of industrial enterprise, and feel far too little apprehension about greener and fresher vegetables. There is a story of an American who carefully studied all the sights of London or Rome or Paris, and came to the conclusion that "it had nothing on Minneapolis." It seems to me that Minneapolis has nothing on Manchester. There were the same grey vistas of shops full of rubber tyres and metallic appliances; a man felt that he might walk a day without seeing a blade of grass; the whole horizon was so infinite with efficiency. The factory chimneys might have been Pittsburgh; the sky-signs might have been New York. One looked up in a sort of despair at the sky, not for a sky-sign but in a sense for a sign, for some sentence of significance and judgment; by the instinct that makes any man in such a scene seek for the only thing that has not been made by men. But even that was illogical, for it was night, and I could only expect to see the stars, which might have reminded me of Old Glory; but that was not the sign that oppressed me. All the ground was a wilderness of stone and all the buildings a forest of brick; I was far in the interior of a labyrinth of lifeless things. Only, looking up, between two black chimneys and a telegraph pole, I saw vast and far and faint, as the first men saw it, the silver pattern of the Plough.

THE FUTURE OF DEMOCRACY

EVERYBODY who goes to America for a short time is expected to write a book; and nearly everybody does. A man who takes a holiday at Trouville or Dieppe is not confronted on his return with the question, "When is your book on France going to appear?" A man who betakes himself to Switzerland for the winter sports is not instantly pinned by the statement, "I suppose your History of the Helvetian Republic is coming out this spring?" Lecturing, at least my kind of lecturing, is not much more serious or meritorious than skiing or sea-bathing; and it happens to afford the holiday-maker far less opportunity of seeing the daily life of the people. Of all this I am only too well aware; and my only defence is that I am at least sincere in my enjoyment and appreciation of America, and equally sincere in my interest in its most serious problem, which I think a very serious problem indeed: the problem of democracy in the modern world. Democracy may be a very obvious and facile affair for plutocrats and politicians who only have to use it as a rhetorical term. But democracy is a very serious problem for democrats. I certainly do not apologise for the word democracy; but I do apologise for the word future. I am no Futurist; and any conjectures I make must be taken with a grain of salt which is indeed the salt of the earth, the descent and moderate humility which comes from a belief in free will. That faith is in itself a divine doubt. I do not believe in any of the scientific predictions about mankind; I notice that they always fail to predict any of the purely human developments of men; I also notice that even their successes prove the same truth as their failures; for their successful predictions are not about men but about machines. But there are two things which a man may reasonably do, in stating the probabilities of a problem, which do not involve any claim to be a prophet. The first is to tell the truth, and especially the neglected truth, about the tendencies that have already accumulated in human history; any miscalculation about which must at least mislead us in any case. We cannot be certain of being right about the future; but we can be almost certain of being wrong about the future, if we are wrong about the past. The other thing that he can do is to note what ideas necessarily go together by their own nature; what ideas will triumph together or fall together. Hence it follows that this chapter must consist of two things. The first is a summary of what has really happened to the idea of democracy in recent times; the second a suggestion of the fundamental doctrine which is necessary for its triumph at any time.

The last hundred years have seen a general decline in the democratic idea. If there be anybody left to whom this historical truth appears a paradox, it is only because during that period nobody has been taught history, least of all the history of ideas. If a sort of intellectual inquisition had been established, for the definition and differentiation of heresies, it would have been found that the original republican orthodoxy had suffered more and more from secessions, schisms and backslidings. The highest point of democratic idealism and conviction was towards the end of the eighteenth century, when the American Republic was "dedicated to the proposition that all men are equal." It was then that the largest number of men had the most serious sort of conviction that the political problem could be solved by the vote of peoples instead of the arbitrary power of princes and privileged orders. These men encountered various difficulties and made various compromises in relation to the practical politics of their time; in England they preserved aristocracy; in America they preserved slavery. But though they had more difficulties, they had less doubt. Since their time democracy has been steadily disintegrated by doubts; and these political doubts have been contemporary with and often identical with religious doubts. This fact could be followed over almost the whole field of the modern world; in this place it will be more appropriate to take the great American example of slavery. I have found traces in all sorts of intelligent quarters of an extraordinary idea that all the Fathers of the Republic owned black men like beasts of burden because they knew no better, until the light of liberty was revealed to them by John Brown and Mrs. Beecher Stowe. One of the best weekly papers in England said recently that even those who drew up the Declaration of Independence did not include negroes in its generalisation about humanity. This is quite consistent with the current convention, in which we were all brought up; the theory that the heart of humanity broadens in ever larger circles of brotherhood, till we pass from embracing a black man to adoring a black beetle. Unfortunately it is quite inconsistent with the facts of American history. The facts show that, in this problem of the Old South, the eighteenth century was *more* liberal than the nineteenth century. There was *more* sympathy for the negro in the school of Jefferson than in the school of Jefferson Davis. Jefferson, in the dark estate of his simple Deism, said the sight of slavery in his country made him tremble, remembering that God is just. His fellow Southerners, after a century of the world's advance, said that slavery in itself was good, when they did not go farther and say that negroes in themselves were bad. And they were supported in this by the great and growing modern suspicion that nature is unjust. Difficulties seemed inevitably to delay justice, to the mind of Jefferson; but so they did to the mind of Lincoln. But that the slave was human and the servitude inhuman—that was, if anything, clearer to Jefferson than to Lincoln. The fact is that the utter separation and subordination of the black like a beast was a *progress;* it was a growth of nineteenth-century enlightenment and experiment; a triumph of science over superstition. It was "the way the world was going," as Matthew Arnold reverentially remarked in some connection; perhaps as part of a definition of God. Anyhow, it was not Jefferson's definition of God. He fancied, in his far-off patriarchal way, a Father who had made all men brothers; and brutally unbrotherly as was the practice, such democratical Deists never dreamed of denying the theory. It was not until the scientific sophistries began that brotherhood was really disputed. Gobineau, who began most of the modern talk about the superiority and inferiority of racial stocks, was seized upon eagerly by the less generous of the slave-owners and trumpeted as a new truth of science and a new defence of slavery. It was not really until the dawn of Darwinism, when all our social relations began to smell of the monkey-house, that men thought of the barbarian as only a first and the baboon as a second cousin. The full servile philosophy has been a modern and even a recent thing; made in an age whose inevitable deity was the Missing Link. The Missing Link was a true metaphor in more ways than one; and most of all in its suggestion of a chain.

By a symbolic coincidence, indeed, slavery grew more brazen and brutal under the encouragement of more than one movement of the progressive sort. Its youth was renewed for it by the industrial prosperity of Lancashire; and under that influence it became a commercial and competitive instead of a patriarchal and customary thing. We may say with no exaggerative irony that the unconscious patrons of slavery were Huxley and Cobden. The machines of Manchester were manufacturing a great many more things than the manufacturers knew or wanted to know; but they were certainly manufacturing the fetters of the slave, doubtless out of the best quality of steel and iron. But this is a minor illustration of the modern tendency, as compared with the main stream of scepticism which was destroying democracy. Evolution became more and more a vision of the break-up of our brotherhood, till by the end of the nineteenth century the genius of its greatest scientific romancer saw it end in the anthropophagous antics of the Time Machine. So far from evolution lifting us above the idea of enslaving men, it was providing us at least with a logical and potential argument for eating them. In the case of the American negroes, it may be remarked, it does at any rate permit the preliminary course of roasting them. All this materialistic hardening, which replaced the remorse of Jefferson, was part of the growing evolutionary suspicion that savages were not a part of the human race, or rather that there was really no such thing

as the human race. The South had begun by agreeing reluctantly
to the enslavement of men. The South ended by agreeing equally
reluctantly to the emancipation of monkeys.

That is what had happened to the democratic ideal in a hundred
years. Anybody can test it by comparing the final phase, I will
not say with the ideal of Jefferson, but with the ideal of Johnson.
There was far more horror of slavery in an eighteenth-century
Tory like Dr. Johnson than in a nineteenth-century democrat like
Stephen Douglas. Stephen Douglas may be mentioned because he
is a very representative type of the age of evolution and expansion; a man thinking in continents, like Cecil Rhodes, human and
hopeful in a truly American fashion, and as a consequence cold
and careless rather than hostile in the matter of the old mystical
doctrines of equality. He "did not care whether slavery was voted
up or voted down." His great opponent Lincoln did indeed care
very much. But it was an intense individual conviction with Lincoln exactly as it was with Johnson. I doubt if the spirit of the
age was not much more behind Douglas and his westward expansion of the white race. I am sure that more and more men were
coming to be in the particular mental condition of Douglas; men
in whom the old moral and mystical ideals had been undermined
by doubt, but only with a negative effect of indifference. Their
positive convictions were all concerned with what some called
progress and some imperialism. It is true that there was a sincere
sectional enthusiasm against slavery in the North; and that the
slaves were actually emancipated in the nineteenth century. But
I doubt whether the Abolitionists would ever have secured Abolition. Abolition was a by-product of the Civil War; which was
fought for quite other reasons. Anyhow, if slavery had somehow
survived to the age of Rhodes and Roosevelt and evolutionary
imperialism, I doubt if the slaves would ever have been emancipated at all. Certainly if it had survived till the modern movement for the Servile State, they would never have been emancipated at all. Why should the world take the chains off the black
man when it was just putting them on the white? And in so far

as we owe the change to Lincoln, we owe it to Jefferson. Exactly what gives its real dignity to the figure of Lincoln is that he stands invoking a primitive first principle of the age of innocence, and holding up the tables of an ancient law, *against* the trend of the nineteenth century; repeating, "We hold these truths to be self-evident; that all men were created equal, being endowed by their Creator, etc.," to a generation that was more and more disposed to say something like this: "We hold these truths to be probable enough for pragmatists; that all things looking like men were evolved somehow, being endowed by heredity and environment with no equal rights, but very unequal wrongs," and so on. I do not believe that creed, left to itself, would ever have founded a state; and I am pretty certain that, left to itself, it would never have overthrown a slave state. What it did do, as I have said, was to produce some very wonderful literary and artistic flights of sceptical imagination. The world did have new visions, if they were visions of monsters in the moon and Martians striding about like spiders as tall as the sky, and the workmen and capitalists becoming two separate species, so that one could devour the other as gaily and greedily as a cat devours a bird. No one has done justice to the meaning of Mr. Wells and his original departure in fantastic fiction; to these nightmares that were the last apocalypse of the nineteenth century. They meant that the bottom had fallen out of the mind at last, that the bridge of brotherhood had broken down in the modern brain, letting up from the chasms this infernal light like a dawn. All had grown dizzy with degree and relativity; so that there would not be so very much difference between eating dog and eating darkie, or between eating darkie and eating dago. There were different sorts of apes; but there was no doubt that we were the superior sort.

Against all this irresistible force stood one immovable post. Against all this dance of doubt and degree stood something that can best be symbolised by a simple example. An ape cannot be a priest, but a negro can be a priest. The dogmatic type of Chris-

tianity, especially the Catholic type of Christianity, had riveted
itself irrevocably to the manhood of all men. Where its faith
was fixed by creeds and councils it could not save itself even
by surrender. It could not gradually dilute democracy, as could
a merely sceptical or secular democrat. There stood, in fact or
in possibility, the solid and smiling figure of a black bishop. And
he was either a man claiming the most towering spiritual privileges of a man, or he was the mere buffoonery and blasphemy of
a monkey in a mitre. That is the point about Christian and Catholic democracy; it is not that it is necessarily at any moment more
democratic, it is that its indestructible minimum of democracy
really is indestructible. And by the nature of things that mystical
democracy was destined to survive, when every other sort of
democracy was free to destroy itself. And whenever democracy
destroying itself is suddenly moved to save itself, it always grasps
at a rag or tag of that old tradition that alone is sure of itself.
Hundreds have heard the story about the mediaeval demagogue
who went about repeating the rhyme

> When Adam delved and Eve span,
> Who was then the gentleman?

Many have doubtless offered the obvious answer to the question, "The Serpent." But few seem to have noticed what would
be the more modern answer to the question, if that innocent
agitator went about propounding it. "Adam never delved and
Eve never span, for the simple reason that they never existed.
They are fragments of a Chaldeo-Babylonian mythos, and Adam
is only a slight variation of Tag-Tug, pronounced Uttu. For the
real beginning of humanity we refer you to Darwin's *Origin of
Species*." And then the modern man would go on to justify plutocracy to the mediaeval man by talking about the Struggle for
Life and the Survival of the Fittest; and how the strongest man
seized authority by means of anarchy, and proved himself a gentleman by behaving like a cad. Now I do not base my beliefs on
the theology of John Ball, or on the literal and materialistic read-

ing of the text of Genesis; though I think the story of Adam and Eve infinitely less absurd and unlikely than that of the prehistoric "strongest man" who could fight a hundred men. But I do note the fact that the idealism of the leveller could be put in the form of an appeal to Scripture, and could not be put in the form of an appeal to Science. And I do note also that democrats were still driven to make the same appeal even in the very century of Science. Tennyson was, if ever there was one, an evolutionist in his vision and an aristocrat in his sympathies. He was always boasting that John Bull was evolutionary and not revolutionary, even as these Frenchmen. He did not pretend to have any creed beyond faintly trusting the larger hope. But when human dignity is really in danger, John Bull has to use the same old argument as John Ball. He tells Lady Clara Vere de Vere that "the gardener Adam and his wife smile at the claim of long descent"; their own descent being by no means long. Lady Clara might surely have scored off him pretty smartly by quoting from "Maud" and "In Memoriam" about evolution and the eft that was lord of valley and hill. But Tennyson has evidently forgotten all about Darwin and the long descent of man. If this was true of an evolutionist like Tennyson, it was naturally ten times truer of a revolutionist like Jefferson. The Declaration of Independence dogmatically bases all rights on the fact that God created all men equal; and it is right; for if they were not created equal, they were certainly evolved unequal.

There is no basis for democracy except in a dogma about the divine origin of man. That is a perfectly simple fact which the modern world will find out more and more to be a fact. Every other basis is a sort of sentimental confusion, full of merely verbal echoes of the older creeds. Those verbal associations are always vain for the vital purpose of constraining the tyrant. An idealist may say to a capitalist, "Don't you sometimes feel in the rich twilight, when the lights twinkle from the distant hamlet in the hills, that all humanity is a holy family?" But it is equally possible for the capitalist to reply with brevity and decision,

"No, I don't," and there is no more disputing about it further than about the beauty of a fading cloud. And the modern world of moods is a world of clouds, even if some of them are thunderclouds.

For I have only taken here, as a convenient working model, the case of negro slavery; because it was long peculiar to America and is popularly associated with it. It is more and more obvious that the line is no longer running between black and white but between rich and poor. It is argued even by industrialists that industrialism has produced a class submerged below the status of emancipated mankind. They imply that the Missing Link is no longer missing, even from England or the Northern States, and that the factories have manufactured their own monkeys. Scientific hypotheses about the feeble-minded and the criminal type will supply the masters of the modern world with more and more excuses for denying the dogma of equality in the case of white labour as well as black. And any man who knows the world knows perfectly well that to tell the millionaires, or their servants, that they are disappointing the sentiments of Thomas Jefferson, or disregarding a creed composed in the eighteenth century, will be about as effective as telling them that they are not observing the creed of St. Athanasius or keeping the rule of St. Benedict.

The world cannot keep its own ideals. The secular order cannot make secure any one of his own noble and natural conceptions of secular perfection. That will be found, as time goes on, the ultimate argument for a Church independent of the world and the secular order. What has become of all those ideal figures from the Wise Man of the Stoics to the democratic Deist of the eighteenth century? What has become of all that purely human hierarchy or chivalry, with its punctilious pattern of the good knight, its ardent ambition in the young squire? The very name of knight has come to represent the petty triumph of a profiteer, and the very word squire the petty tyranny of a landlord. What has become of all that golden liberality of the Humanists, who

found on the high tablelands of the culture of Hellas the very
balance of repose in beauty that is most lacking in the modern
world? The very Greek language that they loved has become a
mere label for snuffy and snobbish dons, and a mere cock-shy
for cheap and half-educated utilitarians, who make it a symbol
of superstition and reaction. We have lived to see a time when
the heroic legend of the Republic and the Citizen, which seemed
to Jefferson the eternal youth of the world, has begun to grow
old in its turn. We cannot recover the earthly estate of knight-
hood, to which all the colours and complications of heraldry
seemed as fresh and natural as flowers. We cannot re-enact the
intellectual experiences of the Humanists, for whom the Greek
grammar was like the song of a bird in spring. The more the
matter is considered the clearer it will seem that these old experiences are now only alive, where they have found a lodgment in
the Catholic tradition of Christendom, and made themselves
friends for ever. St. Francis is the only surviving troubadour.
St. Thomas More is the only surviving Humanist. St. Louis is the
only surviving knight.

It would be the worse sort of insincerity, therefore, to conclude even so hazy an outline of so great and majestic a matter
as the American democratic experiment, without testifying my
belief that to this also the same ultimate test will come. So far as
that democracy becomes or remains Catholic and Christian, that
democracy will remain democratic. In so far it does not, it will
become wildly and wickedly undemocratic. Its rich will riot
with a brutal indifference far beyond the feeble feudalism which
retains some shadow of responsibility or at least of patronage. Its
wage-slaves will either sink into heathen slavery, or seek relief
in theories that are destructive not merely in method but in
aim; since they are but the negations of the human appetites of
property and personality. Eighteenth-century ideals, formulated
in eighteenth-century language, have no longer in themselves the
power to hold all those pagan passions back. Even those documents depended upon Deism; their real strength will survive in

men who are still Deists. And the men who are still Deists are more than Deists. Men will more and more realise that there is no meaning in democracy if there is no meaning in anything; and that there is no meaning in anything if the universe has not a centre of significance and an authority that is the author of our rights. There is truth in every ancient fable, and there is here even something of it in the fancy that finds the symbol of the Republic in the bird that bore the bolts of Jove. Owls and bats may wander where they will in darkness, and for them as for the sceptics the universe may have no centre; kites and vultures may linger as they like over carrion, and for them as for the plutocrats existence may have no origin and no end; but it was far back in the land of legends, where instincts find their true images, that the cry went forth that freedom is an eagle, whose glory is gazing at the sun.

Father Brown Stories

"I try to get inside the murderer. . . .
Indeed it's much more than that, don't
you see? I *am* inside a man. I am always
inside a man, moving his arms and legs;
but I wait till I know I am inside a murderer, thinking his thoughts, wrestling
with his passions; till I have bent myself
into the posture of his hunched and
peering hatred; till I see the world with
his bloodshot and squinting eyes, looking
between the blinkers of his half-witted
concentration; looking up the short and
sharp perspective of a straight road to a
pool of blood. Till I am really a murderer. And when I am quite sure that I
feel exactly like the murderer myself, of
course I know who he is."

THE MAN WHO WAS CHESTERTON

His order was evidently a usual one. "I want, please," he said
with precision, "one halfpenny bun and a small cup of black

THE INVISIBLE MAN

In the cool blue twilight of two steep streets in Camden Town,
the shop at the corner, a confectioner's, glowed like the butt of
a cigar. One should rather say, perhaps, like the butt of a firework, for the light was of many colours and some complexity,
broken up by many mirrors and dancing on many gilt and gaily
coloured cakes and sweetmeats. Against this one fiery glass were
glued the noses of many gutter-snipes, for the chocolates were
all wrapped in those red and gold and green metallic colours
which are almost better than chocolate itself; and the huge white
wedding-cake in the window was somehow at once remote and
satisfying, just as if the whole North Pole were good to eat.
Such rainbow provocations could naturally collect the youth
of the neighbourhood up to the ages of ten or twelve. But this
corner was also attractive to youth at a later stage; and a young
man, not less than twenty-four, was staring into the same shop
window. To him, also, the shop was of fiery charm, but this
attraction was not wholly to be explained by chocolates; which,
however, he was far from despising.

He was a tall, burly, red-haired young man, with a resolute
face but a listless manner. He carried under his arm a flat, grey
portfolio of black-and-white sketches, which he had sold with
more or less success to publishers ever since his uncle (who was
an admiral) had disinherited him for Socialism, because of a
lecture which he had delivered against that economic theory. His
name was John Turnbull Angus.

Entering at last, he walked through the confectioner's shop
to the back room, which was a sort of pastry-cook restaurant,
merely raising his hat to the young lady who was serving there.
She was a dark, elegant, alert girl in black, with a high colour
and very quick, dark eyes; and after the ordinary interval she
followed him into the inner room to take his order.

His order was evidently a usual one. "I want, please," he said with precision, "one halfpenny bun and a small cup of black coffee." An instant before the girl could turn away he added, "Also, I want you to marry me."

The young lady of the shop stiffened suddenly and said, "Those are jokes I don't allow."

The red-haired young man lifted grey eyes of an unexpected gravity.

"Really and truly," he said, "it's as serious—as serious as the halfpenny bun. It is expensive, like the bun; one pays for it. It is indigestible, like the bun. It hurts."

The dark young lady had never taken her dark eyes off him, but seemed to be studying him with almost tragic exactitude. At the end of her scrutiny she had something like the shadow of a smile, and she sat down in a chair.

"Don't you think," observed Angus, absently, "that it's rather cruel to eat these halfpenny buns? They might grow up into penny buns. I shall give up these brutal sports when we are married."

The dark young lady rose from her chair and walked to the window, evidently in a state of strong but not unsympathetic cogitation. When at last she swung round again with an air of resolution she was bewildered to observe that the young man was carefully laying out on the table various objects from the shop-window. They included a pyramid of highly coloured sweets, several plates of sandwiches, and the two decanters containing that mysterious port and sherry which are peculiar to pastry-cooks. In the middle of this neat arrangement he had carefully let down the enormous load of white sugared cake which had been the huge ornament of the window.

"What on earth are you doing?" she asked.

"Duty, my dear Laura," he began.

"Oh, for the Lord's sake, stop a minute," she cried, "and don't talk to me in that way. I mean, what is all that?"

"A ceremonial meal, Miss Hope."

"And what is *that?*" she asked impatiently, pointing to the mountain of sugar.

"The wedding-cake, Mrs. Angus," he said.

The girl marched to that article, removed it with some clatter, and put it back in the shop window; she then returned, and, putting her elegant elbows on the table, regarded the young man not unfavourably but with considerable exasperation.

"You don't give me any time to think," she said.

"I'm not such a fool," he answered; "that's my Christian humility."

She was still looking at him; but she had grown considerably graver behind the smile.

"Mr. Angus," she said steadily, "before there is a minute more of this nonsense I must tell you something about myself as shortly as I can."

"Delighted," replied Angus gravely. "You might tell me something about myself, too, while you are about it."

"Oh, do hold your tongue and listen," she said. "It's nothing that I'm ashamed of, and it isn't even anything that I'm specially sorry about. But what would you say if there were something that is no business of mine and yet is my nightmare?"

"In that case," said the man seriously, "I should suggest that you bring back the cake."

"Well, you must listen to the story first," said Laura, persistently. "To begin with, I must tell you that my father owned the inn called the 'Red Fish' at Ludbury, and I used to serve people in the bar."

"I have often wondered," he said, "why there was a kind of a Christian air about this one confectioner's shop."

"Ludbury is a sleepy, grassy little hole in the Eastern Counties, and the only kind of people who ever came to the 'Red Fish' were occasional commercial travellers, and for the rest, the most awful people you can see, only you've never seen them. I mean little, loungy men, who had just enough to live on and had nothing to do but lean about in bar-rooms and bet on horses, in bad clothes that were just too good for them. Even these wretched young rotters were not very common at our house; but there were two of them that were a lot too common—common in every sort of way. They both lived on money of their own, and were wearisomely idle and over-dressed. But yet I was a bit sorry for them, because I half believed they slunk into our little empty bar because each of them had a slight deformity; the sort of thing that some yokels laugh at. It wasn't exactly a deformity either; it was more an oddity. One of them was a surprisingly small man, something like a dwarf, or at least like a jockey. He was not at all jockeyish to look at, though; he had a round black head and a well-trimmed black beard, bright eyes like a bird's; he jingled money in his pockets; he jangled a great gold watch chain; and he never turned up except dressed just too much like a gentleman to be one. He was no fool though, though a futile idler; he was curiously clever at all kinds of things that couldn't be the slightest use; a sort of impromptu conjuring; making fifteen matches set fire to each other like a regular firework; or cutting a banana or some such thing into a dancing doll. His name was Isidore Smythe; and I can see him still, with his little dark face, just coming up to the counter, making a jumping kangaroo out of five cigars.

"The other fellow was more silent and more ordinary; but somehow he alarmed me much more than poor little Smythe. He was very tall and slight, and light-haired; his nose had a high bridge, and he might almost have been handsome in a spectral sort of way; but he had one of the most appalling squints I have ever seen or heard of. When he looked straight at you, you didn't know where you were yourself, let alone what he was looking at. I fancy this sort of disfigurement embittered the poor chap a little; for while Smythe was ready to show off his monkey tricks anywhere, James Welkin (that was the squinting man's name) never did anything except soak in our bar parlour, and go for great walks by himself in the flat, grey country all round. All the same, I think Smythe, too, was a little sensitive about being so small, though he carried it off more smartly. And so it was that I was really puzzled, as well as startled, and very sorry, when they both offered to marry me in the same week.

"Well, I did what I've since thought was perhaps a silly thing. But, after all, these freaks were my friends in a way; and I had a horror of their thinking I refused them for the real reason, which was that they were so impossibly ugly. So I made up some gas of another sort, about never meaning to marry anyone who hadn't carved his way in the world. I said it was a point of principle with me not to live on money that was just inherited like theirs. Two days after I had talked in this well-meaning sort of way, the whole trouble began. The first thing I heard was that both of them had gone off to seek their fortunes, as if they were in some silly fairy tale.

"Well, I've never seen either of them from that day to this. But I've had two letters from the little man called Smythe, and really they were rather exciting."

"Ever heard of the other man?" asked Angus.

"No, he never wrote," said the girl, after an instant's hesitation. "Smythe's first letter was simply to say that he had started out walking with Welkin to London; but Welkin was such a good walker that the little man dropped out of it, and took a rest by the roadside. He happened to be picked up by some travelling show, and, partly because he was nearly a dwarf, and partly because he was really a clever little wretch, he got on quite well in the show business, and was soon sent up to the Aquarium, to do some tricks that I forget. That was his first letter. His second was much more of a startler, and I only got it last week."

The man called Angus emptied his coffee-cup and regarded her with mild and patient eyes. Her own mouth took a slight twist of laughter as she resumed, "I suppose you've seen on the hoardings all about this 'Smythe's Silent Service'? Or you must be the only person that hasn't. Oh, I don't know much about it, it's some clockwork invention for doing all the housework by machinery. You know the sort of thing: 'Press a button—A Butler who Never Drinks.' 'Turn a Handle—Ten Housemaids who Never Flirt.' You must have seen the advertisements. Well, whatever these machines are, they are making pots of money; and they are making it for that little imp whom I knew down in Ludbury. I can't help feeling pleased the poor little chap has fallen on his feet; but the plain fact is, I'm in terror of his turning up any minute and telling me he's carved his way in the world—as he certainly has."

"And the other man?" repeated Angus with a sort of obstinate quietude.

Laura Hope got to her feet suddenly. "My friend," she said, "I think you are a witch. Yes, you are quite right. I have not seen a line of the other man's writing; and I have no more notion than the dead of what or where he is. But it is of him that I am frightened. It is he who is all about my path. It is he who has half driven me mad. Indeed, I think he has driven me mad; for I have felt him where he could not have been, and I have heard his voice when he could not have spoken."

"Well, my dear," said the young man, cheerfully, "if he were Satan himself, he is done for now you have told somebody. One goes mad all alone, old girl. But when was it you fancied you felt and heard our squinting friend?"

"I heard James Welkin laugh as plainly as I hear you speak," said the girl, steadily. "There was nobody there, for I stood just outside the shop at the corner, and could see down both streets at once. I had forgotten how he laughed, though his laugh was as odd as his squint. I had not thought of him for nearly a year. But it's a solemn truth that a few seconds later the first letter came from his rival."

"Did you ever make the spectre speak or squeak, or anything?" asked Angus, with some interest.

Laura suddenly shuddered, and then said, with an unshaken voice, "Yes. Just when I had finished reading the second letter from Isidore Smythe announcing his success, just then, I heard Welkin say, 'He shan't have you, though.' It was quite plain, as if he were in the room. It is awful; I think I must be mad."

"If you really were mad," said the young man, "you would think you must be sane. But certainly there seems to me to be something a little rum about this unseen gentleman. Two heads are better than one—I spare you allusions to any other organs— and really, if you would allow me, as a sturdy, practical man, to bring back the wedding-cake out of the window—"

Even as he spoke, there was a sort of steely shriek in the street outside, and a small motor, driven at devilish speed, shot up to the door of the shop and stuck there. In the same flash of time a small man in a shiny top hat stood stamping in the outer room.

Angus, who had hitherto maintained hilarious ease from motives of mental hygiene, revealed the strain of his soul by striding abruptly out of the inner room and confronting the new-comer. A glance at him was quite sufficient to confirm the savage guesswork of a man in love. This very dapper but dwarfish figure, with the spike of black beard carried insolently forward, the clever unrestful eyes, the neat but very nervous fingers, could be none other than the man just described to him: Isidore Smythe, who made dolls out of banana skins and match-boxes; Isidore Smythe, who made millions out of undrinking butlers and unflirting housemaids of metal. For a moment the two men, instinctively understanding each other's air of possession, looked at each other with that curious cold generosity which is the soul of rivalry.

Mr. Smythe, however, made no allusion to the ultimate ground of their antagonism, but said simply and explosively, "Has Miss Hope seen that thing on the window?"

"On the window?" repeated the staring Angus.

"There's no time to explain other things," said the small millionaire shortly. "There's some tomfoolery going on here that has to be investigated."

He pointed his polished walking-stick at the window, recently depleted by the bridal preparations of Mr. Angus; and that gentleman was astonished to see along the front of the glass a long strip of paper pasted, which had certainly not been on the window when he had looked through it some time before. Following the energetic Smythe outside into the street, he found that some yard and a half of stamp paper had been carefully gummed along the glass outside, and on this was written in straggly characters, "If you marry Smythe, he will die."

"Laura," said Angus, putting his big red head into the shop, "you're not mad."

"It's the writing of that fellow Welkin," said Smythe gruffly. "I haven't seen him for years, but he's always bothering me. Five times in the last fortnight he's had threatening letters left at my flat, and I can't even find out who leaves them, let alone if it is Welkin himself. The porter of the flats swears that no suspicious characters have been seen, and here he has pasted up a sort of dado on a public shop window, while the people in the shop—"

"Quite so," said Angus modestly, "while the people in the shop were having tea. Well, sir, I can assure you I appreciate your common sense in dealing so directly with the matter. We can talk about other things afterwards. The fellow cannot be very far off yet, for I swear there was no paper there when I went last to the window, ten or fifteen minutes ago. On the other hand, he's too far off to be chased, as we don't even know the direction. If you'll take my advice, Mr. Smythe, you'll put this at once in the hands of some energetic inquiry man, private rather than public. I know an extremely clever fellow, who has set up in business five minutes from here in your car. His name's Flambeau, and though his youth was a bit stormy, he's a strictly honest man now, and his brains are worth money. He lives in Lucknow Mansions, Hampstead."

"That is odd," said the little man, arching his black eyebrows. "I live, myself, in Himylaya Mansions, round the corner. Perhaps you might care to come with me; I can go to my rooms and sort out these queer Welkin documents, while you run round and get your friend the detective."

"You are very good," said Angus politely. "Well, the sooner we act the better."

Both men, with a queer kind of impromptu fairness, took the same sort of formal farewell of the lady, and both jumped into the brisk little car. As Smythe took the handles and they turned the great corner of the street, Angus was amused to see a gigantesque poster of "Smythe's Silent Service," with a picture of a huge headless iron doll, carrying a saucepan with the legend, "A Cook Who Is Never Cross."

"I use them in my own flat," said the little black-bearded man, laughing, "partly for advertisements, and partly for real convenience. Honestly, and all above board, those big clockwork dolls of mine do bring you coals or claret or a time-table quicker than any live servants I've ever known, if you know which knob to press. But I'll never deny, between ourselves, that such servants have their disadvantages, too."

"Indeed?" said Angus; "is there something they can't do?"

"Yes," replied Smythe coolly; "they can't tell me who left those threatening letters at my flat."

The man's motor was small and swift like himself; in fact, like his domestic service, it was of his own invention. If he was an advertising quack, he was one who believed in his own wares. The sense of something tiny and flying was accentuated as they swept up long white curves of road in the dead but open daylight of evening. Soon the white curves came sharper and dizzier; they were upon ascending spirals, as they say in the modern religions. For, indeed, they were cresting a corner of London which is almost as precipitous as Edinburgh, if not quite so picturesque. Terrace rose above terrace, and the special tower of flats they sought, rose above them all to almost Egyptian height, gilt by the level sunset. The change, as they turned the corner and entered the crescent known as Himylaya Mansions, was as abrupt as the opening of a window; for they found that pile of flats sitting above London as above a green sea of slate. Opposite to the mansions, on the other side of the gravel crescent, was a bushy enclosure more like a steep hedge or dyke than a garden, and some way below that ran a strip of artificial water, a sort of canal, like the moat of that embowered fortress. As the car swept round the crescent it passed, at one corner, the stray stall of a man selling chestnuts; and right away at the other end of the curve, Angus could see a dim blue policeman walking slowly. These were the only human shapes in that high suburban solitude; but he had an irrational sense that they expressed the speechless poetry of London. He felt as if they were figures in a story.

The little car shot up to the right house like a bullet, and shot out its owner like a bomb shell. He was immediately inquiring of a tall commissionaire in shining braid, and a short porter in shirt sleeves, whether anybody or anything had been seeking his apartments. He was assured that nobody and nothing had passed these officials since his last inquiries; whereupon he and the slightly bewildered Angus were shot up in the lift like a rocket, till they reached the top floor.

"Just come in for a minute," said the breathless Smythe. "I want to show you those Welkin letters. Then you might run round the corner and fetch your friend." He pressed a button concealed in the wall, and the door opened of itself.

It opened on a long, commodious ante-room, of which the only arresting features, ordinarily speaking, were the rows of tall half-human mechanical figures that stood up on both sides like tailors' dummies. Like tailors' dummies they were headless; and like tailors' dummies they had a handsome unnecessary humpiness in the shoulders, and a pigeon-breasted protuberance of chest; but barring this, they were not much more like a human figure than any automatic machine at a station that is about the human height. They had two great hooks like arms, for carrying trays; and they were painted pea-green, or vermilion, or black for convenience or distinction; in every other way they were only automatic machines and nobody would have looked twice at them. On this occasion, at least, nobody did. For between the two rows of these domestic dummies lay something more interesting than most of the mechanics of the world. It was a white, tattered scrap of paper scrawled with red ink; and the agile inventor had snatched it up almost as soon as the door flew open. He handed it to Angus without a word. The red ink on it actually was not dry, and the message ran, "If you have been to see her today, I shall kill you."

There was a short silence, and then Isidore Smythe said quietly, "Would you like a little whiskey? I rather feel as if I should."

"Thank you; I should like a little Flambeau," said Angus, gloomily. "This business seems to me to be getting rather grave. I'm going round at once to fetch him."

"Right you are," said the other, with admirable cheerfulness. "Bring him round here as quick as you can."

But as Angus closed the front door behind him he saw Smythe push back a button, and one of the clockwork images glided from its place and slid along a groove in the floor carrying a tray with syphon and decanter. There did seem something a trifle weird about leaving the little man alone among those dead servants, who were coming to life as the door closed.

Six steps down from Smythe's landing the man in shirt sleeves was doing something with a pail. Angus stopped to extract a promise, fortified with a prospective bribe, that he would remain in that place until the return with the detective, and would keep count of any kind of stranger coming up those stairs. Dashing down to the front hall he then laid similar charges of vigilance on the commissionaire at the front door, from whom he learned the simplifying circumstances that there was no back door. Not content with this, he captured the floating policeman and induced him to stand opposite the entrance and watch it; and finally paused an instant for a pennyworth of chestnuts, and an inquiry as to the probable length of the merchant's stay in the neighbourhood.

The chestnut seller, turning up the collar of his coat, told him he should probably be moving shortly, as he thought it was going to snow. Indeed, the evening was growing grey and bitter, but Angus, with all his eloquence, proceeded to nail the chest-nut man to his post.

"Keep yourself warm on your own chestnuts," he said ear-nestly. "Eat up your whole stock; I'll make it worth your while. I'll give you a sovereign if you'll wait here till I come back, and then tell me whether any man, woman, or child has gone into that house where the commissionaire is standing."

He then walked away smartly, with a last look at the be-sieged tower.

"I've made a ring round that room, anyhow," he said. "They can't all four of them be Mr. Welkin's accomplices."

Lucknow Mansions were, so to speak, on a lower platform of that hill of houses, of which Himylaya Mansions might be called the peak. Mr. Flambeau's semi-official flat was on the ground floor, and presented in every way a marked contrast to the American machinery and cold hotel-like luxury of the flat of the Silent Service. Flambeau, who was a friend of Angus, re-ceived him in a rococo artistic den behind his office, of which the ornaments were sabres, harquebuses, Eastern curiosities, flasks of Italian wine, savage cooking-pots, a plumy Persian cat, and a small dusty-looking Roman Catholic priest, who looked particu-larly out of place.

"This is my friend Father Brown," said Flambeau. "I've often wanted you to meet him. Splendid weather, this; a little cold for Southerners like me."

"Yes, I think it will keep clear," said Angus, sitting down on a violet-striped Eastern ottoman.

"No," said the priest quietly, "it has begun to snow."

And, indeed, as he spoke, the first few flakes, foreseen by the man of chestnuts, began to drift across the darkening window-pane.

"Well," said Angus heavily, "I'm afraid I've come on busi-ness, and rather jumpy business at that. The fact is, Flambeau, within a stone's throw of your house is a fellow who badly wants your help; he's perpetually being haunted and threatened by an invisible enemy—a scoundrel whom nobody has even seen." As Angus proceeded to tell the whole tale of Smythe and Welkin, beginning with Laura's story, and going on with his own, the supernatural laugh at the corner of two empty streets, the strange distinct words spoken in an empty room, Flambeau grew more and more vividly concerned, and the little priest seemed to be left out of it, like a piece of furniture. When it came to the scribbled stamp-paper pasted on the window, Flambeau rose, seeming to fill the room with his huge shoulders.

"If you don't mind," he said, "I think you had better tell me the rest on the nearest road to this man's house. It strikes me, somehow, that there is no time to be lost."

"Delighted," said Angus, rising also, "though he's safe enough for the present, for I've set four men to watch the only hole to his burrow."

They turned out into the street, the small priest trundling after them with the docility of a small dog. He merely said, in a cheerful way, like one making conversation, "How quick the snow gets thick on the ground."

As they threaded the steep side streets already powdered with silver, Angus finished his story; and by the time they reached the crescent with the towering flats, he had leisure to turn his attention to the four sentinels. The chestnut seller, both before and after receiving a sovereign, swore stubbornly that he had watched the door and seen no visitor enter. The policeman was even more emphatic. He said he had had experience of crooks of all kinds, in top hats and in rags; he wasn't so green as to expect suspicious characters to look suspicious; he looked out for anybody, and, so help him, there had been nobody. And when all three men gathered round the gilded commissionaire, who still stood smiling astride of the porch, the verdict was more final still.

"I've got a right to ask any man, duke or dustman, what he

wants in these flats," said the genial and gold-laced giant, "and I'll swear there's been nobody to ask since this gentleman went away."

The unimportant Father Brown, who stood back, looking modestly at the pavement, here ventured to say meekly, "Has nobody been up and down stairs, then, since the snow began to fall? It began while we were all round at Flambeau's."

"Nobody's been in here, sir, you can take it from me," said the official, with beaming authority.

"Then I wonder what that is?" said the priest, and stared at the ground blankly like a fish.

The others all looked down also; and Flambeau used a fierce exclamation and a French gesture. For it was unquestionably true that down the middle of the entrance guarded by the man in gold lace, actually between the arrogant, stretched legs of that colossus, ran a stringy pattern of grey footprints stamped upon the white snow.

"God!" cried Angus involuntarily, "the Invisible Man!"

Without another word he turned and dashed up the stairs, with Flambeau following; but Father Brown still stood looking about him in the snow-clad street as if he had lost interest in his query.

Flambeau was plainly in a mood to break down the door with his big shoulders; but the Scotchman, with more reason, if less intuition, fumbled about on the frame of the door till he found the invisible button; and the door swung slowly open.

It showed substantially the same serried interior; the hall had grown darker, though it was still struck here and there with the last crimson shafts of sunset, and one or two of the headless machines had been moved from their places for this or that purpose, and stood here and there about the twilit place. The green and red of their coats were all darkened in the dusk; and their likeness to human shapes slightly increased by their very shapelessness. But in the middle of them all, exactly where the paper with the red ink had lain, there lay something that looked like red ink spilt out of its bottle. But it was not red ink.

With a French combination of reason and violence Flambeau simply said "Murder!" and, plunging into the flat, had explored every corner and cupboard of it in five minutes. But if he expected to find a corpse he found none. Isidore Smythe was not in the place, either dead or alive. After the most tearing search the two men met each other in the outer hall, with streaming faces and staring eyes. "My friend," said Flambeau, talking French in his excitement, "not only is your murderer invisible, but he makes invisible also the murdered man."

Angus looked round at the dim room full of dummies, and in some Celtic corner of his Scotch soul a shudder started. One of the life-size dolls stood immediately overshadowing the blood stain, summoned, perhaps, by the slain man an instant before he fell. One of the high-shouldered hooks that served the thing for arms, was a little lifted, and Angus had suddenly the horrid fancy that poor Smythe's own iron child had struck him down. Matter had rebelled, and these machines had killed their master. But even so, what had they done with him?

"Eaten him?" said the nightmare at his ear; and he sickened for an instant at the idea of rent, human remains absorbed and crushed into all that acephalous clockwork.

He recovered his mental health by an emphatic effort, and said to Flambeau, "Well, there it is. The poor fellow has evaporated like a cloud and left a red streak on the floor. The tale does not belong to this world."

"There is only one thing to be done," said Flambeau, "whether it belongs to this world or the other, I must go down and talk to my friend."

They descended, passing the man with the pail, who again asseverated that he had let no intruder pass, down to the commissionaire and the hovering chestnut man, who rigidly reasserted their own watchfulness. But when Angus looked round for his fourth confirmation he could not see it, and called out with some nervousness, "Where is the policeman?"

"I beg your pardon," said Father Brown; "that is my fault. I just sent him down the road to investigate something—that I just thought worth investigating."

"Well, we want him back pretty soon," said Angus abruptly, "for the wretched man upstairs has not only been murdered, but wiped out."

"How?" asked the priest.

"Father," said Flambeau, after a pause, "upon my soul I believe it is more in your department than mine. No friend or foe has entered the house, but Smythe is gone, as if stolen by the fairies. If that is not supernatural, I—"

As he spoke they were all checked by an unusual sight; the big blue policeman came round the corner of the crescent, running. He came straight up to Brown.

"You're right, sir," he panted, "they've just found poor Mr. Smythe's body in the canal down below."

Angus put his hand wildly to his head. "Did he run down and drown himself?" he asked.

"He never came down, I'll swear," said the constable, "and he wasn't drowned either, for he died of a great stab over the heart."

"And yet you saw no one enter?" said Flambeau in a grave voice.

"Let us walk down the road a little," said the priest.

As they reached the other end of the crescent he observed abruptly, "Stupid of me! I forgot to ask the policeman something. I wonder if they found a light brown sack."

"Why a light brown sack?" asked Angus, astonished.

"Because if it was any other coloured sack, the case must begin over again," said Father Brown; "but if it was a light brown sack, why, the case is finished."

"I am pleased to hear it," said Angus with hearty irony. "It hasn't begun, so far as I am concerned."

"You must tell us all about it," said Flambeau with a strange heavy simplicity, like a child.

Unconsciously they were walking with quickening steps down the long sweep of road on the other side of the high crescent, Father Brown leading briskly, though in silence. At last he said with an almost touching vagueness, "Well, I'm afraid you'll think it so prosy. We always begin at the abstract end of things, and you can't begin this story anywhere else.

"Have you ever noticed this—that people never answer what you say? They answer what you mean—or what they think you mean. Suppose one lady says to another in a country house, 'Is anybody staying with you?' the lady doesn't answer 'Yes; the butler, the three footmen, the parlourmaid, and so on,' though the parlourmaid may be in the room, or the butler behind her chair. She says 'There is *nobody* staying with us,' meaning nobody of the sort you mean. But suppose a doctor inquiring into an epidemic asks, 'Who is staying in the house?' then the lady will remember the butler, parlourmaid, and the rest. All language is used like that; you never get a question answered literally, even when you get it answered truly. When those four quite honest men said that no man had gone into the Mansions, they did not really mean that *no man* had gone into them. They meant no man whom they could suspect of being your man. A man did go into the house, and did come out of it, but they never noticed him."

"An invisible man?" inquired Angus, raising his red eyebrows.

"A mentally invisible man," said Father Brown.

A minute or two after he resumed in the same unassuming voice, like a man thinking his way. "Of course you can't think of such a man, until you do think of him. That's where his cleverness comes in. But I came to think of him through two or three little things in the tale Mr. Angus told us. First, there was the fact that this Welkin went for long walks. And then there was the vast lot of stamp paper on the window. And then, most of all, there were the two things the young lady said—things that couldn't be true. Don't get annoyed," he added hastily, noting a sudden movement of the Scotchman's head; "she thought they were true. A person *can't* be quite alone in a street a second before she receives a letter. She can't be quite alone in a street when she starts reading a letter just received. There must be somebody pretty near her; he must be mentally invisible."

"Why must there be somebody near her?" asked Angus.

"Because," said Father Brown, "barring carrier-pigeons, somebody must have brought her the letter."

"Do you really mean to say," asked Flambeau, with energy, "that Welkin carried his rival's letters to his lady?"

"Yes," said the priest. "Welkin carried his rival's letters to his lady. You see, he had to."

"Oh, I can't stand much more of this," exploded Flambeau. "Who is this fellow? What does he look like? What is the usual get-up of a mentally invisible man?"

"He is dressed rather handsomely in red, blue and gold," replied the priest promptly with precision, "and in this striking, and even showy, costume he entered Himylaya Mansions under eight human eyes; he killed Smythe in cold blood, and came down into the street again carrying the dead body in his arms—"

"Reverend sir," cried Angus, standing still, "are you raving mad, or am I?"

"You are not mad," said Brown, "only a little unobservant. You have not noticed such a man as this, for example."

He took three quick strides forward, and put his hand on the shoulder of an ordinary passing postman who had bustled by them unnoticed under the shade of the trees.

"Nobody ever notices postmen somehow," he said thoughtfully; "yet they have passions like other men, and even carry large bags where a small corpse can be stowed quite easily."

The postman, instead of turning naturally, had ducked and tumbled against the garden fence. He was a lean fair-bearded man of very ordinary appearance, but as he turned an alarmed face over his shoulder, all three men were fixed with an almost fiendish squint.

Flambeau went back to his sabres, purple rugs and Persian cat, having many things to attend to. John Turnbull Angus went back to the lady at the shop, with whom that imprudent young man contrives to be extremely comfortable. But Father Brown walked those snow-covered hills under the stars for many hours with a murderer, and what they said to each other will never be known.

THE SINS OF PRINCE SARADINE

WHEN Flambeau took his month's holiday from his office in Westminster he took it in a small sailing-boat, so small that it passed much of its time as a rowing-boat. He took it, moreover, in little rivers in the Eastern counties, rivers so small that the boat looked like a magic boat, sailing on land through meadows and cornfields. The vessel was just comfortable for two people; there was room only for necessities, and Flambeau had stocked it with such things as his special philosophy considered necessary. They reduced themselves, apparently, to four essentials: tins of salmon, if he should want to eat; loaded revolvers, if he should want to fight; a bottle of brandy, presumably in case he should faint; and a priest, presumably in case he should die. With this light luggage he crawled down the little Norfolk rivers, intending to reach the Broads at last, but meanwhile delighting in the overhanging gardens and meadows, the mirrored mansions or villages, lingering to fish in the pools and corners, and in some sense hugging the shore.

Like a true philosopher, Flambeau had no aim in his holiday; but, like a true philosopher, he had an excuse. He had a sort of half purpose, which he took just so seriously that its success would crown the holiday, but just so lightly that its failure would not spoil it. Years ago, when he had been a king of thieves and the most famous figure in Paris, he had often received wild communications of approval, denunciation, or even love; but one had, somehow, stuck in his memory. It consisted simply of a visiting-card, in an envelope with an English postmark. On the back of the card was written in French and in green ink: "If you ever retire and become respectable, come and see me. I want to meet you, for I have met all the other great men of my time. That trick of yours of getting one detective to arrest the other was the most splendid scene in French history." On the front of the card was engraved in the formal fashion, "Prince Saradine, Reed House, Reed Island, Norfolk."

He had not troubled much about the prince then, beyond ascertaining that he had been a brilliant and fashionable figure in southern Italy. In his youth, it was said, he had eloped with a married woman of high rank; the escapade was scarcely startling in his social world, but it had clung to men's minds because of an additional tragedy: the alleged suicide of the insulted husband, who appeared to have flung himself over a precipice in Sicily. The prince then lived in Vienna for a time, but his more recent years seemed to have been passed in perpetual and restless travel. But when Flambeau, like the prince himself, had left European celebrity and settled in England, it occurred to him that he might pay a surprise visit to this eminent exile in the Norfolk Broads. Whether he should find the place he had no idea; and, indeed, it was sufficiently small and forgotten. But, as things fell out, he found it much sooner than he expected.

They had moored their boat one night under a bank veiled in high grasses and short pollarded trees. Sleep, after heavy sculling, had come to them early, and by a corresponding accident they awoke before it was light. To speak more strictly, they awoke before it was daylight; for a large lemon moon was only just setting in the forest of high grass above their heads, and the sky was of a vivid violet-blue, nocturnal but bright. Both men had simultaneously a reminiscence of childhood, of the elfin and adventurous time when tall weeds close over us like woods. Standing up thus against the large low moon, the daisies really seemed to be giant daisies, the dandelions to be giant dandelions. Somehow it reminded them of the dado of a nursery wall-paper. The drop of the river-bed sufficed to sink them under the roots of all shrubs and flowers and make them gaze upwards at the grass.

"By Jove!" said Flambeau, "it's like being in fairyland."

Father Brown sat bolt upright in the boat and crossed himself. His movement was so abrupt that his friend asked him, with a mild stare, what was the matter.

"The people who wrote the mediæval ballads," answered the priest, "knew more about fairies than you do. It isn't only nice things that happen in fairyland."

"Oh, bosh!" said Flambeau. "Only nice things could happen under such an innocent moon. I am for pushing on now and seeing what does really come. We may die and rot before we ever see again such a moon or such a mood."

"All right," said Father Brown. "I never said it was always wrong to enter fairyland. I only said it was always dangerous."

They pushed slowly up the brightening river; the glowing violet of the sky and the pale gold of the moon grew fainter and fainter, and faded into that vast colourless cosmos that precedes the colours of the dawn. When the first faint stripes of red and gold and grey split the horizon from end to end they were broken by the black bulk of a town or village which sat on the river just ahead of them. It was already an easy twilight, in which all things were visible, when they came under the hanging roofs and bridges of this riverside hamlet. The houses, with their long, low, stooping roofs, seemed to come down to drink at the river, like huge grey and red cattle. The broadening and whitening dawn had already turned to working daylight before they saw any living creature on the wharves and bridges of that silent town. Eventually they saw a very placid and prosperous man in his shirt sleeves, with a face as round as the recently sunken moon, and rays of red whisker around the low arc of it, who was leaning on a post above the sluggish tide. By an impulse not to be analysed, Flambeau rose to his full height in the swaying boat and shouted at the man to ask if he knew Reed Island or Reed House. The prosperous man's smile grew slightly more expansive, and he simply pointed up the river towards the next bend of it. Flambeau went ahead without further speech.

The boat took many such grassy corners and followed many such reedy and silent reaches of river; but before the search had become monotonous they had swung round a specially sharp angle and come into the silence of a sort of pool or lake, the sight of which instinctively arrested them. For in the middle of this wider piece of water, fringed on every side with rushes, lay a long, low islet, along which ran a long, low house or bungalow built of bamboo or some kind of tough tropic cane. The up-standing rods of bamboo which made the walls were pale yellow, the sloping rods that made the roof were of darker red or brown, otherwise the long house was a thing of repetition and monot-ony. The early morning breeze rustled the reeds round the is-land and sang in the strange ribbed house as in a giant pan-pipe.

"By George!" cried Flambeau; "here is the place, after all! Here is Reed Island, if ever there was one. Here is Reed House, if it is anywhere. I believe that fat man with whiskers was a fairy."

"Perhaps," remarked Father Brown impartially. "If he was, he was a bad fairy."

But even as he spoke the impetuous Flambeau had run his boat ashore in the rattling reeds, and they stood in the long, quaint islet beside the odd silent house.

The house stood with its back, as it were, to the river and the only landing-stage; the main entrance was on the other side, and looked down the long island garden. The visitors approached it, therefore, by a small path running round nearly three sides of the house, close under the low eaves. Through three different win-dows on three different sides they looked in on the same long, well-lit room, panelled in light wood, with a large number of looking-glasses, and laid out as for an elegant lunch. The front door, when they came round to it at last, was flanked by two turquoise-blue flower pots. It was opened by a butler of the drearier type—long, lean, grey and listless—who murmured that Prince Saradine was from home at present, but was expected hourly; the house being kept ready for him and his guests. The exhibition of the card with the scrawl of green ink awoke a flicker of life in the parchment face of the depressed retainer, and it was with a certain shaky courtesy that he suggested that the strangers should remain. "His Highness may be here any minute," he said, "and would be distressed to have just missed any gentleman he had invited. We have orders always to keep a little cold lunch for him and his friends, and I am sure he would wish it to be offered."

Moved with curiosity to this minor adventure, Flambeau assented gracefully, and followed the old man, who ushered him ceremoniously into the long, lightly panelled room. There was nothing very notable about it, except the rather unusual alternation of many long, low windows with many long, low oblongs of looking-glass, which gave a singular air of lightness and unsubstantialness to the place. It was somehow like lunching out of doors. One or two pictures of a quiet kind hung in the corners, one a large grey photograph of a very young man in uniform, another a red chalk sketch of two long-haired boys. Asked by Flambeau whether the soldierly person was the prince, the butler answered shortly in the negative; it was the prince's younger brother, Captain Stephen Saradine, he said. And with that the old man seemed to dry up suddenly and lose all taste for conversation.

After lunch had tailed off with exquisite coffee and liqueurs, the guests were introduced to the garden, the library, and the housekeeper—a dark, handsome lady, of no little majesty, and rather like a plutonic Madonna. It appeared that she and the butler were the only survivors of the prince's original foreign *ménage*, all the other servants now in the house being new and collected in Norfolk by the housekeeper. This latter lady went by the name of Mrs. Anthony, but she spoke with a slight Italian accent, and Flambeau did not doubt that Anthony was a Norfolk version of some more Latin name. Mr. Paul, the butler, also had a faintly foreign air, but he was in tongue and training English, as are many of the most polished men-servants of the cosmopolitan nobility.

Pretty and unique as it was, the place had about it a curious luminous sadness. Hours passed in it like days. The long, well-windowed rooms were full of daylight, but it seemed a dead daylight. And through all other incidental noises, the sound of talk, the clink of glasses, or the passing feet of servants, they could hear on all sides of the house the melancholy noise of the river.

"We have taken a wrong turning, and come to a wrong place," said Father Brown, looking out of the window at the grey-green sedges and the silver flood. "Never mind; one can sometimes do good by being the right person in the wrong place."

Father Brown, though commonly a silent, was an oddly sympathetic little man, and in those few but endless hours he unconsciously sank deeper into the secrets of Reed House than his professional friend. He had that knack of friendly silence which is so essential to gossip; and saying scarcely a word, he probably obtained from his new acquaintances all that in any case they would have told. The butler indeed was naturally uncommunicative. He betrayed a sullen and almost animal affection for his master; who, he said, had been very badly treated. The chief offender seemed to be his highness's brother, whose name alone would lengthen the old man's lantern jaws and pucker his parrot nose into a sneer. Captain Stephen was a ne'er-do-weel, apparently, and had drained his benevolent brother of hundreds and thousands; forced him to fly from fashionable life and live quietly in this retreat. That was all Paul, the butler, would say, and Paul was obviously a partisan.

The Italian housekeeper was somewhat more communicative, being, as Brown fancied, somewhat less content. Her tone about her master was faintly acid; though not without a certain awe. Flambeau and his friend were standing in the room of the looking-glasses examining the red sketch of the two boys, when the housekeeper swept in swiftly on some domestic errand. It was a peculiarity of this glittering, glass-panelled place that anyone entering was reflected in four or five mirrors at once; and Father Brown, without turning round, stopped in the middle of a sentence of family criticism. But Flambeau, who had his face close up to the picture was already saying in a loud voice, "The

Brothers Saradine, I suppose. They both look innocent enough. It would be hard to say which is the good brother and which the bad." Then, realising the lady's presence, he turned the conversation with some triviality, and strolled out into the garden. But Father Brown still gazed steadily at the red crayon sketch; and Mrs. Anthony still gazed steadily at Father Brown.

She had large and tragic brown eyes, and her olive face glowed darkly with a curious and painful wonder—as of one doubtful of a stranger's identity or purpose. Whether the little priest's coat and creed touched some southern memories of confession, or whether she fancied he knew more than he did, she said to him in a low voice as to a fellow plotter, "He is right enough in one way, your friend. He says it would be hard to pick out the good and bad brothers. Oh, it would be hard, it would be mighty hard, to pick out the good one."

"I don't understand you," said Father Brown, and began to move away.

The woman took a step nearer to him, with thunderous brows and a sort of savage stoop, like a bull lowering his horns.

"There isn't a good one," she hissed. "There was badness enough in the captain taking all that money, but I don't think there was much goodness in the prince giving it. The captain's not the only one with something against him."

A light dawned on the cleric's averted face, and his mouth formed silently the word "blackmail." Even as he did so the woman turned an abrupt white face over her shoulder and almost fell. The door had opened soundlessly and the pale Paul stood like a ghost in the doorway. By the weird trick of the reflecting walls, it seemed as if five Pauls had entered by five doors simultaneously.

"His Highness," he said, "has just arrived."

In the same flash the figure of a man had passed outside the first window, crossing the sunlit pane like a lighted stage. An instant later he passed at the second window and the many mirrors repainted in successive frames the same eagle profile and marching figure. He was erect and alert, but his hair was white and his complexion of an odd ivory yellow. He had that short, curved Roman nose which generally goes with long, lean cheeks and chin, but these were partly masked by moustache and imperial. The moustache was much darker than the beard, giving an effect slightly theatrical, and he was dressed up to the same dashing part, having a white top hat, an orchid in his coat, a yellow waistcoat and yellow gloves which he flapped and swung as he walked. When he came round to the front door they heard the stiff Paul open it, and heard the new arrival say cheerfully, "Well, you see I have come." The stiff Mr. Paul bowed and answered in his inaudible manner; for a few minutes their conversation could not be heard. Then the butler said, "Everything is at your disposal"; and the glove-flapping Prince Saradine came gaily into the room to greet them. They beheld once more that spectral scene—five princes entering a room with five doors.

The prince put the white hat and yellow gloves on the table and offered his hand quite cordially.

"Delighted to see you here, Mr. Flambeau," he said. "Knowing you very well by reputation, if that's not an indiscreet remark."

"Not at all," answered Flambeau, laughing. "I am not sensitive. Very few reputations are gained by unsullied virtue."

The prince flashed a sharp look at him to see if the retort had any personal point; then he laughed also and offered chairs to everyone, including himself.

"Pleasant little place, this, I think," he said with a detached air. "Not much to do, I fear; but the fishing is really good."

The priest, who was staring at him with the grave stare of a baby, was haunted by some fancy that escaped definition. He looked at the grey, carefully curled hair, yellow white visage, and slim, somewhat foppish figure. These were not unnatural, though perhaps a shade *pronouncé*, like the outfit of a figure behind the footlights. The nameless interest lay in something else, in the very framework of the face; Brown was tormented with a half memory of having seen it somewhere before. The man looked like some old friend of his dressed up. Then he suddenly remembered the mirrors, and put his fancy down to some psychological effect of that multiplication of human masks.

Prince Saradine distributed his social attentions between his guests with great gaiety and tact. Finding the detective of a sporting turn and eager to employ his holiday, he guided Flambeau and Flambeau's boat down to the best fishing spot in the stream, and was back in his own canoe in twenty minutes to join Father Brown in the library and plunge equally politely into the priest's more philosophic pleasures. He seemed to know a great deal both about the fishing and the books, though of these not the most edifying; he spoke five or six languages, though chiefly the slang of each. He had evidently lived in varied cities and very motley societies, for some of his cheerfullest stories were about gambling hells and opium dens, Australian bushrangers or Italian brigands. Father Brown knew that the once celebrated Saradine had spent his last few years in almost ceaseless travel, but he had not guessed that the travels were so disreputable or so amusing.

Indeed, with all his dignity of a man of the world, Prince Saradine radiated to such sensitive observers as the priest, a certain atmosphere of the restless and even the unreliable. His face was fastidious, but his eye was wild; he had little nervous tricks, like a man shaken by drink or drugs, and he neither had, nor professed to have, his hand on the helm of household affairs. All these were left to the two old servants, especially to the butler, who was plainly the central pillar of the house. Mr. Paul, indeed, was not so much a butler as a sort of steward or, even, chamberlain; he dined privately, but with almost as much pomp as his master; he was feared by all the servants; and he consulted with the prince decorously, but somewhat unbendingly—rather as if he were the prince's solicitor. The sombre housekeeper was a mere shadow in comparison; indeed, she seemed to efface herself and wait only on the butler, and Brown heard no more of those volcanic whispers which had half told him of the younger brother who blackmailed the elder. Whether the prince was really being thus bled by the absent captain, he could not be certain, but there was something insecure and secretive about Saradine that made the tale by no means incredible.

When they went once more into the long hall with the windows and the mirrors, yellow evening was dropping over the waters and the willowy banks; and a bittern sounded in the distance like an elf upon his dwarfish drum. The same singular sentiment of some sad and evil fairyland crossed the priest's mind again like a little grey cloud. "I wish Flambeau were back," he muttered.

"Do you believe in doom?" asked the restless Prince Saradine suddenly.

"No," answered his guest. "I believe in Doomsday."

The prince turned from the window and stared at him in a singular manner, his face in shadow against the sunset. "What do you mean?" he asked.

"I mean that we here are on the wrong side of the tapestry," answered Father Brown. "The things that happen here do not seem to mean anything; they mean something somewhere else. Somewhere else retribution will come on the real offender. Here it often seems to fall on the wrong person."

The prince made an inexplicable noise like an animal; in his shadowed face the eyes were shining queerly. A new and shrewd thought exploded silently in the other's mind. Was there another meaning in Saradine's blend of brilliancy and abruptness? Was the prince— Was he perfectly sane? He was repeating, "The wrong person—the wrong person," many more times than was natural in a social exclamation.

Then Father Brown awoke tardily to a second truth. In the mirrors before him he could see the silent door standing open, and the silent Mr. Paul standing in it, with his usual pallid impassiveness.

"I thought it better to announce at once," he said, with the same stiff respectfulness as of an old family lawyer, "a boat rowed by six men has come to the landing-stage, and there's a gentleman sitting in the stern."

"A boat!" repeated the prince; "a gentleman?" and he rose to his feet.

There was a startled silence punctuated only by the odd noise of the bird in the sedge; and then, before anyone could speak again, a new face and figure passed in profile round the three sunlit windows, as the prince had passed an hour or two before. But except for the accident that both outlines was aquiline, they had little in common. Instead of the new white topper of Saradine, was a black one of antiquated or foreign shape; under it was a young and very solemn face, clean shaven, blue about its resolute chin, and carrying a faint suggestion of the young Napoleon. The association was assisted by something old and odd about the whole get-up, as of a man who had never troubled to change the fashions of his fathers. He had a shabby blue frock coat, a red, soldierly looking waistcoat, and a kind of coarse white trousers common among the early Victorians, but strangely incongruous to-day. From all this old clothes-shop his olive face stood out strangely young and monstrously sincere.

"The deuce!" said Prince Saradine, and clapping on his white hat he went to the front door himself, flinging it open on the sunset garden.

By that time the new-comer and his followers were drawn up on the lawn like a small stage army. The six boatmen had pulled the boat well up on shore, and were guarding it almost menacingly, holding their oars erect like spears. They were swarthy men, and some of them wore earrings. But one of them stood forward beside the olive-faced young man in the red waistcoat, and carried a large black case of unfamiliar form.

"Your name," said the young man, "is Saradine?"

Saradine assented rather negligently.

The new-comer had dull, dog-like brown eyes, as different as possible from the restless and glittering grey eyes of the prince.

But once again Father Brown was tortured with a sense of having seen somewhere a replica of the face; and once again he remembered the repetitions of the glass-panelled room, and put down the coincidence to that. "Confound this crystal palace!" he muttered. "One sees everything too many times. It's like a dream."

"If you are Prince Saradine," said the young man, "I may tell you that my name is Antonelli."

"Antonelli," repeated the prince languidly. "Somehow I remember the name."

"Permit me to present myself," said the young Italian.

With his left hand he politely took off his old-fashioned top hat; with his right he caught Prince Saradine so ringing a crack across the face that the white top hat rolled down the steps and one of the blue flower-pots rocked upon its pedestal.

The prince, whatever he was, was evidently not a coward; he sprang at his enemy's throat and almost bore him backwards to the grass. But his enemy extricated himself with a singularly inappropriate air of hurried politeness.

"That is all right," he said, panting and in halting English. "I have insulted. I will give satisfaction. Marco, open the case."

The man beside him with the earrings and the big black case proceeded to unlock it. He took out of it two long Italian rapiers, with splendid steel hilts and blades, which he planted point downwards in the lawn. The strange young man standing facing the entrance with his yellow and vindictive face, the two swords standing up in the turf like two crosses in a cemetery, and the line of the ranked towers behind, gave it all an odd appearance of being some barbaric court of justice. But everything else was unchanged, so sudden had been the interruption. The sunset gold still glowed on the lawn, and the bittern still boomed as announcing some small but dreadful destiny.

"Prince Saradine," said the man called Antonelli, "when I was an infant in the cradle you killed my father and stole my mother; my father was the more fortunate. You did not kill him fairly, as

I am going to kill you. You and my wicked mother took him driving to a lonely pass in Sicily, flung him down a cliff, and went on your way. I could imitate you if I chose, but imitating you is too vile. I have followed you all over the world, and you have always fled from me. But this is the end of the world—and of you. I have you now, and I give you the chance you never gave my father. Choose one of those swords."

Prince Saradine, with contracted brows, seemed to hesitate a moment, but his ears were still singing with the blow, and he sprang forward and snatched at one of the hilts. Father Brown had also sprung forward, striving to compose the dispute; but he soon found his personal presence made matters worse. Saradine was a French freemason and a fierce atheist, and a priest moved him by the law of contraries. And for the other man neither priest nor layman moved him at all. This young man with the Bonaparte face and the brown eyes was something far sterner than a puritan—a pagan. He was a simple slayer from the morning of the earth; a man of the stone age—a man of stone.

One hope remained, the summoning of the household; and Father Brown ran back into the house. He found, however, that all the under servants had been given a holiday ashore by the autocrat Paul, and that only the sombre Mrs. Anthony moved uneasily about the long rooms. But the moment she turned a ghastly face upon him, he resolved one of the riddles of the house of mirrors. The heavy brown eyes of Antonelli were the heavy brown eyes of Mrs. Anthony; and in a flash he saw half the story.

"Your son is outside," he said without wasting words; "either he or the prince will be killed. Where is Mr. Paul?"

"He is at the landing-stage," said the woman faintly. "He is—he is—signalling for help."

"Mrs. Anthony," said Father Brown seriously, "there is no time for nonsense. My friend has his boat down the river fishing. Your son's boat is guarded by your son's men. There is only this one canoe; what is Mr. Paul doing with it?"

FATHER BROWN STORIES

"Santa Maria! I do not know," she said; and swooned all her length on the matted floor.

Father Brown lifted her to a sofa, flung a pot of water over her, shouted for help, and then rushed down to the landing-stage of the little island. But the canoe was already in mid-stream, and old Paul was pulling and pushing it up the river with an energy incredible at his years.

"I will save my master," he cried, his eyes blazing maniacally. "I will save him yet!"

Father Brown could do nothing but gaze after the boat as it struggled up-stream and pray that the old man might waken the little town in time.

"A duel is bad enough," he muttered, rubbing up his rough dust-coloured hair, "but there's something wrong about this duel, even as a duel. I feel it in my bones. But what can it be?"

As he stood staring at the water, a wavering mirror of sunset, he heard from the other end of the island garden a small but unmistakable sound—the cold concussion of steel. He turned his head.

Away on the farthest cape or headland of the long islet, on a strip of turf beyond the last rank of roses, the duellists had already crossed swords. Evening above them was a dome of virgin gold, and, distant as they were, every detail was picked out. They had cast off their coats, but the yellow waistcoat and white hair of Saradine, the red waistcoat and white trousers of Antonelli, glittered in the level light like the colours of the dancing clockwork dolls. The two swords sparkled from point to pommel like two diamond pins. There was something frightful in the two figures appearing so little and so gay. They looked like two butterflies trying to pin each other to a cork.

Father Brown ran as hard as he could, his little legs going like a wheel. But when he came to the field of combat he found he was both too late and too early—too late to stop the strife, under the shadow of the grim Sicilians leaning on their oars, and too early to anticipate any disastrous issue of it. For the two men were singularly well matched, the prince using his skill with a sort of cynical confidence, the Sicilian using his with a murderous care. Few finer fencing matches can ever have been seen in crowded amphitheatres than that which tinkled and sparkled on that forgotten island in the reedy river. The dizzy fight was balanced so long that hope began to revive in the protesting priest; by all common probability Paul must soon come back with the police. It would be some comfort even if Flambeau came back from his fishing, for Flambeau, physically speaking, was worth four other men. But there was no sign of Flambeau, and, what was much queerer, no sign of Paul or the police. No other raft or stick was left to float on; in that lost island in that vast nameless pool, they were cut off as on a rock in the Pacific.

Almost as he had the thought the ringing of the rapiers quickened to a rattle, the prince's arms flew up, and the point shot out behind between his shoulder-blades. He went over with a great whirling movement, almost like one throwing the half of a boy's cart-wheel. The sword flew from his hand like a shooting star, and dived into the distant river. And he himself sank with so earth-shaking a subsidence that he broke a big rose-tree with his body and shook up into the sky a cloud of red earth—like the smoke of some heathen sacrifice. The Sicilian had made blood-offering to the ghost of his father.

The priest was instantly on his knees by the corpse; but only to make too sure that it was a corpse. As he was still trying some last hopeless tests he heard for the first time voices from farther up the river, and saw a police boat shoot up to the landing-stage, with constables and other important people, including the excited Paul. The little priest rose with a distinctly dubious grimace.

"Now, why on earth," he muttered, "why on earth couldn't he have come before?"

Some seven minutes later the island was occupied by an invasion of townsfolk and police, and the latter had put their hands on the victorious duellist, ritually reminding him that anything he said might be used against him.

"I shall not say anything," said the monomaniac, with a wonderful and peaceful face. "I shall never say anything more. I am very happy, and I only want to be hanged."

Then he shut his mouth as they led him away, and it is the strange but certain truth that he never opened it again in this world, except to say "Guilty" at his trial.

Father Brown had stared at the suddenly crowded garden, the arrest of the man of blood, the carrying away of the corpse after its examination by the doctor, rather as one watches the break-up of some ugly dream; he was motionless, like a man in a nightmare. He gave his name and address as a witness, but declined their offer of a boat to the shore, and remained alone in the island garden, gazing at the broken rose bush and the whole green theatre of that swift and inexplicable tragedy. The light died along the river; mist rose in the marshy banks; a few belated birds flitted fitfully across.

Stuck stubbornly in his sub-consciousness (which was an unusually lively one) was an unspeakable certainty that there was something still unexplained. This sense that had clung to him all day could not be fully explained by his fancy about "looking-glass land." Somehow he had not seen the real story, but some game or masque. And yet people do not get hanged or run through the body for the sake of a charade.

As he sat on the steps of the landing-stage ruminating he grew conscious of the tall, dark streak of a sail coming silently down the shining river, and sprang to his feet with such a backrush of feeling that he almost wept.

"Flambeau!" he cried, and shook his friend by both hands again and again, much to the astonishment of that sportsman, as he came on shore with his fishing tackle. "Flambeau," he said, "so you're not killed?"

"Killed!" repeated the angler in great astonishment. "And why should I be killed?"

"Oh, because nearly everybody else is," said his companion

rather wildly. "Saradine got murdered, and Antonelli wants to be hanged, and his mother's fainted, and I, for one, don't know whether I'm in this world or the next. But, thank God, you're in the same one." And he took the bewildered Flambeau's arm.

As they turned from the landing-stage they came under the eaves of the low bamboo house, and looked in through one of the windows, as they had done on their first arrival. They beheld a lamp-lit interior well calculated to arrest their eyes. The table in the long dining-room had been laid for dinner when Saradine's destroyer had fallen like a storm-bolt on the island. And the dinner was now in placid progress, for Mrs. Anthony sat somewhat sullenly at the foot of the table, while at the head of it was Mr. Paul, the *major domo*, eating and drinking of the best, his bleared, bluish eyes standing queerly out of his face, his gaunt countenance inscrutable, but by no means devoid of satisfaction.

With a gesture of powerful impatience, Flambeau rattled at the window, wrenched it open, and put an indignant head into the lamp-lit room.

"Well," he cried. "I can understand you may need some refreshment, but really to steal your master's dinner while he lies murdered in the garden—"

"I have stolen a great many things in a long and pleasant life," replied the strange old gentleman placidly; "this dinner is one of the few things I have not stolen. This dinner and this house and garden happen to belong to me."

A thought flashed across Flambeau's face. "You mean to say," he began, "that the will of Prince Saradine—"

"I am Prince Saradine," said the old man, munching a salted almond.

Father Brown, who was looking at the birds outside, jumped as if he were shot, and put in at the window a pale face like a turnip.

"You are *what?*" he repeated in a shrill voice.

"Paul, Prince Saradine, *à vos ordres,*" said the venerable person politely, lifting a glass of sherry. "I live here very quietly, being a domestic kind of fellow; and for the sake of modesty I am called Mr. Paul, to distinguish me from my unfortunate brother Mr. Stephen. He died, I hear, recently—in the garden. Of course, it is not my fault if enemies pursue him to this place. It is owing to the regrettable irregularity of his life. He was not a domestic character."

He relapsed into silence, and continued to gaze at the opposite wall just above the bowed and sombre head of the woman. They saw plainly the family likeness that had haunted them in the dead man. Then his old shoulders began to heave and shake a little, as if he were choking, but his face did not alter.

"My God!" cried Flambeau after a pause, "he's laughing!"

"Come away," said Father Brown, who was quite white. "Come away from this house of hell. Let us get into an honest boat again."

Night had sunk on rushes and river by the time they had pushed off from the island, and they went down-stream in the dark, warming themselves with two big cigars that glowed like crimson ships' lanterns. Father Brown took his cigar out his mouth and said:

"I suppose you can guess the whole story now? After all, it's a primitive story. A man had two enemies. He was a wise man. And so he discovered that two enemies are better than one."

"I do not follow that," answered Flambeau.

"Oh, it's really simple," rejoined his friend. "Simple, though anything but innocent. Both the Saradines were scamps, but the prince, the elder, was the sort of scamp that gets to the top, and the younger, the captain, was the sort that sinks to the bottom. This squalid officer fell from beggar to blackmailer, and one ugly day he got his hold upon his brother, the prince. Obviously it was for no light matter, for Prince Paul Saradine was frankly 'fast,' and had no reputation to lose as to the mere sins of society. In plain fact, it was a hanging matter, and Stephen literally had a rope round his brother's neck. He had somehow discovered the truth about the Sicilian affair, and could prove that Paul murdered old Antonelli in the mountains. The captain raked in the hush money heavily for ten years, until even the prince's splendid fortune began to look a little foolish.

"But Prince Saradine bore another burden besides his blood-sucking brother. He knew that the son of Antonelli, a mere child at the time of the murder, had been trained in savage Sicilian loyalty, and lived only to avenge his father, not with the gibbet (for he lacked Stephen's legal proof), but with the old weapons of vendetta. The boy had practised arms with a deadly perfection, and about the time that he was old enough to use them Prince Saradine began, as the society papers said, to travel. The fact is that he began to flee for his life, passing from place to place like a hunted criminal; but with one relentless man upon his trail. That was Prince Paul's position, and by no means a pretty one. The more money he spent on eluding Antonelli the less he had to silence Stephen. The more he gave to silence Stephen the less chance there was of finally escaping Antonelli. Then it was that he showed himself a great man—a genius like Napoleon.

"Instead of resisting his two antagonists, he surrendered suddenly to both of them. He gave way like a Japanese wrestler, and his foes fell prostrate before him. He gave up the race round the world, and he gave up his address to young Antonelli; then he gave up everything to his brother. He sent Stephen money enough for smart clothes and easy travel, with a letter saying roughly: 'This is all I have left. You have cleaned me out. I still have a little house in Norfolk, with servants and a cellar, and if you want more from me you must take that. Come and take possession if you like, and I will live there quietly as your friend or agent or anything.' He knew that the Sicilian had never seen the Saradine brothers save, perhaps, in pictures; he knew they were somewhat alike, both having grey, pointed beards. Then he shaved his own face and waited. The trap worked. The unhappy captain, in his new clothes, entered the house in triumph as a prince, and walked upon the Sicilian's sword.

"There was one hitch, and it is to the honour of human nature. Evil spirits like Saradine often blunder by never expecting the virtues of mankind. He took it for granted that the Italian's blow, when it came, would be dark, violent and nameless, like the blow it avenged; that the victim would be knifed at night, or shot from behind a hedge, and so die without speech. It was a bad minute for Prince Paul when Antonelli's chivalry proposed a formal duel, with all its possible explanations. It was then that I found him putting off in his boat with wild eyes. He was fleeing, bare-headed, in an open boat before Antonelli should learn who he was.

"But, however agitated, he was not hopeless. He knew the ad-venturer and he knew the fanatic. It was quite probable that Stephen, the adventurer, would hold his tongue, through his mere histrionic pleasure in playing a part, his lust for clinging to his new cosy quarters, his rascal's trust in luck, and his fine fenc-ing. It was certain that Antonelli, the fanatic, would hold his tongue, and be hanged without telling tales of his family. Paul hung about on the river till he knew the fight was over. Then he roused the town, brought the police, saw his two vanquished enemies taken away forever, and sat down smiling to his dinner."

"Laughing, God help us!" said Flambeau with a strong shud-der. "Do they get such ideas from Satan?"

"He got that idea from you," answered the priest.

"God forbid!" ejaculated Flambeau. "From me? What do you mean?"

The priest pulled a visiting-card from his pocket and held it up in the faint glow of his cigar; it was scrawled with green ink.

"Don't you remember his original invitation to you?" he asked, "and the compliment to your criminal exploit? 'That trick of yours,' he says, 'of getting one detective to arrest the other'? He has just copied your trick. With an enemy on each side of him, he slipped swiftly out of the way and let them collide and kill each other."

Flambeau tore Prince Saradine's card from the priest's hands and rent it savagely in small pieces.

"There's the last of that old skull and crossbones," he said as he scattered the pieces upon the dark and disappearing waves of the stream; "but I should think it would poison the fishes."

The last gleam of white card and green ink was drowned and darkened; a faint and vibrant colour as of morning changed the sky, and the moon behind the grasses grew paler. They drifted in silence.

"Father," said Flambeau suddenly, "do you think it was all a dream?"

The priest shook his head, whether in dissent or agnosticism, but remained mute. A smell of hawthorn and of orchards came to them through the darkness, telling them that a wind was awake; the next moment it swayed their little boat and swelled their sail, and carried them onward down the winding river to happier places and the homes of harmless men.

THE SIGN OF THE BROKEN SWORD

The thousand arms of the forest were grey, and its million fingers silver. In a sky of dark green-blue-like slate the stars were bleak and brilliant like splintered ice. All that thickly wooded and sparsely tenanted countryside was stiff with a bitter and brittle frost. The black hollows between the trunks of the trees looked like bottomless, black caverns of that Scandinavian hell, a hell of incalculable cold. Even the square stone tower of the church looked northern to the point of heathenry, as if it were some barbaric tower among the sea rocks of Iceland. It was a queer night for anyone to explore a churchyard. But, on the other hand, perhaps it was worth exploring.

It rose abruptly out of the ashen wastes of forest in a sort of hump or shoulder of green turf that looked grey in the starlight. Most of the graves were on a slant, and the path leading up to the church was as steep as a staircase. On the top of the hill, in the one flat and prominent place, was the monument for which the place was famous. It contrasted strangely with the featureless graves all round, for it was the work of one of the greatest sculptors of modern Europe; and yet his fame was at once forgotten in the fame of the man whose image he had made. It showed, by touches of the small silver pencil of starlight, the massive metal figure of a soldier recumbent, the strong hands sealed in an everlasting worship, the great head pillowed upon a gun. The venerable face was bearded, or rather whiskered, in the old, heavy Colonel Newcome fashion. The uniform, though suggested with the few strokes of simplicity, was that of modern war. By his right side lay a sword, of which the tip was broken off; on the left side lay a Bible. On glowing summer afternoons wagonettes came full of Americans and cultured suburbans to see the sepulchre; but even then they felt the vast forest land with its one dumpy dome of churchyard and church as a place oddly dumb and neglected. In this freezing darkness of mid-winter one would think he might be left alone with the stars. Nevertheless, in the stillness of those stiff woods a wooden gate creaked, and two dim figures dressed in black climbed up the little path to the tomb.

So faint was that frigid starlight that nothing could have been traced about them except that while they both wore black, one man was enormously big, and the other (perhaps by contrast) almost startlingly small. They went up to the great graven tomb of the historic warrior, and stood for a few minutes staring at it. There was no human, perhaps no living, thing for a wide circle; and a morbid fancy might well have wondered if they were human themselves. In any case, the beginning of their conversation might have seemed strange. After the first silence the small man said to the other:

"Where does a wise man hide a pebble?"

And the tall man answered in a low voice: "On the beach."

The small man nodded, and after a short silence said: "Where does a wise man hide a leaf?"

And the other answered: "In the forest."

There was another stillness, and then the tall man resumed: "Do you mean that when a wise man has to hide a real diamond he has been known to hide it among sham ones?"

"No, no," said the little man with a laugh, "we will let bygones be bygones."

He stamped his cold feet for a second or two, and then said: "I'm not thinking of that at all, but of something else; something rather peculiar. Just strike a match, will you?"

The big man fumbled in his pocket, and soon a scratch and a flare painted gold the whole flat side of the monument. On it was cut in black letters the well-known words which so many Americans had reverently read: "Sacred to the Memory of General Sir Arthur St. Clare, Hero and Martyr, who Always Vanquished his Enemies and Always Spared Them, and Was Treacherously Slain by Them At Last. May God in Whom he Trusted both Reward and Revenge him."

The match burnt the big man's fingers, blackened, and dropped. He was about to strike another, but his small companion stopped him. "That's all right, Flambeau, old man; I saw what I wanted. Or, rather, I didn't see what I didn't want. And now we must walk a mile and a half along the road to the next inn, and I will try to tell you all about it. For Heaven knows a man should have a fire and ale when he dares tell such a story."

They descended the precipitous path, they relatched the rusty gate, and set off at a stamping, ringing walk down the frozen forest road. They had gone a full quarter of a mile before the smaller man spoke again. He said: "Yes; the wise man hides a pebble on the beach. But what does he do if there is no beach? Do you know anything of that great St. Clare trouble?"

"I know nothing about English generals, Father Brown," answered the large man, laughing, "though a little about English policemen. I only know that you have dragged me a precious long dance to all the shrines of this fellow, whoever he is. One would think he got buried in six different places. I've seen a memorial to General St. Clare in Westminster Abbey. I've seen a ramping equestrian statue of General St. Clare on the Embankment. I've seen a medallion of General St. Clare in the street he was born in, and another in the street he lived in; and now you drag me after dark to his coffin in the village church-yard. I am beginning to be a bit tired of his magnificent personality, especially as I don't in the least know who he was. What are you hunting for in all these crypts and effigies?"

"I am only looking for one word," said Father Brown. "A word that isn't there."

"Well," asked Flambeau; "are you going to tell me anything about it?"

"I must divide it into two parts," remarked the priest. "First there is what everybody knows; and then there is what I know. Now, what everybody knows is short and plain enough. It is also entirely wrong."

"Right you are," said the big man called Flambeau cheerfully. "Let's begin at the wrong end. Let's begin with what everybody knows, which isn't true."

"If not wholly untrue, it is at least very inadequate," continued Brown; "for in point of fact, all that the public knows amounts precisely to this: The public knows that Arthur St. Clare was a great and successful English general. It knows that after splendid yet careful campaigns both in India and Africa he was in command against Brazil when the great Brazilian patriot Olivier issued his ultimatum. It knows that on that occasion St. Clare with a very small force attacked Olivier with a very large one, and was captured after heroic resistance. And it knows that after his capture, and to the abhorrence of the civilised world, St. Clare was hanged on the nearest tree. He was found swinging there after the Brazilians had retired, with his broken sword hung round his neck."

"And that popular story is untrue?" suggested Flambeau.

"No," said his friend quietly, "that story is quite true, so far as it goes."

"Well, I think it goes far enough!" said Flambeau; "but if the popular story is true, what is the mystery?"

They had passed many hundreds of grey and ghostly trees before the little priest answered. Then he bit his finger reflectively and said: "Why, the mystery is a mystery of psychology. Or, rather, it is a mystery of two psychologies. In that Brazilian business two of the most famous men of modern history acted flat against their characters. Mind you, Olivier and St. Clare were both heroes—the old thing, and no mistake; it was like the fight between Hector and Achilles. Now, what would you say to an affair in which Achilles was timid and Hector was treacherous?"

"Go on," said the large man impatiently as the other bit his finger again.

"Sir Arthur St. Clare was a soldier of the old religious type—the type that saved us during the Mutiny," continued Brown. "He was always more for duty than for dash; and with all his

personal courage was decidedly a prudent commander, particularly indignant at any needless waste of soldiers. Yet in this last
battle he attempted something that a baby could see was absurd.
One need not be a strategist to see it was as wild as wind; just as
one need not be a strategist to keep out of the way of a motor-
bus. Well, that is the first mystery; what had become of the
English general's head? The second riddle is, what had become
of the Brazilian general's heart? President Olivier might be called
a visionary or a nuisance; but even his enemies admitted that he
was magnanimous to the point of knight errantry. Almost every
other prisoner he had ever captured had been set free or even
loaded with benefits. Men who had really wronged him came
away touched by his simplicity and sweetness. Why the deuce
should he diabolically revenge himself only once in his life; and
that for the one particular blow that could not have hurt him?
Well, there you have it. One of the wisest men in the world
acted like an idiot for no reason. One of the best men in the
world acted like a fiend for no reason. That's the long and the
short of it; and I leave it to you, my boy."

"No, you don't," said the other with a snort. "I leave it to
you; and you jolly well tell me all about it."

"Well," resumed Father Brown, "it's not fair to say that the
public impression is just what I've said, without adding that two
things have happened since. I can't say they threw a new light;
for nobody can make sense of them. But they threw a new kind
of darkness; they threw the darkness in new directions. The
first was this. The family physician of the St. Clares quarrelled
with that family, and began publishing a violent series of articles,
in which he said that the late general was a religious maniac; but
as far as the tale went, this seemed to mean little more than a
religious man. Anyhow, the story fizzled out. Everyone knew,
of course, that St. Clare had some of the eccentricities of puritan
piety. The second incident was much more arresting. In the
luckless and unsupported regiment which made that rash attempt
at the Black River there was a certain Captain Keith, who was

at that time engaged to St. Clare's daughter, and who afterwards married her. He was one of those who were captured by Olivier, and, like all the rest except the general, appears to have been bounteously treated and promptly set free. Some twenty years afterwards this man, then Lieutenant-Colonel Keith, published a sort of autobiography called 'A British Officer in Burmah and Brazil.' In the place where the reader looks eagerly for some account of the mystery of St. Clare's disaster may be found the following words: 'Everywhere else in this book I have narrated things exactly as they occurred, holding as I do the old-fashioned opinion that the glory of England is old enough to take care of itself. The exception I shall make is in this matter of the defeat by the Black River; and my reasons, though private, are honourable and compelling. I will, however, add this in justice to the memories of two distinguished men. General St. Clare has been accused of incapacity on this occasion; I can at least testify that this action, properly understood, was one of the most brilliant and sagacious of his life. President Olivier by similar report is charged with savage injustice. I think it due to the honour of an enemy to say that he acted on this occasion with even more than his characteristic good feeling. To put the matter popularly, I can assure my countrymen that St. Clare was by no means such a fool nor Olivier such a brute as he looked. This is all I have to say; nor shall any earthly consideration induce me to add a word to it.' "

A large frozen moon like a lustrous snowball began to show through the tangle of twigs in front of them, and by its light the narrator had been able to refresh his memory of Captain Keith's text from a scrap of printed paper. As he folded it up and put it back in his pocket Flambeau threw up his hand with a French gesture.

"Wait a bit, wait a bit," he cried excitedly. "I believe I can guess it at the first go."

He strode on, breathing hard, his black head and bull neck forward, like a man winning a walking race. The little priest, amused and interested, had some trouble in trotting beside him. Just before them the trees fell back a little to left and right, and the road swept downwards across a clear, moonlit valley, till it dived again like a rabbit into the wall of another wood. The entrance to the farther forest looked small and round, like the black hole of a remote railway tunnel. But it was within some hundred yards, and gaped like a cavern before Flambeau spoke again.

"I've got it," he cried at last, slapping his thigh with his great hand. "Four minutes' thinking, and I can tell your whole story myself."

"All right," assented his friend. "You tell it."

Flambeau lifted his head, but lowered his voice. "General Sir Arthur St. Clare," he said, "came of a family in which madness was hereditary; and his whole aim was to keep this from his daughter, and even, if possible, from his future son-in-law. Rightly or wrongly, he thought the final collapse was close, and resolved on suicide. Yet ordinary suicide would blazen the very idea he dreaded. As the campaign approached the clouds came thicker on his brain; and at last in a mad moment he sacrificed his public duty to his private. He rushed rashly into battle, hoping to fall by the first shot. When he found that he had only attained capture and discredit, the sealed bomb in his brain burst, and he broke his own sword and hanged himself."

He stared firmly at the grey façade of forest in front of him, with the one black gap in it, like the mouth of the grave, into which their path plunged. Perhaps something menacing in the road thus suddenly swallowed reinforced his vivid vision of the tragedy, for he shuddered.

"A horrid story," he said.

"A horrid story," repeated the priest with bent head. "But not the real story."

Then he threw back his head with a sort of despair and cried: "Oh, I wish it had been."

The tall Flambeau faced round and stared at him.

"Yours is a clean story," cried Father Brown, deeply moved. "A sweet, pure, honest story, as open and white as that moon. Madness and despair are innocent enough. There are worse things, Flambeau."

Flambeau looked up wildly at the moon thus invoked; and from where he stood one black tree-bough curved across it exactly like a devil's horn.

"Father—father," cried Flambeau with the French gesture and stepping yet more rapidly forward, "do you mean it was worse than that?"

"Worse than that," said Paul like a grave echo. And they plunged into the black cloister of the woodland, which ran by them in a dim tapestry of trunks, like one of the dark corridors in a dream.

They were soon in the most secret entrails of the wood, and felt close about them foliage that they could not see, when the priest said again:

"Where does a wise man hide a leaf? In the forest. But what does he do if there is no forest?"

"Well, well," cried Flambeau irritably, "what does he do?"

"He grows a forest to hide it in," said the priest in an obscure voice. "A fearful sin."

"Look here," cried his friend impatiently, for the dark wood and the dark saying got a little on his nerves; "will you tell me this story or not? What other evidence is there to go on?"

"There are three more bits of evidence," said the other, "that I have dug up in holes and corners; and I will give them in logical rather than chronological order. First of all, of course, our authority for the issue and event of the battle is in Olivier's own dispatches, which are lucid enough. He was entrenched with two or three regiments on the heights that swept down to the Black River, on the other side of which. was lower and more marshy ground. Beyond this again was gently rising country, on which was the first English outpost, supported by others which lay, however, considerably in its rear. The British forces as a whole were greatly superior in numbers; but this particular regiment was just far enough from its base to make Olivier consider the project of crossing the river to cut it off. By sunset, however, he had decided to retain his own position, which was a specially strong one. At daybreak next morning he was thunderstruck to see that this stray handful of English, entirely unsupported from their rear, had flung themselves across the river, half by a bridge to the right, and the other half by a ford higher up, and were massed upon the marshy bank below him.

"That they should attempt an attack with such numbers against such a position was incredible enough; but Olivier noticed something yet more extraordinary. For instead of attempting to seize more solid ground, this mad regiment, having put the river in its rear by one wild charge, did nothing more, but stuck there in the mire like flies in treacle. Needless to say, the Brazilians blew great gaps in them with artillery, which they could only return with spirited but lessening rifle fire. Yet they never broke; and Olivier's curt account ends with a strong tribute of admiration for the mystic valour of these imbeciles. 'Our line then advanced finally,' writes Olivier, 'and drove them into the river; we captured General St. Clare himself and several other officers. The colonel and the major had both fallen in the battle. I cannot resist saying that few finer sights can have been seen in history than the last stand of this extraordinary regiment; wounded officers picking up the rifles of dead soldiers, and the general himself facing us on horseback bareheaded and with a broken sword.' On what happened to the general afterwards Olivier is as silent as Captain Keith."

"Well," grunted Flambeau, "get on to the next bit of evidence."

"The next evidence," said Father Brown, "took some time to find, but it will not take long to tell. I found at last in an almshouse down in the Lincolnshire Fens an old soldier who not only was wounded at the Black River, but had actually knelt beside the colonel of the regiment when he died. This latter was a certain Colonel Clancy, a big bull of an Irishman; and it would seem that he died almost as much of rage as of bullets. He, at any rate, was not responsible for that ridiculous raid; it must have been imposed on him by the general. His last edifying words, according to my informant, were these: 'And there goes the damned old donkey with the end of his sword knocked off. I wish it was his head.' You will remark that everyone seems to have noticed this detail about the broken sword blade, though most people regard it somewhat more reverently than did the late Colonel Clancy. And now for the third fragment."

Their path through the woodland began to go upward, and the speaker paused a little for breath before he went on. Then he continued in the same business-like tone:

"Only a month or two ago a certain Brazilian official died in England, having quarrelled with Olivier and left his country. He was a well-known figure both here and on the Continent, a Spaniard named Espado; I knew him myself, a yellow-faced old dandy, with a hooked nose. For various private reasons I had permission to see the documents he had left; he was a Catholic, of course, and I had been with him towards the end. There was nothing of his that lit up any corner of the black St. Clare business, except five or six common exercise books filled with the diary of some English soldier. I can only suppose that it was found by the Brazilians on one of those that fell. Anyhow, it stopped abruptly the night before the battle.

"But the account of that last day in the poor fellow's life was certainly worth reading. I have it on me; but it's too dark to read it here, and I will give you a résumé. The first part of that entry is full of jokes, evidently flung about among the men, about somebody called the Vulture. It does not seem as if this person, whoever he was, was one of themselves, nor even an Englishman; neither is he exactly spoken of as one of the enemy. It sounds rather as if he were some local go-between and non-combatant; perhaps a guide or a journalist. He has been closeted with old Colonel Clancy; but is more often seen talking to the major. Indeed, the major is somewhat prominent in this soldier's narrative; a lean, dark-haired man, apparently, of the name of Murray—a north of Ireland man and a Puritan. There are continual jests about the contrast between this Ulsterman's austerity and the conviviality of Colonel Clancy. There is also some joke about the Vulture wearing bright-coloured clothes.

"But all these levities are scattered by what may well be called the note of a bugle. Behind the English camp and almost parallel to the river ran one of the few great roads of that district. Westward the road curved round towards the river, which it crossed by the bridge before mentioned. To the east the road swept backwards into the wilds, and some two miles along it was the next English outpost. From this direction there came along the road that evening a glitter and clatter of light cavalry, in which even the simple diarist could recognise with astonishment the general with his staff. He rode the great white horse which you have seen so often in illustrated papers and Academy pictures; and you may be sure that the salute they gave him was not merely ceremonial. He, at least, wasted no time on ceremony, but, springing from the saddle immediately, mixed with the group of officers, and fell into emphatic though confidential speech. What struck our friend the diarist most was his special disposition to discuss matters with Major Murray; but, indeed, such a selection, so long as it was not marked, was in no way unnatural. The two men were made for sympathy; they were men who 'read their Bibles'; they were both the old Evangelical type of officer. However this may be, it is certain that when the general mounted again he was still talking earnestly to Murray; and that as he walked his horse slowly down the road towards the river, the tall Ulsterman still walked by his bridle rein in earnest debate. The soldiers watched the two until they vanished behind a clump of trees where the road turned towards the river. The colonel had gone back to his tent, and the men to their pickets; the man with the diary lingered for another four minutes, and saw a marvellous sight.

"The great white horse which had marched slowly down the road, as it had marched in so many processions, flew back, galloping up the road towards them as if it were mad to win a race. At first they thought it had run away with the man on its back; but they soon saw that the general, a fine rider, was himself urging it to full speed. Horse and man swept up to them like a whirlwind; and then, reining up the reeling charger, the general turned on them a face like flame, and called for the colonel like the trumpet that wakes the dead.

"I conceive that all the earthquake events of that catastrophe tumbled on top of each other rather like lumber in the minds of men such as our friend with the diary. With the dazed excitement of a dream, they found themselves falling—literally falling —into their ranks, and learned that an attack was to be led at once across the river. The general and the major, it was said, had found out something at the bridge, and there was only just time to strike for life. The major had gone back at once to call up the reserve along the road behind; it was doubtful if even with that prompt appeal help could reach them in time. But they must pass the stream that night, and seize the heights by morning. It is with the very stir and throb of that romantic nocturnal march that the diary suddenly ends."

Father Brown had mounted ahead; for the woodland path grew smaller, steeper, and more twisted, till they felt as if they were ascending a winding staircase. The priest's voice came from above out of the darkness.

"There was one other little and enormous thing. When the general urged them to their chivalric charge he half drew his sword from the scabbard; and then, as if ashamed of such melodrama, thrust it back again. The sword again, you see."

A half-light broke through the network of boughs above them, flinging the ghost of a net about their feet; for they were mounting again to the faint luminosity of the naked night. Flambeau felt truth all round him as an atmosphere, but not as an idea. He answered with bewildered brain: "Well, what's the matter with the sword? Officers generally have swords, don't they?"

"They are not often mentioned in modern war," said the other dispassionately; "but in this affair one falls over the blessed sword everywhere."

"Well, what is there in that?" growled Flambeau; "it was a twopence coloured sort of incident; the old man's blade breaking in his last battle. Anyone might bet the papers would get hold of it, as they have. On all these tombs and things it's shown broken at the point. I hope you haven't dragged me through this Polar expedition merely because two men with an eye for a picture saw St. Clare's broken sword."

"No," cried Father Brown, with a sharp voice like a pistol shot; "but who saw his unbroken sword?"

"What do you mean?" cried the other, and stood still under the stars. They had come abruptly out of the grey gates of the wood.

"I say, who saw his unbroken sword?" repeated Father Brown obstinately. "Not the writer of the diary, anyhow; the general sheathed it in time."

Flambeau looked about him in the moonlight, as a man struck blind might look in the sun; and his friend went on for the first time with eagerness:

"Flambeau," he cried, "I cannot prove it, even after hunting through the tombs. But I am sure of it. Let me add just one more tiny fact that tips the whole thing over. The colonel, by a strange chance, was one of the first struck by a bullet. He was struck long before the troops came to close quarters. But he saw St. Clare's sword broken. Why was it broken? How was it broken? My friend, it was broken before the battle."

"Oh!" said his friend, with a sort of forlorn jocularity; "and pray where is the other piece?"

"I can tell you," said the priest promptly. "In the north-east corner of the cemetery of the Protestant Cathedral at Belfast."

"Indeed?" inquired the other. "Have you looked for it?"

"I couldn't," replied Brown, with frank regret. "There's a great marble monument on top of it; a monument to the heroic Major Murray, who fell fighting gloriously at the famous Battle of the Black River."

Flambeau seemed suddenly galvanised into existence. "You mean," he cried hoarsely, "that General St. Clare hated Murray, and murdered him on the field of battle because—"

"You are still full of good and pure thoughts," said the other. "It was worse than that."

"Well," said the large man, "my stock of evil imagination is used up."

The priest seemed really doubtful where to begin, and at last he said again:

"Where would a wise man hide a leaf? In the forest."

The other did not answer.

"If there were no forest, he would make a forest. And if he wished to hide a dead leaf, he would make a dead forest."

There was still no reply, and the priest added still more mildly and quietly:

"And if a man had to hide a dead body, he would make a field of dead bodies to hide it in."

Flambeau began to stamp forward with an intolerance of delay in time or space; but Father Brown went on as if he were continuing the last sentence:

"Sir Arthur St. Clare, as I have already said, was a man who read his Bible. That was what was the matter with *him*. When will people understand that it is useless for a man to read his Bible unless he also reads everybody else's Bible? A printer reads a Bible for misprints. A Mormon reads his Bible, and finds polygamy; a Christian Scientist reads his, and finds we have no arms and legs. St. Clare was an old Anglo-Indian Protestant soldier. Now, just think what that might mean; and, for Heaven's sake, don't cant about it. It might mean a man physically formidable living under a tropic sun in an Oriental society, and soaking himself without sense or guidance in an Oriental book. Of course, he read the Old Testament rather than the New. Of course, he found in the Old Testament anything that he wanted—lust, tyranny, treason. Oh, I dare say he was honest, as you call it. But what is the good of a man being honest in his worship of dishonesty?"

"In each of the hot and secret countries to which that man went he kept a harem, he tortured witnesses, he amassed shameful gold; but certainly he would have said with steady eyes that he did it to the glory of the Lord. My own theology is sufficiently expressed by asking which Lord? Anyhow, there is this about such evil, that it opens door after door in hell, and always into smaller and smaller chambers. This is the real case against crime, that a man does not become wilder and wilder, but only meaner and meaner. St. Clare was soon suffocated by difficulties of bribery and blackmail; and needed more and more cash. And by the time of the Battle of the Black River he had fallen from world to world to that place which Dante makes the lowest floor of the universe."

"What do you mean?" asked his friend again.

"I mean *that*," retorted the cleric, and suddenly pointed at a puddle sealed with ice that shone in the moon. "Do you remember whom Dante put in the last circle of ice?"

"The traitors," said Flambeau, and shuddered. As he looked around at the inhuman landscape of trees, with taunting and almost obscene outlines, he could almost fancy he was Dante, and the priest with the rivulet of a voice was, indeed, a Virgil leading him through a land of eternal sins.

The voice went on: "Olivier, as you know, was quixotic, and would not permit a secret service and spies. The thing, however, was done, like many other things, behind his back. It was managed by my old friend Espado; he was the bright-clad fop, whose hook nose got him called the Vulture. Posing as a sort of philanthropist at the front, he felt his way through the English Army, and at last got his fingers on its one corrupt man—please God!—and that man at the top. St. Clare was in foul need of money, and mountains of it. The discredited family doctor was threatening those extraordinary exposures that afterwards began and were broken off; tales of monstrous and prehistoric things in Park Lane; things done by an English Evangelical that smelt like human sacrifice and hordes of slaves. Money was wanted, too, for his daughter's dowry; for to him the fame of wealth was as sweet as wealth itself. He snapped the last thread, whispered the word to Brazil, and wealth poured in from the enemies of England. But another man had talked to Espado the Vulture as well as he. Somehow the dark, grim young major from Ulster had guessed the hideous truth; and when they walked slowly together down that road towards the bridge Murray was telling the general that he must resign instantly, or be court-martialled and shot. The general temporised with him till they came to the fringe of tropic trees by the bridge; and there by the singing river and the sunlit palms (for I can see the picture) the general drew his sabre and plunged it through the body of the major."

The wintry road curved over a ridge in cutting frost, with cruel black shapes of bush and thicket; but Flambeau fancied that he saw beyond it faintly the edge of an aureole that was not starlight and moonlight, but some fire such as is made by men. He watched it as the tale drew to its close.

"St. Clare was a hell-hound, but he was a hound of breed. Never, I'll swear, was he so lucid and so strong as when poor Murray lay a cold lump at his feet. Never in all his triumphs, as Captain Keith said truly, was the great man so great as he was in this last world-despised defeat. He looked coolly at his weapon to wipe off the blood; he saw the point he had planted between his victim's shoulders had broken off in the body. He saw quite calmly, as through a club window-pane, all that must follow. He saw that men must find the unaccountable corpse; must extract the unaccountable sword-point; must notice the unaccountable broken sword—or absence of sword. He had killed, but not silenced. But his imperious intellect rose against the facer; there was one way yet. He could make the corpse less unaccountable. He could create a hill of corpses to cover this one. In twenty minutes eight hundred English soldiers were marching down to their death."

The warmer glow behind the black winter wood grew richer and brighter, and Flambeau strode on to reach it. Father Brown also quickened his stride; but he seemed merely absorbed in his tale.

"Such was the valour of that English thousand, and such the genius of their commander, that if they had at once attacked the hill, even their mad march might have met some luck. But the evil mind that played with them like pawns had other aims and reasons. They must remain in the marshes by the bridge at least till British corpses should be a common sight there. Then for the last grand scene; the silver-haired soldier-saint would give up his shattered sword to save further slaughter. Oh, it was well organised for an impromptu. But I think (I cannot prove), I think that it was while they stuck there in the bloody mire that someone doubted—and someone guessed."

He was mute a moment, and then said: "There is a voice from nowhere that tells me the man who guessed was the lover . . . the man to wed the old man's child."

"But what about Olivier and the hanging?" asked Flambeau.

"Olivier, partly from chivalry, partly from policy, seldom encumbered his march with captives," explained the narrator. "He released everybody in most cases. He released everybody in this case."

"Everybody but the general," said the tall man.

"Everybody," said the priest.

Flambeau knitted his black brows. "I don't grasp it all yet," he said.

"There is another picture, Flambeau," said Brown in his more mystical undertone. "I can't prove it; but I can do more—I can see it. There is a camp breaking up on the bare, torrid hills at morning, and Brazilian uniforms massed in blocks and columns to march. There is the red shirt and long black beard of Olivier, which blows as he stands, his broad-brimmed hat in his hand. He is saying farewell to the great enemy he is setting free—the simple, snow-headed English veteran, who thanks him in the name of his men. The English remnant stand behind at attention; beside them are stores and vehicles for the retreat. The drums roll; the Brazilians are moving; the English are still like statues. So they abide till the last hum and flash of the enemy have faded from the tropic horizon. Then they alter their postures all at once, like dead men coming to life; they turn their fifty faces upon the general—faces not to be forgotten."

Flambeau gave a great jump. "Ah," he cried. "You don't mean—"

"Yes," said Father Brown in a deep, moving voice. "It was an English hand that put the rope round St. Clare's neck; I believe the hand that put the ring on his daughter's finger. They were English hands that dragged him up to the tree of shame; the hands of men that had adored him and followed him to victory. And they were English souls (God pardon and endure us all!) who stared at him swinging in that foreign sun on the green gallows of palm, and prayed in their hatred that he might drop off it into hell."

As the two topped the ridge there burst on them the strong scarlet light of a red-curtained English inn. It stood sideways in the road, as if standing aside in the amplitude of hospitality. Its three doors stood open with invitation; and even where they stood they could hear the hum and laughter of humanity happy for a night.

"I need not tell you more," said Father Brown. "They tried him in the wilderness and destroyed him; and then, for the honour of England and of his daughter, they took an oath to seal up for ever the story of the traitor's purse and the assassin's sword blade. Perhaps—Heaven help them—they tried to forget it.

Let us try to forget it, anyhow; here is our inn."

"With all my heart," said Flambeau, and was just striding into the bright, noisy bar when he stepped back and almost fell on the road.

"Look there, in the devil's name!" he cried, and pointed rigidly at the square wooden sign that overhung the road. It showed dimly the crude shape of a sabre hilt and a shortened blade; and was inscribed in false archaic lettering, "The Sign of the Broken Sword."

"Were you not prepared?" asked Father Brown gently. "He is the god of this country; half the inns and parks and streets are named after him and his story."

"I thought we had done with the leper," cried Flambeau, and spat on the road.

"You will never have done with him in England," said the priest, looking down, "while brass is strong and stone abides. His marble statues will erect the souls of proud, innocent boys for centuries, his village tomb will smell of loyalty as of lilies. Millions who never knew him shall love him like a father—this man whom the last few that knew him dealt with like dung. He shall be a saint; and the truth shall never be told of him, because I have made up my mind at last. There is so much good and evil in breaking secrets, that I put my conduct to a test. All these newspapers will perish; the anti-Brazil boom is already over; Olivier is already honoured everywhere. But I told myself that if anywhere, by name, in metal or marble that will endure like the pyramids, Colonel Clancy, or Captain Keith, or President Olivier, or any innocent man was wrongly blamed, then I would speak. If it were only that St. Clare was wrongly praised, I would be silent. And I will."

They plunged into the red-curtained tavern, which was not only cosy, but even luxurious inside. On a table stood a silver model of the tomb of St. Clare, the silver head bowed, the silver sword broken. On the walls were coloured photographs of the same scene, and of the system of wagonettes that took tourists to see it. They sat down on the comfortable padded benches.

"Come, it's cold," cried Father Brown; "let's have some wine or beer."

"Or brandy," said Flambeau.

THE ORACLE OF THE DOG

"Yes," said Father Brown, "I always like a dog so long as he isn't spelt backwards."

Those who are quick in talking are not always quick in listening. Sometimes even their brilliancy produces a sort of stupidity. Father Brown's friend and companion was a young man with a stream of ideas and stories, an enthusiastic young man named Fiennes, with eager blue eyes and blonde hair that seemed to be brushed back, not merely with a hair-brush but with the wind of the world as he rushed through it. But he stopped in the torrent of his talk in a momentary bewilderment before he saw the priest's very simple meaning.

"You mean that people make too much of them?" he said. "Well, I don't know. They're marvellous creatures. Sometimes I think they know a lot more than we do."

Father Brown said nothing; but continued to stroke the head of the big retriever in a half-abstracted but apparently soothing fashion.

"Why," said Fiennes, warming again to his monologue, "there was a dog in the case I've come to see you about; what they call the 'Invisible Murder Case,' you know. It's a strange story, but from my point of view the dog is about the strangest thing in it. Of course, there's the mystery of the crime itself, and how old Druce can have been killed by somebody else when he was all alone in the summer-house—"

The hand stroking the dog stopped for a moment in its rhythmic movement; and Father Brown said calmly, "Oh, it was a summer-house, was it?"

"I thought you'd read all about it in the papers," answered Fiennes. "Stop a minute; I believe I've got a cutting that will give you all the particulars." He produced a strip of newspaper from his pocket and handed it to the priest, who began to read it, and holding it close to his blinking eyes with one hand while the other continued its half-conscious caresses of the dog. It looked like the parable of a man not letting his right hand know what his left hand did.

"Many mystery stories, about men murdered behind locked doors and windows, and murderers escaping without means of entrance and exit, have come true in the course of the extraordinary events at Cranston on the coast of Yorkshire, where Colonel Druce was found stabbed from behind by a dagger that has entirely disappeared from the scene, and apparently even from the neighbourhood.

"The summer-house in which he died was indeed accessible at one entrance, the ordinary doorway which looked down the central walk of the garden towards the house. But by a combination of events almost to be called a coincidence, it appears that both the path and the entrance were watched during the crucial time, and there is a chain of witnesses who confirm each other. The summer-house stands at the extreme end of the garden, where there is no exit or entrance of any kind. The central garden path is a lane between two ranks of tall delphiniums, planted so close that any stray step off the path would leave its traces; and both path and plants run right up to the very mouth of the summer-house, so that no straying from that straight path could fail to be observed, and no other mode of entrance can be imagined.

"Patrick Floyd, secretary of the murdered man, testified that he had been in a position to overlook the whole garden from the time when Colonel Druce last appeared alive in the doorway to the time when he was found dead; as he, Floyd, had been on the top of a step-ladder clipping the garden hedge. Janet Druce, the dead man's daughter, confirmed this, saying that she had sat on the terrace of the house throughout that time and had seen Floyd at his work. Touching some part of the time, this is again supported by Donald Druce, her brother, who overlooked the garden standing at his bedroom window in his dressing-gown, for he had risen late. Lastly the account is consistent with that given by Dr. Valentine, a neighbour, who called for a time to talk with Miss Druce on the terrace, and by the Colonel's solicitor, Mr.

Aubrey Traill, who was apparently the last to see the murdered man alive—presumably with the exception of the murderer.

"All are agreed that the course of events was as follows: about half-past three in the afternoon, Miss Druce went down the path to ask her father when he would like tea; but he said he did not want any and was waiting to see Traill, his lawyer, who was to be sent to him in the summer-house. The girl then came away and met Traill coming down the path; she directed him to her father and he went in as directed. About half an hour afterwards he came out again, the Colonel coming with him to the door and showing himself to all appearance in health and even high spirits. He had been somewhat annoyed earlier in the day by his son's irregular hours, but seemed to recover his temper in a perfectly normal fashion, and had been rather markedly genial in receiving other visitors, including two of his nephews who came over for the day. But as these were out walking during the whole period of the tragedy, they had no evidence to give. It is said, indeed, that the Colonel was not on very good terms with Dr. Valentine, but that gentleman only had a brief interview with the daughter of the house, to whom he is supposed to be paying serious attentions.

"Traill, the solicitor, says he left the Colonel entirely alone in the summer-house, and this is confirmed by Floyd's bird's-eye view of the garden, which showed nobody else passing the only entrance. Ten minutes later Miss Druce again went down the garden and had not reached the end of the path when she saw her father, who was conspicuous by his white linen coat, lying in a heap on the floor. She uttered a scream which brought others to the spot, and on entering the place they found the Colonel lying dead beside his basket-chair, which was also upset. Dr. Valentine, who was still in the immediate neighbourhood, testified that the wound was made by some sort of stiletto, entering under the shoulder-blade and piercing the heart. The police have searched the neighbourhood for such a weapon, but no trace of it can be found."

"So Colonel Druce wore a white coat, did he?" said Father Brown as he put down the paper.

"Trick he learnt in the tropics," replied Fiennes with some wonder. "He'd had some queer adventures there, by his own account; and I fancy his dislike of Valentine was connected with the doctor coming from the tropics too. But it's all an infernal puzzle. The account there is pretty accurate; I didn't see the tragedy, in the sense of the discovery; I was out walking with the young nephews and the dog—the dog I wanted to tell you about. But I saw the stage set for it as described: the straight lane between the blue flowers right up to the dark entrance, and the lawyer going down it in his blacks and his silk hat, and the red head of the secretary showing high above the green hedge as he worked on it with his shears. Nobody could have mistaken that red head at any distance; and if people say they saw it there all the time, you may be sure they did. This red-haired secretary Floyd is quite a character; a breathless, bounding sort of fellow, always doing everybody's work as he was doing the gardener's. I think he is an American; he's certainly got the American view of life; what they call the view-point, bless 'em."

"What about the lawyer?" asked Father Brown.

There was a silence and then Fiennes spoke quite slowly for him. "Traill struck me as a singular man. In his fine black clothes he was almost foppish, yet you can hardly call him fashionable. For he wore a pair of long, luxuriant black whiskers such as haven't been seen since Victorian times. He had rather a fine grave face and a fine grave manner, but every now and then he seemed to remember to smile. And when he showed his white teeth he seemed to lose a little of his dignity and there was something faintly fawning about him. It may have been only embarrassment, for he would also fidget with his cravat and his tie-pin, which were at once handsome and unusual, like himself. If I could think of anybody—but what's the good, when the whole thing's impossible? Nobody knows who did it. Nobody knows how it could be done. At least there's only one exception I'd make, and that's why I really mentioned the whole thing. The dog knows."

Father Brown sighed and then said absently, "You were there as a friend of young Donald, weren't you? He didn't go on your walk with you?"

"No," replied Fiennes smiling. "The young scoundrel had gone to bed that morning and got up that afternoon. I went with his cousins, two young officers from India, and our conversation was trivial enough. I remember the elder, whose name I think is Herbert Druce and who is an authority on horse breeding, talked about nothing but a mare he had bought and the moral character of the man who sold her; while his brother Harry seemed to be brooding on his bad luck at Monte Carlo. I only mention it to show you, in the light of what happened on our walk, that there was nothing psychic about us. The dog was the only mystic in our company."

"What sort of a dog was he?" asked the priest.

"Same breed as that one," answered Fiennes. "That's what started me off on the story, your saying you didn't believe in believing in a dog. He's a big black retriever named Nox, and a suggestive name too; for I think what he did a darker mystery than the murder. You know Druce's house and garden are by the sea; we walked about a mile from it along the sands and then turned back, going the other way. We passed a rather curious rock called the Rock of Fortune, famous in the neighbourhood because it's one of those examples of one stone barely balanced on another, so that a touch would knock it over. It is not really very high, but the hanging outline of it makes it look a little wild and sinister; at least it made it look so to me, for I don't imagine my jolly young companions were afflicted with the picturesque. But it may be that I was beginning to feel an atmosphere; for just then the question arose of whether it was time to go back to tea, and even then I think I had a premonition that time counted for a good deal in the business. Neither Herbert Druce nor I had a watch, so we called out to his brother, who was some paces behind, having stopped to light his pipe under the hedge. Hence it happened that he shouted out the hour, which was twenty past four, in his big voice through the growing twilight; and somehow the loudness of it made it sound like the proclamation of something tremendous. His unconsciousness seemed to make it all the more so; but that was always the way with omens; and particular ticks of the clock were really very ominous things that afternoon. According to Dr. Valentine's testimony, poor Druce had actually died just about half-past four.

"Well, they said we needn't go home for ten minutes and we walked a little farther along the sands, doing nothing in particular—throwing stones for the dog and throwing sticks into the sea for him to swim after. But to me the twilight seemed to grow oddly oppressive and the very shadow of the top-heavy Rock of Fortune lay on me like a load. And then the curious thing happened. Nox had just brought back Herbert's walking stick out of the sea and his brother had thrown his in also. The dog swam out again, but just about what must have been the stroke of the half-hour, he stopped swimming. He came back again on to the shore and stood in front of us. Then he suddenly threw up his head and sent up a howl or wail of woe, if ever I heard one in the world.

"'What the devil's the matter with the dog?' asked Herbert; but none of us could answer. There was a long silence after the brute's wailing and whining died away on the desolate shore; and then the silence was broken. As I live, it was broken by a faint and far-off shriek, like the shriek of a woman from beyond the hedges inland. We didn't know what it was then; but we knew afterwards. It was the cry the girl gave when she first saw the body of her father."

"You went back, I suppose," said Father Brown patiently. "What happened then?"

"I'll tell you what happened then," said Fiennes with a grim emphasis. "When we got back into that garden the first thing we saw was Traill the lawyer; I can see him now with his black hat and black whiskers relieved against the perspective of the blue flowers stretching down to the summer-house, with the sunset and the strange outline of the Rock of Fortune in the distance. His face and figure were in shadow against the sunset; but I swear the white teeth were showing in his head and he was smiling.

"The moment Nox saw that man, the dog dashed forward and stood in the middle of the path barking at him madly, murderously, volleying out curses that were almost verbal in their dreadful distinctness of hatred. And the man doubled up and fled along the path between the flowers."

Father Brown sprang to his feet with a startling impatience.

"So the dog denounced him, did he?" he cried. "The oracle of the dog condemned him. Did you see what birds were flying, and are you sure whether they were on the right hand or the left? Did you consult the augurs about the sacrifices? Surely you didn't omit to cut open the dog and examine his entrails. That is the sort of scientific test you heathen humanitarians seem to trust, when you are thinking of taking away the life and honour of a man."

Fiennes sat gaping for an instant before he found breath to say, "Why, what's the matter with you? What have I done now?"

A sort of anxiety came back into the priest's eyes—the anxiety of a man who has run against a post in the dark and wonders for a moment whether he has hurt it.

"I'm most awfully sorry," he said with sincere distress. "I beg your pardon for being so rude; pray forgive me."

Fiennes looked at him curiously. "I sometimes think you are more of a mystery than any of the mysteries," he said. "But anyhow, if you don't believe in the mystery of the dog, at least you can't get over the mystery of the man. You can't deny that at the very moment when the beast came back from the sea and bellowed, his master's soul was driven out of his body by the blow of some unseen power that no mortal man can trace or even imagine. And as for the lawyer, I don't go only by the dog;

there are other curious details too. He struck me as a smooth, smiling, equivocal sort of person; and one of his tricks seemed like a sort of hint. You know the doctor and the police were on the spot very quickly; Valentine was brought back when walking away from the house, and he telephoned instantly. That, with the secluded house, small numbers, and enclosed space, made it pretty possible to search everybody who could have been near; and everybody was thoroughly searched—for a weapon. The whole house, garden, and shore were combed for a weapon. The disappearance of the dagger is almost as crazy as the disappearance of the man."

"The disappearance of the dagger," said Father Brown, nodding. He seemed to have become suddenly attentive.

"Well," continued Fiennes, "I told you that man Traill had a trick of fidgeting with his tie and tie-pin—especially his tie-pin. His pin, like himself, was at once showy and old-fashioned. It had one of those stones with concentric coloured rings that look like an eye; and his own concentration on it got on my nerves, as if he had been a Cyclops with one eye in the middle of his body. But the pin was not only large but long; and it occurred to me that his anxiety about its adjustment was because it was even longer than it looked; as long as a stiletto in fact."

Father Brown nodded thoughtfully. "Was any other instrument ever suggested?" he asked.

"There was another suggestion," answered Fiennes, "from one of the young Druces—the cousins, I mean. Neither Herbert nor Harry Druce would have struck one at first as likely to be of assistance in scientific detection; but while Herbert was really the traditional type of heavy Dragoon, caring for nothing but horses and being an ornament to the Horse Guards, his younger brother Harry had been in the Indian Police and knew something about such things. Indeed in his own way he was quite clever; and I rather fancy he had been too clever; I mean he had left the police through breaking some red-tape regulations and taking some sort of risk and responsibility of his own. Anyhow, he was in some sense a detective out of work, and threw himself into this business with more than the ardour of an amateur. And it was with him that I had an argument about the weapon—an argument that led to something new. It began by his countering my description of the dog barking at Traill; and he said that a dog at his worst didn't bark, but growled."

"He was quite right there," observed the priest.

"This young fellow went on to say that, if it came to that, he'd heard Nox growling at other people before then; and among others at Floyd the secretary. I retorted that his own argument answered itself; for the crime couldn't be brought home to two or three people, and least of all to Floyd, who was as innocent as a harum-scarum schoolboy, and had been seen by everybody all the time perched above the garden hedge with his fan of red hair as conspicuous as a scarlet cockatoo. 'I know there's difficulties anyhow,' said my colleague, 'but I wish you'd come with me down the garden a minute. I want to show you something I don't think anyone else has seen.' This was on the very day of the discovery, and the garden was just as it had been: the step-ladder was still standing by the hedge, and just under the hedge my guide stooped and disentangled something from the deep grass. It was the shears used for clipping the hedge, and on the point of one of them was a smear of blood."

There was a short silence, and then Father Brown said suddenly, "What was the lawyer there for?"

"He told us the Colonel sent for him to alter his will," answered Fiennes. "And, by the way, there was another thing about the business of the will that I ought to mention. You see, the will wasn't actually signed in the summer-house that afternoon."

"I suppose not," said Father Brown, "there would have to be two witnesses."

"The lawyer actually came down the day before and it was signed then; but he was sent for again next day because the old man had a doubt about one of the witnesses and had to be reassured."

"Who were the witnesses?" asked Father Brown.

"That's just the point," replied his informant eagerly, "the witnesses were Floyd the secretary and this Dr. Valentine, the foreign sort of surgeon or whatever he is; and the two have a quarrel. Now I'm bound to say that the secretary is something of a busybody. He's one of those hot and headlong people whose warmth of temperament has unfortunately turned mostly to pugnacity and bristling suspicion; to distrusting people instead of to trusting them. That sort of red-haired red-hot fellow is always either universally credulous or universally incredulous; and sometimes both. He was not only a Jack of all trades, but he knew better than all tradesmen. He not only knew everything, but he warned everybody against everybody. All that must be taken into account in his suspicions about Valentine; but in that particular case there seems to have been something behind it. He said the name of Valentine was not really Valentine. He said he had seen him elsewhere known by the name of De Villon. He said it would invalidate the will; of course he was kind enough to explain to the lawyer what the law was on that point. They were both in a frightful wax."

Father Brown laughed. "People often are when they are to witness a will," he said. "For one thing it means that they can't have any legacy under it. But what did Dr. Valentine say? No doubt the universal secretary knew more about the doctor's name than the doctor did. But even the doctor might have some information about his own name."

Fiennes paused a moment before he replied.

"Dr. Valentine took it in a curious way. Dr. Valentine is a curious man. His appearance is rather striking but very foreign. He is young but wears a beard cut square; and his face is very pale, dreadfully pale and dreadfully serious. His eyes have a sort of ache in them, as if he ought to wear glasses or had given himself a headache with thinking; but he is quite handsome and always very formally dressed, with a top hat and a dark coat and a little red rosette. His manner is rather cold and haughty, and he has a way of staring at you which is very disconcerting. When thus charged with having changed his name, he merely stared like a sphinx and then said with a little laugh that he supposed Americans had no names to change. At that I think the Colonel also got into a fuss and said all sorts of angry things to the doctor; all the more angry because of the doctor's pretensions to a future place in his family. But I shouldn't have thought much of that but for a few words that I happened to hear later, early in the afternoon of the tragedy. I don't want to make a lot of them, for they weren't the sort of words on which one would like, in the ordinary way, to play the eavesdropper. As I was passing out towards the front gate with my two companions and the dog, I heard voices which told me that Dr. Valentine and Miss Druce had withdrawn for a moment into the shadow of the house, in an angle behind a row of flowering plants, and were talking to each other in passionate whisperings—sometimes almost like hissings; for it was something of a lovers' quarrel as well as a lovers' tryst. Nobody repeats the sorts of things they said for the most part; but in an unfortunate business like this I'm bound to say that there was repeated more than once a phrase about killing somebody. In fact, the girl seemed to be begging him not to kill somebody, or saying that no provocation could justify killing anybody; which seems an unusual sort of talk to address to a gentleman who has dropped in to tea."

"Do you know," asked the priest, "whether Dr. Valentine seemed to be very angry after the scene with the secretary and the Colonel—I mean about witnessing the will?"

"By all accounts," replied the other, "he wasn't half so angry as the secretary was. It was the secretary who went away raging after witnessing the will."

"And now," said Father Brown, "what about the will itself?"

"The Colonel was a very wealthy man, and his will was important. Traill wouldn't tell us the alteration at that stage, but I have since heard, only this morning in fact, that most of the money was transferred from the son to the daughter. I told you that Druce was wild with my friend Donald over his dissipated hours."

"The question of motive has been rather overshadowed by the question of method," observed Father Brown thoughtfully. "At that moment, apparently, Miss Druce was the immediate gainer by the death."

"Good God! What a cold-blooded way of talking," cried Fiennes, staring at him. "You don't really mean to hint that she—"

"Is she going to marry that Dr. Valentine?" asked the other.

"Some people are against it," answered his friend. "But he is liked and respected in the place and is a skilled and devoted surgeon."

"So devoted a surgeon," said Father Brown, "that he had surgical instruments with him when he went to call on the young lady at tea-time. For he must have used a lance or something, and he never seems to have gone home."

Fiennes sprang to his feet and looked at him in a heat of inquiry. "You suggest he might have used the very same lancet—"

Father Brown shook his head. "All these suggestions are fancies just now," he said. "The problem is not who did it or what did it, but how it was done. We might find many men and even many tools—pins and shears and lancets. But how did a man get into the room? How did even a pin get into it?"

He was staring reflectively at the ceiling as he spoke, but as he said the last words his eye cocked in an alert fashion as if he had suddenly seen a curious fly on the ceiling.

"Well, what would you do about it?" asked the young man. "You have a lot of experience, what would you advise now?"

"I'm afraid I'm not much use," said Father Brown with a sigh. "I can't suggest very much without having ever been near the place or the people. For the moment you can only go on with local inquiries. I gather that your friend from the Indian police is more or less in charge of your inquiry down there. I should run down and see how he is getting on. See what he's been doing in the way of amateur detection. There may be news already."

As his guests, the biped and the quadruped, disappeared, Father Brown took up his pen and went back to his interrupted occupation of planning a course of lectures on the Encyclical *Rerum Novarum*. The subject was a large one and he had to recast it more than once, so that he was somewhat similarly employed some two days later when the big black dog again came bounding into the room and sprawled all over him with enthusiasm and excitement. The master who followed the dog shared the excitement if not the enthusiasm. He had been excited in a less pleasant fashion, for his blue eyes seemed to start from his head and his eager face was even a little pale.

"You told me," he said abruptly and without preface, "to find out what Harry Druce was doing. Do you know what he's done?"

The priest did not reply, and the young man went on in jerky tones:

"I'll tell you what he's done. He's killed himself."

Father Brown's lips moved only faintly, and there was nothing practical about what he was saying—nothing that has anything to do with this story or this world.

"You give me the creeps sometimes," said Fiennes. "Did you —did you expect this?"

"I thought it possible," said Father Brown; "that was why I asked you to go and see what he was doing. I hoped you might not be too late."

"It was I who found him," said Fiennes rather huskily. "It was the ugliest and most uncanny thing I ever knew. I went down that old garden again and I knew there was something new and unnatural about it besides the murder. The flowers still tossed about in blue masses on each side of the black entrance into the old gray summer-house; but to me the blue flowers looked like blue devils dancing before some dark cavern of the underworld. I looked all round; everything seemed to be in its ordinary place. But the queer notion grew on me that there was something wrong with the very shape of the sky. And then I saw what it was. The Rock of Fortune always rose in the background beyond the garden hedge and against the sea. And the Rock of Fortune was gone."

Father Brown had lifted his head and was listening intently.

"It was as if a mountain had walked away out of a landscape or a moon fallen from the sky; though I knew, of course, that a touch at any time would have tipped the thing over. Something possessed me and I rushed down that garden path like the wind and went crashing through that hedge as if it were a spider's web. It was a thin hedge really, though its undisturbed trimness had made it serve all the purposes of a wall. On the shore I found the loose rock fallen from its pedestal; and poor Harry Druce lay like a wreck underneath it. One arm was thrown round it in a sort of embrace as if he had pulled it down on himself; and on the broad brown sands beside it, in large crazy lettering he had scrawled the words, 'The Rock of Fortune falls on the Fool.'"

"It was the Colonel's will that did that," observed Father Brown. "The young man had staked everything on profiting himself by Donald's disgrace, especially when his uncle sent for him on the same day as the lawyer, and welcomed him with so much warmth. Otherwise he was done; he'd lost his police job; he was beggared at Monte Carlo. And he killed himself when he found he'd killed his kinsman for nothing."

"Here, stop a minute!" cried the staring Fiennes. "You're going too fast for me."

"Talking about the will, by the way," continued Father Brown calmly, "before I forget it, or we go on to bigger things, there was a simple explanation, I think, of all that business about the doctor's name. I rather fancy I have heard both names before somewhere. The doctor is really a French nobleman with the title of the Marquis de Villon. But he is also an ardent Republican and has abandoned his title and fallen back on the forgotten family surname. 'With your Citizen Riquetti you have puzzled Europe for ten days.' "

"What is that?" asked the young man blankly.

"Never mind," said the priest. "Nine times out of ten it is a rascally thing to change one's name; but this was a piece of fine fanaticism. That's the point of his sarcasm about Americans having no names—that is, no titles. Now in England the Marquis of Hartington is never called Mr. Hartington; but in France the Marquis de Villon is called M. de Villon. So it might well look like a change of name. As for the talk about killing, I fancy that also was a point of French etiquette. The doctor was talking about challenging Floyd to a duel, and the girl was trying to dissuade him."

"Oh, I *see*," cried Fiennes slowly. "Now I understand what she meant."

"And what is that about?" asked his companion smiling.

"Well," said the young man, "it was something that happened to me just before I found that poor fellow's body; only the catastrophe drove it out of my head. I suppose it's hard to remember a little romantic idyll when you've just come on top of a tragedy. But as I went down the lanes leading to the Colonel's old place, I met his daughter walking with Dr. Valentine. She was in mourning of course, and he always wore black as if he were going to a funeral; but I can't say that their faces were very funereal. Never have I seen two people looking in their own way more respectably radiant and cheerful. They stopped and saluted me and then she told me they were married and living in a little house on the outskirts of the town, where the doctor was continuing his practice. This rather surprised me, because I knew that her old father's will had left her his property; and I hinted at it delicately by saying I was going along to her father's old place and had half expected to meet her there. But she only laughed and said, 'Oh, we've given up all that. My husband doesn't like heiresses.' And I discovered with some astonishment they really had insisted on restoring the property to poor Donald; so I hope he's had a healthy shock and will treat it sensibly. There was never much really the matter with him; he was very young and his father was not very wise. But it was in connection with that that she said something I didn't understand at the time; but now I'm sure it must be as you say. She said with a sort of sudden and splendid arrogance that was entirely altruistic:

" 'I hope it'll stop that red-haired fool from fussing any more about the will. Does he think my husband, who has given up a crest and a coronet as old as the Crusades for his principles, would kill an old man in a summer-house for a legacy like that?' Then she laughed again and said, 'My husband isn't killing anybody except in the way of business. Why, he didn't even ask his friends to call on the secretary.' Now, of course, I see what she meant."

"I see part of what she meant, of course," said Father Brown. "What did she mean exactly by the secretary fussing about the will?"

Fiennes smiled as he answered: "I wish you knew the secretary, Father Brown. It would be a joy to you to watch him make things hum, as he calls it. He made the house of mourning hum. He filled the funeral with all the snap and zip of the brightest sporting event. There was no holding him, after something had really happened. I've told you how he used to oversee the gardener as he did the garden, and how he instructed the lawyer in the law. Needless to say, he also instructed the surgeon in the practice of surgery; and as the surgeon was Dr. Valentine, you may be sure it ended in accusing him of something worse than bad surgery. The secretary got it fixed in his red head that the doctor had committed the crime; and when the police arrived he was perfectly sublime. Need I say that he became on the spot the greatest of all amateur detectives? Sherlock Holmes never towered over Scotland Yard with more Titanic intellectual pride and scorn than Colonel Druce's private secretary over the police investigating Colonel Druce's death. I tell you it was a joy to see him. He strode about with an abstracted air, tossing his scarlet crest of hair and giving curt impatient replies. Of course it was his demeanour during these days that made Druce's daughter so wild with him. Of course he had a theory. It's just the sort of theory a man would have in a book; and Floyd is the sort of man who ought to be in a book. He'd be better fun and less bother in a book."

"What was his theory?" asked the other.

"Oh, it was full of pep," replied Fiennes gloomily. "It would have been glorious copy if it could have held together for ten minutes longer. He said the Colonel was still alive when they found him in the summer-house and the doctor killed him with the surgical instrument on pretence of cutting the clothes."

"I see," said the priest. "I suppose he was lying flat on his face on the mud floor as a form of siesta."

"It's wonderful what hustle will do," continued his informant. "I believe Floyd would have got his great theory into the papers at any rate, and perhaps had the doctor arrested, when all these things were blown sky high as if by dynamite by the discovery of that dead body lying under the Rock of Fortune. And that's what we come back to after all. I suppose the suicide is almost a confession. But nobody will ever know the whole story."

There was a silence, and then the priest said modestly, "I rather think I know the whole story."

Fiennes stared. "But look here," he cried, "how do you come to know the whole story, or to be sure it's the true story? You've been sitting here a hundred miles away writing a sermon; do you mean to tell me you really know what happened already? If you've really come to the end, where in the world do you begin? What started you off with your own story?"

Father Brown jumped up with a very unusual excitement and his first exclamation was like an explosion.

"The dog!" he cried. "The dog, of course! You had the whole story in your hands in the business of the dog on the beach, if you'd only noticed the dog properly."

Fiennes stared still more. "But you told me just now that my feelings about the dog were all nonsense, and the dog had nothing to do with it."

"The dog had everything to do with it," said Father Brown, "as you'd have found out, if you'd only treated the dog as a dog and not as God Almighty, judging the souls of men."

He paused in an embarrassed way for a moment, and then said, with a rather pathetic air of apology:

"The truth is, I happen to be awfully fond of dogs. And it seemed to me that in all this lurid halo of dog superstitions nobody was really thinking about the poor dog at all. To begin with a small point, about his barking at the lawyer or growling at the secretary. You asked how I could guess things a hundred miles away; but honestly it's mostly to your credit, for you described people so well that I know the types. A man like Traill who frowns usually and smiles suddenly, a man who fiddles with things, especially at his throat, is a nervous, easily embarrassed man. I shouldn't wonder if Floyd, the efficient secretary, is nervy and jumpy too; those Yankee hustlers often are. Otherwise he wouldn't have cut his fingers on the shears and dropped them when he heard Janet Druce scream.

"Now dogs hate nervous people. I don't know whether they make the dog nervous too; or whether, being after all a brute, he is a bit of a bully; or whether his canine vanity (which is colossal) is simply offended at not being liked. But anyhow there was nothing in poor Nox protesting against those people, except that he disliked them for being afraid of him. Now I know you're awfully clever, and nobody of sense sneers at cleverness. But I sometimes fancy, for instance, that you are too clever to understand animals. Sometimes you are too clever to understand men, especially when they act almost as simply as animals. Animals are very literal; they live in a world of truisms. Take this case; a dog barks at a man and a man runs away from a dog. Now you do not seem to be quite simple enough to see the fact;

that the dog barked because he disliked the man and the man fled because he was frightened of the dog. They had no other motives and they needed none. But you must read psychological mysteries into it and suppose the dog had super-normal vision, and was a mysterious mouthpiece of doom. You must suppose the man was running away, not from the dog but from the hangman. And yet, if you come to think of it, all this deeper psychology is exceedingly improbable. If the dog really could completely and consciously realize the murderer of his master, he wouldn't stand yapping as he might at a curate at a tea-party; he's much more likely to fly at his throat. And on the other hand, do you really think a man who had hardened his heart to murder an old friend and then walk about smiling at the old friend's family, under the eyes of his old friend's daughter and post-mortem doctor—do you think a man like that would be doubled up by mere remorse because a dog barked? He might feel the tragic irony of it; it might shake his soul, like any other tragic trifle. But he wouldn't rush madly the length of a garden to escape from the only witness whom he knew to be unable to talk. People have a panic like that when they are frightened, not of tragic ironies, but of teeth. The whole thing is simpler than you can understand. But when we come to that business by the seashore, things are much more interesting. As you stated them, they were much more puzzling. I didn't understand that tale of the dog going in and out of the water; it didn't seem to me a doggy thing to do. If Nox had been very much upset about something else, he might possibly have refused to go after the stick at all. He'd probably go off nosing in whatever direction he suspected the mischief. But when once a dog is actually chasing a thing, a stone or a stick or a rabbit, my experience is that he won't stop for anything but the most peremptory command, and not always for that. That he should turn round because his mood changed seems to me unthinkable."

"But he did turn round," insisted Fiennes, "and came back without the stick."

"He came back without the stick for the best reason in the world," replied the priest. "He came back because he couldn't find it. He whined because he couldn't find it. That's the sort of thing a dog really does whine about. A dog is a devil of a ritualist. He is as particular about the precise routine of a game as a child about the precise repetition of a fairy-tale. In this case something had gone wrong with the game. He came back to complain seriously of the conduct of the stick. Never had such a thing happened before. Never had an eminent and distinguished dog been so treated by a rotten old walking-stick."

"Why, what had the walking-stick done?" inquired the young man.

"It had sunk," said Father Brown.

Fiennes said nothing, but continued to stare, and it was the priest who continued:

"It had sunk because it was not really a stick, but a rod of steel with a very thin shell of cane and a sharp point. In other words, it was a sword-stick. I suppose a murderer never got rid of a bloody weapon so oddly and yet so naturally as by throwing it into the sea for a retriever."

"I begin to see what you mean," admitted Fiennes; "but even if a sword-stick was used, I have no guess of how it was used."

"I had a sort of guess," said Father Brown, "right at the beginning when you said the word summer-house. And another when you said that Druce wore a white coat. As long as everybody was looking for a short dagger, nobody thought of it; but if we admit a rather long blade like a rapier, it's not so impossible."

He was leaning back, looking at the ceiling, and began like one going back to his own first thoughts and fundamentals.

"All that discussion about detective stories like the Yellow Room, about a man found dead in sealed chambers which no one could enter, does not apply to the present case, because it is a summer-house. When we talk of a Yellow Room, or any room, we imply walls that are really homogeneous and impenetrable.

But a summer-house is not made like that; it is often made, as it was in this case, of closely interlaced but still separate boughs and strips of wood, in which there are chinks here and there. There was one of them just behind Druce's back as he sat in his chair up against the wall. But just as the room was a summer-house, so the chair was a basket-chair. That also was a lattice of loopholes. Lastly, the summer-house was close up under the hedge; and you have just told me that it was really a thin hedge. A man standing outside it could easily see, amid a network of twigs and branches and canes, one white spot of the Colonel's coat as plain as the white of a target.

"Now, you left the geography a little vague; but it was possible to put two and two together. You said the Rock of Fortune was not really high; but you also said it could be seen dominating the garden like a mountain-peak. In other words, it was very near the end of the garden, though your walk had taken you a long way round to it. Also, it isn't likely the young lady really howled so as to be heard half a mile. She gave an ordinary involuntary cry, and yet you heard it on the shore. And among other interesting things that you told me, may I remind you that you said Harry Druce had fallen behind to light his pipe under a hedge."

Fiennes shuddered slightly. "You mean he drew his blade there and sent it through the hedge at the white spot. But surely it was a very odd chance and a very sudden choice. Besides, he couldn't be certain the old man's money had passed to him, and as a fact it hadn't."

Father Brown's face became animated.

"You misunderstand the man's character," he said, as if he himself had known the man all his life. "A curious but not unknown type of character. If he had really *known* the money would come to him, I seriously believe he wouldn't have done it. He would have seen it as the dirty thing it was."

"Isn't that rather paradoxical?" asked the other.

"This man was a gambler," said the priest, "and a man in dis-

grace for having taken risks and anticipated orders. It was probably for something pretty unscrupulous, for every imperial police
is more like a Russian secret police than we like to think. But
he had gone beyond the line and failed. Now, the temptation of
that type of man is to do a mad thing precisely because the risk
will be wonderful in retrospect. He wants to say, 'Nobody but
I could have seized that chance or seen that it was then or never.
What a wild and wonderful guess it was, when I put all those
things together; Donald in disgrace; and the lawyer being sent
for; and Herbert and I sent for at the same time—and then nothing more but the way the old man grinned at me and shook
hands. Anybody would say I was mad to risk it; but that is how
fortunes are made, by the man mad enough to have a little foresight.' In short, it is the vanity of guessing. It is the megalomania
of the gambler. The more incongruous the coincidence, the more
instantaneous the decision, the more likely he is to snatch the
chance. The accident, the very triviality, of the white speck and
the hole in the hedge intoxicated him like a vision of the world's
desire. Nobody clever enough to see such a combination of accidents could be cowardly enough not to use them! That is how
the devil talks to the gambler. But the devil himself would hardly
had induced that unhappy man to go down in a dull, deliberate
way and kill an old uncle from whom he'd always had expecta-
tions. It would be too respectable."

He paused a moment; and then went on with a certain quiet
emphasis.

"And now try to call up the scene, even as you saw it yourself. As he stood there, dizzy with his diabolical opportunity, he
looked up and saw that strange outline that might have been the
image of his own tottering soul—the one great crag poised peri-
lously on the other like a pyramid on its point—and remembered
that it was called the Rock of Fortune. Can you guess how
such a man at such a moment would read such a signal? I think it
strung him up to action and even to vigilance. He who would be
a tower must not fear to be a toppling tower. Anyhow he acted;

his next difficulty was to cover his tracks. To be found with a sword-stick, let alone a blood-stained sword-stick, would be fatal in the search that was certain to follow. If he left it anywhere, it would be found and probably traced. Even if he threw it into the sea the action might be noticed, and thought noticeable—unless indeed he could think of some more natural way of covering the action. As you know, he did think of one, and a very good one. Being the only one of you with a watch, he told you it was not yet time to return, strolled a little farther and started the game of throwing in sticks for the retriever. But how his eyes must have rolled darkly over all that desolate seashore before they alighted on the dog!"

Fiennes nodded, gazing thoughtfully into space. His mind seemed to have drifted back to a less practical part of the narrative.

"It's queer," he said, "that the dog really was in the story after all."

"The dog could almost have told you the story, if he could talk," said the priest. "All I complain of is that because he couldn't talk, you made up his story for him, and made him talk with the tongues of men and angels. It's part of something I've noticed more and more in the modern world, appearing in all sorts of newspaper rumours and conversational catchwords; something that's arbitrary without being authoritative. People readily swallow the untested claims of this, that, or the other. It's drowning all your old rationalism and scepticism, it's coming in like a sea; and the name of it is superstition." He stood up abruptly, his face heavy with a sort of frown, and went on talking almost as if he were alone. "It's the first effect of not believing in God that you lose your common sense, and can't see things as they are. Anything that anybody talks about, and says there's a good deal in it, extends itself indefinitely like a vista in a nightmare. And a dog is an omen and a cat is a mystery and a pig is a mascot and a beetle is a scarab, calling up all the menagerie of polytheism from Egypt and old India; Dog Anubis and great green-eyed Pasht and all the holy howling Bulls of Bashan; reeling back to the bestial gods of the beginning, escaping into elephants and snakes and crocodiles; and all because you are frightened of four words: 'He was made Man.' "

The young man got up with a little embarrassment, almost as if he had overheard a soliloquy. He called to the dog and left the room with vague but breezy farewells. But he had to call the dog twice, for the dog had remained behind quite motionless for a moment, looking up steadily at Father Brown as the wolf looked at St. Francis.

THE QUEER FEET

If you meet a member of that select club, "The Twelve True Fishermen," entering the Vernon Hotel for the annual club dinner, you will observe, as he takes off his overcoat, that his evening coat is green and not black. If (supposing that you have the star-defying audacity to address such a being) you ask him why, he will probably answer that he does it to avoid being mistaken for a waiter. You will then retire crushed. But you will leave behind you a mystery as yet unsolved and a tale worth telling.

If (to pursue the same vein of improbable conjecture) you were to a meet a mild, hard-working little priest, named Father Brown, and were to ask him what he thought was the most singular luck of his life, he would probably reply that upon the whole his best stroke was at the Vernon Hotel, where he had averted a crime and, perhaps, saved a soul, merely by listening to a few footsteps in a passage. He is perhaps a little proud of this wild and wonderful guess of his, and it is possible that he might refer to it. But since it is immeasurably unlikely that you will ever rise high enough in the social world to find "The Twelve True Fishermen," or that you will ever sink low enough among slums and criminals to find Father Brown, I fear you will never hear the story at all unless you hear it from me.

The Vernon Hotel at which The Twelve True Fishermen held their annual dinners was an institution such as can only exist in an oligarchical society which has almost gone mad on good manners. It was that topsy-turvy product—an "exclusive" commercial enterprise. That is, it was a thing which paid not by attracting people, but actually by turning people away. In the heart of a plutocracy tradesmen become cunning enough to be more fastidious than their customers. They positively create difficulties so that their wealthy and weary clients may spend money and diplomacy in overcoming them. If there were a fashionable hotel in London which no man could enter who was under six foot, society would meekly make up parties of six-foot men to dine in it. If there were an expensive restaurant which by a mere caprice of its proprietor was only open on Thursday afternoon, it would be crowded on Thursday afternoon. The Vernon Hotel stood, as if by accident, in the corner of a square in Belgravia. It was a small hotel; and a very inconvenient one. But its very inconveniences were considered as walls protecting a particular class. One inconvenience, in particular, was held to be of vital importance: the fact that practically only twenty-four people could dine in the place at once. The only big dinner table was the celebrated terrace table, which stood open to the air on a sort of veranda overlooking one of the most exquisite old gardens in London. Thus it happened that even the twenty-four seats at this table could only be enjoyed in warm weather; and this making the enjoyment yet more difficult made it yet more desired. The existing owner of the hotel was a Jew named Lever; and he made nearly a million out of it, by making it difficult to get into. Of course he combined with this limitation in the scope of his enterprise the most careful polish in its performance. The wines and cooking were really as good as any in Europe, and the demeanour of the attendants exactly mirrored the fixed mood of the English upper class. The proprietor knew all his waiters like the fingers on his hand; there were only fifteen of them all told. It was much easier to become a Member of Parliament than to become a waiter in that hotel. Each waiter was trained in terrible silence and smoothness, as if he were a gentleman's servant. And, indeed, there was generally at least one waiter to every gentleman who dined.

The club of the Twelve True Fishermen would not have consented to dine anywhere but in such a place, for it insisted on a luxurious privacy; and would have been quite upset by the mere thought that any other club was even dining in the same building. On the occasion of their annual dinner the Fishermen were in the habit of exposing all their treasures, as if they were in a private house, especially the celebrated set of fish knives and forks which were, as it were, the insignia of the society, each being exquisitely wrought in silver in the form of a fish, and each loaded at the hilt with one large pearl. These were always laid out for the fish course, and the fish course was always the most magnificent in that magnificent repast. The society had a vast number of ceremonies and observances, but it had no history and no object; that was where it was so very aristocratic. You did not have to be anything in order to be one of the Twelve Fishers; unless you were already a certain sort of person, you never even heard of them. It had been in existence twelve years. Its president was Mr. Audley. Its vice-president was the Duke of Chester.

If I have in any degree conveyed the atmosphere of this appalling hotel, the reader may feel a natural wonder as to how I came to know anything about it, and may even speculate as to how so ordinary a person as my friend Father Brown came to find himself in that golden galley. As far as that is concerned, my story is simple, or even vulgar. There is in the world a very aged rioter and demagogue who breaks into the most refined retreats with the dreadful information that all men are brothers, and wherever this leveller went on his pale horse it was Father Brown's trade to follow. One of the waiters, an Italian, had been struck down with a paralytic stroke that afternoon; and his Jewish employer, marvelling mildly at such superstitions, had consented to send for the nearest Popish priest. With what the waiter confessed to Father Brown we are not concerned, for the excellent reason that that cleric kept it to himself; but apparently it involved him in writing out a note or statement for the conveying of some message or the righting of some wrong. Father Brown, therefore, with a meek impudence which he would have shown equally in Buckingham Palace, asked to be provided with a room and writing materials. Mr. Lever was torn in two. He was a kind man, and had also that bad imitation of kindness, the dislike of any difficulty or scene. At the same time the presence of one unusual stranger in his hotel that evening was like a speck of dirt on something just cleaned. There was never any borderland or anteroom in the Vernon Hotel, no people waiting in the hall, no customers coming in on chance. There were fifteen waiters. There were twelve guests. It would be as startling to find a new guest in the hotel that night as to find a new brother taking breakfast or tea in one's own family. Moreover, the priest's appearance was second-rate and his clothes muddy; a mere glimpse of him afar off might precipitate a crisis in the club. Mr. Lever at last hit on a plan to cover, since he might not obliterate, the disgrace. When you enter (as you never will) the Vernon Hotel, you pass down a short passage decorated with a few dingy but important pictures, and come to the main vestibule and lounge which opens on your right into passages leading to the public rooms, and on your left to a similar passage pointing to the kitchens and offices of the hotel. Immediately on your left hand is the corner of a glass office, which abuts upon the lounge—a house within a house, so to speak, like the old hotel bar which probably once occupied its place.

In this office sat the representative of the proprietor (nobody in this place ever appeared in person if he could help it), and just beyond the office, on the way to the servants' quarters, was the gentlemen's cloak room, the last boundary of the gentlemen's domain. But between the office and the cloak room was a small private room without other outlet, sometimes used by the proprietor for delicate and important matters such as lending a duke a thousand pounds or declining to lend him sixpence. It is a mark of the magnificent tolerance of Mr. Lever that he permitted this holy place to be for about half an hour profaned by a mere priest, scribbling away on a piece of paper. The story which Father Brown was writing down was very likely a much better story than this one, only it will never be known. I can merely state that it was very nearly as long, and that the last two or three paragraphs of it were the least exciting and absorbing.

For it was by the time that he had reached these that the priest began a little to allow his thoughts to wander and his animal

senses, which were commonly keen, to awaken. The time of
darkness and dinner was drawing on; his own forgotten little
room was without a light, and perhaps the gathering gloom, as
occasionally happens, sharpened the sense of sound. As Father
Brown wrote the last and least essential part of his document, he
caught himself writing to the rhythm of a recurrent noise outside, just as one sometimes thinks to the tune of a railway train.
When he became conscious of the thing he found what it was:
only the ordinary patter of feet passing the door, which in an
hotel was no very unlikely matter. Nevertheless, he stared at the
darkened ceiling, and listened to the sound. After he had listened for a few seconds dreamily, he got to his feet and listened
intently, with his head a little on one side. Then he sat down
again and buried his brow in his hands, now not merely listening
but listening and thinking also.

The footsteps outside at any given moment were such as one
might hear in any hotel; and yet, taken as a whole, there was
something very strange about them. There were no other footsteps. It was always a very silent house, for the few familiar
guests went at once to their own apartments, and the well-
trained waiters were told to be almost invisible until they were
wanted. One could not conceive any place where there was less
reason to apprehend anything irregular. But these footsteps were
so odd that one could not decide to call them regular or irregular. Father Brown followed them with his finger on the edge of
the table, like a man trying to learn a tune on the piano.

First, there came a long rush of rapid little steps, such as a light
man might make in winning a walking race. At a certain point
they stopped and changed to a sort of slow, swinging stamp,
numbering not a quarter of the steps, but occupying about the
same time. The moment the last echoing stamp had died away
would come again the run or ripple of light, hurrying feet, and
then again the thud of the heavier walking. It was certainly the
same pair of boots, partly because (as has been said) there were
no other boots about, and partly because they had a small but

unmistakable creak in them. Father Brown had the kind of head that cannot help asking questions; and on this apparently trivial question his head almost split. He had seen men run in order to jump. He had seen men run in order to slide. But why on earth should a man run in order to walk? Or, again, why should he walk in order to run? Yet no other description would cover the antics of this invisible pair of legs. The man was either walking very fast down one half of the corridor in order to walk very slow down the other half; or he was walking very slow at one end to have the rapture of walking fast at the other. Neither suggestion seemed to make much sense. His brain was growing darker and darker, like his room.

Yet, as he began to think steadily, the very blackness of his cell seemed to make his thoughts more vivid; he began to see as in a kind of vision the fantastic feet capering along the corridor in unnatural or symbolic attitudes. Was it a heathen religious dance? Or some entirely new kind of scientific exercise? Father Brown began to ask himself with more exactness what the steps suggested. Taking the slow step first: it certainly was not the step of the proprietor. Men of his type walk with a rapid waddle, or they sit still. It could not be any servant or messenger waiting for directions. It did not sound like it. The poorer orders (in an oligarchy) sometimes lurch about when they are slightly drunk, but generally, and especially in such gorgeous scenes, they stand or sit in constrained attitudes. No; that heavy yet springy step, with a kind of careless emphasis, not specially noisy, yet not caring what noise it made, belonged to only one of the animals of this earth. It was a gentleman of western Europe, and probably one who had never worked for his living.

Just as he came to this solid certainty, the step changed to the quicker one, and ran past the door as feverishly as a rat. The listener remarked that though this step was much swifter it was also much more noiseless, almost as if the man were walking on tiptoe. Yet it was not associated in his mind with secrecy, but with something else—something that he could not remember. He was maddened by one of those half-memories that make a man feel half-witted. Surely he had heard that strange, swift walking somewhere. Suddenly he sprang to his feet with a new idea in his head, and walked to the door. His room had no direct outlet on the passage, but let on one side into the glass office, and on the other into the cloak room beyond. He tried the door into the office, and found it locked. Then he looked at the window, now a square pane full of purple cloud cleft by livid sunset, and for an instant he smelt evil as a dog smells rats.

The rational part of him (whether the wiser or not) regained its supremacy. He remembered that the proprietor had told him that he should lock the door, and would come later to release him. He told himself that twenty things he had not thought of might explain the eccentric sounds outside; he reminded himself that there was just enough light left to finish his own proper work. Bringing his paper to the window so as to catch the last stormy evening light, he resolutely plunged once more into the almost completed record. He had written for about twenty minutes, bending closer and closer to his paper in the lessening light; then suddenly he sat upright. He had heard the strange feet once more.

This time they had a third oddity. Previously the unknown man had walked, with levity indeed and lightning quickness, but he had walked. This time he ran. One could hear the swift, soft, bounding steps coming along the corridor, like the pads of a fleeing and leaping panther. Whoever was coming was a very strong, active man, in still yet tearing excitement. Yet, when the sound had swept up to the office like a sort of whispering whirlwind, it suddenly changed again to the old slow, swaggering stamp.

Father Brown flung down his paper, and, knowing the office door to be locked, went at once into the cloak room on the other side. The attendant of this place was temporarily absent, probably because the only guests were at dinner and his office was a sinecure. After groping through a grey forest of overcoats, he found that the dim cloak room opened on the lighted corridor in the form of a sort of counter of half-door, like most of the counters across which we have all handed umbrellas and received tickets. There was a light immediately above the semicircular arch of this opening. It threw little illumination on Father Brown himself, who seemed a mere dark outline against the dim sunset window behind him. But it threw an almost theatrical light on the man who stood outside the cloak room in the corridor.

He was an elegant man in very plain evening dress; tall, but with an air of not taking up much room; one felt that he could have slid along like a shadow where many smaller men would have been obvious and obstructive. His face, now flung back in the lamplight, was swarthy and vivacious, the face of a foreigner. His figure was good, his manners good humoured and confident; a critic could only say that his black coat was a shade below his figure and manners, and even bulged and bagged in an odd way. The moment he caught sight of Brown's black silhouette against the sunset, he tossed down a scrap of paper with a number and called out with amiable authority: "I want my hat and coat, please; I find I have to go away at once."

Father Brown took the paper without a word, and obediently went to look for the coat; it was not the first menial work he had done in his life. He brought it and laid it on the counter; meanwhile, the strange gentleman who had been feeling in his waist-coat pocket, said laughing: "I haven't got any silver; you can keep this." And he threw down half a sovereign, and caught up his coat.

Father Brown's figure remained quite dark and still; but in that instant he had lost his head. His head was always most valuable when he had lost it. In such moments he put two and two together and made four million. Often the Catholic Church (which is wedded to common sense) did not approve of it. Often he did not approve of it himself. But it was real inspiration—important at rare crises—when whosoever shall lose his head the same shall save it.

"I think, sir," he said civilly, "that you have some silver in your pocket."

The tall gentleman stared. "Hang it," he cried, "if I choose to give you gold, why should you complain?"

"Because silver is sometimes more valuable than gold," said the priest mildly; "that is, in large quantities."

The stranger looked at him curiously. Then he looked still more curiously up the passage towards the main entrance. Then he looked back at Brown again, and then he looked very carefully at the window beyond Brown's head, still coloured with the after-glow of the storm. Then he seemed to make up his mind. He put one hand on the counter, vaulted over as easily as an acrobat and towered above the priest, putting one tremendous hand upon his collar.

"Stand still," he said, in a hacking whisper. "I don't want to threaten you, but—"

"I do want to threaten you," said Father Brown, in a voice like a rolling drum, "I want to threaten you with the worm that dieth not, and the fire that is not quenched."

"You're a rum sort of cloak-room clerk," said the other.

"I am a priest, Monsieur Flambeau," said Brown, "and I am ready to hear your confession."

The other stood gasping for a few moments, and then staggered back into a chair.

The first two courses of the dinner of the Twelve True Fishermen had proceeded with placid success. I do not possess a copy of the menu; and if I did it would not convey anything to anybody. It was written in a sort of super-French employed by cooks, but quite unintelligible to Frenchmen. There was a tradition in the club that the *hors d'œuvres* should be various and manifold to the point of madness. They were taken seriously because they were avowedly useless extras, like the whole dinner and the whole club. There was also a tradition that the soup course should be light and unpretending—a sort of simple and austere vigil for the feast of fish that was to come. The talk was that strange, slight talk which governs the British Empire, which governs it in secret, and yet would scarcely enlighten an ordinary Englishman even if he could overhear it. Cabinet ministers on both sides were alluded to by their Christian names with a sort of bored benignity. The Radical Chancellor of the Exchequer, whom the whole Tory party was supposed to be cursing for his extortions, was praised for his minor poetry, or his saddle in the hunting field. The Tory leader, whom all Liberals were supposed to hate as a tyrant, was discussed and, on the whole, praised—as a Liberal. It seemed somehow that politicians were very important. And yet, anything seemed important about them except their politics. Mr. Audley, the chairman, was an amiable, elderly man who still wore Gladstone collars; he was a kind of symbol of all that phantasmal and yet fixed society. He had never done anything—not even anything wrong. He was not fast; he was not even particularly rich. He was simply in the thing; and there was an end of it. No party could ignore him, and if he had wished to be in the Cabinet he certainly would have been put there. The Duke of Chester, the vice-president, was a young and rising politician. That is to say, he was a pleasant youth, with flat, fair hair and a freckled face, with moderate intelligence and enormous estates. In public his appearances were always successful and his principle was simple enough. When he thought of a joke he made it, and was called brilliant. When he could not think of a joke he said that this was no time for trifling, and was called able. In private, in a club of his own class, he was simply quite pleasantly frank and silly, like a schoolboy. Mr. Audley, never having been in politics, treated them a little more seriously. Sometimes he even embarrassed the company by phrases suggesting that there was some difference between a Liberal and a Conservative. He himself was a Conservative, even in private life. He had a roll of grey hair over the back of his collar, like certain old-fashioned statesmen, and seen from behind he looked like the man the empire wants. Seen from the front he looked like a mild, self-indulgent bachelor, with rooms in the Albany—which he was.

As has been remarked, there were twenty-four seats at the terrace table, and only twelve members of the club. Thus they could occupy the terrace in the most luxurious style of all, being ranged along the inner side of the table, with no one opposite, commanding an uninterrupted view of the garden, the colours of which were still vivid, though evening was closing in somewhat luridly for the time of year. The chairman sat in the centre of the line, and the vice-president at the right-hand end of it. When the twelve guests first trooped into their seats it was the custom (for some unknown reason) for all the fifteen waiters to stand lining the wall like troops presenting arms to the king, while the fat proprietor stood and bowed to the club with radiant surprise, as if he had never heard of them before. But before the first chink of knife and fork this army of retainers had vanished, only the one or two required to collect and distribute the plates darting about in deathly silence. Mr. Lever, the proprietor, of course had disappeared in convulsions of courtesy long before. It would be exaggerative, indeed irreverent, to say that he ever positively appeared again. But when the important course, the fish course, was being brought on, there was—how shall I put it?—a vivid shadow, a projection of his personality, which told that he was hovering near. The sacred fish course consisted (to the eyes of the vulgar) in a sort of monstrous pudding, about the size and shape of a wedding cake, in which some considerable number of interesting fishes had finally lost the shapes which God had given to them. The Twelve True Fishermen took up their celebrated fish knives and fish forks, and approached it as gravely as if every inch of the pudding cost as much as the silver fork it was eaten with. So it did, for all I know. This course was dealt with in eager and devouring silence; and it was only when his plate was nearly empty that the young duke made the ritual remark: "They can't do this anywhere but here."

"Nowhere," said Mr. Audley, in a deep bass voice, turning to the speaker and nodding his venerable head a number of times. "Nowhere, assuredly, except here. It was represented to me that at the Café Anglais—"

Here he was interrupted and even agitated for a moment by the removal of his plate, but he recaptured the valuable thread of his thoughts. "It was represented to me that the same could be done at the Café Anglais. Nothing like it, sir," he said, shaking his head ruthlessly, like a hanging judge. "Nothing like it."

"Overrated place," said a certain Colonel Pound, speaking (by the look of him) for the first time for some months.

"Oh, I don't know," said the Duke of Chester, who was an optimist, "it's jolly good for some things. You can't beat it at—"

A waiter came swiftly along the room, and then stopped dead. His stoppage was as silent as his tread; but all those vague and kindly gentlemen were so used to the utter smoothness of the unseen machinery which surrounded and supported their lives, that a waiter doing anything unexpected was a start and a jar. They felt as you and I would feel if the inanimate world disobeyed—if a chair ran away from us.

The waiter stood staring a few seconds, while there deepened on every face at table a strange shame which is wholly the product of our time. It is the combination of modern humanitarianism with the horrible modern abyss between the souls of the rich and poor. A genuine historic aristocrat would have thrown things at the waiter, beginning with empty bottles, and very probably ending with money. A genuine democrat would have asked him, with a comrade-like clearness of speech, what the devil he was doing. But these modern plutocrats could not bear a poor man near to them, either as a slave or as a friend. That something had gone wrong with the servants were merely a dull, hot embarrassment. They did not want to be brutal, and they dreaded the need to be benevolent. They wanted the thing, whatever it was, to be over. It was over. The waiter, after standing for some seconds rigid, like a cataleptic, turned round and ran madly out of the room.

When he reappeared in the room, or rather in the doorway, it was in company with another waiter, with whom he whispered and gesticulated with southern fierceness. Then the first waiter went away, leaving the second waiter, and reappeared with a third waiter. By the time a fourth waiter had joined this hurried synod, Mr. Audley felt it necessary to break the silence in the interests of Tact. He used a very loud cough, instead of a presidential hammer, and said: "Splendid work young Moocher's doing in Burmah. Now, no other nation in the world could have—"

A fifth waiter had sped towards him like an arrow, and was whispering in his ear: "So sorry. Important! Might the proprietor speak to you?"

The chairman turned in disorder, and with a dazed stare saw Mr. Lever coming towards them with his lumbering quickness. The gait of the good proprietor was indeed his usual gait, but his face was by no means usual. Generally it was a genial copper-brown; now it was a sickly yellow.

"You will pardon me, Mr. Audley," he said, with asthmatic breathlessness. "I have great apprehensions. Your fish-plates, they are cleared away with the knife and fork on them!"

"Well, I hope so," said the chairman, with some warmth.

"You see him?" panted the excited hotel keeper; "you see the waiter who took them away? You know him?"

"Know the waiter?" answered Mr. Audley indignantly. "Certainly not!"

Mr. Lever opened his hands with a gesture of agony. "I never send him," he said. "I know not when or why he come. I send my waiter to take away the plates, and he find them already away."

Mr. Audley still looked rather too bewildered to be really the man the empire wants; none of the company could say anything except the man of wood—Colonel Pound—who seemed galvanised into an unnatural life. He rose rigidly from his chair, leaving all the rest sitting, screwed his eyeglass into his eye, and spoke in a raucous under-tone as if he had half-forgotten how to speak. "Do you mean," he said, "that somebody has stolen our silver fish service?"

The proprietor repeated the open-handed gesture with even greater helplessness; and in a flash all the men at the table were on their feet.

"Are all your waiters here?" demanded the colonel, in his low, harsh accent.

"Yes; they're all here. I noticed it myself," cried the young duke, pushing his boyish face into the inmost ring. "Always count 'em as I come in; they look so queer standing up against the wall."

"But surely one cannot exactly remember," began Mr. Audley, with heavy hesitation.

"I remember exactly, I tell you," cried the duke excitedly. "There never have been more than fifteen waiters at this place, and there were no more than fifteen to-night, I'll swear; no more and no less."

The proprietor turned upon him, quaking in a kind of palsy of surprise. "You say—you say," he stammered, "that you see all my fifteen waiters?"

"As usual," assented the duke. "What is the matter with that?"

"Nothing," said Lever, with a deepening accent, "only you did not. For one of zem is dead upstairs."

There was a shocking stillness for an instant in that room. It may be (so supernatural is the word death) that each of those idle men looked for a second at his soul, and saw it as a small dried pea. One of them—the duke, I think—even said with the idiotic kindness of wealth: "Is there anything we can do?"

"He has had a priest," said the Jew, not untouched.

Then, as to the clang of doom, they awoke to their own position. For a few weird seconds they had really felt as if the fifteenth waiter might be the ghost of the dead man upstairs. They had been dumb under that oppression, for ghosts were to them an embarrassment, like beggars. But the remembrance of the silver broke the spell of the miraculous; broke it abruptly and with a brutal reaction. The colonel flung over his chair and strode to the door. "If there was a fifteenth man here, friends," he said, "that fifteenth fellow was a thief. Down at once to the front and back doors and secure everything; then we'll talk. The twenty-four pearls of the club are worth recovering."

Mr. Audley seemed at first to hesitate about whether it was gentlemanly to be in such a hurry about anything; but, seeing the duke dash down the stairs with youthful energy, he followed with a more mature motion.

At the same instant a sixth waiter ran into the room, and declared that he had found the pile of fish plates on a sideboard, with no trace of the silver.

The crowd of diners and attendants that tumbled helter-skelter down the passages divided into two groups. Most of the Fishermen followed the proprietor to the front room to demand news of any exit. Colonel Pound, with the chairman, the vice-president, and one or two others darted down the corridor leading to the servants' quarters, as the more likely line of escape. As they did so they passed the dim alcove or cavern of the cloak room, and saw a short, black-coated figure, presumably an attendant, standing a little way back in the shadow of it.

"Hallo, there!" called out the duke. "Have you seen anyone pass?"

The short figure did not answer the question directly, but merely said: "Perhaps I have got what you are looking for, gentlemen."

They paused, wavering and wondering, while he quietly went to the back of the cloak room, and came back with both hands full of shining silver, which he laid out on the counter as calmly as a salesman. It took the form of a dozen quaintly shaped forks and knives.

"You—you—" began the colonel, quite thrown off his balance at last. Then he peered into the dim little room and saw two things: first, that the short, black-clad man was dressed like a clergyman; and, second, that the window of the room behind him was burst, as if someone had passed violently through.

"Valuable things to deposit in a cloak room, aren't they?" remarked the clergyman, with cheerful composure.

"Did—did you steal those things?" stammered Mr. Audley, with staring eyes.

"If I did," said the cleric pleasantly, "at least I am bringing them back again."

"But you didn't," said Colonel Pound, still staring at the broken window.

"To make a clean breast of it, I didn't," said the other, with some humour. And he seated himself quite gravely on a stool.

"But you know who did," said the colonel.

"I don't know his real name," said the priest placidly, "but I know something of his fighting weight, and a great deal about his spiritual difficulties. I formed the physical estimate when he was trying to throttle me, and the moral estimate when he repented."

"Oh, I say—repented!" cried young Chester, with a sort of crow of laughter.

Father Brown got to his feet, putting his hands behind him. "Odd, isn't it," he said, "that a thief and a vagabond should repent, when so many who are rich and secure remain hard and frivolous, and without fruit for God or man? But there, if you will excuse me, you trespass a little upon my province. If you doubt the penitence as a practical fact, there are your knives and forks. You are the Twelve True Fishers, and there are all your silver fish. But He has made me a fisher of men."

"Did you catch this man?" asked the colonel, frowning.

Father Brown looked him full in his frowning face. "Yes," he said, "I caught him, with an unseen hook and an invisible line which is long enough to let him wander to the ends of the world, and still to bring him back with a twitch upon the thread."

There was a long silence. All the other men present drifted away to carry the recovered silver to their comrades, or to consult the proprietor about the queer condition of affairs. But the grim-faced colonel still sat sideways on the counter, swinging his long, lank legs and biting his dark moustache.

At last he said quietly to the priest: "He must have been a clever fellow, but I think I know a cleverer."

"He was a clever fellow," answered the other, "but I am not quite sure of what other you mean."

"I mean you," said the colonel, with a short laugh. "I don't want to get the fellow jailed; make yourself easy about that. But I'd give a good many silver forks to know exactly how you fell into this affair, and how you got the stuff out of him. I reckon you're the most up-to-date devil of the present company."

Father Brown seemed rather to like the saturnine candour of the soldier. "Well," he said, smiling, "I mustn't tell you anything of the man's identity, or his own story, of course; but there's no particular reason why I shouldn't tell you of the mere outside facts which I found out for myself."

He hopped over the barrier with unexpected activity, and sat beside Colonel Pound, kicking his short legs like a little boy on a gate. He began to tell the story as easily as if he were telling it to an old friend by a Christmas fire.

"You see, colonel," he said, "I was shut up in that small room there doing some writing, when I heard a pair of feet in this passage doing a dance that was as queer as the dance of death. First came quick, funny little steps, like a man walking on tiptoe for a wager; then came slow, careless, creaking steps, as of a big man walking about with a cigar. But they were both made by the same feet, I swear, and they came in rotation; first the run and then the walk, and then the run again. I wondered at first idly and then wildly why a man should act these two parts at once. One walk I knew; it was just like yours, colonel. It was the walk of a well-fed gentleman waiting for something, who strolls about rather because he is physically alert than because he is mentally impatient. I knew that I knew the other walk, too, but I could not remember what it was. What wild creature had I met on my travels that tore along on tiptoe in that extraordinary style? Then I heard a clink of plates somewhere; and the answer stood up as plain as St. Peter's. It was the walk of a waiter—that walk with the body slanted forward, the eyes looking down, the ball of the toe spurning away the ground, the coat tails and napkin flying. Then I thought for a minute and a half more. And I believe I saw the manner of the crime, as clearly as if I were going to commit it."

Colonel Pound looked at him keenly, but the speaker's mild grey eyes were fixed upon the ceiling with almost empty wistfulness.

"A crime," he said slowly, "is like any other work of art. Don't look surprised; crimes are by no means the only works of art that come from an infernal workshop. But every work of art, divine or diabolic, has one indispensable mark—I mean, that the centre of it is simple, however much the fulfilment may be complicated. Thus, in *Hamlet*, let us say, the grotesqueness of the grave-digger, the flowers of the mad girl, the fantastic finery of Osric, the pallor of the ghost and the grin of the skull are all oddities in a sort of tangled wreath round one plain tragic figure of a man in black. Well, this also," he said, getting slowly down from his seat with a smile, "this also is the plain tragedy of a man in black. Yes," he went on, seeing the colonel look up in some wonder, "the whole of this tale turns on a black coat. In this, as in *Hamlet*, there are the rococo excrescences—yourselves, let us say. There is the dead waiter, who was there when he could not be there. There is the invisible hand that swept your table clear of silver and melted into air. But every clever crime is founded ultimately on some one quite simple fact—some fact that is not itself mysterious. The mystification comes in covering it up, in leading men's thoughts away from it. This large and subtle and (in the ordinary course) most profitable crime, was built on the plain fact that a gentleman's evening dress is the same as a waiter's. All the rest was acting, and thundering good acting, too."

"Still," said the colonel, getting up and frowning at his boots,

"I am not sure that I understand."

"Colonel," said Father Brown, "I tell you that this archangel of impudence who stole your forks walked up and down this passage twenty times in the blaze of all the lamps, in the glare of all the eyes. He did not go and hide in dim corners where suspicion might have searched for him. He kept constantly on the move in the lighted corridors, and everywhere that he went he seemed to be there by right. Don't ask me what he was like; you have seen him yourself six or seven times to-night. You were waiting with all the other grand people in the reception room at the end of the passage there, with the terrace just beyond. Whenever he came among you gentlemen, he came in the lightning style of a waiter, with bent head, flapping napkin and flying feet. He shot out on to the terrace, did something to the table cloth, and shot back again towards the office and the waiters' quarters. By the time he had come under the eye of the office clerk and the waiters he had become another man in every inch of his body, in every instinctive gesture. He strolled among the servants with the absent-minded insolence which they have all seen in their patrons. It was no new thing to them that a swell from the dinner party should pace all parts of the house like an animal at the Zoo; they know that nothing marks the Smart Set more than a habit of walking where one chooses. When he was magnificently weary of walking down that particular passage he would wheel round and pace back past the office; in the shadow of the arch just beyond he was altered as by a blast of magic, and went hurrying forward again among the Twelve Fishermen, an obsequious attendant. Why should the gentlemen look at a chance waiter? Why should the waiters suspect a first-rate walking gentleman? Once or twice he played the coolest tricks. In the proprietor's private quarters he called out breezily for a syphon of soda water, saying he was thirsty. He said genially that he would carry it himself, and he did; he carried it quickly and correctly through the thick of you, a waiter with an obvious errand. Of course, it could not have been kept up long, but it only had to be kept up till the end of the fish course.

"His worst moment was when the waiters stood in a row; but even then he contrived to lean against the wall just round the corner in such a way that for that important instant the waiters thought him a gentleman, while the gentlemen thought him a waiter. The rest went like winking. If any waiter caught him away from the table, that waiter caught a languid aristocrat. He had only to time himself two minutes before the fish was cleared, become a swift servant, and clear it himself. He put the plates down on a sideboard, stuffed the silver in his breast pocket, giving it a bulgy look, and ran like a hare (I heard him coming) till he came to the cloak room. There he had only to be a plutocrat again—a plutocrat called away suddenly on business. He had only to give his ticket to the cloak-room attendant, and go out again elegantly as he had come in. Only—only I happened to be the cloak-room attendant."

"What did you do to him?" cried the colonel, with unusual intensity. "What did he tell you?"

"I beg your pardon," said the priest immovably, "that is where the story ends."

"And the interesting story begins," muttered Pound. "I think I understand his professional trick. But I don't seem to have got hold of yours."

"I must be going," said Father Brown.

They walked together along the passage to the entrance hall, where they saw the fresh, freckled face of the Duke of Chester, who was bounding buoyantly along towards them.

"Come along, Pound," he cried breathlessly. "I've been looking for you everywhere. The dinner's going again in spanking style, and old Audley has got to make a speech in honour of the forks being saved. We want to start some new ceremony, don't you know, to commemorate the occasion. I say, you really got the goods back, what do you suggest?"

"Why," said the colonel, eyeing him with a certain sardonic approval, "I should suggest that henceforward we wear green coats, instead of black. One never knows what mistakes may arise when one looks so like a waiter."

"Oh, hang it all," said the young man, "a gentleman never looks like a waiter."

"Nor a waiter like a gentleman, I suppose," said Colonel Pound, with the same lowering laughter on his face. "Reverend sir, your friend must have been very smart to act the gentleman."

Father Brown buttoned up his commonplace overcoat to the neck, for the night was stormy, and took his commonplace umbrella from the stand.

"Yes," he said; "it must be very hard work to be a gentleman; but, do you know, I have sometimes thought that it may be almost as laborious to be a waiter."

And saying "Good evening," he pushed open the heavy doors of that palace of pleasures. The golden gates closed behind him, and he went at a brisk walk through the damp, dark streets in search of a penny omnibus.

The Everlasting Man

"For religion all men are equal, as all
pennies are equal, because the only value
in any of them is that they bear the image of the King."

THE END OF THE WORLD

I WAS once sitting on a summer day in a meadow in Kent under
the shadow of a little village church, with a rather curious companion with whom I had just been walking through the woods.
He was one of a group of eccentrics I had come across in my
wanderings who had a new religion called Higher Thought; in
which I had been so far initiated as to realise a general atmosphere of loftiness or height, and was hoping at some later and more
esoteric stage to discover the beginnings of thought. My companion was the most amusing of them, for however he may have
stood towards thought, he was at least very much their superior
in experience, having travelled beyond the tropics while they
were meditating in the suburbs; though he had been charged
with excess in telling travellers' tales. In spite of anything said
against him, I preferred him to his companions and willingly
went with him through the wood; where I could not but feel
that his sunburnt face and fierce tufted eyebrows and pointed
beard gave him something of the look of Pan. Then we sat down
in the meadow and gazed idly at the tree-tops and the spire of the
village church; while the warm afternoon began to mellow into
early evening and the song of a speck of a bird was faint far up
in the sky and no more than a whisper of breeze soothed rather
than stirred the ancient orchards of the garden of England. Then
my companion said to me: "Do you know why the spire of that
church goes up like that?" I expressed a respectable agnosticism,
and he answered in an off-hand way, "Oh, the same as the
obelisks; the Phallic Worship of antiquity." Then I looked across
at him suddenly as he lay there leering above his goatlike beard;
and for the moment I thought he was not Pan but the Devil. No
mortal words can express the immense, the insane incongruity
and unnatural perversion of thought involved in saying such a
thing at such a moment and in such a place. For one moment I

was in the mood in which men burned witches; and then a sense of absurdity equally enormous seemed to open about me like a dawn. "Why, of course," I said after a moment's reflection, "if it hadn't been for phallic worship, they would have built the spire pointing downwards and standing on its own apex." I could have sat in that field and laughed for an hour. My friend did not seem offended, for indeed he was never thin-skinned about his scientific discoveries. I had only met him by chance and I never met him again, and I believe he is now dead; but though it has nothing to do with the argument, it may be worth while to mention the name of this adherent of Higher Thought and interpreter of primitive religious origins; or at any rate the name by which he was known. It was Louis de Rougemont.

That insane image of the Kentish church standing on the point of its spire, as in some old rustic topsy-turvy tale, always comes back into my imagination when I hear these things said about pagan origins; and calls to my aid the laughter of the giants. Then I feel as genially and charitably to all other scientific investigators, higher critics, and authorities on ancient and modern religion, as I do to poor Louis de Rougemont. But the memory of that immense absurdity remains as a sort of measure and check by which to keep sane, not only on the subject of Christian churches, but also on the subject of heathen temples. Now a great many people have talked about heathen origins as the distinguished traveller talked about Christian origins. Indeed a great many modern heathens have been very hard on heathenism. A great many modern humanitarians have been very hard on the real religion of humanity. They have represented it as being everywhere and from the first rooted only in these repulsive arcana; and carrying the character of something utterly shameless and anarchical. Now I do not believe this for a moment. I should never dream of thinking about the whole worship of Apollo what De Rougemont could think about the worship of Christ. I would never admit that there was such an atmosphere in a Greek city as that madman was able to smell in a Kentish

village. On the contrary, it is the whole point of this chapter
upon the final decay of paganism, to insist once more that the
worst sort of paganism had already been defeated by the best
sort. It was the best sort of paganism that conquered the gold of
Carthage. It was the best sort of paganism that wore the laurels
of Rome. It was the best thing the world had yet seen, all things
considered and on any large scale, that ruled from the wall of
the Grampians to the garden of the Euphrates. It was the best
that conquered; it was the best that ruled; and it was the best
that began to decay.

Unless this broad truth be grasped, the whole story is seen
askew. Pessimism is not in being tired of evil but in being tired
of good. Despair does not lie in being weary of suffering, but in
being weary of joy. It is when for some reason or other the good
things in a society no longer work that the society begins to decline; when its food does not feed, when its cures do not cure,
when its blessings refuse to bless. We might almost say that in a
society without such good things we should hardly have any test
by which to register a decline; that is why some of the static
commercial oligarchies like Carthage have rather an air in history
of standing and staring like mummies, so dried up and swathed
and embalmed that no man knows when they are new or old.
But Carthage at any rate was dead, and the worst assault ever
made by the demons on mortal society had been defeated. But
how much would it matter that the worst was dead if the best
was dying?

To begin with, it must be noted that the relation of Rome to
Carthage was partially repeated and extended in her relations to
nations more normal and more nearly akin to her than Carthage.
I am not here concerned to controvert the merely political view
that Roman statesmen acted unscrupulously towards Corinth or
the Greek cities. But I am concerned to contradict the notion
that there was nothing but a hypocritical excuse in the ordinary
Roman dislike of Greek vices. I am not presenting these pagans
as paladins of chivalry, with a sentiment about nationalism never

known until Christian times. But I am presenting them as men with the feelings of men; and those feelings were not a pretence. The truth is that one of the weaknesses in nature-worship and mere mythology had already produced a perversion among the Greeks, due to the worst sophistry; the sophistry of simplicity. Just as they became unnatural by worshipping nature, so they actually became unmanly by worshipping man. If Greece led her conqueror, she might have misled her conqueror; but these were things he did originally wish to conquer—even in himself. It is true that in one sense there was less inhumanity even in Sodom and Gomorrah than in Tyre and Sidon. When we consider the war of the demons on the children, we cannot compare even Greek decadence to Punic devil worship. But it is not true that the sincere revulsion from either need be merely pharisaical. It is not true to human nature or to common sense. Let any lad who has had the luck to grow up sane and simple in his day-dreams of love hear for the first time of the cult of Ganymede; he will not be merely shocked but sickened. And that first impression, as has been said here so often about first impressions, will be right. Our cynical indifference is an illusion; it is the greatest of all illusions; the illusion of familiarity. It is right to conceive the more or less rustic virtues of the ruck of the original Romans as reacting against the very rumour of it, with complete spontaneity and sincerity. It is right to regard them as reacting, if in a lesser degree, exactly as they did against the cruelty of Carthage. Because it was in a less degree they did not destroy Corinth as they destroyed Carthage. But if their attitude and action was rather destructive, in neither case need their indignation have been mere self-righteousness covering mere selfishness. And if anybody insists that nothing could have operated in either case but reasons of state and commercial conspiracies, we can only tell him that there is something which he does not understand; something which possibly he will never understand; something which, until he does understand, he will never understand the Latins. That something is called democracy. He has probably heard the word a good many times and even used it himself; but he has no notion of what it means. All through the revolutionary history of Rome there was an incessant drive towards democracy; the state and the statesman could do nothing without a considerable backing of democracy; the sort of democracy that never has anything to do with diplomacy. It is precisely because of the presence of Roman democracy that we hear so much about Roman oligarchy. For instance, recent historians have tried to explain the valour and victory of Rome in terms of that detestable and detested usury which was practised by some of the Patricians; as if Curius had conquered the men of the Macedonian phalanx by lending them money; or the Consul Nero had negotiated the victory of Metaurus at five per cent. But we realise the usury of the Patricians because of the perpetual revolt of the Plebeians. The rule of the Punic merchant princes had the very soul of usury. But there was never a Punic mob that dared to call them usurers.

Burdened like all mortal things with all mortal sin and weakness, the rise of Rome had really been the rise of normal and especially of popular things; and in nothing more than in the thoroughly normal and profoundly popular hatred of perversion. Now among the Greeks a perversion had become a convention. It is true that it had become so much of a convention, especially a literary convention, that it was sometimes conventionally copied by Roman literary men. But this is one of those complications that always arise out of conventions. It must not obscure our sense of the difference of tone in the two societies as a whole. It is true that Virgil would once in a way take over a theme of Theocritus; but nobody can get the impression that Virgil was particularly fond of that theme. The themes of Virgil were specially and notably the normal themes and nowhere more than in morals; piety and patriotism and the honor of the countryside. And we may well pause upon the name of the poet as we pass into the autumn of antiquity; upon his name who was in so supreme a sense the very voice of autumn, of its maturity and its melancholy; of its fruits of fulfilment and its prospect of decay. Nobody who reads even a few lines of Virgil can doubt that he understood what moral sanity means to mankind. Nobody can doubt his feelings when the demons were driven in flight before the household gods. But there are two particular points about him and his work which are particularly important to the main thesis here. The first is that the whole of his great patriotic epic is in a very peculiar sense founded upon the fall of Troy; that is upon an avowed pride in Troy although she had fallen. In tracing to Trojans the foundation of his beloved race and republic, he began what may be called the great Trojan tradition which runs through medieval and modern history. We have already seen the first hint of it in the pathos of Homer about Hector. But Virgil turned it not merely into a literature but into a legend. And it was a legend of the almost divine dignity that belongs to the defeated. This was one of the traditions that did truly prepare the world for the coming of Christianity and especially of Christian chivalry. This is what did help to sustain civilisation through the incessant defeats of the Dark Ages and the barbarian wars; out of which what we call chivalry was born. It is the moral attitude of the man with his back to the wall; and it was the wall of Troy. All through medieval and modern times this version of the virtues in the Homeric conflict can be traced in a hundred ways co-operating with all that was akin to it in Christian sentiment. Our own countrymen, and the men of other countries, loved to claim like Virgil that their own nation was descended from the heroic Trojans. All sorts of people thought it the most superb sort of heraldry to claim to be descended from Hector. Nobody seems to have wanted to be descended from Achilles. The very fact that the Trojan name has become a Christian name, and been scattered to the last limits of Christendom, to Ireland or the Gaelic Highlands, while the Greek name has remained relatively rare and pedantic, is a tribute to the same truth. Indeed it involves a curiosity of language almost in the nature of a joke. The name has been turned into a verb; and the very phrase about hectoring, in the sense of swaggering, suggests the myriads of soldiers who have taken the fallen Trojan for a model. As a matter of fact, nobody in antiquity was less given to hectoring than Hector. But even the bully pretending to be a conqueror took his title from the conquered. That is why the popularisation of the Trojan origin by Virgil has a vital relation to all those elements that have made men say that Virgil was almost a Christian. It is almost as if two great tools or toys of the same timber, the divine and the human, had been in the hands of Providence; and the only thing comparable to the Wooden Cross of Calvary was the Wooden Horse of Troy. So, in some wild allegory, pious in purpose if almost profane in form, the Holy Child might have fought the Dragon with a wooden sword and a wooden horse.

The other element in Virgil which is essential to the argument is the particular nature of his relation to mythology; or what may here in a special sense be called folklore, the faiths and fancies of the populace. Everybody knows that his poetry at its most perfect is less concerned with the pomposity of Olympus than with the *numina* of natural and agricultural life. Everyone knows where Virgil looked for the causes of things. He speaks of finding them not so much in cosmic allegories of Uranus and Chronos; but rather in Pan and the sisterhood of the nymphs and Sylvanus the old man of the forest. He is perhaps most himself in some passages of the Eclogues, in which he has perpetuated for ever the great legend of Arcadia and the shepherds. Here again it is easy enough to miss the point with petty criticism about all the things that happen to separate his literary convention from ours. There is nothing more artificial than the cry of artificiality as directed against the old pastoral poetry. We have entirely missed all that our fathers meant by looking at the externals of what they wrote. People have been so much amused with the mere fact that the china shepherdess was made of china that they have not even asked why she was made at all. They have been so content to consider the Merry Peasant as a figure in an opera that they have not asked even how he came to go to the opera, or how he strayed on to the stage.

In short, we have only to ask why there is a china shepherdess and not a china shopkeeper. Why were not mantelpieces adorned with figures of city merchants in elegant attitudes; of ironmasters wrought in iron or gold speculators in gold? Why did the opera exhibit a Merry Peasant and not a Merry Politician? Why was there not a ballet of bankers, pirouetting upon pointed toes? Because the ancient instinct and humour of humanity have always told them, under whatever conventions, that the conventions of complex cities were less really healthy and happy than the customs of the countryside. So it is with the eternity of the Eclogues. A modern poet did indeed write things called Fleet Street Eclogues, in which poets took the place of the shepherds. But nobody has yet written anything called Wall Street Eclogues, in which millionaires should take the place of the poets. And the reason is that there is a real if only a recurrent yearning for that sort of simplicity; and there is never that sort of yearning for that sort of complexity. The key to the mystery of the Merry Peasant is that the peasant often is merry. Those who do not believe it are simply those who do not know anything about him, and therefore do not know which are his times for merriment. Those who do not believe in the shepherd's feast or song are merely ignorant of the shepherd's calendar. The real shepherd is indeed very different from the ideal shepherd, but that is no reason for forgetting the reality at the root of the ideal. It needs a truth to make a tradition. It needs a tradition to make a convention. Pastoral poetry is certainly often a convention, especially in a social decline. It was in a social decline that Watteau shepherds and shepherdesses lounged about the gardens of Versailles. It was also in a social decline that shepherds and shepherdesses continued to pipe and dance through the most faded imitations of Virgil. But that is no reason for dismissing the dying paganism without ever understanding its life. It is no reason for forgetting that the very word Pagan is the same as the word Peasant. We

may say that this art is only artificiality; but it is not a love of
the artificial. On the contrary, it is in its very nature only the
failure of nature worship, or the love of the natural.

For the shepherds were dying because their gods were dying.
Paganism lived upon poetry; that poetry already considered under the name of mythology. But everywhere, and especially in
Italy, it had been a mythology and a poetry rooted in the countryside; and that rustic religion had been largely responsible for
the rustic happiness. Only as the whole society grew in age and
experience, there began to appear that weakness in all mythology
already noted in the chapter under that name. This religion was
not quite a religion. In other words, this religion was not quite a
reality. It was the young world's riot with images and ideas like
a young man's riot with wine or love-making; it was not so much
immoral as irresponsible; it had no foresight of the final test of
time. Because it was creative to any extent it was credulous to
any extent. It belonged to the artistic side of man, yet even considered artistically it had long become overloaded and entangled.
The family trees sprung from the seed of Jupiter were a jungle
rather than a forest; the claims of the gods and demigods seemed
like things to be settled rather by a lawyer or a professional
herald than by a poet. But it is needless to say that it was not
only in the artistic sense that these things had grown more
anarchic. There had appeared in more and more flagrant fashion
that flower of evil that is really implicit in the very seed of
nature-worship, however natural it may seem. I have said that I
do not believe that natural worship necessarily begins with this
particular passion; I am not of the De Rougemont school of
scientific folk-lore. I do not believe that mythology must begin
with eroticism. But I do believe that mythology must end in it.
I am quite certain that mythology did end in it. Moreover, not
only did the poetry grow more immoral, but the immorality
grew more indefensible. Greek vices, oriental vices, hints of the
old horrors of the Semitic demons, began to fill the fancies of
decaying Rome, swarming like flies on a dung-heap. The psy-

chology of it is really human enough, to anyone who will try that experiment of seeing history from the inside. There comes an hour in the afternoon when the child is tired of "pretending"; when he is weary of being a robber or a Red Indian. It is then that he torments the cat. There comes a time in the routine of an ordered civilisation when the man is tired at playing at mythology and pretending that a tree is a maiden or that the moon made love to a man. The effect of this staleness is the same everywhere; it is seen in all drug-taking and dram-drinking and every form of the tendency to increase the dose. Men seek stranger sins or more startling obscenities as stimulants to their jaded sense. They seek after mad oriental religions for the same reason. They try to stab their nerves to life, if it were with the knives of the priests of Baal. They are walking in their sleep and try to wake themselves up with nightmares.

At that stage even of paganism therefore the peasant songs and dances sound fainter and fainter in the forest. For one thing the peasant civilisation was fading, or had already faded from the whole countryside. The Empire at the end was organised more and more on that servile system which generally goes with the boast of organisation; indeed it was almost as servile as the modern schemes for the organisation of industry. It is proverbial that what would once have been a peasantry became a mere populace of the town dependent for bread and circuses; which may again suggest to some a mob dependent upon doles and cinemas. In this as in many other respects, the modern return to heathenism has been a return not even to the heathen youth but rather to the heathen old age. But the causes of it were spiritual in both cases; and especially the spirit of paganism had departed with its familiar spirits. The heart had gone out of it with its household gods, who went along with the gods of the garden and the field and the forest. The Old Man of the Forest was too old; he was already dying. It is said truly in a sense that Pan died because Christ was born. It is almost as true in another sense that men knew that Christ was born because Pan was already dead. A void was made by the vanishing of the whole mythology of mankind, which would have asphyxiated like a vacuum if it had not been filled with theology. But the point for the moment is that the mythology could not have lasted like a theology in any case. Theology is thought, whether we agree with it or not. Mythology was never thought, and nobody could really agree with it or disagree with it. It was a mere mood of glamour and when the mood went it could not be recovered. Men not only ceased to believe in the gods, but they realised that they had never believed in them. They had sung their praises; they had danced round their altars. They had played the flute; they had played the fool.

So came the twilight upon Arcady and the last notes of the pipe sound sadly from the beechen grove. In the great Virgilian poems there is already something of the sadness; but the loves and the household gods linger in lovely lines like that which Mr. Belloc took for a test of understanding; *incipe parve puer risu cognoscere matrem.* But with them as with us, the human family itself began to break down under servile organisation and the herding of the towns. The urban mob became enlightened; that is it lost the mental energy that could create myths. All round the circle of the Mediterranean cities the people mourned for the loss of gods and were consoled with gladiators. And meanwhile something similar was happening to that intellectual aristocracy of antiquity that had been walking about and talking at large ever since Socrates and Pythagoras. They began to betray to the world the fact that they were walking in a circle and saying the same thing over and over again. Philosophy began to be a joke; it also began to be a bore. That unnatural simplification of everything into one system or another, which we have noted as the fault of the philosopher, revealed at once its finality and its futility. Everything was virtue or everything was happiness or everything was fate or everything was good or everything was bad; anyhow, everything was everything and there was no more to be said; so they said it. Everywhere the sages had degenerated into sophists; that is, into hired rhetoricians or askers of riddles. It is one of the symptoms of this that the sage begins to turn not only into a sophist but into a magician. A touch of oriental occultism is very much appreciated in the best houses. As the philosopher is already a society entertainer, he may as well also be a conjurer.

Many moderns have insisted on the smallness of that Mediterranean world; and the wider horizons that might have awaited it with the discovery of the other continents. But this is an illusion; one of the many illusions of materialism. The limits that paganism had reached in Europe were the limits of human existence; at its best it had only reached the same limits anywhere else. The Roman stoics did not need any Chinamen to teach them stoicism. The Pythagoreans did not need any Hindus to teach them about recurrence or the simple life or the beauty of being a vegetarian. In so far as they could get these things from the East, they had already got rather too much of them from the East. The Syncretists were as convinced as Theosophists that all religions are really the same. And how else could they have extended philosophy merely by extending geography? It can hardly be proposed that they should learn a purer religion from the Aztecs or sit at the feet of the Incas of Peru. All the rest of the world was a welter of barbarism. It is essential to recognise that the Roman Empire was recognised as the highest achievement of the human race; and also as the broadest. A dreadful secret seemed to be written as in obscure hieroglyphics across those mighty works of marble and stone, those colossal amphitheatres and aqueducts. Man could do no more.

For it was not the message blazed on the Babylonian wall, that one king was found wanting or his one kingdom given to a stranger. It was no such good news as the news of invasion and conquest. There was nothing left that could conquer Rome; but there was also nothing left that could improve it. It was the strongest thing that was growing weak. It was the best thing that was going to the bad. It is necessary to insist again and again that many civilisations had met in one civilisation of the Mediterranean sea; that it was already universal with a stale and sterile universality. The peoples had pooled their resources and still there was not enough. The empires had gone into partnership and they were still bankrupt. No philosopher who was really philosophical could think anything except that, in that central sea, the wave of the world had risen to its highest, seeming to touch the stars. But the wave was already stooping; for it was only the wave of the world.

That mythology and that philosophy into which paganism has already been analysed had thus both of them been drained most literally to the dregs. If with the multiplication of magic the third department, which we have called the demons, was even increasingly active, it was never anything but destructive. There remains only the fourth element or rather the first; that which had been in a sense forgotten because it was the first. I mean the primary and overpowering yet impalpable impression that the universe after all has one origin and one aim; and because it has an aim must have an author. What became of this great truth in the background of men's minds, at this time, it is perhaps more difficult to determine. Some of the Stoics undoubtedly saw it more and more clearly as the clouds of mythology cleared and thinned away; and great men among them did much even to the last to lay the foundations of a concept of the moral unity of the world. The Jews still held their secret certainty of it jealously behind high fences of exclusiveness; yet it is intensely characteristic of the society and the situation that some fashionable figures, especially fashionable ladies, actually embraced Judaism. But in the case of many others I fancy there entered at this point a new negation. Atheism became really possible in that abnormal time; for atheism is abnormality. It is not merely the denial of a dogma. It is the reversal of a subconscious assumption in the soul; the sense that there is a meaning and a direction in the world it sees. Lucretius, the first evolutionist who endeavored to substitute Evolution for God, had already dangled before men's eyes his dance of glittering atoms, by which he conceived cosmos as created by chaos. But it was not his strong poetry or his sad philosophy, as I fancy, that made it possible for men to entertain such a vision. It was something in the sense of impotence and despair with which men shook their fists vainly at the stars, as they saw all the best work of humanity sinking slowly and helplessly into a swamp. They could easily believe that even creation itself was not a creation but a perpetual fall, when they saw that the weightiest and worthiest of all human creations was falling by its own weight. They could fancy that all the stars were falling stars; and that the very pillars of their own solemn porticos were bowed under a sort of gradual Deluge. To men in that mood there was a reason for atheism that is in some sense reasonable. Mythology might fade and philosophy might stiffen; but if behind these things there was a reality, surely that reality might have sustained things as they sank. There was no God; if there had been a God, surely this was the very moment when He would have moved and saved the world.

The life of the great civilisation went on with dreary industry and even with dreary festivity. It was the end of the world, and the worst of it was that it need never end. A convenient compromise had been made between all the multitudinous myths and religions of the Empire; that each group should worship freely and merely give a sort of official flourish of thanks to the tolerant Emperor, by tossing a little incense to him under his official title of Divus. Naturally there was no difficulty about that; or rather it was a long time before the world realised that there ever had been even a trivial difficulty anywhere. The members of some Eastern sect or secret society or other seemed to have made a scene somewhere; nobody could imagine why. The incident occurred once or twice again and began to arouse irritation out of proportion to its insignificance. It was not exactly what these provincials said; though of course it sounded queer enough. They seemed to be saying that God was dead and that they themselves had seen him die. This might be one of the many manias produced by the despair of the age; only they did not seem particularly despairing. They seem quite unnaturally joyful about it, and gave the reason that the death of God had allowed them to eat him and drink his blood. According to other accounts God was not exactly dead after all; there trailed through the bewildered imagination some sort of fantastic procession of the funeral of God, at which the sun turned black, but which ended with the dead omnipotence breaking out of the tomb and rising again like the sun. But it was not the strange story to which anybody paid any particular attention; people in that world had seen queer religions enough to fill a madhouse. It was something in the tone of the madmen and their type of formation. They were a scratch company of barbarians and slaves and poor and unimportant people; but their formation was military; they moved together and were very absolute about who and what was really a part of their little system; and about what they said, however mildly, there was a ring like iron. Men used to many mythologies and moralities could make no analysis of the mystery, except the curious conjecture that they meant what they said. All attempts to make them see reason in the perfectly simple matter of the Emperor's statue seemed to be spoken to deaf men. It was as if a new meteoric metal had fallen on the earth; it was a difference of substance to the touch. Those who touched their foundation fancied they had struck a rock.

With a strange rapidity, like the changes of a dream, the proportions of things seemed to change in their presence. Before most men knew what had happened, these few men were palpably present. They were important enough to be ignored. People became suddenly silent about them and walked stiffly past them. We see a new scene, in which the world has drawn its skirts away from these men and women and they stand in the centre of a great space like lepers. The scene changes again and the great space where they stand is overhung on every side with a cloud of witnesses, interminable terraces full of faces looking down towards them intently; for strange things are happening to them. New tortures have been invented for the madmen who have brought good news. That sad and weary society seems almost to find a new energy in establishing its first religious persecution. Nobody yet knows very clearly why that level world has thus lost its balance about the people in its midst; but they stand unnaturally still while the arena and the world seem to revolve round them. And there shone on them in that dark hour a light that has never been darkened; a white fire clinging to that group like an unearthly phosphorescence, blazing its track through the twilights of history and confounding every effort to confound it with the mists of mythology and theory; that shaft of light or lightening by which the world itself has struck and isolated and crowned it; by which its own enemies have made it more illustrious and its own critics have made it more inexplicable; the halo of hatred around the Church of God.

THE purpose of these pages is to fix the falsity of certain vague and vulgar assumptions; and we have here one of the most false. There is a sort of notion in the air everywhere that all the religions are equal because all the religious founders were rivals; that they are all fighting for the same starry crown. It is quite false. The claim to that crown, or anything like that crown, is really so rare as to be unique. Mahomet did not make it any more than Micah or Malachi. Confucius did not make it any more than Plato or Marcus Aurelius. Buddha never said he was Bramah. Zoroaster no more claimed to be Ormuz than to be Ahriman. The truth is that, in the common run of cases, it is just as we should expect it to be, in common sense and certainly in Christian philosophy. It is exactly the other way. Normally speaking, the greater a man is, the less likely he is to make the very greatest claim. Outside the unique case we are considering, the only kind of man who ever does make that kind of claim is a very small man; a secretive or self-centered monomaniac. No-body can imagine Aristotle claiming to be the father of gods and men, come down from the sky; though we might imagine some insane Roman Emperor like Caligula claiming it for him, or more probably for himself. Nobody can imagine Shake-speare talking as if he were literally divine; though we might imagine some crazy American crank finding it as a cryptogram in Shakespeare's works, or preferably in his own works. It is possible to find here and there human beings who make this su-premely superhuman claim. It is possible to find them in lunatic asylums; in padded cells; possibly in strait waistcoats. But what is much more important than their mere materialistic fate in our very materialistic society, under very crude and clumsy laws about lunacy, the type we know as tinged with this, or tending towards it, is a diseased and disproportionate type; narrow yet swollen and morbid to monstrosity. It is by rather an unlucky metaphor that we talk of a madman as cracked; for in a sense he is not cracked enough. He is cramped rather than cracked; there are not enough holes in his head to ventilate it. This impossibility of letting in daylight on a delusion does sometimes cover and conceal a delusion of divinity. It can be found, not among prophets and sages and founders of religions, but only among a low set of lunatics. But this is exactly where the argument becomes intensely interesting; because the argument proves too much. For nobody supposes that Jesus of Nazareth was *that* sort of person. No modern critic in his five wits thinks that the preacher of the Sermon on the Mount was a horrible half-witted imbecile that might be scrawling stars on the walls of a cell. No atheist or blasphemer believes that the author of the Parable of the Prodigal Son was a monster with one mad idea like a cyclops with one eye. Upon any possible historical criticism, he must be put higher in the scale of human beings than that. Yet by all analogy we have really to put him there or else in the highest place of all.

In fact, those who can really take it (as I here hypothetically take it) in a quite dry and detached spirit, have here a most curious and interesting human problem. It is so intensely interesting, considered as a human problem, that it is in a spirit quite disinterested, so to speak, that I wish some of them had turned that intricate human problem into something like an intelligible human portrait. If Christ was simply a human character, he really was a highly complex and contradictory human character. For he combined exactly the two things that lie at the two extremes of human variation. He was exactly what the man with a delusion never is; he was wise; he was a good judge. What he said was always unexpected; but it was always unexpectedly magnanimous and often unexpectedly moderate. Take a thing like the point of the parable of the tares and the wheat. It has the quality that unites sanity and subtlety. It has not the simplicity of a madman. It has not even the simplicity of a fanatic. It might be uttered by a philosopher a hundred years old, at the end of a century of Utopias. Nothing could be less like this quality of seeing beyond and all round obvious things, than the condition of the ego-maniac with the one sensitive spot on his brain. I really do not see how these two characters could be convincingly combined, except in the astonishing way in which the creed combines them. For until we reach the full acceptance of the fact as a fact, how-ever marvellous, all mere approximations to it are actually further and further away from it. Divinity is great enough to be divine; it is great enough to call itself divine. But as humanity grows greater, it grows less and less likely to do so. God is God, as the Moslems say; but a great man knows he is not God, and the greater he is the better he knows it. That is the paradox; every-thing that is merely approaching to that point is merely receding from it. Socrates, the wisest man, knows that he knows nothing. A lunatic may think he is omniscience, and a fool may talk as if he were omniscient. But Christ is in another sense omniscient if he not only knows, but knows that he knows.

Even on the purely human and sympathetic side, therefore, the Jesus of the New Testament seems to me to have in a great many ways the note of something superhuman; that is of some-thing human and more than human. But there is another quality running through all his teachings which seems to me neglected in most modern talk about them as teachings; and that is the per-sistent suggestion that he has not really come to teach. If there is one incident in the record which affects me personally as grandly and gloriously human, it is the incident of giving wine for the wedding-feast. That is really human in the sense in which a whole crowd of prigs, having the appearance of human beings, can hardly be described as human. It rises superior to all supe-rior persons. It is as human as Herrick and as democratic as Dickens. But even in that story there is something else that has that note of things not fully explained; and in a way here very relevant. I mean the first hesitation, not on any ground touching the nature of the miracle, but on that of the propriety of working any miracles at all, at least at that stage; "my time is not yet come." What did that mean? At least it certainly meant a general plan or purpose in the mind, with which certain things did or did not fit in. And if we leave out that solitary strategic plan, we not only leave out the point of the story, but the story.

We often hear of Jesus of Nazareth as a wandering teacher; and there is a vital truth in that view in so far as it emphasises an attitude towards luxury and convention which most respectable people would still regard as that of a vagabond. It is expressed in his own great saying about the holes of the foxes and the nests of the birds, and, like many of his great sayings, it is felt as less powerful than it is, through lack of appreciation of that great paradox by which he spoke of his own humanity as in some way collectively and representatively human; calling himself simply the Son of Man; that is, in effect, calling himself simply Man. It is fitting that the New Man or the Second Adam should repeat in so ringing a voice and with so arresting a gesture the great fact which came first in the original story; that man differs from the brutes by everything, even by deficiency; that he is in a sense less normal and even less native; a stranger upon the earth. It is well to speak of his wanderings in this sense and in the sense that he shared the drifting life of the most homeless and hopeless of the poor. It is assuredly well to remember that he would quite certainly have been moved on by the police and almost certainly arrested by the police, for having no visible means of subsistence. For our law has in it a turn of humour or touch of fancy which Nero and Herod never happened to think of; that of actually punishing homeless people for not sleeping at home.

But in another sense the word "wandering" as applied to his life is a little misleading. As a matter of fact, a great many of the pagan sages and not a few of the pagan sophists might truly be described as wandering teachers. In some of them their rambling journeys were not altogether without a parallel in their rambling remarks. Apollonius of Tyana, who figured in some fashion-

able cults as a sort of ideal philosopher, is represented as rambling
as far as the Ganges and Ethiopia, more or less talking all the
time. There was actually a school of philosophers called the
Peripatetics; and most even of the great philosophers give us a
vague impression of having very little to do except to walk and
talk. The great conversations which give us our glimpses of the
great minds of Socrates or Buddha or even Confucius often seem
to be parts of a never-ending picnic; and especially, which is the
important point, to have neither beginning nor end. Socrates did
indeed find the conversation interrupted by the incident of his
execution. But it is the whole point, and the whole particular
merit, of the position of Socrates that death was only an interruption and an incident. We miss the real moral importance of
the great philosopher if we miss that point; that he stares at the
executioner with an innocent surprise, and almost an innocent
annoyance, at finding anyone so unreasonable as to cut short a
little conversation for the elucidation of truth. He is looking for
truth and not looking for death. Death is but a stone in the road
which can trip him up. His work in life is to wander on the roads
of the world and talk about truth for ever. Buddha, on the other
hand, did arrest attention by one gesture; it was the gesture of
renunciation, and therefore in a sense of denial. But by one dramatic negation he passed into a world of negation that was not
dramatic; which he would have been the first to insist was not
dramatic. Here again we miss the particular moral importance of
the great mystic if we do not see the distinction; that it was his
whole point that he had done with drama, which consists of
desire and struggle and generally of defeat and disappointment.
He passes into peace and lives to instruct others how to pass into
it. Henceforth his life is that of the ideal philosopher; certainly
a far more really ideal philosopher than Apollonius of Tyana;
but still a philosopher in the sense that it is not his business to do
anything but rather to explain everything; in his case, we might
almost say, mildly and softly to explode everything. For the
messages are basically different. Christ said "Seek first the king-

dom, and all these things shall be added unto you." Buddha said "Seek first the kingdom, and then you will need none of these things."

Now compared to these wanderers the life of Jesus went as swift and straight as a thunderbolt. It was above all things dramatic; it did above all things consist in doing something that had to be done. It emphatically would not have been done, if Jesus had walked about the world for ever doing nothing except tell the truth. And even the external movement of it must not be described as a wandering in the sense of forgetting that it was a journey. This is where it was a fulfilment of the myths rather than of the philosophies; it is a journey with a goal and an object, like Jason going to find the Golden Fleece, or Hercules the golden apples of the Hesperides. The gold that he was seeking was death. The primary thing that he was going to do was to die. He was going to do other things equally definite and objective; we might almost say equally external and material. But from first to last the most definite fact is that he is going to die. No two things could possibly be more different than the death of Socrates and the death of Christ. We are meant to feel that the death of Socrates was, from the point of view of his friends at least, a stupid muddle and miscarriage of justice interfering with the flow of a humane and lucid, I had almost said a light philosophy. We are meant to feel that Death was the bride of Christ as Poverty was the bride of St. Francis. We are meant to feel that his life was in that sense a sort of love-affair with death, a romance of the pursuit of the ultimate sacrifice. From the moment when the star goes up like a birthday rocket to the moment when the sun is extinguished like a funeral torch, the whole story moves on wings with the speed and direction of a drama, ending in an act beyond words.

Therefore the story of Christ is the story of a journey, almost in the manner of a military march; certainly in the manner of the quest of a hero moving to his achievement or his doom. It is a story that begins in the paradise of Galilee, a pastoral and peaceful land having really some hint of Eden, and gradually climbs the rising country into the mountains that are nearer to the storm-clouds and the stars, as to a Mountain of Purgatory. He may be met as if straying in strange places, or stopped on the way for discussion or dispute; but his face is set towards the mountain city. That is the meaning of that great culmination when he crested the ridge and stood at the turning of the road and suddenly cried aloud, lamenting over Jerusalem. Some light touch of that lament is in every patriotic poem; or if it is absent, the patriotism stinks with vulgarity. That is the meaning of the stirring and startling incident at the gates of the Temple, when the tables were hurled like lumber down the steps, and the rich merchants driven forth with bodily blows; the incident that must be at least as much of a puzzle to the pacifists as any paradox about non-resistance can be to any of the militarists. I have compared the quest to the journey of Jason, but we must never forget that in a deeper sense it is rather to be compared to the journey of Ulysses. It was not only a romance of travel but a romance of return; and of the end of a usurpation. No healthy boy reading the story regards the rout of the Ithacan suitors as anything but a happy ending. But there are doubtless some who regard the rout of the Jewish merchants and money changers with that refined repugnance which never fails to move them in the presence of violence, and especially of violence against the well-to-do. The point, here however, is that all these incidents have in them a character of mounting crisis. In other words, these incidents are not incidental. When Apollonius the ideal philosopher is brought before the judgment-seat of Domitian and vanishes by magic, the miracle is entirely incidental. It might have occurred at any time in the wandering life of the Tyanean; indeed, I believe it is doubtful in date as well as in substance. The ideal philosopher merely vanished, and resumed his ideal existence somewhere else for an indefinite period. It is characteristic of the contrast perhaps that Apollonius was supposed to have lived to an almost miraculous old age. Jesus of Nazareth was less prudent in his miracles. When Jesus was brought before the judgment-seat of Pontius Pilate, he did not vanish. It was the crisis and the goal; it was the hour and the power of darkness. It was the supremely supernatural act, of all his miraculous life, that he did not vanish.

Every attempt to amplify that story has diminished it. The task has been attempted by many men of real genius and eloquence as well as by only too many vulgar sentimentalists and self-conscious rhetoricians. The tale has been retold with patronising pathos by elegant sceptics and with fluent enthusiasm by boisterous best-sellers. It will not be retold here. The grinding power of the plain words of the Gospel story is like the power of mill-stones; and those who can read them simply enough will feel as if rocks had been rolled upon them. Criticism is only words about words; and of what use are words about such words as these? What is the use of word-painting about the dark garden filled suddenly with torchlight and furious faces? "Are you come out with swords and staves as against a robber? All day I sat in your temple teaching, and you took me not." Can anything be added to the massive and gathered restraint of that irony; like a great wave lifted to the sky and refusing to fall? "Daughters of Jerusalem, weep not for me but weep for yourselves and for your children." As the High Priest asked what further need he had of witnesses, we might well ask what further need we have of words. Peter in a panic repudiated him: "and immediately the cock crew; and Jesus looked upon Peter, and Peter went out and wept bitterly." Has anyone any further remarks to offer? Just before the murder he prayed for all the murderous race of men, saying, "They know not what they do"; is there anything to say to that, except that we know as little what we say? Is there any need to repeat and spin out the story of how the tragedy trailed up the Via Dolorosa and how they threw him in haphazard with two thieves in one of the ordinary batches of execution; and how in all that horror and howling wilderness of desertion one voice spoke in homage, a startling voice from the very last place where it was looked for, the gibbet of the criminal; and he said to that nameless ruffian, "This night shalt thou be with me in Paradise"? Is there anything to put after that but a full-stop? Or is anyone prepared to answer adequately that farewell gesture to all flesh which created for his Mother a new Son?

It is more within my powers, and here more immediately to my purpose, to point out that in that scene were symbolically gathered all the human forces that have been vaguely sketched in this story. As kings and philosophers and the popular element had been symbolically present at his birth, so they were more practically concerned in his death; and with that we come face to face with the essential fact to be realised. All the great groups that stood about the Cross represent in one way or another the great historical truth of the time; that the world could not save itself. Man could do no more. Rome and Jerusalem and Athens and everything else were going down like a sea turned into a slow cataract. Externally indeed the ancient world was still at its strongest; it is always at that moment that the inmost weakness begins. But in order to understand that weakness we must repeat what has been said more than once; that it was not the weakness of a thing originally weak. It was emphatically the strength of the world that was turned to weakness and the wisdom of the world that was turned to folly.

In this story of Good Friday it is the best things in the world that are at their worst. That is what really shows us the world at its worst. It was, for instance, the priests of a true monotheism and the soldiers of an international civilisation. Rome, the legend, founded upon fallen Troy and triumphant over fallen Carthage, had stood for a heroism which was the nearest that any pagan ever came to chivalry. Rome had defended the household gods and the human decencies against the ogres of Africa and the hermaphrodite monstrosities of Greece. But in the lightning flash of this incident, we see great Rome, the imperial republic, going downward under her Lucretian doom. Scepticism has eaten away even the confident sanity of the conquerors of the world. He who is enthroned to say what is justice can only ask, "What is truth?" So in that drama which decided the whole fate of antiquity, one of the central figures is fixed in what seems the reverse of his true rôle. Rome was almost another name for responsibility. Yet he stands for ever as a sort of rocking statue of the irresponsible. Man could do no more. Even the practical had become the impracticable. Standing between the pillars of his own judgment-seat, a Roman had washed his hands of the world.

There too were the priests of that pure and original truth that was behind all the mythologies like the sky behind the clouds. It was the most important truth in the world; and even that could not save the world. Perhaps there is something overpowering in pure personal theism; like seeing the sun and moon and sky come together to form one staring face. Perhaps the truth is too tremendous when not broken by some intermediaries divine or human; perhaps it is merely too pure and far away. Anyhow it could not save the world; it could not even convert the world. There were philosophers who held it in its highest and noblest form; but they not only could not convert the world, but they never tried. You could no more fight the jungle of popular mythology with a private opinion than you could clear away a forest with a pocket-knife. The Jewish priests had guarded it jealously in the good and the bad sense. They had kept it as a gigantic secret. As savage heroes might have kept the sun in a box, they kept the Everlasting in the tabernacle. They were proud that they alone could look upon the blinding sun of a single deity; and they did not know that they had themselves gone blind. Since that day their representatives have been like blind men in broad daylight, striking to right and left with their staffs, and cursing the darkness. But there has been that in their monumental monotheism that it has at least remained like a monument, the last thing of its kind, and in a sense motionless in the more restless world which it cannot satisfy. For it is certain that for some reason it cannot satisfy. Since that day it has never been quite enough to say that God is in his heaven and all is right with the world; since the rumour that God had left his heavens to set it right.

And as it was with these powers that were good, or at least had once been good, so it was with the element which was perhaps the best, or which Christ himself seems certainly to have felt as the best. The poor to whom he preached the good news, the common people who heard him gladly, the populace that had made so many popular heroes and demigods in the old pagan world, showed also the weaknesses that were dissolving the world. They suffered the evils often seen in the mob of the city, and especially the mob of the capital, during the decline of a society. The same thing that makes the rural population live on tradition makes the urban population live on rumour. Just as its myths at the best had been irrational, so its likes and dislikes are easily changed by baseless assertion that is arbitrary without being authoritative. Some brigand or other was artificially turned into a picturesque and popular figure and run as a kind of candidate against Christ. In all this we recognise the urban population that we know, with its newspaper scares and scoops. But there was present in this ancient population an evil more peculiar to the ancient world. We have noted it already as the neglect of the individual, even of the individual voting the condemnation and still more of the individual condemned. It was the soul of the hive; a heathen thing. The cry of this spirit also was heard in that hour, "It is well that one man die for the people." Yet this spirit in antiquity of devotion to the city and to the state had also been in itself and in its time a noble spirit. It had its poets and its martyrs; men still to be honoured for ever. It was failing through its weakness in not seeing the separate soul of a man, the shrine of all mysticism; but it was only failing as everything else was failing. The mob went along with the Sadducees and the Pharisees, the philosophers and the moralists. It went along with the imperial magistrates and the sacred priests, the scribes and the soldiers, that the one universal human spirit might suffer a universal condemnation; that there might be one deep, unanimous chorus of approval and harmony when Man was rejected of men.

There were solitudes beyond where none shall follow. There were secrets in the inmost and invisible part of that drama that have no symbol in speech; or in any severance of a man from men. Nor is it easy for any words less stark and single-minded than those of the naked narrative even to hint at the horror of exaltation that lifted itself above the hill. Endless expositions have not come to the end of it, or even to the beginning. And if there be any sound that can produce a silence, we may surely be silent about the end and the extremity; when a cry was driven out of that darkness in words dreadfully distinct and dreadfully unintelligible, which man shall never understand in all the eternity they have purchased for him; and for one annihilating instant an abyss that is not for our thoughts had opened even in the unity of the absolute; and God had been forsaken of God.

They took the body down from the cross and one of the few rich men among the first Christians obtained permission to bury it in a rock tomb in his garden; the Romans setting a military guard lest there should be some riot and attempt to recover the body. There was once more a natural symbolism in these natural proceedings; it was well that the tomb should be sealed with all the secrecy of ancient eastern sepulture and guarded by the authority of the Caesars. For in that second cavern the whole of that great and glorious humanity which we call antiquity was gathered up and covered over; and in that place it was buried. It was the end of a very great thing called human history; the history that was merely human. The mythologies and the philosophies were buried there, the gods and the heroes and the sages. In the great Roman phrase, they had lived. But as they could only live, so they could only die; and they were dead.

On the third day the friends of Christ coming at daybreak to the place found the grave empty and the stone rolled away. In varying ways they realised the new wonder; but even they hardly realised that the world had died in the night. What they were looking at was the first day of a new creation, with a new heaven and a new earth; and in a semblance of the gardener God walked again in the garden, in the cool not of the evening but the dawn.

THE ROMANCE OF ORTHODOXY

IT is customary to complain of the bustle and strenuousness of our epoch. But in truth the chief mark of our epoch is a profound laziness and fatigue; and the fact is that the real laziness is the cause of the apparent bustle. Take one quite external case; the streets are noisy with taxicabs and motor-cars; but this is not due to human activity but to human repose. There would be less bustle if there were more activity, if people were simply walking about. Our world would be more silent if it were more strenuous. And this which is true of the apparent physical bustle is true also of the apparent bustle of the intellect. Most of the machinery of modern language is labour-saving machinery; and it saves mental labour very much more than it ought. Scientific phrases are used like scientific wheels and piston-rods to make swifter and smoother yet the path of the comfortable. Long words go rattling by us like long railway trains. We know they are carrying thousands who are too tired or too indolent to walk and think for themselves. It is a good exercise to try for once in a way to express any opinion one holds in words of one syllable. If you say "The social utility of the indeterminate sentence is recognized by all criminologists as a part of our sociological evolution towards a more humane and scientific view of punishment," you can go on talking like that for hours with hardly a movement of the gray matter inside your skull. But if you begin "I wish Jones to go to gaol and Brown to say when Jones shall come out," you will discover, with a thrill of horror, that you are obliged to think. The long words are not the hard words, it is the short words that are hard. There is much more metaphysical subtlety in the word "damn" than in the word "degeneration."

But these long comfortable words that save modern people the toil of reasoning have one particular aspect in which they are

386

especially ruinous and confusing. This difficulty occurs when
the same long word is used in different connections to mean
quite different things. Thus, to take a well-known instance, the
word "idealist" has one meaning as a piece of philosophy and
quite another as a piece of moral rhetoric. In the same way the
scientific materialists have had just reason to complain of people
mixing up "materialist" as a term of cosmology with "materialist" as a moral taunt. So, to take a cheaper instance, the man
who hates "progressives" in London always calls himself a "progressive" in South Africa.

A confusion quite as unmeaning as this has arisen in connection with the word "liberal" as applied to religion and as applied
to politics and society. It is often suggested that all Liberals ought
to be freethinkers, because they ought to love everything that is
free. You might just as well say that all idealists ought to be
High Churchmen, because they ought to love everything that is
high. You might as well say that Low Churchmen ought to like
Low Mass, or that Broad Churchmen ought to like broad jokes.
The thing is a mere accident of words. In actual modern Europe
a freethinker does not mean a man who thinks for himself. It
means a man who, having thought for himself, has come to one
particular class of conclusions, the material origin of phenomena,
the impossibility of miracles, the improbability of personal immortality and so on. And none of these ideas are particularly
liberal. Nay, indeed almost all these ideas are definitely illiberal,
as it is the purpose of this chapter to show.

In the few following pages I propose to point out as rapidly
as possible that on every single one of the matters most strongly
insisted on by liberalisers of theology their effect upon social
practice would be definitely illiberal. Almost every contemporary proposal to bring freedom into the church is simply a proposal to bring tyranny into the world. For freeing the church
now does not even mean freeing it in all directions. It means
freeing that peculiar set of dogmas loosely called scientific, dogmas of monism, of pantheism, or of Arianism, or of necessity.

And every one of these (and we will take them one by one) can be shown to be the natural ally of oppression. In fact, it is a remarkable circumstance (indeed not so very remarkable when one comes to think of it) that most things are the allies of oppression. There is only one thing that can never go past a certain point in its alliance with oppression—and that is orthodoxy. I may, it is true, twist orthodoxy so as partly to justify a tyrant. But I can easily make up a German philosophy to justify him entirely.

Now let us take in order the innovations that are the notes of the new theology or the modernist church. We concluded the last chapter with the discovery of one of them. The very doctrine which is called the most old-fashioned was found to be the only safeguard of the new democracies of the earth. The doctrine seemingly most unpopular was found to be the only strength of the people. In short, we found that the only logical negation of oligarchy was in the affirmation of original sin. So it is, I maintain, in all the other cases.

I take the most obvious instance first, the case of miracles. For some extraordinary reason, there is a fixed notion that it is more liberal to disbelieve in miracles than to believe in them. Why, I cannot imagine, nor can anybody tell me. For some inconceivable cause a "broad" or "liberal" clergyman always means a man who wishes at least to diminish the number of miracles; it never means a man who wishes to increase that number. It always means a man who is free to disbelieve that Christ came out of His grave; it never means a man who is free to believe that his own aunt came out of her grave. It is common to find trouble in a parish because the parish priest cannot admit that St. Peter walked on water; yet how rarely do we find trouble in a parish because the clergyman says that his father walked on the Serpentine? And this is not because (as the swift secularist debater would immediately retort) miracles cannot be believed in our experience. It is not because "miracles do not happen," as in the dogma which Matthew Arnold recited with simple faith. More

supernatural things are *alleged* to have happened in our time than
would have been possible eighty years ago. Men of science believe in such marvels much more than they did: the most perplexing, and even horrible, prodigies of mind and spirit are always being unveiled in modern psychology. Things that the
old science at least would frankly have rejected as miracles are
hourly being asserted by the new science. The only thing which
is still old-fashioned enough to reject miracles is the New Theology. But in truth this notion that it is "free" to deny miracles
has nothing to do with the evidence for or against them. It is
a lifeless verbal prejudice of which the original life and beginning was not in the freedom of thought, but simply in the dogma
of materialism. The man of the nineteenth century did not disbelieve in the Resurrection because his liberal Christianity allowed him to doubt it. He disbelieved in it because his very strict
materialism did not allow him to believe it. Tennyson, a very
typical nineteenth century man, uttered one of the instinctive
truisms of his contemporaries when he said that there was faith
in their honest doubt. There was indeed. Those words have a
profound and even a horrible truth. In their doubt of miracles
there was a faith in a fixed and godless fate; a deep and sincere
faith in the incurable routine of the cosmos. The doubts of the
agnostic were only the dogmas of the monist.

Of the fact and evidence of the supernatural I will speak
afterwards. Here we are only concerned with this clear point;
that in so far as the liberal idea of freedom can be said to be on
either side in the discussion about miracles, it is obviously on the
side of miracles. Reform or (in the only tolerable sense) progress
means simply the gradual control of matter by mind. A miracle
simply means the swift control of matter by mind. If you wish
to feed the people, you may think that feeding them miracu-
lously in the wilderness is impossible—but you cannot think it
illiberal. If you really want poor children to go to the seaside,
you cannot think it illiberal that they should go there on flying
dragons; you can only think it unlikely. A holiday, like Liberal-

ism, only means the liberty of man. A miracle only means the liberty of God. You may conscientiously deny either of them, but you cannot call your denial a triumph of the liberal idea. The Catholic Church believed that man and God both had a sort of spiritual freedom. Calvinism took away the freedom from man, but left it to God. Scientific materialism binds the Creator Himself; it chains up God as the Apocalypse chained the devil. It leaves nothing free in the universe. And those who assist this process are called the "liberal theologians."

This, as I say, is the lightest and most evident case. The assumption that there is something in the doubt of miracles akin to liberality or reform is literally the opposite of the truth. If a man cannot believe in miracles there is an end of the matter; he is not particularly liberal, but he is perfectly honourable and logical, which are much better things. But if he can believe in miracles, he is certainly the more liberal for doing so; because they mean first, the freedom of the soul, and secondly, its control over the tyranny of circumstance. Sometimes this truth is ignored in a singularly naïve way, even by the ablest men. For instance, Mr. Bernard Shaw speaks with hearty old-fashioned contempt for the idea of miracles, as if they were a sort of breach of faith on the part of nature: he seems strangely unconscious that miracles are only the final flowers of his own favourite tree, the doctrine of the omnipotence of will. Just in the same way he calls the desire for immortality a paltry selfishness, forgetting that he has just called the desire for life a healthy and heroic selfishness. How can it be noble to wish to make one's life infinite and yet mean to wish to make it immortal? No, if it is desirable that man should triumph over the cruelty of nature or custom, then miracles are certainly desirable; we will discusss afterwards whether they are possible.

But I must pass on to the larger cases of this curious error; the notion that the "liberalising" of religion in some way helps the liberation of the world. The second example of it can be found in the question of pantheism—or rather of a certain modern attitude which is often called immanentism, and which often is Buddhism. But this is so much more difficult a matter that I must approach it with rather more preparation.

The things said most confidently by advanced persons to crowded audiences are generally those quite opposite to the fact; it is actually our truisms that are untrue. Here is a case. There is a phrase of facile liberality uttered again and again at ethical societies and parliaments of religion: "the religions of the earth differ in rites and forms, but they are the same in what they teach." It is false; it is the opposite of the fact. The religions of the earth do *not* greatly differ in rites and forms; they do greatly differ in what they teach. It is as if a man were to say, "Do not be misled by the fact that the *Church Times* and the *Freethinker* look utterly different, that one is painted on vellum and the other carved on marble, that one is triangular and the other hectagonal; read them and you will see that they say the same thing." The truth is, of course, that they are alike in everything except in the fact that they don't say the same thing. An atheist stockbroker in Surbiton looks exactly like a Swedenborgian stockbroker in Wimbledon. You may walk round and round them and subject them to the most personal and offensive study without seeing anything Swedenborgian in the hat or anything particularly godless in the umbrella. It is exactly in their souls that they are divided. So the truth is that the difficulty of all the creeds of the earth is not as alleged in this cheap maxim: that they agree in meaning, but differ in machinery. It is exactly the opposite. They agree in machinery; almost every great religion on earth works with the same external methods, with priests, scriptures, altars, sworn brotherhoods, special feasts. They agree in the mode of teaching; what they differ about is the thing to be taught. Pagan optimists and Eastern pessimists would both have temples, just as Liberals and Tories would both have newspapers. Creeds that exist to destroy each other both have scriptures, just as armies that exist to destroy each other both have guns.

The great example of this alleged identity of all human religions is the alleged spiritual identity of Buddhism and Christianity. Those who adopt this theory generally avoid the ethics of most other creeds, except, indeed, Confucianism, which they like because it is not a creed. But they are cautious in their praises of Mahommedanism, generally confining themselves to imposing its morality only upon the refreshment of the lower classes. They seldom suggest that Mahommedan view of marriage (for which there is a great deal to be said), and towards Thugs and fetish worshippers their attitude may even be called cold. But in the case of the great religion of Gautama they feel sincerely a similarity.

Students of popular science, like Mr. Blatchford, are always insisting that Christianity and Buddhism are very much alike, especially Buddhism. This is generally believed, and I believed it myself until I read a book giving the reasons for it. The reasons were of two kinds: resemblances that meant nothing because they were common to all humanity, and resemblances which were not resemblances at all. The author solemnly explained that the two creeds were alike in things in which all creeds are alike, or else he described them as alike in some point in which they are quite obviously different. Thus, as a case of the first class, he said that both Christ and Buddha were called by the divine voice coming out of the sky, as if you would expect the divine voice to come out of the coal-cellar. Or, again, it was gravely urged that these two Eastern teachers, by a singular coincidence, both had to do with the washing of feet. You might as well say that it was a remarkable coincidence that they both had feet to wash. And the other class of similarities were those which simply were not similar. Thus this reconciler of the two religions draws earnest attention to the fact that at certain religious feasts the robe of the Lama is rent in pieces out of respect, and the remnants highly valued. But this is the reverse of a resemblance, for the garments of Christ were not rent in pieces out of respect, but out of derision; and the remnants were not highly valued except

for what they would fetch in the rag shops. It is rather like al-
luding to the obvious connection between the two ceremonies
of the sword: when it taps a man's shoulder, and when it cuts
off his head. It is not at all similar for the man. These scraps of
puerile pedantry would indeed matter little if it were not also
true that the alleged philosophical resemblances are also of these
two kinds, either proving too much or not proving anything.
That Buddhism approves of mercy or of self-restraint is not
to say that it is specially like Christianity; it is only to say that
it is not utterly unlike all human existence. Buddhists disapprove
in theory of cruelty or excess because all sane human beings disapprove in theory of cruelty or excess. But to say that Buddhism
and Christianity give the same philosophy of these things is
simply false. All humanity does agree that we are in a net of sin.
Most of humanity agrees that there is some way out. But as to
what is the way out, I do not think that there are two institutions
in the universe which contradict each other so flatly as Buddhism
and Christianity.

Even when I thought, with most other well-informed, though
unscholarly, people, that Buddhism and Christianity were alike,
there was one thing about them that always perplexed me; I mean
the startling difference in their type of religious art. I do not
mean in its technical style of representation, but in the things
that it was manifestly meant to represent. No two ideals could be
more opposite than a Christian saint in a Gothic cathedral and
a Buddhist saint in a Chinese temple. The opposition exists at
every point; but perhaps the shortest statement of it is that the
Buddhist saint always has his eyes shut, while the Christian saint
always has them very wide open. The Buddhist saint has a sleek
and harmonious body, but his eyes are heavy and sealed with sleep.
The mediæval saint's body is wasted to its crazy bones, but his
eyes are frightfully alive. There cannot be any real community
of spirit between forces that produce symbols so different as
that. Granted that both images are extravagances, are perversions
of the pure creed, it must be a real divergence which could

produce such opposite extravagances. The Buddhist is looking with a peculiar intentness inwards. The Christian is staring with a frantic intentness outwards. If we follow that clue steadily we shall find some interesting things.

A short time ago Mrs. Besant, in an interesting essay, announced that there was only one religion in the world, that all faiths were only versions or perversions of it, and that she was quite prepared to say what it was. According to Mrs. Besant this universal Church is simply the universal self. It is the doctrine that we are really all one person; that there are no real walls of individuality between man and man. If I may put it so, she does not tell us to love our neighbours; she tells us to be our neighbours. That is Mrs. Besant's thoughtful and suggestive description of the religion in which all men must find themselves in agreement. And I never heard of any suggestion in my life with which I more violently disagree. I want to love my neighbour not because he is I, but precisely because he is not I. I want to adore the world, not as one likes a looking-glass, because it is one's self, but as one loves a woman, because she is entirely different. If souls are separate love is possible. If souls are united love is obviously impossible. A man may be said loosely to love himself, but he can hardly fall in love with himself, or, if he does, it must be a monotonous courtship. If the world is full of real selves, they can be really unselfish selves. But upon Mrs. Besant's principle the whole cosmos is only one enormously selfish person.

It is just here that Buddhism is on the side of modern pantheism and immanence. And it is just here that Christianity is on the side of humanity and liberty and love. Love desires personality; therefore love desires division. It is the instinct of Christianity to be glad that God has broken the universe into little pieces, because they are living pieces. It is her instinct to say "little children love one another" rather than to tell one large person to love himself. This is the intellectual abyss between Buddhism and Christianity; that for the Buddhist or Theosophist personality is the fall of man, for the Christian it is the purpose of God, the whole point of his cosmic idea. The world-soul of the Theosophists asks man to love it only in order that man may throw himself into it. But the divine centre of Christianity actually threw man out of it in order that he might love it. The oriental deity is like a giant who should have lost his leg or hand and be always seeking to find it; but the Christian power is like some giant who in a strange generosity should cut off his right hand, so that it might of its own accord shake hands with him. We come back to the same tireless note touching the nature of Christianity; all modern philosophies are chains which connect and fetter; Christianity is a sword which separates and sets free. No other philosophy makes God actually rejoice in the separation of the universe into living souls. But according to orthodox Christianity this separation between God and man is sacred, because this is eternal. That a man may love God it is necessary that there should be not only a God to be loved, but a man to love him. All those vague theosophical minds for whom the universe is an immense melting-pot are exactly the minds which shrink instinctively from that earthquake saying of our Gospels, which declare that the Son of God came not with peace but with a sundering sword. The saying rings entirely true even considered as what it obviously is; the statement that any man who preaches real love is bound to beget hate. It is as true of democratic fraternity as a divine love; sham love ends in compromise and common philosophy; but real love has always ended in bloodshed. Yet there is another and yet more awful truth behind the obvious meaning of this utterance of our Lord. According to Himself the Son was a sword separating brother and brother that they should for an æon hate each other. But the Father also was a sword, which in the black beginning separated brother and brother, so that they should love each other at last.

This is the meaning of that almost insane happiness in the eyes of the mediæval saint in the picture. This is the meaning of the sealed eyes of the superb Buddhist image. The Christian saint is happy because he has verily been cut off from the world; he is separate from things and is staring at them in astonishment. But why should the Buddhist saint be astonished at things?—since there is really only one thing, and that being impersonal can hardly be astonished at itself. There have been many pantheist poems suggesting wonder, but no really successful ones. The pantheist cannot wonder, for he cannot praise God or praise anything as really distinct from himself. Our immediate business here, however, is with the effect of this Christian admiration (which strikes outwards, towards a deity distinct from the worshipper) upon the general need for ethical activity and social reform. And surely its effect is sufficiently obvious. There is no real possibility of getting out of pantheism any special impulse to moral action. For pantheism implies in its nature that one thing is as good as another; whereas action implies in its nature that one thing is greatly preferable to another. Swinburne in the high summer of his scepticism tried in vain to wrestle with this difficulty. In "Songs before Sunrise," written under the inspiration of Garibaldi and the revolt of Italy he proclaimed the newer religion and the purer God which should wither up all the priests of the world:

> "What doest thou now
> Looking Godward to cry
> I am I, thou art thou,
> I am low, thou art high,
> I am thou that thou seekest to find him, find
>   thou but thyself, thou art I."

Of which the immediate and evident deduction is that tyrants are as much the sons of God as Garibaldis; and that King Bomba of Naples having, with the utmost success, "found himself" is identical with the ultimate good in all things. The truth is that the western energy that dethrones tyrants has been directly due to the western theology that says "I am I, thou art thou." The same spiritual separation which looked up and saw a good king in the universe looked up and saw a bad king in Naples. The worshippers of Bomba's god dethroned Bomba. The worshippers of Swinburne's god have covered Asia for centuries and have never dethroned a tyrant. The Indian saint may reasonably shut his eyes because he is looking at that which is I and Thou and We and They and It. It is a rational occupation: but it is not true in theory and not true in fact that it helps the Indian to keep an eye on Lord Curzon. That external vigilance which has always been the mark of Christianity (the command that we should *watch* and pray) has expressed itself both in typical western orthodoxy and in typical western politics: but both depend on the idea of a divinity transcendent, different from ourselves, a deity that disappears. Certainly the most sagacious creeds may suggest that we should pursue God into deeper and deeper rings of the labyrinth of our own ego. But only we of Christendom have said that we should hunt God like an eagle upon the mountains: and we have killed all monsters in the chase.

Here again, therefore, we find that in so far as we value democracy and the self-renewing energies of the west, we are much more likely to find them in the old theology than the new. If we want reform, we must adhere to orthodoxy; especially in this matter (so much disputed in the counsels of Mr. R. J. Campbell), the matter of insisting on the immanent or the transcendent deity. By insisting specially on the immanence of God we get introspection, self-isolation, quietism, social indifference—Tibet. By insisting specially on the transcendence of God we get wonder, curiosity, moral and political adventure, righteous indignation—Christendom. Insisting that God is inside man, man is always inside himself. By insisting that God transcends man, man has transcended himself.

If we take any other doctrine that has been called old-fashioned we shall find the case the same. It is the same, for instance, in the deep matter of the Trinity. Unitarians (a sect never to be mentioned without a special respect for their distinguished intellectual dignity and high intellectual honour) are often reformers by the accident that throws so many small sects into such an attitude. But there is nothing in the least liberal or akin to reform in the substitution of pure monotheism for the Trinity. The complex God of the Athanasian Creed may be an enigma for the intellect; but He is far less likely to gather the mystery and cruelty of a Sultan than the lonely god of Omar or Mahomet. The god who is a mere awful unity is not only a king but an Eastern king. The *heart* of humanity, especially of European humanity, is certainly much more satisfied by the strange hints and symbols that gather round the Trinitarian idea, the image of a council at which mercy pleads as well as justice, the conception of a sort of liberty and variety existing even in the inmost chamber of the world. For Western religion has always felt keenly the idea "it is not well for man to be alone." The social instinct asserted itself everywhere as when the Eastern idea of hermits was practically expelled by the Western idea of monks. So even asceticism became brotherly; and the Trappists were sociable even when they were silent. If this love of a living complexity be our test, it is certainly healthier to have the Trinitarian religion than the Unitarian. For to us Trinitarians (if I may say it with reverence)—to us God Himself is a society. It is indeed a fathomless mystery of theology, and even if I were theologian enough to deal with it directly, it would not be relevant to do so here. Suffice it to say here that this triple enigma is as comforting as wine and open as an English fireside; that this thing that bewilders the intellect utterly quiets the heart: but out of the desert, from the dry places and the dreadful suns, come the cruel children of the lonely God; the real Unitarians who with scimitar in hand have laid waste the world. For it is not well for God to be alone.

Again, the same is true of that difficult matter of the danger of the soul, which has unsettled so many just minds. To hope for all souls is imperative; and it is quite tenable that their salvation is inevitable. It is tenable, but it is not specially favourable to activity or progress. Our fighting and creative society ought rather to insist on the danger of everybody, on the fact that every man is hanging by a thread or clinging to a precipice. To say that all will be well anyhow is a comprehensible remark: but it cannot be called the blast of a trumpet. Europe ought rather to emphasize possible perdition; and Europe always has emphasized it. Here its highest religion is at one with all its cheapest romances. To the Buddhist or the eastern fatalist existence is a science or a plan, which must end up in a certain way. But to a Christian existence is a *story*, which may end up in any way. In a thrilling novel (that purely Christian product) the hero is not eaten by cannibals; but it is essential to the existence of the thrill that he *might* be eaten by cannibals. The hero must (so to speak) be an eatable hero. So Christian morals have always said to the man, not that he would lose his soul, but that he must take care that he didn't. In Christian morals, in short, it is wicked to call a man "damned": but it is strictly religious and philosophic to call him damnable.

All Christianity concentrates on the man at the cross-roads. The vast and shallow philosophies, the huge syntheses of humbug, all talk about ages and evolution and ultimate developments. The true philosophy is concerned with the instant. Will a man take this road or that?—that is the only thing to think about, if you enjoy thinking. The æons are easy enough to think about, any one can think about them. The instant is really awful: and it is because our religion has intensely felt the instant, that it has in literature dealt much with battle and in theology dealt much with hell. It is full of *danger*, like a boy's book: it is at an immortal crisis. There is a great deal of real similarity between popular fiction and the religion of the western people. If you say that popular fiction is vulgar and tawdry, you only say what the dreary and well-informed say also about the images in the Catholic churches. Life (according to the faith) is very like a serial story in a magazine: life ends with the promise (or menace) "to be continued in our next." Also, with a noble vulgarity, life imitates the serial and leaves off at the exciting moment. For death is distinctly an exciting moment.

But the point is that a story is exciting because it has in it so strong an element of will, of what theology calls free-will. You cannot finish a sum how you like. But you can finish a story how you like. When somebody discovered the Differential Calculus there was only one Differential Calculus he could discover. But when Shakespeare killed Romeo he might have married him to Juliet's old nurse if he had felt inclined. And Christendom has excelled in the narrative romance exactly because it has insisted on the theological free will. It is a large matter and too much to one side of the road to be discussed adequately here; but this is the real objection to that torrent of modern talk about treating crime as disease, about making a prison merely a hygienic environment like a hospital, of healing sin by slow scientific methods. The fallacy of the whole thing is that evil is a matter of active choice whereas disease is not. If you say that you are going to cure a profligate as you cure an asthmatic, my cheap and obvious answer is, "Produce the people who want to be asthmatics as many people want to be profligates." A man may lie still and be cured of a malady. But he must not lie still if he wants to be cured of a sin; on the contrary, he must get up and jump about violently. The whole point indeed is perfectly expressed in the very word which we use for a man in hospital; "patient" is in the passive mood; "sinner" is in the active. If a man is to be saved from influenza, he may be a patient. But if he is to be saved from forging, he must be not a patient but an *impatient*. He must be personally impatient with forgery. All moral reform must start in the active not the passive will.

Here again we reach the same substantial conclusion. In so far as we desire the definite reconstructions and the dangerous revolutions which have distinguished European civilization, we shall not discourage the thought of possible ruin; we shall rather encourage it. If we want, like the Eastern saints, merely to contemplate how right things are, of course we shall only say that they must go right. But if we particularly want to *make* them go right, we must insist that they may go wrong.

Lastly, this truth is yet again true in the case of the common modern attempts to diminish or to explain away the divinity of Christ. The thing may be true or not; that I shall deal with before I end. But if the divinity is true it is certainly terribly revolutionary. That a good man may have his back to the wall is no more than we knew already; but that God could have his back to the wall is a boast for all insurgents for ever. Christianity is the only religion on earth that has felt that omnipotence made God incomplete. Christianity alone has felt that God, to be wholly God, must have been a rebel as well as a king. Alone of all creeds, Christianity has added courage to the virtues of the Creator. For the only courage worth calling courage must necessarily mean that the soul passes a breaking point—and does not break. In this indeed I approach a matter more dark and awful than it is easy to discuss; and I apologise in advance if any of my phrases fall wrong or seem irreverent touching a matter which the greatest saints and thinkers have justly feared to approach. But in that terrific tale of the Passion there is a distinct emotional suggestion that the author of all things (in some unthinkable way) went not only through agony, but through doubt. It is written, "Thou shalt not tempt the Lord thy God." No; but the Lord thy God may tempt Himself; and it seems as if this was what happened in Gethsemane. In a garden Satan tempted man: and in a garden God tempted God. He passed in some superhuman manner through our human horror of pessimism. When the world shook and the sun was wiped out of heaven, it was not at the crucifixion, but at the cry from the cross: the cry which confessed that God was forsaken of God. And now let the revolutionists choose a creed from all the creeds and a god from all the gods of the world, carefully weighing all the gods of inevitable recurrence and of unalterable power. They will not find another god who has himself been in revolt. Nay, (the matter grows too difficult for human speech,) but let the atheists themselves choose a god. They will find only one divinity who ever uttered their isolation; only one religion in which

God seemed for an instant to be an atheist.

These can be called the essentials of the old orthodoxy, of which the chief merit is that it is the natural fountain of revolution and reform; and of which the chief defect is that it is obviously only an abstract assertion. Its main advantage is that it is the most adventurous and manly of all theologies. Its chief disadvantage is simply that it is a theology. It can always be urged against it that it is in its nature arbitrary and in the air. But it is not so high in the air but that great archers spend their whole lives in shooting arrows at it—yes, and their last arrows; there are men who will ruin themselves and ruin their civilization if they may ruin also this old fantastic tale. This is the last and most astounding fact about this faith; that its enemies will use any weapon against it, the swords that cut their own fingers, and the firebrands that burn their own homes. Men who begin to fight the Church for the sake of freedom and humanity end by flinging away freedom and humanity if only they may fight the Church. This is no exaggeration; I could fill a book with the instances of it. Mr. Blatchford set out, as an ordinary Bible-smasher, to prove that Adam was guiltless of sin against God; in manœuvring so as to maintain this he admitted, as a mere side issue, that all the tyrants, from Nero to King Leopold, were guiltless of any sin against humanity. I know a man who has such a passion for proving that he will have no personal existence after death that he falls back on the position that he has no personal existence now. He invokes Buddhism and says that all souls fade into each other; in order to prove that he cannot go to heaven he proves that he cannot go to Hartlepool. I have known people who protested against religious education with arguments against any education, saying that the child's mind must grow freely or that the old must not teach the young. I have known people who showed that there could be no divine judgment by showing that there can be no human judgment, even for practical purposes. They burned their own corn to set fire to the church; they smashed their own tools to smash it; any stick was good enough to beat it with, though it were the last stick of their own dismembered furniture. We do not admire, we hardly excuse, the fanatic who wrecks this world for love of the other. But what are we to say of the fanatic who wrecks this world out of hatred of the other? He sacrifices the very existence of humanity to the non-existence of God. He offers his victims not to the altar, but merely to assert the idleness of the altar and the emptiness of the throne. He is ready to ruin even that primary ethic by which all things live, for his strange and eternal vengeance upon some one who never lived at all.

And yet the thing hangs in the heavens unhurt. Its opponents only succeed in destroying all that they themselves justly hold dear. They do not destroy orthodoxy; they only destroy political and common courage sense. They do not prove that Adam was not responsible to God; how could they prove it? They only prove (from their premises) that the Czar is not responsible to Russia. They do not prove that Adam should not have been punished by God; they only prove that the nearest sweater should not be punished by men. With their oriental doubts about personality they do not make certain that we shall have no personal life hereafter; they only make certain that we shall not have a very jolly or complete one here. With their paralysing hints of all conclusions coming out wrong they do not tear the book of the Recording Angel; they only make it a little harder to keep the books of Marshall & Snelgrove. Not only is the faith the mother of all worldly energies, but its foes are the fathers of all worldly confusion. The secularists have not wrecked divine things; but the secularists have wrecked secular things, if that is any comfort to them. The Titans did not scale heaven; but they laid waste the world.

THE ETHICS OF ELFLAND

When the business man rebukes the idealism of his office-boy, it is commonly in some such speech as this: "Ah, yes, when one is young, one has these ideals in the abstract and these castles in the air; but in middle age they all break up like clouds, and one comes down to a belief in practical politics, to using the machinery one has and getting on with the world as it is." Thus, at least, venerable and philanthropic old men now in their honoured graves used to talk to me when I was a boy. But since then I have grown up and have disovered that these philanthropic old men were telling lies. What has really happened is exactly the opposite of what they said would happen. They said that I should lose my ideals and begin to believe in the methods of practical politicians. Now, I have not lost my ideals in the least; my faith in fundamentals is exactly what it always was. What I have lost is my old childlike faith in practical politics. I am still as much concerned as ever about the Battle of Armageddon; but I am not so much concerned about the General Election. As a babe I leapt up on my mother's knee at the mere mention of it. No; the vision is always solid and reliable. The vision is always a fact. It is the reality that is often a fraud. As much as I ever did, more than I ever did, I believe in Liberalism. But there was a rosy time of innocence when I believed in Liberals.

I take this instance of one of the enduring faiths because, having now to trace the roots of my personal speculation, this may be counted, I think, as the only positive bias. I was brought up a Liberal, and have always believed in democracy, in the elementary liberal doctrine of a self-governing humanity. If any one finds the phrase vague or threadbare, I can only pause for a moment to explain that the principle of democracy, as I mean it, can be stated in two propositions. The first is this: that the things common to all men are more important than the things peculiar to any men. Ordinary things are more valuable than extraordinary things; nay, they are more extraordinary. Man is something more awful than men; something more strange. The sense of the miracle of humanity itself should be always more vivid to us than any marvels of power, intellect, art, or civilization. The mere man on two legs, as such, should be felt as something more heart-breaking than any music and more startling than any caricature. Death is more tragic even than death by starvation. Having a nose is more comic even than having a Norman nose.

This is the first principle of democracy: that the essential things in men are the things they hold in common, not the things they hold separately. And the second principle is merely this: that the political instinct or desire is one of these things which they hold in common. Falling in love is more poetical than dropping into poetry. The democratic contention is that government (helping to rule the tribe) is a thing like falling in love, and not a thing like dropping into poetry. It is not something analogous to playing the church organ, painting on vellum, discovering the North Pole (that insidious habit), looping the loop, being Astronomer Royal, and so on. For these things we do not wish a man to do at all unless he does them well. It is, on the contrary, a thing analogous to writing one's own love-letters or blowing one's own nose. These things we want a man to do for himself, even if he does them badly. I am not here arguing the truth of any of these conceptions; I know that some moderns are asking to have their wives chosen by scientists, and they may soon be asking, for all I know, to have their noses blown by nurses. I merely say that mankind does recognize these universal human functions, and that democracy classes government among them. In short, the democratic faith is this: that the most terribly important things must be left to ordinary men themselves—the mating of the sexes, the rearing of the young, the laws of the state. This is democracy; and in this I have always believed.

But there is one thing that I have never from my youth up

been able to understand. I have never been able to understand where people got the idea that democracy was in some way opposed to tradition. It is obvious that tradition is only democracy extended through time. It is trusting to a consensus of common human voices rather than to some isolated or arbitrary record. The man who quotes some German historian against the tradition of the Catholic Church, for instance, is strictly appealing to aristocracy. He is appealing to the superiority of one expert against the awful authority of a mob. It is quite easy to see why a legend is treated, and ought to be treated, more respectfully than a book of history. The legend is generally made by the majority of people in the village, who are sane. The book is generally written by the one man in the village who is mad. Those who urge against tradition that men in the past were ignorant may go and urge it at the Carlton Club, along with the statement that voters in the slums are ignorant. It will not do for us. If we attach great importance to the opinion of ordinary men in great unanimity when we are dealing with daily matters, there is no reason why we should disregard it when we are dealing with history or fable. Tradition may be defined as an extension of the franchise. Tradition means giving votes to the most obscure of all classes, our ancestors. It is the democracy of the dead. Tradition refuses to submit to the small and arrogant oligarchy of those who merely happen to be walking about. All democrats object to men being disqualified by the accident of birth; tradition objects to their being disqualified by the accident of death. Democracy tells us not to neglect a good man's opinion, even if he is our groom; tradition asks us not to neglect a good man's opinion, even if he is our father. I, at any rate, cannot separate the two ideas of democracy and tradition; it seems evident to me that they are the same idea. We will have the dead at our councils. The Ancient Greeks voted by stones; these shall vote by tombstones. It is all quite regular and official, for most tombstones, like most ballot papers, are marked with a cross.

I have first to say, therefore, that if I have had a bias, it was always a bias in favour of democracy, and therefore of tradition. Before we come to any theoretic or logical beginnings I am content to allow for that personal equation; I have always been more inclined to believe the ruck of hard-working people than to believe that special and troublesome literary class to which I belong. I prefer even the fancies and prejudices of the people who see life from the inside to the clearest demonstrations of the people who see life from the outside. I would always trust the old wives' fables against the old maids' facts. As long as wit is mother wit it can be as wild as it pleases.

Now, I have to put together a general position, and I pretend to no training in such things. I propose to do it, therefore, by writing down one after another the three or four fundamental ideas which I have found for myself, pretty much in the way that I found them. Then I shall roughly synthesise them, summing up my personal philosophy or natural religion; then I shall describe my startling discovery that the whole thing had been discovered before. It had been discovered by Christianity. But of these profound persuasions which I have to recount in order, the earliest was concerned with this element of popular tradition. And without the foregoing explanation touching tradition and democracy I could hardly make my mental experience clear. As it is, I do not know whether I can make it clear, but I now propose to try.

My first and last philosophy, that which I believe in with unbroken certainty, I learnt in the nursery. I generally learnt it from a nurse; that is, from the solemn and star-appointed priestess at once of democracy and tradition. The things I believed most then, the things I believe most now, are the things called fairy tales. They seem to me to be the entirely reasonable things. They are not fantasies: compared with them other things are fantastic. Compared with them religion and rationalism are both abnormal, though religion is abnormally right and rationalism abnormally wrong. Fairyland is nothing but the sunny country of common sense. It is not earth that judges heaven, but heaven

that judges earth; so for me at least it was not earth that criticised elfland, but elfland that criticised the earth. I knew the
magic beanstalk before I had tasted beans; I was sure of the
Man in the Moon before I was certain of the moon. This was
at one with all popular tradition. Modern minor poets are natu-
ralists, and talk about the bush or the brook; but the singers of
the old epics and fables were supernaturalists, and talked about
the gods of brook and bush. That is what the moderns mean
when they say that the ancients did not "appreciate Nature,"
because they said that Nature was divine. Old nurses do not
tell children about the grass, but about the fairies that dance
on the grass; and the old Greeks could not see the trees for the
dryads.

But I deal here with what ethic and philosophy come from
being fed on fairy tales. If I were describing them in detail I
could note many noble and healthy principles that arise from
them. There is the chivalrous lesson of "Jack the Giant Killer";
that giants should be killed because they are gigantic. It is a
manly mutiny against pride as such. For the rebel is older than
all the kingdoms, and the Jacobin has more tradition than the
Jacobite. There is the lesson of "Cinderella," which is the same
as that of the Magnificat—*exaltavit humiles*. There is the great
lesson of "Beauty and the Beast"; that a thing must be loved *before* it is loveable. There is the terrible allegory of the "Sleeping
Beauty," which tells how the human creature was blessed with
all birthday gifts, yet cursed with death; and how death also may
perhaps be softened to a sleep. But I am not concerned with any
of the separate statutes of elfland, but with the whole spirit of
its law, which I learnt before I could speak, and shall retain
when I cannot write. I am concerned with a certain way of looking at life, which was created in me by the fairy tales, but has
since been meekly ratified by the mere facts.

It might be stated this way. There are certain sequences or developments (cases of one thing following another), which are,
in the true sense of the word, reasonable. They are, in the true

sense of the word, necessary. Such are mathematical and merely
logical sequences. We in fairyland (who are the most reasonable
of all creatures) admit that reason and that necessity. For instance, if the Ugly Sisters are older than Cinderella, it is (in an
iron and awful sense) *necessary* that Cinderella is younger than
the Ugly Sisters. There is no getting out of it. Haeckel may talk
as much fatalism about that fact as he pleases: it really must be.
If Jack is the son of a miller, a miller is the father of Jack. Cold
reason decrees it from her awful throne: and we in fairyland
submit. If the three brothers all ride horses, there are six animals
and eighteen legs involved: that is true rationalism, and fairyland
is full of it. But as I put my head over the hedge of the elves
and began to take notice of the natural world, I observed an
extraordinary thing. I observed that learned men in spectacles
were talking of the actual things that happened—dawn and death
and so on—as if *they* were rational and inevitable. They talked
as if the fact that trees bear fruit were just as *necessary* as the
fact that two and one trees make three. But it is not. There
is an enormous difference by the test of fairyland; which is the
test of the imagination. You cannot *imagine* two and one not
making three. But you can easily imagine trees not growing
fruit; you can imagine them growing golden candlesticks or
tigers hanging on by the tail. These men in spectacles spoke
much of a man named Newton, who was hit by an apple, and
who discovered a law. But they could not be got to see the
distinction between a true law, a law of reason, and the mere
fact of apples falling. If the apple hit Newton's nose, Newton's
nose hit the apple. That is a true necessity: because we cannot
conceive the one occurring without the other. But we can quite
well conceive the apple not falling on his nose; we can fancy it
flying ardently through the air to hit some other nose, of which
it had a more definite dislike. We have always in our fairy tales
kept this sharp distinction between the science of mental relations, in which there really are laws, and the science of physical
facts, in which there are no laws, but only weird repetitions. We

believe in bodily miracles, but not in mental impossibilities. We believe that a Bean-stalk climbed up to Heaven; but that does not at all confuse our convictions on the philosophical question of how many beans make five.

Here is the peculiar perfection of tone and truth in the nursery tales. The man of science says, "Cut the stalk, and the apple will fall"; but he says it calmly, as if the one idea really led up to the other. The witch in the fairy tale says, "Blow the horn, and the ogre's castle will fall"; but she does not say it as if it were something in which the effect obviously arose out of the cause. Doubtless she has given the advice to many champions, and has seen many castles fall, but she does not lose either her wonder or her reason. She does not muddle her head until it imagines a necessary mental connection between a horn and a falling tower. But the scientific men do muddle their heads, until they imagine a necessary mental connection between an apple leaving the tree and an apple reaching the ground. They do really talk as if they had found not only a set of marvellous facts, but a truth connecting those facts. They do talk as if the connection of two strange things physically connected them philosophically. They feel that because one incomprehensible thing constantly follows another incomprehensible thing the two together somehow make up a comprehensible thing. Two black riddles make a white answer.

In fairyland we avoid the word "law"; but in the land of science they are singularly fond of it. Thus they will call some interesting conjecture about how forgotten folks pronounced the alphabet, Grimm's Law. But Grimm's Law is far less intellectual than Grimm's Fairy Tales. The tales are, at any rate, certainly tales; while the law is not a law. A law implies that we know the nature of the generalisation and enactment; not merely that we have noticed some of the effects. If there is a law that pick-pockets shall go to prison, it implies that there is an imaginable mental connection between the idea of prison and the idea of picking pockets. And we know what the idea is. We can say why we take liberty from a man who takes liberties. But we cannot say why an egg can turn into a chicken any more than we can say why a bear could turn into a fairy prince. As *ideas*, the egg and the chicken are further off from each other than the bear and the prince; for no egg in itself suggests a chicken, whereas some princes do suggest bears. Granted, then, that certain transformations do happen, it is essential that we should regard them in the philosophic manner of fairy tales, not in the unphilosophic manner of science and the "Laws of Nature." When we are asked why eggs turn to birds or fruits fall in autumn, we must answer exactly as the fairy godmother would answer if Cinderella asked her why mice turned to horses or her clothes fell from her at twelve o'clock. We must answer that it is *magic*. It is not a "law," for we do not understand its general formula. It is not a necessity, for though we can count on it happening practically, we have no right to say that it must always happen. It is no argument for unalterable law (as Huxley fancied) that we count on the ordinary course of things. We do not count on it; we bet on it. We risk the remote possibility of a miracle as we do that of a poisoned pancake or a world-destroying comet. We leave it out of account, not because it is a miracle, and therefore an impossibility, but because it is a miracle, and therefore an exception. All the terms used in the science books, "law," "necessity," "order," "tendency," and so on, are really unintellectual, because they assume an inner synthesis, which we do not possess. The only words that ever satisfied me as describing Nature are the terms used in the fairy books, "charm," "spell," "enchantment." They express the arbitrariness of the fact and its mystery. A tree grows fruit because it is a *magic* tree. Water runs downhill because it is bewitched. The sun shines because it is bewitched.

I deny altogether that this is fantastic or even mystical. We may have some mysticism later on; but this fairy-tale language about things is simply rational and agnostic. It is the only way I can express in words my clear and definite perception that one

thing is quite distinct from another; that there is no logical connection between flying and laying eggs. It is the man who talks
about "a law" that he has never seen who is the mystic. Nay, the
ordinary scientific man is strictly a sentimentalist. He is a sentimentalist in this essential sense, that he is soaked and swept away
by mere associations. He has so often seen birds fly and lay eggs
that he feels as if there must be some dreamy, tender connection
between the two ideas, whereas there is none. A forlorn lover
might be unable to dissociate the moon from lost love; so
the materialist is unable to dissociate the moon from the tide. In
both cases there is no connection, except that one has seen them
together. A sentimentalist might shed tears at the smell of apple-
blossom, because, by a dark association of his own, it reminded
him of his boyhood. So the materialist professor (though he conceals his tears) is yet a sentimentalist, because, by a dark association of his own, apple-blossoms remind him of apples. But the
cool rationalist from fairyland does not see why, in the abstract,
the apple tree should not grow crimson tulips; it sometimes does
in his country.

This elementary wonder, however, is not a mere fancy derived
from the fairy tales; on the contrary, all the fire of the fairy tales
is derived from this. Just as we all like love tales because there
is an instinct of sex, we all like astonishing tales because they
touch the nerve of the ancient instinct of astonishment. This is
proved by the fact that when we are very young children we do
not need fairy tales: we only need tales. Mere life is interesting
enough. A child of seven is excited by being told that Tommy
opened a door and saw a dragon. But a child of three is excited
by being told that Tommy opened a door. Boys like romantic
tales; but babies like realistic tales—because they find them romantic. In fact, a baby is about the only person, I should think,
to whom a modern realistic novel could be read without boring
him. This proves that even nursery tales only echo an almost pre-
natal leap of interest and amazement. These tales say that apples
were golden only to refresh the forgotten moment when we

found that they were green. They make rivers run with wine only to make us remember, for one wild moment, that they run with water. I have said that this is wholly reasonable and even agnostic. And, indeed, on this point I am all for the higher agnosticism; its better name is Ignorance. We have all read in scientific books, and, indeed, in all romances, the story of the man who has forgotten his name. This man walks about the streets and can see and appreciate everything; only he cannot remember who he is. Well, every man is that man in the story. Every man has forgotten who he is. One may understand the cosmos, but never the ego; the self is more distant than any star. Thou shalt love the Lord thy God; but thou shalt not know thyself. We are all under the same mental calamity; we have all forgotten our names. We have all forgotten what we really are. All that we call common sense and rationality and practicality and positivism only means that for certain dead levels of our life we forget that we have forgotten. All that we call spirit and art and ecstacy only means that for one awful instant we remember that we forget.

But though (like the man without memory in the novel) we walk the streets with a sort of half-witted admiration, still it is admiration. It is admiration in English and not only admiration in Latin. The wonder has a positive element of praise. This is the next milestone to be definitely marked on our road through fairyland. I shall speak in the next chapter about optimists and pessimists in their intellectual aspect, so far as they have one. Here I am only trying to describe the enormous emotions which cannot be described. And the strongest emotion was that life was as precious as it was puzzling. It was an ecstacy because it was an adventure; it was an adventure because it was an opportunity. The goodness of the fairy tale was not affected by the fact that there might be more dragons than princesses; it was good to be in a fairy tale. The test of all happiness is gratitude; and I felt grateful, though I hardly knew to whom. Children are grateful when Santa Claus puts in their stockings gifts of toys or sweets.

Could I not be grateful to Santa Claus when he put in my stockings the gift of two miraculous legs? We thank people for birthday presents of cigars and slippers. Can I thank no one for the birthday present of birth?

There were, then, these two first feelings, indefensible and indisputable. The world was a shock, but it was not merely shocking; existence was a surprise, but it was a pleasant surprise. In fact, all my first views were exactly uttered in a riddle that stuck in my brain from boyhood. The question was, "What did the first frog say?" And the answer was, "Lord, how you made me jump!" That says succinctly all that I am saying. God made the frog jump; but the frog prefers jumping. But when these things are settled there enters the second great principle of the fairy philosophy.

Any one can see it who will simply read "Grimm's Fairy Tales" or the fine collections of Mr. Andrew Lang. For the pleasure of pedantry I will call it the Doctrine of Conditional Joy. Touchstone talked of much virtue in an "if"; according to elfin ethics all virtue is in an "if." The note of the fairy utterance always is, "You may live in a palace of gold and sapphire, *if* you do not say the word 'cow' "; or "You may live happily with the King's daughter, *if* you do not show her an onion." The vision always hangs upon a veto. All the dizzy and colossal things conceded depend upon one small thing withheld. All the wild and whirling things that are let loose depend upon one thing that is forbidden. Mr. W. B. Yeats, in his exquisite and piercing elfin poetry, describes the elves as lawless; they plunge in innocent anarchy on the unbridled horses of the air—

> "Ride on the crest of the dishevelled tide,
> And dance upon the mountains like a flame."

It is a dreadful thing to say that Mr. W. B. Yeats does not understand fairyland. But I do say it. He is an ironical Irishman, full of intellectual reactions. He is not stupid enough to understand fairyland. Fairies prefer people of the yokel type like myself;

people who gape and grin and do as they are told. Mr. Yeats reads into elfland all the righteous insurrection of his own race. But the lawlessness of Ireland is a Christian lawlessness, founded on reason and justice. The Fenian is rebelling against something he understands only too well; but the true citizen of fairyland is obeying something that he does not understand at all. In the fairy tale an incomprehensible happiness rests upon an incomprehensible condition. A box is opened, and all evils fly out. A word is forgotten, and cities perish. A lamp is lit, and love flies away. A flower is plucked, and human lives are forfeited. An apple is eaten, and the hope of God is gone.

This is the tone of fairy tales, and it is certainly not lawlessness or even liberty, though men under a mean modern tyranny may think it liberty by comparison. People out of Portland Gaol might think Fleet Street free; but closer study will prove that both fairies and journalists are the slaves of duty. Fairy god-mothers seem at least as strict as other god-mothers. Cinderella received a coach out of Wonderland and a coachman out of no-where, but she received a command—which might have come out of Brixton—that she should be back by twelve. Also, she had a glass slipper; and it cannot be a coincidence that glass is so common a substance in folk-lore. This princess lives in a glass castle, that princess on a glass hill; this one sees all things in a mirror; they may all live in glass houses if they will not throw stones. For this thin glitter of glass everywhere is the expression of the fact that the happiness is bright but brittle, like the substance most easily smashed by a housemaid or a cat. And this fairy-tale sentiment also sank into me and became my sentiment towards the whole world. I felt and feel that life itself is as bright as the diamond, but as brittle as the window-pane; and when the heavens were compared to the terrible crystal I can remember a shudder. I was afraid that God would drop the cosmos with a crash.

Remember, however, that to be breakable is not the same as to be perishable. Strike a glass, and it will not endure an instant; simply do not strike it, and it will endure a thousand years. Such, it seemed, was the joy of man, either in elfland or on earth; the happiness depended on *not doing something* which you could at any moment do and which, very often, it was not obvious why you should not do. Now, the point here is that to *me* this did not seem unjust. If the miller's third son said to the fairy, "Explain why I must not stand on my head in the fairy palace," the other might fairly reply, "Well, if it comes to that, explain the fairy palace." If Cinderella says, "How is it that I must leave the ball at twelve?" her godmother might answer, "How is it that you are going there till twelve?" If I leave a man in my will ten talking elephants and a hundred winged horses, he cannot complain if the conditions partake of the slight eccentricity of the gift. He must not look a winged horse in the mouth. And it seemed to me that existence was itself so very eccentric a legacy that I could not complain of not understanding the limitations of the vision when I did not understand the vision they limited. The frame was no stranger than the picture. The veto might well be as wild as the vision; it might be as startling as the sun, as elusive as the waters, as fantastic and terrible as the towering trees.

For this reason (we may call it the fairy-god-mother philosophy) I never could join the young men of my time in feeling what they called the general sentiment of *revolt*. I should have resisted, let us hope, any rules that were evil, and with these and their definition I shall deal in another chapter. But I did not feel disposed to resist any rule merely because it was mysterious. Estates are sometimes held by foolish forms, the breaking of a stick or the payment of a peppercorn: I was willing to hold the huge estate of earth and heaven by any such feudal fantasy. It could not well be wilder than the fact that I was allowed to hold it at all. At this stage I give only one ethical instance to show my meaning. I could never mix in the common murmur of that rising generation against monogamy, because no restriction on sex seemed so odd and unexpected as sex itself. To be allowed, like Endymion, to make love to the moon and then to complain that Jupiter kept his own moons in a harem seemed to me (bred on fairy tales like Endymion's) a vulgar anti-climax. Keeping to one woman is a small price for so much as seeing one woman. To complain that I could only be married once was like complaining that I had only been born once. It was incommensurate with the terrible excitement of which one was talking. It showed, not an exaggerated sensibility to sex, but a curious insensibility to it. A man is a fool who complains that he cannot enter Eden by five gates at once. Polygamy is a lack of the realization of sex; it is like a man plucking five pears in mere absence of mind. The æsthetes touched the last insane limits of language in their eulogy on lovely things. The thistledown made them weep; a burnished beetle brought them to their knees. Yet their emotion never impressed me for an instant, for this reason, that it never occurred to them to pay for their pleasure in any sort of symbolic sacrifice. Men (I felt) might fast forty days for the sake of hearing a blackbird sing. Men might go through fire to find a cowslip. Yet these lovers of beauty could not even keep sober for the blackbird. They would not go through common Christian marriage by way of recompense to the cowslip. Surely one might pay for extraordinary joy in ordinary morals. Oscar Wilde said that sunsets were not valued because we could not pay for sunsets. Oscar Wilde was wrong; we can pay for sunsets. We can pay for them by not being Oscar Wilde.

Well, I left the fairy tales lying on the floor of the nursery, and I have not found any books so sensible since. I left the nurse guardian of tradition and democracy, and I have not found any modern type so sanely radical or so sanely conservative. But the matter for important comment was here: that when I first went out into the mental atmosphere of the modern world, I found that the modern world was positively opposed on two points to my nurse and to the nursery tales. It has taken me a long time to find out that the modern world is wrong and my nurse was right. The really curious thing was this: that modern thought contradicted this basic creed of my boyhood on its two most essential doctrines. I have explained that the fairy tales founded in me two convictions; first, that this world is a wild and startling place, which might have been quite different, but which is quite delightful; second, that before this wildness and delight one may well be modest and submit to the queerest limitations of so queer a kindness. But I found the whole modern world running like a high tide against both my tendernesses; and the shock of that collision created two sudden and spontaneous sentiments, which I have had ever since and which, crude as they were, have since hardened into convictions.

First, I found the whole modern world talking scientific fatalism; saying that everything is as it must always have been, being unfolded without fault from the beginning. The leaf on the tree is green because it could never have been anything else. Now, the fairy-tale philosopher is glad that the leaf is green precisely because it might have been scarlet. He feels as if it had turned green an instant before he looked at it. He is pleased that snow is white on the strictly reasonable ground that it might have been black. Every colour has in it a bold quality as of choice; the red of garden roses is not only decisive but dramatic, like suddenly spilt blood. He feels that something has been *done*. But the great determinists of the nineteenth century were strongly against this native feeling that something had happened an instant before. In fact, according to them, nothing ever really had happened since the beginning of the world. Nothing ever had happened since existence had happened; and even about the date of that they were not very sure.

The modern world as I found it was solid for modern Calvinism, for the necessity of things being as they are. But when I came to ask them I found they had really no proof of this unavoidable repetition in things except the fact that the things were repeated. Now, the mere repetition made the things to me rather more weird than more rational. It was as if, having seen a curiously shaped nose in the street and dismissed it as an accident, I had then seen six other noses of the same astonishing shape. I should have fancied for a moment that it must be some local secret society. So one elephant having a trunk was odd; but all elephants having trunks looked like a plot. I speak here only of an emotion, and of an emotion at once stubborn and subtle. But the repetition in Nature seemed sometimes to be an excited repetition, like that of an angry schoolmaster saying the same thing over and over again. The grass seemed signalling to me with all its fingers at once; the crowded stars seemed bent upon being understood. The sun would make me see him if he rose a thousand times. The recurrences of the universe rose to the maddening rhythm of an incantation, and I began to see an idea.

All the towering materialism which dominates the modern mind rests ultimately upon one assumption; a false assumption. It is supposed that if a thing goes on repeating itself it is probably dead; a piece of clockwork. People feel that if the universe was personal it would vary; if the sun were alive it would dance. This is a fallacy even in relation to known fact. For the variation in human affairs is generally brought into them, not by life, but by death; by the dying down or breaking off of their strength or desire. A man varies his movements because of some slight element of failure or fatigue. He gets into an omnibus because he is tired of walking; or he walks because he is tired of sitting still. But if his life and joy were so gigantic that he never tired of going to Islington, he might go to Islington as regularly as the Thames goes to Sheerness. The very speed and ecstacy of his life would have the stillness of death. The sun rises every morning. I do not rise every morning; but the variation is due not to my activity, but to my inaction. Now, to put the matter in a popular phrase, it might be true that the sun rises regularly because he never gets tired of rising. His routine might be due, not to a lifelessness, but to a rush of life. The thing I mean can be seen, for instance, in children, when they find some game or joke that they specially enjoy. A child kicks his legs rhythmically through excess, not absence, of life. Because children have abounding vitality, because they are in spirit fierce and free, therefore they want things repeated and unchanged. They always say, "Do it again"; and the grown-up person does it again until he is nearly dead. For grown-up people are not strong enough to exult in monotony. But perhaps God is strong enough to exult in monotony. It is possible that God says every morning, "Do it again" to the sun; and every evening, "Do it again" to the moon. It may not be automatic necessity that makes all daisies alike; it may be that God makes every daisy separately, but has never got tired of making them. It may be that He has the eternal appetite of infancy; for we have sinned and grown old, and our Father is younger than we. The repetition in Nature may not be a mere recurrence; it may be a theatrical *encore*. Heaven may *encore* the bird who laid an egg. If the human being conceives and brings forth a human child instead of bringing forth a fish, or a bat, or a griffin, the reason may not be that we are fixed in an animal fate without life or purpose. It may be that our little tragedy has touched the gods, that they admire it from their starry galleries, and that at the end of every human drama man is called again and again before the curtain. Repetition may go on for millions of years, by mere choice, and at any instant it may stop. Man may stand on the earth generation after generation, and yet each birth be his positively last appearance.

This was my first conviction; made by the shock of my childish emotions meeting the modern creed in mid-career. I had always vaguely felt facts to be miracles in the sense that they are wonderful: now I began to think them miracles in the stricter sense that they were *wilful*. I mean that they were, or might be, repeated exercises of some will. In short, I had always believed that the world involved magic: now I thought that perhaps it involved a magician. And this pointed a profound emotion always present and sub-conscious; that this world of ours has some purpose; and if there is a purpose, there is a person. I had always felt life first as a story: and if there is a story there is a story-teller.

But modern thought also hit my second human tradition. It went against the fairy feeling about strict limits and conditions. The one thing it loved to talk about was expansion and large-

ness. Herbert Spencer would have been greatly annoyed if any
one had called him an imperialist, and therefore it is highly regrettable that nobody did. But he was an imperialist of the lowest
type. He popularized this contemptible notion that the size of the
solar system ought to over-awe the spiritual dogma of man. Why
should a man surrender his dignity to the solar system any more
than to a whale? If mere size proves that man is not the image of
God, then a whale may be the image of God; a somewhat formless image; what one might call an impressionist portrait. It is
quite futile to argue that man is small compared to the cosmos;
for man was always small compared to the nearest tree. But Herbert Spencer, in his headlong imperialism, would insist that we
had in some way been conquered and annexed by the astronomical universe. He spoke about men and their ideals exactly as the
most insolent Unionist talks about the Irish and their ideals. He
turned mankind into a small nationality. And his evil influence
can be seen even in the most spirited and honourable of later
scientific authors; notably in the early romances of Mr. H. G.
Wells. Many moralists have in an exaggerated way represented
the earth as wicked. But Mr. Wells and his school made the
heavens wicked. We should lift up our eyes to the stars from
whence would come our ruin.

But the expansion of which I speak was much more evil than
all this. I have remarked that the materialist, like the madman, is
in prison; in the prison of one thought. These people seemed to
think it singularly inspiring to keep on saying that the prison was
very large. The size of this scientific universe gave one no novelty, no relief. The cosmos went on for ever, but not in its wildest constellation could there be anything really interesting; anything, for instance, such as forgiveness or free will. The grandeur
or infinity of the secret of its cosmos added nothing to it. It was
like telling a prisoner in Reading gaol that he would be glad to
hear that the gaol now covered half the county. The warder
would have nothing to show the man except more and more long
corridors of stone lit by ghastly lights and empty of all that is

human. So these expanders of the universe had nothing to show us except more and more infinite corridors of space lit by ghastly suns and empty of all that is divine.

In fairyland there had been a real law; a law that could be broken, for the definition of a law is something that can be broken. But the machinery of this cosmic prison was something that could not be broken; for we ourselves were only a part of its machinery. We were either unable to do things or we were destined to do them. The idea of the mystical condition quite disappeared; one can neither have the firmness of keeping laws nor the fun of breaking them. The largeness of this universe had nothing of that freshness and airy outbreak which we have praised in the universe of the poet. This modern universe is literally an empire; that is, it was vast, but it is not free. One went into larger and larger windowless rooms, rooms big with Babylonian perspective; but one never found the smallest window or a whisper of outer air.

Their infernal parallels seemed to expand with distance; but for me all good things come to a point, swords for instance. So finding the boast of the big cosmos so unsatisfactory to my emotions I began to argue about it a little; and I soon found that the whole attitude was even shallower than could have been expected. According to these people the cosmos was one thing since it had one unbroken rule. Only (they would say) while it is one thing it is also the only thing there is. Why, then, should one worry particularly to call it large? There is nothing to compare it with. It would be just as sensible to call it small. A man may say, "I like this vast cosmos, with its throng of stars and its crowd of varied creatures." But if it comes to that why should not a man say, "I like this cosy little cosmos, with its decent number of stars and as neat a provision of live stock as I wish to see"? One is as good as the other; they are both mere sentiments. It is mere sentiment to rejoice that the sun is larger than the earth; it is quite as sane a sentiment to rejoice that the sun is no larger than it is. A man chooses to have an emotion about the largeness of

the world; why should he not choose to have an emotion about
its smallness?

It happened that I had that emotion. When one is fond of anything one addresses it by diminutives, even if it is an elephant or
a life guardsman. The reason is, that anything, however huge,
that can be conceived of as complete, can be conceived of as
small. If military moustaches did not suggest a sword or tusks a
tail, then the object would be vast because it would be immeasurable. But the moment you can imagine a guardsman you can
imagine a small guardsman. The moment you really see an elephant you can call it "Tiny." If you can make a statue of a thing
you can make a statuette of it. These people professed that the
universe was one coherent thing; but they were not fond of the
universe. But I was frightfully fond of the universe and wanted
to address it by a diminutive. I often did so; and it never seemed
to mind. Actually and in truth I did feel that these dim dogmas
of vitality were better expressed by calling the world small than
by calling it large. For about infinity there was a sort of carelessness which was the reverse of the fierce and pious care which I
felt touching the pricelessness and the peril of life. They showed
only a dreary waste; but I felt a sort of sacred thrift. For economy is far more romantic than extravagance. To them stars were
an unending income of halfpence; but I felt about the golden
sun and the silver moon as a schoolboy feels if he has one sovereign and one shilling.

These subconscious convictions are best hit off by the colour
and tone of certain tales. Thus I have said that stories of magic
alone can express my sense that life is not only a pleasure but a
kind of eccentric privilege. I may express this other feeling of
cosmic cosiness by allusion to another book always read in boyhood, "Robinson Crusoe," which I read about this time, and
which owes its eternal vivacity to the fact that it celebrates the
poetry of limits, nay, even the wild romance of prudence. Crusoe
is a man on a small rock with a few comforts just snatched from
the sea: the best thing in the book is simply the list of things

saved from the wreck. The greatest of poems is an inventory. Every kitchen tool becomes ideal because Crusoe might have dropped it in the sea. It is a good exercise, in empty or ugly hours of the day, to look at anything, the coal-scuttle or the book-case, and think how happy one could be to have brought it out of the sinking ship on to the solitary island. But it is a better exercise still to remember how all things have had this hairbreadth escape: everything has been saved from a wreck. Every man has had one horrible adventure: as a hidden untimely birth he had not been, as infants that never see the light. Men spoke much in my boyhood of restricted or ruined men of genius: and it was common to say that many a man was a Great Might-Have-Been. To me it is a more solid and startling fact that any man in the street is a Great Might-Not-Have-Been.

But I really felt (the fancy may seem foolish) as if all the order and number of things were the romantic remnant of Crusoe's ship. That there are two sexes and one sun, was like the fact that there were two guns and one axe. It was poignantly urgent that none should be lost; but somehow, it was rather fun that none could be added. The trees and the planets seemed like things saved from the wreck: and when I saw the Matterhorn I was glad that it had not been overlooked in the confusion. I felt economical about the stars as if they were sapphires (they are called so in Milton's Eden): I hoarded the hills. For the universe is a single jewel, and while it is a natural cant to talk of a jewel as peerless and priceless, of this jewel it is literally true. This cosmos is indeed without peer and without price: for there cannot be another one.

Thus ends, in unavoidable inadequacy, the attempt to utter the unutterable things. These are my ultimate attitudes towards life; the soils for the seeds of doctrine. These in some dark way I thought before I could write, and felt before I could think: that we may proceed more easily afterwards, I will roughly recapitulate them now. I felt in my bones; first, that this world does not explain itself. It may be a miracle with a supernatural explanation; it may be a conjuring trick, with a natural explanation. But the explanation of the conjuring trick, if it is to satisfy me, will have to be better than the natural explanations I have heard. The thing is magic, true or false. Second, I came to feel as if magic must have a meaning, and meaning must have some one to mean it. There was something personal in the world, as in a work of art; whatever it meant it meant violently. Third, I thought this purpose beautiful in its old design, in spite of its defects, such as dragons. Fourth, that the proper form of thanks to it is some form of humility and restraint: we should thank God for beer and Burgundy by not drinking too much of them. We owed, also, an obedience to whatever made us. And last, and strangest, there had come into my mind a vague and vast impression that in some way all good was a remnant to be stored and held sacred out of some primordial ruin. Man had saved his good as Crusoe saved his goods: he had saved them from a wreck. All this I felt and the age gave me no encouragement to feel it. And all this time I had not even thought of Christian theology.

THE FLAG OF THE WORLD

WHEN I was a boy there were two curious men running about who were called the optimist and the pessimist. I constantly used the words myself, but I cheerfully confess that I never had any very special idea of what they meant. The only thing which might be considered evident was that they could not mean what they said; for the ordinary verbal explanation was that the optimist thought this world as good as it could be, while the pessimist thought it as bad as it could be. Both these statements being obviously raving nonsense, one had to cast about for other explanations. An optimist could not mean a man who thought everything right and nothing wrong. For that is meaningless; it is like calling everything right and nothing left. Upon the whole, I came to the conclusion that the optimist thought everything good except the pessimist, and that the pessimist thought everything bad, except himself. It would be unfair to omit altogether from the list the mysterious but suggestive definition said to have been given by a little girl, "An optimist is a man who looks after your eyes, and a pessimist is a man who looks after your feet." I am not sure that this is not the best definition of all. There is even a sort of allegorical truth in it. For there might, perhaps, be a profitable distinction drawn between that more dreary thinker who thinks merely of our contact with the earth from moment to moment, and that happier thinker who considers rather our primary power of vision and of choice of road.

But this is a deep mistake in this alternative of the optimist and the pessimist. The assumption of it is that a man criticises this world as if he were house-hunting, as if he were being shown over a new suite of apartments. If a man came to this world from some other world in full possession of his powers he might discuss whether the advantage of midsummer woods made up for the disadvantage of mad dogs, just as a man looking for lodgings might balance the presence of a telephone against the absence of a sea view. But no man is in that position. A man belongs to this world before he begins to ask if it is nice to belong to it. He has fought for the flag, and often won heroic victories for the flag long before he has ever enlisted. To put shortly what seems the essential matter, he has a loyalty long before he has any admiration.

In the last chapter it has been said that the primary feeling that this world is strange and yet attractive is best expressed in fairy tales. The reader may, if he likes, put down the next stage to that bellicose and even jingo literature which commonly comes next in the history of a boy. We all owe much sound morality to the penny dreadfuls. Whatever the reason, it seemed and still seems to me that our attitude towards life can be better expressed in terms of a kind of military loyalty than in terms of criticism and approval. My acceptance of the universe is not optimism, it is more like patriotism. It is a matter of primary loyalty. The world is not a lodging-house at Brighton, which we are to leave because it is miserable. It is the fortress of our family, with the flag flying on the turret, and the more miserable it is the less we should leave it. The point is not that this world is too sad to love or too glad not to love; the point is that when you do love a thing, its gladness is a reason for loving it, and its sadness a reason for loving it more. All optimistic thoughts about England and all pessimistic thoughts about her are alike reasons for the English patriot. Similarly, optimism and pessimism are alike arguments for the cosmic patriot.

Let us suppose we are confronted with a desperate thing—say Pimlico. If we think what is really best for Pimlico we shall find the thread of thought leads to the throne or the mystic and the arbitrary. It is not enough for a man to disapprove of Pimlico: in that case he will merely cut his throat or move to Chelsea. Nor, certainly, is it enough for a man to approve of Pimlico: for then it will remain Pimlico, which would be awful. The only way out of it seems to be for somebody to love Pimlico: to love it with a transcendental tie and without any earthly reason. If there arose a man who loved Pimlico, then Pimlico would rise into ivory towers and golden pinnacles; Pimlico would attire herself as a woman does when she is loved. For decoration is not given to hide horrible things: but to decorate things already adorable. A mother does not give her child a blue bow because he is so ugly without it. A lover does not give a girl a necklace to hide her neck. If men loved Pimlico as mothers love children, arbitrarily, because it is *theirs*, Pimlico in a year or two might be fairer than Florence. Some readers will say that this is a mere fantasy. I answer that this is the actual history of mankind. This, as a fact, is how cities did grow great. Go back to the darkest roots of civilization and you will find them knotted round some sacred stone or encircling some sacred well. People first paid honour to a spot and afterwards gained glory for it. Men did not love Rome because she was great. She was great because they had loved her.

The eighteenth-century theories of the social contract have been exposed to much clumsy criticism in our time; in so far as they meant that there is at the back of all historic government an idea of content and co-operation, they were demonstrably right. But they really were wrong in so far as they suggested that men had ever aimed at order or ethics directly by a conscious exchange of interests. Morality did not begin by one man saying to another, "I will not hit you if you do not hit me"; there is no trace of such a transaction. There *is* a trace of both men having said, "We must not hit each other in the holy place." They gained their morality by guarding their religion. They did not cultivate courage. They fought for the shrine, and found they had become courageous. They did not cultivate cleanliness. They purified themselves for the altar, and found that they were clean. The history of the Jews is the only early document known to most Englishmen, and the facts can be judged sufficiently from that. The Ten Commandments which have been found substantially common to mankind were merely military commands; a code of regimental orders, issued to protect a certain ark across a certain desert. Anarchy was evil because it endangered the sanctity. And only when they made a holy day for God did they find they had made a holiday for men.

If it be granted that this primary devotion to a place or thing is a source of creative energy, we can pass on to a very peculiar fact. Let us reiterate for an instant that the only right optimism is a sort of universal patriotism. What is the matter with the pessimist? I think it can be stated by saying that he is the cosmic anti-patriot. And what is the matter with the anti-patriot? I think it can be stated, without undue bitterness, by saying that he is the candid friend. And what is the matter with the candid friend. There we strike the rock of real life and immutable human nature.

I venture to say that what is bad in the candid friend is simply that he is not candid. He is keeping something back—his own gloomy pleasure in saying unpleasant things. He has a secret desire to hurt, not merely to help. This is certainly, I think, what makes a certain sort of anti-patriot irritating to healthy citizens. I do not speak (of course) of the anti-patriotism which only irritates feverish stockbrokers and gushing actresses; that is only patriotism speaking plainly. A man who says that no patriot should attack the Boer War until it is over is not worth answering intelligently; he is saying that no good son should warn his mother of a cliff until she has fallen over it. But there is an anti-patriot who honestly angers honest men, and the explanation of him is, I think, what I have suggested: he is the uncandid candid friend; the man who says, "I am sorry to say we are ruined," and is not sorry at all. And he may be said, without rhetoric, to be a traitor; for he is using that ugly knowledge which was allowed him to strengthen the army, to discourage people from joining it. Because he is allowed to be pessimistic as a military adviser he is being pessimistic as a recruiting sergeant. Just in the same way the pessimist (who is the cosmic anti-patriot) uses the freedom that life allows to her counsellors to lure away the people from her flag. Granted that he states only facts, it is still essential to know what are his emotions, what is his motive. It may be that twelve hundred men in Tottenham are down with smallpox; but we want to know whether this is stated by some great philosopher who wants to curse the gods, or only by some common clergyman who wants to help the men.

The evil of the pessimist is, then, not that he chastises gods and men, but that he does not love what he chastises—he has not this primary and supernatural loyalty to things. What is the evil of the man commonly called an optimist? Obviously, it is felt that the optimist, wishing to defend the honour of this world, will defend the indefensible. He is the jingo of the universe; he will say, "My cosmos, right or wrong." He will be less inclined to the reform of things; more inclined to a sort of front-bench official answer to all attacks, soothing every one with assurances. He will not wash the world, but whitewash the world. All this (which is true of a type of optimist) leads us to the one really interesting point of psychology, which could not be explained without it.

We say there must be a primal loyalty to life: the only question is, shall it be a natural or a supernatural loyalty? If you like to put it so, shall it be a reasonable or an unreasonable loyalty? Now, the extraordinary thing is that the bad optimism (the whitewashing, the weak defence of everything) comes in with the reasonable optimism. Rational optimism leads to stagnation: it is irrational optimism that leads to reform. Let me explain by using once more the parallel of patriotism. The man who is most likely to ruin the place he loves is exactly the man who loves it with a reason. The man who will improve the place is the man who loves it without a reason. If a man loves some feature of Pimlico (which seems unlikely), he may find himself defending that feature against Pimlico itself. But if he simply loves Pimlico itself, he may lay it waste and turn it into the New Jerusalem. I do not deny that reform may be excessive; I only say that it is the mystic patriot who reforms. Mere jingo self-contentment is commonest among those who have some pedantic reason for their patriotism. The worst jingoes do not love England, but a theory of England. If we love England for being an empire, we may overrate the success with which we rule the Hindoos. But if we love it only for being a nation, we can face all events: for it would be a nation even if the Hindoos ruled us. Thus also only those will permit their patriotism to falsify history whose patriotism depends on history. A man who loves England for being English will not mind how she arose. But a man who loves England for being Anglo-Saxon may go against all facts for his fancy. He may end (like Carlyle and Freeman) by maintaining that the Norman Conquest was a Saxon Conquest. He may end in utter unreason—because he has a reason. A man who loves France for being military will palliate the army of 1870. But a man who loves France for being France will improve the army of 1870. This is exactly what the French have done, and France is a good instance of the working paradox. Nowhere else is patriotism more purely abstract and arbitrary; and nowhere else is reform more drastic and sweeping. The more transcendental is your patriotism, the more practical are your politics.

Perhaps the most everyday instance of this point is in the case of women; and their strange and strong loyalty. Some stupid people started the idea that because women obviously back up their own people through everything, therefore women are blind and do not see anything. They can hardly have known any women. The same women who are ready to defend their men through thick and thin are (in their personal intercourse with the man) almost morbidly lucid about the thinness of his excuses or the thickness of his head. A man's friend likes him but leaves him as he is: his wife loves him and is always trying to turn him into somebody else. Women who are utter mystics in their creed are utter cynics in their criticism. Thackeray expressed this well when he made Pendennis' mother, who worshipped her son as a god, yet assume that he would go wrong as a man. She underrated his virtue, though she overrated his value.

The devotee is entirely free to criticise; the fanatic can safely be a sceptic. Love is not blind; that is the last thing that it is. Love is bound; and the more it is bound the less it is blind.

This at least had come to be my position about all that was called optimism, pessimism, and improvement. Before any cosmic act of reform we must have a cosmic oath of allegiance. A man must be interested in life, then he could be disinterested in his views of it. "My son give me thy heart"; the heart must be fixed on the right thing: the moment we have a fixed heart we have a free hand. I must pause to anticipate an obvious criticism. It will be said that a rational person accepts the world as mixed of good and evil with a decent satisfaction and a decent endurance. But this is exactly the attitude which I maintain to be defective. It is, I know, very common in this age; it was perfectly put in those quiet lines of Matthew Arnold which are more piercingly blasphemous than the shrieks of Schopenhauer—

> "Enough we live:—and if a life,
> With large results so little rife,
> Though bearable, seem hardly worth
> This pomp of worlds, this pain of birth."

I know this feeling fills our epoch, and I think it freezes our epoch. For our Titanic purposes of faith and revolution, what we need is not the cold acceptance of the world as a compromise, but some way in which we can heartily hate and heartily love it. We do not want joy and anger to neutralize each other and produce a surly contentment; we want a fiercer delight and a fiercer discontent. We have to feel the universe at once as an ogre's castle, to be stormed, and yet as our own cottage, to which we can return at evening.

No one doubts that an ordinary man can get on with this world: but we demand not strength enough to get on with it, but strength enough to get it on. Can he hate it enough to change it, and yet love it enough to think it worth changing? Can he look up at its colossal good without once feeling acquiescence?

Can he look up at its colossal evil without once feeling despair? Can he, in short, be at once not only a pessimist and an optimist, but a fanatical pessimist and a fanatical optimist? Is he enough of a pagan to die for the world, and enough of a Christian to die to it? In this combination, I maintain, it is the rational optimist who fails, the irrational optimist who succeeds. He is ready to smash the whole universe for the sake of itself.

I put these things not in their mature logical sequence, but as they came: and this view was cleared and sharpened by an accident of the time. Under the lengthening shadow of Ibsen, an argument arose whether it was not a very nice thing to murder one's self. Grave moderns told us that we must not even say "poor fellow," of a man who had blown his brains out, since he was an enviable person, and had only blown them out because of their exceptional excellence. Mr. William Archer even suggested that in the golden age there would be penny-in-the-slot machines, by which a man could kill himself for a penny. In all this I found myself utterly hostile to many who called themselves liberal and humane. Not only is suicide a sin, it is the sin. It is the ultimate and absolute evil, the refusal to take an interest in existence; the refusal to take the oath of loyalty to life. The man who kills a man, kills a man. The man who kills himself, kills all men; as far as he is concerned he wipes out the world. His act is worse (symbolically considered) than any rape or dynamite outrage. For it destroys all buildings: it insults all women. The thief is satisfied with diamonds; but the suicide is not: that is his crime. He cannot be bribed, even by the blazing stones of the Celestial City. The thief compliments the things he steals, if not the owner of them. But the suicide insults everything on earth by not stealing it. He defiles every flower by refusing to live for its sake. There is not a tiny creature in the cosmos at whom his death is not a sneer. When a man hangs himself on a tree, the leaves might fall off in anger and the birds fly away in fury: for each has received a personal affront. Of course there may be pathetic emotional excuses for the act. There often are for rape, and there

almost always are for dynamite. But if it comes to clear ideas and
the intelligent meaning of things, then there is much more rational and philosophic truth in the burial at the cross-roads and
the stake driven through the body, than in Mr. Archer's suicidal
automatic machines. There is a meaning in burying the suicide
apart. The man's crime is different from other crimes—for it
makes even crimes impossible.

About the same time I read a solemn flippancy by some free
thinker: he said that a suicide was only the same as a martyr.
The open fallacy of this helped to clear the question. Obviously
a suicide is the opposite of a martyr. A martyr is a man who cares
so much for something outside him, that he forgets his own personal life. A suicide is a man who cares so little for anything
outside him, that he wants to see the last of everything. One
wants something to begin: the other wants everything to end. In
other words, the martyr is noble, exactly because (however he
renounces the world or execrates all humanity) he confesses this
ultimate link with life; he sets his heart outside himself: he dies
that something may live. The suicide is ignoble because he has
not this link with being: he is a mere destroyer; spiritually, he
destroys the universe. And then I remembered the stake and the
cross-roads, and the queer fact that Christianity had shown this
weird harshness to the suicide. For Christianity had shown a wild
encouragement of the martyr. Historic Christianity was accused,
not entirely without reason, of carrying martyrdom and asceticism to a point, desolate and pessimistic. The early Christian
martyrs talked of death with a horrible happiness. They blas-
phemed the beautiful duties of the body: they smelt the grave
afar off like a field of flowers. All this has seemed to many the
very poetry of pessimism. Yet there is the stake at the cross-
roads to show what Christianity thought of the pessimist.

This was the first of the long train of enigmas with which
Christianity entered the discussion. And there went with it a
peculiarity of which I shall have to speak more markedly, as a
note of all Christian notions, but which distinctly began in this

one. The Christian attitude to the martyr and the suicide was not what is so often affirmed in modern morals. It was not a matter of degree. It was not that a line must be drawn somewhere, and that the self-slayer in exaltation fell within the line, the self-slayer in sadness just beyond it. The Christian feeling evidently was not merely that the suicide was carrying martyrdom too far. The Christian feeling was furiously for one and furiously against the other: these two things that looked so much alike were at opposite ends of heaven and hell. One man flung away his life; he was so good that his dry bones could heal cities in pestilence. Another man flung away life; he was so bad that his bones would pollute his brethren's. I am not saying this fierceness was right; but why was it so fierce?

Here it was that I first found that my wandering feet were in some beaten track. Christianity had also felt this opposition of the martyr to the suicide: had it perhaps felt it for the same reason? Had Christianity felt what I felt, but could not (and cannot) express—this need for a first loyalty to things, and then for a ruinous reform of things? Then I remembered that it was actually the charge against Christianity that it combined these two things which I was wildly trying to combine. Christianity was accused, at one and the same time, of being too optimistic about the universe and of being too pessimistic about the world. The coincidence made me suddenly stand still.

An imbecile habit has arisen in modern controversy of saying that such and such a creed can be held in one age but cannot be held in another. Some dogma, we are told, was credible in the twelfth century, but is not credible in the twentieth. You might as well say that a certain philosophy can be believed on Mondays, but cannot be believed on Tuesdays. You might as well say of a view of the cosmos that it was suitable to half-past three, but not suitable to half-past four. What a man can believe depends upon his philosophy, not upon the clock or the century. If a man believes in unalterable natural law, he cannot believe in any miracle in any age. If a man believes in a will behind law, he can believe in any miracle in any age. Suppose, for the sake of argument, we are concerned with a case of thaumaturgic healing. A materialist of the twelfth century could not believe it any more than a materialist of the twentieth century. But a Christian Scientist of the twentieth century can believe it as much as a Christian of the twelfth century. It is simply a matter of a man's theory of things. Therefore in dealing with any historical answer, the point is not whether it was given in our time, but whether it was given in answer to our question. And the more I thought about when and how Christianity had come into the world, the more I felt that it had actually come to answer this question.

It is commonly the loose and latitudinarian Christians who pay quite indefensible compliments to Christianity. They talk as if there had never been any piety or pity until Christianity came, a point on which any mediæval would have been eager to correct them. They represent that the remarkable thing about Christianity was that it was the first to preach simplicity or self-restraint, or inwardness and sincerity. They will think me very narrow (whatever that means) if I say that the remarkable thing about Christianity was that it was the first to preach Christianity. Its peculiarity was that it was peculiar, and simplicity and sincerity are not peculiar, but obvious ideals for all mankind. Christianity was the answer to a riddle, not the last truism uttered after a long talk. Only the other day I saw in an excellent weekly paper of Puritan tone this remark, that Christianity when stripped of its armour of dogma (as who should speak of a man stripped of his armour of bones), turned out to be nothing but the Quaker doctrine of the Inner Light. Now, if I were to say that Christianity came into the world specially to destroy the doctrine of the Inner Light, that would be an exaggeration. But it would be very much nearer to the truth. The last Stoics, like Marcus Aurelius, were exactly the people who did believe in the Inner Light. Their dignity, their weariness, their sad external care for others, their incurable internal care for themselves, were all due to the

Inner Light, and existed only by that dismal illumination. Notice that Marcus Aurelius insists, as such introspective moralists always do, upon small things done or undone; it is because he has not hate or love enough to make a moral revolution. He gets up early in the morning, just as our own aristocrats living the Simple Life get up early in the morning; because such altruism is much easier than stopping the games of the amphitheatre or giving the English people back their land. Marcus Aurelius is the most intolerable of human types. He is an unselfish egoist. An unselfish egoist is a man who has pride without the excuse of passion. Of all conceivable forms of enlightenment the worst is what these people call the Inner Light. Of all horrible religions the most horrible is the worship of the god within. Any one who knows any body knows how it would work; any one who knows any one from the Higher Thought Centre knows how it does work. That Jones shall worship the god within him turns out ultimately to mean that Jones shall worship Jones. Let Jones worship the sun or moon, anything rather than the Inner Light; let Jones worship cats or crocodiles, if he can find any in his street, but not the god within. Christianity came into the world firstly in order to assert with violence that a man had not only to look inwards, but to look outwards, to behold with astonishment and enthusiasm a divine company and a divine captain. The only fun of being a Christian was that a man was not left alone with the Inner Light, but definitely recognized an outer light, fair as the sun, clear as the moon, terrible as an army with banners.

All the same, it will be as well if Jones does not worship the sun and moon. If he does, there is a tendency for him to imitate them; to say, that because the sun burns insects alive, he may burn insects alive. He thinks that because the sun gives people sun-stroke, he may give his neighbour measles. He thinks that because the moon is said to drive men mad, he may drive his wife mad. This ugly side of mere external optimism had also shown itself in the ancient world. About the time when the Stoic idealism had begun to show the weaknesses of pessimism, the old nature worship of the ancients had begun to show the enormous weaknesses of optimism. Nature worship is natural enough while the society is young, or, in other words, Pantheism is all right as long as it is the worship of Pan. But Nature has another side which experience and sin are not slow in finding out, and it is no flippancy to say of the god Pan that he soon showed the cloven hoof. The only objection to Natural Religion is that somehow it always becomes unnatural. A man loves Nature in the morning for her innocence and amiability, and at nightfall, if he is loving her still, it is for her darkness and her cruelty. He washes at dawn in clear water as did the Wise Man of the Stoics, yet, somehow at the dark end of the day, he is bathing in hot bull's blood, as did Julian the Apostate. The mere pursuit of health always leads to something unhealthy. Physical nature must not be made the direct object of obedience; it must be enjoyed, not worshipped. Stars and mountains must not be taken seriously. If they are, we end where the pagan nature worship ended. Because the earth is kind, we can imitate all her cruelties. Because sexuality is sane, we can all go mad about sexuality. Mere optimism had reached its insane and appropriate termination. The theory that everything was good had become an orgy of everything that was bad.

On the other side our idealist pessimists were represented by the old remnant of the Stoics. Marcus Aurelius and his friends had really given up the idea of any god in the universe and looked only to the god within. They had no hope of any virtue in nature, and hardly any hope of any virtue in society. They had not enough interest in the outer world really to wreck or revolutionise it. They did not love the city enough to set fire to it. Thus the ancient world was exactly in our own desolate dilemma. The only people who really enjoyed this world were busy breaking it up; and the virtuous people did not care enough about them to knock them down. In this dilemma (the same as ours) Christianity suddenly stepped in and offered a singular answer, which the world eventually accepted as *the* answer. It was the answer then, and I think it is the answer now.

This answer was like the slash of a sword; it sundered; it did not in any sense sentimentally unite. Briefly, it divided God from the cosmos. That transcendence and distinctness of the deity which some Christians now want to remove from Christianity, was really the only reason why any one wanted to be a Christian. It was the whole point of the Christian answer to the unhappy pessimist and the still more unhappy optimist. As I am here only concerned with their particular problem, I shall indicate only briefly this great metaphysical suggestion. All descriptions of the creating or sustaining principle in things must be metaphorical, because they must be verbal. Thus the pantheist is forced to speak of God *in* all things as if he were in a box. Thus the evolutionist has, in his very name, the idea of being unrolled like a carpet. All terms, religious and irreligious, are open to this charge. The only question is whether all terms are useless, or whether one can, with such a phrase, cover a distinct *idea* about the origin of things. I think one can, and so evidently does the evolutionist, or he would not talk about evolution. And the root phrase for all Christian theism was this, that God was a creator, as an artist is a creator. A poet is so separate from his poem that he himself speaks of it as a little thing he has "thrown off." Even in giving it forth he has flung it away. This principle that all creation and procreation is a breaking off is at least as consistent through the cosmos as the evolutionary principle that all growth is a branching out. A woman loses a child even in having a child. All creation is separation. Birth is as solemn a parting as death.

It was the prime philosophic principle of Christianity that this divorce in the divine act of making (such as severs the poet from the poem or the mother from the new-born child) was the true description of the act whereby the absolute energy made the world. According to most philosophers, God in making the world enslaved it. According to Christianity, in making it, He set it free. God has written, not so much a poem, but rather a play; a play he had planned as perfect, but which had necessarily been left to human actors and stage-managers, who had since made a great mess of it. I will discuss the truth of this theorem later. Here I have only to point out with what a startling smoothness it passed the dilemma we have discussed in this chapter. In this way at least one could be both happy and indignant without degrading one's self to be either a pessimist or an optimist. On this system one could fight all the forces of existence without deserting the flag of existence. One could be at peace with the universe and yet be at war with the world. St. George could still fight the dragon, however big the monster bulked in the cosmos, though he were bigger than the mighty cities or bigger than the everlasting hills. If he were as big as the world he could yet be killed in the name of the world. St. George had not to consider any obvious odds or proportions in the scale of things, but only the original secret of their design. He can shake his sword at the dragon, even if it is everything; even if the empty heavens over his head are only the huge arch of its open jaws.

And then followed an experience impossible to describe. It was as if I had been blundering about since my birth with two huge and unmanageable machines, of different shapes and without apparent connection—the world and the Christian tradition. I had found this hole in the world: the fact that one must somehow find a way of loving the world without trusting it; somehow one must love the world without being worldly. I found this projecting feature of Christian theology, like a sort of hard spike, the dogmatic insistence that God was personal, and had made a world separate from Himself. The spike of dogma fitted exactly into the hole in the world—it had evidently been meant to go there—and then the strange thing began to happen. When once these two parts of the two machines had come together, one after another, all the other parts fitted and fell in with an eerie exactitude. I could hear bolt after bolt over all the machinery falling into its place with a kind of click of relief. Having got one part right, all the other parts were repeating that rectitude, as clock after clock strikes noon. Instinct after instinct was answered by doctrine after doctrine. Or, to vary the metaphor, I was like one who had advanced into a hostile country to take one high fortress. And when that fort had fallen the whole country surrendered and turned solid behind me. The whole land was lit up, as it were, back to the first fields of my childhood. All those blind fancies of boyhood which in the fourth chapter I have tried in vain to trace on the darkness, became suddenly transparent and sane. I was right when I felt that roses were red by some sort of choice: it was the divine choice. I was right when I felt that I would almost rather say that grass was the wrong colour than say it must by necessity have been that colour: it might verily have been any other. My sense that happiness hung on the crazy thread of a condition did mean something when all was said: it meant the whole doctrine of the Fall. Even those dim and shapeless monsters of notions which I have not been able to describe, much less defend, stepped quietly into their places like colossal caryatides of the creed. The fancy that the cosmos was not vast and void, but small and cosy, had a fulfilled significance now, for anything that is a work of art must be small in the sight of the artist; to God the stars might be only small and dear, like diamonds. And my haunting instinct that somehow good was not merely a tool to be used, but a relic to be guarded, like the goods from Crusoe's ship—even that had been the wild whisper of something originally wise, for, according to Christianity, we were indeed the survivors of a wreck, the crew of a golden ship that had gone down before the beginning of the world.

But the important matter was this, that it entirely reversed the reason for optimism. And the instant the reversal was made it felt like the abrupt ease when a bone is put back in the socket. I had often called myself an optimist, to avoid the too evident blasphemy of pessimism. But all the optimism of the age had been false and disheartening for this reason, that it had always been trying to prove that we fit in to the world. The Christian optimism is based on the fact that we do *not* fit in to the world. I had tried to be happy by telling myself that man is an animal, like any other which sought its meat from God. But now I really was happy, for I had learnt that man is a monstrosity. I had been right in feeling all things as odd, for I myself was at once worse and better than all things. The optimist's pleasure was prosaic, for it dwelt on the naturalness of everything; the Christian pleasure was poetic, for it dwelt on the unnaturalness of everything in the light of the supernatural. The modern philosopher had told me again and again that I was in the right place, and I had still felt depressed even in acquiescence. But I had heard that I was in the *wrong* place, and my soul sang for joy, like a bird in spring. The knowledge found out and illuminated forgotten chambers in the dark house of infancy. I knew now why grass had always seemed to me as queer as the green beard of a giant, and why I could feel homesick at home.

A Grammar of Distributism

"I observe that the social prophets are still offering the homeless something much higher and purer than a home, and promising a supernormal superiority to people who are not allowed to be normal. I am quite content to dream of the old drudgery of democracy, by which as much as possible of a human life should be given to every human being. And indeed I do believe that when they lose the pride of personal ownership they will lose something that belongs to their erect posture and to their footing and poise upon the planet. Meanwhile I sit amid droves of overdriven clerks and underpaid workmen in a tube or a train; I read of the great conception of Men Like Gods and I wonder when men will be like men."

A Grammar of Distributism

THE BLUFF OF THE BIG SHOPS

TWICE in my life has an editor told me in so many words that he dared not print what I had written, because it would offend the advertisers in his paper. The presence of such pressure exists everywhere in a more silent and subtle form. But I have a great respect for the honesty of this particular editor; for it was evidently as near to complete honesty as the editor of an important weekly magazine can possibly go. He told the truth about the falsehood he had to tell.

On both those occasions he denied me liberty of expression because I said that the widely advertised stores and large shops were really worse than little shops. That, it may be interesting to note, is one of the things that a man is now forbidden to say; perhaps the only thing he is really forbidden to say. If it had been an attack on Government, it would have been tolerated. If it had been an attack on God, it would have been respectfully and tactfully applauded. If I had been abusing marriage or patriotism or public decency, I should have been heralded in headlines and allowed to sprawl across Sunday newspapers. But the big newspaper is not likely to attack the big shop; being itself a big shop in its way and more and more a monument of monopoly. But it will be well if I repeat here in a book what I found it impossible to repeat in an article. I think the big shop is a bad shop. I think it bad not only in a moral but a mercantile sense; that is, I think shopping there is not only a bad action but a bad bargain. I think the monster emporium is not only vulgar and insolent, but incompetent and uncomfortable; and I deny that its large organization is efficient. Large organization is loose organization. Nay, it would be almost as true to say that organization is always disorganization. The only thing perfectly organic is an organism; like that grotesque and obscure organism called a man. He alone can be quite certain of doing what he wants; beyond

445

him, every extra man may be an extra mistake. As applied to things like shops, the whole thing is an utter fallacy. Some things like armies *have* to be organized; and therefore do their very best to be well organized. You must have a long rigid line stretched out to guard a frontier; and therefore you stretch it tight. But it is not true that you must have a long rigid line of people trimming hats or tying bouquets, in order that they may be trimmed or tied neatly. The work is much more likely to be neat if it is done by a particular craftsman for a particular customer with particular ribbons and flowers. The person told to trim the hat will never do it quite suitably to the person who wants it trimmed; and the hundredth person told to do it will do it badly; as he does. If we collected all the stories from all the housewives and householders about the big shops sending the wrong goods, smashing the right goods, forgetting to send any sort of goods, we should behold a welter of inefficiency. There are far more blunders in a big shop than ever happen in a small shop, where the individual customer can curse the individual shopkeeper. Confronted with modern efficiency the customer is silent; well aware of that organization's talent for sacking the wrong man. In short, organization is a necessary evil—which in this case is not necessary.

I have begun these notes with a note on the big shops because they are things near to us and familiar to us all. I need not dwell on other and still more entertaining claims made for the colossal combination of departments. One of the funniest is the statement that it is convenient to get everything in the same shop. That is to say, it is convenient to walk the length of the street, so long as you walk indoors, or more frequently underground, instead of walking the same distance in the open air from one little shop to another. The truth is that the monopolists' shops are really very convenient—to the monopolist. They have all the advantage of concentrating business as they concentrate wealth, in fewer and fewer of the citizens. Their wealth sometimes permits them to pay tolerable wages; their wealth also permits them to buy up better businesses and advertise worse goods. But that their own goods are better nobody has ever even begun to show; and most of us know any number of concrete cases where they are definitely worse. Now I expressed this opinion of my own (so shocking to the magazine editor and his advertisers) not only because it is an example of my general thesis that small properties should be revived, but because it is essential to the realization of another and much more curious truth. It concerns the psychology of all these things: of mere size, of mere wealth, of mere advertisement and arrogance. And it gives us the first working model of the way in which things are done to-day and the way in which (please God) they may be undone to-morrow.

There is one obvious and enormous and entirely neglected general fact to be noted before we consider the laws chiefly needed to renew the State. And that is the fact that one considerable revolution could be made without any laws at all. It does not concern any existing law, but rather an existing superstition. And the curious thing is that its upholders boast that it is a superstition. The other day I saw and very thoroughly enjoyed a popular play called *It Pays to Advertise;* which is all about a young business man who tries to break up the soap monopoly of his father, a more old-fashioned business man, by the wildest application of American theories of the psychology of advertising. One thing that struck me as rather interesting about it was this. It was quite good comedy to give the old man and the young man our sympathy in turn. It was quite good farce to make the old man and the young man each alternately look a fool. But nobody seemed to feel what I felt to be the most outstanding and obvious points of folly. They scoffed at the old man because he was old; because he was old-fashioned; because he himself was healthy enough to scoff at the monkey tricks of their mad advertisements. But nobody really criticized him for having made a corner, for which he might once have stood in a pillory. Nobody seemed to have enough instinct for independence and human dignity to be irritated at the idea that one purse-proud old man could prevent us all from having an ordinary human commodity if he chose. And as with the old man, so it was with the young man. He had been taught by his American friend that advertisement can hypnotize the human brain; that people are dragged by a deadly fascination into the doors of a shop as into the mouth of a snake; that the subconscious is captured and the will paralysed by repetition; that we are all made to move like mechanical dolls when a Yankee advertiser says, "Do It Now." But it never seemed to occur to anybody to resent this. Nobody seemed sufficiently alive to be annoyed. The young man was made game of because he was poor; because he was bankrupt; because he was driven to the shifts of bankruptcy; and so on. But he did not seem to know he was something much worse than a swindler, a sorcerer. He did not know he was by his own boast a mesmerist and a mystagogue; a destroyer of reason and will; an enemy of truth and liberty.

I think such people exaggerate the extent to which it pays to advertise; even if there is only the devil to pay. But in one sense this psychological case for advertising is of great practical importance to any programme of reform. The American advertisers have got hold of the wrong end of the stick; but it is a stick that can be used to beat something else besides their own absurd big drum. It is a stick that can be used also to beat their own absurd business philosophy. They are always telling us that the success of modern commerce depends on creating an atmosphere, on manufacturing a mentality, on assuming a point of view. In short, they insist that their commerce is not merely commercial, or even economic or political, but purely psychological. I hope they will go on saying it; for then some day everybody may suddenly see that it is true.

For the success of big shops and such things really is psychology; not to say psycho-analysis; or, in other words, nightmare. It is not real and, therefore, not reliable. This point concerns merely our immediate attitude, at the moment and on the spot, towards the whole plutocratic occupation of which such publicity is the gaudy banner. The very first thing to do, before we come to any of our proposals that are political and legal, is something that really is (to use their beloved word) entirely psychological. The very first thing to do is to tell these American poker-players that they do not know how to play poker. For they not only bluff, but they boast that they are bluffing. In so far as it really is a question of an instant psychological method, there must be, and there is, an immediate psychological answer. In other words, because they are admittedly bluffing, we can call their bluff.

I said recently that any practical programme for restoring normal property consists of two parts, which current cant would call destructive and constructive; but which might more truly be called defensive and offensive. The first is stopping the mere mad stampede towards monopoly, before the last traditions of property and liberty are lost. It is with that preliminary problem of resisting the world's trend towards being more monopolist, that I am first of all dealing here. Now, when we ask what we can do, here and now, against the actual growth of monopoly, we are always given a very simple answer. We are told that we can do nothing. By a natural and inevitable operation the large things are swallowing the small, as large fish might swallow little fish. The trust can absorb what it likes, like a dragon devouring what it likes, because it is already the largest creature left alive in the land. Some people are so finally resolved to accept this result that they actually condescend to regret it. They are so convinced that it is fate that they will even admit that it is fatality. The fatalists almost become sentimentalists when looking at the little shop that is being bought up by the big company. They are ready to weep, so long as it is admitted that they weep because they weep in vain. They are willing to admit that the loss of a little toy-shop of their childhood, or a little tea-shop of their youth, is even in the true sense a tragedy. For a tragedy means always a man's struggle with that which is stronger than man. And it is the feet of the gods themselves that are here trampling on our traditions; it is death and doom themselves that have broken our little toys like sticks; for against the stars of destiny none shall prevail. It is amazing what a little bluff will do in this world.

For they go on saying that the big fish eats the little fish, without asking whether little fish swim up to big fish and ask to be eaten. They accept the devouring dragon without wondering whether a fashionable crowd of princesses ran after the dragon to be devoured. They have never heard of a fashion; and do not know the difference between fashion and fate. The necessitarians have here carefully chosen the one example of something that is certainly *not* necessary, whatever else is necessary. They have chosen the one thing that does happen still to be free, as a proof of the unbreakable chains in which all things are bound. Very little is left free in the modern world; but private buying and selling are still supposed to be free; and indeed still are free; if anyone has a will free enough to use his freedom. Children may be driven by force to a particular school. Men may be driven by force away from a public-house. All sorts of people, for all sorts of new and nonsensical reasons, may be driven by force to a prison. But nobody is yet driven by force to a particular shop.

I shall deal later with some practical remedies and reactions against the rush towards rings and corners. But even before we consider these, it is well to have paused a moment on the moral fact which is so elementary and so entirely ignored. Of all things in the world, the rush to the big shops is the thing that could be most easily stopped—by the people who rush there. We do not know what may come later; but they cannot be driven there by bayonets just yet. American business enterprise, which has already used British soldiers for purposes of advertisement, may doubtless in time use British soldiers for purposes of coercion. But we cannot yet be dragooned by guns and sabres into Yankee shops or international stores. The alleged economic attraction, with which I will deal in due course, is quite a different thing: I am merely pointing out that if we came to the conclusion that big shops ought to be boycotted, we could boycott them as easily as we should (I hope) boycott shops selling instruments of torture or poisons for private use in the home. In other words, this first and fundamental question is not a question of necessity but of will. If we chose to make a vow, if we chose to make a league, for dealing only with little local shops and never with large centralized shops, the campaign could be every bit as practical as the Land Campaign in Ireland. It would probably be nearly as successful. It will be said, of course, that people will go to the best shop. I deny it; for Irish boycotters did not take the best offer. I deny that the big shop is the best shop; and I especially deny that people go there because it is the best shop. And if I be asked why, I answer at the end with the unanswerable fact with which I began at the beginning. I know it is not merely a matter of business, for the simple reason that the business men themselves tell me it is merely a matter of bluff. It is they who say that nothing succeeds like a mere appearance of success. It is *they* who say that publicity influences us without our will or knowledge. It is they who say that "It Pays to Advertise"; that is, to tell people in a bullying way that they must "Do It Now," when they need not do it at all.

A MISUNDERSTANDING ABOUT METHOD

BEFORE I go any further with this sketch, I find I must pause upon a parenthesis touching the nature of my task, without which the rest of it may be misunderstood. As a matter of fact, without pretending to any official or commercial experience, I am here doing a great deal more than has ever been asked of most of the mere men of letters (if I may call myself for the moment a man of letters) when they confidently conducted social movements or set up social ideals. I will promise that, by the end of these notes, the reader shall know a great deal more about how men might set about making a Distributive State than the readers of Carlyle ever knew about how they should set about finding a Hero King or a Real Superior. I think we can explain how to make a small shop or a small farm a common feature of our society better than Matthew Arnold explained how to make the State the organ of Our Best Self. I think the farm will be marked on some sort of rude map more clearly than the Earthly Paradise on the navigation chart of William Morris; and I think that in comparison with his News from Nowhere this might fairly be called News from Somewhere. Rousseau and Ruskin were often much more vague and visionary than I am; though Rousseau was even more rigid in abstractions, and Ruskin was sometimes very much excited about particular details. I need not say that I am not comparing myself to these great men; I am only pointing out that even from these, whose minds dominated so much wider a field, and whose position as publicists was much more respected and responsible, nothing was as a matter of fact asked beyond the general principles we are accused of giving. I am merely pointing out that the task has fallen to a very minor poet when these very major prophets were not required to carry out and complete the fulfilment of their own prophecies. It would seem that our fathers did not think it quite so futile to have a clear vision of the goal with or without a detailed map of the road; or to be able to describe a scandal without going on to describe a substitute. Anyhow, for whatever reason, it is quite certain that if I really were great enough to deserve the reproaches of the utilitarians, if I really were as merely idealistic or imaginative as they make me out, if I really did confine myself to describing a direction without exactly measuring a road, to pointing towards home or heaven and telling men to use their own good sense in getting there—if this were really all that I could do, it would be all that men immeasurably greater than I am were ever expected to do; from Plato and Isaiah to Emerson and Tolstoy.

But it is not all that I can do; even though those who did not do it did so much more. I can do something else as well; but I can only do it if it be understood what I am doing. At the same time I am well aware that, in explaining the improvement of so elaborate a society, a man may often find it very difficult to explain exactly what he is doing, until it is done. I have considered and rejected half a dozen ways of approaching the problem, by different roads that all lead to the same truth. I had thought of beginning with the simple example of the peasant; and then I knew that a hundred correspondents would leap upon me, accusing me of trying to turn all of them into peasants. I thought of beginning with describing a decent Distributive State in being, with all its balance of different things; just as the Socialists describe their Utopia in being, with its concentration in one thing. Then I knew a hundred correspondents would call me Utopian; and say it was obvious my scheme could not work, because I could only describe it when it was working. But what they would really mean by my being Utopian, would be this: that until that scheme was working, there was no work to be done. I have finally decided to approach the social solution in this fashion: to point out first that the monopolist momentum is not irresistible; that even here and now much could be done to modify it, much by anybody, almost everything by everybody.

Then I would maintain that on the removal of that particular plutocratic pressure, the appetite and appreciation of natural property would revive, like any other natural thing. Then, I say, it will be worth while to propound to people thus returning to sanity, however sporadically, a sane society that could balance property and control machinery. With the description of that ultimate society, with its laws and limitations, I would conclude.

Now that may or may not be a good arrangement or order of ideas; but it is an intelligible one; and I submit with all humility that I have a right to arrange my explanations in that order, and no critic has a right to complain that I do not disarrange them in order to answer questions out of their order. I am willing to write him a whole Encyclopædia of Distributism if he has the patience to read it; but he must have the patience to read it. It is unreasonable for him to complain that I have not dealt adequately with Zoology, State Provision For, under the letter B; or described the honourable social status of the Guild of the Xylographers while I am still dealing alphabetically with the Guild of Architects. I am willing to be as much of a bore as Euclid; but the critic must not complain that the forty-eighth proposition of the second book is not a part of the *Pons Asinorum*. The ancient Guild of Bridge-Builders will have to build many such bridges.

Now from comments that have come my way, I gather that the suggestions I have already made may not altogether explain their own place and purpose in this scheme. I am merely pointing out that monopoly is not omnipotent even now and here; and that anybody could think, on the spur of the moment, of many ways in which its final triumph can be delayed and perhaps defeated. Suppose a monopolist who is my mortal enemy endeavours to ruin me by preventing me from selling eggs to my neighbours, I can tell him I shall live on my own turnips in my own kitchen garden. I do not mean to tie myself to turnips; or swear never to touch my own potatoes or beans. I mean the turnips as an example; something to throw at him. Suppose the wicked millionaire in question comes and grins over my garden wall and says, "I perceive by your starved and emaciated appearance that you are in immediate need of a few shillings; but you can't possibly get them," I may possibly be stung into retorting, "Yes, I can. I could sell my first edition of *Martin Chuzzlewit*." I do not necessarily mean that I see myself already in a pauper's grave unless I can sell *Martin Chuzzlewit*; I do not mean that I have nothing else to suggest except selling *Martin Chuzzlewit*; I do not mean to brag like any common politician that I have nailed my colours to the *Martin Chuzzlewit* policy. I mean to tell the offensive pessimist that I am not at the end of my resources; that I can sell a book or even, if the case grows desperate, write a book. I could do a great many things before I came to definitely anti-social action like robbing a bank or (worse still) working in a bank. I could do a great many things of a great many kinds, and I give an example at the start to suggest that there are many more of them, not that there are no more of them. There are a great many things of a great many kinds in my house, besides the copy of a *Martin Chuzzlewit*. Not many of them are of great value except to me; but some of them are of some value to anybody. For the whole point of a home is that it is a hotch-potch. And mine, at any rate, rises to that austere domestic ideal. The whole point of one's own house is that it is not only a number of totally different things, which are nevertheless one thing, but it is one in which we still value even the things that we forget. If a man has burnt my house to a heap of ashes, I am none the less justly indignant with him for having burnt everything, because I cannot at first even remember everything he has burnt. And as it is with the household gods, so it is with the whole of that household religion, or what remains of it, to offer resistance to the destructive discipline of industrial capitalism. In a simpler society, I should rush out of the ruins, calling for help on the Commune or the King, and crying out, "Haro; a robber has burnt my house." I might, of course, rush down the street crying in one passionate breath, "Haro! a robber has burnt my front door of seasoned oak with the usual fittings, fourteen window frames, nine curtains, five and a half carpets, 753 books, of which four were *éditions de luxe*, one portrait of my great-grandmother," and so on through all the items; but something would be lost of the fierce and simple feudal cry. And in the same way I could have begun this outline with an inventory of all the alterations I should like to see in the laws, with the object of establishing some economic justice in England. But I doubt whether the reader would have had any better idea of what I was ultimately driving at; and it would not have been the approach by which I propose at present to drive. I shall have occasion later to go into some slight detail about these things; but the cases I give are merely illustrations of my first general thesis: that we are not even at the moment doing everything that could be done to resist the rush of monopoly; and that when people talk as if nothing could now be done, that statement is false at the start; and that all sorts of answers to it will immediately occur to the mind.

Capitalism is breaking up; and in one sense we do not pretend to be sorry it is breaking up. Indeed, we might put our own point pretty correctly by saying that we would help it to break up; but we do not want it merely to break down. But the first fact to realize is precisely that; that it is a choice between its breaking up and its breaking down. It is a choice between its being voluntarily resolved into its real component parts, each taking back its own, and its merely collapsing on our heads in a crash or confusion of all its component parts, which some call communism and some call chaos. The former is the one thing all sensible people should try to procure. The latter is the one thing that all sensible people should try to prevent. That is why they are often classed together.

I have mainly confined myself to answering what I have always found to be the first question, "What are we to do now?" To that I answer, "What we must do now is to stop the other people from doing what they are doing now." The initiative is with the enemy. It is he who is already doing things, and will have done them long before we can begin to do anything, since he has the money, the machinery, the rather mechanical majority, and other things which we have first to gain and then to use. He has nearly completed a monopolist conquest, but not quite; and he can still be hampered and halted. The world has woken up very late; but that is not our fault. That is the fault of all the fools who told us for twenty years that there could never be any Trusts; and are now telling us, equally wisely, that there can never be anything else.

There are other things I ask the reader to bear in mind. The first is that this outline is only an outline, though one that can hardly avoid some curves and loops. I do not profess to dispose of all the obstacles that might arise in this question, because so many of them would seem to many to be quite a different question. I will give one example of what I mean. What would the critical reader have thought, if at the very beginning of this sketch I had gone off into a long disputation about the Law of Libel? Yet, if I were strictly practical, I should find that one of the most practical obstacles. It is the present ridiculous position that monopoly is not resisted as a social force but can still be resented as a legal imputation. If you try to stop a man cornering milk, the first thing that happens will be a smashing libel action for calling it a corner. It is manifestly mere common sense that if the thing is not a sin it is not a slander. As things stand, there is no punishment for the man who does it; but there is a punishment for the man who discovers it. I do not deal here (though I am quite prepared to deal elsewhere) with all these detailed difficulties which a society as now constituted would raise against such a society as we want to constitute. If it were constituted on the principles I suggest, those details would be dealt with on those principles as they arose. For instance, it would put an end to the nonsense whereby men, who are more powerful than emperors, pretend to be private tradesmen suffering from private malice; it will assert that those who are in practice public men must be criticized as potential public evils. It would destroy the absurdity by which an "important case" is tried by a "special jury"; or, in other words, that any serious issue between rich and poor is tried by the rich. But the reader will see that I cannot here rule out all the ten thousand things that might trip us up; I must assume that a people ready to take the larger risks would also take the smaller ones.

Now this outline is an outline; in other words, it is a design, and anybody who thinks we can have practical things without theoretical designs can go and quarrel with the nearest engineer or architect for drawing thin lines on thin paper. But there is another and more special sense in which my suggestion is an outline; in the sense that it is deliberately drawn as a large limitation within which there are many varieties. I have long been acquainted, and not a little amused, with the sort of practical man who will certainly say that I generalize because there is no practical plan. The truth is that I generalize because there are so many practical plans. I myself know four or five schemes that have been drawn up, more or less drastically, for the diffusion of capital. The most cautious, from a capitalist standpoint, is the gradual extension of profit-sharing. A more stringently democratic form of the same thing is the management of every business (if it *cannot* be a small business) by a guild or group clubbing their contributions and dividing their results. Some Distributists dislike the idea of the workman having shares only where he has work; they think he would be more independent if his little capital were invested elsewhere; but they all agree that he ought to have the capital to invest. Others continue to call themselves Distributists because they would give every citizen a dividend out of much larger national systems of production. I deliberately draw out my general principles so as to cover as many as possible of these alternative business schemes. But I object to being told that I am covering so many because I know there are none. If I tell a man he is too luxurious and extravagant, and that he ought to economize in something, I am not bound to give him a list of his luxuries. The point is that he will be all the better for cutting down any of his luxuries. And my point is that modern society would be all the better for cutting up property by any of these processes. This does not mean that I have not my own favourite form; personally I prefer the second type of division given in the above list of examples. But my main business is to point out that *any* reversal of the rush to concentrate property will be an improvement on the present state of things. If I tell a man his house is burning down in Putney, he may thank me even if I do not give him a list of all the vehicles which go to Putney, with the numbers of all the taxicabs and the time-table of all the trams. It is enough that I know there are a great many vehicles for him to choose from, before he is reduced to the proverbial adventure of going to Putney on a pig. It is enough that any one of those vehicles is on the whole less uncomfortable than a house on fire or even a heap of ashes. I admit I might be called unpractical if impenetrable forests and destructive floods lay between here and Putney; it might then be as merely idealistic to praise Putney as to praise Paradise. But I do not admit that I am unpractical because I know there are half a dozen practical ways which are more practical than the present state of things. But it does not follow, in fact, that I do not know how to get to Putney. Here, for instance, are half a dozen things which would help the process of Distributism, apart from those on which I shall have occasion to touch as points of principle. Not all Distributists would agree with all of them; but all would agree that they are in the direction of Distributism. (1) The taxation of contracts so as to discourage the sale of small property to big proprietors and encourage the break-up of big property among small proprietors. (2) Something like the Napoleonic testamentary law and the destruction of primogeniture. (3) The establishment of free law for the poor, so that small property could always be defended against great. (4) The deliberate protection of certain experiments in small property, if necessary by tariffs and even local tariffs. (5) Subsidies to foster the starting of such experiments. (6) A league of voluntary dedication, and any number of other things of the same kind. But I have inserted this chapter here in order to explain that this is a sketch of the first principles of Distributism and not of the last details, about which even Distributists might dispute. In such a statement, examples are given as examples, and not as exact and exhaustive lists of all the cases covered by the rule. If this elementary principle of exposition be not understood I must be content to be called an unpractical person by that sort of practical man. And indeed in his sense there is something in his accusation. Whether or no I am a practical man, I am not what is called a practical politician, which means a professional politician. I can claim no part in the glory of having brought our country to its present promising and hopeful condition. Harder heads than mine have established the present prosperity of coal. Men of action, of a more rugged energy, have brought us to the comfortable condition of living on our capital. I have had no part in the great industrial revolution which has increased the beauties of nature and reconciled the classes of society; nor must the too enthusiastic reader think of thanking *me* for this more enlightened England, in which the employee is living on a dole from the State and the employer on an overdraft at the Bank.

A CASE IN POINT

IT is as natural to our commercial critics to argue in a circle as to travel on the Inner Circle. It is not mere stupidity, but it is mere habit; and it is not easy either to break into or to escape from that iron ring. When we say things can be done, we commonly mean either that they could be done by the mass of men, or else by the ruler of the State. I gave an example of something that could be done quite easily by the mass; and here I will give an example of something that could be done quite easily by the ruler. But we must be prepared for our critics beginning to argue in a circle and saying that the present populace will never agree or the present ruler act in that way. But this complaint is a confusion. We are answering people who call our ideal impossible in itself. If you do not want it, of course, you will not try to get it; but do not say that because you do not want it, it follows that you could not get it if you did want it. A thing does not become intrinsically impossible merely by a mob not trying to obtain it; nor does a thing cease to be practical politics because no politician is practical enough to do it.

I will start with a small and familiar example. In order to ensure that our huge proletariat should have a holiday, we have a law obliging all employers to shut their shops for half a day once a week. Given the proletarian principle, it is a healthy and necessary thing for a proletarian state; just as the saturnalia is a healthy and necessary thing for a slave state. Given this provision for the proletariat, a practical person will naturally say: "It has other advantages, too; it will be a chance for anybody who chooses to do his own dirty work; for the man who can manage without servants." That degraded being who actually knows how to do things himself, will have a look in at last. That isolated crank, who can really work for his own living, may possibly have a chance to live. A man does not need to be a Distributist to say

461

this; it is the ordinary and obvious thing that anybody would say. The man who has servants must cease to work his servants. Of course, the man who has no servants to work cannot cease to work them. But the law is actually so constructed that it forces this man also to give a holiday to the servants he has not got. He proclaims a saturnalia that never happens to a crowd of phantom slaves that have never been there. Now there is not a rudiment of reason about this arrangement. In every possible sense, from the immediate material to the abstract and mathematical sense, it is quite mad. We live in days of dangerous division of interests between the employer and the employed. Therefore, even when the two are not divided, but actually united in one person, we must divide them again into two parties. We coerce a man into giving himself something he does not want, because somebody else who does not exist might want it. We warn him that he had better receive a deputation from himself, or he might go on strike against himself. Perhaps he might even become a Bolshevist, and throw a bomb at himself; in which case he would have no other course left to his stern sense of law and order but to read the Riot Act and shoot himself. They call us unpractical; but we have not yet produced such an academic fantasy as this. They sometimes suggest that our regret for the disappearance of the yeoman or the apprentice in a mere matter of sentiment. Sentimental! We have not quite sunk to such sentimentalism as to be sorry for apprentices who never existed at all. We have not quite reached that richness of romantic emotion that we are capable of weeping more copiously for an imaginary grocer's assistant than for a real grocer. We are not quite so maudlin yet as to see double when we look into our favourite little shop; or to set the little shopkeeper fighting with his own shadow. Let us leave these hard-headed and practical men of business shedding tears over the sorrows of a non-existent office boy, and proceed upon our own wild and erratic path, that at least happens to pass across the land of the living.

Now if so small a change as that were made tomorrow, it

would make a difference: a considerable and increasing difference. And if any rash apologist of Big Business tells me that a little thing like that could make very little difference, let him beware. For he is doing the one thing which such apologists commonly avoid above all things: he is contradicting his masters. Among the thousand things of interest, which are lost in the million things of no interest, in the newspaper reports of Parliament and public affairs, there really was one delightful little comedy dealing with this point. Some man of normal sense and popular instincts, who had strayed into Parliament by some mistake or other, actually pointed out this plain fact: that there was no need to protect the proletariat where there was no proletariat to protect; and that the lonely shopkeeper might, therefore, remain in his lonely shop. And the Minister in charge of the matter actually replied, with a ghastly innocence, that it was impossible; for it would be unfair to the big shops. Tears evidently flow freely in such circles, as they did from the rising politician, Lord Lundy; and in this case it was the mere thought of the possible sufferings of the millionaires that moved him. There rose before his imagination Mr. Selfridge in his agony, and the groans of Mr. Woolworth, of the Woolworth Tower, thrilled through the kind hearts to which the cry of the sorrowing rich will never come in vain. But whatever we may think of the sensibility needed to regard the big store-owners as objects of sympathy, at any rate it disposes at a stroke of all the fashionable fatalism that sees something inevitable in their success. It is absurd to tell us that our attack is bound to fail; and then that there would be something quite unscrupulous in its so immediately succeeding. Apparently Big Business must be accepted because it is invulnerable, and spared because it is vulnerable. This big absurd bubble can never conceivably be burst; and it is simply cruel that a little pin-prick of competition can burst it.

I do not know whether the big shops are quite so weak and wobbly as their champion said. But whatever the immediate effect on the big shops, I am sure there would be an immediate effect on the little shops. I am sure that if they could trade on the general holiday, it would not only mean that there would be more trade for them, but that there would be more of them trading. It might mean at last a large class of little shopkeepers; and that is exactly the sort of thing that makes all the political difference, as it does in the case of a large class of little farmers. It is not in the merely mechanical sense a matter of numbers. It is a matter of the presence and pressure of a particular social type. It is not a question merely of how many noses are counted; but in the more real sense whether the noses count. If there were anything that could be called a class of peasants, or a class of small shopkeepers, they would make their presence felt in legislation, even if it were what is called class legislation. And the very existence of that third class would be the end of what is called the class war; in so far as its theory divides all men into employers and employed. I do not mean, of course, that this little legal alteration is the only one I have to propose; I mention it first because it is the most obvious. But I mention it also because it illustrates very clearly what I mean by the two stages: the nature of the negative and positive reform. If little shops began to gain custom and big shops began to lose it, it would mean two things, both indeed preliminary but both practical. It would mean that the mere centripetal rush was slowed down, if not stopped, and might at last change to a centrifugal movement. And it would mean that there were a number of new citizens in the State to whom all the ordinary Socialist or servile arguments were inapplicable. Now when you have got your considerable sprinkling of small proprietors, of men with the psychology and philosophy of small property, *then* you can begin to talk to them about something more like a just general settlement upon their own lines; something more like a land fit for Christians to live in. You can make *them* understand, as you cannot make plutocrats or proletarians understand, why the machine must not exist save as the servant of the man, why the things we produce ourselves are precious like our own children, and why we can pay too dearly for the possession of luxury by the loss of liberty. If bodies of men only begin to be detached from the servile settlements, they will begin to form the body of *our* public opinion. Now there are a large number of other advantages that could be given to the small man, which can be considered in their place. In all of them I presuppose a deliberate policy of favouring the small man. But in the primary example here given we can hardly even say that there is any question of favour. You make a law that slave-owners shall free their slaves for a day: the man who has no slaves is outside the thing entirely; he does not come under it in law, because he does not come into it in logic. He has been deliberately dragged into it; not in order that all slaves shall be free for a day, but in order that all free men shall be slaves for a lifetime. But while some of the expedients are only common justice to small property, and others are deliberate protection of small property, the point at the moment is that it will be worth while at the beginning to create small property though it were only on a small scale. English citizens and yeomen would once more exist; and wherever they exist they count. There are many other ways, which can be briefly described, by which the break-up of property can be encouraged on the legal and legislative side. I shall deal with some of them later, and especially with the real responsibility which Government might reasonably assume in a financial and economic condition which is becoming quite ludicrous. From the standpoint of any sane person, in any other society, the present problem of capitalist concentration is not only a question of law but of criminal law, not to mention criminal lunacy.

Of that monstrous megalomania of the big shops, with their blatant advertisements and stupid standardization, something is said elsewhere. But it may be well to add, in the matter of the small shops, that when once they exist they generally have an organization of their own which is much more self-respecting and much less vulgar. This voluntary organization, as every one knows, is called a Guild; and it is perfectly capable of doing everything that really needs to be done in the way of holidays and popular festivals. Twenty barbers would be quite capable of arranging with each other not to compete with each other on a particular festival or in a particular fashion. It is amusing to note that the same people who say that a Guild is a dead medieval thing that would never work are generally grumbling against the power of a Guild as a living modern thing where it is actually working. In the case of the Guild of the Doctors, for instance, it is made a matter of reproach in the newspapers, that the confederation in question refuses to "make medical discoveries accessible to the general public." When we consider the wild and unbalanced nonsense that is made accessible to the general public by the public press, perhaps we have some reason to doubt whether our souls and bodies are not at least as safe in the hands of a Guild as they are likely to be in the hands of a Trust. For the moment the main point is that small shops can be governed even if they are not bossed by the Government. Horrible as this may seem to the democratic idealists of the day, they can be governed by themselves.

THE FREE MAN AND THE FORD CAR

I AM not a fanatic; and I think that machines may be of considerable use in destroying machinery. I should generously accord them a considerable value in the work of exterminating all that they represent. But to put the truth in those terms is to talk in terms of the remote conclusion of our slow and reasonable revolution. In the immediate situation the same truth may be stated in a more moderate way. Towards all typical things of our time we should have a rational charity. Machinery is not wrong; it is only absurd. Perhaps we should say it is merely childish, and can even be taken in the right spirit by a child. If, therefore, we find that some machine enables us to escape from an inferno of machinery, we cannot be committing a sin though we may be cutting a silly figure, like a dragoon rejoining his regiment on an old bicycle. What is essential is to realize that there is something ridiculous about the present position, something wilder than any Utopia. For instance, I shall have occasion here to note the proposal of centralized electricity, and we could justify the use of it so long as we see the joke of it. But, in fact, we do not even see the joke of the waterworks and the water company. It is almost too broadly comic that an essential of life like water should be pumped to us from nobody knows where, by nobody knows whom, sometimes nearly a hundred miles away. It is every bit as funny as if air were pumped to us from miles away, and we all walked about like divers at the bottom of the sea. The only reasonable person is the peasant who owns his own well. But we have a long way to go before we begin to think about being reasonable.

There are at present some examples of centralization of which the effects may work for decentralization. An obvious case is that recently discussed in connection with a common plant of electricity. I think it is broadly true that if electricity could be cheapened, the chances of a very large number of small independent shops, especially workshops, would be greatly improved. At the same time, there is no doubt at all that such dependence for essential power on a central plant is a real dependence, and is therefore a defect in any complete scheme of independence. On this point I imagine that many Distributists might differ considerably; but, speaking for myself, I am inclined to follow the more moderate and provisional policy that I have suggested more than once in this place I think the first necessity is to make sure of any small properties obtaining any success in any decisive or determining degree. Above all, I think it is vital to create the experience of small property, the psychology of small property, the sort of man who is a small proprietor. When once men of that sort exist, they will decide, in a manner very different from any modern mob, how far the central power-house is to dominate their own private house, or whether it need dominate at all. They will perhaps discover the way of breaking up and individualizing that power. They will sacrifice, if there is any need to sacrifice, even the help of science to the hunger for possession. So that I am disposed at the moment to accept any help that science and machinery can give in creating small property, without in the least bowing down to such superstitions where they only destroy it. But we must keep in mind the peasant ideal as the motive and the goal; and most of those who offer us mechanical help seem to be blankly ignorant of what we regard it as helping. A well-known name will illustrate both the thing being done and the man being ignorant of what he is doing.

The other day I found myself in a Ford car, like that in which I remember riding over Palestine, and in which (I suppose) Mr. Ford would enjoy riding over Palestinians. Anyhow, it reminded me of Mr. Ford, and that reminded me of Mr. Penty and his views upon equality and mechanical civilization. The Ford car (if I may venture on one of those new ideas urged upon us in newspapers) is a typical product of the age. The best thing about it is the thing for which it is despised; that it is small. The worst thing about it is the thing for which it is praised; that it is standardized. Its smallness is, of course, the subject of endless American jokes, about a man catching a Ford like a fly or possibly a flea. But nobody seems to notice how this popularization of motoring (however wrong in motive or in method) really is a complete contradiction to the fatalistic talk about inevitable combination and concentration. The railway is fading before our eyes—birds nesting, as it were, in the railway signals, and wolves howling, so to speak, in the waiting-room. And the railway really was a communal and concentrated mode of travel like that in a Utopia of the Socialists. The free and solitary traveller is returning before our very eyes; not always (it is true) equipped with scrip or scallop, but having recovered to some extent the freedom of the King's highway in the manner of Merry England. Nor is this the only ancient thing such travel has revived. While Mugby Junction neglected its refreshment-rooms, Hugby-in-the-Hole has revived its inns. To that limited extent the Ford motor is already a reversion to the free man. If he has not three acres and a cow, he has the very inadequate substitute of three hundred miles and a car. I do not mean that this development satisfies my theories. But I do say that it destroys other people's theories; all the theories about the collective thing as a thing of the future and the individual thing as a thing of the past. Even in their own special and stinking way of science and machinery, the facts are very largely going against their theories.

Yet I have never seen Mr. Ford and his little car really and intelligently praised for this. I have often, of course, seen him praised for all the conveniences of what is called standardization The argument seems to be more or less to this effect. When your car breaks down with a loud crash in the middle of Salisbury Plain, though it is not very likely that any fragments of other ruined motor cars will be lying about amid the ruins of Stonehenge, yet if they are, it is a great advantage to think that they will probably be of the same pattern, and you can take them to mend your own car. The same principle applies to persons motoring in Tibet, and exulting in the reflection that if another motorist from the United States did happen to come along, it would be possible to exchange wheels or footbrakes in token of amity. I may not have got the details of the argument quite correct; but the general point of it is that if anything goes wrong with parts of a machine, they can be replaced with identical machinery. And anyhow the argument could be carried much further; and used to explain a great many other things. I am not sure that it is not the clue to many mysteries of the age. I begin to understand, for instance, why magazine stories are all exactly alike; it is ordered so that when you have left one magazine in a railway carriage in the middle of a story called "Pansy Eyes," you may go on with exactly the same story in another magazine under the title of "Dandelion Locks." It explains why all leading articles on The Future of the Churches are exactly the same; so that we may begin reading the article in the *Daily Chronicle* and finish it in the *Daily Express*. It explains why all the public utterances urging us to prefer new things to old never by any chance say anything new; they mean that we should go to a new paper-stall and read it in a new newspaper. This is why all American caricatures repeat themselves like a mathematical pattern; it means that when we have torn off a part of the picture to wrap up sandwiches, we can tear off a bit of another picture and it will always fit in. And this is also why American millionaires all look exactly alike; so that when the bright, resolute expression of one of them has led us to do serious damage to his face with a heavy blow of the fist, it is always possible to mend it with noses and jaw-bones taken from other millionaires, who are exactly similarly constituted.

Such are the advantages of standardization; but, as may be suspected, I think the advantages are exaggerated; and I agree with Mr. Penty in doubting whether all this repetition really corresponds to human nature. But a very interesting question was raised by Mr. Ford's remarks on the difference between men and men; and his suggestion that most men preferred mechanical action or were only fitted for it. About all those arguments affecting human equality, I myself always have one feeling, which finds expression in a little test of my own. I shall begin to take seriously those classifications of superiority and inferiority, when I find a man classifying himself as inferior. It will be noted that Mr. Ford does not say that *he* is only fitted to mind machines; he confesses frankly that he is too fine and free and fastidious a being for such tasks. I shall believe the doctrine when I hear somebody say: "I have only got the wits to turn a wheel." That would be real, that would be realistic, that would be scientific. That would be independent testimony that could not easily be disputed. It is exactly the same, of course, with all the other superiorities and denials of human equality that are so specially characteristic of a scientific age. It is so with the men who talk about superior and inferior races; I never heard a man say: "Anthropology shows that I belong to an inferior race." If he did, he might be talking like an anthropologist; as it is, he is talking like a man, and not unfrequently like a fool. I have long hoped that I might some day hear a man explaining on scientific principles his own unfitness for any important post or privilege, say: "The world should belong to the free and fighting races, and not to persons of that servile disposition that you will notice in myself; the intelligent will know how to form opinions, but the weakness of intellect from which I so obviously suffer renders my opinions manifestly absurd on the face of them: there are indeed stately and godlike races—but look at me! Observe my shapeless and fourth-rate features! Gaze, if you can bear it, on my commonplace and repulsive face!" If I heard a man making a scientific demonstration in that style, I might admit that he was really scientific. But as it invariably happens, by a curious coincidence, that the superior race is his own race, the superior type is his own type, and the superior preference for work the sort of work he happens to prefer—I have come to the conclusion that there is a simpler explanation.

Now Mr. Ford is a good man, so far as it is consistent with

being a good millionaire. But he himself will very well illustrate where the fallacy of his argument lies. It is probably quite true that, in the making of motors, there are a hundred men who can work a motor and only one man who can design a motor. But of the hundred men who could work a motor, it is very probable that one could design a garden, another design a charade, another design a practical joke or a derisive picture of Mr. Ford. I do not mean, of course, in anything I say here, to deny differences of intelligence, or to suggest that equality (a thing wholly religious) depends on any such impossible denial. But I do mean that men are nearer to a level than anybody will discover by setting them all to make one particular kind of runabout clock. Now Mr. Ford himself is a man of defiant limitations. He is so indifferent to history, for example, that he calmly admitted in the witness-box that he had never heard of Benedict Arnold. An American who has never heard of Benedict Arnold is like a Christian who has never heard of Judas Iscariot. He is rare. I believe that Mr. Ford indicated in a general way that he thought Benedict Arnold was the same as Arnold Bennett. Not only is this not the case, but it is an error to suppose that there is no importance in such an error. If he were to find himself, in the heat of some controversy, accusing Mr. Arnold Bennett of having betrayed the American President and ravaged the South with an Anti-American army, Mr. Bennett might bring an action. If Mr. Ford were to suppose that the lady who recently wrote revelations in the *Daily Express* was old enough to be the widow of Benedict Arnold, the lady might bring an action. Now it is not impossible that among the workmen whom Mr. Ford perceives (probably quite truly) to be only suited to the mechanical part of the construction of mechanical things, there might be a man who was fond of reading all the history he could lay his hands on; and who had advanced step by step, by painful efforts of self-education, until the difference between Benedict Arnold and Arnold Bennett was quite clear in his mind. If his employer did not care about the difference, of course, he would not consult him about the difference, and the man would remain to all appearance a mere cog in the machine; there would be no reason for finding out that he was a rather cogitating cog. Anybody who knows anything of modern business knows that there are any number of such men who remain in subordinate and obscure positions because their private tastes and talents have no relation to the very stupid business in which they are engaged. If Mr. Ford extends his business over the Solar System, and gives cars to the Martians and the Man in the Moon, he will not be an inch nearer to the mind of the man who is working his machine for him, and thinking about something more sensible. Now all human things are imperfect; but the condition in which such hobbies and secondary talents do to some extent come out is the condition of small independence. The peasant almost always runs two or three sideshows and lives on a variety of crafts and expedients. The village shopkeeper will shave travellers and stuff weasels and grow cabbages and do half a dozen such things, keeping a sort of balance in his life like the balance of sanity in the soul. The method is not perfect; but it is more intelligent than turning him into a machine in order to find out whether he has a soul above machinery.

Upon this point of immediate compromise with machinery, therefore, I am inclined to conclude that it is quite right to use the existing machines in so far as they do create a psychology that can despise machines; but not if they create a psychology that respects them. The Ford car is an excellent illustration of the question; even better than the other illustration I have given of an electrical supply for small workshops. If possessing a Ford car means rejoicing in a Ford car, it is melancholy enough; it does not bring us much farther than Tooting or rejoicing in a Tooting tramcar. But if possessing a Ford car means rejoicing in a field of corn or clover, in a fresh landscape and a free atmosphere, it may be the beginning of many things—and even the end of many things. It may be, for instance, the end of the car and the beginning of the cottage. Thus we might almost say that

the final triumph of Mr. Ford is not when the man gets into the
car, but when he enthusiastically falls out of the car. It is when
he finds somewhere, in remote and rural corners that he could
not normally have reached, that perfect poise and combination of
hedge and tree and meadow in the presence of which any modern machine seems suddenly to look an absurdity; yes, even an
antiquated absurdity. Probably that happy man, having found
the place of his true home, will proceed joyfully to break up
the car with a large hammer, putting its iron fragments for the
first time to some real use, as kitchen utensils or garden tools.
That is using a scientific instrument in the proper way; for it is
using it as an instrument. The man has used modern machinery
to escape from modern society; and the reason and rectitude of
such a course commends itself instantly to the mind. It is not so
with the weaker brethren who are not content to trust Mr.
Ford's car, but also trust Mr. Ford's creed. If accepting the car
means accepting the philosophy I have just criticized, the notion
that some men are born to make cars, or rather small bits of cars,
then it will be far more worthy of a philosopher to say frankly
that men never needed to have cars at all. It is only because the
man had been sent into exile in a railway-train that he has to be
brought back home in a motor-car. It is only because all machinery has been used to put things wrong that some machinery
may now rightly be used to put things right. But I conclude
upon the whole that it may so be used; and my reason is that
which I considered on a previous page under the heading of
"The Chance of Recovery." I pointed out that our ideal is so
sane and simple, so much in accord with the ancient and general
instincts of men, that when once it is given a chance anywhere
it will improve that chance by its own inner vitality because
there is some reaction towards health whenever disease is removed. The man who has used his car to find his farm will be
more interested in the farm than in the car; certainly more interested than in the shop where he once bought the car. Nor will
Mr. Ford always woo him back to that shop, even by telling him

tenderly that he is not fitted to be a lord of land, a rider of horses, or a ruler of cattle; since his deficient intellect and degraded anthropological type fit him only for mean and mechanical operations. If anyone will try saying this (tenderly, of course) to any considerable number of large farmers, who have lived for some time on their own farms with their own families, he will discover the defects of the approach.

Tales and Short Stories

THE SHADOW OF THE SHARK

It is notable that the late Mr. Sherlock Holmes, in the course of those inspiring investigations for which we can never be sufficiently grateful to their ingenious author, seems only twice to have ruled out an explanation as intrinsically impossible. And it is curious to notice that in both cases the distinguished author himself has since come to regard that impossible thing as possible, and even as positively true. In the first case the great detective declared that he never knew a crime committed by a flying creature. Since the development of aviation, and especially the development of German aviation, Sir Arthur Conan Doyle, patriot and war historian, has seen a good many crimes committed by flying creatures. And in the other case the detective implied that no deed need be attributed to spirits or supernatural beings; in short, to any of the agencies to which Sir Arthur is now the most positive and even passionate witness. Presumably, in his present mood and philosophy the Hound of the Baskervilles might well have been a really ghostly hound; at least, if the optimism which seems to go with spiritualism would permit him to believe in such a thing as a hell-hound. It may be worth while to note this coincidence, however, in telling a tale in which both these explanations necessarily played a part. The scientists were anxious to attribute it to aviation, and the spiritualists to attribute it to spirits; though it might be questioned whether either the spirit or the flying-man should be congratulated on his utility as an assassin.

A mystery which may yet linger as a memory, but which was in its time a sensation, revolved round the death of a certain Sir Owen Cram, a wealthy eccentric, chiefly known as a patron of learning and the arts. And the peculiarity of the case was that he was found stabbed in the middle of a great stretch of yielding sand by the sea-shore, on which there was absolutely no trace

of any foot-prints but his own. It was admitted that the wound
could not have been self-inflicted; and it grew more and more
difficult even to suggest how it could have been inflicted at all.
Many theories were suggested, ranging, as we have said, from
that of the enthusiasts for aviation to that of the enthusiasts for
psychical research; it being evidently regarded as a feather in the
cap either of science or spiritualism to have effected so neat an
operation. The true story of this strange business has never been
told; it certainly contained elements which, if not supernatural,
were at least supernormal. But to make it clear, we must go back
to the scene with which it began; the scene on the lawn of Sir
Owen's seaside residence, where the old gentleman acted as a
sort of affable umpire in the disputes of the young students who
were his favourite company; the scene which led up to the
singular silence and isolation, and ultimately to the rather eccentric exit of Mr. Amos Boon.

Mr. Amos Boon had been a missionary, and still dressed like
one; at any rate, he dressed like nothing else. His sturdy, full-
bearded figure carried a broad-brimmed hat combined with a
frock-coat; which gave him an air at once outlandish and dowdy.
Though he was no longer a missionary, he was still a traveller.
His face was brown and his long beard was black; there was a
furrow of thought in his brow and a rather strained look in his
eyes, one of which sometimes looked a little larger than the
other, giving a sinister touch to what was in some ways so commonplace. He had ceased to be a missionary through what he
himself would have called the broadening of his mind. Some
said there had been a broadening of his morals as well as of his
mind; and that the South Sea Islands, where he had lived, had
seen not a little of such ethical emancipation. But this was possibly a malicious misrepresentation of his very human curiosity
and sympathy in the matter of the customs of the savages; which
to the ordinary prejudice was indistinguishable from a white man

going *fantee*. Anyhow, travelling about alone with nothing but a big Bible, he had learned to study it minutely, first for oracles and commandments, and afterwards for errors and contradictions; for the Bible-smasher is only the Bible-worshipper turned upside down. He pursued the not very arduous task of proving that David and Saul did not on all occasions merit the Divine favour; and always concluded by roundly declaring that he preferred the Philistines. Boon and his Philistines were already a byword of some levity among the young men who, at that moment, were arguing and joking around him.

At that moment Sir Owen Cram was playfully presiding over a dispute between two or three of his young friends about science and poetry. Sir Owen was a little restless man, with a large head, a bristly grey moustache, and a grey fan of hair like the crest of a cockatoo. There was something sprawling and splay-footed about his continuous movement which was compared by thoughtless youth to that of a crab; and it corresponded to a certain universal eagerness which was really ready to turn in all directions. He was a typical amateur, taking up hobby after hobby with equal inconsistency and intensity. He had impetuously left all his money to a museum of natural history, only to become immediately swallowed up in the single pursuit of landscape painting; and the groups around him largely represented the stages of his varied career. At the moment a young painter, who was also by way of being a poet, was defending some highly poetical notions against the smiling resistance of a rising doctor, whose hobby was biology. The data of agreement would have been difficult to find, and few save Sir Owen could have claimed any common basis of sympathy; but the important matter just then was the curious effect of the young men's controversy upon Mr. Boon.

"The subject of flowers is hackneyed, but the flowers are not," the poet was insisting. "Tennyson was right about the flower in the crannied wall; but most people don't look at flowers in a wall, but only in a wall-paper. If you generalize them, they are dull, but if you simply see them they are always startling. If there's a special providence in a falling star, there's more in a rising star; and a live star at that."

"Well, I can't see it," said the man of science, good-humouredly; he was a red-haired, keen-faced youth in pince-nez, by the name of Wilkes. "I'm afraid we fellows grow out of the way of seeing it like that. You see, a flower is only a growth like any other, with organs and all that; and its inside isn't any prettier or uglier than an animal's. An insect is much the same pattern of rings and radiations. I'm interested in it as I am in an octopus or any sea-beast you would think a monster."

"But why should you put it that way round?" retorted the poet. "Why isn't it quite as logical the other way round? Why not say the octopus is as wonderful as the flower, instead of the flower as ordinary as the octopus? Why not say that crackens and cuttles and all the sea-monsters are themselves flowers; fearful and wonderful flowers in that terrible twilight garden of God. I do not doubt that God can be as fond of a shark as I am of a buttercup."

"As to God, my dear Gale," began the other quietly, and then he seemed to change his form of words. "Well, I am only a man —nay, only a scientific man, which you may think lower than a sea-beast. And the only interest I have in a shark is to cut him up; always on the preliminary supposition that I have prevented him from cutting me up."

"Have you ever met a shark?" asked Amos Boon, intervening suddenly.

"Not in society," replied the poet with a certain polite discomposure, looking round with something like a flush under his fair hair; he was a long, loose-limbed man named Gabriel Gale, whose pictures were more widely known than his poems.

"You've seen them in the tanks, I suppose," said Boon; "but I've seen them in the sea. I've seen them where they are lords of the sea, and worshipped by the people as great gods. I'd as soon worship those gods as any other."

Gale the poet was silent, for his mind always moved in a sort of sympathy with merely imaginative pictures; and he instantly saw, as in a vision, boiling purple seas and plunging monsters. But another young man standing near him, who had hitherto been rather primly silent, cut in quietly; a theological student, named Simon, the deposit of some epoch of faith in Sir Owen's stratified past. He was a slim man with sleek, dark hair and darting, mobile eyes, in spite of his compressed lips. Whether in caution or contempt, he had left the attack on medical material-ism to the poet, who was always ready to plunge into an endless argument with anybody. Now he intervened merely to say:

"Do they only worship a shark? It seems rather a limited sort of religion."

"Religion!" repeated Amos Boon, rudely; "what do you peo-ple know about religion? You pass the plate round, and when Sir Owen puts a penny in it, you put up a shed where a curate can talk to a congregation of maiden aunts. These people have got something like a religion. They sacrifice things to it—their beasts, their babies, their lives. I reckon you'd turn green with fear if you'd ever so much as caught a glimpse of Religion. Oh, it's not just a fish in the sea; rather it's the sea round a fish. The sea is the blue cloud he moves in, or the green veil or curtain hung about him, the skirts of which trail with thunder."

All faces were turned towards him, for there was something about him beyond his speech. Twilight was spreading over the garden, which lay near the edge of a chalk cliff above the shore, but the last light of sunset still lay on a part of the lawn, paint-ing it yellow rather than green, and glowing almost like gold against the last line of the sea, which was a sombre indigo and violet, changing nearer land to a lurid, pale green. A long cloud of a jagged shape happened to be trailing across the sun; and the broad-hatted, hairy man from the South Seas suddenly pointed at it.

"I know where the shape of that cloud would be called the shadow of the shark," he cried, "and a thousand men would fall on their faces ready to fast or fight, or die. Don't you see the great black dorsal fin, like the peak of a moving mountain? And then you lads discuss him as if he were a stroke at golf; and one of you says he would cut him up like birthday cake; and the other says your Jewish Jehovah would condescend to pat him like a pet rabbit."

"Come, come," said Sir Owen, with a rather nervous waggishness, "we mustn't have any of your broad-minded blasphemies."

Boon turned on him a baneful eye; literally an eye, for one of his eyes grew larger till it glowed like the eye of the Cyclops. His figure was black against the fiery turf, and they could almost hear his beard bristling.

"Blasphemy!" he cried in a new voice, with a crack in it. "Take care it is not you who blaspheme."

And then, before anyone could move, the black figure against the patch of gold had swung round and was walking away from the house, so impetuously that they had a momentary fear that he would walk over the cliff. However, he found the little wooden gate that led to a flight of wooden steps; and they heard him stumbling down the path to the fishing village below.

Sir Owen seemed suddenly to shake off a paralysis like a fit of slumber. "My old friend is a little eccentric," he said. "Don't go, gentlemen; don't let him break up the party. It is early yet."

But growing darkness and a certain social discomfort had already begun to dissolve the group on the lawn; and the host was soon left with a few of the most intimate of his guests. Simon and Gale, and his late antagonist, Dr. Wilkes, were staying to dinner; the darkness drove them indoors, and eventually found them sitting round a flask of green Chartreuse on the table; for Sir Owen had his expensive conventions as well as his expensive eccentricities. The talkative poet, however, had fallen silent, and was staring at the green liquid in his glass as if it were the green depth of the sea. His host attacked with animation the other ordinary topics of the day.

"I bet I'm the most industrious of the lot of you," he said. "I've been at my easel on the beach all day, trying to paint this blessed cliff, and make it look like chalk and not cheese."

"I saw you, but I didn't like to disturb you," said Wilkes. "I generally try to put in an hour or so looking for specimens at high tide: I suppose most people think I'm shrimping or only paddling and doing it for my health. But I've got a pretty good nucleus of that museum we were talking about, or at least the aquarium part of it. I put in most of the rest of the time arranging the exhibits; so I deny the implication of idleness. Gale was on the sea-shore too. He was doing nothing as usual; and now he's saying nothing, which is much more uncommon."

"I have been writing letters," said Simon, in his precise way, "but letters are not always trivial. Sometimes they are rather tremendous."

Sir Owen glanced at him for a moment, and a silence followed, which was broken by a thud and a rattle of glasses as Gale brought his fist down on the table like a man who had thought of something suddenly.

"Dagon!" he cried, in a sort of ecstasy.

Most of the company seemed but little enlightened; perhaps they thought that saying "Dagon" was his poetical and professional fashion of saying "Damn." But the dark eyes of Simon brightened, and he nodded quickly.

"Why, of course you're right," he said. "That must be why Mr. Boon is so fond of the Philistines."

In answer to a general state of inquiry, he said smoothly: "The Philistines were a people from Crete, probably of Hellenic origin, who settled on the coast of Palestine, carrying with them a worship which may very well have been that of Poseidon, but which their enemies, the Israelites, described as that of Dagon. The relevant matter here is that the carved or painted symbol of the god seems always to have been a fish."

The mention of the new matter seemed to reawaken the tendency of the talk to turn into a wrangle between the poet and the professional scientist.

"From my point of view," said the latter, "I must confess my-self somewhat disappointed with your friend Mr. Boon. He represented himself as a rationalist like myself, and seemed to have made some scientific studies of folklore in the South Seas. But he seemed a little unbalanced; and surely he made a curious fuss about some sort of a fetish, considering it was only a fish."

"No, no, no!" cried Gale, almost with passion. "Better make a fetish of the fish. Better sacrifice yourself and everybody else on the horrible huge altar of the fish. Better do anything than utter the star-blasting blasphemy of saying it is *only* a fish. It's as bad as saying the other thing is only a flower."

"All the same, it *is* only a flower," answered Wilkes, "and the advantage of looking at these things in a cool and rational way from the outside is that you can—"

He stopped a moment and remained quite still, as if he were watching something. Some even fancied that his pale, aquiline face looked paler as well as sharper.

"What was that at the window?" he asked. "Is anybody out-side this house?"

"What's the matter? What did you see?" asked his host, in abrupt agitation.

"Only a face," replied the doctor, "but it was not—it was not like a man's face. Let's get outside and look into this."

Gabriel Gale was only a moment behind the doctor, who had impetuously dashed out of the room. Despite his lounging de-meanour, the poet had already leapt to his feet with his hand on the back of the chair, when he stiffened where he stood; for he had seen it. The faces of the others showed that they had seen it too.

Pressed against the dark window-pane, but only wanly lumi-nous as it protruded out of the darkness, was a large face look-ing at first rather like a green goblin mask in a pantomime. Yet it was in no sense human; its eyes were set in large circles, rather in the fashion of an owl. But the glimmering covering that faintly showed on it was not of feathers, but of scales.

The next moment it had vanished. The mind of the poet, which made images as rapidly as a cinema, even in a crisis of action, had already imagined a string of fancies about the sort of creature he saw it to be. He had thought involuntarily of some great flying fish winging its way across the foam, and the flat sand and the spire and roofs of the fishing village. He had half-imagined the moist sea air thickening in some strange way to a greener and more liquid atmosphere in which the marine monsters could swim about in the streets. He had entertained the fancy that the house itself stood in the depths of the sea, and that the great goblin-headed fishes were nosing round it, as round the cabin windows of a wreck.

At that moment a loud voice was heard outside crying in distinct accents:

"The fish has legs."

For that instant, it seemed to give the last touch to the monstrosity. But the meaning of it came back to them, a returning reality, with the laughing face of Dr. Wilkes as he reappeared in the doorway, panting.

"Our fish had two legs, and used them," he said. "He ran like a hare when he saw me coming; but I could see plainly enough it was a man, playing you a trick of some sort. So much for that psychic phenomenon."

He paused and looked at Sir Owen Cram with a smile that was keen and almost suspicious.

"One thing is very clear to me," he said. "You have an enemy."

The mystery of the human fish, however, did not long remain even a primary topic of conversation in a social group that had so many topics of conversation. They continued to pursue their hobbies and pelt each other with their opinions; even the smooth and silent Simon being gradually drawn into the discussions, in which he showed a dry and somewhat cynical dexterity. Sir Owen continued to paint with all the passion of an amateur.

Gale continued to neglect to paint, with all the nonchalance of a painter. Mr. Boon was presumably still as busy with his wicked Bible and his good Philistines as Dr. Wilkes with his museum and his microscopic marine animals, when the little seaside town was shaken as by an earthquake with the incomprehensible calamity which spread its name over all the newspapers of the country.

Gabriel Gale was scaling the splendid swell of turf that terminated in the great chalk cliff above the shore, in a mood consonant to the sunrise that was storming the skies above him. Clouds haloed with sunshine were already sailing over his head as if sent flying from a flaming wheel; and when he came to the brow of the cliff he saw one of those rare revelations when the sun does not seem to be merely the most luminous object in a luminous landscape, but itself the solitary focus and streaming fountain of all light. The tide was at the ebb, and the sea was only a strip of delicate turquoise over which rose the tremendous irradiation. Next to the strip of turquoise was a strip of orange sand, still wet, and nearer the sand was a desert of a more dead yellow or brown, growing paler in the increasing light. And as he looked down from the precipice upon that plain of pale gold, he saw two black objects lying in the middle of it. One was a small easel, still standing, with a camp-stool fallen beside it; the other was the flat and sprawling figure of a man.

The figure did not move, but as he stared he became conscious that another human figure was moving, was walking over the flat sands towards it from under the shadow of the cliff. Looking at it steadily, he saw that it was the man called Simon; and in an instant he seemed to realize that the motionless figure was that of Sir Owen Cram. He hastened to the stairway down the cliff and so to the sands; and soon stood face to face with Simon; for they both looked at each other for a moment before they both looked down at the body. The conviction was already cold in his heart that it was a dead body. Nevertheless, he said sharply: "We must have a doctor; where is Dr. Wilkes?"

"It is no good, I fear," said Simon, looking away at the sea.

"Wilkes may only confirm our fears that he is dead," said Gale, "but he may have something to say about how he died."

"True," said the other, "I will go for him myself." And he walked back rapidly towards the cliff in the track of his own foot-prints.

Indeed, it was at the foot-prints that Gale was gazing in a bemused fashion at that moment. The tracks of his own coming were clear enough, and the tracks of Simon's coming and going; and the third rather more rambling track of the unmistakable boots of the unfortunate Sir Owen, leading up to the spot where his easel was planted. And that was all. The sand was soft, so that the lightest foot would disturb it; it was well above the tides; and there was not the faintest trace of any other human being having been near the body. Yet the body had a deep wound under the angle of the jaw; and there was no sign of any weapon of suicide.

Gabriel Gale was a believer in commonsense, in theory if not always in practice. He told himself repeatedly that these things were the practical clues in such a case; the wound, the weapon or absence of weapon, the foot-prints or absence of foot-prints. But there was also a part of his mind which was always escaping from his control and playing tricks; fixing on his memory meaningless things as if they were symbols, and then haunting him with them as mysteries. He made no point of it; it was rather sub-conscious than self-conscious; but the parts of any living picture that he saw were seldom those that others saw, or that it seemed sensible to see. And there were one or two details in the tragedy before him that haunted him then and long afterwards. Cram had fallen backwards in a rather twisted fashion, with his feet towards the shore; and a few inches from the left foot lay a star-fish. He could not say whether it was merely the bright orange colour of the creature that irrationally riveted his eye, or merely some obscure fancy of repetition, in that the human figure was itself spread and sprawling flat like a star-fish, with four limbs instead of five. Nor did he attempt to analyze this æsthetic antic of his psychology; it was a suppressed part of his mind which still repeated that the mystery of the untrodden sands would turn out to be something quite simple; but that the star-fish possessed the secret.

He looked up to see Simon returning with the doctor, indeed with two doctors; for there was more than one medical representative in the mob of Sir Owen's varied interests. The other was a Dr. Garth, a little man with an angular and humorous face; he was an old friend of Gale's, but the poet's greeting was rather *distrait*. Garth and his colleagues, however, got to work on a preliminary examination, which made further talk needless. It could not be a full examination till the arrival of the police, but it was sufficient to extinguish any hope of life, if any such had lingered. Garth, who was bent over the body in a crouching posture, spoke to his fellow physician without raising his head.

"There seems to be something rather odd about this wound. It goes almost straight upwards, as if it was struck from below. But Sir Owen was a very small man; and it seems queer that he should be stabbed by somebody smaller still."

Gale's sub-consciousness exploded with a strange note of harsh mockery.

"What," he cried, "you don't think the starfish jumped up and killed him?"

"No, of course not," said Garth, with his gruff good humour. "What on earth is the matter with you?"

"Lunacy, I think," said the poet, and began to walk slowly towards the shore.

As time went on he almost felt disposed to fancy that he had correctly diagnosed his own complaint. The image began to figure even in his dreams, but not merely as a natural nightmare about the body on the sea-shore. The significant sea creature seemed more vivid even than the body. As he had originally seen the corpse from above, spread flat out beneath him, he saw it in his visions as something standing, as if propped against a wall or even merely drawn or graven on a wall. Sometimes the sandy ground had become a ground of old gold in some decoration of the Dark Ages, with the figure in the stiff agonies of a martyr, but the red star always showed like a lamp by his feet. Sometimes it was a hieroglyphic of a more Eastern sort, as of some stone god rigidly dancing; but the five-pointed star was always in the same place below. Sometimes it seemed a rude, red-sandstone sort of drawing; yet more archaic; but the star was always the reddest spot in it. Now and again, while the human figure was as dry and dark as a mummy, the star would seem to be literally alive, waving its flaming fingers as if it were trying to tell him something. Now and then even the whole figure was upside down, as if to restore the star to its proper place in the skies.

"I told Wilkes that a flower was a living star," he said to himself. "A starfish is more literally a living star. But this is like going crazy. And if there is one thing I strongly object to, it is going crazy. What use should I be to all my brother lunatics, if I once really lost my balance on the tight-rope over the abyss?"

He sat staring into vacancy for some time, trying to fit in this small and stubborn fancy with a much steadier stream of much deeper thoughts that were already driving in a certain direction. At last, the light of a possibility began to dawn in his eyes; and it was evidently something very simple when it was realized; something which he felt he ought to have thought of before; for he laughed shortly and scornfully at himself as he rose to his feet.

"If Boon goes about everywhere introducing his shark and I go into society always attended by my starfish," he murmured to himself, "we shall turn the world into an aquarium bigger and better than Dr. Wilkes is fixing up. I'm going down to make some inquiries in the village."

Returning thence across the sands at evening, after several conversations with skippers and fishermen, he wore a more satisfied expression.

"I always did believe," he reflected, "that the foot-print business would be the simplest thing in the affair. But there are some things in it that are by no means simple."

Then he looked up, and saw far off on the sands, lonely and dark against the level evening light, the strange hat and stumpy figure of Amos Boon.

He seemed to consider for a moment the advisability of a meeting; then he turned away and moved towards the stairway up the cliff. Mr. Boon was apparently occupied in idly drawing lines on the sand with his shabby umbrella; like one drawing plans for a child's sand-castle, but apparently without any such intelligent object or excuse. Gale had often seen the man mooning about with equally meaningless and automatic gestures; but as the poet mounted the rocky steps, climbing higher and higher, he had a return of the irrational feeling of a visionary vertigo. He told himself again, as if in warning, that it was his whole duty in life to walk on a tight-rope above a void in which many imaginative men were swallowed up. Then he looked down again at the drop of the dizzy cliffs to the flats that seemed to be swimming below him like a sea. And he saw the long, loose lines drawn in the sand unified into a shape, as flat as a picture on a wall. He had often seen a child, in the same fashion, draw on the sand a pig as large as a house. But in this case he could not shake off his former feeling of something archaic, like a palæolithic drawing, about the scratching of the brown sand. And Mr. Boon had not drawn a pig, but a shark; conspicuous with its jagged teeth and fin like a horn exalted.

But he was not the only person overlooking this singular decorative scheme. When he came to the short railings along the brow of the cliff in which the stairway terminated, he found three figures leaning on it and looking down; and instantly realized how the case was closing in. For even in their outlines against the sky he had recognized the two doctors and an inspector of police.

"Hullo, Gale," observed Wilkes, "may I present you to Inspector Davies; a very active and successful officer."

Garth nodded. "I understand the inspector will soon make an arrest," he said.

"The inspector must be getting back to his work and not talking about it," said that official good-humouredly. "I'm going down to the village. Anybody coming my way?"

Dr. Wilkes assented and followed him, but Dr. Garth stopped a moment, being detained by the poet, who caught hold of his sleeve with unusual earnestness.

"Garth," he said, "I want to apologize. I'm afraid I was wool-gathering when we met the other day, and didn't hail you as I ought to hail an old friend. You and I have been in one or two queer affairs together, and I want to talk to you about this one. Shall we sit down on that seat over there?"

They seated themselves on an iron seat set up on the picturesque headland; and Gale added, "I wish you could tell me roughly how you got as far as you seem to have got."

Garth gazed silently out to sea, and said at last:

"Do you know that man Simon?"

"Yes," replied the poet, "that's the way it works, is it?"

"Well, the investigation soon began to show that Simon knew rather more than he said. He was on the spot before you; and for some time he wouldn't admit what it was he saw before you turned up. We guessed it was because he was afraid to tell the truth; and in one sense he was."

"Simon doesn't talk enough," said Gale thoughtfully. "He doesn't talk about himself enough; so he thinks about himself too much. A man like that always gets secretive; not necessarily in the sense of being criminal, or even of being malicious, but merely of being morbid. He is the sort that is ill-treated at school and never says so. As long as a thing terrified him, he couldn't talk about it."

"I don't know how you guessed it," said Garth, "but that is something like the line of discoveries. At first they thought that Simon's silence was guilt, but it was only a fear of something more than guilt; of some diabolic destiny and entanglement. The truth is, that when he went up before you to the cliff-head at daybreak, he saw something that hag-rode his morbid spirit ever since. He saw the figure of this man Boon poised on the brink of the precipice, black against the dawn, and waving his arms in some unearthly fashion as if he were going to fly. Simon thought the man was talking to himself, and perhaps even singing. Then the strange creature passed on towards the village and was lost in the twilight; but when Simon came to the edge of the cliff he saw Sir Owen lying dead far out on the sands below, beside his easel."

"And ever since, I suppose," observed Gale, "Simon has seen sharks everywhere."

"You are right again," said the doctor. "He has admitted since that a shadow on the blind or a cloud on the moon would have the unmistakable shape of the fish with the fin erect. But, in fact, it is a very mistakable shape; anything with a triangular top to it would suggest it to a man on his state of nerves. But the truth is that so long as he thought Boon had dealt death from a distance by some sort of curse or spell, we could get nothing out of him. Our only chance was to show him that Boon might have done it even by natural means. And we did show it, after all."

"What is your theory, then?" asked the other.

"It is too general to be called a theory yet," replied the doctor; "but, honestly, I do not think it at all impossible that Boon might have killed a man on the sands from the top of a cliff, without falling back on any supernatural stuff. You've got to consider it like this: Boon has been very deep in the secrets of savages, especially in that litter of islands that lie away towards Australia. Now, we know that such savages, for all they are called ignorant, have developed many dexterities and many unique tools. They have blow-pipes that kill at a considerable distance; they harpoon and lasso things, and draw them in on a line. Above all, the Australian savages have discovered the boomerang, that actually returns to the hand. Is it quite so inconceivable that Boon might know some way of sending a penetrating projectile from a distance, and even possibly of recovering it in some way? Dr. Wilkes and I, on examining the wound, found it a very curious one: it was made by some tapering, pointed tool, with a slight curve; and it not only curved upwards, but even slightly outwards, as if the curve were returning on itself. Does not that suggest to you some outlandish weapon of a strange shape, and possibly with strange properties? And always remember that such an explanation would explain something else as well, which is generally regarded as the riddle. It would explain why the murderer left no foot-prints round the body."

Gale gazed out to sea in silence, as if considering; then he said simply:

"An extremely shrewd argument. But I know why he left no foot-prints. It is a much simpler explanation than that."

Garth stared at him for a few moments; and then observed gravely:

"May I then ask, in return, what is your theory?"

"My theory will seem a maze of theories, and nothing else," said Gale. "It is, as many would say, of such stuff as dreams are made of. Most modern people have a curious contradiction; they abound in theories, yet they never see the part that theories play in practical life. They are always talking about temperament and circumstances and accident; but most men are what their theories make them; most men go in for murder or marriage, or mere lounging because of some theory of life, asserted or assumed. So I can never manage to begin my explanations in that brisk, pointed, practical way that you doctors and detectives do. I see a man's mind first, sometimes almost without any particular man attached to it. I could only begin this business by describing a mental state—which can't be described. Our murderer or maniac, or whatever you call him, is certainly affected by some of the elements attributed to him. His view has reached an insane degree of simplicity, and in that sense of savagery. But I doubt whether he would necessarily transfer the savagery from the end to the means. In one sense, indeed, his view might be compared to the barbaric. He saw every creature and even every object naked. He did not understand that what clothes a thing is sometimes the most real part of it. Have you ever noticed how true is that old phrase, 'clothed and in his right mind'? Man is not in his right mind when he is not clothed with the symbols of his social dignity. Humanity is not even human when it is naked. But in a lower sense it is so of lesser things, even of lifeless things. A lot of nonsense is talked about auras; but this is the truth behind it. Everything has a halo. Everything has a sort of atmosphere of what it signifies, which makes it sacred. Even the little creatures he studied had each of them its halo; but he would not see it."

"But what little creatures did Boon study?" asked Garth in some wonder. "Do you mean the cannibals?"

"I was not thinking about Boon," replied Gabriel Gale.

"What do you mean?" cried the other, in sudden excitement. "Why, Boon is almost in the hands of the police."

"Boon is a good man," said Gale, calmly; "he is very stupid; that is why he is an atheist. There are intelligent atheists, as we shall see presently; but that stunted, stupid sort is much commoner, and much nicer. But he is a good man; his motive is good; he originally talked all that tosh of the superiority of the savage because he thought he was the underdog. He may be a trifle cracked, by now, about sharks and other things; but that's only because his travels have been too much for his intellect. They say travel broadens the mind; but you must have the mind. He had a mind for a suburban chapel, and there passed before it all the panorama of gilded nature-worship and purple sacrifice. He doesn't know if he's on his head or his heels, any more than a good many others. But I shouldn't wonder if heaven is largely populated with atheists of that sort, scratching their heads and wondering where they are.

"But Boon is a parenthesis; that is all he is. The man I am talking about is very much the point, and a sharp one at that. He dealt in something very different from muddled mysticism about human sacrifice. Human sacrifice is quite a human weakness. He

dealt in assassination; direct, secret, straight from a head as inhuman as hell. And I knew it when I first talked to him over the
tea-cups and he said he saw nothing pretty in a flower."

"My dear fellow!" remonstrated Dr. Garth.

"I don't mean that a man merely dissecting a daisy must be on
the road to the gallows," conceded the poet, magnanimously,
"but I do say that to mean it as he meant it is to be on a straight
road of logic that leads there if he chooses to follow it. God is
inside everything. But this man wanted to be outside everything;
to see everything hung in a vacuum, simply its own dead self.
It's not only not the same, it's almost the opposite of scepticism
in the sense of Boon or the Book of Job. That's a man over-
whelmed by the mysteries; but this man denies that there are any
mysteries. It's not, in the ordinary sense, a matter of theology,
but psychology. Most good pagans and pantheists might talk of
the miracles of nature; but this man denies that there are any
miracles, even in the sense of marvels. Don't you see that dreadful dry light shed on things must at last wither up the moral
mysteries as illusions, respect for age, respect for property, and
that the sanctity of life will be a superstition? The men in the
street are only organisms, with their organs more or less displayed. For such a one there is no longer any terror in the touch
of human flesh, nor does he see God watching him out of the
eyes of a man."

"He may not believe in miracles, but he seems to work them,"
remarked the doctor. "What else was he doing, when he struck
a man down on the sand without leaving a mark to show where
he stood?"

"He was paddling," answered Gale.

"As high up on the shore as that?" inquired the other.

Gale nodded. "That was what puzzled me; till something I
saw on the sand started a train of thought that led to my asking
the seafaring people about the tides. It's very simple; the night
before we found the body was a flood-tide, and the sea came up
higher than usual; not quite to where Cram was sitting, but

pretty near. So that was the way that the real human fish came out of the sea. That was the way the divine shark really devoured the sacrifice. The man came paddling in the foam, like a child on a holiday."

"Who came?" asked Garth; but he shuddered.

"Who did go dredging for sea-beasts with a sort of shrimping-net along the shore every evening? Who did inherit the money of the old man for his ambitious museum and his scientific career? Who did tell me in the garden that a cowslip was only a growth like a cancer?"

"I am compelled to understand you," said the doctor gloomily. "You mean that very able young man named Wilkes?"

"To understand Wilkes you must understand a good deal," continued his friend. "You must reconstruct the crime, as they say. Look out over that long line of darkening sea and sand, where the last light runs red as blood; that is where he came dredging every day, in the same bloodshot dusk, looking for big beasts and small; and in a true sense everything was fish that came to his net. He was constructing his museum as a sort of cosmos; with everything traced from the fossil to the flying fish. He had spent enormous sums on it, and had got quite distinterestedly into debt; for instance he had had magnificent models made, in wax or papier maché, of small fish magnified, or extinct fish restored; things that South Kensington cannot afford, and certainly Wilkes could not afford. But he had persuaded Cram to leave his money to the museum, as you know; and for him Cram was simply a silly old fool, who painted pictures he couldn't paint, and talked of sciences he didn't understand; and whose only natural function was to die and save the museum. Well, when every morning Wilkes had done polishing the glass cases of his masks and models, he came round by the cliff and took a turn at the fossils in the chalk with his geological hammer; then he put it back in that great canvas bag of his, and unslung his long shrimping net and began to wade. This is where I want you to look at that dark red sand and see the picture; one never un-

derstands anything till one sees the picture. He went for miles
along the shallows of that desolate shore, long inured to seeing
one queer creature or another stranded on the sand; here a sea-
hedgehog, and there a starfish, and then a crab, and then another creature. I have told you he had reached a stage when he
would have looked at an angel with the eye of an ornithologist.
What would he think of a man, and a man looking like that?
Don't you see that poor Cram must have looked like a crab or a
sea-urchin; his dwarfed, hunched figure seen from behind, with
his fan of bristling whiskers, his straggling bow legs and restless
twisting feet all tangled up with the three legs of his stool; making him look as if he had five limbs like a starfish? Don't you see
he looked like a Common Object of the Seashore? And Wilkes
had only to collect this specimen, and all his other specimens
were safe. Everything was fish that came to his net, and . . .

"He stretched out the long pole in his hand to its full extent,
and drew the net over the old man's head as if he were catching
a great grey moth. He plucked him backwards off his stool so
that he lay kicking on his back on the sand; and doubtless looking more like a large insect than ever. Then the murderer bent
forward, propped by one hand upon his pole, and the other
armed with his geological hammer. With the pick at the back of
that instrument he struck in what he well knew to be a vital spot.
The curve you noticed in the wound is due to that sharp side of
the hammer being shaped like a pickaxe. But the unusual position
of it, and the puzzle of how such a blow could be struck upwards, was due to the queer posture of the two figures. The murderer struck at a head that was upside down. It could only occur
as a rule if the victim were standing on his head, a posture in
which few persons await the assassin. But with the flourish and
sweep of the great net, I fancy a starfish caught in it fell out of
it, just beyond the dead man's foot. At any rate, it was that starfish and the accident of its flying so high on the shore, that set
my mind drifting in the general direction of tides; and the possibility of the murderer having been moving about in the water.

If he made any prints the breakers washed them out; and I should never have begun to think of it but for that red five-fingered little monster."

"Then do you mean to tell me," demanded Garth, "that all this business about the shadow of the shark had nothing to do with it?"

"The shadow of the shark had everything to do with it," replied Gale. "The murderer hid in the shadow of the shark, and struck from under the shadow of the shark. I doubt if he would have struck at all, if he had not had the shadow of that fantastic fin in which to hide. And the proof is that he himself took the trouble to emphasize and exaggerate the legend of poor Boon dancing before Dagon. Do you remember that queer incident of the fish's face at the window? How did anybody merely playing a practical joke get hold of a fish's face? It was very life-like; for it was one of the masks modelled for the Wilkes museum; and Wilkes had left it in the hall in his great canvas bag. It seems simple, doesn't it, for a man to raise an alarm inside a house, walk out to see, and instantly put on a mask and look in at a window? That's all he did; and you can see his idea, from the fact that he proceeded to warn Sir Owen of an enemy. He wanted all this idolatrous and mystical murder business worked for all it was worth, that his own highly reasonable murder might not be noticed. And you see he has succeeded. You tell me that Boon is in the hands of the police."

Garth sprang to his feet. "What is to be done?" he said.

"You will know what to do," said the poet. "You are a good and just man, and a practical man, too. I am not a practical man." He rose with a certain air of apology. "You see, you want an unpractical man for finding out this sort of thing."

And once more he gazed down from the precipice into the abysses below.

THE CRIME OF GABRIEL GALE

Dr. Butterworth, the famous London physician, was sitting in
his summer-house in his shirt sleeves, for it was a hot day and he
had been playing tennis on the sunny lawns outside. He had a
solid face and figure and carried everywhere an atmosphere of
bodily health and good humour which helped him not a little in
his profession; but he was not serious or self-conscious about it.
He was not one of those in whom health has degenerated into
hygiene. He played tennis when he felt inclined and left off
when he felt inclined; as on the present occasion, when he had
retired to smoke a pipe in the shade. He enjoyed a game as he
enjoyed a joke; which was interpreted by some as meaning that
he would never be a player, and by himself as meaning that he
would always be able to play. And he enjoyed a joke very much,
even the most minute and trivial joke that his roving eye encountered; and at this moment it encountered a quaint detail,
which was something of a quaint contrast, in the glowing garden outside. Framed in the dark doorway of the summer-house,
like a lighted scene on the stage, was the perspective of a garden path, bordered with very gay and flamboyant beds of tulips,
having something of the gorgeous formality of the borders of a
Persian illumination. And down the centre of the central path
was advancing a figure that looked by comparison almost completely black, with black top-hat, black clothes and black umbrella; it might have been the mythical Black Tulip come to life
and a walking parody of the tall, top-heavy garden flowers. The
next moment all such fancies had faded from the doctor's day-
dream; for he had recognized a familiar face under the top-hat;
he knew that the contrast was not merely grotesque; and was
shocked with the gravity of the visitor's eyes.

"Hullo, Garth," he said in a hearty manner, "sit down and tell
us all about yourself. You look as if you were going to a funeral."

"So I am," replied Dr. Garth, putting his black hat on a chair; he was a small, red-haired, shrewd-faced man and he looked pale and harassed.

"I am so sorry," said Butterworth quickly, "if I spoke without thinking. I'm afraid you're really rather cut up."

"I am going to a queer sort of funeral," said Dr. Garth grimly; "the sort of funeral where we take special precautions to ensure premature burial."

"What in the world do you mean?" asked his colleague, staring.

"I mean I've got to bury a man alive," said Garth with a ghastly calm. "But it's the sort of burial that requires two doctors' certificates instead of one."

Butterworth stared at the patch of sunlight and sucked in his cheeks with a soundless whistle. "Oh . . . I see," he said.

Then he added abruptly: "Of course it's always a sad business; but I'm afraid it's rather personal for you. A friend of yours?"

"One of my best friends, I think, barring yourself," replied Garth; "and one of the best and brightest young men of our time as well. I was afraid something of the sort might happen; but I hoped it wouldn't be so bad as this." He stopped for an instant and then said almost explosively:

"It's poor old Gale; and he's done it once too often."

"Done what?" asked Dr. Butterworth.

"It's rather difficult to explain, unless you know him," said Garth. "Gabriel Gale is a poet, also a painter and other wild things of that sort; but he has also a wild theory of his own about how to cure lunatics. In short, the amateur set up as a mad doctor and now the doctor is really mad. It's a horrid tragedy; but really he was asking for it."

"I don't yet understand what it's all about," said the other doctor patiently.

"I tell you he had a theory," said Garth. "He thought he could cure cracked people by what he called sympathy. But it didn't mean what you would mean by sympathy; he meant following their thoughts and going half-way with them, or all the way with them if he could. I used to joke with him, poor fellow, and say that if a lunatic thought he was made of glass, Gale would try hard to feel a little transparent. Anyhow, that was his notion, that he could really look at things to some extent from the lunatic's point of view; and talk to him in his own language. He admitted himself that it was a risky business, to walk on the edge of the precipice like that; and now, as I say, he's done it once too often. I always distrusted it myself."

"I should think so," said Dr. Butterworth, all his solid sanity stiffening against the suggestion. "He might as well say that a doctor ought to limp all the way to cure a lame man, or shut his eyes in order to help the blind."

"If the blind lead the blind," assented the other gloomily. "Well, he's fallen into the ditch this time."

"Why especially this time?" asked Butterworth.

"Well, if he doesn't go to an asylum, he'll go to jail," said Garth grimly. "That's why I'm in such a hurry to have him certified; God knows I don't like doing that. But he's broken out this time in a way he never did before. He was always fanciful and eccentric, of course; but I'm bound to say he had a very sane streak in him somewhere. It's exactly because he's never done anything like this before that I'm sure the end has really come. For one thing, he's committed a perfectly crazy assault and apparently tried to murder a man with a pitchfork. But what hits me much harder, who knew him, is that he tried to murder a perfectly mild and shy and inoffensive person; in fact a rather gauche youth from Cambridge, half developed into a curate. Now that's quite unlike Gabriel, even at his maddest. The men with whom he wrestled in spirit, if not in body, were intellectual bullies or mesmerists, the sort of men who wanted somebody to stand up to them; like that thin-lipped Dr. Wilkes, or that Russian Professor. I can no more see him savaging somebody like poor young Saunders than I can see him kicking a crippled child. And yet I *did* see him do it. The only explanation is that he wasn't himself.

"There was another thing which made me sure he wasn't himself. The weather had been very trying for everybody for some time; hot and stormy and electric; but it was the first time I've ever known him upset by such storms. I've known him to do the silliest things; I've known him stand on his head in the garden; but that was only showing that he was *not* affected by the storm. But this time I'm sure these queer semi-tropical tempests have been too much for him; so that even the very subject of the storm upset him in some way. For this tragedy arose out of the most trivial sort of triviality. The whole terrible unnatural business began with talking about the weather.

"Lady Flamborough said to a guest at her rather damp garden-party, 'You brought bad weather with you.' Anybody might say that to anybody; but she did say it to young Herbert Saunders, who is awfully awkward and shy, one of those long, loose boys with large feet, who seem to have outgrown their clothes and their wits; the last sort of person who would want to be singled out by any remark, however trifling. So Saunders only gaped and gurgled or was dumb, but somehow the lady's remark seemed to get on Gale's nerves from the first. A little while afterwards Gale met Lady Flamborough again, at another reception where it was raining, and he suddenly pointed, like some comic conspirator, at the tall ungainly figure of Saunders in the distance and said: 'He still brings bad weather.' Then happened one of those co-incidences that are quite natural but seem to drive madmen really mad. The next time all that set happened to get together was on a really beautiful afternoon at Mrs. Blakeney's; with a clear blue sky without a cloud in it, so that old Blakeney went pottering round and showed all the first comers his gardens and glass-houses. But after that they all went in to tea, which was served in the great peacock-green drawing room in the middle of the house; and so it happened that Saunders came late and there was

a good deal of laughter as he sat down, much to his embarrassment; because the weather joke had been repeated and people
were quite pleased to see it falsified for once. Then they all went
out into the rooms nearer the entrance; and Gabriel Gale was
walking towards the doorway. Between two pillars he caught
sight of one of the outer windows and stood rooted to the spot,
rigidly pointing with one arm. That gesture alone warned me
that something was really rather wrong with him; but when I
looked I could hardly help sharing his shock of surprise. For the
windows that had been painted blue with summer sky were
painted black with rain. On every side of the house the rain
dripped and pattered as dismally as if it had been raining for a
hundred years. And ten minutes before the whole garden had
seemed a garden of gold like the Hesperides. Gale stood staring
at this flying storm from nowhere, that had so suddenly struck
the house; then he turned slowly and looked, with an expression
not to be forgotten, at the man who was standing a few yards
away. It was Herbert Saunders.

"You can imagine it's not much in my line to believe in witch-
craft or magicians who control the elements; but there did really
seem something funny about that cloudless day having so rapidly overclouded, with the coming of the one man whose name
was already associated with it, if only by a jest. It was a mere
coincidence, of course; but what worried me was the possible
effect on my friend's already rather rickety psychology. He and
Saunders were both standing and staring out of the same wide
window, looking at the deluge-darkened garden and the swaying
and tormented trees; but Saunders's simple face seemed to express only amiable bewilderment; indeed, he was smiling vaguely
and shyly, as he did when he received a compliment. For he was
one of those whose face after a compliment always looks as if it
has received a buffet. He obviously saw nothing in it but a repetition of the joke; perhaps he thought that the English climate
was keeping up the joke. And, compared with his face, the face
of Gabriel was like the face of a fiend. So it seemed at least, as it

sprang white out of the growing dark to meet the first white burst of the lightning; then there followed only thunder and the noise of the roaring rain; but I knew that he stood there rocking with that inexplicable excitement. Through the thunder I heard his voice saying, 'It makes one feel like God.'

"Immediately under the windows a little path ran on the edge of some meadow land attached to the garden, where the Blakeneys had been getting in their hay; and a moderately large mound of hay looked almost mountainously dark against that low and lowering sky; a two-pronged pitchfork lying across it had certainly something grim about its black outline, which may have captured poor Gale's fancy; for he was always prone to be taken by odd sights as if they were signals. Anyhow at that moment the host and hostess and other guests came hurrying by; the old man lamenting over the ruin of his hay; but the lady of the house apparently much more concerned about the fate of some highly ornamental garden-chairs, which had apparently been left out on the lawn just adjoining the meadow, under the large apple tree whose boughs were now tossing and twisting in the storm.

"Gabriel Gale, when in his right mind, is the most chivalrous of men, and would have regained the lady's chairs at a bound. But now he could do nothing but glare at the unfortunate Saunders; who awoke trembling to his social duties, in that agony of self-consciousness in which a man is afraid to do the right thing and afraid not to do it. At length, however, he jerked himself forward, fumbled with the door, flung it open and ran out into the reverberating rain. Then Gale followed him to the open door and shouted something after him. For most of the company, I think, it was lost in the din; but even if they had heard it, they certainly could not have understood it. I heard it; and I thought I understood it only too well. For what Gale shouted through the storm was, 'Why don't you call the chairs and they'll come to you.'

"A second or so afterwards he added, as if it were an after-

thought, 'You might as well tell the tree to come here as well.'
Naturally there was no answer; and indeed Saunders, partly by
his natural clumsiness and partly in the distraction of the driving
elements, seemed for the moment to have lost his way and was
staggering up the steeper path of the meadow some way to the
left of the tree. I could just see his long figure and angular awkward elbows traced against the sky. Then followed the sudden,
violent and utterly unintelligible incident. A rope happened to
lie half round one of the swathes in the foreground; and Gale,
leaping out of the door, caught it up and seemed to be knotting
it in a sort of savage haste. The next moment there swept across
the sky the great swirling curves of a noose thrown in the manner of a lasso. And I could see the wavering figure on the dark
ridge alter its attitude and rear up as against an invisible obstacle,
as the rope tightened and tugged it back.

"I looked round for assistance; and was surprised and somewhat alarmed to find I was alone. The host and hostess, and the
others, having despatched the obliging Saunders after the chairs,
had rushed off to summon the servants or secure other doors and
windows, or look after other fittings threatened by the weather;
and there was no one but myself to watch the unmeaning and
apparently imbecile tragedy outside. I saw Gale drag Saunders
like a sack at the end of a rope along the whole length of windows and disappear round a corner of the house. But I turned
cold with a new fear when, even as he rushed past, he snatched
the hay-fork from the mound and seemed to disappear brandish-
ing it, like the fabulous fork of a demon. I rushed after them, but
slipping on the wet stones, hurt my foot and had to limp; the
raving storm seemed to have swallowed up that lunatic and all
his antics; and it was not until some time afterwards that men
found how that dance had ended. Herbert Saunders was found
tied to a tree, still alive and even unwounded, but presenting the
appearance of having barely missed a murderous attack; for the
prongs of the pitchfork were driven by sheer fury into the tree
on each side of his neck, holding him pinned there as by an iron

ring. Gabriel Gale was not found for nearly a day, until after the storm was spent and the sunshine had returned; and he was loitering about in an adjoining meadow blowing the clocks off dandelions. I have seldom known him so serene."

There was a short silence. "How is the other fellow—Saunders?" asked Butterworth, after a pause of frowning consideration. "Was he much hurt?"

"Had a shock and is still shaky, of course," answered Garth. "Had to go for a rest-cure or something; but I believe he's all right now. Only you can hardly expect a harmless person who's been half murdered in a raving attack like that to feel very friendly or forgiving. So I'm afraid they will make it a case of attempted murder unless we can get our friend off on medical grounds. As a matter of fact, I have him waiting outside in the car."

"Very well," said the London doctor, rising with abrupt composure and buttoning up his coat. "We had better go along to see him now and get it over."

The interview between Gale and the two doctors, at an adjacent hotel, was so short and so extraordinary that they went away with their very level heads turning like wind-mills. For Gale displayed nothing even of the merely childish innocence of levity attributed to him in the tale of the dandelions. He listened with patience, and a humorous and benevolent mildness which made the two doctors, who were considerably his seniors, feel as if they were being treated as juniors. When Garth began to break it to him gently that some sort of rest-cure was required in his own interests, he laughed heartily and anticipated all such periphrases.

"Don't be nervous, old man," he said, "you mean I ought to be in a madhouse; and I'm sure you mean well."

"You know I am your friend," said Garth earnestly; "and all your friends would say what I say."

"Indeed," said Gale, smiling. "Well, if that is the opinion of my friends, perhaps it would be better to get the opinion of my enemies."

"What do you mean," demanded the other. "Of your enemies?"

"Shall we say of my enemy?" continued Gale in level tones. "Of the man to whom I have done this perfectly outrageous thing. Well, really, that is all I ask; that before you lock me up for this outrage, you ask Herbert Saunders himself what he thinks about it."

"Do you mean," broke in Butterworth rather impatiently, "that we are to ask him whether he liked being half-throttled and impaled on a pitchfork?"

"Yes," said Gale, nodding, "I want you to ask him whether he liked being half throttled and impaled on a pitchfork."

He slightly knitted his brows as if considering a new and merely practical point and then added:

"I should send him a telegram now . . . say anything . . . 'How do you like being lassoed,' or, 'What price pitchforks,' or something playful of that sort."

"We could telephone, if it comes to that," said Garth.

The poet shook his head. "No," he said, "that sort of man feels much more free in writing. He will only stammer on the telephone. He won't stammer anything like what you imagine, even then; but he will stammer. But writing with his head in one of those little cubicles at the telegraph office, he will feel as free as in a confessional box."

The two doctors, when they parted in some bewilderment, but tacitly accepting this suggestion of a respite, lost no time in fulfilling the condition required. They sent off a carefully worded telegram to Saunders, who had now returned home to his mother's house, asking him what were his impressions and views about the extraordinary conduct of Gabriel Gale. The reply came back with remarkable promptitude; and Garth came to Butterworth with the open telegram in his hand and a rather dazed expression on his face. For the exact terms of the message were:

"Can never be sufficiently grateful to Gale for his great kindness which more than saved my life."

The two doctors looked at each other in silence; and in almost as complete a silence got into a car and drove across the hills once more to the Blackeney's house, where Gale was still staying.

They drove across the hilly country and descended into the wide and shallow valley where stood the house which sheltered that dangerous character, Mr. Gabriel Gale. Garth could recall, and Butterworth could imagine, all the irony suggested to the imagination by such a story about such a scene. The house of the Blackeneys stood high and plain just beyond the river; it was one of those houses that strike the eye as old-fashioned and yet not old. Certainly it was not old enough to be beautiful; but it had everything that recalls, to those that faintly remember them, the last traditions of Early Victorian lingering into Mid-Victorian times. The tall pillars looked so very pallid; the long plain windows looked in dismally upon high-ceilinged rooms; the curtains that hung parallel with the pillars were strips of dull red; and even from that distance the humorous Butterworth was certain that they had heavy and quite useless tassels. It was a strange house to have been the scene of an incredible crime or lunacy. It was an even stranger house to have been, as was alleged, the scene of a yet more incredible or mysterious mercy. All about it lay its ordered gardens and its mown or unmown meadows; its plantations of trees and deep alleys and shrubberies; all the things which on that wild night had been given over to the withering splendour of the lightning and the wind. Now the whole landscape was laid bare in a golden calm of summer; and the blue heavens above it were so deep and still that the sound of a humming fly hung there and was heard as far away as the skylark. Thus glittered in the sun, all solid and objective, the stage properties of that hideous farce. Garth saw all the blank and staring windows which he had last beheld streaming with rain and swept by the wind and the wild dance of the lunatic and his victim. He saw the forked tree to which the victim had been bound, still with the two black holes in it where the fork had pierced it, looking like the hollow eyes of a skull, and making the whole seem like some horned goblin. There was the heaped up hay, still to some extent disordered and scattered as by the dizzy dance of a small cyclone; and beyond it rose the high green wall of the unmown and standing grass of the next meadow. From the very thick of this mild jungle or miniature forest, a long thin line of smoke was drawn up into the sky; as if from a very small fire of weeds. Nothing else human or alive was visible in the sultry summer landscape; but Garth seemed to know and recognize the significance of the smoke. He sent a far halloo across the fields, calling out, "Is that you, Gale?"

Two feet pointed skyward and two long legs upside down rose vertically out of the tall grass, just beyond the smoke; and waved to them like arms, as if according to a preconcerted science of signalling. Then the legs seemed to give a leap and dive and the owner of the legs came the right side up and rose or surged slowly out of the depths of green, gazing across at them with a misty and benevolent expression. He was smoking a long thin cigar: the fire behind the smoke.

He received them and their news with no air of triumph, still less of surprise. Abandoning his grassy nest, he sat down with them on the garden chairs which had also played their part in the mystery; and only smiled a little as he handed back the telegram.

"Well," he said; "do you still think I am mad?"

"Well," said Butterworth, "I can't help wondering whether he is."

Gale leaned across, showing his first eagerness, and said, "He isn't. But he jolly nearly was."

Then he leaned slowly back again and stared abstractedly at a daisy on the lawn, almost as if he had forgotten their presence.

When he spoke again it was in a clear but rather colourless tone, like a lecturer:

"A very large number of young men nearly go mad. But nearly all of them only nearly do it; and normally they recover the normal. You might almost say it's normal to have an abnormal period. It comes when there's a lack of adjustment in the scale of things outside and within. Lots of those boys, those big healthy schoolboys you hear about, who care for nothing but cricket or the tuck-shop, are bursting with a secret and swelling morbidity. But in this young man it was rather symbolically expressed even in the look of him. It was like his growing out of his clothes, or being too big for his boots. The inside gets too big for the outside. He doesn't know how to relate the two things; and generally he doesn't relate them at all. In one way his own mind and self seem to be colossal and cosmic and everything outside them small or distant. In another way the world is much too big for him; and his thoughts are fragile things to be hidden away. There are any number of cases of that disproportionate secretiveness. You know how silent boys have been about incredible abuses in bad schools. Whether or no it's false to say a girl can't keep a secret, it's often really the ruin of a boy that he can keep a secret.

"Now in that dangerous time, there's a dreadfully dangerous moment; when the first connexion is made between the subjective and objective: the first real bridge between the brain and real things. It all depends what it is; because, while it confirms his self-consciousness, it may happen to confirm his self-deception. That young man had never really been noticed by anybody until Lady Flamborough happened to tell him that he had brought the bad weather. It came just at the moment when his whole sense of proportions and possibilities had gone wild. I think the first thing that made me suspect he was . . . By the way," added Gale abruptly, "what was it that made you first suspect *me* of being mad?"

"I think," said Garth slowly, "it was when you were staring

out of the window at the storm."

"The storm? Was there a storm?" asked Gale vaguely. "Oh, yes, now I come to think of it, there was."

"But, hang it all," replied the doctor, "what else could you have been staring out of the window at, except the storm?"

"I wasn't staring out of the window," answered Gale.

"Really, my dear fellow," remonstrated Dr. Garth.

"I was staring at the window," said the poet. "I often stare at windows. So few people ever look at windows, unless they are stained glass windows. But glass is a very beautiful thing, like diamonds; and transparency is a sort of transcendental colour. Besides, in this case there was something else; and something far more awful and thrilling than a thunderstorm."

"Well, what *were* you looking at, that was more awful than a thunderstorm?"

"I was looking at two raindrops running down the pane," said Gale. "And so was Saunders."

Seeing the others staring at him, he continued: "Oh, yes, it's quite true; as the poet says," and he recited with great and unusual gravity:

> " 'Little drops of water,
> Little grains of sand,
> Make the soul to stagger
> Till the stars can hardly stand.'

"Haven't I told you a thousand times," he continued with increasing earnestness and animation, "that I always find myself looking at some little thing, a stone or a starfish or what not, and that's the only way I can ever learn anything? But when I looked at Saunders, I saw his eyes were fixed on the same spot on the window-pane; and I shuddered from head to foot, for I knew I had guessed right. He was wearing a certain kind of unobtrusive smile.

"You know that incurable gamblers sometimes bet on a race between two raindrops. But there is this specially about the

sport; that it is abstract and equal and gives one a sense of impartiality. If you bet on a dog-fight, you may find you really
sympathize with a Scotch terrier against an Irish terrier, or *vice
versa;* you may like the look of a billiard player or even the
colours of a jockey. Therefore the event may go *against* your
sympathies; and you will realize your limitations. But in the case
of those two crystal spheres hung in a void of transparency,
there is something like the equal scales of an abstract justice; you
feel that whichever wins might be the one you had chosen. You
may easily, in a certain secret megalomania, persuade yourself it
is the one you have chosen. It is easy to imagine oneself controlling things hung so evenly. That was when I said to him, to test
whether I was following his train of thought, 'It makes you feel
like God.' Did you think I was talking about the storm? Storm!
Pooh! Why should a storm make a man think he's God? If he'd
got any sense it might make him feel he wasn't. But I knew that
Saunders was just at the delicate crisis, where he was half trying
to believe he was. He was half trying to think he had really
changed the weather and might change everything; and a game
like that of the raindrops was just the thing to encourage him.
He really felt as if he were Omnipotence looking at two falling
stars: and he was the special providence in them.

"Remember that there is always something double about morbidity; the sound old popular phrase said the madman was 'beside himself.' There is a part of him encouraging itself to go
mad; and a part that still doesn't quite believe in the mania. He
would delight in easy self-deceptions, as in the raindrops. He
would also subconsciously *avoid* tests too decisive. He would
avoid *wanting* to want something incredible; as that a tree should
dance. He would avoid it; partly for fear it should and partly for
fear it shouldn't. And I was suddenly and furiously certain, with
every cell of my brain, that he must stop himself instantly,
violently, by telling the tree to dance; and finding it wouldn't.

"That was when I shouted to him to tell the chairs and the
tree to move. I was certain that unless he learnt his human limita-

tions sharply and instantly, something illimitable and inhuman would take hold of him in that very hour. He took no notice; he rushed out into the garden; he forgot all about the chairs; he ran up that steep meadow with a leap like that of a wild goat; and I knew he had broken loose from reality and was out of the world. He would go careering through waste places, with the storm within and without; and when he returned from that country walk he would never be the same again. He would leap and dance on that lonely road; he would be horribly happy; nothing would stop him. I was already resolved that something must stop him. It must be something abrupt, arresting, revealing the limit of real things; the throttling shock with which a thing comes to the end of its tether. Then I saw the rope and threw it, catching him back like a wild horse. Somehow there rose in my imagination the image of the pagan Centaur rearing backwards, bridled, and rampant against heaven: for the Centaur, like all paganism, is at once natural and unnatural; a part of nature-worship and yet a monster.

"I went through with the whole wild business; and I was sure I was right; as he himself is now sure I was right. Nobody knew but I how far he had already gone along that road; and I knew that there was nothing for it but acute, practical, painful discovery that he could not control matter or the elements; that he could not move trees or remove pitchforks; that he could struggle for two hours with a rope and a pair of prongs and still be bound.

"It was certainly rather a desperate remedy; there is really nothing to be said for it except that it was a remedy. And I believe profoundly that there was no other remedy. Anything in the nature of soothing or quieting him would only have made him yet more secretive and yet more swollen-headed. As for humouring him, it's the very worst thing to do with people who are losing their sense of humour. No; there was something he was beginning to believe about himself; and it was still possible to prove that it wasn't true."

"Do you think," asked Dr. Butterworth, frowning, "that there was really anything in that theological imagery in the matter? Do you suppose *he* put it in the form that he could bring the rain and thunder because he was God Almighty? Of course there are cases of religious mania that are rather like that."

"You must remember," said Gale, "that he was a theological student and was going to be a clergyman; and he may have brooded upon doubt and inspiration and prophecy till they began to work the wrong way. The worst is always very near the best; there is something much worse than atheism which is Satanism; otherwise known as Being God. But as a matter of mere philosophy, apart from theology, the thing is much nearer to the nerve of all thinking than you might think. That's why it was so insinuating and so difficult to see or to stop. That's what I mean when I say I had a sympathy with the young lunatic. After all, it was a very natural mistake."

"My dear Gale," protested his friend Garth. "You are getting a little too fond of paradox. A young tadpole of a curate thinks he can control the skies and uproot trees and call up the thunder and you call it a natural mistake."

"Have you ever lain on your back in a field and stared at the sky and kicked your heels in the air?" asked the poet.

"Not in a public or professional way," answered the doctor. "It's not generally considered the best bedside manner. But suppose I did?"

"If you think like that, and go back to primitive things," said Gale, "you will find yourself wondering why you can control some things and not others. After all, your legs look a long way off when you wave them in the sky. You can wave legs about, but you can't wave trees about. I'm not sure it's so unnatural, in the abstract, for a man to fancy the whole material universe is his own body; since it all seems equally, in one sense, to be outside his own mind. But when he is in hell is when he fancies it is inside his own mind."

"I'm afraid I don't bother much about all this metaphysical

business," said Butterworth. "I suppose I really don't understand it. I know what I mean by a man being outside his mind in the sense of being out of his mind; and I suppose you're right in saying that Saunders was morbid enough to be nearly out of his mind. And as for being outside his body, I know what it means in the sense of his blowing his brains out or his body being left for dead. And really, to be candid, you seem to have come precious near to knocking him out of his body to cure him of being out of his mind. It certainly was an exceedingly desperate remedy; and though it may have been defensible, I shouldn't much like to have to go into a law-court as an expert witness to defend it. I can only go by results, and he certainly seems to be all the better for it. But when it comes to all your mystical explanations, about how it is hell to have everything inside your mind, frankly I give up trying to follow. I'm afraid I'm rather a materialist."

"Afraid!" cried Gale, as if with indignation; "*afraid* you are a materialist! You haven't got much notion of what there really is to be afraid of! Materialists are all right; they are at least near enough to heaven to accept the earth and not imagine they made it. The dreadful doubts are not the doubts of the materialist. The dreadful doubts, the deadly and damnable doubts, are the doubts of the idealist."

"I always imagined you were an idealist," said Garth.

"I use the word idealist in its philosophical sense. I mean the real sceptic who doubts matter and the minds of others and everything except his own ego. I have been through it myself; as I have been through nearly every form of infernal idiocy. That is the only use I am in the world; having been every kind of idiot. But believe me, the worst and most miserable sort of idiot is he who seems to create and contain all things. Man is a creature; all his happiness consists in being a creature; or, as the Great Voice commanded us, in becoming a child. All his fun is in having a gift or present; which the child, with profound understanding, values because it is 'a surprise.' But surprise implies that a thing came from outside ourselves; and gratitude that it comes from someone other than ourselves. It is thrust through the letter-box; it is thrown in at the window; it is thrown over the wall. Those limits are the lines of the very plan of human pleasure.

"I also dreamed that I had dreamed of the whole creation. I had given myself the stars for a gift; I had handed myself the sun and moon. I had been behind and at the beginning of all things; and without me nothing was made that was made. Anybody who has been in that centre of the cosmos knows that it is to be in hell. And there is only one cure for it. Oh, I know that people have written all kinds of cant and false comfort about the cause of evil; and of why there is pain in the world. God forbid that we should add ourselves to such a chattering monkey-house of moralists. But for all that, this truth is true; objectively and experimentally true. There is no cure for that nightmare of omnipotence except pain; because that is the thing a man *knows* he would not tolerate if he could really control it. A man must be in some place from which he would certainly escape if he could, if he is really to realize that all things do not come from within. That is the meaning of that mad parable or mystery play you have seen acted here like an allegory. I doubt whether any of our action is really anything but an allegory. I doubt whether any truth can be told except in a parable. There was a man who saw himself sitting in the sky; and his servants the angels went to and fro in coloured garments of cloud and flame and the pageant of the seasons; but he was over all and his face seemed to fill the heavens. And, God forgive me for blasphemy, but I nailed him to a tree."

He had risen to his feet in a suppressed and very unusual excitement; and his face was pale in the sunlight. For he spoke indeed in parables; and the things of which he was thinking were far away from that garden or even from that tale. There swelled up darkly and mountainously in his memory the slopes of another garden against another storm. The skeleton arch of a

ruined abbey stood gaunt against the ghastly light, and beyond
the racing river was the low and desolate inn among the reeds;
and all that grey landscape was to him one purple patch of Paradise—and of Paradise Lost.

"It is the only way," he kept repeating; "it is the only answer
to the heresy of the mystic; which is to fancy that mind is all. It
is to break your heart. Thank God for hard stones; thank God
for hard facts; thank God for thorns and rocks and deserts and
long years. At least I know now that I am not the best or strongest thing in the world. At least I know now that I have not
dreamed of everything."

"You look very strange," said his friend Garth.

"I know it now," said Gale. "For there is one who would be
here, if dreaming could do it."

There was again an utter stillness in which the fly could be
heard buzzing in the blue; and when he spoke again, though in
the same brooding vein, they had an indescribable intuition that
a door in his mind had stood open for an instant and had now
again closed finally with a clang. He said after the long silence:

"We are all tied to trees and pinned with pitchforks. And as
long as these are solid we know the stars will stand and the hills
will not melt at our word. Can't you imagine the huge tide of
healthy relief and thanks, like a hymn of praise from all nature,
that went up from that captive nailed to the tree, when he had
wrestled till the dawn and received at last the great and glorious
news; the news that he was only a man?"

Dr. Butterworth was looking across the table with a restrained
but somewhat amused expression; for the poet's eyes were shining like lamps and he was speaking on a note not often heard in
any man speaking prose.

"If I hadn't got a good deal of special knowledge and experience," he said, rising, "I should think there was a bit of a doubt
about you after all."

Gabriel Gale looked sharply over his shoulder and the note of his voice changed once more.

"Don't say that," he said rather curtly. "That's the only sort of danger I really run."

"I don't understand," said Butterworth. "Do you mean the danger of being certified?"

"Certify me till all is blue," said Gale contemptuously. "Do you suppose I should particularly mind if you did? Do you suppose I couldn't be reasonably happy in a lunatic asylum, so long as there was dust in a sunbeam or shadows on a wall—so long as I could look at ordinary things and think how extraordinary they are? Do you suppose I couldn't praise God with tolerable piety for the shape of my keeper's nose or anything else calculated to give pleasure to a thoughtful mind? I should imagine that a madhouse would be an excellent place to be sane in. I'd a long sight rather live in a nice quiet secluded madhouse than in intellectual clubs full of unintellectual people, all chattering nonsense about the newest book of philosophy; or in some of those earnest, elbowing sort of Movements that want you to go in for Service and help to take away somebody else's toys. I don't much mind to what place I may wander to think in, before I die; so long as the thoughts do not wander too much; or wander down the wrong road. And what you said just now does touch the real danger. It does touch the danger that Garth was really thinking about, when he suggested that I had reclaimed lunatics and might myself become a castaway. If people tell me they really do not understand what I mean—if they say they cannot see so simple a truth as that it is best for a man to be a man, that it is dangerous to give oneself divine honours—if they say they do not see *that* for themselves, but imagine it to be some sort of mysticism out of my own head, *then* I am myself again in peril. I am in peril of thinking something that may be wilder and worse than thinking I am God Almighty."

"And still I don't understand," said the smiling physician.

"I shall think I am the only sane man," said Gabriel Gale.

There was a sort of sequel which came to Garth's ears long afterwards; an epilogue to the crazy comedy of the pitchfork and the apple-tree. Garth differed from Gale in having a more obvious turn for the rational, or at least the rationalistic; and he often found himself debating with the sceptics of various scientific clubs and groups; finding them a very worthy race, often genuinely hard-headed and sometimes tending rather to be wooden-headed. In a particular country place, the name of which is not material, the post of village atheist had become vacant, so to speak, by the regrettable perversity of the cobbler in being a Congregationalist. His official functions were performed by a more prosperous person named Pond, a worthy hatter who was rather more famous as a cricketer. On the cricket field he was often pitted against another excellent cricketer, who was Vicar of the parish; indeed they contended more frequently on the field of cricket than on the field of spiritual speculation. For the clergyman was one of the type that is uproariously popular and successful chiefly by his proficiency in such sports. He was the sort of parson whom people praise by saying he is not a bit like a parson. He was a big, beefy, jolly man, red-faced and resolute of manner; still young but the father of a boisterous family of boys, and in most ways very like a boy himself. Nevertheless, as was natural, certain passages of chaff, that could hardly be called controversy, occasionally passed between the parson and the village atheist. There was no need to commiserate the clergyman upon the pin-pricks of the scientific materialist; for a pin has no effect on a pachyderm. The parson was the sort of man who seems to be rolled in layers within layers of solid substance resisting anything outside his own cheery and sensible mode of life. But one curious episode had clung to the memory of Pond, and he recounted it to Garth, in something of the puzzled tone in which a materialist tells a ghost story. The rival cricketers had been chipping each other in the usual friendly fashion, which did not go very much below the surface. The Vicar was doubtless a sincere Christian, though chiefly what used to be called a muscular Christian. But it is not unfair to him to say that he was more deeply moved in saying that some action was not Cricket than in saying it was not Christianity. On this and other occasions, however, he relied chiefly on ragging his opponent with rather obvious jokes; such as the oft-repeated inquiry as to how often the hatter might be expected to do the hat-trick. Perhaps the repetition of this epigram eventually annoyed the worthy freethinker; or perhaps there was something in the deeper and more positive tones with which the parson dealt with more serious matters, that had the same effect. It was with more than his usual breeziness that the reverend gentleman on this occasion affirmed the philosophy of his life. "God wants you to play the game," he said. "That's all that God wants; people who will play the game."

"How do you know?" asked Mr. Pond rather snappishly and in unusual irritation. "How do you know what God wants? You never were God, were you?"

There was a silence; and the atheist was seen to be staring at the red face of the parson in a somewhat unusual fashion.

"Yes," said the clergyman in a queer quiet voice. "I was God once; for about fourteen hours. But I gave it up. I found it was too much of a strain."

With these words the Rev. Herbert Saunders went back to the cricket tent, where he mingled with Boy Scouts and village girls with all his usual heartiness and hilarity. But Mr. Pond, the atheist, sat for some time staring, like one who has seen a miracle. And he afterwards confided to Garth that for a moment the eyes of Saunders had looked out of his red, good-humoured face as out of a mask; with an instantaneous memory of something awful and appalling, and at the same time empty; something the other man could only figure to himself in vague thoughts of some flat stark building with blank windows in a blind alley; and peering out of one of the windows the pale face of an idiot.

THE PURPLE JEWEL

GABRIEL GALE was a painter and poet; he was the last person to pretend to be even a very private detective. It happened that he had solved several mysteries; but most of them were the sort of mysteries more attractive to a mystic. Nevertheless, it also happened once or twice that he had to step out of the clouds of mysticism into the more brisk and bracing atmosphere of murder. Sometimes he succeeded in showing that a murder was a suicide, sometimes that a suicide was a murder; sometimes he was even involved in the study of lighter occupations like forgery and fraud. But the connection was generally a coincidence; it concerned some point at which his imaginative interest in men's strange motives and moods happened to lead him, or at any rate them, across the border-line of legality. And in most cases, as he himself pointed out, the motives of murderers and thieves are perfectly sane and even conventional.

"I am no good at such a sensible job," he would say. "The police could easily make me look a fool in any practical matter such as they discuss in detective stories. What is the good of asking me to measure the marks made by somebody's feet all over the ground, to show why he was walking about, or where he was going? If you will show me the marks of somebody's hands all over the ground, I will tell you why he was walking upside down. But I shall find it out in the only way I ever do find out anything. And that is simply because I am mad, too, and often do it myself."

A similar brotherhood in folly probably led him into the very baffling mystery of the disappearance of Phineas Salt, the famous author and dramatist. Some of the parties involved may have accepted the parallel of setting a thief to catch a thief, when they set a poet to find a poet. For the problem did involve, in all probability, some of the purely poetical motives of a poet. And even practical people admitted that these might possibly be more familiar to a poet than to a policeman.

Phineas Salt was the sort of man whose private life was rather a public life; like that of Byron or d'Annunzio. He was a remarkable man, and perhaps rather remarkable than respectable. But there was much to be really admired in him; and there were of course any number of people who admired even what was not so admirable. The pessimistic critics claimed him as a great pessimist; and this was widely quoted in support of the theory that his disappearance was in fact a suicide. But the optimistic critics had always obstinately maintained that he was a True Optimist (whatever that may be) and these in their natural rosy rapture of optimism, dwelt rather on the idea that he had been murdered. So lurid and romantic had his whole career been made in the eyes of all. Europe, that very few people kept their heads enough to reflect, or summoned their courage to suggest, that there is no particular principle in the nature of things to prevent a great poet falling down a well or being attacked by cramp while swimming at Felixstowe. Most of his admirers, and all those who were by profession journalists, preferred more sublime solutions.

He left no family, of the regular sort, except a brother in a small commercial way in the Midlands, with whom he had had very little to do; but he left a number of other people who stood to him in conspicuous spiritual or economic relations. He left a publisher, whose emotions were of mingled grief and hope in the cessation of his production of books and the high-class advertisement given to those already produced. The publisher was himself a man of considerable social distinction, as such distinctions go to-day; a certain Sir Walter Drummond, the head of a famous and well-established firm; and a type of a certain kind of successful Scotchman who contradicts the common tradition by combining being business-like with being extremely radiant and benevolent. He left a theatrical manager in the very act of launching his great poetical play about Alexander and the Persians; this was an artistic but adaptable Jew, named Isidore Marx, who was similarly balanced between the advantages and disadvantages of an inevitable silence following the cry of "Author." He left a beautiful but exceedingly bad-tempered leading actress, who was about to gain fresh glory in the part of the Persian Princess; and who was one of the persons, not indeed few, with whom (as the quaint phrase goes) his name had been connected. He left a number of literary friends; some at least of whom were really literary and a few of whom had really been friendly. But his career had been itself so much like a sensational drama on the stage that it was surprising, when it came to real calculations about his probable conduct, how little anybody seemed to know about the essentials of his real character. And without any such clue, the circumstances seemed to make the poet's absence as disturbing and revolutionary as his presence.

Gabriel Gale, who also moved in the best literary circles, knew all this side of Phineas Salt well enough. He also had been in literary negotiations with Sir Walter Drummond. He also had been approached for poetical plays by Mr. Isidore Marx. He had managed to avoid having "his name connected" with Miss Hertha Hathaway, the great Shakespearean actress; but he knew her well enough, in a world where everybody knows everybody. But being somewhat carelessly familiar with these noisy outer courts of the fame of Phineas, it gave him a mild shock of irony to pass into the more private and prosaic interior. He owed his connection with the case, not to this general knowledge he shared with the world of letters, but to the accident that his friend, Dr. Garth, had been the family physician of the Salts. And he could not but be amused, when he attended a sort of family council of the matter, to discover how very domestic and even undistinguished the family council was; and how different from the atmosphere of large rumour and loose reputation that roared like a great wind without. He had to remind himself that it is only natural, after all, that anybody's private affairs should be private. It was absurd to expect that a wild poet would have a wild solicitor or a strange and fantastic doctor or dentist. But Dr. Garth, in the very professional black suit he always wore, looked such a very family physician. The solicitor looked such a very family solicitor. He was a square-faced, silver-haired gentleman named Gunter; it seemed impossible that his tidy, legal files and strong-boxes could contain such material as the prolonged scandal of Phineas Salt. Joseph Salt, the brother of Phineas Salt, came up specially from the provinces, seemed so very provincial. It was hard to believe that this silent, sandy-haired, big, embarrassed tradesman, in his awkward clothes, was the one other remaining representative of such a name. The party was completed by Salt's secretary, who also seemed disconcertingly secretarial to be closely connected with such an incalculable character. Again Gale had to remind himself that even poets can only go mad on condition that a good many people connected with them remain sane. He reflected, with a faint and dawning interest, that Byron probably had a butler; and possibly even a good butler. The disconnected fancy crossed his mind that even Shelley may have gone to the dentist. He also reflected that Shelley's dentist was probably rather like any other dentist.

Nevertheless, he did not lose the sense of contrast in stepping into this inner chamber of immediate and practical responsibilities. He felt rather out of place in it; for he had no illusions about himself as a business adviser, or one to settle things with the private secretary and the family lawyer. Garth had asked him to come and he sat patiently looking at Garth; while Gunter, the solicitor, laid the general state of things before the informal committee.

"Mr. Hatt has been telling us," said the lawyer, glancing for a moment at the secretary who sat opposite, "that he last saw Mr. Phineas Salt at his own flat two hours after lunch on Friday last. Until about an hour ago, I should have said that this interview (which was apparently very short) was the last occasion on which the missing man had been seen. Rather more than an hour ago, however, I was rung up by a person, a complete stranger to me, who declared that he had been with Phineas Salt for the six or seven hours following on that meeting at the flat and that he was coming round to this office as soon as possible, to lay all the facts before us. This evidence, if we find it in any way worthy of credit, will at least carry the story a considerable stage further and perhaps provide us with some important hint about Mr. Salt's whereabouts or fate. I do not think we can say much more about it until he comes."

"I rather fancy he has come," said Dr. Garth. "I heard somebody answering the door; and that sounds like boots scaling these steep legal stairs"; for they had met in the solicitor's office in Lincoln's Inn.

The next moment a slim, middle-aged man slipped rather than stepped into the room; there was indeed something smooth and unobtrusive about the very look of his quiet grey suit, at once shabby and shiny and yet carrying something like the last glimmer of satin and elegance. The only other seizable thing about him was that he not only had rather long dark hair parted down the middle, but his long olive face was fringed with a narrow dark beard, which was also parted in the middle, drooping in two separated strands. But as he entered he laid on a chair a soft black hat with a very large brim and a very low crown; which somehow called up instantly to the fancy the cafés and the coloured lights of Paris.

"My name is James Florence," he said in a cultivated accent. "I was a very old friend of Phineas Salt; and in our younger days I have often travelled about Europe with him. I have every reason to believe that I travelled with him on his last journey."

"His last journey," repeated the lawyer, looking at him with frowning attention; "are you prepared to say that Mr. Salt is dead, or are you saying this for sensationalism?"

"Well, he is either dead or something still more sensational," said Mr. James Florence.

"What do you mean?" asked the other sharply. "What could be more sensational than his death?"

The stranger looked at him with a fixed and very grave expression and then said simply, "I cannot imagine."

Then, when the lawyer made an angry movement, as if suspecting a joke, the man added equally gravely, "I am still trying to imagine."

"Well," said Gunter, after a pause, "perhaps you had better tell your story and we will put the conversation on a regular footing. As you probably know, I am Mr. Salt's legal adviser; this is his brother, Mr. Joseph Salt, whom I am advising also; this is Dr. Garth, his medical adviser. This is Mr. Gabriel Gale."

The stranger bowed to the company and took a seat with quiet confidence.

"I called on my old friend Salt last Friday afternoon about five o'clock. I think I saw this gentleman leaving the flat as I came in." He looked across at the secretary, Mr. Hatt, a hard-faced and reticent man, who concealed with characteristic discretion, the American name of Hiram; but could not quite conceal a certain American keenness about the look of his long chin and his spectacles. He regarded the newcomer with a face of wood, and said nothing as usual.

"When I entered the flat, I found Phineas in a very disordered and even violent condition, even for him. In fact somebody seemed to have been breaking the furniture; a statuette was knocked off its pedestal and a bowl of irises upset; and he was striding up and down the room like a roaring lion with his red mane rampant and his beard a bonfire. I thought it might be merely an artistic mood, a fine shade of poetical feeling; but he told me he had been entertaining a lady. Miss Hertha Hathaway, the actress, had only just left."

"Here, wait a minute," interposed the solicitor. "It would appear that Mr. Hatt, the secretary, had also only just left. But I don't think you said anything about a lady, Mr. Hatt."

"It's a pretty safe rule," said the impenetrable Hiram. "You never asked me about any lady. I've got my own work to do and I told you how I left when I'd done it."

"This is rather important, though," said Gunter doubtfully. "If Salt and the actress threw bowls and statues at each other—well, I suppose we may cautiously conclude there was some slight difference of opinion."

"There was a final smash-up," said Florence frankly. "Phineas told me he was through with all that sort of thing and, as far as I could make out, with everything else as well. He was in a pretty wild state; I think he had been drinking a little already; then he routed out a dusty old bottle of absinthe and said that he and I must drink it again in memory of old days in Paris; for it was the last time, or the last day, or some expression of that sort. Well, I hadn't drunk it myself for a long time; but I knew enough about it to know that he was drinking a great deal too much, and it's not a thing like ordinary wine or brandy; the state it can get you into is quite extraordinary; more like the clear madness that comes from hashish. And he finally rushed out of the house with that green fire in his brain and began to get out his car; starting it quite correctly and even driving it well, for there is a lucidity in such intoxication; but driving it faster and faster down the dreary vistas of the Old Kent Road and out into the country towards the south-east. He had dragged me with him with the same sort of hypnotic energy and uncanny conviviality; but I confess I felt pretty uncomfortable spinning out along the country roads with twilight turning to dark. We were nearly killed several times; but I don't think he was trying to be killed—at least not there on the road by an ordinary motor accident. For he kept on crying out that he wanted the high and perilous places of the earth; peaks and precipices and towers; that he would like to take his last leap from some such pinnacle and either fly like an eagle or fall like a stone. And all that seemed the more blind and grotesque because we were driving further and further into some of the flattest country in England, where he certainly would never find any mountains such as towered and toppled in his dream. And then, after I don't know how many hours, he gave a new sort of cry; and I saw, against the last grey strip of the gloaming and all the flat land towards the east, the towers of Canterbury."

"I wonder," said Gabriel Gale suddenly, like a man coming out of a dream, "how they did upset the statuette. Surely the woman threw it, if anybody did. He'd hardly have done a thing like that, even if he was drunk."

Then he turned his head slowly and stared rather blankly at the equally blank face of Mr. Hatt; but he said no more and, after a slightly impatient silence, the man called Florence went on with his narrative.

"Of course I knew that the moment he saw the great Gothic towers of the cathedral they would mingle with his waking nightmare and in a way fulfil and crown it. I cannot say whether he had taken that road in order to reach the cathedral; or whether it was merely a coincidence; but there was naturally nothing else in all that landscape that could so fit in with his mood about steep places and dizzy heights. And so of course he took up his crazy parable again and talked about riding upon gargoyles, as upon demon horses, or hunting with hell-hounds above the winds of heaven. It was very late before we reached the cathedral; and though it stands more deeply embedded in the town than is common in cathedral cities, it so happened that the houses nearest to us were all barred and silent and we stood in a deep angle of the building, which had something of seclusion and was covered with the vast shadow of the tower. For a strong moon was already brightening behind the cathedral and I remember the light of it made a sort of ring in Salt's ragged red hair like a dull crimson fire. It seemed a rather unholy halo; and it is a detail I remember the more, because he himself was declaiming in praise of moonshine and especially of the effect of stained-glass windows seen against the moon rather than the sun, as in the famous lines in Keats. He was wild to get inside the building and see the coloured glass, which he swore was the only really successful thing religion ever did; and when he found the cathedral was locked up (as was not unusual at that hour) he had a grand final reaction of rage and scorn and began to curse the dean and chapter and everyone else. Then a blast of boyish historical reminiscence seemed to sweep through his changing mind; and he caught up a great ragged stone from the border of the turf and struck thunderous blows on the door with it, as with a hammer, and shouted aloud, 'King's men! King's men! Where is the traitor? We have come to kill the archbishop.' Then he laughed groggily and said, 'Fancy killing Dr. Randall Davidson . . . But Becket was really worth killing. He had lived, by God! He had really made the best of both worlds, in a bigger sense than they use the phrase for. Not both at once and both tamely, as the snobs do. But one at a time and both wildly and to the limit. He went clad in crimson and gold and gained laurels and overthrew great knights in tournaments; and then suddenly became a saint, giving his goods to the poor, fasting, dying a martyr. Ah, that is the right way to do it! The right way to live a Double Life! No wonder miracles were worked at his tomb.' Then he hurled the heavy flint from him: and suddenly all the laughter and historical rant seemed to die out of his face and to leave it rather sad and sober; and as stony as one of the stone faces carved above the Gothic doors. 'I shall work a miracle to-night,' he said stolidly, 'after I have died.'

"I asked him what in the world he meant; and he made no answer. But he began abruptly to talk to me in quite a quiet and friendly and even affectionate way; thanking me for my companionship on this and many occasions; and saying that we must part; for his time was come. But when I asked him where he was going, he only pointed a finger upwards; and I could not make out at all whether he meant metaphorically that he was going to heaven or materially that he was going to scale the high tower. Anyhow, the only stairway for scaling it was inside and I could not imagine how he could reach it. I tried to question him and he answered, 'I shall ascend . . . ; I shall be lifted up . . . but no miracles will be worked at my tomb. For my body will never be found.'

"And then, before I could move, and without a gesture of warning, he leapt up and caught a stone bracket by the gateway; in another second he was astride it; in a third standing on it; and in a fourth vanished utterly in the vast shadow of the wall above. Once again I heard his voice, much higher up and even far away, crying, 'I shall ascend.' Then all was silence and solitude. I cannot undertake to say whether he did ascend. I can only say with tolerable certainty that he did not descend."

"You mean," said Gunter gravely, "that you have never seen him since."

"I mean," answered James Florence equally gravely, "that I doubt whether anybody on earth has seen him since."

"Did you make inquiries on the spot?" pursued the lawyer.

The man called Florence laughed in a rather embarrassed fashion. "The truth is," he said, "that I knocked up the neighbours and even questioned the police; and I couldn't get anybody to believe me. They said I had had something to drink, which was true enough; and I think they fancied I had seen myself double, and was trying to chase my own shadow over the cathedral roofs. I daresay they know better now there has been a hue and cry in the newspapers. As for me, I took the last train back to London."

"What about the car?" asked Garth, sharply; and a light of wonder or consternation came over the stranger's face.

"Why, hang it all!" he cried, "I forgot all about poor Salt's car! We left it backed into a crack between two old houses just by the cathedral. I never thought of it again till this minute."

Gunter got up from his desk and went into the inner room, in which he was heard obscurely telephoning. When he came back, Mr. Florence had already picked up his round black hat in his usual unembarrassed manner and suggested that he had better be going; for he had told all that he knew about the affair. Gunter watched him walking away with an interested expression; as if he were not quite so certain of the last assertion as he would like to be. Then he turned to the rest of the company and said:

"A curious yarn. A very curious yarn. But there's another

curious thing you ought to know, that may or may not be connected with it." For the first time he seemed to take notice of the worthy Joseph Salt, who was present as the nearest surviving relative of the deceased or disappearing person. "Do you happen to know, Mr. Salt, what was your brother's exact financial position?"

"I don't," said the provincial shopkeeper shortly, and contrived to convey an infinite degree of distance and distaste. "Of course you understand, gentlemen, that I'm here to do anything I can for the credit of the family. I wish I could feel quite certain that finding poor Phineas will be for the credit of the family. He and I hadn't much in common, as you may imagine; and to tell the truth, all these newspaper stories don't do a man like me very much good. Men may admire a poet for drinking green fire or trying to fly from a church tower; but they don't order their lunch from a pastry-cook's shop kept by his brother; they get a fancy there might be a little too much green fire in the gingerale. And I've only just opened my shop in Croydon; that is, I've bought a new business there. Also," and he looked down at the table with an embarrassment rather rustic but not unmanly, "I'm engaged to be married; and the young lady is very active in church work."

Garth could not suppress a smile at the incongruous lives of the two brothers; but he saw that there was, after all, a good deal of common sense in the more obscure brother's attitude.

"Yes," he said, "I quite see that; but you can hardly expect the public not to be interested."

"The question I wanted to ask," said the solicitor, "has a direct bearing on something I have just discovered. Have you any notion, even a vague one, of what Phineas Salt's income was, or if he had any capital?"

"Well," said Joseph Salt reflectively, "I don't think he really had much capital; he may have had the five thousand we each of us got from the old Dad's business. In fact, I think he had; but I think he lived up to the edge of his income and a bit beyond. He sometimes made big scoops on a successful play or so; but you know the sort of fellow he was; and the big scoop went in a big splash. I should guess he had two or three thousand in the bank when he disappeared."

"Quite so," said the solicitor gravely. "He had two thousand five hundred in the bank on the day he disappeared. And he drew it all out on the day he disappeared. And it entirely disappeared on the day he disappeared."

"Do you think he's bolted to foreign climes or something?" asked the brother.

"Ah," answered the lawyer, "he may have done so. Or he may have intended to do so and not done so."

"Then how did the money disappear?" asked Garth.

"It may have disappeared," replied Gunter, "while Phineas was drunk and talking nonsense to a rather shady Bohemian acquaintance, with a remarkable gift of narration."

Garth and Gale both glanced sharply across at the speaker; and both, observant in such different ways, realized that the lawyer's face was a shade too grim to be called merely cynical.

"Ah," cried the doctor with something like a catch in his breath. "And you mean something worse than theft."

"I have no right to assert even theft," said the lawyer, without relaxing his sombre expression, "but I have a right to suspect things that go rather deep. To begin with, there is some evidence for the start of Mr. Florence's story, but none for its conclusion. Mr. Florence met Mr. Hatt; I take it, from the absence of contradiction, that Mr. Hatt also met Mr. Florence."

On the poker face of Mr. Hatt there was still an absence of contradiction; that might presumably be taken for confirmation.

"Indeed, I have found some evidence corroborating the story of Salt starting with Florence in the car. There is no evidence corroborating all that wild moonlight antic on the roads of Kent; and if you ask me, I think it very likely that this particular joy-ride ended in some criminal den in the Old Kent Road. I telephoned a moment ago to ask about the car left in Canterbury;

and they cannot at present find traces of any such car. Above all, there is the damning fact that this fellow Florence forgot all about his imaginary car, and contradicted himself by saying that he went back by train. That alone makes me think his story is false."

"Does it?" asked Gale, looking at him with childlike wonder. "Why, that alone makes me think his story is true."

"How do you mean?" asked Gunter, "that alone?"

"Yes," said Gale; "that one detail is so true that I could almost believe the truth of all the rest, if he'd described Phineas as flying from the tower on a stone dragon."

He sat frowning and blinking for a moment and then said rather testily, "Don't you see it's just the sort of mistake that would be made by that sort of man? A shabby, impecunious man, a man who never travels far except in trains, is caught up for one wild ride in a rich friend's car, drugged into a sort of dream of absinthe, dragged into a topsy-turvy mystery like a nightmare, wakes up to find his friend caught up into the sky and everybody, in broad daylight, denying that the thing had ever happened. In that sort of chilly, empty awakening, a poor man talking to a contemptuous policeman, he would no more have remembered any responsibility for the car than if it had been a fairy chariot drawn by griffins. It was part of the dream. He would automatically fall back on his ordinary way of life and take a third-class ticket home. But he would never make such a blunder in a story he had entirely made up for himself. The instant I heard him make that howler, I knew he was telling the truth."

The others were gazing at the speaker in some mild surprise, when the telephone bell, strident and prolonged, rang in the adjoining office. Gunter got hastily to his feet and went to answer it, and for a few moments there was no sound but the faint buzz of his questions and replies. Then he came back into the room, his strong face graven with a restrained stupefaction.

"This is a most remarkable coincidence," he said; "and, I must admit, a confirmation of what you say. The police down there have found the marks of a car, with tyres and general proportions like Phineas Salt's, evidently having stood exactly where James Florence professed to have left it standing. But what is even more odd, it has gone; the tracks show it was driven off down the road to the south-east by somebody. Presumably by Phineas Salt."

"To the south-east," cried Gale, and sprang to his feet. "I thought so!"

He took a few strides up and down the room and then said, "But we mustn't go too fast. There are several things. To begin with, any fool can see that Phineas would drive to the east; it was nearly daybreak when he disappeared. Of course, in that state, he would drive straight into the sunrise. What else could one do? Then, if he was really full of that craze for crags or towers, he would find himself leaving the last towers behind and driving into flatter and flatter places; for that road leads down into Thanet. What would he do? He must make for the chalk cliffs and look down at least on sea and sand; but I fancy he would want to look down on people too; just as he might have looked down on the people of Canterbury from the cathedral tower. . . . I know that south-eastern road. . . ."

Then he faced them solemnly and, like one uttering a sacred mystery, said, "Margate."

"And why?" asked the staring Garth.

"A form of suicide, I suppose," said the solicitor dryly. "What could a man of that sort want to do at Margate except commit suicide?"

"What could any man want at Margate except suicide?" asked Dr. Garth, who had a prejudice against such social resorts.

"A good many millions of God's images go there simply for fun," said Gale; "but it remains to be shown why one of them should be Phineas Salt . . . there are possibilities . . . those black crawling masses seen from the white cliffs might be a sort of vision for a pessimist; possibly a dreadful destructive vision

of shutting the gates in the cliffs and inundating them all in the
ancient awful sea . . . or could he have some cranky notion of
making Margate glorious by his creative or destructive acts;
changing the very sound of the name, making it heroic or tragic
for ever? There have been such notions in such men . . . but
wherever this wild road leads, I am sure it ends in Margate."

The worthy tradesman of Croydon was the first to get to his
feet after Gale had risen, and he fingered the lapels of his outlandish coat with all his native embarrassment. "I'm afraid all this
is beyond me, gentlemen," he said, "gargoyles and dragons and
pessimists and such are not in my line. But it does seem that
the police have got a clue that points down the Margate road;
and if you ask me, I think we'd better discuss this matter again
when the police have investigated a little more."

"Mr. Salt is perfectly right," said the lawyer heartily. "See
what it is to have a business man to bring us back to business. I
will go and make some more inquiries; and soon, perhaps, I may
have a little more to tell you."

If Gabriel Gale was, and felt himself to be, an incongruous
figure in the severe framework of leather and parchment, of law
and commerce, represented by the office of Mr. Gunter, it
might well have been supposed that he would feel even more of
a fish out of water in the scene of the second family council.
For it was held at the new headquarters of the family, or all that
remained of the family; the little shop in Croydon over which
the lost poet's very prosaic brother was presiding with a mixture
of the bustle of a new business and the last lingering formalities
of a funeral. Mr. J. Salt's suburban shop was a very suburban
shop. It was a shop for selling confectionery and sweetmeats and
similar things; with a sort of side-show of very mild refresh-
ments, served on little round shiny tables and apparently chiefly
consisting of pale green lemonade. The cakes and sweets were
arranged in decorative patterns in the window, to attract the eye
of Croydon youth, and as the building consisted chiefly of windows, it seemed full of a sort of cold and discolouring light. A

parlour behind, full of neat but illogical knicknacks and mementoes, was not without a sampler, a testimonial from a Provident Society and a portrait of George V. But it was never easy to predict in what place or circumstances Mr. Gale would find a certain intellectual interest. He generally looked at objects, not objectively in the sense of seeing them as themselves, but in connection with some curious trains of thought of his own; and, for some reason or other, he seemed to take quite a friendly interest in Mr. Salt's suburban shop. Indeed, he seemed to take more interest in this novel scene than in the older and more serious problem which he had come there to solve. He gazed entranced at the china dogs and pink pincushions on the parlour mantelpiece; he was with difficulty drawn away from a rapt contemplation of the diamond pattern of lemon-drops and raspberry-drops which decorated the window; and he looked even at the lemonade as if it were as important as that pale green wine of wormwood, which had apparently played a real part in the tragedy of Phineas Salt.

He had been indeed unusually cheerful all the morning, possibly because it was a beautiful day, possibly for more personal reasons; and had drawn near to the rendezvous through the trim suburban avenues with a step of unusual animation. He saw the worthy confectioner himself, stepping out of a villa of a social shade faintly superior to his own; a young woman with a crown of braided brown hair, and a good grave face, came with him down the garden path. Gale had little difficulty in identifying the young lady interested in church work. The poet gazed at the pale squares of lawn and the few thin and dwarfish trees with quite a sentimental interest, almost as if it were a romance of his own; nor did his universal good humour fail him even when he encountered, a few lamp-posts further down the road, the saturnine and somewhat unsympathetic countenance of Mr. Hiram Hatt. The lover was still lingering at the garden gate, after the fashion of his kind, and Hatt and Gale walked more briskly ahead of him towards his home. To Hatt the poet made the somewhat irrelevant remark, "Do you understand that desire to be one of the lovers of Cleopatra?"

Mr. Hatt, the secretary, indicated that, had he nourished such a desire, his appearance on the historical scene would have lacked something of true American hustle and punctuality.

"Oh, there are plenty of Cleopatras still," answered Gale; "and plenty of people who have that strange notion of being the hundredth husband of an Egyptian cat. What could have made a man of real intellect, like that fellow's brother, break himself all up for a woman like Hertha Hathaway?"

"Well, I'm all with you there," said Hatt. "I didn't say anything about the woman, because it wasn't my business; but I tell you, sir, she was just blue ruin and vitriol. Only the fact that I didn't mention her seems to have set your friend the solicitor off on another dance of dark suspicion. I swear he fancies she and I were mixed up in something; and probably had to do with the disappearance of Phineas Salt."

Gale looked hard at the man's hard face for a moment and then said irrelevantly: "Would it surprise you to find him at Margate?"

"No; nor anywhere else," replied Hatt. "He was restless just then and drifted about into the commonest crowds. He did no work lately; sometimes sat and stared at a blank sheet of paper as if he had no ideas."

"Or as if he had too many," said Gabriel Gale.

With that they turned in at the confectioner's door; and found Dr. Garth already in the outer shop, having only that moment arrived. But when they penetrated to the parlour, they came on a figure that gave them, indescribably, a cold shock of sobriety. The lawyer was already seated in that gim-crack room, resolutely and rather rudely, with his top hat on his head, like a bailiff in possession; but they all sensed something more sinister, as of the bearer of the bowstring.

"Where is Mr. Joseph Salt?" he asked. "He said he would be home at eleven."

Gale smiled faintly and began to fiddle with the funny little ornaments on the mantelpiece. "He is saying farewell," he said. "Sometimes it is rather a long word to say."

"We must begin without him," said Gunter. "Perhaps it is just as well."

"You mean you have bad news for him?" asked the doctor, lowering his voice. "Have you the last news of his brother?"

"I believe it may fairly be called the last news," answered the lawyer dryly. "In the light of the latest discoveries— Mr. Gale, I should be much obliged if you would leave off fidgeting with those ornaments and sit down. There is something that somebody has got to explain."

"Yes," replied Gale rather hazily. "Isn't *this* what he has got to explain?"

He picked up something from the mantelpiece and put it on the central table. It was a very absurd object to be stared at thus, as an exhibit in a grim museum of suicide or crime. It was a cheap, childish, pink and white mug, inscribed in large purple letters, "A Present from Margate."

"There is a date inside," said Gale, looking down dreamily into the depths of this remarkable receptacle. "This year. And we're still at the beginning of the year, you know."

"Well, it may be one of the things," said the solicitor. "But I have got some other Presents from Margate."

He took a sheaf of papers from his breast-pocket and laid them out thoughtfully on the table before he spoke.

"Understand, to begin with, that there really is a riddle and the man really has vanished. Don't imagine a man can easily melt into a modern crowd; the police have traced his car on the road and could have traced him, if he had left it. Don't imagine anybody can simply drive down country roads throwing corpses out of cars. There are always a lot of fussy people about, who notice a little thing like that. Whatever he did, sooner or later the explanation would probably be found; and we have found it."

Gale put down the mug abruptly and stared across, still open-mouthed, but as it were more dry-throated, coughing and stammering now with a real eagerness.

"Have you really found out?" he asked. "Do you know all about the Purple Jewel?"

"Look here!" cried the doctor, as if with a generous indignation; "this is getting too thick. I don't mind being in a mystery, but it needn't be a melodrama. Don't say that we are after the Rajah's Ruby. Don't say, oh, don't say, that it is in the eye of the god Vishnu."

"No," replied the poet. "It is in the eye of the Beholder."

"And who's he?" asked Gunter. "I don't know exactly what you're talking about, but there may have been a theft involved. Anyhow, there was more than a theft."

He sorted out from his papers two or three photographs of the sort that are taken casually with hand cameras in a holiday crowd. As he did so he said:

"Our investigations at Margate have not been fruitless; in fact they have been rather fruitful. We have found a witness, a photographer on Margate beach, who testifies to having seen a man corresponding to Phineas Salt, burly and with a big red beard and long hair, who stood for some time on an isolated crag of white chalk, which stands out from the cliff, and looked down at the crowds below. Then he descended by a rude stairway cut in the chalk and, crossing a crowded part of the beach, spoke to another man who seemed to be an ordinary clerk or commonplace holiday-maker; and, after a little talk, they went up to the row of bathing-sheds, apparently for the purpose of having a dip in the sea. My informant thinks they did go into the sea; but cannot be quite so certain. What he is quite certain of is that he never saw the red-bearded man again, though he did see the commonplace clean-shaven man, both when he returned in his bathing-suit and when he resumed his ordinary, his very ordinary, clothes. He not only saw him, but he actually took a snapshot of him, and there he is."

He handed the photograph to Garth, who gazed at it with

slowly rising eyebrows. The photograph represented a sturdy man with a bulldog jaw but rather blank eyes, with his head lifted, apparently staring out to sea. He wore very light holiday clothes, but of a clumsy, unfashionable cut; and, so far as he could be seen under the abrupt shadow and rather too jaunty angle of his stiff straw hat, his hair was of some light colour. Only, as it happened, the doctor had no need to wait for the development of colour photography. For he knew exactly what colour it was. He knew it was a sort of sandy red; he had often seen it, not in the photograph, but on the head where it grew. For the man in the stiff straw hat was most unmistakably Mr. Joseph Salt, the worthy confectioner and new social ornament to the suburb of Croydon.

"So Phineas went down to Margate to meet his brother," said Garth. "After all, that's natural enough in one way. Margate is exactly the sort of place his brother would go to."

"Yes; Joseph went there on one of those motor-char-à-banc expeditions, with a whole crowd of other trippers, and he seems to have returned the same night on the same vehicle. But nobody knows when, where or *if* his brother Phineas returned."

"I rather gather from your tone," said Garth very gravely, "that you think his brother Phineas never did return."

"I think his brother never will return," said the lawyer, "unless it happens (by a curious coincidence) that he was drowned while bathing and his body is some day washed up on the shore. But there's a strong current running just there that would carry it far away."

"The plot thickens, certainly," said the doctor. "All this bathing business seems to complicate things rather."

"I am afraid," said the lawyer, "that it simplifies them very much."

"What," asked Garth sharply. "Simplifies?"

"Yes," said the other, gripping the arms of his chair and rising abruptly to his feet. "I think this story is as simple as the story of Cain and Abel. And rather like it."

There was a shocked silence, which was at length broken by
Gale, who was peering into the Present from Margate, crying or
almost crowing, in the manner of a child.

"Isn't it a funny little mug! He must have bought it before
he came back in the char-à-banc. Such a jolly thing to buy, when
you have just murdered your own brother."

"It does seem a queer business," said Dr. Garth, frowning. "I
suppose one might work out some explanation of how he did it.
I suppose a man might drown another man while they were
bathing, even off a crowded beach like that. But I'm damned if
I can understand why he did it. Have you discovered a motive
as well as a murder?"

"The motive is old enough and I think obvious enough," answered Gunter. "We have in this case all the necessary elements
of a hatred, of that slow and corroding sort that is founded on
jealousy. Here you had two brothers, sons of the same insignificant Midland tradesman; having the same education, environment, opportunities; very nearly of an age, very much of one
type, even of one physical type, rugged, red-haired, rather plain
and heavy, until Phineas made himself a spectacle with that big
Bolshevist beard and bush of hair; not so different in youth but
that they must have had ordinary rivalries and quarrels on fairly
equal terms. And then see the sequel. One of them fills the world
with his name, wears a laurel like the crown of Petrarch, dines
with kings and emperors and is worshipped by women like a
hero on the films. The other—isn't it enough to say that the other
has had to go on slaving all his life in a room like this?"

"Don't you like the room?" inquired Gale with the same
simple eagerness. "Why, I think some of the ornaments are so
nice!"

"It is not yet quite clear," went on Gunter, ignoring him,
"how the pastry-cook lured the poet down to Margate and a
dip in the sea. But the poet was admittedly rather random in his
movements just then, and too restless to work; and we have no
reason to suppose that he knew of the fraternal hatred or that he

in any way reciprocated it. I don't think there would be much difficulty in swimming with a man beyond the crowd of bathers and holding him under water, till you could send his body adrift on a current flowing away from the shore. Then he went back and dressed and calmly took his place in the char-à-banc."

"Don't forget the dear little mug," said Gale softly. "He stopped to buy that and then went home. Well, it's a very able and thorough explanation and reconstruction of the crime, my dear Gunter, and I congratulate you. Even the best achievements have some little flaw; and there's only one trifling mistake in yours. You've got it the wrong way round."

"What do you mean?" asked the other quickly.

"Quite a small correction," explained Gale. "You think that Joseph was jealous of Phineas. As a matter of fact, Phineas was jealous of Joseph."

"My dear Gale, you are simply playing the goat," said the doctor very sharply and impatiently. "And let me tell you I don't think it's a decent occasion for doing it. I know all about your jokes and fancies and paradoxes, but we're all in a damned hard position, sitting here in the man's own house, and knowing we're in the house of a murderer."

"I know—it's simply infernal," said Gunter, his stiffness shaken for the first time; and he looked up with a shrinking jerk, as if he half expected to see the rope hanging from that dull and dusty ceiling.

At the same moment the door was thrown open and the man they had convicted of murder stood in the room. His eyes were bright like a child's over a new toy, his face was flushed to the roots of his fiery hair, his broad shoulders were squared backwards like a soldier's; and in the lapel of his coat was a large purple flower, of a colour that Gale remembered in the garden-beds of the house down the road. Gale had no difficulty in guessing the reason of this triumphant entry.

Then the man with the buttonhole saw the tragic faces on the other side of the table and stopped, staring.

"Well," he said at last, in a rather curious tone. "What about your search?"

The lawyer was about to open his locked lips with some such question as was once asked of Cain by the voice out of the cloud, when Gale interrupted him by flinging himself backwards in a chair and emitting a short but cheery laugh.

"I've given up the search," said Gale gaily. "No need to bother myself about that any more."

"Because you know you will never find Phineas Salt," said the tradesman steadily.

"Because I have found him," said Gabriel Gale.

Dr. Garth got to his feet quickly and remained staring at them with bright eyes.

"Yes," said Gale, "because I am talking to him." And he smiled across at his host, as if he had just been introduced.

Then he said rather more gravely, "Will you tell us all about it, Mr. Phineas Salt? Or must I guess it for you all the way through?"

There was a heavy silence.

"You tell the story," said the shopkeeper at last. "I am quite sure you know all about it."

"I only know about it," answered Gale gently, "because I think I should have done the same thing myself. It's what some call having a sympathy with lunatics—including literary men."

"Hold on for a moment," interposed the staring Mr. Gunter. "Before you get too literary, am I to understand that this gentleman, who owns this shop, actually is the poet, Phineas Salt? In that case, where is his brother?"

"Making the Grand Tour, I imagine," said Gale. "Gone abroad for a holiday, anyhow; a holiday which will be not the less enjoyable for the two thousand five hundred pounds that his brother gave him to enjoy himself with. His slipping away was easy enough; he only swam a little bit further along the shore to where they had left another suit of clothes. Meanwhile our friend here went back and shaved off his beard and effected the

change of appearance in the bathing-tent. He was quite sufficiently like his brother to go back with a crowd of strangers.
And then, you will doubtless note, he opened a new shop in an
entirely new neighbourhood."

"But *why?*" cried Garth in a sort of exasperation. "In the
name of all the saints and angels, why? That's what I can't
make any sense of."

"I will tell you why," said Gabriel Gale, "but you won't make
any sense of it."

He stared at the mug on the table for a moment and then said:
"This is what you would call a nonsense story; and you can only
understand it by understanding nonsense; or, as some politely
call it, poetry. The poet Phineas Salt was a man who had made
himself master of everything, in a sort of frenzy of freedom and
omnipotence. He had tried to feel everything, experience everything, imagine everything that could be or could not be. And
he found, as all such men have found, that that illimitable liberty
is itself a limit. It is like the circle, which is at once an eternity
and a prison. He not only wanted to do everything. He wanted
to be everybody. To the Pantheist God is everybody; to the
Christian He is also somebody. But this sort of Pantheist will not
narrow himself by a choice. To want everything is to will nothing. Mr. Hatt here told me that Phineas would sit staring at a
blank sheet of paper; and I told him it was not because he had
nothing to write about, but because he could write about anything. When he stood on that cliff and looked down on that
mazy crowd, so common and yet so complex, he felt he could
write ten thousand tales and then that he could write none; because there was no reason to choose one more than another.

"Well, what is the step beyond that? What comes next? I tell
you there are only two steps possible after that. One is the step
over the cliff; to cease to be. The other is to *be* somebody, instead of writing about everybody. It is to become incarnate as
one real human being in that crowd; to begin all over again as a
real person. Unless a man be born again—

"He tried it and found that this was what he wanted; the things he had not known since childhood; the silly little lower middle-class things; to have to do with lollipops and ginger-beer; to fall in love with a girl round the corner and feel awkward about it; to be young. That was the only paradise still left virgin and unspoilt enough, in the imagination of a man who has turned the seven heavens upside down. That is what he tried as his last experiment, and I think we can say it has been a success."

"Yes," said the confectioner with a stony satisfaction, "it has been a great success."

Mr. Gunter, the solicitor, rose also with a sort of gesture of despair. "Well, I don't think I understand it any better for knowing all about it," he said; "but I suppose it must be as you say. But how in the world did you know it yourself?"

"I think it was those coloured sweets in the window that set me off," said Gale. "I couldn't take my eyes off them. They were so pretty. Sweets are better than jewelry: the children are right. For they have the fun of eating rubies and emeralds. I felt sure they were speaking to me in some way. And then I realized what they were saying. Those violet or purple raspberry drops were as vivid and glowing as amethysts, when you saw them from *inside* the shop; but from outside, with the light on them, they would look quite dingy and dark. Meanwhile, there were plenty of other things, gilded or painted with opaque colours, that would have looked much more gay in the shop-window, to the customer looking in at it. Then I remembered the man who said he must break into the cathedral to see the coloured windows from inside, and I knew it in an instant. The man who had arranged the shop-window was not a shopkeeper. He was not thinking of how things looked from the street, but of how they looked to his own artistic eye from inside. From there he saw purple jewels. And then, thinking of the cathedral, of course I remembered something else. I remembered what the poet had said about the Double Life of St. Thomas of Canterbury; and how when he had all the earthly glory, he had to have the exact opposite. St. Phineas of Croydon is also living a Double Life."

"Well," broke out Gunter, heaving with a sort of heavy gasp, "with all respect to him, if he has done all this, I can only say that he must have gone mad."

"No," said Gale, "a good many of my friends have gone mad and I am by no means without sympathy with them. But you can call this the story of 'The Man Who Went Sane.'"

THE THREE HORSEMEN OF APOCALYPSE

THE curious and sometimes creepy effect which Mr. Pond produced upon me, despite his commonplace courtesy and dapper
decorum, was possibly connected with some memories of childhood; and the vague verbal association of his name. He was a
Government official who was an old friend of my father; and I
fancy my infantile imagination had somehow mixed up the name
of Mr. Pond with the pond in the garden. When one came to
think of it, he was curiously like the pond in the garden. He was
so quiet at all normal times, so neat in shape and so shiny, so to
speak, in his ordinary reflections of earth and sky and the common daylight. And yet I knew there were some queer things in
the pond in the garden. Once in a hundred times, on one or two
days during the whole year, the pond would look oddly different; or there would come a flitting shadow or a flash in its
flat serenity; and a fish or a frog or some more grotesque creature
would show itself to the sky. And I knew there were monsters
in Mr. Pond also: monsters in his mind which rose only for a
moment to the surface and sank again. They took the form of
monstrous remarks, in the middle of all his mild and rational
remarks. Some people thought he had suddenly gone mad in the
midst of his sanest conversation. But even they had to admit
that he must have suddenly gone sane again.

Perhaps, again, this foolish fantasy was fixed in the youthful
mind because, at certain moments, Mr. Pond looked rather like
a fish himself. His manners were not only quite polite but quite
conventional; his very gestures were conventional, with the exception of one occasional trick of plucking at his pointed beard
which seemed to come on him chiefly when he was at last forced
to be serious about one of his strange and random statements.
At such moments he would stare owlishly in front of him and
pull his beard, which had a comic effect of pulling his mouth

open, as if it were the mouth of a puppet with hairs for wires. This odd, occasional opening and shutting of his mouth, without speech, had quite a startling similarity to the slow gaping and gulping of a fish. But it never lasted for more than a few seconds, during which, I suppose, he swallowed the unwelcome proposal of explaining what on earth he meant.

He was talking quite quietly one day to Sir Hubert Wotton, the well-known diplomatist; they were seated under gaily-striped tents or giant parasols in our own garden, and gazing towards the pond which I had perversely associated with him. They happened to be talking about a part of the world that both of them knew well, and very few people in Western Europe at all: the vast flats fading into fens and swamps that stretch across Pomerania and Poland and Russia and the rest; right away, for all I know, into the Siberian deserts. And Mr. Pond recalled that, across a region where the swamps are deepest and intersected by pools and sluggish rivers, there runs a single road raised on a high causeway with steep and sloping sides: a straight path safe enough for the ordinary pedestrian, but barely broad enough for two horsemen to ride abreast. That is the beginning of the story.

It concerned a time not very long ago, but a time in which horsemen were still used much more than they are at present, though already rather less as fighters than as couriers. Suffice it to say that it was in one of the many wars that have laid waste that part of the world—in so far as it is possible to lay waste such a wilderness. Inevitably it involved the pressure of the Prussian system on the nation of the Poles, but beyond that it is not necessary to expound the politics of the matter, or discuss its rights and wrongs here. Let us merely say, more lightly, that Mr. Pond amused the company with a riddle.

"I expect you remember hearing," said Pond, "of all the excitement there was about Paul Petrowski, the poet from Cracow, who did two things rather dangerous in those days: moving from Cracow and going to live in Poznan; and trying to combine being a poet with being a patriot. The town he was living in was held at the moment by the Prussians, it was situated exactly at the eastern end of the long causeway; the Prussian command having naturally taken care to hold the bridgehead of such a solitary bridge across such a sea of swamps. But their base for that particular operation was at the western end of the causeway; the celebrated Marshal Von Grock was in general command; and, as it happened, his own old regiment, which was still his favourite regiment, the White Hussars, was posted nearest to the beginning of the great embanked road. Of course, everything was spick and span, down to every detail of the wonderful white uniforms, with the flame-coloured baldrick slung across them; for this was just before the universal use of colours like mud and clay for all the uniforms in the world. I don't blame them for that; I sometimes feel the old epoch of heraldry was a finer thing than all that epoch of imitative colouring, that came in with natural history and the worship of chameleons and beetles. Anyhow, this crack regiment of cavalry in the Prussian service still wore its own uniform; and, as you will see, that was another element in the fiasco. But it wasn't only the uniforms; it was the uniformity. The whole thing went wrong because the discipline was too good. Grock's soldiers obeyed him too well; so he simply couldn't do a thing he wanted."

"I suppose that's a paradox," said Wotton, heaving a sigh. "Of course, it's very clever and all that; but really, it's all nonsense, isn't it? Oh, I know people say in a general way that there's too much discipline in the German army. But you can't have too much discipline in an army."

"But I don't say it in a general way," said Pond plaintively. "I say it in a particular way, about this particular case. Grock failed because his soldiers obeyed him. Of course, if *one* of his soldiers had obeyed him, it wouldn't have been so bad. But when *two* of his soldiers obeyed him—why, really, the poor old devil had no chance."

Wotton laughed in a guttural fashion. "I'm glad to hear your new military theory. You'd allow one soldier in a regiment to obey orders; but two soldiers obeying orders strikes you as carrying Prussian discipline a bit too far."

"I haven't got any military theory. I'm talking about a military fact," replied Mr. Pond placidly. "It is a military fact that Grock failed, because two of his soldiers obeyed him. It is a military fact that he might have succeeded, if one of them had disobeyed him. You can make up what theories you like about it afterwards."

"I don't go in much for theories myself," said Wotton rather stiffly, as if he had been touched by a trivial insult.

At this moment could be seen striding across the sun-chequered lawn, the large and swaggering figure of Captain Gahagan, the highly incongruous friend and admirer of little Mr. Pond. He had a flaming flower in his buttonhole and a grey top-hat slightly slanted upon his ginger-haired head; and he walked with a swagger that seemed to come out of an older period of dandies and duellists, though he himself was comparatively young. So long as his tall, broad-shouldered figure was merely framed against the sunlight, he looked like the embodiment of all arrogance. When he came and sat down, with the sun on his face, there was a sudden contradiction of all this in his very soft brown eyes, which looked sad and even a little anxious.

Mr. Pond, interrupting his monologue, was almost in a twitter of apologies: "I'm afraid I'm talking too much, as usual; the truth is I was talking about that poet, Petrowski, who was nearly executed in Poznan—quite a long time ago. The military authorities on the spot hesitated and were going to let him go, unless they had direct orders from Marshal Von Grock or higher; but Marshal Von Grock was quite determined on the poet's death; and sent orders for his execution that very evening. A reprieve was sent afterwards to save him; but as the man carrying the reprieve died on the way, the prisoner was released, after all."

"But as—" repeated Wotton mechanically.

"The man carrying the *reprieve*," added Gahagan somewhat

sarcastically.

"Died on the way," muttered Wotton.

"Why then, of course, the prisoner was released," observed Gahagan in a loud and cheerful voice. "All as clear as clear can be. Tell us another of those stories, Grandpapa."

"It's a perfectly true story," protested Pond, "and it happened exactly as I say. It isn't any paradox or anything like that. Only, of course, you have to know the story to see how simple it is."

"Yes," agreed Gahagan. "I think I should have to know the story, before realizing how simple it is."

"Better tell us the story and have done with it," said Wotton shortly.

Paul Petrowski was one of those utterly unpractical men who are of prodigious importance in practical politics. His power lay in the fact that he was a national poet but an international singer. That is, he happened to have a very fine and powerful voice, with which he sang his own patriotic songs in half the concert halls of the world. At home, of course, he was a torch and trumpet of revolutionary hopes, especially then, in the sort of international crisis in which practical politicians disappear, and their place is taken by men either more or less practical than themselves. For the true idealist and the real realist have at least the love of action in common. And the practical politician thrives by offering practical objections to any action. What the idealist does may be unworkable, and what the man of action does may be unscrupulous; but in neither trade can a man win a reputation by doing nothing. It is odd that these two extreme types stood at the two extreme ends of that one ridge and road among the marshes—the Polish poet a prisoner in the town at one end, the Prussian soldier a commander in the camp at the other.

For Marshal Von Grock was a true Prussian, not only entirely practical but entirely prosaic. He had never read a line of poetry himself; but he was no fool. He had the sense of reality which belongs to soldiers; and it prevented him from falling into the asinine error of the practical politician. He did not scoff at visions; he only hated them. He knew that a poet or a prophet could be as dangerous as an army. And he was resolved that the poet should die. It was his one compliment to poetry; and it was sincere.

He was at the moment sitting at a table in his tent; the spiked helmet that he always wore in public was lying in front of him; and his massive head looked quite bald, though it was only closely shaven. His whole face was also shaven; and had no covering but a pair of very strong spectacles, which alone gave an enigmatic look to his heavy and sagging visage. He turned to a Lieutenant standing by, a German of the pale-haired and rather pudding-faced variety, whose blue saucer-eyes were staring vacantly.

"Lieutenant Von Hocheimer," he said, "did you say His Highness would reach the camp to-night?"

"Seven forty-five, Marshal," replied the Lieutenant, who seemed rather reluctant to speak at all, like a large animal learning a new trick of talking.

"Then there is just time," said Grock, "to send you with that order for execution, before he arrives. We must serve His Highness in every way, but especially in saving him needless trouble. He will be occupied enough reviewing the troops; see that everything is placed at His Highness's disposal. He will be leaving again for the next outpost in an hour."

The large Lieutenant seemed partially to come to life and made a shadowy salute. "Of course, Marshal, we must all obey His Highness."

"I said we must all serve His Highness," said the Marshal.

With a sharper movement than usual, he unhooked his heavy spectacles and rapped them down upon the table. If the pale blue eyes of the Lieutenant could have seen anything of the sort, or if they could have opened any wider even if they had, they might as well have opened wide enough at the transformation

made by the gesture. It was like the removal of an iron mask.
An instant before, Marshal Von Grock had looked uncommonly
like a rhinoceros, with his heavy folds of leathery cheek and jaw.
Now he was a new kind of monster: a rhinoceros with the eyes
of an eagle. The bleak blaze of his old eyes would have told almost anybody that he had something within that was not merely
heavy; at least, that there was a part of him made of steel and
not only of iron. For all men live by a spirit, though it were an
evil spirit, or one so strange to the commonalty of Christian men
that they hardly know whether it be good or evil.

"I said we must all serve His Highness," repeated Grock. "I
will speak more plainly, and say we must all save His Highness.
Is it not enough for our kings that they should be our gods? Is
it not enough for them to be served and saved? It is we who must
do the serving and saving."

Marshal Von Grock seldom talked, or even thought, as more
theoretical people would count thinking. And it will generally
be found that men of his type, when they do happen to think
aloud, very much prefer to talk to the dog. They have even a
certain patronizing relish in using long words and elaborate
arguments before the dog. It would be unjust to compare Lieutenant Von Hocheimer to a dog. It would be unjust to the dog,
who is a much more sensitive and vigilant creature. It would be
truer to say that Grock in one of his rare moments of reflection,
had the comfort and safety of feeling that he was reflecting aloud
in the presence of a cow or a cabbage.

"Again and again, in the history of our Royal House, the
servant has saved the master," went on Grock, "and often got
little but kicks for it, from the outer world at least, which always
whines sentimentalism against the successful and the strong. But
at least we were successful and we were strong. They cursed
Bismarck for deceiving even his own master over the Ems telegram; but it made that master the master of the world. Paris was
taken; Austria dethroned; and we were safe. To-night Paul Petrowski will be dead; and we shall again be safe. That is why

I am sending you with his death-warrant at once. You understand that you are bearing the order for Petrowski's instant execution—and that you must remain to see it obeyed?"

The inarticulate Hocheimer saluted; he could understand that
all right. And he had some qualities of a dog, after all: he was as
brave as a bulldog; and he could be faithful to the death.

"You must mount and ride at once," went on Grock, "and see
that nothing delays or thwarts you. I know for a fact that fool
Arnheim is going to release Petrowski to-night, if no message
comes. Make all speed."

And the Lieutenant again saluted and went out into the night;
and mounting one of the superb white chargers that were part
of the splendour of that splendid corps, began to ride along the
high, narrow road along the ridge, almost like the top of a wall,
which overlooked the dark horizon, the dim patterns and decaying colours of those mighty marshes.

Almost as the last echoes of his horse's hoofs died away along
the causeway, Von Grock rose and put on his helmet and his
spectacles and came to the door of his tent; but for another reason. The chief men of his staff, in full dress, were already approaching him; and all along the more distant lines there were
the sounds of ritual salutation and the shouting of orders. His
Highness the Prince had come.

His Highness the Prince was something of a contrast, at least
in externals, to the men around him; and, even in other things,
something of an exception in his world. He also wore a spiked
helmet, but that of another regiment, black with glints of blue
steel; and there was something half incongruous and half imaginatively appropriate, in some antiquated way, in the combination of that helmet with the long, dark, flowing beard, amid all
those shaven Prussians. As if in keeping with the long, dark,
flowing beard, he wore a long, dark, flowing cloak, blue with one
blazing star on it of the highest Royal Order; and under the
blue cloak he wore a black uniform. Though as German as any

man, he was a very different kind of German; and something in his proud but abstracted face was consonant with the legend that the one true passion of his life was music.

In truth, the grumbling Grock was inclined to connect with that remote eccentricity the, to him, highly irritating and exasperating fact that the Prince did not immediately proceed to the proper review and reception by the troops, already drawn out in all the labyrinthine parade of the military etiquette of their nation; but plunged at once impatiently into the subject which Grock most desired to see left alone: the subject of this infernal Pole, his popularity and his peril; for the Prince had heard some of the man's songs sung in half the opera-houses of Europe.

"To talk of executing a man like that is madness," said the Prince, scowling under his black helmet. "He is not a common Pole. He is a European institution. He would be deplored and deified by our allies, by our friends, even by our fellow-Germans. Do you want to be the mad women who murdered Orpheus?"

"Highness," said the Marshal, "he would be deplored; but he would be dead. He would be deified; but he would be dead. Whatever he means to do, he would never do it. Whatever he is doing, he would do no more. Death is the fact of all facts; and I am rather fond of facts."

"Do you know nothing of the world?" demanded the Prince.

"I care nothing for the world," answered Grock, "beyond the last black and white post of the Fatherland."

"God in heaven," cried His Highness, "you would have hanged Goethe for a quarrel with Weimar!"

"For the safety of your Royal House," answered Grock, "without one instant's hesitation."

There was a short silence and the Prince said sharply and suddenly: "What does this mean?"

"It means that I had not an instant's hesitation," replied the Marshal steadily. "I have already myself sent orders for the execution of Petrowski."

The Prince rose like a great dark eagle, the swirl of his cloak like the sweep of mighty wings; and all men knew that a wrath beyond mere speech had made him a man of action. He did not even speak to Von Grock; but talking across him, at the top of his voice, called out to the second in command, General Von Voglen, a stocky man with a square head, who had stood in the background as motionless as a stone.

"Who has the best horse in your cavalry division, General? Who is the best rider?"

"Arnold Von Schacht has a horse that might beat a race-horse," replied the General promptly. "And rides it as well as a jockey. He is of the White Hussars."

"Very well," said the Prince, with the same new ring in his voice. "Let him ride at once after the man with this mad message and stop him. I will give him authority, which I think the distin-guished Marshal will not dispute. Bring me pen and ink."

He sat down, shaking out the cloak, and they brought him writing materials; and he wrote firmly and with a flourish the order, overriding all other orders, for the reprieve and release of Petrowski the Pole.

*   *   *   *

Then amid a dead silence, in the midst of which old Grock stood with an unblinking stare like a stone idol of prehistoric times, he swept out of the room, trailing his mantle and sabre. He was so violently displeased that no man dared to remind him of the formal reviewing of the troops. But Arnold Von Schacht, a curly-haired active youth, looking more like a boy, but wear-ing more than one medal on the white uniform of the Hussars, clicked his heels, and received the folded paper from the Prince; then, striding out, he sprang on his horse and flew along the high, narrow road like a silver arrow or a shooting star.

The old Marshal went back slowly and calmly to his tent, slowly and calmly removed his spiked helmet and his spectacles, and laid them on the table as before. Then he called out to an orderly just outside the tent; and bade him fetch Sergeant

Schwartz of the White Hussars immediately.

A minute later, there presented himself before the Marshal a gaunt and wiry man, with a great scar across his jaw, rather dark for a German, unless all his colours had been changed by years of smoke and storm and bad weather. He saluted and stood stiffly at attention, as the Marshal slowly raised his eyes to him. And vast as was the abyss between the Imperial Marshal, with Generals under him, and that one battered non-commissioned officer, it is true that of all the men who have talked in this tale, these two men alone looked and understood each other without words.

"Sergeant," said the Marshal, curtly, "I have seen you twice before. Once, I think, when you won the prize of the whole army for marksmanship with the carbine."

The sergeant saluted and said nothing.

"And once again," went on Von Grock, "when you were questioned for shooting that damned old woman who would not give us information about the ambush. The incident caused considerable comment at the time even in some of our own circles. Influence, however, was exerted on your side. My influence."

The sergeant saluted again; and was still silent. The Marshal continued to speak in a colourless but curiously candid way.

"His Highness the Prince has been misinformed and deceived on a point essential to his own safety and that of the Fatherland. Under this error, he has rashly sent a reprieve to the Pole Petrowski, who is to be executed to-night. I repeat: who is to be executed to-night. You must immediately ride after Von Schacht, who carried the reprieve, and stop him."

"I can hardly hope to overtake him, Marshal," said Sergeant Schwartz. "He has the swiftest horse in the regiment, and is the finest rider."

"I did not tell you to overtake him. I told you to stop him," said Grock. Then he spoke more slowly: "A man may often be stopped or recalled by various signals: by shouting or shooting." His voice dragged still more ponderously, but without a pause.

"The discharge of a carbine might attract his attention."

And then the dark sergeant saluted for the third time; and his grim mouth was again shut tight.

"The world is changed," said Grock, "not by what is said, or what is blamed or praised, but by what is done. The world never recovers from what is done. At this moment the killing of a man is a thing that must be done." He suddenly flashed his brilliant eyes of steel at the other, and added: "I mean, of course, Petrowski."

And Sergeant Schwartz smiled still more grimly; and he also, lifting the flap of the tent, went out into the darkness and mounted his horse and rode.

The last of the three riders was even less likely than the first to indulge in imaginative ideas for their own sake. But because he also was in some imperfect manner human, he could not but feel, on such a night and such an errand, the oppressiveness of that inhuman landscape. While he rode along that one abrupt ridge, there spread out to infinity all round him something a myriad times more inhuman than the sea. For a man could not swim in it, nor sail boats on it, nor do anything human with it; he could only sink in it and practically without a struggle. The sergeant felt vaguely the presence of some primordial slime that was neither solid nor liquid nor capable of any form; and he felt its presence behind the forms of all things.

He was atheist, like so many thousands of dull, clever men in Northern Germany; but he was not that happier sort of pagan who can see in human progress a natural flowering of the earth. That world before him was not a field in which green or living things evolved and developed and bore fruit; it was only an abyss in which all living things would sink for ever as in a bottomless pit; and the thought hardened him for all the strange duties he had to do in so hateful a world. The grey-green blotches of flattened vegetation, seen from above like a sprawling map, seemed more like the chart of a disease than a development; and the land-locked pools might have been of poison rather than water.

He remembered some humanitarian fuss or other about the poisoning of pools.

But the reflections of the sergeant, like most reflections of men not normally reflective, had a root in some subconscious strain on his nerves and his practical intelligence. The truth was that the straight road before him was not only dreary, but seemed interminably long. He would never have believed he could have ridden so far without catching some distant glimpse of the man he followed. Von Schacht must indeed have the fleetest of horses to have got so far ahead already; for, after all, he had only started, at whatever speed, within a comparatively short time. As Schwartz had said, he hardly expected to overtake him; but a very realistic sense of the distances involved had told him that he must very soon come in sight of him. And then, just as despair was beginning to descend and spread itself vaguely over the desolate landscape, he saw him at last.

A white spot, which slightly, slowly, enlarged into something like a white figure, appeared far ahead, riding furiously. It enlarged to that extent because Schwartz managed a spurt of riding furiously himself; but it was large enough to show the faint streak of orange across the white uniform that marked the regiment of the Hussars. The winner of the prize for shooting, in the whole army, had hit the white of smaller targets than that.

He unslung his carbine; and a shock of unnatural noise shook up all the wild fowl for miles upon the silent marshes. But Sergeant Schwartz did not trouble about them. What interested him was that, even at such a distance, he could see the straight, white figure turn crooked and alter in shape, as if the man had suddenly grown deformed. He was hanging like a humpback over the saddle; and Schwartz, with his exact eye and long experience, was certain that his victim was shot through the body; and almost certain that he was shot through the heart. Then he brought the horse down with a second shot; and the whole equestrian group heeled over and slipped and slid and vanished in one white flash into the dark fenland below.

The hard-headed sergeant was certain that his work was done. Hard-headed men of his sort are generally very precise about what they are doing; that is why they are so often quite wrong about what they do. He had outraged the comradeship that is the soul of armies; he had killed a gallant officer who was in the performance of his duty; he had deceived and defied his sovereign and committed a common murder without excuse of personal quarrel; but he had obeyed his superior officer and he had helped to kill a Pole. These two last facts for the moment filled his mind; and he rode thoughtfully back again to make his report to Marshal Von Grock. He had no doubts about the thoroughness of the work he had done. The man carrying the reprieve was certainly dead; and even if by some miracle he were only dying, he could not conceivably have ridden his dead or dying horse to the town in time to prevent the execution. No; on the whole it was much more practical and prudent to get back under the wing of his protector, the author of the desperate project. With his whole strength he leaned on the strength of the great Marshal.

And truly the great Marshal had this greatness about him: that after the monstrous thing he had done, or caused to be done, he disdained to show any fear of facing the facts on the spot or the compromising possibilities of keeping in touch with his tool. He and the sergeant, indeed, an hour or so later, actually rode along the ridge together, till they came to a particular place where the Marshal dismounted, but bade the other ride on. He wished the sergeant to go forward to the original goal of the riders, and see if all was quiet in the town after the execution, or whether there remained some danger from popular resentment.

"Is it here, then, Marshal?" asked the sergeant in a low voice. "I fancied it was further on; but it's a fact the infernal road seemed to lengthen out like a nightmare."

"It is here," answered Grock, and swung himself heavily from saddle and stirrup, and then went to the edge of the long parapet and looked down.

The moon had risen over the marshes and gone up strengthening in splendour and gleaming on dark waters and green scum; and in the nearest clump of reeds, at the foot of the slope, there lay, as in a sort of luminous and radiant ruin, all that was left of one of those superb white horses and white horsemen of his old brigade. Nor was the identity doubtful; the moon made a sort of aureole of the curled golden hair of young Arnold, the second rider and the bearer of the reprieve; and the same mystical moonshine glittered not only on baldrick and buttons, but on the special medals of the young soldier and the stripes and signs of his degree. Under such a glamorous veil of light, he might almost have been in the white armour of Sir Galahad; and there could scarcely have been a more horrible contrast than that between such fallen grace and youth below and the rocky and grotesque figure looking down from above. Grock had taken off his helmet again; and though it is possible that this was the vague shadow of some funereal form of respect, its visible effect was that the queer naked head and neck like that of a pachyderm glittered stonily in the moon, like the hairless head and neck of some monster of the Age of Stone. Rops, or some such etcher of the black, fantastic German schools, might have drawn such a picture: of a huge beast as inhuman as a beetle looking down on the broken wings and white and golden armour of some defeated champion of the Cherubim.

Grock said no prayer and uttered no pity; but in some dark way his mind was moved, as even the dark and mighty swamp will sometimes move like a living thing; and as such men will, when feeling for the first time faintly on their defence before they know not what, he tried to formulate his only faith and confront it with the stark universe and the staring moon.

"After and before the deed the German Will is the same. It cannot be broken by changes and by time, like that of those others who repent. It stands outside time like a thing of stone, looking forward and backward with the same face."

The silence that followed lasted long enough to please his cold vanity with a certain sense of portent; as if a stone figure had spoken in a valley of silence. But the silence began to thrill once more with a distant whisper which was the faint throb of horse-hoofs; and a moment later the sergeant came galloping, or rather racing, back along the uplifted road, and his scarred and swarthy visage was no longer merely grim but ghastly in the moon.

"Marshal," he said, saluting with a strange stiffness, "I have seen Petrowski the Pole!"

"Haven't they buried him yet?" asked the Marshal, still staring down and in some abstraction.

"If they have," said Schwartz, "he has rolled the stone away and risen from the dead."

He stared in front of him at the moon and marshes; but, indeed, though he was far from being a visionary character, it was not these things that he saw, but rather the things he had just seen. He had, indeed, seen Paul Petrowski walking alive and alert down the brilliantly illuminated main avenue of that Polish town to the very beginning of the causeway; there was no mistaking the slim figure with plumes of hair and tuft of Frenchified beard which figured in so many private albums and illustrated magazines. And behind him he had seen that Polish town aflame with flags and firebrands and a population boiling with triumphant hero-worship, though perhaps less hostile to the government than it might have been, since it was rejoicing at the release of its popular hero.

"Do you mean," cried Grock with a sudden croaking stridency of voice, "that they have dared to release him in defiance of my message?"

Schwartz saluted again and said:

"They had already released him and they have received no message."

"Do you ask me, after all this," said Grock, "to believe that no messenger came from our camp at all?"

"No messenger at all," said the sergeant.

There was a much longer silence, and then Grock said, hoarsely: "What in the name of hell has happened? Can you think of anything to explain it all?"

"I have seen something," said the sergeant, "which I think does explain it all."

When Mr. Pond had told the story up to this point, he paused with an irritating blankness of expression.

"Well," said Gahagan impatiently, "and do *you* know anything that would explain it all?"

"Well, I think I do," said Mr. Pond meekly. "You see, I had to worry it out for myself, when the report came round to my department. It really did arise from an excess of Prussian obedience. It also arose from an excess of another Prussian weakness: contempt. And of all the passions that blind and madden and mislead men, the worst is the coldest: contempt.

"Grock had talked much too comfortably before the cow, and much too confidently before the cabbage. He despised stupid men even on his own staff; and treated Von Hocheimer, the first messenger, as a piece of furniture merely because he looked like a fool; but the Lieutenant was not such a fool as he looked. He also understood what the great Marshal meant, quite as well as the cynical sergeant, who had done such dirty work all his life. Hochmeimer also understood the Marshal's peculiar moral philosophy: that an act is unanswerable even when it is indefensible. He knew that what his commander wanted was simply the corpse of Petrowski; that he wanted it anyhow, at the expense of any deception of princes or destruction of soldiers And when he heard a swifter horseman behind him, riding to overtake him, he knew as well as Grock himself that the new messenger must be carrying with him the message of the mercy of the Prince. Von Schacht, that very young but gallant officer, looking like the very embodiment of all that more generous tradition of Germany that has been too much neglected in this tale, was worthy of the accident that made him the herald of a more generous policy. He came with the speed of that noble horsemanship that has left behind it in Europe the very name of chivalry, calling out to the other in a tone like a herald's trumpet to stop and stand and turn. And Von Hocheimer obeyed. He stopped, he reined in his horse, he turned in his saddle; but his hand held the carbine levelled like a pistol, and he shot the boy between the eyes.

"Then he turned again and rode on, carrying the death-warrant of the Pole. Behind him horse and man had crashed over the edge of the embankment, so that the whole road was clear. And along that clear and open road toiled in his turn the third messenger, marvelling at the interminable length of his journey; till he saw at last the unmistakable uniform of a Hussar like a white star disappearing in the distance, and he shot also. Only he did not kill the second messenger, but the first.

"That was why no messenger came alive to the Polish town that night. That was why the prisoner walked out of his prison alive. Do you think I was quite wrong in saying that Von Grock had two faithful servants, and one too many?"

Poems

Poems.

LEPANTO

White founts falling in the courts of the sun,
And the Soldan of Byzantium is smiling as they run;
There is laughter like the fountains in that face of all men feared,
It stirs the forest darkness, the darkness of his beard,
It curls the blood-red crescent, the crescent of his lips,
For the inmost sea of all the earth is shaken with his ships.
They have dared the white republics up the capes of Italy,
They have dashed the Adriatic round the Lion of the Sea,
And the Pope has cast his arms abroad for agony and loss,
And called the kings of Christendom for swords about the Cross,
The cold queen of England is looking in the glass;
The shadow of the Valois is yawning at the Mass;
From evening isles fantastical rings faint the Spanish gun,
And the Lord upon the Golden Horn is laughing in the sun.

Dim drums throbbing, in the hills half heard,
Where only on a nameless throne a crownless prince has stirred,
Where, risen from a doubtful seat and half-attainted stall,
The last knight of Europe takes weapons from the wall,
The last and lingering troubadour to whom the bird has sung,
That once went singing southward when all the world was
     young,
In that enormous silence, tiny and unafraid,
Comes up along a winding road the noise of the Crusade.
Strong gongs groaning as the guns boom far,
Don John of Austria is going to the war,
Stiff flags straining in the night-blasts cold
In the gloom black-purple, in the glint old-gold,
Torchlight crimson on the copper kettle-drums,
Then the tuckets, then the trumpets, then the cannon, and he
     comes.

Don John laughing in the brave beard curled,
Spurning of his stirrups like the thrones of all the world,
Holding his head up for a flag of all the free.
Love-light of Spain—hurrah!
Death-light of Africa!
Don John of Austria
Is riding to the sea.

Mahound is in his paradise above the evening star,
(*Don John of Austria is going to the war.*)
He moves a mighty turban on the timeless houri's knees,
His turban that is woven of the sunset and the seas.
He shakes the peacock gardens as he rises from his ease,
And he strides among the tree-tops and is taller than the trees,
And his voice through all the garden is a thunder sent to bring
Black Azrael and Ariel and Ammon on the wing.
Giants and the Genii,
Multiplex of wing and eye,
Whose strong obedience broke the sky
When Solomon was king.

They rush in red and purple from the red clouds of the morn,
From temples where the yellow gods shut up their eyes in scorn;
They rise in green robes roaring from the green hells of the sea
Where fallen skies and evil hues and eyeless creatures be;
On them the sea-valves cluster and the grey sea-forests curl,
Splashed with a splendid sickness, the sickness of the pearl;
They swell in sapphire smoke out of the blue cracks of the
    ground,—
They gather and they wonder and give worship to Mahound.
And he saith, "Break up the mountains where the hermit-folk
    may hide,
And sift the red and silver sands lest bone of saint abide,
And chase the Giaours flying night and day, not giving rest,
For that which was our trouble comes again out of the west.

We have set the seal of Solomon on all things under sun,
Of knowledge and of sorrow and endurance of things done,
But a noise is in the mountains, in the mountains, and I know
The voice that shook our palaces—four hundred years ago:
It is he that saith not "Kismet"; it is he that knows not Fate;
It is Richard, it is Raymond, it is Godfrey in the gate!
It is he whose loss is laughter when he counts the wager worth,
Put down your feet upon him, that our peace be on the earth."
For he heard drums groaning and he heard guns jar,
(*Don John of Austria is going to the war.*)
Sudden and still—hurrah!
Bolt from Iberia!
Don John of Austria
Is gone by Alcalar.

St. Michael's on his Mountain in the sea-roads of the north
(*Don John of Austria is girt and going forth.*)
Where the grey seas glitter and the sharp tides shift
And the sea folk labour and the red sails lift.
He shakes his lance of iron and he claps his wings of stone;
The noise is gone through Normandy; the noise is gone alone;
The North is full of tangled things and texts and aching eyes
And dead is all the innocence of anger and surprise,
And Christian killeth Christian in a narrow dusty room,
And Christian dreadeth Christ that hath a newer face of doom,
And Christian hateth Mary that God kissed in Galilee,
But Don John of Austria is riding to the sea.
Don John calling through the blast and the eclipse
Crying with the trumpet, with the trumpet of his lips,
Trumpet that sayeth ha!
Domino Gloria!
Don John of Austria
Is shouting to the ships.

King Philip's in his closet with the Fleece about his neck
(*Don John of Austria is armed upon the deck.*)

The walls are hung with velvet that is black and soft as sin,
And little dwarfs creep out of it and little dwarfs creep in.
He holds a crystal phial that has colours like the moon,
He touches, and it tingles, and he trembles very soon,
And his face is as a fungus of a leprous white and grey
Like plants in the high houses that are shuttered from the day,
And death is in the phial, and the end of noble work,
But Don John of Austria has fired upon the Turk.
Don John's hunting, and his hounds have bayed—
Booms away past Italy the rumour of his raid.
Gun upon gun, ha! ha!
Gun upon gun, hurrah!
Don John of Austria
Has loosed the cannonade.

The Pope was in his chapel before day or battle broke,
(*Don John of Austria is hidden in the smoke.*)
The hidden room in a man's house where God sits all the year,
The secret window whence the world looks small and very dear.
He sees as in a mirror on the monstrous twilight sea
The crescent of his cruel ships whose name is mystery;
They fling great shadows foe-wards, making Cross and Castle
    dark,
They veil the plumèd lions on the galleys of St. Mark;
And above the ships are palaces of brown, black-bearded chiefs,
And below the ships are prisons, where with multitudinous griefs,
Christian captives sick and sunless, all a labouring race repines
Like a race in sunken cities, like a nation in the mines.
They are lost like slaves that swat, and in the skies of morning
    hung
The stairways of the tallest gods when tyranny was young.
They are countless, voiceless, hopeless as those fallen or fleeing
    on
Before the high Kings' horses in the granite of Babylon.
And many a one grows witless in his quiet room in hell

Where a yellow face looks inward through the lattice of his cell,
And he finds his God forgotten, and he seeks no more a sign—
(*But Don John of Austria has burst the battle-line!*)
Don John pounding from the slaughter-painted poop,
Purpling all the ocean like a bloody pirate's sloop,
Scarlet running over on the silvers and the golds,
Breaking of the hatches up and bursting of the holds,
Thronging of the thousands up that labour under sea
White for bliss and blind for sun and stunned for liberty.
Vivat Hispania!
Domino Gloria!
Don John of Austria
Has set his people free!

Cervantes on his galley sets the sword back in the sheath
(*Don John of Austria rides homeward with a wreath.*)
And he sees across a weary land a straggling road in Spain,
Up which a lean and foolish knight forever rides in vain,
And he smiles, but not as Sultans smile, and settles back the
        blade. . . .
(*But Don John of Austria rides home from the Crusade.*)

THE DONKEY

When fishes flew and forests walked
    And figs grew upon thorn,
Some moment when the moon was blood
    Then surely I was born.

With monstrous head and sickening cry
    And ears like errant wings,
The devil's walking parody
    On all four-footed things.

The tattered outlaw of the earth,
   Of ancient crooked will;
Starve, scourge, deride me: I am dumb,
   I keep my secret still.

Fools! For I also had my hour;
   One far fierce hour and sweet:
There was a shout about my ears,
   And palms before my feet.

THE BEATIFIC VISION

Through what fierce incarnations, furled
   In fire and darkness, did I go,
Ere I was worthy in the world
   To see a dandelion grow?

Well, if in any woes or wars
   I bought my naked right to be,
Grew worthy of the grass, nor gave
   The wren, my brother, shame for me.

But what shall God not ask of him
   In the last time when all is told,
Who saw her stand beside the hearth,
   The firelight garbing her in gold?

THE PRAISE OF DUST

"What of vile dust?" the preacher said.
   Methought the whole world woke,
The dead stone lived beneath my foot,
   And my whole body spoke.

"You, that play tyrant to the dust,
    And stamp its wrinkled face,
This patient star that flings you not
    Far into homeless space.

"Come down out of your dusty shrine
    The living dust to see,
The flowers that at your sermon's end
    Stand blazing silently.

"Rich white and blood-red blossoms; stones,
    Lichens like fire encrust;
A gleam of blue, a glare of gold,
    The vision of the dust.

"Pass them all by: till, as you come
    Where, at a city's edge,
Under a tree—I know it well—
    Under a lattice ledge,

"The sunshine falls on one brown head.
    You, too, O cold of clay,
Eater of stones, may haply hear
    The trumpets of that day.

"When God to all his paladins
    By his own splendour swore
To make a fairer face than heaven,
    Of dust and nothing more."

WINE AND WATER

Old Noah he had an ostrich farm and fowls on the largest scale,
He ate his egg with a ladle in a egg-cup big as a pail,

And the soup he took was Elephant Soup and the fish he took
    was Whale,
But they all were small to the cellar he took when he set out to
    sail,
And Noah he often said to his wife when he sat down to dine,
"I don't care where the water goes if it doesn't get into the wine."

The cataract of the cliff of heaven fell blinding off the brink
As if it would wash the stars away as suds go down a sink,
The seven heavens came roaring down for the throats of hell to
    drink,
And Noah he cocked his eye and said, "It looks like rain, I think,
The water has drowned the Matterhorn as deep as a Mendip
    mine,
But I don't care where the water goes if it doesn't get into the
    wine."

But Noah he sinned, and we have sinned; on tipsy feet we trod,
Till a great big black teetotaller was sent to us for a rod,
And you can't get wine at a P.S.A., or chapel, or Eisteddfod,
For the Curse of Water has come again because of the wrath of
    God,
And water is on the Bishop's board and the Higher Thinker's
    shrine,
But I don't care where the water goes if it doesn't get into the
    wine.

BALLADE D'UNE GRANDE DAME

Heaven shall forgive you Bridge at dawn,
The clothes you wear—or do not wear—
And Ladies' Leap-frog on the lawn
And dyes and drugs and *petits verres*.
Your vicious things shall melt in air . . . . . .

. . . But for the Virtuous Things you do,
The Righteous Work, the Public Care,
It shall not be forgiven you.

Because you could not even yawn
When your Committees would prepare
To have the teeth of paupers drawn
Or strip the slums of Human Hair;
Because a Doctor Otto Maehr
Spoke of "a segregated few"—
And you sat smiling in your chair—
It shall not be forgiven you.

Though your sins cried to—Father Vaughan,
These desperate you could not spare
Who steal, with nothing left to pawn;
You caged a man up like a bear
For ever in a jailer's care
Because his sins were more than *two* . . .
. . . I know a house in Hoxton where
It shall not be forgiven you.

ENVOI

Princess, you trapped a guileless Mayor
To meet some people that you knew . . .
When the last trumpet rends the air
It shall not be forgiven you.

A BALLADE OF SUICIDE

The gallows in my garden, people say,
Is new and neat and adequately tall.
I tie the noose on in a knowing way

As one that knots his necktie for a ball;
But just as all the neighbours—on the wall—
Are drawing a long breath to shout "Hurray!"
The strangest whim has seized me. . . . After all
I think I will not hang myself to-day.

To-morrow is the time I get my pay—
My uncle's sword is hanging in the hall—
I see a little cloud all pink and grey—
Perhaps the Rector's mother will *not* call—
I fancy that I heard from Mr. Gall
That mushrooms could be cooked another way—
I never read the works of Juvenal—
I think I will not hang myself to-day.

The world will have another washing day;
The decadents decay; the pedants pall;
And H. G. Wells has found that children play,
And Bernard Shaw discovered that they squall;
Rationalists are growing rational—
And through thick woods one finds a stream astray,
So secret that the very sky seems small—
I think I will not hang myself to-day.

ENVOI

Prince, I can hear the trumpet of Germinal,
The tumbrils toiling up the terrible way;
Even to-day your royal head may fall—
I think I will not hang myself to-day.

ELEGY IN A COUNTRY CHURCHYARD

The men that worked for England
They have their graves at home:

And bees and birds of England
About the cross can roam.

But they that fought for England,
Following a falling star,
Alas, alas for England
They have their graves afar.

And they that rule in England,
In stately conclave met,
Alas, alas for England
They have no graves as yet.

SONNET

ON HEARING A LANDLORD ACCUSED (FALSELY, FOR ALL THE BARD
CAN SAY) OF NEGLECTING ONE OF THE NUMEROUS WHITE
HORSES THAT WERE OR WERE NOT CONNECTED WITH
ALFRED THE GREAT

If you have picked your lawn of leaves and snails,
If you have told your valet, even with oaths,
Once a week or so, to brush your clothes,
If you have dared to clean your teeth, or nails,
While the Horse upon the holy mountain fails—
Then God that Alfred to his earth betrothes
Send on you screaming all that honour loathes,
Horsewhipping, Houndsditch, debts, and *Daily Mails*.

Can you not even conserve? For if indeed
The White Horse fades; then closer creeps the fight
When we shall scour the face of England white,
Plucking such men as you up like a weed,
And fling them far beyond a shaft shot right
When Wessex went to battle for the Creed.

THE JUDGMENT OF ENGLAND

"Ill fares the land, to hastening ills a prey
Where Wealth accumulates and Men decay."
So rang of old the noble voice in vain
O'er the Last Peasants wandering on the plain,
Doom has reversed the riddle and the rhyme,
While sinks the commerce reared upon that crime,
The thriftless towns litter with lives undone,
To whom our madness left no joy but one;
And irony that glares like Judgment Day
See Men accumulate and Wealth decay.

THE WORLD STATE

Oh, how I love Humanity,
   With love so pure and pringlish,
And how I hate the horrid French,
   Who never will be English!

The International Idea,
   The largest and the clearest,
Is welding all the nations now,
   Except the one that's nearest.

This compromise has long been known,
   This scheme of partial pardons,
In ethical societies
   And small suburban gardens—

The villas and the chapels where
   I learned with little labour

The way to love my fellow-man
And hate my next-door neighbour.

MEMORY

If I ever go back to Baltimore,
The City of Maryland,
I shall miss again as I missed before
A thousand things of the world in store,
The story standing in every door
That beckons on every hand.

I shall not know where the bonds were riven,
And a hundred faiths set free,
Where a wandering cavalier had given
Her hundredth name to the Queen of Heaven,
And made oblation of feuds forgiven
To Our Lady of Liberty.

I shall not travel the tracks of fame
Where the war was not to the strong;
Where Lee the last of the heroes came
With the Men of the South and a flag like flame,
And called the land by its lovely name
In the unforgotten song.

If ever I cross the sea and stray
To the city of Maryland,
I will sit on a stone and watch or pray
For a stranger's child that was there one day:
And the child will never come back to play,
And no one will understand.

TO HILAIRE BELLOC

The Dedication of *The Napoleon of Notting Hill*

For every tiny town or place
   God made the stars especially;
Babies look up with owlish face
   And see them tangled in a tree:
You saw a moon from Sussex Downs,
   A Sussex moon, untravelled still,
I saw a moon that was the town's,
   The largest lamp on Campden Hill.

Yea, Heaven is everywhere at home,
   The big blue cap that always fits,
And so it is (be calm; they come
   To goal at last, my wandering wits),
So is it with the heroic thing;
   This shall not end for the world's end,
And though the sullen engines swing,
   Be you not much afraid, my friend.

This did not end by Nelson's urn
   Where an immortal England sits—
Nor where our tall young men in turn
   Drank death like wine at Austerlitz.
And when the pedants bade us mark
   What cold mechanic happenings
Must come; our souls said in the dark,
   "Belike; but there are likelier things."

Likelier across these flats afar,
   These sulky levels smooth and free,
The drums shall crash a waltz of war
   And Death shall dance with Liberty;

Likelier the barricades shall blare
    Slaughter below and smoke above,
And death and hate and hell declare
    That men have found a thing to love.

Far from your sunny uplands set
    I saw the dream; the streets I trod,
The lit straight streets shot out and met
    The starry streets that point to God;
The legend of an epic hour
    A child I dreamed, and dream it still,
Under the great grey water tower
    That strikes the stars on Campden Hill.

THE DELUGE

Though giant rains put out the sun,
    Here stand I for a sign.
Though Earth be filled with waters dark,
    My cup is filled with wine.
Tell to the trembling priests that here
    Under the deluge rod,
One nameless, tattered, broken man
    Stood up and drank to God.

Sun has been where the rain is now,
    Bees in the heat to hum,
Haply a humming maiden came,
    Now let the deluge come:
Brown of aureole, green of garb,
    Straight as a golden rod,
Drink to the throne of thunder now!
    Drink to the wrath of God.

High in the wreck I held the cup,
  I clutched my rusty sword,
I cocked my tattered feather
  To the glory of the Lord.
Not undone were the heaven and earth,
  This hollow world thrown up,
Before one man had stood up straight,
  And drained it like a cup.

THE GREAT MINIMUM

It is something to have wept as we have wept,
It is something to have done as we have done,
It is something to have watched when all men slept,
And seen the stars which never see the sun.

It is something to have smelt the mystic rose,
Although it break and leave the thorny rods,
It is something to have hungered once as those
Must hunger who have ate the bread of gods.

To have seen you and your unforgotten face,
Brave as a blast of trumpets for the fray,
Pure as white lilies in a watery space,
It were something, though you went from me to-day.

To have known the things that from the weak are furled,
Perilous ancient passions, strange and high;
It is something to be wiser than the world,
It is something to be older than the sky.

In a time of sceptic moths and cynic rusts,
And fatted lives that of their sweetness tire,

In a world of flying loves and fading lusts,
It is something to be sure of a desire.

Lo, blessed are our ears for they have heard;
Yea, blessed are our eyes for they have seen:
Let thunder break on man and beast and bird
And the lightning. It is something to have been.

THE SONG OF QUOODLE

They haven't got no noses,
The fallen sons of Eve;
Even the smell of roses
Is not what they supposes;
But more than mind discloses
And more than men believe.

They haven't got no noses,
They cannot even tell
When door and darkness closes
The park a Jew encloses,
Where even the law of Moses
Will let you steal a smell.

The brilliant smell of water,
The brave smell of a stone,
The smell of dew and thunder,
The old bones buried under,
Are things in which they blunder
And err, if left alone.

The wind from winter forests,
The scent of scentless flowers,

The breath of brides' adorning,
The smell of snare and warning,
The smell of Sunday morning,
God gave to us for ours.
· · · ·

And Quoodle here discloses
All things that Quoodle can,
They haven't got no noses,
They haven't got no noses,
And goodness only knowses
The Noselessness of Man.

ECCLESIASTES

There is one sin: to call a green leaf grey,
    Whereat the sun in heaven shuddereth.
There is one blasphemy: for death to pray,
    For God alone knoweth the praise of death.

There is one creed: 'neath no world-terror's wing
    Apples forget to grow on apple-trees.
There is one thing is needful—everything—
    The rest is vanity of vanities.

ETERNITIES

I cannot count the pebbles in the brook.
    Well hath He spoken: "Swear not by thy head,
    Thou knowest not the hairs," though He, we read,
Writes that wild number in His own strange book.

I cannot count the sands or search the seas,
    Death cometh, and I leave so much untrod.

Grant my immortal aureole, O my God,
And I will name the leaves upon the trees.

In heaven I shall stand on gold and glass,
　Still brooding earth's arithmetic to spell;
　Or see the fading of the fires of hell
Ere I have thanked my God for all the grass.

A CHRISTMAS CAROL

The Christ-child lay on Mary's lap,
　His hair was like a light.
(O weary, weary were the world,
　But here is all aright.)

The Christ-child lay on Mary's breast,
　His hair was like a star.
(O stern and cunning are the kings,
　But here the true hearts are.)

The Christ-child lay on Mary's heart,
　His hair was like a fire.
(O weary, weary is the world,
　But here the world's desire.)

The Christ-child stood at Mary's knee,
　His hair was like a Crown,
And all the flowers looked up at Him,
　And all the stars looked down.

THE HOUSE OF CHRISTMAS

There fared a mother driven forth
Out of an inn to roam;

In the place where she was homeless
All men are at home.
The crazy stable close at hand,
With shaking timber and shifting sand,
Grew a stronger thing to abide and stand
Than the square stones of Rome.

For men are homesick in their homes,
And strangers under the sun,
And they lay their heads in a foreign land
Whenever the day is done.
Here we have battle and blazing eyes,
And chance and honour and high surprise,
But our homes are under miraculous skies
Where the yule tale was begun.

A Child in a foul stable,
Where the beasts feed and foam;
Only where He was homeless
Are you and I at home;
We have hands that fashion and heads that know,
But our hearts we lost—how long ago!
In a place no chart nor ship can show
Under the sky's dome.

This world is wild as an old wives' tale,
And strange the plain things are,
The earth is enough and the air is enough
For our wonder and our war;
But our rest is as far as the fire-drake swings
And our peace is put in impossible things
Where clashed and thundered unthinkable wings
Round an incredible star.

To an open house in the evening
Home shall men come,

To an older place than Eden
And a taller town than Rome.
To the end of the way of the wandering star,
To the things that cannot be and that are,
To the place where God was homeless
And all men are at home.

Further Essays

"I cannot understand the people who take literature seriously; but I can love them, and I do. Out of my love I warn them to keep clear of this book. It is a collection of papers upon current or rather flying subjects. Their chief vice is that so many of them are very serious; because I had no time to make them flippant. It is so easy to be solemn; it is so hard to be frivolous. That is why so many tired, elderly, and wealthy men go in for politics. They are responsible, because they have not the strength of mind left to be irresponsible. It is also easier. So in these easy pages I keep myself on the whole on the level of the *Times:* it is only occasionally that I leap upwards almost to the level of *Tit-Bits*."

IN certain endless uplands, uplands like great flats gone dizzy, slopes that seem to contradict the idea that there is even such a thing as a level, and make us all realize that we live on a planet with a sloping roof, you will come from time to time upon whole valleys filled with loose rocks and boulders, so big as to be like mountains broken loose. The whole might be an experimental creation shattered and cast away. It is often difficult to believe that such cosmic refuse can have come together except by human means. The mildest and most cockney imagination conceives the place to be the scene of some war of giants. To me it is always associated with one idea, recurrent and at last instinctive. The scene was the scene of the stoning of some prehistoric prophet, a prophet as much more gigantic than after-prophets as the boulders are more gigantic than the pebbles. He spoke some words—words that seemed shameful and tremendous —and the world, in terror, buried him under a wilderness of stones. The place is the monument of an ancient fear.

If we followed the same mood of fancy, it would be more difficult to imagine what awful hint or wild picture of the universe called forth that primal persecution, what secret of sensational thought lies buried under the brutal stones. For in our time the blasphemies are threadbare. Pessimism is now patently, as it always was essentially, more commonplace than piety. Profanity is now more than an affectation—it is a convention. The curse against God is Exercise I, in the primer of minor poetry. It was not, assuredly, for such babyish solemnities that our imaginary prophet was stoned in the morning of the world. If we weigh the matter in the faultless scales of imagination, if we see what is the real trend of humanity, we shall feel it most probable that he was stoned for saying that the grass was green and that the birds sang in spring; for the mission of all the prophets from the beginning has not been so much the pointing out of heavens or hells as primarily the pointing out of the earth.

Religion has had to provide that longest and strangest tele-scope—the telescope through which we could see the star upon which we dwelt. For the mind and eyes of the average man this world is as lost as Eden and as sunken as Atlantis. There runs a strange law through the length of human history—that men are continually tending to undervalue their environment, to under-value their happiness, to undervalue themselves. The great sin of mankind, the sin typified by the fall of Adam, is the tendency, not towards pride, but towards this weird and horrible hu-mility.

This is the great fall, the fall by which the fish forgets the sea, the ox forgets the meadow, the clerk forgets the city, every man forgets his environment and, in the fullest and most literal sense, forgets himself. This is the real fall of Adam, and it is a spiritual fall. It is a strange thing that many truly spiritual men, such as General Gordon, have actually spent some hours in speculating upon the precise location of the Garden of Eden. Most probably we are in Eden still. It is only our eyes that have changed.

The pessimist is commonly spoken of as the man in revolt. He is not. Firstly, because it requires some cheerfulness to con-tinue in revolt, and secondly, because pessimism appeals to the weaker side of everybody, and the pessimist, therefore, drives as roaring a trade as the publican. The person who is really in revolt is the optimist, who generally lives and dies in a desperate and suicidal effort to persuade all the other people how good they are. It has been proved a hundred times over that if you really wish to enrage people and make them angry, even unto death, the right way to do it is to tell them that they are all the sons of God. Jesus Christ was crucified, it may be remembered, not because of anything he said about God, but on a charge of saying that a man could in three days pull down and rebuild the Temple. Every one of the great revolutionists, from Isaiah to Shelley, have been optimists. They have been indignant, not about the badness of existence, but about the slowness of men in realizing its goodness. The prophet who is stoned is not a brawler or a marplot. He is simply a rejected lover. He suffers from an unrequited attachment to things in general.

It becomes increasingly apparent, therefore that the world is in a permanent danger of being misjudged. That this is no fanciful or mystical idea may be tested by simple examples. The two absolutely basic words "good" and "bad," descriptive of two primal and inexplicable sensations, are not, and never have been, used properly. Things that are bad are not called good by any people who experience them; but things that are good are called bad by the universal verdict of humanity.

Let me explain a little: Certain things are bad so far as they go, such as pain, and no one, not even a lunatic, calls a toothache good in itself; but a knife which cuts clumsily and with difficulty is called a bad knife, which it certainly is not. It is only not so good as other knives to which men have grown accustomed. A knife is never bad except on such rare occasions as that in which it is neatly and scientifically planted in the middle of one's back. The coarsest and bluntest knife which ever broke a pencil into pieces instead of sharpening it is a good thing in so far as it is a knife. It would have appeared a miracle in the Stone Age. What we call a bad knife is a good knife not good enough for us; what we call a bad hat is a good hat not good enough for us; what we call bad cookery is good cookery not good enough for us; what we call a bad civilization is a good civilization not good enough for us. We choose to call the great mass of the history of mankind bad, not because it is bad, but because we are better. This is palpably an unfair principle. Ivory may not be so white as snow, but the whole Arctic continent does not make ivory black.

Now it has appeared to me unfair that humanity should be engaged perpetually in calling all those things bad which have been good enough to make other things better, in everlastingly kicking down the ladder by which it has climbed. It has appeared to me that progress should be something else besides a continual parricide; therefore I have investigated the dust-heaps of humanity, and found a treasure in all of them. I have found that humanity is not incidentally engaged, but eternally and systematically engaged, in throwing gold into the gutter and diamonds into the sea. I have found that every man is disposed to call the green leaf of the tree a little less green than it is, and the snow of Christmas a little less white than it is; therefore I have imagined that the main business of a man, however humble, is defence. I have conceived that a defendant is chiefly required when worldlings despise the world—that a counsel for the defence would not have been out of place in that terrible day when the sun was darkened over Calvary and Man was rejected of men.

A DEFENCE OF SKELETONS

SOME little time ago I stood among immemorial English trees that seemed to take hold upon the stars like a brood of Ygdrasils. As I walked among these living pillars I became gradually aware that the rustics who lived and died in their shadow adopted a very curious conversational tone. They seemed to be constantly apologizing for the trees, as if they were a very poor show. After elaborate investigation, I discovered that their gloomy and penitent tone was traceable to the fact that it was winter and all the trees were bare. I assured them that I did not resent the fact that it was winter, that I knew the thing had happened before, and that no forethought on their part could have averted this blow of destiny. But I could not in any way reconcile them to the fact that it *was* winter. There was evidently a general feeling that I had caught the trees in a kind of disgraceful deshabille, and that they ought not to be seen until, like the first human sinners, they had covered themselves with leaves. So it is quite clear that, while very few people appear to know anything of how trees look in winter, the actual foresters know less than anyone. So far from the line of the tree when it is bare appearing harsh and severe, it is luxuriantly indefinable to an unusual degree; the fringe of the forest melts away like a vignette. The tops of two or three high trees when they are leafless are so soft that they seem like the gigantic brooms of that fabulous lady who was sweeping the cobwebs off the sky. The outline of a leafy forest is in comparison hard, gross and blotchy; the clouds of night do not more certainly obscure the moon than those green and monstrous clouds obscure the tree; the actual sight of the little wood, with its gray and silver sea of life, is entirely a winter vision. So dim and delicate is the heart of the winter woods, a kind of glittering gloaming, that a figure stepping towards us in the chequered twilight seems as if he were breaking through unfathomable depths of spiders' webs.

But surely the idea that its leaves are the chief grace of a tree is a vulgar one, on a par with the idea that his hair is the chief grace of a pianist. When winter, that healthy ascetic, carries his gigantic razor over hill and valley, and shaves all the trees like monks, we feel surely that they are all the more like trees if they are shorn, just as so many painters and musicians would be all the more like men if they were less like mops. But it does appear to be a deep and essential difficulty that men have an abiding terror of their own structure, or of the structure of things they love. This is felt dimly in the skeleton of the tree: it is felt profoundly in the skeleton of the man.

The importance of the human skeleton is very great, and the horror with which it is commonly regarded is somewhat mysterious. Without claiming for the human skeleton a wholly conventional beauty, we may assert that he is certainly not uglier than a bull-dog, whose popularity never wanes, and that he has a vastly more cheerful and ingratiating expression. But just as man is mysteriously ashamed of the skeletons of the trees in winter, so he is mysteriously ashamed of the skeleton of himself in death. It is a singular thing altogether, this horror of the archi-

tecture of things. One would think it would be most unwise in
a man to be afraid of a skeleton, since Nature has set curious and
quite insuperable obstacles to his running away from it.

One ground exists for this terror: a strange idea has infected
humanity that the skeleton is typical of death. A man might as
well say that a factory chimney was typical of bankruptcy. The
factory may be left naked after ruin, the skeleton may be left
naked after bodily dissolution; but both of them have had a
lively and workmanlike life of their own, all the pulleys creaking, all the wheels turning, in the House of Livelihood as in the
House of Life. There is no reason why this creature (new, as I
fancy, to art), the living skeleton, should not become the essential symbol of life.

The truth is that man's horror of the skeleton is not horror of
death at all. It is man's eccentric glory that he has not, generally
speaking, any objection to being dead, but has a very serious objection to being undignified. And the fundamental matter which
troubles him in the skeleton is the reminder that the ground-
plan of his appearance is shamelessly grotesque. I do not know
why he should object to this. He contentedly takes his place in
a world that does not pretend to be genteel—a laughing, working, jeering world. He sees millions of animals carrying, with
quite a dandified levity, the most monstrous shapes and ap-
pendages, the most preposterous horns, wings, and legs, when
they are necessary to utility. He sees the good temper of the
frog, the unaccountable happiness of the hippopotamus. He sees
a whole universe which is ridiculous, from the animalcule, with
a head too big for its body, up to the comet, with a tail too big
for its head. But when it comes to the delightful oddity of his
own inside, his sense of humour rather abruptly deserts him.

In the Middle Ages and in the Renaissance (which was, in
certain times and respects, a much gloomier period) this idea of
the skeleton had a vast influence in freezing the pride out of all
earthly pomps and the fragrance out of all fleeting pleasures.
But it was not, surely, the mere dread of death that did this, for

these were ages in which men went to meet death singing; it was the idea of the degradation of man in the grinning ugliness of his structure that withered the juvenile insolence of beauty and pride. And in this it almost assuredly did more good than harm. There is nothing so cold or so pitiless as youth, and youth in aristocratic stations and ages tended to an impeccable dignity, an endless summer of success which needed to be very sharply reminded of the scorn of the stars. It was well that such flamboyant prigs should be convinced that one practical joke, at least, would bowl them over, that they would fall into one grinning man-trap, and not rise again. That the whole structure of their existence was as wholesomely ridiculous as that of a pig or a parrot they could not be expected to realize; that birth was humorous, coming of age humorous, drinking and fighting humorous, they were far too young and solemn to know. But at least they were taught that death was humorous.

There is a peculiar idea abroad that the value and fascination of what we call Nature lie in her beauty. But the fact that Nature is beautiful in the sense that a dado or a Liberty curtain is beautiful, is only one of her charms, and almost an accidental one. The highest and most valuable quality in Nature is not her beauty, but her generous and defiant ugliness. A hundred instances might be taken. The croaking noise of the rooks is, in itself, as hideous as the whole hell of sounds in a London railway tunnel. Yet it uplifts us like a trumpet with its coarse kindliness and honesty, and the lover in "Maud" could actually persuade himself that this abominable noise resembled his ladylove's name. Has the poet, for whom Nature means only roses and lilies, ever heard a pig grunting? It is a noise that does a man good—a strong, snorting, imprisoned noise, breaking its way out of unfathomable dungeons through every possible outlet and organ. It might be the voice of the earth itself, snoring in its mighty sleep. This is the deepest, the oldest, the most wholesome and religious sense of the value of Nature—the value which comes from her immense babyishness. She is as top-heavy, as grotesque, as solemn and as happy as a child. The mood does come when we see all her shapes like shapes that a baby scrawls upon a slate—simple, rudimentary, a million years older and stronger than the whole disease that is called Art. The objects of earth and heaven seem to combine into a nursery tale, and our relation to things seems for a moment so simple that a dancing lunatic would be needed to do justice to its lucidity and levity. The tree above my head is flapping like some gigantic bird standing on one leg; the moon is like the eye of a cyclops. And, however much my face clouds with sombre vanity, or vulgar vengeance, or contemptible contempt, the bones of my skull beneath it are laughing for ever.

A DEFENCE OF PUBLICITY

It is a very significant fact that the form of art in which the modern world has certainly not improved upon the ancient is what may roughly be called the art of the open air. Public monuments have certainly not improved, nor has the criticism of them improved, as is evident from the fashion of condemning such a large number of them as pompous. An interesting essay might be written on the enormous number of words that are used as insults when they are really compliments. It is in itself a singular study in that tendency which, as I have said, is always making things out worse than they are, and necessitating a systematic attitude of defence. Thus, for example, some dramatic critics cast contempt upon a dramatic performance by calling it theatrical, which simply means that it is suitable to a theatre, and is as much a compliment as calling a poem poetical. Similarly we speak disdainfully of a certain kind of work as sentimental, which simply means possessing the admirable and essential quality of sentiment. Such phrases are all parts of one peddling and cowardly philosophy, and remind us of the days when 'enthusiast' was a term of reproach. But of all this vocabulary of unconscious eulogies nothing is more striking than the word 'pompous.'

Properly speaking, of course, a public monument ought to be pompous. Pomp is its very object; it would be absurd to have columns and pyramids blushing in some coy nook like violets in the woods of spring. And public monuments have in this matter a great and much-needed lesson to teach. Valour and mercy and the great enthusiasms ought to be a great deal more public than they are at present. We are too fond nowadays of committing the sin of fear and calling it the virtue of reverence. We have forgotten the old and wholesome morality of the Book of Proverbs, "Wisdom crieth without; her voice is heard in the streets." In Athens and Florence her voice was heard in the streets. They had an outdoor life of war and argument, and they had what modern commercial civilization has never had—an outdoor art. Religious services, the most sacred of all things, have always been held publicly; it is entirely a new and debased notion that sanctity is the same as secrecy. A great many modern poets, with the most abstruse and delicate sensibilities, love darkness, when all is said and done, much for the same reason that thieves love it. The mission of a great spire or statue should be to strike the spirit with a sudden sense of pride as with a thunder-bolt. It should lift us with it into the empty and ennobling air. Along the base of every noble monument, whatever else may be written there, runs in invisible letters the lines of Swinburne:

"This thing is God:
To be man with thy might,
To go straight in the strength of thy spirit, and live out thy life
    in the light."

If a public monument does not meet this first supreme and obvious need, that it should be public and monumental, it fails from the outset.

There has arisen lately a school of realistic sculpture, which may perhaps be better described as a school of sketchy sculpture. Such a movement was right and inevitable as a reaction from the mean and dingy pomposity of English Victorian statuary. Perhaps the most hideous and depressing object in the universe—far more hideous and depressing than one of Mr. H. G. Wells's shapeless monsters of the slime (and not at all unlike them)—is the statue of an English philanthropist. Almost as bad, though, of course, not quite as bad, are the statues of English politicians in Parliament Fields. Each of them is cased in a cylindrical frock-coat, and each carries either a scroll or a dubious-looking garment over the arm that might be either a bathing-towel or a light great-coat. Each of them is in an oratorical attitude, which has all the disadvantage of being affected without even any of the advantages of being theatrical. Let no one suppose that such abortions arise merely from technical demerit. In every line of those leaden dolls is expressed the fact that they were not set up with any heat of natural enthusiasm for beauty or dignity. They were set up mechanically, because it would seem indecorous or stingy if they were not set up. They were even set up sulkily, in a utilitarian age which was haunted by the thought that there were a great many more sensible ways of spending money. So long as this is the dominant national sentiment, the land is barren, statues and churches will not grow—for they have to grow, as much as trees and flowers. But this moral disadvantage which lay so heavily upon the early Victorian sculpture lies in a modified degree upon that rough, picturesque, commonplace sculpture which has begun to arise, and of which the statue of Darwin in the South Kensington Museum and the statue of Gordon in Trafalgar Square are admirable examples. It is not enough for a popular monument to be artistic, like a black charcoal sketch; it must be striking; it must be in the highest sense of the word sensational; it must stand for humanity; it must speak for us to the stars; it must declare in the face of all the heavens that when the longest and blackest catalogue has been made of all our crimes and follies there are some things of which we men are not ashamed.

The two modes of commemorating a public man are a statue and a biography. They are alike in certain respects, as, for example, in the fact that neither of them resembles the original, and that both of them commonly tone down not only all a man's vices, but all the more amusing of his virtues. But they are treated in one respect differently. We never hear anything about biography without hearing something about the sanctity of private life and the necessity for suppressing the whole of the most important part of a man's existence. The sculptor does not work at this disadvantage. The sculptor does not leave out the nose of an eminent philanthropist because it is too beautiful to be given to the public; he does not depict a statesman with a sack over his head because his smile was too sweet to be endurable in the light of day. But in biography the thesis is popularly and solidly maintained, so that it requires some courage even to hint a doubt of it, that the better a man was, the more truly human life he led, the less should be said about it.

For this idea, this modern idea that sanctity is identical with secrecy, there is one thing at least to be said. It is for all practical purposes an entirely new idea; it was unknown to all the ages in which the idea of sanctity really flourished. The record of the great spiritual movements of mankind is dead against the idea that spirituality is a private matter. The most awful secret of every man's soul, its most lonely and individual need, its most primal and psychological relationship, the thing called worship, the communication between the soul and the last reality—this most private matter is the most public spectacle in the world. Anyone who chooses to walk into a large church on Sunday morning may see a hundred men each alone with his Maker. He stands, in truth, in the presence of one of the strangest spectacles in the world—a mob of hermits. And in thus definitely espousing publicity by making public the most internal mystery, Christianity acts in accordance with its earliest origins and its

terrible beginning. It was surely by no accident that the spectacle which darkened the sun at noonday was set upon a hill.
The martyrdoms of the early Christians were public not only
by the caprice of the oppressor, but by the whole desire and
conception of the victims.

The mere grammatical meaning of the word "martyr" breaks
into pieces at a blow the whole notion of the privacy of goodness. The Christian martyrdoms were more than demonstrations: they were advertisements. In our day the new theory of
spiritual delicacy would desire to alter all this. It would permit
Christ to be crucified if it was necessary to His Divine nature,
but it would ask in the name of good taste why He could not
be crucified in a private room. It would declare that the act of a
martyr in being torn in pieces by lions was vulgar and sensational, though, of course, it would have no objection to being
torn in pieces by a lion in one's own parlour before a circle of
really intimate friends.

It is, I am inclined to think, a decadent and diseased purity
which has inaugurated this notion that the sacred object must be
hidden. The stars have never lost their sanctity, and they are
more shameless and naked and numerous than advertisements of
Pears' soap. It would be a strange world indeed if Nature was
suddenly stricken with this ethereal shame, if the trees grew
with their roots in the air and their load of leaves and blossoms
underground, if the flowers closed at dawn and opened at sunset,
if the sunflower turned towards the darkness, and the birds flew,
like bats, by night.

A DEFENCE OF NONSENSE

THERE are two equal and eternal ways of looking at this twilight
world of ours: we may see it as the twilight of evening or the
twilight of morning; we may think of anything, down to a

fallen acorn, as a descendant or as an ancestor. There are times when we are almost crushed, not so much with the load of the evil as with the load of the goodness of humanity, when we feel that we are nothing but the inheritors of a humiliating splendour. But there are other times when everything seems primitive, when the ancient stars are only sparks blown from a boy's bonfire, when the whole earth seems so young and experimental that even the white hair of the aged, in the fine Biblical phrase, is like almond-trees that blossom, like the white hawthorn grown in May. That it is good for a man to realize that he is "the heir of all the ages" is pretty commonly admitted; it is a less popular but equally important point that it is good for him sometimes to realize that he is not only an ancestor, but an ancestor of primal antiquity; it is good for him to wonder whether he is not a hero, and to experience ennobling doubts as to whether he is not a solar myth.

The matters which most thoroughly evoke this sense of the abiding childhood of the world are those which are really fresh, abrupt and inventive in any age; and if we were asked what was the best proof of this adventurous youth in the nineteenth century we should say, with all respect to its portentous sciences and philosophies, that it was to be found in the rhymes of Mr. Edward Lear and in the literature of nonsense. "The Dong with the Luminous Nose," at least, is original, as the first ship and the first plough were original.

It is true in a certain sense that some of the greatest writers the world has seen—Aristophanes, Rabelais and Sterne—have written nonsense; but unless we are mistaken, it is in a widely different sense. The nonsense of these men was satiric—that is to say, symbolic; it was a kind of exuberant capering round a discovered truth. There is all the difference in the world between the instinct of satire, which, seeing in the Kaiser's moustaches something typical of him, draws them continually larger and larger; and the instinct of nonsense which, for no reason whatever, imagines what those moustaches would look like on the present Archbishop of Canterbury if he grew them in a fit of absence of mind. We incline to think that no age except our own could have understood that the Quangle-Wangle meant absolutely nothing, and the Lands of the Jumblies were absolutely nowhere. We fancy that if the account of the knave's trial in "Alice in Wonderland" had been published in the seventeenth century it would have been bracketed with Bunyan's "Trial of Faithful" as a parody on the State prosecutions of the time. We fancy that if "The Dong with the Luminous Nose" had appeared in the same period every one would have called it a dull satire on Oliver Cromwell.

It is altogether advisedly that we quote chiefly from Mr. Lear's "Nonsense Rhymes." To our mind he is both chronologically and essentially the father of nonsense; we think him superior to Lewis Carroll. In one sense, indeed, Lewis Carroll has a great advantage. We know what Lewis Carroll was in daily life: he was a singularly serious and conventional don, universally respected, but very much of a pedant and something of a Philistine. Thus his strange double life in earth and in dreamland emphasizes the idea that lies at the back of nonsense—the idea of *escape*, of escape into a world where things are not fixed horribly in an eternal appropriateness, where apples grow on pear-trees, and any odd man you meet may have three legs. Lewis Carroll, living one life in which he would have thundered morally against any one who walked on the wrong plot of grass, and another life in which he would cheerfully call the sun green and the moon blue, was, by his very divided nature, his one foot on both worlds, a perfect type of the position of modern nonsense. His Wonderland is a country populated by insane mathematicians. We feel the whole is an escape into a world of masquerade; we feel that if we could pierce their disguises, we might discover that Humpty Dumpty and the March Hare were Professors and Doctors of Divinity enjoying a mental holiday. This sense of escape is certainly less emphatic in Edward Lear, because of the completeness of his citizenship in the world of unreason. We do not know his prosaic biography as we know Lewis Carroll's. We accept him as a purely fabulous figure, on his own description of himself:

> "His body is perfectly spherical,
>   He weareth a runcible hat."

While Lewis Carroll's Wonderland is purely intellectual, Lear introduces quite another element—the element of the poetical and even emotional. Carroll works by the pure reason, but this is not so strong a contrast; for, after all, mankind in the main has always regarded reason as a bit of a joke. Lear introduces his unmeaning words and his amorphous creatures not with the pomp of reason, but with the romantic prelude of rich hues and haunting rhythms.

> "Far and few, far and few,
>   Are the lands where the Jublies live,"

is an entirely different type of poetry to that exhibited in "Jabberwocky." Carroll, with a sense of mathematical neatness, makes his whole poem a mosaic of new and mysterious words. But Edward Lear, with more subtle and placid effrontery, is always introducing scraps of his own elvish dialect into the middle of simple and rational statements, until we are almost stunned into admitting that we know what they mean. There is a genial ring of common sense about such lines as,

> "For his aunt Jobiska said 'Every one knows
>   That a Pobble is better without his toes,' "

which is beyond the reach of Carroll. The poet seems so easy on the matter that we are almost driven to pretend that we see his meaning, that we know the peculiar difficulties of a Pobble, that we are as old travellers in the "Gromboolian Plain" as he is.

Our claim that nonsense is a new literature (we might almost say a new sense) would be quite indefensible if nonsense were nothing more than a mere æsthetic fancy. Nothing sublimely artistic has ever arisen out of mere art, any more than anything essentially reasonable has ever arisen out of the pure reason. There must always be a rich moral soil for any great æsthetic growth. The principle of *art for art's sake* is a very good principle if it means that there is a vital distinction between the earth and the tree that has its roots in the earth; but it is a very bad principle if it means that the tree could grow just as well with its roots in the air. Every great literature has always been allegorical—allegorical of some view of the whole universe. The "Iliad" is only great because all life is a battle, the "Odyssey" because all life is a journey, the Book of Job because all life is a riddle. There is one attitude in which we think that all existence is summed up in the word "ghosts"; another, and somewhat better one, in which we think it is summed up in the words "A Midsummer Night's Dream." Even the vulgarest melodrama or detective story can be good if it expresses something of the delight in sinister possibilities—the healthy lust for darkness and terror which may come on us any night in walking down a dark lane. If, therefore, nonsense is really to be the literature of the future, it must have its own version of the Cosmos to offer; the world must not only be the tragic, romantic, and religious, it must be nonsensical also. And here we fancy that nonsense will, in a very unexpected way, come to the aid of the spiritual view of things. Religion has for centuries been trying to make men exult in the "wonders" of creation, but it has forgotten that a thing cannot be completely wonderful so long as it remains sensible. So long as we regard a tree as an obvious thing, naturally and reasonably created for a giraffe to eat, we cannot properly wonder at it. It is when we consider it as a prodigious wave of the living soil sprawling up to the skies for no reason in particular that we take off our hats, to the astonishment of the park keeper. Everything has in fact another side to it, like the moon, the patroness of nonsense. Viewed from that other side, a bird is a blossom broken loose from its chain of stalk, a man a quadruped begging on its hind legs, a house a gigantesque hat to cover a man from the sun, a chair an apparatus of four wooden legs for a cripple with only two.

This is the side of things which tends most truly to spiritual wonder. It is significant that in the greatest religious poem existent, the Book of Job, the argument which convinces the infidel is not (as has been represented by the merely rational religionism of the eighteenth century) a picture of the ordered beneficence of the Creation; but, on the contrary, a picture of the huge and undecipherable unreason of it. "Hast Thou sent the rain upon the desert where no man is?" This simple sense of wonder at the shapes of things, and at their exuberant independence of our intellectual standards and our trivial definitions, is the basis of spirituality as it is the basis of nonsense. Nonsense and faith (strange as the conjunction may seem) are the two supreme symbolic assertions of the truth that to draw out the soul of things with a syllogism is as impossible as to draw out Leviathan with a hook. The well-meaning person who, by merely studying the logical side of things, has decided that "faith is nonsense," does not know how truly he speaks; later it may come back to him in the form that nonsense is faith.

A DEFENCE OF USEFUL INFORMATION

IT is natural and proper enough that the masses of explosive ammunition stored up in detective stories and the replete and solid sweet-stuff shops which are called sentimental novelettes should be popular with the ordinary customer. It is not difficult to realize that all of us, ignorant or cultivated, are primarily interested in murder and love-making. The really extraordinary thing is that the most appalling fictions are not actually so popular as that literature which deals with the most undisputed and depressing facts. Men are not apparently so interested in murder and love-making as they are in the number of different forms of latchkey which exist in London or the time that it would take a grasshopper to jump from Cairo to the Cape. The enormous mass of fatuous and useless truth which fills the most widely-circulated papers, such as *Tit-Bits, Science Siftings,* and many of the illustrated magazines, is certainly one of the most extraordinary kinds of emotional and mental pabulum on which man ever fed. It is almost incredible that these preposterous statistics should actually be more popular than the most blood-curdling mysteries and the most luxurious debauches of sentiment. To imagine it is like imagining the humorous passages in Bradshaw's Railway Guide read aloud on winter evenings. It is like conceiving a man unable to put down an advertisement of Mother Seigel's Syrup because he wished to know what eventually happened to the young man who was extremely ill at Edinburgh. In the case of cheap detective stories and cheap novelettes, we can most of us feel, whatever our degree of education, that it might be possible to read them if we gave full indulgence to a lower and more facile part of our natures; at the worst we feel that we might enjoy them as we might enjoy bull-baiting or getting drunk. But the literature of information is absolutely mysterious to us. We can no more think of amusing ourselves with it than of reading whole pages of a Surbiton local directory. To read such things would not be a piece of vulgar indulgence; it would be a highly arduous and meritorious enterprise. It is this fact which constitutes a profound and almost unfathomable interest in this particular branch of popular literature.

Primarily, at least, there is one rather peculiar thing which must in justice be said about it. The readers of this strange science must be allowed to be, upon the whole, as disinterested as a prophet seeing visions or a child reading fairy-tales. Here, again, we find, as we so often do, that whatever view of this matter of popular literature we can trust, we can trust least of all the comment and censure current among the vulgar educated. The ordinary version of the ground of this popularity for information, which would be given by a person of greater cultivation, would be that common men are chiefly interested in those sordid facts that surround them on every side. A very small degree of examination will show us that whatever ground there is for the popularity of these insane encyclopædias, it cannot be the ground of utility. The version of life given by a penny novelette may be very moonstruck and unreliable, but it is at least more likely to contain facts relevant to daily life than computations on the subject of the number of cows' tails that would reach the North Pole. There are many more people who are in love than there are people who have any intention of counting or collecting cows' tails. It is evident to me that the grounds of this widespread madness of information for information's sake must be sought in other and deeper parts of human nature than those daily needs which lie so near the surface that even social philosophers have discovered them somewhere in that profound and eternal instinct for enthusiasm and minding other people's business which made great popular movements like the Crusades or the Gordon Riots.

I once had the pleasure of knowing a man who actually talked in private life after the manner of these papers. His conversation consisted of fragmentary statements about height and weight and depth and time and population, and his conversation was a nightmare of dulness. During the shortest pause he would ask whether his interlocutors were aware how many tons of rust were scraped every year off the Menai Bridge, and how many rival shops Mr. Whiteley had bought up since he opened his business. The attitude of his acquaintances towards this inexhaustible entertainer varied according to his presence or absence between indifference and terror. It was frightful to think of a man's brain being stocked with such inexpressibly profitless treasures. It was like visiting some imposing British Museum and finding its galleries and glass cases filled with specimens of London mud, of common mortar, of broken walking-sticks and cheap tobacco. Years afterwards I discovered that this intolerable prosaic bore had been, in fact, a poet. I learnt that every

item of this multitudinous information was totally and unblush-
ingly untrue, that for all I knew he had made it up as he went
along; that no tons of rust are scraped off the Menai Bridge, and
that the rival tradesmen and Mr. Whiteley were creatures of the
poet's brain. Instantly I conceived consuming respect for the
man who was so circumstantial, so monotonous, so entirely pur-
poseless a liar. With him it must have been a case of art for art's
sake. The joke sustained so gravely through a respected lifetime
was of that order of joke which is shared with omniscience. But
what struck me more cogently upon reflection was the fact that
these immeasurable trivialities, which had struck me as utterly
vulgar and arid when I thought they were true, immediately
became picturesque and almost brilliant when I thought they
were inventions of the human fancy. And here, as it seems to
me, I laid my finger upon a fundamental quality of the cultivated
class which prevents it, and will, perhaps, always prevent it
from seeing with the eyes of popular imagination. The merely
educated can scarcely ever be brought to believe that this world
is itself an interesting place. When they look at a work of art,
good or bad, they expect to be interested, but when they look
at a newspaper advertisement or a group in the street, they do
not, properly and literally speaking, expect to be interested. But
to common and simple people this world is a work of art, though
it is, like many great works of art, anonymous. They look to life
for interest with the same kind of cheerful and uneradicable as-
surance with which we look for interest at a comedy for which
we have paid money at the door. To the eyes of the ultimate
school of contemporary fastidiousness, the universe is indeed an
ill-drawn and over-coloured picture, the scrawlings in circles of
a baby upon the slate of night; its starry skies are a vulgar pattern which they would not have for a wallpaper, its flowers and
fruits have a cockney brilliancy, like the holiday hat of a flower-
girl. Hence, degraded by art to its own level, they have lost
altogether that primitive and typical taste of man—the taste for
news. By this essential taste for news, I mean the pleasure in

hearing the mere fact that a man has died at the age of 110 in South Wales, or that the horses ran away at a funeral in San Francisco. Large masses of the early faiths and politics of the world, numbers of the miracles and heroic anecdotes, are based primarily upon this love of something that has just happened, this divine institution of gossip. When Christianity was named the good news, it spread rapidly, not only because it was good, but also because it was news. So it is that if any of us have ever spoken to a navvy in a train about the daily paper, we have generally found the navvy interested, not in those struggles of Parliaments and trades unions which sometimes are, and are always supposed to be, for his benefit; but in the fact that an unusually large whale has been washed up on the coast of Orkney, or that some leading millionaire like Mr. Harmsworth is reported to break a hundred pipes a year. The educated classes, cloyed and demoralized with the mere indulgence of art and mood, can no longer understand the idle and splendid disinterestedness of the reader of *Pearson's Weekly*. He still keeps something of that feeling which should be the birthright of men—the feeling that this planet is like a new house into which we have just moved our baggage. Any detail of it has a value, and, with a truly sportsmanlike instinct, the average man takes most pleasure in the details which are most complicated, irrelevant, and at once difficult and useless to discover. Those parts of the newspaper which announce the giant gooseberry and the raining frogs are really the modern representatives of the popular tendency which produced the hydra and the werewolf and the dog-headed men. Folk in the Middle Ages were not interested in a dragon or a glimpse of the devil because they thought that it was a beautiful prose idyll, but because they thought that it had really just been seen. It was not like so much artistic literature, a refuge indicating the dulness of the world: it was an incident pointedly illustrating the fecund poetry of the world.

That much can be said, and is said, against the literature of information, I do not for a moment deny. It is shapeless, it is trivial, it may give an unreal air of knowledge, it unquestionably lies along with the rest of popular literature under the general indictment that it may spoil the chance of better work, certainly by wasting time, possibly by ruining taste. But these obvious objections are the objections which we hear so persistently from everyone that one cannot help wondering where the papers in question procure their myriads of readers. The natural necessity and natural good underlying such crude institutions is far less often a subject of speculation; yet the healthy hungers which lie at the back of the habits of modern democracy are surely worthy of the same sympathetic study that we give to the dogmas of the fanatics long dethroned and the intrigues of commonwealths long obliterated from the earth. And this is the base and consideration which I have to offer: that perhaps the taste for shreds and patches of journalistic science and history is not, as is continually asserted, the vulgar and senile curiosity of a people that has grown old, but simply the babyish and indiscriminate curiosity of a people still young and entering history for the first time. In other words, I suggest that they only tell each other in magazines the same kind of stories of commonplace portents and conventional eccentricities which, in any case, they would tell each other in taverns. Science itself is only the exaggeration and specialization of this thirst for useless fact, which is the mark of the youth of man. But science has become strangely separated from the mere news and scandal of flowers and birds; men have ceased to see that a pterodactyl was as fresh and natural as a flower, that a flower is as monstrous as a pterodactyl. The rebuilding of this bridge between science and human nature is one of the greatest needs of mankind. We have all to show that before we go on to any visions or creations we can be contented with a planet of miracles.

A DEFENCE OF PENNY DREADFULS

ONE of the strangest examples of the degree to which ordinary life is under-valued is the example of popular literature, the vast mass of which we contentedly describe as vulgar. The boy's novelette may be ignorant in a literary sense, which is only like saying that a modern novel is ignorant in the chemical sense, or the economic sense, or the astronomical sense; but it is not vulgar intrinsically—it is the actual centre of a million flaming imaginations.

In former centuries the educated class ignored the ruck of vulgar literature. They ignored, and therefore did not, properly speaking, despise it. Simple ignorance and indifference does not inflate the character with pride. A man does not walk down the street giving a haughty twirl to his moustaches at the thought of his superiority to some variety of deep-sea fishes. The old scholars left the whole under-world of popular compositions in a similar darkness.

To-day, however, we have reversed this principle. We do despise vulgar compositions, and we do not ignore them. We are in some danger of becoming petty in our study of pettiness; there is a terrible Circean law in the background that if the soul stoops too ostentatiously to examine anything it never gets up again. There is no class of vulgar publications about which there is, to my mind, more utterly ridiculous exaggeration and misconception than the current boys' literature of the lowest stratum. This class of composition has presumably always existed, and must exist. It has no more claim to be good literature than the daily conversation of its readers to be fine oratory, or the lodging-houses and tenements they inhabit to be sublime architecture. But people must have conversation, they must have houses, and they must have stories. The simple need for some kind of ideal world in which fictitious persons play an unhampered part is infinitely deeper and older than the rules of good art, and much more important. Every one of us in childhood has constructed such an invisible *dramatis personæ*, but it never occurred to our nurses to correct the composition by careful comparison with Balzac. In the East the professional story-teller goes from village to village with a small carpet; and I wish sincerely that anyone had the moral courage to spread that carpet and sit on it in Ludgate Circus. But it is not probable that all the tales of the carpet-bearer are little gems of original artistic workmanship. Literature and fiction are two entirely different things. Literature is a luxury; fiction is a necessity. A work of art can hardly be too short, for its climax is its merit. A story can never be too long, for its conclusion is merely to be deplored, like the last halfpenny or the last pipelight. And so, while the increase of the artistic conscience tends in more ambitious works to brevity and impressionism, voluminous industry still marks the producer of the true romantic trash. There was no end to the ballads of Robin Hood; there is no end to the volumes about Dick Deadshot and the Avenging Nine. These two heroes are deliberately conceived as immortal.

But instead of basing all discussion of the problem upon the common-sense recognition of this fact—that the youth of the lower orders always has had and always must have formless and endless romantic reading of some kind, and then going on to make provision for its wholesomeness—we begin, generally speaking, by fantastic abuse of this reading as a whole and indignant surprise that the errand-boys under discussion do not read "The Egoist" and "The Master Builder." It is the custom, particularly among magistrates, to attribute half the crimes of the Metropolis to cheap novelettes. If some grimy urchin runs away with an apple, the magistrate shrewdly points out that the child's knowledge that apples appease hunger is traceable to some curious literary researches. The boys themselves, when penitent, frequently accuse the novelettes with great bitterness, which is only to be expected from young people possessed of no little native humour. If I had forged a will, and could obtain sympathy by tracing the incident to the influence of Mr. George Moore's novels, I should find the greatest entertainment in the diversion. At any rate, it is firmly fixed in the minds of most people that gutter-boys, unlike everybody else in the community, find their principal motives for conduct in printed books.

Now it is quite clear that this objection, the objection brought by magistrates, has nothing to do with literary merit. Bad story writing is not a crime. Mr. Hall Caine walks the streets openly, and cannot be put in prison for an anticlimax. The objection rests upon the theory that the tone of the mass of boys' novelettes is criminal and degraded, appealing to low cupidity and low cruelty. This is the magisterial theory, and this is rubbish.

So far as I have seen them, in connection with the dirtiest book-stalls in the poorest districts, the facts are simply these: The whole bewildering mass of vulgar juvenile literature is concerned with adventures, rambling, disconnected and endless. It does not express any passion of any sort, for there is no human character of any sort. It runs eternally in certain grooves of local and historical type: the medieval knight, the eighteenth-century duellist, and the modern cowboy, recur with the same stiff simplicity as the conventional human figures in an Oriental pattern. I can quite as easily imagine a human being kindling wild appetites by the contemplation of his Turkey carpet as by such dehumanized and naked narrative as this.

Among these stories there are a certain number which deal sympathetically with the adventures of robbers, outlaws and pirates, which present in a dignified and romantic light thieves and murderers like Dick Turpin and Claude Duval. That is to say, they do precisely the same thing as Scott's "Ivanhoe," Scott's "Rob Roy," Scott's "Lady of the Lake," Byron's "Corsair," Wordsworth's "Rob Roy's Grave," Stevenson's "Macaire," Mr. Max Pemberton's "Iron Pirate," and a thousand more works distributed systematically as prizes and Christmas presents. Nobody imagines that an admiration of Locksley in "Ivanhoe" will lead a boy to shoot Japanese arrows at the deer in Richmond

Park; no one thinks that the incautious opening of Wordsworth at the poem on Rob Roy will set him up for life as a blackmailer. In the case of our own class, we recognise that this wild life is contemplated with pleasure by the young, not because it is like their own life, but because it is different from it. It might at least cross our minds that, for whatever other reason the errand-boy reads "The Red Revenge," it really is not because he is dripping with the gore of his own friends and relatives.

In this matter, as in all such matters, we lose our bearings entirely by speaking of the "lower classes" when we mean humanity minus ourselves. This trivial romantic literature is not especially plebeian: it is simply human. The philanthropist can never forget classes and callings. He says, with a modest swagger, "I have invited twenty-five factory hands to tea." If he said, "I have invited twenty-five chartered accountants to tea," everyone would see the humour of so simple a classification. But this is what we have done with this lumberland of foolish writing: we have probed, as if it were some monstrous new disease, what is, in fact, nothing but the foolish and valiant heart of man. Ordinary men will always be sentimentalists: for a sentimentalist is simply a man who has feelings and does not trouble to invent a new way of expressing them. These common and current publications have nothing essentially evil about them. They express the sanguine and heroic truisms on which civilization is built; for it is clear that unless civilization is built on truisms, it is not built at all. Clearly, there could be no safety for a society in which the remark by the Chief Justice that murder was wrong was regarded as an original and dazzling epigram.

If the authors and publishers of "Dick Deadshot," and such remarkable works, were suddenly to make a raid upon the educated class, were to take down the names of every man, however distinguished, who was caught at a University Extension Lecture, were to confiscate all our novels and warn us all to correct our lives, we should be seriously annoyed. Yet they have far more right to do so than we; for they, with all their idiocy, are normal and we are abnormal. It is the modern literature of the educated, not of the uneducated, which is avowedly and aggressively criminal. Books recommending profligacy and pessimism, at which the high-souled errand-boy would shudder, lie upon all our drawing-room tables. If the dirtiest old owner of the dirtiest old bookstall in Whitechapel dared to display works really recommending polygamy or suicide, his stock would be seized by the police. These things are our luxuries. And with a hypocrisy so ludicrous as to be almost unparalleled in history, we rate the gutter-boys for their immorality at the very time that we are discussing (with equivocal German Professors) whether morality is valid at all. At the very instant that we curse the Penny Dreadful for encouraging thefts upon property, we canvass the proposition that all property is theft. At the very instant we accuse it (quite unjustly) of lubricity and indecency, we are cheerfully reading philosophies which glory in lubricity and indecency. At the very instant that we charge it with encouraging the young to destroy life, we are placidly discussing whether life is worth preserving.

But it is we who are the morbid exceptions; it is we who are the criminal class. This should be our great comfort. The vast mass of humanity, with their vast mass of idle books and idle words, have never doubted and never will doubt that courage is splendid, that fidelity is noble, that distressed ladies should be rescued, and vanquished enemies spared. There are a large number of cultivated persons who doubt these maxims of daily life, just as there are a large number of persons who believe they are the Prince of Wales; and I am told that both classes of people are entertaining conversationalists. But the average man or boy writes daily in these great gaudy diaries of his soul, which we call Penny Dreadfuls, a plainer and better gospel than any of those iridescent ethical paradoxes that the fashionable change as often as their bonnets. It may be a very limited aim in morality to shoot a "many-faced and fickle traitor," but at least it is a better aim than to be a many-faced and fickle traitor, which is a simple summary of a good many modern systems from Mr. d'Annunzio's downwards. So long as the coarse and thin texture of mere current popular romance is not touched by a paltry culture it will never be vitally immoral. It is always on the side of life. The poor—the slaves who really stoop under the burden of life—have often been mad, scatter-brained and cruel, but never hopeless. That is a class privilege, like cigars. Their drivelling literature will always be a "blood and thunder" literature, as simple as the thunder of heaven and the blood of men.

A DEFENCE OF UGLY THINGS

THERE are some people who state that the exterior, sex, or physique of another person is indifferent to them, that they care only for the communion of mind with mind; but these people need not detain us. There are some statements that no one ever thinks of believing, however often they are made.

But while nothing in this world would persuade us that a great friend of Mr. Forbes Robertson, let us say, would experience no surprise or discomfort at seeing him enter the room in the bodily form of Mr. Chaplin, there is a confusion constantly made between being attracted by exterior, which is natural and universal, and being attracted by what is called physical beauty, which is not entirely natural and not in the least universal. Or rather, to speak more strictly, the conception of physical beauty has been narrowed to mean a certain kind of physical beauty which no more exhausts the possibilities of external attractiveness than the respectability of a Clapham builder exhausts the possibilities of moral attractiveness.

The tyrants and deceivers of mankind in this matter have been the Greeks. All their splendid work for civilization ought not to have wholly blinded us to the fact of their great and terrible sin against the variety of life. It is a remarkable fact that while the Jews have long ago been rebelled against and accused of blighting the world with a stringent and one-sided ethical standard, nobody has noticed that the Greeks have committed us to an infinitely more horrible asceticism—an asceticism of the fancy, a worship of one æsthetic type alone. Jewish severity had at least common-sense as its basis; it recognised that men lived in a world of fact, and that if a man married within the degrees of blood certain consequences might follow. But they did not starve their instinct for contrasts and combinations; their prophets gave two wings to the ox and any number of eyes to the cherubim with all the riotous ingenuity of Lewis Carroll. But the Greeks carried their police regulation into elfland; they vetoed not the actual adulteries of the earth but the wild weddings of ideas, and forbade the banns of thought.

It is extraordinary to watch the gradual emasculation of the monsters of Greek myth under the pestilent influence of the Apollo Belvedere. The chimæra was a creature of whom any healthy-minded people would have been proud; but when we see it in Greek pictures we feel inclined to tie a ribbon round its neck and give it a saucer of milk. Who ever feels that the giants in Greek art and poetry were really big—big as some folk-lore giants have been? In some Scandinavian story a hero walks for miles along a mountain ridge, which eventually turns out to be the bridge of the giant's nose. That is what we should call, with a calm conscience, a large giant. But this earthquake fancy terrified the Greeks, and their terror has terrified all mankind out of their natural love of size, vitality, variety, energy, ugliness. Nature intended every human face, so long as it was forcible, individual, and expressive, to be regarded as distinct from all others, as a poplar is distinct from an oak, and an apple-tree from a willow. But what the Dutch gardeners did for trees the Greeks did for the human form; they lopped away its living and sprawling features to give it a certain academic shape; they hacked off noses and pared down chins with a ghastly horticultural calm. And they have really succeeded so far as to make us call some of the most powerful and endearing faces ugly, and some of the most silly and repulsive faces beautiful. This disgraceful *via media*, this pitiful sense of dignity, has bitten far deeper into the soul of modern civilization than the external and practical Puritanism of Israel. The Jew at the worst told a man to dance in fetters; the Greek put an exquisite vase upon his head and told him not to move.

Scripture says that one star differeth from another in glory, and the same conception applies to noses. To insist that one type of face is ugly because it differs from that of the Venus of Milo is to look at it entirely in a misleading light. It is strange that we should resent people differing from ourselves; we should resent much more violently their resembling ourselves. This principle has made a sufficient hash of literary criticism, in which it is always the custom to complain of the lack of sound logic in a fairy tale, and the entire absence of true oratorical power in a three-act farce. But to call another man's face ugly because it powerfully expresses another man's soul is like complaining that a cabbage has not two legs. If we did so, the only course for the cabbage would be to point out with severity, but with some show of truth, that we were not a beautiful green all over.

But this frigid theory of the beautiful has not succeeded in conquering the art of the world, except in name. In some quarters, indeed, it has never held sway. A glance at Chinese dragons or Japanese gods will show how independent are Orientals of the conventional idea of facial and bodily regularity, and how keen and fiery is their enjoyment of real beauty, of goggle eyes, of sprawling claws, of gaping mouths and writhing coils. In the Middle Ages men broke away from the Greek standard of beauty, and lifted up in adoration to heaven great towers, which seemed alive with dancing apes and devils. In the full summer of technical artistic perfection the revolt was carried to its real consummation in the study of the faces of men. Rembrandt declared the sane and manly gospel that a man was dignified, not when he was like a Greek god, but when he had a strong, square nose like a cudgel, a boldly-blocked head like a helmet, and a jaw like a steel trap.

This branch of art is commonly dismissed as the grotesque. We have never been able to understand why it should be humiliating to be laughable, since it is giving an elevated artistic pleasure to others. If a gentleman who saw us in the street were suddenly to burst into tears at the mere thought of our existence, it might be considered disquieting and uncomplimentary; but laughter is not uncomplimentary. In truth, however, the phrase "grotesque" is a misleading description of ugliness in art. It does not follow that either the Chinese dragons or the Gothic gargoyles or the goblinish old women of Rembrandt were in the least intended to be comic. Their extravagance was not the extravagance of satire, but simply the extravagance of vitality; and here lies the whole key of the place of ugliness in æsthetics. We like to see a crag jut out in shameless decision from the cliff, we like to see the red pines stand up hardily upon a high cliff, we like to see a chasm cloven from end to end of a mountain. With equally noble enthusiasm we like to see a nose jut out decisively, we like to see the red hair of a friend stand up hardily in bristles upon his head, we like to see his mouth broad and clean cut like the mountain crevasse. At least some of us like all this; it is not a question of humour. We do not burst with amusement at the first sight of the pines or the chasm; but we like them because they are expressive of the dramatic stillness of Nature, her bold experiments, her definite departures, her fearlessness and savage pride in her children. The moment we have snapped the spell of conventional beauty, there are a million beautiful faces waiting for us everywhere, just as there are a million beautiful spirits.

THE PERFECT GAME

WE have all met the man who says that some odd things have happened to him, but that he does not really believe that they were supernatural. My own position is the opposite of this. I believe in the supernatural as a matter of intellect and reason, not as a matter of personal experience. I do not see ghosts; I only see their inherent probability. But it is entirely a matter of the mere intelligence, not even of the motions; my nerves and body are altogether of this earth, very earthy. But upon people of this temperament one weird incident will often leave a peculiar impression. And the weirdest circumstance that ever occurred to me occurred a little while ago. It consisted in nothing less than my playing a game, and playing it quite well for some seventeen consecutive minutes. The ghost of my grandfather would have astonished me less.

On one of these blue and burning afternoons I found myself, to my inexpressible astonishment, playing a game called croquet. I had imagined that it belonged to the epoch of Leach and Anthony Trollope, and I had neglected to provide myself with those very long and luxuriant side whiskers which are really essential to such a scene. I played it with a man whom we will call Parkinson, and with whom I had a semi-philosophical argument which lasted through the entire contest. It is deeply implanted in my mind that I had the best of the argument; but it is certain and beyond dispute that I had the worst of the game.

"Oh, Parkinson, Parkinson!" I cried, patting him affectionately on the head with a mallet, "how far you really are from the pure love of the sport—you who can play. It is only we who play badly who love the Game itself. You love glory; you love applause; you love the earthquake voice of victory; you do not love croquet. You do not love croquet until you love being beaten at croquet. It is we the bunglers who adore the occupation in the abstract. It is we to whom it is art for art's sake. If we may see the face of Croquet herself (if I may so express myself) we are content to see her face turned upon us in anger. Our play is called amateurish; and we wear proudly the name of amateur, for amateurs is but the French for Lovers. We accept all adventures from our Lady, the most disastrous or the most dreary. We wait outside her iron gates (I allude to the hoops), vainly essaying to enter. Our devoted balls, impetuous and full of chivalry, will not be confined within the pedantic boundaries of the mere croquet ground. Our balls seek honour in the ends of the earth; they turn up in the flower-beds and the conservatory; they are to be found in the front garden and the next street. No, Parkinson! The good painter has skill. It is the bad painter who loves his art. The good musician loves being a musician, the bad musician loves music. With such a pure and hopeless passion do I worship croquet. I love the game itself. I love the parallelogram of grass marked out with chalk or tape, as if its limits were the frontiers of my sacred Fatherland, the four seas of Britain. I love the mere swing of the mallets, and the click of the balls is music. The four colours are to me sacramental and symbolic, like the red of martyrdom, or the white of Easter Day. You lose all this, my poor Parkinson. You have to solace yourself for the absence of this vision by the paltry consolation of being able to go through hoops and to hit the stick."

And I waved my mallet in the air with a graceful gaiety.

"Don't be too sorry for me," said Parkinson, with his simple sarcasm. "I shall get over it in time. But it seems to me that the more a man likes a game the better he would want to play it. Granted that the pleasure in the thing itself comes first, does not the pleasure of success come naturally and inevitably afterwards? Or, take your own simile of the Knight and his Lady-love. I admit the gentleman does first and foremost want to be in the lady's presence. But I never yet heard of a gentleman who wanted to look an utter ass when he was there."

"Perhaps not; though he generally looks it," I replied. "But the truth is that there is a fallacy in the simile, although it was my own. The happiness at which the lover is aiming is an infinite happiness, which can be extended without limit. The more he is loved, normally speaking, the jollier he will be. It is definitely true that the stronger the love of both lovers, the stronger will be the happiness. But it is not true that the stronger the play of both croquet players the stronger will be the game. It is log-ically possible—(follow me closely here, Parkinson!)—it is log-ically possible, to play croquet too well to enjoy it at all. If you could put this blue ball through that distant hoop as easily as you could pick it up with your hand, then you would not put it through that hoop any more than you pick it up with your hand; it would not be worth doing. If you could play unerringly you would not play at all. The moment the game is perfect the game disappears."

"I do not think, however," said Parkinson, "that you are in any immediate danger of effecting that sort of destruction. I do not think your croquet will vanish through its own faultless ex-cellence. You are safe for the present."

I again caressed him with the mallet, knocked a ball about, wired myself, and resumed the thread of my discourse.

The long, warm evening had been gradually closing in, and by this time it was almost twilight. By the time I had delivered four more fundamental principles, and my companion had gone through five more hoops, the dusk was verging upon dark.

"We shall have to give this up," said Parkinson, as he missed a ball almost for the first time, "I can't see a thing."

"Nor can I," I answered, "and it is a comfort to reflect that I could not hit anything if I saw it."

With that I struck a ball smartly, and sent it away into the darkness towards where the shadowy figure of Parkinson moved in the hot haze. Parkinson immediately uttered a loud and dramatic cry. The situation, indeed, called for it. I had hit the right ball.

Stunned with astonishment, I crossed the gloomy ground, and hit my ball again. It went through a hoop. I could not see the hoop; but it was the right hoop. I shuddered from head to foot.

Words were wholly inadequate, so I slouched heavily after that impossible ball. Again I hit it away into the night, in what I supposed was the vague direction of the quite invisible stick. And in the dead silence I heard the stick rattle as the ball struck it heavily.

I threw down my mallet. "I can't stand this," I said. "My ball has gone right three times. These things are not of this world."

"Pick your mallet up," said Parkinson, "have another go."

"I tell you I daren't. If I made another hoop like that I should see all the devils dancing there on the blessed grass."

"Why devils?" asked Parkinson; "they may be only fairies making fun of you. They are sending you the 'Perfect Game,' which is no game."

I looked about me. The garden was full of a burning darkness, in which the faint glimmers had the look of fire. I stepped across the grass as if it burnt me, picked up the mallet, and hit the ball somewhere—somewhere where another ball might be. I heard the dull click of the balls touching, and ran into the house like one pursued.

ON FLAGS

IN recent times the flags of all nations have tended to run to stripes, whether they were the narrow stripes of the American flag or the broad stripes of the French flag. Despite all we say, often truly enough, about the complexity of the modern world, there is a real sense in which modern things tend to simplicity; and sometimes to too much simplicity. In that fashion of tricolours which was started by the more or less rationalistic revolt of the French nation at the end of the eighteenth century, there is much of such harsh simplicity. There is something perhaps of the mathematical spirit of the pure logician; marching into battle under a banner that is like a diagram of Euclid. His nearest approach to heraldry is a picture of parallel straight lines which cannot meet. It is as if there were lifted above the lances and the sabres an ensign in the form of an isosceles triangle or a flag cut in a pattern to illustrate the square on the hypotenuse.

That French flag of the three colours has been so gloriously coloured with heroism and martyrdom and the romance of revolution; with splendid victories and with defeats more splendid than victories, that it has become vividly romantic in retrospect; and more magnificent than all the eagles and leopards of the kings. But it is not at all improbable that those who originally designed it were men moving about in the cold innocence of the dawn of nationalism, who supposed that they were planning something as purely rational as the pattern of a machine. They may have cut up the flag into sections as they cut up the country into departments, ignoring the romantic traditions of the old provinces of France. They may have done it as calmly and confidently as they broke up the old crowns and coins of the great duchies into the exact equality of the decimal system. But romance has reappeared, not only in spite of the rational republic, but actually in the form of the rational republic. And the other nations, that have copied France in this as in so many other things, have varied the conception and the colours in ways that are more symbolic than anything required for the practical numbering of the nation. The black and gold and scarlet of the flag of Flanders carries the memory of the lion of Brabant; there is a significant hope of unity in the orange strip at the end of the new Irish flag; it might be called the Unceltic Fringe. And it was not for nothing, nor without another and even better sort of hope in the augury, that even into the new tricolour of Cavour and Garibaldi there crept a chivalric shield bearing the symbol of the cross.

Perhaps this modern simplification in political symbols might be compared not only to the simplification in science but to the simplification in art. Stevenson said that a geometrical problem was an exact and luminous parallel to a work of art; and many of the artists of his period undoubtedly loved to simplify their art to such an extreme. In those days the critics often complained that the pictures of Whistler were mere bands of flat colour, a slab of grey for the sky and a slab of green for the sea; the whole having indeed something of the same flatness as the flags. Whistler, that very militant person, might well be said to have marched into battle waving a tri-colour of grey, black and Chinese white. But here again the same general principle holds; and even simplicity preserved the tendency to variety; and especially to national variety. It was soon found that character could not be simplified for nothing or rationalized out of existence. And in no case was this more marked than in the very countries where science was supposed to be most abstract or art most impersonal. Nothing, for instance, could be more impersonal than impressionism; but anybody studying its origins will receive a very French impression. Both in science and art it was found that even a universal simplification did not get rid of a fundamental division, like the three divisions in the simplest tricolour flag.

But there is a special truth in this symbol which specially affects the intercourse of nations. It may be stated under the same figure of speech. The Belgian flag may be, as Whistler would put it, an arrangement in black and yellow and red, or the Italian a different effect produced by the introduction of white and green. But there are flags that are arrangements in the same colours; only that they are differently arranged. And this is perhaps the nearest metaphor by which we can describe a very vital and even dangerous similarity and dissimilarity. The French republican flag is of red, white, and blue; but so, for that matter, is the Union Jack; so also is the Stars and Stripes. When Napoleon forced the English out of Toulon, when Nelson broke the French at Trafalgar, the glorious battle-flags reared against each other in that heroic combat were both tricolours of the same blended hues. When the victory of the *Chesapeake* raised Old Glory for a moment above the mistress of the seas, it was still a new flag but an old tricolour. And the hearty old English Tories, who loved to sing over their port the patriotic song which ran "Three Cheers for the Red, White, and Blue," would have been considerably annoyed, not to say agitated, if some polite Frenchman had bowed in acknowledgment of this compliment to the Republic and the Revolution. They would have been still more annoyed if some breezy and brotherly Anglo-Saxon from Alabama had expressed his gratification at finding that the old country had got wise to the go-ahead virtues of the Stars and Stripes. All the colours would indeed be the same; all would be familiar with the look of blue or red; and any Anglo-Saxon might, if he liked, compare the blue to the sea which was common to the two nations or the red to the blood that is thicker than water. But the fact remains that what affects people in practice is not the tints they use but the pictures that they make. In this sense form is much more powerful than colour. Men see a sign, an emblem, an object, before they see the polychrome elements that make it up. And, as I have already suggested, these things are an allegory.

What affects men sharply about a foreign nation is not so much finding or not finding familiar things; it is rather not finding them in the familiar place. It is not so much that he cannot find red, white, and blue on the French or American flag; but that he always finds red where he expects blue and blue where he expects white. The actual mixture of human and ethical elements in the different countries is not so very different. The amount of good and evil is pretty much what it is everywhere in the moral balance and mortal battle of the soul of man. In that sense we may say that every nation is an arrangement in black and white. Perhaps it is rather like an unkind historical allusion to say that American history has been written in black and white. And yet that historical allusion would be an excellent historical illustration. All through the eighteenth and early nineteenth centuries America and England were astonished at each other; not because either was complete or consistent, but because each had inequality where the other expected equality. The English knew that they had not got rid of a squirearchy, which many of them already wanted to get rid of; but they said to themselves with satisfaction that if they had squires, at least they did not have slaves. The Americans admitted that they had not got rid of the slaves; many of them admitted it with regret or shame; but they felt that if they had slaves, at least they also had citizens. They felt that, in comparison, England had no notion even of the nature of citizens. These cross purposes can be seen in the great national figures of both nations. An advanced democrat like Jefferson still has slaves. An antiquated Tory like Johnson is yet horrified at slavery. But Jefferson could not conceive how Johnson could submit to an old fool like George III. Still less could he understand the acceptation of aristocracy; as little as the other could understand the acceptation of slavery. We might almost say that in the one case there were lords and no slaves and in the other slaves and no lords. But that sort of misunderstanding always perplexes the mutual understanding of nations. And in no case is this stronger than in the present relations of England and America. I have deliberately taken an old and familiar example, as I have taken an obvious and popular metaphor, to make clear this point about the difference between elements and the relation of elements, between colours and the arrangement of colours. And in these days when people are talking so much about the necessity of peace and international sympathy, I suggest it as one of the problems on which there has been much talking and perhaps not quite enough thinking.

MILTON AND MERRY ENGLAND

MR. FREEMAN, in contributing to the "London Mercury" some of those critical analyses which we all admire, remarked about myself (along with compliments only too generous and strictures almost entirely just) that there was very little autobiography in my writings. I hope the reader will not have reason to curse him for this kindly provocation, watching me assume the graceful poses of Marie Bashkirtseff, but I feel tempted to plead it in extenuation or excuse for this article, which can hardly

avoid being egotistical. For though it concerns one of those
problems of literature, of philosophy and of history that certainly interest me more than my own psychology, it is one on
which I can hardly explain myself without seeming to expose
myself.

That valuable public servant, "The Gentleman with the
Duster," has passed on from Downing Street, from polishing up
the Mirrors and polishing off the Ministers, to a larger world of
reflections in "The Glass of Fashion." I call the glass a world of
reflections rather than a world of shadows: especially as I myself
am one of those tenuous shades. And the matter which interests
me here is that the critic in question complains that I have been
very unjust to Puritans and Puritanism, and especially to a certain ethical idealism in them, which he declares to have been
more essential than the Calvinism of which I "make so much."
He puts the point in a genial but somewhat fantastic fashion by
saying that the world owes something to the jokes of Mr. G. K.
Chesterton, but more to the moral earnestness of John Milton.
This involves rather a dizzy elevation than a salutary depression; and the comparison is rather too overwhelming to be
crushing. For I suppose the graceful duster of mirrors himself
would hardly feel crushed if I told him he did not hold the
mirror up to Nature quite so successfully as Shakespeare. Nor
can I be described as exactly reeling from the shock of being
informed that I am a less historic figure than Milton. I know not
how to answer, unless it be in the noble words of Sam Weller:
"That's what we call a self-evident proposition, as the cats'-
meat-man said to the housemaid when she said he was no gentleman." But for all that I have a controversial issue with the critic
about the moral earnestness of Milton, and I have a confession
to make which will seem to many only too much in the personal manner referred to by Mr. Freeman.

My first impulse to write, and almost my first impulse to
think, was a revolt of disgust with the Decadents and the æsthetic pessimism of the 'nineties. It is now almost impossible

to bring home to anybody, even to myself, how final that *fin de siècle* seemed to be; not the end of the century but the end of the world. To a boy his first hatred is almost as immortal as his first love. He does not realize that the objects of either can alter; and I did not know that the twilight of the gods was only a᾿ mood. I thought that all the wit and wisdom in the world were banded together to slander and depress the world, and in becoming an optimist I had the feelings of an outlaw. Like Prince Florizel of Bohemia, I felt myself to be alone in a luxurious Suicide Club. But even the death seemed to be a living or rather everlasting death. To-day the whole thing is merely dead; it was not sufficiently immortal to be damned, but then the image of Dorian Gray was really an idol, with something of the endless youth of a god. To-day the picture of Dorian Gray has really grown old. Dodo then was not merely an amusing female; she was the eternal feminine. To-day the Dodo is extinct. Then, above all, everyone claiming intelligence insisted on what was called "Art for art's sake." To-day even the biographer of Oscar Wilde proposes to abandon "art for art's sake," and to substitute "art for life's sake." But at the time I was more inclined to substitute "no art, for God's sake." I would rather have had no art at all than one which occupies itself in matching shades of peacock and turquoise for a decorative scheme of blue devils. I started to think it out, and the more I thought of it the more certain I grew that the whole thing was a fallacy; that art could not exist apart from, still less in opposition to, life; especially the life of the soul, which is salvation; and that great art never had been so much detached as that from conscience and common sense, or from what my critic would call moral earnestness. Unfortunately, by the time I had exposed it as a fallacy it had entirely evaporated as a fashion. Since then I have taken universal annihilations more lightly. But I can still be stirred, as man always can be by memories of their first excitements or ambitions, by anything that shows the cloven hoof of that particular blue devil. I am still ready to knock him about, though I no longer think he has a cloven hoof or even a lame leg to stand on. But for all that there is one real argument which I still recognize on his side; and that argument is in a single word. There is still one word which the æsthete can whisper; and the whisper will bring back all my childish fears that the æsthete may be right after all. There is one name that does seem to me a strong argument for the decadent doctrine that "art is unmoral." When that name is uttered, the world of Wilde and Whistler comes back with all its cold levity and cynical connoisseurship; the butterfly becomes a burden, and the green carnation flourishes like the green bay-tree. For the moment I do believe in "art for art's sake." And that name is John Milton.

It does really seem to me that Milton was an artist, and nothing but an artist; and yet so great an artist as to sustain by his own strength the idea that art can exist alone. He seems to me an almost solitary example of a man of magnificent genius whose greatness does not depend at all upon moral earnestness, or upon anything connected with morality. His greatness is in a style, and a style which seems to me rather unusually separate from its substance. What is the exact nature of the pleasure which I, for one, take in reading and repeating some such lines, for instance, as those familiar ones:

> Dying put on the weeds of Dominic
> Or in Franciscan think to pass disguised.

So far as I can see, the whole effect is in a certain unexpected order and arrangement of words, independent and distinguished, like the perfect manners of an eccentric gentleman. Say instead "Put on in death the weeds of Dominic," and the whole unique dignity of the line has broken down. It is something in the quiet but confident inversion of "Dying put on" which exactly achieves that perpetual slight novelty which Aristotle profoundly said was the language of poetry. The idea itself is at best an obvious and even conventional condemnation of superstition, and in the ultimate sense a rather superficial one. Coming where it does, indeed, it does not so much suggest moral earnestness as rather a moralizing priggishness. For it is dragged in very laboriously into the very last place where it is wanted, before a splendidly large and luminous vision of the world newly created, and the first innocence of earth and sky. It is that passage in which the wanderer through space approaches Eden; one of the most unquestionable triumphs of all human literature. That one book at least of "Paradise Lost" could claim the more audacious title of "Paradise Found." But if it was necessary for the poet going to Eden to pass through Limbo, why was it necessary to pass through Lambeth and Little Bethel? Why should he go there via Rome and Geneva? Why was it necessary to compare the débris of Limbo to the details of ecclesiastical quarrels in the seventeenth century, when he was moving in a world before the dawn of all the centuries, or the shadow of the first quarrel? Why did he talk as if the Church was reformed before the world was made, or as if Latimer lit his candle before God made the sun and moon? Matthew Arnold made fun of those who claimed divine sanction for episcopacy by suggesting that when God said, "Let there be light," He also said "Let there be Bishops." But his own favourite Milton went very near suggesting that when God said, "Let there be light," He soon afterwards remarked, "Let there be Nonconformists," I do not feel this merely because my own religious sympathies happen to be rather on the other side. It is indeed probable that Milton did not appreciate a whole world of ideas on which he saw merely the corruptions: the idea of relics and symbolic acts and the drama of the deathbed. It does not enlarge his place in the philosophy of history that this should be his only relation either to the divine demagogy of the Dogs of God or to the fantastical fraternity of the Jugglers of God. But I should feel exactly the same incongruity if the theological animus were the other way. It would be equally disproportionate if the approach to Eden were interrupted with jokes against Puritans, or if Limbo were littered with steeple-crowned hats and the scrolls of interminable

Calvinistic sermons. We should still feel that a book of "Paradise Lost" was not the right place for a passage from Hudibras. So far from being morally earnest, in the best sense, there is something almost philosophically frivolous in the incapacity to think firmly and magnanimously about the First Things, and the primary colours of the creative palette, without spoiling the picture with this ink-slinging of sectarian politics. Speaking from the standpoint of moral earnestness, I confess it seems to me trivial and spiteful and even a little vulgar. After which impertinent criticism, I will now repeat in a loud voice, and for the mere lust of saying it as often as possible:

> Dying put on the weeds of Dominic
> Or in Franciscan think to pass disguised.

And the exuberant joy I take in it is the nearest thing I have ever known to art for art's sake.

In short it seems to me that Milton was a great artist, and that he was also a great accident. It was rather in the same sense that his master Cromwell was a great accident. It is not true that all the moral virtues were crystallized in Milton and his Puritans. It is not true that all the military virtues were concentrated in Cromwell and his Ironsides. There were masses of moral devotion on the one side, and masses of military valour on the other side. But it did so happen that Milton had more ability and success in literary expression, and Cromwell more ability and success in military science, than any of their many rivals. To represent Cromwell as a fiend or Milton as a hypocrite is to rush to another extreme and be ridiculous; they both believed sincerely enough in certain moral ideas of their time. Only they were not, as seems to be supposed, the only moral ideas of their time. And they were not, in my private opinion, the best moral ideas of their time. One of them was the idea that wisdom is more or less weakened by laughter and a popular taste in pleasure; and we may call this moral earnestness if we like. But the point is that Cromwell did not succeed by his moral earnestness, but by his strategy; and Milton did not succeed by his moral earnestness, but by his style.

And, first of all, let me touch on the highest form of moral earnestness and the relation of Milton to the religious poetry of his day. "Paradise Lost" is certainly a religious poem; but, for many of its admirers, the religion is the least admirable part of it. The poet professes indeed to justify the ways of God to men; but I never heard of any men who read it in order to have them justified, as men do still read a really religious poem, like the dark and almost sceptical Book of Job. A poem can hardly be said to justify the ways of God, when its most frequent effect is admittedly to make people sympathize with Satan. In all this I am in a sense arguing against myself; for all my instincts, as I have said, are against the æsthetic theory that art so great can be wholly irreligious. And I agree that even in Milton there are gleams of Christianity. Nobody quite without them could have written the single line: "By the dear might of Him that walked the waves." But it is hardly too much to say that it is the one place where that Figure walks in the whole world of Milton. Nobody, I imagine, has ever been able to recognize Christ in the cold conqueror who drives a chariot in the war in Heaven, like Apollo warring on the Titans. Nobody has ever heard Him in the stately disquisitions either of the Council in Heaven or of "Paradise Regained." But apart from all these particular problems, it is surely the general truth that the great religious epic strikes us with a sense of disproportion; the sense of how little it is religious considering how manifestly it is great. It seems almost strange that a man should have written so much and so well without stumbling on Christian tradition.

Now in the age of Milton there was a riot of religious poetry. Most of it had moral earnestness, and much of it had splendid spiritual conviction. But most of it was not the poetry of the Puritans; on the contrary, it was mostly the poetry of the Cavaliers. The most real religion—we might say the most realistic religion—is not to be found in Milton, but in Vaughan, in Traherne, in Crashaw, in Herbert, and even in Herrick. The best proof of it is that the religion is alive to-day, as religion and not merely as literature. A Roman Catholic can read Crashaw, an Anglo-Catholic can read Herbert, in a direct devotional spirit; I gravely doubt whether many modern Congregationalists read the theology of "Paradise Lost" in that spirit. For the moment I mention only this purely religious emotion; I do not deny that Milton's poetry, like all great poetry, can awaken other great emotions. For instance, a man bereaved by one of the tragedies of the Great War might well find a stoical serenity in the great lines beginning, "Nothing is here, for tears." That sort of consolation is uttered, as nobly as it could be uttered, by Milton; but it might be uttered by Sophocles or Goethe, or even by Lucretius or Voltaire. But supposing that a man were seeking a more Christian kind of consolation, he would not find it in Milton at all, as he would find it in the lines beginning, "They are all gone into the world of light." The whole of the two great Puritan epics does not contain all that is said in saying, "O holy hope and high humility." Neither hope nor humility were Puritan specialties.

But it was not only in devotional mysticism that these Cavaliers could challenge the great Puritan; it was in a mysticism more humanistic and even more modern. They shine with that white mystery of daylight which many suppose to have dawned with Wordsworth and with Blake. In that sense they make earth mystical where Milton only made Heaven material. Nor are they inferior in philosophic freedom; the single line of Crashaw, addressed to a woman, "By thy large draughts of intellectual day," is less likely, I fancy, to have been addressed by Adam to Eve, or by Milton to Mrs. Milton. It seems to me that these men were superior to Milton in magnanimity, in chivalry, in joy of life, in the balance of sanity and subtlety, in everything except the fact (not wholly remote from literary criticism) that they did not write so well as he did. But they wrote well enough to lift the load of materialism from the English name and show us the shining fields of a Paradise that is not wholly lost.

Of such was the anti-Puritan party; and the reader may learn more about it from the author of "The Glass of Fashion." There he may form a general idea of how, but for the Puritans, England would have been abandoned to mere ribaldry and licence; blasted by the blasphemies of George Herbert; rolled in the mire of the vile materialism of Vaughan; tickled to ribald laughter by the cheap cynicism and tap-room familiarities of Crashaw and Traherne. But the same Cavalier tradition continued into the next age, and indeed into the next century; and the critic must extend his condemnation to include the brutal buffooneries of Bishop Ken or the gay and careless worldliness of Jeremy Collier. Nay, he must extend it to cover the last Tories who kept the tradition of the Jacobites; the careless merriment of Dean Swift, the godless dissipation of Dr. Johnson. None of these men were Puritans; all of them were strong opponents of political and religious Puritanism. The truth is that English literature bears a very continuous and splendid testimony to the fact that England was not merely Puritan. Ben Jonson in "Bartholomew Fair" spoke for most English people, and certainly for most English poets. Anti-Puritanism was the one thing common to Shakespeare and Dryden, to Swift and Jonson, to Cobbett and Dickens. And the historical bias the other way has come, not from Puritan superiority, but simply from Puritan success. It was the political triumph of the party, in the Revolution and the resultant commercial industrialism, that suppressed the testimony of the populace and the poets. Loyalty died away in a few popular songs; the Cromwellians never had any popular song to die. English history has moved away from English literature. Our culture, like our agriculture, is at once very native and very neglected. And as this neglect is regrettable, if only as neglect of literature, I will pause in conclusion upon the later period, two generations after Milton, when the last of the true Tories drank wine with Bolingbroke or tea with Johnson.

The truth that is missed about the Tories of this tradition is that they were rebels. They had the virtues of rebels; they also had the vices of rebels. Swift had the fury of a rebel; Johnson the surliness of a rebel; Goldsmith the morbid sensibility of a rebel; and Scott, at the end of the process, something of the despair and mere retrospection of a defeated rebel. And the Whig school of literary criticism, like the Whig school of political history, has omitted or missed this truth about them, because it necessarily omitted the very existence of the thing against which they rebelled. For Macaulay and Thackeray and the average of Victorian liberality the Revolution of 1688 was simply an emancipation, the defeat of the Stuarts was simply a downfall of tyranny and superstition; the politics of the eighteenth century were simply a progress leading up to the pure and happy politics of the nineteenth century; freedom slowly broadening down, etc., etc. This makes the attitude of the Tory rebels entirely meaningless; so that the critics in question have been forced to represent some of the greatest Englishmen who ever lived as a mere procession of lunatics and ludicrous eccentrics. But these rebels, right or wrong, can only be understood in relation to the real power against which they were rebelling; and their titanic figures can best be traced in the light of the lightning which they defied. That power was a positive thing; it was anything but a mere negative emancipation of everybody. It was as definite as the monarchy which it had replaced; for it was an aristocracy that replaced it. It was the oligarchy of the great Whig families, a very close corporation indeed, having Parliament for its legal form, but the new wealth for its essential substance. That is why these lingering Jacobites appear most picturesque when they are pitted against some of the princes of the new aristocratic order. That is why Bolingbroke remains in the memory, standing in his box at the performance of "Cato," and flinging forth his defiance to Marlborough. That is why Johnson remains rigid in his magnificent disdain, hurling his defiance at Chesterfield. Churchill and

Chesterfield were not small men, either in personality or in power; they were brilliant ornaments of the triumph of the world. They represented the English governing class when it could really govern; the modern plutocracy when it still deserved to be called an aristocracy also. And the whole point of the position of these men of letters is that they were denying, and denouncing something which was growing every day in prestige and prosperity; which seemed to have, and indeed had, not only the present but the future on its side. The only thing it had not got on its side was the ancient tradition of the English populace. That populace was being more and more harried by evictions and enclosures, that its old common lands and yeomen freeholds might be added to the enormous estates of the all-powerful aristocracy. One of the Tory rebels has himself made that infamy immortal in the great lines of the "Deserted Village." At least, it is immortal in the sense that it can never now be lost for lovers of English literature; but even this record was for a long time lost to the public by under-valuation and neglect. In recent times the "Deserted Village" was very much of a deserted poem. But of that I may have occasion to speak later. The point for the moment is that the psychology of these men, in its evil as well as its good, is to be interpreted not so much in terms of a lingering loyalty as of a frustrated revolution. Some of them had, of course, elements of extravagance and morbidity peculiar to their own characters; but they grew ten times more extravagant and more morbid as their souls swelled within them at the success of the shameless and the insolence of the fortunate. I doubt whether anybody ever felt so bitter against the Stuarts. Now this misunderstanding has made a very regrettable gap in literary criticism. The masterpieces of these men are represented as much more crabbed or cranky or inconsequent than they really were, because their objective is not seen objectively. It is like judging the raving of some Puritan preacher without allowing for the fact that the Pope or the King had ever possessed any power at all. To ignore the fact

of the great Whig families because of the legal fiction of a free
Parliament is like ignoring the feelings of the Christian martyrs
about Nero, because of the legal fiction that the Imperator was
only a military general. These fictions do not prevent imaginative persons from writing books like the "Apocalypse" or books
like "Gulliver's Travels."

I will take only one example of what I mean by this purely
literary misunderstanding: an example from "Gulliver's Travels"
itself. The case of the under-valuation of Swift is a particularly
subtle one, for Swift was really unbalanced as an individual,
which has made it much easier for critics not to keep the rather
delicate balance of justice about him. There is a superficial case
for saying he was mad, apart from the physical accident of his
madness; but the point is that even those who have realized
that he was sometimes mad with rage have not realized what he
was in a rage with. And there is a curious illustration of this in
the conclusion of the story of Gulliver. Everyone remembers the
ugly business about the Yahoos, and the still uglier business
about the real human beings who reminded the returned traveller
of Yahoos; how Gulliver shrank at first from his friends, and
would only gradually consent to sit near his wife. And everybody remembers the picturesque but hostile sketch which
Thackeray gives of the satire and the satirist; of Swift as the
black and evil blasphemer sitting down to write his terrible allegory, of which the only moral is that all things are, and always
must be, valueless and vile. I say that everybody remembers both
these literary passages; but, indeed, I fear that many remember
the critical who do not really remember the creative passage, and
that many have read Thackeray who have not read Swift.

Now it is here that purely literary criticism has a word to
say. A man of letters may be mad or sane in his cerebral constitution; he may be right or wrong in his political antipathies; he
may be anything we happen to like or dislike from our own individual standpoint. But there is one thing to which a man of
letters has a right, whatever he is, and that is a fair critical com-

prehension of any particular literary effect which he obviously aims at and achieves. He has a right to his climax, and a right not to be judged without reference to his climax. It would not be fair to leave out the beautiful last lines of "Paradise Lost" as mere bathos; without realizing that the poet had a fine intention in allowing that conclusion, after all the thunder and the trumps of doom, to fall and fade away on a milder note of mercy and reasonable hope. It would not be fair to stigmatize the incident of Ignorance, damned at the very doors of Heaven at the end of Bunyan's book, as a mere blot of black Calvinist cruelty and spite, without realizing that the writer fully intended its fearful irony, like a last touch of the finger of fear. But this justice which is done to the Puritan masters of imagination has hardly been done to the great Tory masters of irony. No critic I have read has noticed the real point and climax of that passage about the Yahoos. Swift leads up to it ruthlessly enough, for an artist of that sort is often ruthless; and it is increased by his natural talent for a sort of mad reality of detail, as in his description of the slowly diminished distance between himself and his wife at the dinner-table. But he was working up to something that he really wished to say, something which was well worth saying, but which few seem to have thought worth hearing. He suggests that he gradually lost the loathing for humanity with which the Yahoo parallel had inspired him, that although men are in many ways petty and animal, he came to feel them to be normal and tolerable; that the sense of their unworthiness now very seldom returns; and indeed that there is only one thing that revives it. If one of these creatures exhibits Pride.

That is the voice of Swift; and the cry arraigning aristocracy. It is natural for a monkey to collect nuts, and it may be pardonable for John Churchill to collect guineas. But to think that John Churchill can be proud of his heap of guineas, can convert them into stars and coronets, and can carry that calm and classic face disdainful above the multitude! It is natural for she-monkeys to be mated somehow; but to think that the Duchess of Yarmouth is proud of being the Duchess of Yarmouth! It may not be surprising that the nobility should have scrambled like screaming Yahoos for the rags and ribbons of the Revolution, tripping up and betraying anybody and everybody in turn, with every dirty trick of treason, for anything and everything they could get. But that those of them who had got everything should then despise those who had got nothing, that the rich should sneer at the poor for having no part of the plunder, that this oligarchy of Yahoos should actually feel superior to any-thing or anybody—that does move the prophet of the losing side to an indignation which is something much deeper and nobler than the negative flippancies that we call blasphemy. Swift was perhaps more of a Jeremiah than an Isaiah, and a faulty Jeremiah at that; but in his great climax of his grim satire he is none the less a seer and a speaker of the things of God; because he gives the testimony of the strongest and most searching of human intellects to the profound truth of the meanness and imbecility of pride.

And the other men of the same tradition had essentially the same instinct. Johnson was in many ways unjust to Swift, just as Cobbett was afterwards unjust to Johnson. But looking back up the perspective of history we can all see that those three great men were all facing the same way; that they all regretted the rise of a rapacious and paganized commercial aristocracy, and its conquest over the old popular traditions, which some would call popular prejudices. When Johnson said that the devil was the first Whig, he might have merely varied the phrase by saying that he was the first aristocrat. For the men of this Tory tradi-tion, in spirit if not in definition, distinguished between the privilege of monarchy and that of the new aristocracy by a very tenable test. The mark of aristocracy is ambition. The king can-not be ambitious. We might put it now by saying that mon-archy is authority; but in its essence aristocracy is always an-archy. But the men of that school did not criticize the oligarch merely as a rebel against those above; they were well aware of his activities as an oppressor of those below. This aspect, as has already been noted, was best described by a friend of Johnson, for whom Johnson had a very noble and rather unique appreciation—Oliver Goldsmith.

I hope that the author of an admirable study of Mr. Belloc in the "London Mercury" will not think that I am merely traversing one of his criticisms if I venture to add something to it. He used the phrase that Mr. Belloc had been anticipated by Disraeli in his view of England as having evolved into a Venetian oligarchy. The truth is that Disraeli was anticipated by Bolingbroke and the many highly intelligent men who agreed with him; and not least by Goldsmith. The whole view, including the very parallel with Venice, can be found stated with luminous logic and cogency in the "Vicar of Wakefield." And Goldsmith attacked the problem entirely from the popular side. Nobody can mistake his Toryism for a snobbish submission to a privilege or title:

> Princes and lords may flourish or may fade—
> A breath can make them, as a breath has made:
> But a bold peasantry, their country's pride,
> When once destroy'd can never be supplied.

I hope he was wrong; but I sometimes have a horrible feeling that he may have been right.

But I have here, thank God, no cause for touching upon modern politics. I was educated, as much as my critic, in the belief that Whiggism was a pure deliverance; and I hope I am still as willing as he to respect Puritans for their individual virtue as well as for their individual genius. But it moves all my memories of the unmorality of the 'nineties to be charged with indifference to the importance of being earnest. And it is for the sake of English literature that I protest against the suggestion that we had no purity except Puritanism, or that only a man like the author of "Paradise Lost" could manage to be on the side of the angels.

On Peace Day I set up outside my house two torches, and twined them with laurel; because I thought at least there was nothing pacifist about laurel. But that night, after the bonfire and the fireworks had faded, a wind grew and blew with gathering violence, blowing away the rain. And in the morning I found one of the laurelled posts torn off and lying at random on the rainy ground; while the other still stood erect, green and glittering in the sun. I thought that the pagans would certainly have called it an omen; and it was one that strangely fitted my own sense of some great work half fulfilled and half frustrated. And I thought vaguely of that man in Virgil, who prayed that he might slay his foe and return to his country; and the gods heard half the prayer, and the other half was scattered to the winds. For I knew we were right to rejoice; since the tyrant was indeed slain and his tyranny fallen for ever; but I know not when we shall find our way back to our own land.

THE GARDEN OF THE SEA

ONE sometimes hears from persons of the chillier type of culture the remark that plain country people do not appreciate the beauty of the country. This is an error rooted in the intellectual pride of mediocrity; and is one of the many examples of a truth in the idea that extremes meet. Thus, to appreciate the virtues of the mob one must either be on a level with it (as I am) or be really high up, like the saints. It is roughly the same with æsthetics; slang and rude dialect can be relished by a really literary taste, but not by a merely bookish taste. And when these cultivated cranks say that rustics do not talk of Nature in an appreciative way, they really mean that they do not talk in a bookish way. They do not talk bookishly about clouds or stones, or pigs or slugs, or horses or anything you please. They talk piggishly about pigs; and sluggishly, I suppose, about slugs; and are refreshingly horsy about horses. They speak in a stony way of stones; they speak in a cloudy way of clouds; and this is surely the right way. And if by any chance a simple intelligent person from the country comes in contact with any aspect of Nature unfamiliar and arresting, such a person's comment is always worth remark. It is sometimes an epigram, and at worst it is never a quotation.

Consider, for instance, what wastes of wordy imitation and ambiguity the ordinary educated person in the big towns could pour out on the subject of the sea. A country girl I know in the county of Buckingham had never seen the sea in her life until the other day. When she was asked what she thought of it she said it was like cauliflowers. Now that is a piece of pure literature—vivid, entirely independent and original, and perfectly true. I had always been haunted with an analogous kinship which I could never locate; cabbages always remind me of the sea and the sea always reminds me of cabbages. It is partly, perhaps, the veined mingling of violet and green, as in the sea a purple that is almost dark red may mix with a green that is almost yellow, and still be the blue sea as a whole. But it is more the grand curves of the cabbage that curl over cavernously like waves, and it is partly again that dreamy repetition, as of a pattern, that made two great poets, Æschylus and Shakespeare, use a word like "multitudinous" of the ocean. But just where my fancy halted the Buckinghamshire young woman rushed (so to speak) to my imaginative rescue. Cauliflowers are twenty times better than cabbages, for they show the wave breaking as well as curling, and the efflorescence of the branching foam, blind, bubbling, and opaque. Moreover, the strong lines of life are suggested; the arches of the rushing waves have all the rigid energy of green stalks, as if the whole sea were one great green plant with one immense white flower rooted in the abyss.

Now, a large number of delicate and superior persons would refuse to see the force in that kitchen garden comparison, because it is not connected with any of the ordinary maritime sentiments as stated in books and songs. The æsthetic amateur would say that he knew what large and philosophical thoughts he ought to have by the boundless deep. He would say that he was not a greengrocer who would think first of greens. To which I should reply, like Hamlet, apropos of a parallel profession, "I would you were so honest a man." The mention of "Hamlet" reminds me, by the way, that besides the girl who had never seen the sea, I knew a girl who had never seen a stage-play. She was taken to "Hamlet," and she said it was very sad. There is another case of going to the primordial point which is overlaid by learning and secondary impressions. We are so used to thinking of "Hamlet" as a problem that we sometimes quite forget that it is a tragedy, just as we are so used to thinking of the sea as vast and vague, that we scarcely notice when it is white and green.

But there is another quarrel involved in which the young gentleman of culture comes into violent collision with the young lady of the cauliflowers. The first essential of the merely bookish view of the sea is that it is boundless, and gives a sentiment of infinity. Now it is quite certain, I think, that the cauliflower simile was partly created by exactly the opposite impression, the impression of boundary and of barrier. The girl thought of it as a field of vegetables, even as a yard of vegetables. The girl was right. The ocean only suggests infinity when you cannot see it; a sea mist may seem endless, but not a sea. So far from being vague and vanishing, the sea is the one hard straight line in Nature. It is the one plain limit; the only thing that God has made that really looks like a wall. Compared to the sea, not only sun and cloud are chaotic and doubtful, but solid mountains and standing forests may be said to melt and fade and flee in the presence of that lonely iron line. The old naval phrase, that the seas are England's bulwarks, is not a frigid and artificial metaphor; it came into the head of some genuine sea-dog, when he was genuinely looking at the sea. For the edge of the sea is like the edge of a sword; it is sharp, military, and decisive; it really looks like a bolt or bar, and not like a mere expansion. It hangs in heaven, grey, or green, or blue, changing in colour, but changeless in form, behind all the slippery contours of the land and all the savage softness of the forests, like the scales of God held even. It hangs, a perpetual reminder of that divine reason and justice which abides behind all compromises and all legitimate variety; the one straight line; the limit of the intellect; the dark and ultimate dogma of the world.

THE WRONG INCENDIARY

I STOOD looking at the Coronation Procession—I mean the one in Beaconsfield; not the rather elephantine imitation of it which, I believe, had some success in London—and I was seriously impressed. Most of my life is passed in discovering with a deathly surprise that I was quite right. Never before had I realised how right I was in maintaining that the small area expresses the real patriotism: the smaller the field the taller the tower. There were things in our local procession that did not (one might even reverently say, could not) occur in the London procession. One of the most prominent citizens in our procession (for instance) had his face blacked. Another rode on a pony which wore pink and blue trousers. I was not present at the Metropolitan affair, and therefore my assertion is subject to such correction as the eyewitness may always offer to the absentee. But I believe with some firmness that no such features occurred in the London pageant.

But it is not of the local celebration that I would speak, but of something that occurred before it. In the field beyond the end of my garden the materials for a bonfire had been heaped; a hill of every kind of rubbish and refuse and things that nobody wants; broken chairs, dead trees, rags, shavings, newspapers, new religions, in pamphlet form, reports of the Eugenic Congress, and so on. All this refuse, material and mental, it was our purpose to purify and change to holy flame on the day when the King was crowned. The following is an account of the rather strange thing that really happened. I do not know whether it was any sort of symbol; but I narrate it just as it befell.

In the middle of the night I woke up slowly and listened to what I supposed to be the heavy crunching of a cart-wheel along a road of loose stones. Then it grew louder, and I thought somebody was shooting out cartloads of stones; then it seemed as if the shock was breaking big stones into pieces. Then I realised that under this sound there was also a strange, sleepy, almost inaudible roar; and that on top of it every now and then came pigmy pops like a battle of penny pistols. Then I knew what it was. I went to the window; and a great firelight flung across two meadows smote me where I stood. "Oh, my holy aunt," I thought, "they've mistaken the Coronation Day."

And yet when I eyed the transfigured scene it did not seem exactly like a bonfire or any ritual illumination. It was too chaotic, and too close to the houses of the town. All one side of a cottage was painted pink with the giant brush of flame; the next side, by contrast, was painted as black as tar. Along the front of this ran a blackening rim or rampart edged with a restless red ribbon that danced and doubled and devoured like a scarlet snake; and beyond it was nothing but a deathly fulness of light.

I put on some clothes and went down the road; all the dull or startling noises in that din of burning growing louder and louder as I walked. The heaviest sound was that of an incessant cracking and crunching, as if some giant with teeth of stone was breaking up the bones of the world. I had not yet come within sight of the real heart and habitat of the fire; but the strong red light, like an unnatural midnight sunset, powdered the greyest grass with gold and flushed the few tall trees up to the last fingers of their foliage. Behind them the night was black and cavernous; and one could only trace faintly the ashen horizon beyond the dark and magic Wilton Woods. As I went, a workman on a bicycle shot a rood past me; then staggered from his machine and shouted to me to tell him where the fire was. I answered that I was going to see, but thought it was the cottages by the wood-yard. He said, "My God!" and vanished.

A little farther on I found grass and pavement soaking and flooded, and the red and yellow flames repainted in pools and puddles. Beyond were dim huddles of people and a small distant voice shouting out orders. The fire-engines were at work. I went on among the red reflections, which seemed like subterranean fires; I had a singular sensation of being in a very important dream. Oddly enough, this was increased when I found that most of my friends and neighbours were entangled in the crowd. Only in dreams do we see familiar faces so vividly against a black background of midnight. I was glad to find (for the workman cyclist's sake) that the fire was not in the houses by the wood-yard, but in the wood-yard itself. There was no fear for human life, and the thing was seemingly accidental; though there were the usual ugly whispers about rivalry and revenge. But for all that I could not shake off my dream-drugged soul a swollen, tragic, portentous sort of sensation, that it all had something to do with the crowning of the English King, and the glory or the end of England. It was not till I saw the puddles and the ashes in broad daylight next morning that I was fundamentally certain that my midnight adventure had not happened outside this world.

But I was more arrogant than the ancient Emperors Pharaoh or Nebuchadnezzar; for I attempted to interpret my own dream. The fire was feeding upon solid stacks of unused beech or pine, grey and white piles of virgin wood. It was an orgy of mere waste; thousands of good things were being killed before they had ever existed. Doors, tables, walking-sticks, wheelbarrows, wooden swords for boys, Dutch dolls for girls—I could hear the cry of each uncreated thing as it expired in the flames. And then I thought of that other noble tower of needless things that stood

in the field beyond my garden; the bonfire, the mountain of
vanities, that is meant for burning; and how it stood dark and
lonely in the meadow, and the birds hopped on its corners and
the dew touched and spangled its twigs. And I remembered that
there are two kinds of fires, the Bad Fire and the Good Fire—the
last must surely be the meaning of Bonfire. And the paradox is
that the Good Fire is made of bad things, of things that we do
not want; but the Bad Fire is made of good things, of things that
we do want; like all that wealth of wood that might have made
dolls and chairs and tables, but was only making a hueless ash.

And then I saw, in my vision, that just as there are two fires,
so there are two revolutions. And I saw that the whole mad modern world is a race between them. Which will happen first—the
revolution in which bad things shall perish, or that other revolution, in which good things shall perish also? One is the riot that all
good men, even the most conservative, really dream of, when
the sneer shall be struck from the face of the well-fed; when the
wine of honour shall be poured down the throat of despair;
when we shall, so far as to the sons of flesh is possible, take
tyranny and usury and public treason and bind them into bun-
dles and burn them. And the other is the disruption that may
come prematurely, negatively, and suddenly in the night; like
the fire in my little town.

It may come because the mere strain of modern life is unbearable; and in it even the things that men do desire may break
down; marriage and fair ownership and worship and the mysterious worth of man. The two revolutions, white and black, are
racing each other like two railway trains; I cannot guess the
issue . . . but even as I thought of it, the tallest turret of the
timber stooped and faltered and came down in a cataract of
noises. And the fire, finding passage, went up with a spout like
a fountain. It stood far up among the stars for an instant, a blazing pillar of brass fit for a pagan conqueror, so high that one
could fancy it visible away among the goblin trees of Burnham
or along the terraces of the Chiltern Hills.

THE DICKENS PERIOD

MUCH of our modern difficulty, in religion and other things, arises merely from this, that we confuse the word "indefinable" with the word "vague." If some one speaks of a spiritual fact as "indefinable" we promptly picture something misty, a cloud with indeterminate edges. But this is an error even in commonplace logic. The thing that cannot be defined is the first thing; the primary fact. It is our arms and legs, our pots and pans, that are indefinable. The indefinable is the indisputable. The man next door is indefinable, because he is too actual to be defined. And there are some to whom spiritual things have the same fierce and practical proximity; some to whom God is too actual to be defined.

But there is a third class of primary terms. There are popular expressions which every one uses and no one can explain; which the wise man will accept and reverence, as he reverences desire or darkness or any elemental thing. The prigs of the debating club will demand that he should define his terms. And being a wise man he will flatly refuse. This first inexplicable term is the most important term of all. The word that has no definition is the word that has no substitute. If a man falls back again and again on some such word as "vulgar" or "manly" do not suppose that the word means nothing because he cannot say what it means. If he could say what the word means he would say what it means instead of saying the word. When the Game Chicken (that fine thinker) kept on saying to Mr. Toots, "It's mean. That's what it is—it's mean," he was using language in the wisest possible way. For what else could he say? There is no word for mean except mean. A man must be very mean himself before he comes to defining meanness. Precisely because the word is indefinable, the word is indispensable.

In everyday talk, or in any of our journals, we may find the loose but important phrase, "Why have we no great men to-day? Why have we no great men like Thackeray, or Carlyle, or Dickens?" Do not let us dismiss this expression, because it appears loose or arbitrary. "Great" does mean something, and the test of its actuality is to be found by noting how instinctively and decisively we do apply it to some men and not to others; above all how instinctively and decisively we do apply it to four or five men in the Victorian era, four or five men of whom Dickens was not the least. The term is found to fit a definite thing. Whatever the word "great" means, Dickens was what it means. Even the fastidious and unhappy who cannot read his books without a continuous critical exasperation, would use the word of him without stopping to think. They feel that Dickens is a great writer even if he is not a good writer. He is treated as a classic; that is, as a king who may now be deserted, but who cannot now be dethroned. The atmosphere of this word clings to him; and the curious thing is that we cannot get it to cling to any of the men of our own generation. "Great" is the first adjective which the most supercilious modern critic would apply to Dickens. And "great" is the last adjective that the most supercilious modern critic would apply to himself. We dare not claim to be great men, even when we claim to be superior to them.

Is there, then, any vital meaning in this idea of "greatness" or in our laments over its absence in our own time? Some people say, indeed, that this sense of mass is but a mirage of distance, and that men always think dead men great and live men small. They seem to think that the law of perspective in the mental world is the precise opposite to the law of perspective in the physical world. They think that figures grow larger as they walk away. But this theory cannot be made to correspond with the facts. We do not lack great men in our own day because we decline to look for them in our own day; on the contrary, we are looking for them all day long. We are not, as a matter of fact, mere examples of those who stone the prophets and leave it to their posterity to build their sepulchres. If the world would only produce our perfect prophet, solemn, searching, universal,

nothing would give us keener pleasure than to build his sepulchre. In our eagerness we might even bury him alive. Nor is it
true that the great men of the Victorian era were not called
great in their own time. By many they were called great from
the first. Charlotte Brontë held this heroic language about
Thackeray. Ruskin held it about Carlyle. A definite school regarded Dickens as a great man from the first days of his fame:
Dickens certainly belonged to this school.

In reply to this question, "Why have we no great men to-
day?" many modern explanations are offered. Advertisement,
cigarette-smoking, the decay of religion, the decay of agriculture, too much humanitarianism, too little humanitarianism, the
fact that people are educated insufficiently, the fact that they
are educated at all, all these are reasons given. If I give my own
explanation, it is not for its intrinsic value; it is because my answer to the question, "Why have we no great men?" is a short
way of stating the deepest and most catastrophic difference between the age in which we live and the early nineteenth century;
the age under the shadow of the French Revolution, the age in
which Dickens was born.

The soundest of the Dickens critics, a man of genius, Mr.
George Gissing, opens his criticism by remarking that the world
in which Dickens grew up was a hard and cruel world. He notes
its gross feeding, its fierce sports, its fighting and foul humour,
and all this he summarizes in the words hard and cruel. It is
curious how different are the impressions of men. To me this old
English world seems infinitely less hard and cruel than the world
described in Gissing's own novels. Coarse external customs are
merely relative, and easily assimilated. A man soon learnt to
harden his hands and harden his head. Faced with the world of
Gissing, he can do little but harden his heart. But the fundamental difference between the beginning of the nineteenth century and the end of it is a difference simple but enormous. The
first period was full of evil things, but it was full of hope. The
second period, the *fin de siècle*, was even full (in some sense) of

good things. But it was occupied in asking what was the good of good things. Joy itself became joyless; and the fighting of Cobbett was happier than the feasting of Walter Pater. The men of Cobbett's day were sturdy enough to endure and inflict brutality; but they were also sturdy enough to alter it. This "hard and cruel" age was, after all, the age of reform. The gibbet stood up black above them; but it was black against the dawn.

This dawn, against which the gibbet and all the old cruelties stood out so black and clear, was the developing idea of liberalism, the French Revolution. It was a clear and a happy philosophy. And only against such philosophies do evils appear evident at all. The optimist is a better reformer than the pessimist; and the man who believes life to be excellent is the man who alters it most. It seems a paradox, yet the reason of it is very plain. The pessimist can be enraged at evil. But only the optimist can be surprised at it. From the reformer is required a simplicity of surprise. He must have the faculty of a violent and virgin astonishment. It is not enough that he should think injustice distressing; he must think injustice *absurd*, an anomaly in existence, a matter less for tears than for a shattering laughter. On the other hand, the pessimists at the end of the century could hardly curse even the blackest thing; for they could hardly see it against its black and eternal background. Nothing was bad, because everything was bad. Life in prison was infamous—like life anywhere else. The fires of persecution were vile—like the stars. We perpetually find this paradox of a contented discontent. Dr. Johnson takes too sad a view of humanity, but he is also too satisfied a Conservative. Rousseau takes too rosy a view of humanity, but he causes a revolution. Swift is angry, but a Tory. Shelley is happy, and a rebel. Dickens, the optimist, satirizes the Fleet, and the Fleet is gone. Gissing, the pessimist, satirizes Suburbia, and Suburbia remains.

Mr. Gissing's error, then, about the early Dickens period we may put thus: in calling it hard and cruel he omits the wind of hope and humanity that was blowing through it. It may have been full of inhuman institutions, but it was full of humanitarian people. And this humanitarianism was very much the better (in my view) because it was a rough and even rowdy humanitarianism. It was free from all the faults that cling to the name. It was, if you will, a coarse humanitarianism. It was a shouting, fighting, drinking philanthropy—a noble thing. But, in any case, this atmosphere was the atmosphere of the Revolution; and its main idea was the idea of human equality. I am not concerned here to defend the egalitarian idea against the solemn and babyish attacks made upon it by the rich and learned of to-day. I am merely concerned to state one of its practical consequences. One of the actual and certain consequences of the idea that all men are equal is immediately to produce very great men. I would say superior men, only that the hero thinks of himself as great, but not as superior. This has been hidden from us of late by a foolish worship of sinister and exceptional men, men without comradeship, or any infectious virtue. This type of Cæsar does exist. There is a great man who makes every man feel small. But the real great man is the man who makes every man feel great.

The spirit of the early century produced great men, because it believed that men were great. It made strong men by encouraging weak men. Its education, its public habits, its rhetoric, were all addressed towards encouraging the greatness in everybody. And by encouraging the greatness in everybody, it naturally encouraged superlative greatness in some. Superiority came out of the high rapture of equality. It is precisely in this sort of passionate unconsciousness and bewildering community of thought that men do become more than themselves. No man by taking thought can add one cubit to his stature; but a man may add many cubits to his stature by not taking thought. The best men of the Revolution were simply common men at their best. This is why our age can never understand Napoleon. Because he was something great and triumphant, we suppose that he must have been something extraordinary, something inhuman. Some say he was the Devil; some say he was the Superhuman.

Was he a very, very bad man? Was he a good man with some greater moral code? We strive in vain to invent the mysteries behind that immortal mask of brass. The modern world with all its subtleness will never guess his strange secret; for his strange secret was that he was very like other people.

And almost without exception all the great men have come out of this atmosphere of equality. Great men may make despotisms; but democracies make great men. The other main factory of heroes besides a revolution is a religion. And a religion again, is a thing which, by its nature, does not think of men as more or less valuable, but of men as all intensely and painfully valuable, a democracy of eternal danger. For religion all men are equal, as all pennies are equal, because the only value in any of them is that they bear the image of the King. This fact has been quite insufficiently observed in the study of religious heroes. Piety produces intellectual greatness precisely because piety in itself is quite indifferent to intellectual greatness. The strength of Cromwell was that he cared for religion. But the strength of religion was that it did not care for Cromwell; did not care for him, that is, any more than for anybody else. He and his footman were equally welcomed to warm places in the hospitality of hell. It has often been said, very truly, that religion is the thing that makes the ordinary man feel extraordinary; it is an equally important truth that religion is the thing that makes the extraordinary man feel ordinary.

Carlyle killed the heroes; there have been none since his time. He killed the heroic (which he sincerely loved) by forcing upon each man this question: "Am I strong or weak?" To which the answer from any honest man whatever (yes, from Cæsar or Bismarck) would certainly be "weak." He asked for candidates for a definite aristocracy, for men who should hold themselves consciously above their fellows. He advertised for them, so to speak; he promised them glory; he promised them omnipotence. They have not appeared yet. They never will. For the real heroes of whom he wrote had appeared out of an ecstacy of the ordinary.

I have already instanced such a case as Cromwell. But there is no need to go through all the great men of Carlyle. Carlyle himself was as great as any of them; and if ever there was a typical child of the French Revolution, it was he. He began with the wildest hopes from the Reform Bill, and although he soured afterwards, he had been made and moulded by those hopes. He was disappointed with Equality; but Equality was not disappointed with him. Equality is justified of all her children.

But we, in the post-Carlylean period, have become fastidious about great men. Every man examines himself, every man examines his neighbours, to see whether they or he quite come up to the exact line of greatness. The answer is, naturally, "No." And many a man calls himself contentedly "a minor poet" who would then have been inspired to be a major prophet. We are hard to please and of little faith. We can hardly believe that there is such a thing as a great man. They could hardly believe there was such a thing as a small one. But we are always praying that our eyes may behold greatness, instead of praying that our hearts may be filled with it. Thus, for instance, the Liberal party (to which I belong) was, in its period of exile, always saying, "O for a Gladstone!" and such things. We were always asking that it might be strengthened from above, instead of ourselves strengthening it from below, with our hope and our anger and our youth. Every man was waiting for a leader. Every man ought to be waiting for a chance to lead. If a god does come upon the earth, he will descend at the sight of the brave. Our protestations and litanies are of no avail; our new moons and our sabbaths are an abomination. The great man will come when all of us are feeling great, not when all of us are feeling small. He will ride in at some splendid moment when we all feel that we could do without him.

We are then able to answer in some manner the question, "Why have we no great men?" We have no great men chiefly because we are always looking for them. We are connoisseurs of greatness, and connoisseurs can never be great; we are fastidious, that is, we are small. When Diogenes went about with a lantern looking for an honest man, I am afraid he had very little time to be honest himself. And when anybody goes about on his hands and knees looking for a great man to worship, he is making sure that one man at any rate shall not be great. Now, the error of Diogenes is evident. The error of Diogenes lay in the fact that he omitted to notice that every man is both an honest man and a dishonest man. Diogenes looked for his honest man inside every crypt and cavern; but he never thought of looking inside the thief. And that is where the Founder of Christianity found the honest man; He found him on a gibbet and promised him Paradise. Just as Christianity looked for the honest man inside the thief, democracy looked for the wise man inside the fool. It encouraged the fool to be wise. We can call this thing sometimes optimism, sometimes equality; the nearest name for it is encouragement. It had its exaggerations—failure to understand original sin, notions that education would make all men good, the childlike yet pedantic philosophies of human perfectibility. But the whole was full of a faith in the infinity of human souls, which is in itself not only Christian but orthodox; and this we have lost amid the limitations of a pessimistic science. Christianity said that any man could be a saint if he chose; democracy, that any man could be a citizen if he chose. The note of the last few decades in art and ethics has been that a man is stamped with an irrevocable psychology, and is cramped for perpetuity in the prison of his skull. It was a world that expected everything of everybody. It was a world that encouraged anybody to be anything. And in England and literature its living expression was Dickens.

Dickens may be considered in many other capacities, but let us put this one first. He was the voice in England of this humane intoxication and expansion, this encouraging of anybody to be anything. His best books are a carnival of liberty, and there is more of the real spirit of the French Revolution in "Nicholas Nickleby" than in "The Tale of Two Cities." His work has the great glory of the Revolution, the bidding of every man to be himself; it has also the revolutionary deficiency; it seems to think that this mere emancipation is enough. No man *encouraged* his characters so much as Dickens. "I am an affectionate father," he says, "to every child of my fancy." He was not only an affectionate father, he was an everindulgent father. The children of his fancy are spoilt children. They shake the house like heavy and shouting schoolboys; they smash the story to pieces like so much furniture. When we moderns write stories our characters are better controlled. But, alas! our characters are rather easier to control. We are in no danger from the gigantic gambols of creatures like Mantalini and Micawber. We are in no danger of giving our readers too much Weller or Wegg. We have not got it to give. When we experience the ungovernable sense of life which goes along with the old Dickens sense of liberty, we experience the best of the revolution. We are filled with the first of all democratic doctrines, that all men are interesting; Dickens tried to make some of his people appear dull people, but he could not keep them dull. He could not make a monotonous man. The bores in his books are brighter than the wits in other books.

I have put this position first for a defined reason. It is useless for us to attempt to imagine Dickens and his life unless we are able at least to imagine this old atmosphere of a democratic optimism—a confidence in common men. Dickens depends upon such a comprehension in a rather unusual manner, a manner worth explanation, or at least remark.

The disadvantage under which Dickens has fallen, both as an artist and a moralist, is very plain. His misfortune is that neither of the two last movements in literary criticism has done him any good. He has suffered alike from his enemies, and from the enemies of his enemies. The facts to which I refer are familiar. When the world first awoke from the mere hypnotism of Dickens, from the direct tyranny of his temperament, there was, of course, a reaction. At the head of it came the Realists, with their documents. They declared that scenes and types in Dickens were wholly impossible (in which they were perfectly right), and on this rather paradoxical ground objected to them as literature. They were not "like life," and there, they thought, was an end of the matter. The Realist for a time prevailed. But Realists did not enjoy their victory (if they enjoyed anything) very long. A more symbolic school of criticism soon arose. Men saw that it was necessary to give a much deeper and more delicate meaning to the expression "like life." Streets are not life, cities and civilizations are not life, faces even and voices are not life itself. Life is within, and no man hath seen it at any time. As for our meals, and our manners, and our daily dress, these are things exactly like sonnets; they are random symbols of the soul. One man tried to express himself in books, another in boots; both probably fail. Our solid houses and square meals are in the strict sense fiction. They are things made up to typify our thoughts. The coat a man wears may be wholly fictitious; the movement of his hands may be quite unlike life.

This much the intelligence of men soon perceived. And by this much Dickens's fame should have greatly profited. For Dickens is "like life" in the truer sense, in the sense that he is akin to the living principle in us and in the universe; he is like life, at least in this detail, that he is alive. His art is like life, because, like life, it cares for nothing outside itself, and goes on its way rejoicing. Both produce monsters with a kind of carelessness, like enormous by-products; life producing the rhinoceros, and art Mr. Bunsby. Art indeed copies life in not copying life, for life copies nothing. Dickens's art is like life because, like life, it is irresponsible, because, like life, it is incredible.

Yet the return of this realization has not greatly profited Dickens, the return of romance has been almost useless to this great romantic. He has gained as little from the fall of the Realists as from their triumph; there has been a revolution, there has been a counter revolution, there has been no restoration. And the reason of this brings us back to that atmosphere of popular optimism of which I spoke. And the shortest way of expressing the more recent neglect of Dickens is to say that for our time and taste he exaggerates the wrong thing.

Exaggeration is the definition of Art. That both Dickens and the moderns understood Art is, in its inmost nature, fantastic. Time brings queer revenges, and while the Realists were yet living, the art of Dickens was justified by Aubrey Beardsley. But men like Aubrey Beardsley were allowed to be fantastic, because the mood which they overstrained and overstated was a mood which their period understood. Dickens overstrains and overstates a mood our period does not understand. The truth he exaggerates is exactly this old Revolution sense of infinite opportunity and boisterous brotherhood. And we resent his undue sense of it, because we ourselves have not even a due sense of it. We feel troubled with too much where we have too little; we wish he would keep it within bounds. For we are all exact and scientific on the subjects we do not care about. We all immediately detect exaggeration in an exposition of Mormonism or a patriotic speech from Paraguay. We all require sobriety on the subject of the sea serpent. But the moment we begin to believe a thing ourselves, that moment we begin easily to overstate it; and the moment our souls become serious, our words become a little wild. And certain moderns are thus placed towards exaggeration. They permit any writer to emphasize doubts, for instance, for doubts are their religion, but they permit no man to emphasize dogmas. If a man be the mildest Christian, they smell "cant"; but he can be a raving windmill of pessimism, and they call it "temperament." If a moralist paints a wild picture of immorality, they doubt its truth, they say that devils are not so black as they are painted. But if a pessimist paints a wild picture of melancholy, they accept the whole horrible psychology, and they never ask if devils are as blue as they are painted.

It is evident, in short, why even those who admire exaggeration do not admire Dickens. He is exaggerating the wrong thing. They know what it is to feel a sadness so strange and deep that only impossible characters can express it: they do not know what it is to feel a joy so vital and violent that only impossible characters can express that. They know that the soul can be so sad as to dream naturally of the blue faces of the corpses of Baudelaire: they do not know that the soul can be so cheerful as to dream naturally of the blue face of Major Bagstock. They know that there is a point of depression at which one believes in Tintagiles: they do not know that there is a point of exhilaration at which one believes in Mr. Wegg. To them the impossibilities of Dickens seem much more impossible than they really are, because they are already attuned to the opposite impossibilities of Maeterlinck. For every mood there is an appropriate impossibility—a decent and tactful impossibility—fitted to the frame of mind. Every train of thought may end in an ecstasy, and all roads lead to Elfland. But few now walk far enough along the street of Dickens to find the place where the cockney villas grow so comic that they become poetical. People do not know how far mere good spirits will go. For instance, we never think (as the old folk-lore did) of good spirits reaching to the spiritual world. We see this in the complete absence from modern, popular supernaturalism of the old popular mirth. We hear plenty to-day of the wisdom of the spiritual world; but we do not hear, as our fathers did, of the folly of the spiritual world, of the tricks of the gods, and the jokes of the patron saints. Our popular tales tell us of a man who is so wise that he touches the supernatural, like Dr. Nikola; but they never tell us (like the popular tales of the past) of a man who was so silly that he touched the supernatural, like Bottom the Weaver. We do not understand the dark and transcendental sympathy between fairies and fools. We understand a devout occultism, an evil occultism, a tragic occultism, but a farcical occultism is beyond us. Yet a farcical occultism is the very essence of "The Midsummer Night's Dream." It is also the right and credible essence of "The Christmas Carol." Whether we understand it depends upon whether we can understand that exhilaration is not a physical accident, but a mystical fact; that exhilaration can be infinite, like sorrow;

that a joke can be so big that it breaks the roof of the stars. By simply going on being absurd, a thing can become godlike; there is but one step from the ridiculous to the sublime.

Dickens was great because he was immoderately possessed with all this; if we are to understand him at all we must also be moderately possessed with it. We must understand this old limitless hilarity and human confidence, at least enough to be able to endure it when it is pushed a great deal too far. For Dickens did push it too far; he did push the hilarity to the point of incredible character-drawing; he did push the human confidence to the point of an unconvincing sentimentalism. You can trace, if you will, the revolutionary joy till it reaches the incredible Sapsea epitaph; you can trace the revolutionary hope till it reaches the repentance of Dombey. There is plenty to carp at in this man if you are inclined to carp; you may easily find him vulgar if you cannot see that he is divine; and if you cannot laugh with Dickens, undoubtedly you can laugh at him.

I believe myself that this braver world of his will certainly return; for I believe that it is bound up with realities, like morning and the spring. But for those who beyond remedy regard it as an error, I put this appeal before any other observations on Dickens. First let us sympathize, if only for an instant, with the hopes of the Dickens period, with that cheerful trouble of change. If democracy has disappointed you, do not think of it as a burst bubble, but at least as a broken heart, an old love-affair. Do not sneer at the time when the creed of humanity was on its honeymoon; treat it with the dreadful reverence that is due to youth. For you, perhaps, a drearier philosophy has covered and eclipsed the earth. The fierce poet of the Middle Ages wrote, "Abandon hope all ye who enter here" over the gates of the lower world. The emancipated poets of to-day have written it over the gates of this world. But if we are to understand the story of Dickens, we must erase that apocalyptic writing, if only for an hour. We must recreate the faith of our fathers, if only as an artistic atmosphere. If, then, you are a pessimist, in reading

this story, forego for a little the pleasures of pessimism. Dream
for one mad moment that the grass is green. Unlearn that sinister
learning that you think so clear; deny that deadly knowledge
that you think you know. Surrender the very flower of your
culture; give up the very jewel of your pride; abandon hope-
lessness, all ye who enter here.

BERNARD SHAW AND AMERICA

WHEREVER I wandered in the United States people leapt out
upon me from holes and hedges with the question pointed like a
pistol, with all the promptitude of a gun in the hand of a gun-
man: "How is Bernard Shaw?" It is not surprising that they
should be interested in Bernard Shaw; so are we all, however
much we disagree with him, interested in that now thoroughly
enthroned and authoritative Grand Old Man; and there is some
truth in his own theory that the Americans are especially interested in him because he abuses Americans. It is not surprising, I
say, that they should be intensely interested in Bernard Shaw;
what is extraordinary is that they should be so intensely interested in me in connexion with Bernard Shaw. They seem to suppose that I am his brother or his keeper; though I admit that, if
we travelled together, there might be a dispute among the
schools as to which was the keeper and which the lunatic. Sometimes I am almost tempted to think that Shaw and I are the only
Britishers they have heard of; or perhaps because one of us is
thin and the other fat we figure as buffoons in an eternal dust
and dance, like Dan Leno and Herbert Campbell. By this time I
am driven to go about declaring that I am Bernard Shaw; the
difference is a mere matter of two disguises: of alternative
cushions and a beard.

Well, I hope the association of ideas may be connected with
the cordial admiration and affection I have always felt for the

most genial and generous of Puritans. But, with all that admiration, I cannot deny that in considering America, and comparing it with Shaw, I have sometimes had darker thoughts. I think, I might say I fear, that Mr. Shaw's refusal to visit America extensively is a bad thing for America but rather a good thing for Mr. Shaw. With a sort of filial piety I would keep from him, if I could, the awful truth of how large a part of America shares some of his Shavian notions; and how very common, not to say vulgar, those notions are when seen on so large a scale. The very things which in aristocratic England seem like the rather distinguished oddities of a sage have, in democratic America, become the dull prejudices of a society. Total abstinence in a man like Shaw is an almost elegant eccentricity; but there was nothing elegant about Prohibition, and it was not an eccentricity but a convention. Shaw would find thousands of Americans to take quite seriously his prejudice against tea or tobacco; but their seriousness would only serve to make him absurd.

In that sense, we may even say that Shaw does well to keep out of America; because he is the only American in England. The great Fabian faddist would be horrified if he knew how much of America follows his fads; for these things when they begin really to exist, are not fads but fanaticism. Sometimes I think that if Mr. Shaw did come to America he would take to drink, or rather he would take to drinking; a totally different thing. He would walk down Main Street puffing smoke from an enormous pipe which would not, perhaps, prove to be altogether the pipe of peace. For those old nineteenth-century negations of his, those mere distinctions of disgust, would not long retain their dignity in a world where their ubiquity makes them themselves disgusting.

Mr. Shaw, in his amusing confession concerning his habit of abusing America, says with great pride that he has always denounced America as a civilization of villages or a nation of villagers. I am astounded not at the disrespect to America but at the disrespect to villages. I can imagine no more splendid or soaring compliment to any society of sinful men than to say that it is a civilization of villages. I only feel that it is a much more splendid and soaring compliment than modern America deserves. But in so far as it does deserve it, it is in that fact that it retains some of the democratic tradition, or, as some would say, some of the democratic dream. It is true that a peculiar Puritan type of religion has come to stiffen the village life of America, but it is equally true and very important to notice that this Puritan religion did not originally come from the village life of England, still less from the village life of Europe. Puritanism was originally a thing of the towns, especially of the rich merchants and the first modern capitalists. In fact, the Puritan chapels were distributed then just as the petrol pumps are distributed now. That is, they became numerous, but they never became natural. They never, in the true historic sense, became normal. Puritanism always stood toward paganism or papistry as a petrol pump stands to a tree; it may have a reason, but it has not a root; nor can it grow anywhere of itself.

Anyhow, in spite of this artificial admixture in the ancient agricultural life of mankind, the modern agricultural life of America is still the only real life there is. It is, especially, all that remains of the real popular life. Exactly in so far as men are villagers, men are democrats; in so far as they still live in villages, they are citizens: citizenship has vanished from the cities.

Here indeed appears the whole fallacy of Business Training. The weakness of what is called "useful education" is that it does not propose to teach these villagers something that will widen them, but something that will keep them narrow, or even make them more narrow. It will replace Niagara with a petrol pump; a trickle of oil for a torrent of water. Utilitarianism will limit and localize, exactly as Puritanism did limit and localize, the natural universality of the village. So long as the village is merely the ancient human village, it is dealing with elemental and universal things; with water and fire and the watching of stars and winds, the bearing of children, the mourning for the dead, the whole naked and abstract grandeur of the death and life of men. But so soon as it becomes a modern industrial city, still more a modern technical school, it shrinks and dwindles to little and local things; things peculiar to a particular and already passing epoch; the particular mechanical toys of our time; the particular medical antidotes to our diseases. And the proof of all this is in the practical fact, which almost all intelligent Americans are already beginning to lament.

It can be stated in half a hundred different ways, but perhaps the simplest way of stating it is to say that a perfectly vigorous and intelligent young American, equipped with all the latest devices of mechanics and chemistry, bursting with all the latest business tips about salesmanship and mass psychology, is not an educated man. He is not educated because he has only been educated in all modern things, and not even in all mortal, let alone all immortal, things. In a word, he has not been made acquainted with human things, and that is what we mean when we say that he has neglected the humanities.

Thus Mr. Bernard Shaw's charge of mere rustic and rudimentary ignorance does not really hit the weak point of America; though it may in a sense hit the weak point of Mr. Bernard Shaw. Now I come to think of it, it is odd that a Vegetarian, who lives on the fruits of the earth, should be so much cut off from the earth. It is curious that a man who must often consume the same sort of roots and salads as a peasant, should be so ignorant of a peasantry. True, I do not quite know what food Mr. Bernard Shaw ought to eat, unless it be salt and star-dust and pure oxygen. But anyhow, in regarding America as merely rustic, he does not so much condemn it unfairly as compliment it too much. In so far as America retains certain rural truths and traditions, it is exactly by those, as I shall point out later, that she may yet survive and succeed. But the obvious and outstanding American feature is that even the ruralism is not rural. Something may be due to the omnipresence of machinery; much to the omnipresence of newspapers with their note of town life;

more to the habit of treating a farm not as a farm to feed people, but as a shop from which to sell food. But anyhow the
stranger misses what is meant in Europe by the rural note. Men
are not talking about Land, as they are talking from Siberia to
Connaught about Land; they are talking about Real Estate. I
know it is often insisted that the celebrated Main Street was only
a village; that is exactly what I mean by my much criticized remark that America does not contain a village. In that sense, Main
Street is as urban as Wall Street. The tone of discussion, the type
of success that is discussed, even the type and look and dress of
the men who join in the discussion, strike a European as belonging entirely to the town. I have read in American comic fiction
of the Hick and Hayseed; but I have never seen them in America. Therefore, in the two essays which follow, I must be excused if I use the name of Main Street to express the main bulk
of American popular life. I must be pardoned if I am quite sure
that Main Street is a Street: much more certain than I am that
Gopher Prairie is a Prairie. I may be wrong; but I am not quite
so wrong as Mr. Shaw, when he makes the two monstrous suggestions; first, that America is a world of villages; and second,
that it would be any the worse if it were.

THE CASE AGAINST MAIN STREET

THERE is one aspect of the great American quarrel between Puritans and Pagans, with the Humanists and the Catholics intervening, in which I have a pretty complete sympathy with Mr.
Sinclair Lewis and the attack on Main Street. Mr. Lewis seems to
have lived for a long time on the shady side of Main Street; and
most streets have a shady and a sunny side. I myself have only
lived for a short time on what seemed to me the sunnier side of
Main Street; and I was pretty contented with such a place in the
sun. But there is a shady side; there is even a dark side. And upon

one point the criticism advanced by this famous critic is a fair one.

It was stated to me with great spirit and sincerity by a young journalist from Wisconsin, who told me that he agreed with Sinclair Lewis because the old generation in the Middle West had despised him for liking music and poetry, and considered such things effeminate and even cowardly. Now, in that attitude there really is, or was, a most dangerous delusion, which greatly concerns the fashions and false values of our time. There certainly does or did exist a dim idea, in the minds of many Americans, that a business man is in a special sense a man. It is what is really implied in praising him as a Regular Guy, or a Red-Blooded He-Man, or a hundred per cent. American. Because he has been dealing with materialistic things, there clings to him a faint suggestion of that very different thing: a mastery of materials.

Man subduing matter is rightly regarded as man asserting himself as man. But man dealing in modern commerce is not man subduing matter. He is, on the contrary, a man more analogous to a mathematician or an astronomer, in that he is dealing with things generally abstract and almost invariably remote. If the enterprising huckster who has just sold a hundred shares in rubber were one who had just been hacking his way through a rubber forest, we might excuse, though we might not admire, his masculine swagger at the expense of an intellectual Jew merely playing on a Jew's harp. But even playing on a Jew's harp might be regarded as an athletic and even an acrobatic feat, compared with merely mentioning in Wall Street that a transaction was to be recorded at a certain figure. If a big business man having a big jeweller's shop on Fifth Avenue could be supposed to have dived for all the pearls in the Pacific Ocean, or even climbed the mountains to find rubies and emeralds in their caverns, he might call himself a He-Man and be pardoned for his simplicity in regarding a violinist as less conspicuously He. But a violinist is much more like a smith or a swordsman or a strong manual craftsman than is a man who merely dresses up in shiny clothes and a smile, and buys and sells pearls that other men have dived for and rubies that other men have dug from the mine. This illusion of a sort of strength or sanity in modern business operations is in fact the chief falsity which poisons our present society.

It was all implied, and summed up, in the remark of a typical plutocratic politician, when he called it Normalcy. That famous phrase did contain the whole false suggestion: that the present buying and selling is normal, as the primitive hunting and fishing were normal. As a matter of fact, they are far less normal than modern fiddling or fretwork. The arts are nearer to the crafts, and the crafts are nearer to the soil, than any of them are to the ghastly abstractions and wild unrealities of speculation and finance. In so far as this was an attitude encouraged among Regular Guys, the Guys were really as irregular as a Guy on Guy Fawkes day in England; they were like a Guy made of paper, or stuffed with straw, or wearing merely a mask for a face. In so far as this was the charge brought by men like Mr. Sinclair Lewis against the Regular Guys, the charge was justified. It was not wholly justified; because there were and are other manlier elements in Main Street; and especially a tradition, not altogether dead, of the pioneering and the personal adventures of the days of Huckleberry Finn. But I cannot insist too strongly on this point, for it is the whole point of my political thesis: that the current commercial mode of life is not common human welfare, or even common human warfare. It is a process at best indirect and at worst crooked; often a nightmare and always a dream.

Some Englishmen, I believe, have always been in favour of what they called an Anglo-American alliance. All Englishmen, I hope, have always been in favour of an Anglo-American friendship. Above all, all Englishmen, I most ardently hope, will always be opposed to that most dangerous and degrading of all relations: an alliance without a friendship. Personally, and for reasons related to much deeper matters of national and international dignity, I should be very well contented with a friendship without an alliance. But it is another matter, for any one who understands either national or international things, to make sure that a friendship is really friendly. And in this matter as in many similar matters, there is a bad principle which often expresses itself in even worse practice.

Some people seem to believe that it is possible for any person to steer his way through this world, in perfect sympathy and safety, so long as he selects occasions for praise and not occasions for blame. Unfortunately, the principle of praise, in preference to blame, very often works out like this. The foreign critic, being forbidden to blame anybody, really decides not to criticize or even consider anybody. And then the foreign critic, being forced to praise somebody, judiciously decides to praise himself. This is sometimes called Optimism, and is supposed to be a very cheering sight. In plain fact, the critic gives far more offence by praising himself than by abusing all the aliens in the world. Of this kind, for instance, are the Englishmen who praise everything by calling it English. Such a one is certain that any foreigner will dance with delight on being told that his house or church is really quite English; though he ought to know with exactly what amount of delight he would himself be dancing if he were told that Westminster Abbey is quite Turkish or that Shakespeare's cottage is entirely Prussian.

Another way of falling into the same folly is to declare that the Englishman has all good things, and therefore has goodwill; even goodwill to Americans. Many a worthy sympathizer has supposed that he was praising foreigners when he was obviously only praising English charity to foreigners. Doubtless there are plenty of foreign diplomatists who make the same blunder in the process of praising England; but it is a blunder to be avoided by anybody who is praising anything. It would be almost better to impute ill to our neighbours than always to impute good to our neighbours with an air of imputing good nature to ourselves.

But there is one form of this fallacy which is really a practical obstacle to international sympathy. It is even a practical obstacle to international criticism. It is essentially this: that a man will actually be unable to criticize a foreign nation, because he is unwilling to criticize his own nation, in so far as it is subject to the same criticism. If he began by frankly confessing that his own country had to some extent made the same mistake, he could probably go ahead and really and conclusively prove that the foreigner was mistaken. As it is, he will sometimes be forced cravenly to admit that the foreigner is right, because he is afraid to admit that he himself has ever been wrong.

There are several very practical examples of this very practical problem. For instance, an Englishman, as a European, has a right to complain of the bumptious and purse-proud swagger of some Yankee globe-trotters in Europe. Only he ought to preface his protest by admitting that the same sort of complaint was made about Englishmen in Europe in the days when England had the same mercantile supremacy and the same materialistic mood. After he has said that, he can say anything; he can pursue the vulgar and offensive American with fire and swore of satire and derision and denunciation, and probably find most sensible and responsible Americans agreeing with him. What irritates the normal or rational American is not that he should think Americans blamable, but that he should think himself blameless. I believe this to be a very vital principle of the peace and friendship of nations.

It is therefore essential that Englishmen should be very careful to admit that the real American evil is not so much the result of America breaking away from England as of its having remained only too English. This is so in part, in the *fanciful* nature of finance and commerce. The American tradesman is every bit as romantic as an Englishman. He is in some aspects more than enough of a realist; and yet it is the nature of contemporary commerce that this sort of unreality is a part of reality. We, who propose a return to simpler social relations are always described as reomantics and visionaries and idealists of the impossible. But the truth is that we are the only realists, and the adherents of Big Business are by their very nature unrealists. They have to be unrealists, because so many of their dealings are in unreal wealth or unreal wares. It is of the very nature of finance and speculation to be perpetually taking money out of Lunar Green-Cheeses and putting them into Sunbeam Cucumbers; gambling in Moonshine Consolidated and Mares'-Nests, Ltd.; making profits on merely getting, and then getting rid of, various projects for obtaining figs from thistles and blood from stones. This unreality, in the sense of the remoteness of the ultimate material test, marks a mass of ordinary quite respectable stock-broking; quite apart from any that can be considered in any way disreputable. It is not merely a question of those who start baseless companies, but of those who profit by them in passing without ever knowing for certain if they are baseless or not; without ever dreaming of dealing with the realities they are supposed to represent. But even over and above this question of the unreality of speculation, there is an interesting question involved in the other unreality which is called Optimism. The truth is that the commercialists have to be optimists,—because they live in a world that can so easily go wrong. The business men live in a world of notions; they live in a world of fictions; they live in a world of dreams.

There is a proverb to the effect that farmers always grumble; and it is true that peasants often strike a superficial observer as pessimists. People living close to the land, especially their own land, have a way of talking candidly and caustically about their experiences of life, which does seem almost sulky compared to the sentimental self-encouragement we are used to in journalism and professional politics. It is only when the peasant is known a little better, that it becomes apparent that his free cursing and criticizing of conditions covers a real love of the permanent facts behind them; a solid tenderness for his own soil, a talkative pride in his own knowledge of the tricks of weather or animal life; in

short, that sense of being quite at home which is the origin of
his grumbling as well as of his contentment. But the vital point
is that he is a realist, dealing with realities, and therefore certain that they will remain the same whatever he says about them.
He does not think that a cloud will come across the sun because
he curses the unsufficiency of sunlight; he does not think he will
bring on a thunderstorm by being in a bad temper; he does not
imagine that he can change the wind with a word, or dry up the
dew by confessing to a fit of depression. But the business man
does believe these things, and in his own mad business world he
is right. He knows he *can* cloud the fortunes of some speculation, by speaking against it, or bring on a crisis by permitting a
criticism; or ruin a prosperous season with a whisper, or create a
depression merely by being depressed. Therefore he has to be
an Optimist, poor devil; poor, dear, dreary, miserable devil.

Moses in *The Vicar of Wakefield* has become the type of all
that is unbusiness-like, because he bought a gross of green spectacles. But the Trust Magnate, the type of all that is business-
like, really does have to buy a gross of rose-coloured spectacles.
To see everything pink and pretty is really a necessity of his
nonsensical existence. Hence we find that in America, the home
of this kind of colossal commerce and combination, practically
all their strange sects agree about this strange philosophy of Optimism. Everybody is educated in a sort of permanent ethic of
unmeaning hopefulness, or, as the idiom of the civilization goes,
the duty of "being as cheerful as the cheerfullest man in sight."
There is a great deal in the American character that really does
cheer the soul of man by spirit and example; a great deal of social courage in the way of the self-organization of the populace;
a great deal of instinctive consideration of men as men; a great
deal of honourable pride in hard work; a certain absence of
fundamental cynicism; a certain presence of casual confidence in
strangers. But though I really like Americans myself, I think
their cheerfulness is the most dismal thing about them.

At least it has become a dismal thing, in so far as it no longer refers to the old realities of democracy, but rather to the new unrealities of plutocracy and publicity. It is a proverb that this kind of Yankee is considered very wide-awake. But what is now the matter with him is that he is asleep and dreaming; his wealth is such stuff as dreams are made of, and his little life is rounded with a slump. But the same criticism applies to English Business Government, and generally to that cosmopolitan business Government which now rules us all. Where it differs from a true system of Property, the real condition of Hormatcy to which some give the name of Distributism, is in the simple fact that Distributism is not a dream. It is a project, which may or may not be found practicable by particular people at a particular time. But when it is established, its fundamental facts, like the land or the family, are not affected by what other people say about them. They do not vanish as the result of a rumour or roll away like clouds because somebody relaxes the rigid strain of being optimistic about them. They have a life of their own, and they go on of themselves; and when they are in vigour, there is a free and happy society; in which men are liberated from the horrible slavery of smiling.

THE CASE FOR MAIN STREET

I AM on the side of Main Street in the main. I mean by the statement, not that I prefer Main Street as it is to Main Street as it ought to be, but that I prefer even Main Street as it is to the views of those who think it ought not to be. I mean that if I were driven to the awful—nay, ghastly—alternative of choosing between its critics and itself, I should prefer that it should remain itself. If I were absolutely forced to choose between being a Methodist real estate agent in Gopher Prairie or being an artist, anarchist and atheist in Greenwich Village, I should (in the stern spirit of one bracing himself to terrible renunciations and the facing of a dreadful doom) decide to be a real estate agent. And I should say this even with every sympathy for the artist, because simple people may be at the beginning of beauty, whereas sophisticated people have come to the end of beauty and the end of everything. But when it comes to describing the positive virtues of Main Street, I am in a difficulty, because Main Streeters are unconscious of their virtues. That is the greatest of all their virtues.

There is a difficulty in this sort of international explanation. If I suggest even vaguely that Gopher Prairie is a virtuous village I can see Mr. Sinclair Lewis watching me with irony kindling in his eye and ready to launch the most brilliant wit and blasting satire for my extinction. But the truth is that he and I not only mean two different things by the word "virtuous," but we mean two different things by the word "village." Nothing marks as more absolute the abyss of the Atlantic than the colour and connotation of the word "village." There is no such thing in England, let alone Europe, as a Puritan village. There is such a thing as a Pagan village.

The penetrating pen of the author of *The Spoon River Anthology* noted down as one of the few good points in that rather unpleasing community that the Irish priest had helped those who sought to save the village from the bleak bigotry of "village morality." In that sense there is no such thing in England as village morality. In that sense there is very little except village immorality. Yet Mr. Masters or Mr. Lewis, coming into an English village, would instantly feel the virtues of a pagan village. They would feel a freedom, a good nature, a toleration of the village drunkard and the village idiot. I feel bound, on my side, to see and salute the virtues of a Puritan village. I can see for myself that it is not only Puritan, but also, in the real sense, Republican.

Men imagine their own virtues much more universal than they really are. If the foreigner tells them they are absent from foreign countries, they revolt into a curious error. With the very paradox of humility, they suppose the foreigners to be specially vicious, rather than suppose themselves to be specially virtuous. As I say, it is a beautiful innocence in human nature, but it leads to some very ugly imaginations about human beings. If a Norman peasant works hard, he thinks little of hard work. He even takes hard work lightly. But if he is told that Neapolitan peasants work less hard, he cannot take that lightly, and he generally imagines that the Neapolitans are much lazier than they are.

So it is with the American, if he is congratulated by the Englishman on the very real elements of equality and fraternity that are instantly felt by a man entering America. It is strictly true that an Englishman of any liberality does feel a certain kind of fresh air, from which a certain kind of smell has departed, and the thing that has vanished is snobbishness. But the American will be wildly wrong if he infers from this that the atmosphere of England is merely snobbish. The atmosphere of England is an extremely subtle blend of liberty and aristocracy and a universal belief in courtesy, with a sort of by-product of snobbishness; but a by-product which smells to heaven. But the American says to himself, "What snobs these people must be if they think it odd that folks should be friendly." And he immediately makes a picture of feudal England which is no more like England than William the Conqueror in a waxwork show is like George V taking tea in the drawing-room.

It is always easier to explain these complex cross purposes by concrete cases. I found an exact illustration of what I really like in America. It occurred in a country town where there is a college or university in which I had just lectured. One of the professors was kind enough to say that he liked my line of argument and that it had contained one point that had not occurred to him before. A minute or two later, as I was standing waiting outside the hall, the same professor's chauffeur came up to me in exactly the same manner and said almost exactly the same thing. He said he agreed upon that particular point, but was doubtful upon some other point of controversy. There was absolutely no difference between the tone and gesture and bodily carriage of the professor and his servant. Neither was aggressive; neither was apologetic; neither thought it anything but natural to say something that had just come into his head.

That is what I like in America. That is what is nearly impossible in England. But the trouble is this: that if I say that such an incident in England would be impossible, crowds of untravelled Americans will instantly make up pictures of an arrogant aristocratic England which would be far more impossible. Many might be left with a vague idea that English chauffeurs are not admitted to lectures; or that English chauffeurs cannot read or write and are incapable of understanding lectures; or that English chauffeurs are silent out of terror of their haughty and highborn masters; or that English gentlemen strut about like Prussian Junkers, twirling military moustaches and shouting military orders to miserable chauffeurs.

Nothing of this sort could possibly happen; any more than the other thing could happen. I know exactly what would happen. It is a matter of tone; of social atmosphere; of something that can generally be better conveyed by a novelist than an essayist. Most probably the lady of the house, radiantly receiving the lecturer, might even notice the presence of the chauffeur, or the butler or the gamekeeper or the gardener or some other upper servant. And she would very probably say, with a curious sort of foggy affection in her mind, "Wiggins will take care of you. I do hope you will be comfortable." Then with a sort of running up the scale of laughter, "Wiggins went to your lecture. Wiggins reads quite a lot of books"; all with a curious warmth of pride in her tone, as if she owned the learned pig or the calculating horse or some quite exceptional animal of whom she was rather fond. And Wiggins would at first look sheepish, as if he had been caught stealing books from the library, and grin in an apologetic but speechless manner. And only afterwards when you had agreed with Wiggins about a hundred times that it was a fine day, might he begin to make fragmentary human noises, and you might learn something of what he thought of the lecture. But, anyhow, that is the difference. There is no question, in the ordinary sense, of being overbearing or brutal with such servants. One of the very first things that the small squire will be taught at the age of six is the sacred necessity of being polite to Wiggins. But he will never be the equal of Wiggins; and Wiggins will never act as if he were. That they should both comment on a strange gentleman's lecture, independently, simultaneously, spontaneously, in the same tone and at the same time —that is what does not happen in England and that is what does happen in America.

To say that America is more democratic lets loose a wild confusion of tongues. For democracy, strictly speaking, does not mean ease or equality or comradeship among the people. It means direct government by the people. Now government by the people is a devilish difficult thing to establish at all, at least in a modern complicated industrial State. It is supposed to exist in America; for that matter, it is supposed to exist in England; but its existence can be very easily doubted or disputed anywhere. It is not of the political conception of popular rule that I am talking just now. What exists in America is not democracy, which may or may not be possible. It is equality, which was always supposed to be much more impossible. It is not impossible. As an atmosphere, but an actual atmosphere, the sense of social equality (or if you prefer the phrase, the absence of rank) does exist in America, as it does not exist in Europe. It is not an impossibility; it is not a possibility; it is a positive fact. It exists to show that Jefferson did something, as Islam exists to show that Mahomet did something. It is mixed up with all sorts of abuses and abominations, like other human achievements; but it is achieved.

I will mention another incident which illustrates another aspect of the same thing. It illustrates something impossible in England and possible in America; but the moral is so much more subtle that it might not be understood by Americans any more than by Englishmen. It is only fair to say that it occurred in a

682 THE MAN WHO WAS CHESTERTON

town with no university, a place the reverse of academic. It may be that the man I met was only a freak or adventurer, but I do not think so. Anyhow, I have never met such a freak or had such an adventure in any other land, least of all in my own land. He seemed to think it was quite natural and, if the American reader thinks it was nothing except trivial, my point about the difference is proved.

I had come out of my hotel and was walking, I trust inoffensively, down the street, when a young man stopped and spoke to me. He was shabby, not so shabby as I was, but with that indescribably genuine air suggesting that his shabbiness was due to poverty and not like mine, to natural inefficiency. He was not obtrusive or vulgar; he had a sharp, refined face; he spoke quite quietly and in my own beloved island would have been in some danger of being removed as a lunatic. He said, "Pardon me. May I ask if you are one of our local statesmen?"

I replied politely that I was not one of his local statesmen. I added that if his locality possessed any statesmen, it was more fortunate than most localities are just now. He replied:

"Pardon my curiosity, but something about your appearance suggested to me that you must be a statesman—or else a writer."

This shaft struck nearer home, and I admitted that I had once or twice written things. At this he got quite excited and said, "I also am a writer"; and produced sheafs of papers from his pocket, including press cuttings presumably appreciative of what he wrote. I stood looking through them with blear-eyed urbanity, and we remained thus in conference in the middle of the street, holding up the traffic as it were, while the endless local processions of gangsters or oil magnates streamed or struggled past us. Then he asked, still with a certain delicacy, whether I would mind telling him what sort of things I wrote. I replied vaguely that I had written a lot of rather different things, from shockers and murder mysteries to some little trifles on topics of theology and philosophy.

He held up his hand suddenly, like a traffic signal, and said,

"That's my subject!"

Then he dived again into the sheaf of papers and brought out a photograph of an old man with a very big beard and very big feet, in sandals, walking in the sunlight; a sort of parody of Walt Whitman.

"If you want any philosophy," said my mad friend confidentially, tapping the photograph and talking like a man recommending a tobacconist, "if ever you want any philosophy, that's the man. He lives at Apocalypse Villa on Revelation Hill," or some such address.

I was ashamed of my lack of enthusiasm; one glance at the venerable humbug in the photograph had told me, child of an older and wearier civilization, what sort of philosophy I should get from him. Doubtless there are hundreds like him in all countries, if a few more thousands like him in that country; and it may be that there are thousands like his conversational admirer. He concluded with a truly human touch, by producing a photograph of his son in uniform, a student at West Point. But I was not at that moment thinking of what was curious about him. I was thinking of something much more curious about myself. And I suddenly saw, in a lightning-flash not perhaps to be recovered, what I really like in America—and even in Main Street.

I am not saying anything here about what I like in England. I leave it to be understood how massive and manifold are the great qualities that I should praise in my own house and people; the largesse, the uncommanded charity, the understanding of loneliness and liberty, the humour and the deep soil from which the poets sprang. But there is in the English atmosphere a certain evil, and the mere absence of that atmosphere, when I realized it, startled me like a strange smell. I suddenly remembered, like something a thousand miles away, that if a shabby man had begun to talk to me like that in Fleet Street, I should not even have thought he was a lunatic; I should have thought nothing so noble. I should have thought, I should have been unable to prevent myself from thinking, that he wanted me to give or lend him money.

When I remembered those shamefaced approaches there fell on me from afar the shame that lies heavier on the rich than the poor, and heavier on the lender than the borrower. I remembered a sordid something, and I remembered that I had not remembered it before. A thousand things had crossed my mind while conversing with that amiable lunatic in the street, but it had never even crossed my mind that he merely wanted money. It had never crossed my mind, and it had never crossed his mind. He did not know that there is an atmosphere where such sudden buttonholings are suspect. He did not want anything out of me, except the time and attention of a total stranger; and he never so much as thought that I could think he did.

What could be more natural than telling a total stranger in the street all about your favourite philosophy and your soldier son? He certainly made no attempt to draw any practical advantage from that extraordinary conversation; and I do not think it was ever in his mind. Nor, in that place and time, was it in my mind. And that fact means something if it were rightly studied; something about a social atmosphere that has never been rightly named. There had gone completely out of my head the memory of a certain sort of harassed and humiliated relation of rich and poor. Every genuine Englishman will know what I mean. Every truthful Englishman will agree with what I say.

Now this note, though it be only negative, is very queer; is on the face of it a paradox. There is much more talking about money in America than in England; there is any amount of worrying about money, groping for money, grabbing, stealing and swindling for money in America and everywhere else. A man would be likely enough to stop me in that street to sell me a gold brick or a vanishing oil field; I would not put it past him, in the American phrase, to stick me up for any blackguard form of blackmail or bribery. All those crude forms of crime were potentially there, but there was something that was not there. It was a sort of uncomfortable convention, painfully familiar to more stratified social systems, that the shabby man does not stop the more prosperous unless he is, if not a sort of black-mailer, at least a sort of beggar. That is really the bad side of inequality. It is rather worse when it is a sort of undefined or informal inequality; and the poor man sometimes spoke more freely when he was a slave.

These problems, indeed, can only be dealt with in paradoxes. Listening to the mere talk of Englishmen, a stranger might suppose that nobody ever thought about rank. Listening to the mere talk of Americans, a stranger might suppose that everybody always thought about money. But I believe these impressions are not only profoundly untrue, but pretty nearly the reverse of the truth. Lord Palmerston, when asked to define a gentleman, very shrewdly replied, "a man who never uses the word." Every Englishman knows that it is caddish to be always talking about being gentlemanly. But it is none the less true that the ideal thus protected from verbal vulgarization runs through all modern English history and is the cue to it. We might almost say that the romance of the gentleman has been the religion of the Englishman.

On the other hand, the ordinary American seems ready to talk about dollars to any stray stranger. But he is not always trying to get dollars out of the stray stranger. If he were, the whole social habit would very rapidly be abandoned. In some cases he talks for the sake of good fellowship. In some cases he talks for the sake of talking. Readers of Mr. Lewis will remember that *The Man Who Knew Coolidge* did not exactly imitate the al-leged silence of Coolidge. He talked through a whole book, and he talked a great deal about his business, which was, if I remem-ber right, the furnishing of office fittings. But Mr. Lewis, though a realist, cannot entirely escape reality. A highly intelligent though perhaps unconscious instinct made him pay the poor traveller a very true though perhaps unintentional compliment. It will be remarked that, though *The Man Who Knew Coolidge* talks incessantly and interminably about selling the goods, he does not apparently sell any goods. Still less does he beg or borrow any money. He is an artist inspired by a sort of art for art's sake. He talks for the love of talking; which is something much more generous than the love of money.

That disinterested directness, that assumption that any American can talk to anybody else and talk about money as much as about anything else, is the key to my odd psychological experience in the street. That is why I did in some way feel at ease with the strange man in California, as I might not have felt at ease with a strange man in Camden Town. All nations naturally laugh at each other, and I can, of course, find much that strikes me as odd about that friendly footpad, with his private press cuttings and his photograph of a philosopher. Apparently he found much that was odd about me. He must have looked at me much as he would have looked at a hippopotamus passing placidly through his town, or he would hardly have so wantonly arrested me and accused me of being a statesman.

But, with all my English amusement at his American abruptness, I can see that there was in it a great quality of truth and candour and that my very acceptance of it was an unconscious tribute to something unspoiled and healthy in his strange sociability. It is the breath of something not quite broken or stifled even by the brutalities and trickeries of all that materialism which is the burden of America and the whole modern world; a memory of brotherhood, an assumption of manhood, a sort of good and golden simplicity and spontaneity that recalls even yet the ancient visions of Atlantis as a sort of Utopia and the hope that filled the founding of the Western republics; something not altogether unworthy of that golden Californian air. For the golden age only comes to men when they have, if only for a moment, forgotten gold.

There are men in Main Street, there are men in America, who can forget money even when they are talking about money. They are not expecting money; they are not asking for money; they are not cadging for money. They are talking about money.

It is their subject but not their object. This is their great virtue and I hasten to veil it from them, for it is not good for men to know how good they are.

THE ROMANCE OF RHYME

THE poet in the comic opera, it will be remembered (I hope), claimed for his æsthetic authority that "Hey diddle diddle will rank as an idyll, if I pronounce it chaste." In face of a satire which still survives the fashion it satirized, it may require some moral courage seriously to pronounce it chaste, or to suggest that the nursery rhyme in question has really some of the qualities of an idyll. Of its chastity, in the vulgar sense, there need be little dispute, despite the scandal of the elopement of the dish with the spoon, which would seem as free from grossness as the loves of the triangles. And though the incident of the cow may have something of the moonstruck ecstasy of Endymion, that also has a silvery coldness about it worthy of the wilder aspects of Diana. The truth more seriously tenable is that this nursery rhyme is a complete and compact model of the nursery short story. The cow jumping over the moon fulfils to perfection the two essentials of such a story for children. It makes an effect that is fantastic out of objects that are familiar; and it makes a picture that is at once incredible and unmistakable. But it is yet more tenable, and here more to the point, that this nursery rhyme is emphatically a rhyme. Both the lilt and the jingle are just right for their purpose, and are worth whole libraries of elaborate literary verse for children. And the best proof of its vitality is that the satirist himself has unconsciously echoed the jingle even in making the joke. The metre of that nineteenth-century satire is the metre of the nursery rhyme. "Hey diddle diddle, the cat and the fiddle" and "Hey diddle diddle will rank as an idyll" are obviously both dancing to the same ancient tune;

and that by no means the tune the old cow died of, but the more exhilarating air to which she jumped over the moon.

The whole history of the thing called rhyme can be found between those two things: the simple pleasure of rhyming "diddle" to "fiddle," and the more sophisticated pleasure of rhyming "diddle" to "idyll." Now the fatal mistake about poetry, and more than half of the fatal mistake about humanity, consists in forgetting that we should have the first kind of pleasure as well as the second. It might be said that we should have the first pleasure as the basis of the second; or yet more truly, the first pleasure inside the second. The fatal metaphor of progress, which means leaving things behind us, has utterly obscured the real idea of growth, which means leaving things inside us. The heart of the tree remains the same, however many rings are added to it; and a man cannot leave his heart behind by running hard with his legs. In the core of all culture are the things that may be said, in every sense, to be learned by heart. In the innermost part of all poetry is the nursery rhyme, the nonsense that is too happy even to care about being nonsensical. It may lead on to the more elaborate nonsense of the Gilbertian line, or even the far less poetic nonsense of some of the Browningesque rhymes. But the true enjoyment of poetry is always in having the simple pleasure as well as the subtle pleasure. Indeed it is on this primary point that so many of our artistic and other reforms seem to go wrong. What is the matter with the modern world is that it is trying to get simplicity in everything except the soul. Where the soul really has simplicity it can be grateful for anything—even complexity. Many peasants have to be vegetarians, and their ordinary life is really a simple life. But the peasants do not despise a good dinner when they can get it; they wolf it down with enthusiasm, because they have not only the simple life but the simple spirit. And it is so with the modern modes of art which revert, very rightly, to what is "primitive." But their moral mistake is that they try to combine the ruggedness that should belong to simplicity with a superciliousness that should only belong to satiety. The last Futurist draughtsmanship, for instance, evidently has the aim of drawing a tree as it might be drawn by a child of ten. I think the new artists would admit it; nor do I merely sneer at it. I am willing to admit, especially for the sake of argument, that there is a truth of philosophy and psychology in this attempt to attain the clarity even through the crudity of childhood. In this sense I can see what a man is driving at when he draws a tree merely as a stick with smaller sticks standing out of it. He may be trying to trace in black and white or grey a primeval and almost pre-natal illumination; that it is very remarkable that a stick should exist, and still more remarkable that a stick should stick up or stick out. He may be similarly enchanted with his own stick of charcoal or grey chalk; he may be enraptured, as a child is, with the mere fact that it makes a mark on the paper—a highly poetic fact in itself. But the child does not despise the real tree for being different from his drawing of the tree. He does not despise Uncle Humphrey because that talented amateur can really draw a tree. He does not think less of the real sticks because they are live sticks, and can grow and branch and curve in a way uncommon in walking sticks. Because he has a single eye he can enjoy a double pleasure. This distinction, which seems strangely neglected, may be traced again in the drama and most other domains of art. Reformers insist that the audiences of simpler ages were content with bare boards or rudimentary scenery if they could hear Sophocles or Shakespeare talking a language of the gods. They were very properly contented with plain boards. But they were not discontented with pageants. The people who appreciated Antony's oration as such would have appreciated Aladdin's palace as such. They did not think gilding and spangles substitutes for poetry and philosophy, because they are not. But they did think gilding and spangles great and admirable gifts of God, because they are.

But the application of this distinction here is to the case of rhyme in poetry. And the application of it is that we should never be ashamed of enjoying a thing as a rhyme as well as enjoying it as a poem. And I think the modern poets who try to escape from the rhyming pleasure, in pursuit of a freer poetical pleasure, are making the same fundamentally fallacious attempt to combine simplicity with superiority. Such a poet is like a child who could take no pleasure in a tree because it looked like a tree, or a playgoer who could take no pleasure in the Forest of Arden because it looked like a forest. It is not impossible to find a sort of prig who professes that he could listen to literature in any scenery, but strongly objects to good scenery. And in poetical criticism and creation there has also appeared the prig who insists that any new poem must avoid the sort of melody that makes the beauty of any old song. Poets must put away childish things, including the child's pleasure in the mere sing-song of irrational rhyme. It may be hinted that when poets put away childish things they will put away poetry. But it may be well to say a word in further justification of rhyme as well as poetry, in the child as well as the poet. Now, the neglect of this nursery instinct would be a blunder, even if it were merely an animal instinct or an automatic instinct. If a rhyme were to a man merely what a bark is to a dog, or a crow to a cock, it would be clear that such natural things cannot be merely neglected. It is clear that a canine epic, about Argus instead of Ulysses, would have a beat ultimately consisting of barks. It is clear that a long poem like "Chantecler," written by a real cock, would be to the tune of Cock-a-doodle-doo. But in truth the nursery rhyme has a nobler origin; if it be ancestral it is not animal; its principle is a primary one, not only in the body but in the soul.

Milton prefaced "Paradise Lost" with a ponderous condemnation of rhyme. And perhaps the finest and even the most familiar line in the whole of "Paradise Lost" is really a glorification of rhyme. "Seasons return, but not to me return," is not only an echo that has all the ring of rhyme in its form, but it happens to contain nearly all the philosophy of rhyme in its spirit. The wonderful word "return" has, not only in its sound but in its sense, a hint of the whole secret of song. It is not merely that its very form is a fine example of a certain quality in English. It is that it also describes poetry itself, not only in a mechanical but a moral sense. Song is not only a recurrence, it is a return. It does not merely, like the child in the nursery, take pleasure in seeing the wheels go round. It also wishes to go back as well as round; to go back to the nursery where such pleasures are found. Or to vary the metaphor slightly, it does not merely rejoice in the rotation of a wheel on the road, as if it were a fixed wheel in the air. It is not only the wheel but the wagon that is returning. That labouring caravan is always travelling towards some camping-ground that it has lost and cannot find again. No lover of poetry needs to be told that all poems are full of that noise of returning wheels; and none more than the poems of Milton himself. The whole truth is obvious, not merely in the poem, but even in the two words of the title. All poems might be bound in one book under the title of "Paradise Lost." And the only object of writing "Paradise Lost" is to turn it, if only by a magic and momentary illusion, into "Paradise Regained."

It is in this deeper significance of return that we must seek for the peculiar power in the recurrence we call rhyme. It would be easy enough to reply to Milton's strictures on rhyme in the spirit of a sensible if superficial liberality by saying that it takes all sorts to make a world, and especially the world of the poets. It is evident enough that Milton might have been right to dispense with rhyme without being right to despise it. It is obvious that the peculiar dignity of his religious epic would have been weakened if it had been a rhymed epic, beginning:—

> Of man's first disobedience and the fruit
> Of that forbidden tree whose mortal root.

But it is equally obvious that Milton himself would not have tripped on the light fantastic toe with quite so much charm and cheerfulness in the lines:—

> But come thou Goddess fair and free
> In heaven yclept Euphrosyne

if the goddess had been yclept something else, as, for the sake
of argument, Syrinx. Milton in his more reasonable moods
would have allowed rhyme in theory a place in all poetry, as he
allowed it in practice in his own poetry. But he would certainly
have said at this time, and possibly at all times, that he allowed it
an inferior place, or at least a secondary place. But is its place
secondary; and is it in any sense inferior?

The romance of rhyme does not consist merely in the pleasure of a jingle, though this is a pleasure of which no man should
be ashamed. Certainly most men take pleasure in it, whether
or not they are ashamed of it. We see it in the older fashion of
prolonging the chorus of a song with syllables like "rumty
tumty" or "tooral looral." We see it in the similar but later
fashion of discussing whether a truth is objective or subjective,
or whether a reform is constructive or destructive, or whether
an argument is deductive or inductive: all bearing witness to a
very natural love for those nursery rhyme recurrences which
make a sort of song without words, or at least without any kind
of intellectual significance. But something much deeper is involved in the love of rhyme as distinct from other poetic forms,
something which is perhaps too deep and subtle to be described.
The nearest approximation to the truth I can think of is something like this: that while all forms of genuine verse recur, there
is in rhyme a sense of return to exactly the same place. All modes
of song go forward and backward like the tides of the sea; but
in the great sea of Homeric or Virgilian hexametres, the sea that
carried the labouring ships of Ulysses and Æneas, the thunder of
the breakers is rhythmic, but the margin of the foam is necessarily irregular and vague. In rhyme there is rather a sense of
water poured safely into one familiar well, or (to use a nobler
metaphor) of ale poured safely into one familiar flagon. The
armies of Homer and Virgil advance and retreat over a vast

country, and suggest vast and very profound sentiments about it, about whether it is their own country or only a strange country. But when the old nameless ballad boldly rhymes "the bonny ivy tree" to "my ain countree" the vision at once dwindles and sharpens to a very vivid image of a single soldier passing under the ivy that darkens his own door. Rhythm deals with similarity, but rhyme with identity. Now in the one word identity are involved perhaps the deepest and certainly the dearest human things. He who is homesick does not desire houses or even homes. He who is lovesick does not want to see all the women with whom he might have fallen in love. Only he who is seasick, perhaps, may be said to have a cosmopolitan craving for all lands or any kind of land. And this is probably why seasickness, like cosmopolitanism, has never yet been a high inspiration to song. Songs, especially the most poignant of them, generally refer to some absolute, to some positive place or person for whom no similarity is a substitute. In such a case all approximation is merely asymptotic. The prodigal returns to his father's house and not the house next door, unless he is still an imperfectly sober prodigal; the lover desires his lady and not her twin sister, except in old complications of romance; and even the spiritualist is generally looking for a ghost and not merely for ghosts. I think the intolerable torture of spiritualism must be a doubt about identity. Anyhow, it will generally be found that where this call for the identical has been uttered most ringingly and unmistakably in literature, it has been uttered in rhyme. Another purpose for which this pointed and definite form is very much fitted is the expression of dogma, as distinct from doubt or even opinion. This is why, with all allowance for a decline in the most classical effects of the classical tongue, the rhymed Latin of the mediæval hymns does express what it had to express in a very poignant poetical manner, as compared with the reverent agnosticism so nobly uttered in the rolling unrhymed metres of the ancients. For even if we regard the matter of the mediæval verses as a dream, it was at least a vivid dream, a dream full of faces, a dream of love and of lost things. And something of the same spirit runs in a vaguer way through proverbs and phrases that are not exactly religious, but rather in a rude sense philosophical, but which all move with the burden of returning; things to be felt only in familiar fragments . . . *on revient toujours* . . . it's the old story—it's love that makes the world go round; and all roads lead to Rome: we might almost say that all roads lead to Rhyme.

Milton's revolt against rhyme must be read in the light of history. Milton is the Renascence frozen into a Puritan form; the beginning of a period which was in a sense classic, but was in a still more definite sense aristocratic. There the Classicist was the artistic aristocrat because the Calvinist was the spiritual aristocrat. The seventeenth century was intensely individualistic; it had both in the noble and the ignoble sense a respect for persons. It had no respect whatever for popular traditions; and it was in the midst of its purely logical and legal excitement that most of the popular traditions died. The Parliament appeared and the people disappeared. The arts were put under patrons, where they had once been under patron saints. The schools and colleges at once strengthened and narrowed the New Learning, making it something rather peculiar to one country and one class. A few men talked a great deal of good Latin, where all men had once talked a little bad Latin. But they talked even the good Latin so that no Latinist in the world could understand them. They confined all study of the classics to that of the most classical period, and grossly exaggerated the barbarity and barrenness of patriotic Greek or mediæval Latin. It is as if a man said that because the English translation of the Bible is perhaps the best English in the world, therefore Addison and Pater and Newman are not worth reading. We can imagine what men in such a mood would have said of the rude rhymed hexametres of the monks; and it is not unnatural that they should have felt a reaction against rhyme itself. For the history of rhyme is the history of something else, very vast and sometimes invisible, certainly somewhat indefinable, against which they were in aristocratic rebellion.

That thing is difficult to define in impartial modern terms. It might well be called Romance, and that even in a more technical sense, since it corresponds to the rise of the Romance languages as distinct from the Roman language. It might more truly be called Religion, for historically it was the gradual re-emergence of Europe through the Dark Ages, because it still had one religion, though no longer one rule. It was, in short, the creation of Christendom. It may be called Legend, for it is true that the most overpowering presence in it is that of omnipresent and powerful popular Legend; so that things that may never have happened, or, as some say, could never have happened, are nevertheless rooted in our racial memory like things that have happened to ourselves. The whole Arthurian Cycle, for instance, seems something more real than reality. If the faces in that darkness of the Dark Ages, Lancelot and Arthur and Merlin and Modred, are indeed faces in a dream, they are like faces in a real dream: a dream in a bed and not a dream in a book. Subconsciously at least, I should be much less surprised if Arthur was to come again than I should be if the Superman were to come at all. Again, the thing might be called Gossip: a noble name, having in it the name of God and one of the most generous and genial of the relations of men. For I suppose there has seldom been a time when such a mass of culture and good traditions of craft and song have been handed down orally, by one universal buzz of conversation, through centuries of ignorance down to centuries of greater knowledge. Education must have been an eternal *viva voce* examination; but the men passed their examination. At least they went out in such rude sense masters of art as to create the Song of Roland and the round Roman arches that carry the weight of so many Gothic towers. Finally, of course, it can be called ignorance, barbarism, black superstition, a reaction towards obscurantism and old night; and such a view is eminently complete and satisfactory, only that it leaves behind it a sort of weak wonder as to why the very youngest poets do still go on writing poems about the sword of Arthur and the horn of Roland.

All this was but the beginning of a process which has two great points of interest. The first is the way in which the mediæval movement did rebuild the old Roman civilization; the other was the way in which it did not. A strange interest attaches to the things which had never existed in the pagan culture and did appear in the Christian culture. I think it is true of most of them that they had a quality that can very approximately be described as popular, or perhaps as vulgar, as indeed we still talk of the languages which at that time liberated themselves from Latin as the vulgar tongues. And to many Classicists these things would appear to be vulgar in a more vulgar sense. They were vulgar in the sense of being vivid almost to excess, of making a very direct and unsophisticated appeal to the emotions. The first law of heraldry was to wear the heart upon the sleeve. Such mediævalism was the reverse of mere mysticism, in the sense of mere mystery; it might more truly be described as sensationalism. One of these things, for instance, was a hot and even an impatient love of colour. It learned to paint before it could draw, and could afford the twopence coloured long before it could manage the penny plain. It culminated at last, of course, in the energy and gaiety of the Gothic; but even the richness of Gothic rested on a certain psychological simplicity. We can contrast it with the classic by noting its popular passion for telling a story in stone. We may admit that a Doric portico is a poem, but no one would describe it as an anecdote. The time was to come when much of the imagery of the cathedrals was to be lost; but it would have mattered the less that it was defaced by its enemies if it had not been already neglected by its friends. It would have mattered less if the whole tide of taste among the rich had not turned against the old popular masterpieces. The Puritans defaced them, but the Cavaliers did not truly defend them. The Cavaliers were also aristocrats of the new classical culture, and used the word Gothic in the sense of barbaric. For the benefit of the Teutonists we may note in parenthesis that, if this phrase meant that Gothic was despised, it also meant that the Goths were despised. But when the Cavaliers came back, after the Puritan interregnum, they restored not in the style of Pugin but in the style of Wren. The very thing we call the Restoration, which was the restoration of King Charles, was also the restoration of St. Paul's. And it was a very modern restoration.

So far we might say that simple people do not like simple things. This is certainly true if we compare the classic with these highly coloured things of mediævalism, or all the vivid visions which first began to glow in the night of the Dark Ages. Now one of these things was the romantic expedient called rhyme. And even in this, if we compare the two, we shall see something of the same paradox by which the simple like complexities and the complex like simplicities. The ignorant like rich carvings and melodious and often ingenious rhymes. The learned like bare walls and blank verse. But in the case of rhyme it is peculiarly difficult to define the double and yet very definite truth. It is difficult to define the sense in which rhyme is artificial and the sense in which it is simple. In truth it is simple because it is artificial. It is an artifice of the kind enjoyed by children and other poetic people; it is a toy. As a technical accomplishment it stands at the same distance from the popular experience as the old popular sports. Like swimming, like dancing, like drawing the bow, anybody can do it, but nobody can do it without taking the trouble to do it; and only a few can do it very well. In a hundred ways it was akin to that simple and even humble energy that made all the lost glory of the guilds. Thus their rhyme was useful as well as ornamental. It was not merely a melody but also a mnemonic; just as their towers were not merely trophies but beacons and belfries. In another aspect rhyme is akin to rhetoric, but of a very positive and emphatic sort: the coincidence of sound giving the effect of saying, "It is certainly so." Shakespeare realized this when he rounded off a fierce or romantic scene with a rhymed couplet. I know that some critics do not like this, but I think there is a moment when a drama ought to become a melodrama. Then there is a much older effect of rhyme that can only be called mystical, which may seem the very opposite of the utilitarian, and almost equally remote from the rhetorical. Yet it shares with the former the tough texture of something not easily forgotten, and with the latter the touch of authority which is the aim of all oratory. The thing I mean may be found in the fact that so many of the old proverbial prophecies, from Merlin to Mother Shipton, were handed down in rhyme. It can be found in the very name of Thomas the Rhymer.

But the simplest way of putting this popular quality is in a single word: it is a song. Rhyme corresponds to a melody so simple that it goes straight like an arrow to the heart. It corresponds to a chorus so familiar and obvious that all men can join in it. I am not disturbed by the suggestion that such an arrow of song, when it hits the heart, may entirely miss the head. I am not concerned to deny that the chorus may sometimes be a drunken chorus, in which men have lost their heads to find their tongues. I am not defending but defining; I am trying to find words for a large but elusive distinction between certain things that are certainly poetry and certain other things which are also song. Of course it is only an accident that Horace opens his greatest series of odes by saying that he detests the profane populace and wishes to drive them from his temple of poetry. But it is the sort of accident that is almost an allegory. There is even a sense in which it has a practical side. When all is said, *could* a whole crowd of men sing the "Descende Cœlo," that noble ode, as a crowd can certainly sing the "Dies Irae," or for that matter "Down among the Dead Men"? Did Horace himself sing the Horatian odes in the sense in which Shakespeare could sing, or could hardly help singing, the Shakespearean songs. I do not know, having no kind of scholarship on these points. But I do not feel that it could

have been at all the same thing; and my only purpose is to attempt a rude description of that thing. Rhyme is consonant to
the particular kind of song that can be a popular song, whether
pathetic or passionate or comic; and Milton is entitled to his
true distinction; nobody is likely to sing "Paradise Lost" as if it
were a song of that kind. I have tried to suggest my sympathy
with rhyme, in terms true enough to be accepted by the other
side as expressing their antipathy for it. I have admitted that
rhyme is a toy and even a trick, of the sort that delights children.
I have admitted that every rhyme is a nursery rhyme. What I
will never admit is that anyone who is too big for the nursery is
big enough for the Kingdom of God, though the God were only
Apollo.

A good critic should be like God in the great saying of a
Scottish mystic. George Macdonald said that God was easy to
please and hard to satisfy. That paradox is the poise of all good
artistic appreciation. Without the first part of the paradox appreciation perishes, because it loses the power to appreciate. Good
criticism, I repeat, combines the subtle pleasure in a thing being
done well with the simple pleasure in it being done at all. It
combines the pleasure of the scientific engineer in seeing how
the wheels work together to a logical end with the pleasure of
the baby in seeing the wheels go round. It combines the pleasure
of the artistic draughtsman in the fact that his lines of charcoal,
light and apparently loose, fall exactly right and in a perfect
relation with the pleasure of the child in the fact that the charcoal makes marks of any kind on the paper. And in the same
fashion it combines the critic's pleasure in a poem with the
child's pleasure in a rhyme. The historical point about this kind
of poetry, the rhymed romantic kind, is that it rose out of the
Dark Ages with the whole of this huge popular power behind
it, the human love of a song, a riddle, a proverb, a pun or a
nursery rhyme; the sing-song of innumerable children's games,
the chorus of a thousand camp-fires and a thousand taverns.
When poetry loses its link with all these people who are easily

pleased it loses all its power of giving pleasure. When a poet looks down on a rhyme it is, I will not say as if he looked down on a daisy (which might seem possible to the more literal-minded), but rather as if he looked down on a lark because he had been up in a balloon. It is cutting away the very roots of poetry; it is revolting against nature because it is natural, against sunshine because it is bright, or mountains because they are high, or moonrise because it is mysterious. The freezing process began after the Reformation with a fastidious search for finer yet freer forms; to-day it has ended in formlessness.

But the joke of it is that even when it is formless it is still fastidious. The new anarchic artists are not ready to accept everything. They are not ready to accept anything except anarchy. Unless it observes the very latest conventions of unconventionality, they would rule out anything classic as coldly as any classic ever ruled out anything romantic. But the classic was a form; and there was even a time when it was a new form. The men who invented Sapphics did invent a new metre; the introduction of Elizabethan blank verse was a real revolution in literary form. But *vers libre*, or nine-tenths of it, is not a new metre any more than sleeping in a ditch is a new school of architecture. It is no more a revolution in literary form than eating meat raw is an innovation in cookery. It is not even original, because it is not creative; the artist does not invent anything, but only abolishes something. But the only point about it that is to my present purpose is expressed in the word "pride." It is not merely proud in the sense of being exultant, but proud in the sense of being disdainful. Such outlaws are more exclusive than aristocrats; and their anarchical arrogance goes far beyond the pride of Milton and the aristocrats of the New Learning. And this final refinement has completed the work which the saner aristocrats began, the work now most evident in the world: the separation of art from the people. I need not insist on the sensational and self-evident character of that separation. I need not recommend the modern poet to attempt to sing his *vers libres* in a public house. I need not even urge the young Imagist to read out a number of his disconnected Images to a public meeting. The thing is not only admitted but admired. The old artist remained proud in spite of his unpopularity; the new artist is proud because of his unpopularity; perhaps it is his chief ground for pride.

Dwelling as I do in the Dark Ages, or at latest along the mediæval fairy-tales, I am yet moved to remember something I once read in a modern fairy-tale. As it happens, I have already used the name of George Macdonald; and in the best of his books there is a description of how a young miner in the mountains could always drive away the subterranean goblins if he could remember and repeat any kind of rhyme. The impromptu rhymes were often doggerel, as was the dog-Latin of many monkish hexametres or the burden of many rude Border ballads. But I have a notion that they drove away the devils, blue devils of pessimism and black devils of pride. Anyhow Madame Montessori, who has apparently been deploring the educational affects of fairy-tales, would probably see in me a pitiable example of such early perversion, for that image which was one of my first impressions seems likely enough to be one of my last; and when the noise of many new and original musical instruments, with strange shapes and still stranger noises, has passed away like a procession, I shall hear in the succeeding silence only a rustle and scramble among the rocks and a boy singing on the mountain.

THE FEAR OF THE FILM

Long lists are being given of particular cases in which children have suffered in spirits or health from alleged horrors of the kinema. One child is said to have had a fit after seeing a film; another to have been sleepless with some fixed idea taken from a film; another to have killed his father with a carving-knife through having seen a knife used in a film. This may possibly have occurred; though if it did, anybody of common sense would prefer to have details about that particular child, rather than about that particular picture. But what is supposed to be the practical moral of it, in any case? Is it that the young should never see a story with a knife in it? Are they to be brought up in complete ignorance of "The Merchant of Venice" because Shylock flourishes a knife for a highly disagreeable purpose? Are they never to hear of Macbeth, lest it should slowly dawn upon their trembling intelligence that it is a dagger that they see before them? It would be more practical to propose that a child should never see a real carving-knife, and still more practical that he should never see a real father. All that may come; the era of preventive and prophetic science has only begun. We must not be impatient. But when we come to the cases of morbid panic after some particular exhibition, there is yet more reason to clear the mind of cant. It is perfectly true that a child will have the horrors after seeing some particular detail. It is quite equally true that nobody can possibly predict what that detail will be. It certainly need not be anything so obvious as a murder or even a knife. I should have thought anybody who knew anything about children, or for that matter anybody who had been a child, would know that these nightmares are quite incalculable. The hint of horror may come by any chance in any connexion. If the kinema exhibited nothing but views of country vicarages or vegetarian restaurants, the ugly fancy is as likely to be stim-ulated by these things as by anything else. It is like seeing a face in the carpet; it makes no difference that it is the carpet at the vicarage.

I will give two examples from my own most personal circle; I could give hundreds from hearsay. I know a child who screamed steadily for hours if he had been taken past the Albert Memorial. This was not a precocious precision or excellence in his taste in architecture. Nor was it a premature protest against all that gimcrack German culture which nearly entangled us in

the downfall of the barbaric tyranny. It was the fear of something which he himself described with lurid simplicity as "The
Cow with the India-rubber Tongue." It sounds rather a good
title for a creepy short story. At the base of the Albert Memorial
(I may explain for those who have never enjoyed that monument) are four groups of statuary representing Europe, Asia,
Africa, and America. America especially is very overwhelming;
borne onward on a snorting bison who plunges forward in a
fury of western progress, and is surrounded with Red Indians,
Mexicans, and all sorts of pioneers, O pioneers, armed to the
teeth. The child passed this transatlantic tornado with complete
coolness and indifference. Europe however is seated on a bull
so mild as to look like a cow; the tip of its tongue is showing
and happened to be discoloured by weather; suggesting, I suppose, a living thing coming out of the dead marble. Now nobody
could possibly foretell that a weather-stain would occur in that
particular place, and fill that particular child with that particular
fancy. Nobody is likely to propose meeting it by forbidding
graven images, like the Moslems and the Jews. Nobody has said
(as yet) that it is bad morals to make a picture of a cow. Nobody has even pleaded that it is bad manners for a cow to put
its tongue out. These things are utterly beyond calculation; they
are also beyond counting, for they occur all over the place, not
only to morbid children but to any children. I knew this particular child very well, being a rather older child myself at the
time. He certainly was not congenitally timid or feeble-minded;
for he risked going to prison to expose the Marconi Scandal and
died fighting in the Great War.

Here is another example out of scores. A little girl, now a very
normal and cheerful young lady, had an insomnia of insane
terror entirely arising from the lyric of "Little Bo-Peep." After
an inquisition like that of the confessor or the psycho-analyst,
it was found that the word "bleating" had some obscure connexion in her mind with the word "bleeding." There was thus
perhaps an added horror in the phrase "heard"; in hearing rather

than seeing the flowing of blood. Nobody could possibly provide against that sort of mistake. Nobody could prevent the little girl from hearing about sheep, any more than the little boy from hearing about cows. We might abolish all nursery rhymes; and as they are happy and popular and used with universal success, it is very likely that we shall. But the whole point of the mistake about that phrase is that it might have been a mistake about any phrase. We cannot foresee all the fancies that might arise, not only out of what we say, but of what we do not say. We cannot avoid promising a child a caramel lest he should think we say cannibal, or conceal the very word "hill" lest it should sound like "hell."

All the catalogues and calculations offered us by the party of caution in this controversy are therefore quite worthless. It is perfectly true that examples can be given of a child being frightened of this, that or the other. But we can never be certain of his being frightened of the same thing twice. It is not on the negative side, by making lists of vetoes, that the danger can be avoided; it can never indeed be entirely avoided. We can only fortify the child on the positive side by giving him health and humour and a trust in God; not omitting (what will much mystify the moderns) an intelligent appreciation of the idea of authority, which is only the other side of confidence, and which alone can suddenly and summarily cast out such devils. But we may be sure that most modern people will not look at it in this way. They will think it more scientific to attempt to calculate the incalculable. So soon as they have realized that it is not so simple as it looks, they will try to map it out, however complicated it may be. When they discover that the terrible detail need not be a knife, but might just as well be a fork, they will only say there is a fork complex as well as a knife complex. And that increasing complexity of complexes is the net in which liberty will be taken.

Instead of seeing in the odd cases of the cow's tongue or the bleating sheep the peril of their past generalizations, they will see them only as starting points for new generalizations. They will get yet another theory out of it. And they will begin acting on the theory long before they have done thinking about it. They will start out with some new and crude conception that sculpture has made children scream or that nursery rhymes have made children sleepless; and the thing will be a clause in a programme of reform before it has begun to be a conclusion in a serious study of psychology. That is the practical problem about modern liberty which the critics will not see; of which eugenics is one example and all this amateur child-psychology is another. So long as an old morality was in black and white like a chessboard, even a man who wanted more of it made white was certain that no more of it would be made black. Now he is never certain what vices may not be released, but neither is he certain what virtues may be forbidden. Even if he did not think it wrong to run away with a married woman, he knew that his neighbours only thought it wrong because the woman was married. They did not think it wrong to run away with a redhaired woman, or a left-handed woman, or a woman subject to headaches. But when we let loose a thousand eugenical speculations, all adopted before they are verified and acted on even before they are adopted, he is just as likely as not to find himself separated from the woman for those or any other reasons. Similarly there was something to be said for restrictions, even rather puritanical and provincial restrictions, upon what children should read or see, so long as they fenced in certain fixed departments like sex or sensational tortures. But when we begin to speculate on whether other sensations may not stimulate as dangerously as sex, those other sensations may be as closely controlled as sex. When, let us say, we hear that the eye and brain are weakened by the rapid turning of wheels as well as by the most revolting torturing of men, we have come into a world in which cart-wheels and steam-engines may become as obscene as racks and thumbscrews. In short, so long as we *combine* ceaseless and often reckless scientific speculation with rapid and often random social reform, the result must inevitably be not anarchy but ever-increasing tyranny. There must be a ceaseless and almost mechanical multiplication of things forbidden. The resolution to cure all the ills that flesh is heir to, combined with the guesswork about all possible ills that flesh and nerve and brain-cell may be heir to—these two things conducted simultaneously must inevitably spread a sort of panic of prohibition. Scientific imagination and social reform between them will quite logically and almost legitimately have made us slaves. This seems to me a very clear, a very fair and a very simple point of public criticism; and I am much mystified about why so many publicists cannot even see what it is, but take refuge in charges of anarchism, which firstly are not true, and secondly have nothing to do with it.

THE GLORY OF GREY

I SUPPOSE that, taking this summer as a whole, people will not call it an appropriate time for praising the English climate. But for my part I will praise the English climate till I die—even if I die of the English climate. There is no weather so good as English weather. Nay, in a real sense there is no weather at all anywhere but in England. In France you have much sun and some rain; in Italy you have hot winds and cold winds; in Scotland and Ireland you have rain, either thick or thin; in America you have hells of heat and cold, and in the Tropics you have sunstrokes varied by thunderbolts. But all these you have on a broad and brutal scale, and you settle down into contentment or despair. Only in our own romantic country do you have the strictly romantic thing called Weather; beautiful and changing as a woman. The great English landscape painters (neglected now like everything that is English) have this salient distinction: that the Weather is not the atmosphere of their pictures; it is the subject of their pictures. They paint portraits of the

Weather. The Weather sat to Constable. The Weather posed for Turner; and a deuce of a pose it was. This cannot truly be said of the greatest of their continental models or rivals. Poussin and Claude painted objects, ancient cities or perfect Arcadian shepherds through a clear medium of the climate. But in the English painters Weather is the hero; with Turner an Adelphi hero, taunting, flashing and fighting, melodramatic but really magnificent. The English climate, a tall and terrible protagonist, robed in rain and thunder and snow and sunlight, fills the whole canvas and the whole foreground. I admit the superiority of many other French things besides French art. But I will not yield an inch on the superiority of English weather and weather-painting. Why, the French have not even got a word for Weather: and you must ask for the weather in French as if you were asking for the time in English.

Then, again, variety of climate should always go with stability of abode. The weather in the desert is monotonous; and as a natural consequence the Arabs wander about, hoping it may be different somewhere. But an Englishman's house is not only his castle; it is his fairy castle. Clouds and colours of every varied dawn and eve are perpetually touching and turning it from clay to gold, or from gold to ivory. There is a line of woodland beyond a corner of my garden which is literally different on every one of the three hundred and sixty-five days. Sometimes it seems as near as a hedge, and sometimes as far as a faint and fiery evening cloud. The same principle (by the way) applies to the difficult problem of wives. Variability is one of the virtues of a woman. It avoids the crude requirement of polygamy. So long as you have one good wife you are sure to have a spiritual harem.

Now, among the heresies that are spoken in this matter is the habit of calling a grey day a "colourless" day. Grey is a colour, and can be a very powerful and pleasing colour. There is also an insulting style of speech about "one grey day just like another." You might as well talk about one green tree just like another. A grey clouded sky is indeed a canopy between us and the sun; so is a green tree, if it comes to that. But the grey umbrellas differ as much as the green in their style and shape, in their tint and tilt. One day may be grey like steel, and another grey like dove's plumage. One may seem grey like the deathly frost, and another grey like the smoke of substantial kitchens. No things could seem further apart than the doubt of grey and the decision of scarlet. Yet grey and red can mingle, as they do in the morning clouds: and also in a sort of warm smoky stone of which they build the little towns in the west country. In those towns even the houses that are wholly grey have a glow in them as if their secret firesides were such furnaces of hospitality as faintly to transfuse the walls like walls of cloud. And wandering in those westland parts I did once really find a signpost pointing up a steep crooked path to a town that was called Clouds. I did not climb up to it; I feared that either the town would not be good enough for the name, or I should not be good enough for the town. Anyhow, the little hamlets of the warm grey stone have a geniality which is not achieved by all the artistic scarlet of the suburbs; as if it were better to warm one's hands at the ashes of Glastonbury than at the painted flames of Croydon.

Again, the enemies of grey (those astute, daring and evil-minded men) are fond of bringing forward the argument that colours suffer in grey weather, and that strong sunlight is necessary to all the hues of heaven and earth. Here again there are two words to be said; and it is essential to distinguish. It is true that sun is needed to burnish and bring into bloom the tertiary and dubious colours; the colour of peat, pea-soup, Impressionist sketches, brown velvet coats, olives, grey and blue slates, the complexions of vegetarians, the tints of volcanic rock, chocolate, cocoa, mud, soot, slime, old boots; the delicate shades of these do need the sunlight to bring out the faint beauty that often clings to them. But if you have a healthy negro taste in colour, if you choke your garden with poppies and geraniums, if you paint your house sky-blue and scarlet, if you wear, let us say, a golden top-hat and a crimson frock-coat, you will not only be visible on the greyest day, but you will notice that your costume and environment produce a certain singular effect. You will find, I mean, that rich colours actually look more luminous on a grey day, because they are seen against a sombre background and seem to be burning with a lustre of their own. Against a dark sky all flowers look like fireworks. There is something strange about them, at once vivid and secret, like flowers traced in fire in the phantasmal garden of a witch. A bright blue sky is necessarily the high light of the picture; and its brightness kills all the bright blue flowers. But on a grey day the larkspur looks like fallen heaven; the red daisies are really the red lost eyes of day; and the sunflower is the vice-regent of the sun.

Lastly, there is this value about the colour that men call colourless; that it suggests in some way the mixed and troubled average of existence, especially in its quality of strife and expectation and promise. Grey is a colour that always seems on the eve of changing to some other colour; of brightening into blue or blanching into white or bursting into green and gold. So we may be perpetually reminded of the indefinite hope that is in doubt itself; and when there is grey weather in our hills or grey hairs in our heads, perhaps they may still remind us of the morning.

ON MALTREATING WORDS

I READ a phrase in a newspaper the other day, printed in very large letters at the top of a column, which ran as follows: "Crusade to Reform Auction Bridge." And I mused, in a slightly melancholy mood, upon the destiny and the decline of human words; and how clearly the fate of words illustrates the fall of man.

Surely anyone will see something a little strange in that remarkable combination of terms and topics; anyone at least who knows what has been for mankind the meaning of the Crusade, not to speak of the meaning of the Cross. Indeed it is quite equally incongruous whether our sympathies are with the Cross or the Crescent. A Moslem of any historical imagination might well be annoyed at such treatment of the tremendous and heroic trial, through which his own creed and culture passed. And when we consider what the Crusade meant to the men of our own race, the fathers and founders of us all, it will indeed seem a steep and staggering disproportion; when we call up all the imagery which was familiar for so long in all European history and poetry and all the stages of that marvellous story; the first vast movement, anonymous and almost anarchical, moving by mere popular impulse across the world, the mightiest mob in history. For no revolutionary movement of republicans or communists was ever so international as the First Crusade; few were so popular, for it is said that in all that wild democracy there were only nine knights. Then their destruction in the desert and the revenge or recovery, when the despair and darkness opened before the glory of Godfrey's ride; when the toppling battle-towers swayed and sank in flames around the city as Godfrey leapt upon the wall; the high place where he refused the crown of gold under the shadow of the crown of thorns; the return of a deeper darkness, and the last stand under the Horns of Hattin, where the knights died around the True Cross; the rush of the rescuer upon Acre and that vain victory after which the Lion Heart threw his lance to earth and turned his back on Jerusalem, that he might not see what he must not save; the strange and gloomy story of the Fourth Crusade and old Simon de Montfort riding away alone because he would not draw the sword against Christian men; the way in which that golden or crimson thread was woven into the tapestries of every land; whether they showed Douglas hurling the heart of Bruce before him in battle with the Saracens, or old Barbarossa sunken under the river but still waiting with his hand on his barbaric sword, or a light that shone in the desert where St. Louis lay like one dying and mingling the Crucifixion with the Crusade. If we have any sense of the historic influence of these images among men, of how Godfrey blazed among the Nine Worthies or what it was that lingered on the lyre of Tasso, we shall perhaps repeat to ourselves in a curious and meditative voice those simple words, "Crusade to Reform Auction Bridge."

Of course this loss of verbal values comes gradually; and at the beginning may even be a tribute of the lesser thing to the greater. Somebody talks naturally enough about a crusade for liberty or a crusade for knowledge; then the hunt is up and everybody who honestly believes in anything uses the term as a cliché; and we are all made familiar with the rush and hustle of a crusade for vaccination or against vivisection. In fact, the word "crusade" begins by meaning "movement" and ends with meaning merely "proposal," when it does not mean merely "fuss." We receive leaflets about a crusade against waste paper: leaflets that are decidedly waste paper. We receive visitors with a crusade against muzzling dogs: visitors whom we ardently desire to muzzle. Crusades for painting the lamp-posts green or putting the costermongers into livery follow each other with unabated enthusiasm; and we have already a crusade to reform auction bridge, and shall doubtless have another to improve ping-pong. *Dieu le Veult.*

Of course there are a great many other examples in every-day English, which may be represented as every bit as bad. We talk about a man being a martyr to indigestion, without being haunted or shamed by the burning shades of St. Lawrence or St. Sebastian. We say that Pebbleswick-on-Sea is a God-forsaken place, without committing ourselves to the highly heretical dogma that it is really forsaken of God. For it is heresy to suggest that even a successful watering-place can really be an exception, either to the divine omnipresence or to the divine charity and forgiveness. But that single phrase "God-forsaken," in itself so tragic, is also in itself a tragedy. I mean it is a marked example of this tragedy of the gradual weakening of words. For it is in itself a very powerful and even appalling phrase. It is not a piece of sound theology, but it is a piece of vigorous and vivid literature. It reminds us of some great phrase in "Paradise Lost," giving a glimpse of a sort of lurid negation and ruinous quiet; not light, but rather darkness visible. Yet, strange to say, a human being can say this awful thing about Pebbleswick without shuddering. Doubtless there are any number of other examples, which I could think of if I stopped to think. Perhaps there is some touch of such levity even in saying that a thing is "crucial" or in declaring that it is the crux of the question. Perhaps there is a grim reminder of it in the fact that "a Resurrectionist" generally means a body-snatcher and not a believer in the Resurrection.

But my wandering thoughts have strayed rather backwards to the origins of these things than outwards to the numberless examples of them. I think it obvious that the tendency is a general one, apart from extreme examples; though I would still lift a faint and feeble protest against the reformer of auction bridge being literally elevated to the position of Pontifex Maximus. But though we may reasonably remonstrate with some very abrupt accelerations of the process, it may be that it generally goes on as a slow process; and especially as a sleepy process. Most thoroughly bad processes are slow and sleepy; which is why I have sometimes been found wanting in a full and fanatical faith in evolution. And it seems to me that the moral of all these things is the very opposite of that which is offered to us by many evolutionists. There are indeed many of them so clear-headed as not to confuse strictly scientific evolution with a vague notion of ethical exaltation or expansion. But others do ask us to accept a sort of general upward tendency; and it seems to me that in these things there is a general downward tendency. In the matter of language, which is the main matter of literature, it is clear that words are perpetually falling below themselves. They are ceasing to say what they mean or to mean what they say; they are always beginning to mean something that is not only quite different, but much less definite and strong. And, in this fall of man's chosen symbols, there may well be a symbol of his own fall. He has a difficulty in ruling his tongue; not only in the sense of the talking organ, but in the sense of the language that he talks. Almost when he is not looking, it is always running wild; or, worse still, running weak.

Now this distinction directly concerns all the talk about new art or experiments in literature. It does not make me believe in these things as a progress; but it does in a sense make me believe in them as a change. I am at once more tolerant of them and less trustful of them. I can see that people must be allowed to play about with human language to a certain extent; because unless it is kept stirring it goes stale. But I do not think a thing is necessarily great because we feel it as fresh; or necessarily small because we feel it as stale. All we are doing, when we pick our words or try our experiments, is resisting the general trend of all style towards staleness. Some traditionalists do go a little too stale. Many get a great deal too fresh, as the landladies were supposed to say. But their mistake is merely in supposing that they have any claim to progress or claim to pride. What they are doing, at the best, is to resist retrogression, the retrogression that simply goes with repetition. In other words, all artists are dedicated to an eternal struggle against the downward tendency of their own method and medium. For this reason they must sometimes be fresh; but there is no reason why they should not also be modest. There is nothing to brag about, in the mere fact that your only mode of expression is perpetually going to the dogs. The dignity of the artist lies in his duty of keeping awake the sense of wonder in the world. In this long vigil he often has to vary his methods of stimulation; but in this long vigil he is also himself striving against a continual tendency to sleep. There are some to whom this may even seem a sombre version of human existence; but not to me; for I have long believed that the only really happy and hopeful faith is a faith in the Fall of Man.

THE TERROR OF A TOY

It would be too high and hopeful a compliment to say that the world is becoming absolutely babyish. For its chief weak-mindedness is an inability to appreciate the intelligence of babies. On every side we hear whispers and warnings that would have appeared half-witted to the Wise Men of Gotham. Only this Christmas I was told in a toy-shop that not so many bows and arrows were being made for little boys; because they were considered dangerous. It might in some circumstances be dangerous to have a little bow. It is always dangerous to have a little boy. But no other society, claiming to be sane, would have dreamed of supposing that you could abolish all bows unless you could abolish all boys. With the merits of the latter reform I will not deal here. There is a great deal to be said for such a course; and perhaps we shall soon have an opportunity of considering it. For the modern mind seems quite incapable of distinguishing between the means and the end, between the organ and the disease, between the use and the abuse; and would doubtless break the boy along with the bow, as it empties out the baby with the bath.

But let us, by way of a little study in this mournful state of things, consider this case of the dangerous toy. Now the first and most self-evident truth is that, of all the things a child sees and touches, the most dangerous toy is about the least dangerous thing. There is hardly a single domestic utensil that is not much more dangerous than a little bow and arrow. He can burn himself in the fire, he can boil himself in the bath, he can cut his throat with the carving-knife, he can scald himself with the kettle, he can choke himself with anything small enough, he can break his neck off anything high enough. He moves all day long amid a murderous machinery, as capable of killing and maiming as the wheels of the most frightful factory. He plays all day in a house fitted up with engines of torture like the Spanish Inquisition. And while he thus dances in the shadow of death, he is to be saved from all the perils of possessing a piece of string, tied to a bent bough or twig. When he is a little boy it generally takes him some time even to learn how to hold the bow. When he does hold it, he is delighted if the arrow flutters for a few yards like a feather or an autumn leaf. But even if he grows a little older and more skilful, and has yet not learned to despise arrows in favour of aeroplanes, the amount of damage he could conceivably do with his little arrows would be about one hundredth part of the damage that he could always in any case have done by simply picking up a stone in the garden.

Now you do not keep a little boy from throwing stones by preventing him from ever seeing stones. You do not do it by locking up all the stones in the Geological Museum, and only issuing tickets of admission to adults. You do not do it by trying to pick up all the pebbles on the beach, for fear he should practise throwing them into the sea. You do not even adopt so obvious and even pressing a social reform as forbidding roads to be made of anything but asphalt, or directing that all gardens shall be made on clay and none on gravel. You neglect all these great opportunities opening before you; you neglect all these inspiring vistas of social science and enlightenment. When you want to prevent a child from throwing stones, you fall back on the stalest and most sentimental and even most superstitious methods. You do it by trying to preserve some reasonable authority and influence over the child. You trust to your private relation with the boy, and not to your public relation with the stone. And what is true of the natural missile is just as true, of course, of the artificial missile; especially as it is a very much more ineffectual and therefore innocuous missile. A man could be really killed, like St. Stephen, with the stones in the road. I doubt if he could be really killed, like St. Sebastian, with the arrows in the toyshop. But anyhow the very plain principle is the same. If you can teach a child not to throw a stone, you can teach him when to shoot an arrow; if you cannot teach him anything, he will always have something to throw. If he can be persuaded not to smash the Archdeacon's hat with a heavy flint, it will probably be possible to dissuade him from transfixing that head-dress with a toy arrow. If his training deters him from heaving half a brick at the postman, it will probably also warn him against constantly loosening shafts of death against the policeman. But the notion that the child depends upon particular implements, labelled dangerous, in order to be a danger to himself and other people, is a notion so nonsensical that it is hard to see how any human mind can entertain it for a moment. The truth is that all sorts of faddism, both official and theoretical, have broken down the natural authority of the domestic institution, especially among the poor; and the faddists are now casting about desperately for a substitute for the thing they have themselves destroyed. The normal thing is for the parents to prevent a boy from doing more than a reasonable amount of damage with his bow and arrow; and for the rest, to leave him to a reasonable enjoyment of them. Officialism cannot thus follow the life of the individual boy, as can the individual guardian. You cannot appoint a particular policeman for each boy, to pursue him when he climbs trees or falls into ponds. So the modern spirit has descended to the indescribable mental degradation of trying to abolish the abuse of things by abolishing the things themselves; which is as if it were to abolish ponds or abolish trees. Perhaps it will have a try at that before long. Thus we have all heard of savages who try a tomahawk for murder, or burn a wooden club for the damage it has done to society. To such intellectual levels may the world return.

There are indeed yet lower levels. There is a story from America about a little boy who gave up his toy cannon to assist the disarmament of the world. I do not know if it is true, but on the whole I prefer to think so; for it is perhaps more tolerable to imagine one small monster who could do such a thing than many more mature monsters who could invent or admire it. There were some doubtless who neither invented nor admired. It is one of the peculiarities of the Americans that they combine a power of producing what they satirize as "sob-stuff" with a parallel power of satirizing it. And of the two American tall stories, it is sometimes hard to say which is the story and which the satire. But it seems clear that some people did really repeat this story in a reverential spirit. And it marks, as I have said, another stage of cerebral decay. You can (with luck) break a window with a toy arrow; but you can hardly bombard a town with a toy gun. If people object to the mere model of a cannon, they must equally object to the picture of a cannon, and so to every picture in the world that depicts a sword or a spear. There would be a splendid clearance of all the great art-galleries of the world. But it would be nothing to the destruction of all the great libraries of the world, if we logically extended the principle to all the literary masterpieces that admit the glory of arms. When this progress had gone on for a century or two, it might begin to dawn on people that there was something wrong with their moral principle. What is wrong with their moral principle is that it is immoral. Arms, like every other adventure or art of man, have two sides according as they are invoked for the infliction or the defiance of wrong. They have also an element of real poetry and an element of realistic and therefore repulsive prose. The child's symbolic sword and bow are simply the poetry without the prose; the good without the evil. The toy sword is the abstraction and emanation of the heroic, apart from all its horrible accidents. It is the soul of the sword, that will never be stained with blood.

THE CHORUS

ONE of the most marked instances of the decline of true popular sympathy is the gradual disappearance in our time of the habit of singing in chorus. Even when it is done nowadays it is done tentatively and sometimes inaudibly; apparently upon some preposterous principle (which I have never clearly grasped) that singing is an art. In the new aristocracy of the drawing-room a lady is actually asked whether she sings. In the old democracy of the dinner table a man was simply told to sing, and he had to do it. I like the atmosphere of those old banquets. I like to think of my ancestors, middle-aged or venerable gentlemen, all sitting round a table and explaining that they would never forget old days or friends with a rumpty-iddity-iddity, or letting it be known that they would die for England's glory with their tooral ooral, etc. Even the vices of that society (which sometimes, I fear, rendered the narrative portions of the song almost as cryptic and inarticulate as the chorus) were displayed with a more human softening than the same vices in the saloon bars of our own time. I greatly prefer Mr. Richard Swiveller to Mr. Stanley Ortheris. I prefer the man who exceeded in rosy wine in order that the wing of friendship might never moult a feather to the man who exceeds quite as much in whiskies and sodas, but declares all the time that he's for number one, and that you don't catch him paying for other men's drinks. The old men of pleasure (with their tooral ooral) got at least some social and communal virtue out of pleasure. The new men of pleasure (without the slightest vestige of a tooral ooral) are simply hermits of irreligion instead of religion, anchorites of atheism, and they might as well be drugging themselves with hashish or opium in a wilderness.

But the chorus of the old songs had another use besides this obvious one of asserting the popular element in the arts. The chorus of a song, even of a comic song, has the same purpose as the chorus in a Greek tragedy. It reconciles men to the gods. It connects this one particular tale with the cosmos and the philosophy of common things. Thus we constantly find in the old ballads, especially the pathetic ballads, some refrain about the grass growing green, or the birds singing, or the woods being merry in spring. These are windows opened in the house of tragedy; momentary glimpses of larger and quieter scenes, of more ancient and enduring landscapes. Many of the country songs describing crime and death have refrains of a startling joviality like cock crow, just as if the whole company were coming in with a shout of protest against so sombre a view of existence. There is a long and gruesome ballad called "The Berkshire Tragedy," about a murder committed by a jealous sister, for the consummation of which a wicked miller is hanged, and the chorus (which should come in a kind of burst) runs:

"And I'll be true to my love
If my love'll be true to me."

The very reasonable arrangement here suggested is introduced, I think, as a kind of throw back to the normal; a reminder that even "The Berkshire Tragedy" does not fill the whole of Berkshire. The poor young lady is drowned, and the wicked miller (to whom we may have been affectionately attached) is hanged; but still a ruby kindles in the vine, and many a garden by the water blows. Not that Omar's type of hedonistic resignation is at all the same as the breezy impatience of the Berkshire refrain; but they are alike in so far as they gaze out beyond the particular complication to more open plains of peace. The chorus of the ballad looks past the drowning maiden and the miller's gibbet, and sees the lanes full of lovers.

This use of the chorus to humanise and dilute a dark story is strongly opposed to the modern view of art. Modern art has to be what is called "intense." It is not easy to define being intense; but, roughly speaking, it means saying only one thing at a time, and saying it wrong. Modern tragic writers have to write

THE MAN WHO WAS CHESTERTON

short stories; if they wrote long stories (as the man said of philosophy) cheerfulness would creep in. Such stories are like stings; brief, but purely painful. And doubtless they bore some resemblance to some lives lived under our successful scientific civilisation; lives which tend in any case to be painful, and in many cases to be brief. But when the artistic people passed beyond the poignant anecdote and began to write long books full of poignancy, then the reading public began to rebel and to demand the recall of romance. The long books about the black poverty of cities became quite insupportable. The Berkshire tragedy had a chorus; but the London tragedy has no chorus. Therefore people welcomed the return of adventurous novels about alien places and times, the trenchant and swordlike stories of Stevenson. But I am not narrowly on the side of the romantics. I think that glimpses of the gloom of our civilisation ought to be recorded. I think that the bewilderments of the solitary and sceptical soul ought to be preserved, if it be only for the pity (yes, and the admiration) of the happier time. But I wish that there were some way in which the chorus could enter. I wish that at the end of each chapter of stiff agony or insane terror the choir of humanity could come in with a crash of music and tell both the reader and the author that this is not the whole of human experience. Let them go on recording hard scenes or hideous questions, but let there be a jolly refrain.

Thus we might read: "As Honoria laid down the volume of Ibsen and went wearily to her window, she realised that life must be to her not only harsher, but colder than it was to the comfortable and the weak. With her tooral ooral, etc."; or, again: "The young curate smiled grimly as he listened to his great-grandmother's last words. He knew only too well that since Phogg's discovery of the hereditary hairiness of goats religion stood on a very different basis from that which it had occupied in his childhood. With his rumpty-iddity, rumpty-iddity"; and so on. Or we might read: "Uriel Maybloom stared gloomily down at his sandals, as he realised for the first time how senseless and anti-social are all ties between man and woman; how each must go his or her way without any attempt to arrest the head-long separation of their souls." And then would come in one deafening chorus of everlasting humanity "But I'll be true to my love, if my love'll be true to me."

In the records of the first majestic and yet fantastic developments of the foundation of St. Francis of Assisi is an account of a certain Blessed Brother Giles. I have forgotten most of it, but I remember one fact: that certain students of theology came to ask him whether he believed in free will, and, if so, how he could reconcile it with necessity. On hearing the question St. Francis's follower reflected a little while and then seized a fiddle and began capering and dancing about the garden, playing a wild tune and generally expressing a violent and invigorating indifference. The tune is not recorded, but it is the eternal chorus of mankind, that modifies all the arts and mocks all the individualisms, like the laughter and thunder of some distant sea.

THE RED ANGEL

I FIND that there really are human beings who think fairy tales bad for children. I do not speak of the man in the green tie, for him I can never count truly human. But a lady has written me an earnest letter saying that fairy tales ought not to be taught to children even if they are true. She says that it is cruel to tell children fairy tales, because it frightens them. You might just as well say that it is cruel to give girls sentimental novels because it makes them cry. All this kind of talk is based on that complete forgetting of what a child is like which has been the firm foundation of so many educational schemes. If you keep bogies and goblins away from children they would make them up for themselves. One small child in the dark can invent more hells than Swedenborg. One small child can imagine monsters too big and black to get into any picture, and give them names too unearthly and cacophonous to have occurred in the cries of any lunatic. The child, to begin with, commonly likes horrors, and he continues to indulge in them even when he does not like them. There is just as much difficulty in saying exactly where pure pain begins in his case, as there is in ours when we walk of our own free will into the torture-chamber of a great tragedy. The fear does not come from fairy tales; the fear comes from the universe of the soul.

. . . . .

The timidity of the child or the savage is entirely reasonable; they are alarmed at this world, because this world is a very alarming place. They dislike being alone because it is verily and indeed an awful idea to be alone. Barbarians fear the unknown for the same reason that Agnostics worship it—because it is a fact. Fairy tales, then, are not responsible for producing in children fear, or any of the shapes of fear; fairy tales do not give the child the idea of the evil or the ugly; that is in the child already, because it is in the world already. Fairy tales do not give a child his first idea of bogey. What fairy tales give the child is his first clear idea of the possible defeat of bogey. The baby has known the dragon intimately ever since he had an imagination. What the fairy tale provides for him is a St. George to kill the dragon.

Exactly what the fairy tale does is this: it accustoms him for a series of clear pictures to the idea that these limitless terrors had a limit, that these shapeless enemies have enemies, that these strong enemies of man have enemies in the knights of God, that there is something in the universe more mystical than darkness, and stronger than strong fear. When I was a child I have stared at the darkness until the whole black bulk of it turned into one negro giant taller than heaven. If there was one star in the sky it only made him a Cyclops. But fairy tales restored my mental health, for next day I read an authentic account of how a negro

giant with one eye, of quite equal dimensions, had been baffled
by a little boy like myself (of similar inexperience and even
lower social status) by means of a sword, some bad riddles, and
a brave heart. Sometimes the sea at night seemed as dreadful as
any dragon. But then I was acquainted with many youngest sons
and little sailors to whom a dragon or two was as simple as the
sea.

Take the most horrible of Grimm's tales in incident and
imagery, the excellent tale of the "Boy who Could not Shudder," and you will see what I mean. There are some living shocks
in that tale. I remember specially a man's legs which fell down
the chimney by themselves and walked about the room, until
they were rejoined by the severed head and body which fell
down the chimney after them. That is very good. But the point
of the story and the point of the reader's feelings is not that these
things were frightening, but the far more striking fact that the
hero was not frightened at them. The most fearful of all these
fearful wonders was his own absence of fear. He slapped the
bogies on the back and asked the devils to drink wine with him;
many a time in my youth, when stifled with some modern morbidity, I have prayed for a double portion of his spirit. If you
have not read the end of his story, go and read it; it is the wisest
thing in the world. The hero was at last taught to shudder by
taking a wife, who threw a pail of cold water over him. In that
one sentence there is more of the real meaning of marriage than
in all the books about sex that cover Europe and America.

. . . . .

At the four corners of a child's bed stand Perseus and Roland,
Sigurd and St. George. If you withdraw the guard of heroes
you are not making him rational; you are only leaving him to
fight the devils alone. For the devils, alas, we have always believed in. The hopeful element in the universe has in modern
times continually been denied and reasserted; but the hopeless
element has never for a moment been denied. The one thing

modern people really do believe in is damnation. The greatest of purely modern poets summed up the really modern attitude in that fine Agnostic line—

"There may be Heaven; there must be Hell."

The gloomy view of the universe has been a continuous tradition; and the new types of spiritual investigation or conjecture all begin by being gloomy. A little while ago men believed in no spirits. Now they are beginning rather slowly to believe in rather slow spirits.

Some people objected to spiritualism, table rapping, and such things, because they were undignified, because the ghosts cracked jokes or waltzed with dinner-tables. I do not share this objection in the least. I wish the spirits were more farcical than they are. That they should make more jokes and better ones, would be my suggestion. For almost all the spiritualism of our time, in so far as it is new, is solemn and sad. Some Pagan gods were lawless, and some Christian saints were a little too serious; but the spirits of modern spiritualism are both lawless and serious—a disgusting combination. The specially contemporary spirits are not only devils, they are blue devils. This is, first and last, the real value of Christmas; in so far as the mythology remains at all it is a kind of happy mythology. Personally, of course, I believe in Santa Claus; but it is the season of forgiveness, and I will forgive others for not doing so. But if there is anyone who does not comprehend the defect in our world which I am civilising, I should recommend him, for instance, to read a story by Mr. Henry James, called "The Turn of the Screw." It is one of the most powerful things ever written, and it is one of the things about which I doubt most whether it ought ever to have been written at all. It describes two innocent children gradually growing at once omniscient and half-witted under the influence of the foul ghosts of a groom and a governess. As I say, I doubt whether Mr. Henry James ought to have published it (no, it is not indecent, do not buy it; it is a spiritual matter), but I think the question so doubtful that I will give that truly great man a chance. I will approve the thing as well as admire it if he will write another tale just as powerful about two children and Santa Claus. If he will not, or cannot, then the conclusion is clear; we can deal strongly with gloomy mystery, but not with happy mystery; we are not rationalists, but diabolists.

I have thought vaguely of all this staring at a great red fire that stands up in the room like a great red angel. But, perhaps, you have never heard of a red angel. But you have heard of a blue devil. That is exactly what I mean.

THE UNPSYCHOLOGICAL AGE

As I began these essays in the hope of irritating everybody by impartiality, which is the most irritating thing I can think of, I propose to conclude them on the same quiet but none the less discordant note. In a recent article, on the one side, I denied that the Victorian Age was the Age of Virtue. I shall here deny that the period of the present generation is in any sense whatever the Age of Pleasure. I think there is a great deal less actual pleasure at this moment than there was in the days of my youth or in most of the days of my ancestors. It is true that a great many worthy moralists denounce the present time because of the prevalence of pleasure-seeking. It may be true, indeed it probably is true, that there is a great deal of pleasure-seeking. But there is a great deal of difference between pleasure-seeking and pleasure-finding. Indeed it might be maintained that the very fury with which people go on seeking pleasure is a proof that they have not found it.

But this generation is full of such depressing paradoxes. The first and most comic is the thing they call Psychology. This gen-

eration is everlastingly talking about Psychology. This generation knows nothing whatever about Psychology. It knows far
less about Psychology than any generation of our civilized past;
possibly even any of our savage past. It does not know, for
instance, the perfectly simple meaning of the Greek word, still
less the profound meaning of the Greek myth. I suppose these
psychologists have heard of the legend of Cupid and Psyche;
but I doubt whether it has ever occurred to them to connect
it with their own monstrous Goddess called Psychology. Anyhow, even in that case, it is significant that they would understand the grosser better than the more delicate element in the
story. Many of the modern fashion may be said to know, or at
least to claim to know, rather more about Cupid than about
Psyche.

But the point here is their comic ignorance of the very idea
they are always talking about. They even use the word wrong.
They talk about it as if it were a particular disease and not a
general science. If we read a passionate and heart-searching modern novel (which God forbid) we may open any page and come
on a sentence like this: "Maurice fascinated Daphne by his exquisite understanding of her psychology." This is exactly as if
I were to say: "I should like to meet Maurice and give him a
good hearty kick in the physiology." So indeed I should; but I
should not express my just and natural aspiration in such illogical terms. Physiology is not his body, but the study of his
body; and Psychology is not his mind, but the study of his mind.
Understanding Daphne's Psychology ought not to mean understanding her character, but understanding the books she has
written, the lectures she has delivered or the theories she has held
on Psychology in general. And if I know anything of Daphne,
she has never meddled with such nonsense. Or somebody will
say, in a more scholarly work: "The Psychology of Attila, the
Hun, has never been scientifically studied." Which is like saying
that his Geology has never been adequately studied. The Hun,
happy fellow, had no Psychology and no Geology. He could

lay waste the earth without asking what it was made of and enjoy himself without asking what he himself was made of. Many human beings, without being Huns, have in the past managed to enjoy themselves a great deal without bothering about Psychology. Still, if a whole human generation is going to bother and bewilder itself with Psychology, it might as well know something about it. The present generation knows nothing about it.

What the present generation knows is a number of catch phrases taken from one particular theory, which happens to be the last theory, and which will therefore be blown to bits by the next theory. But even before it is blown to bits, the culture of our time has never had anything except bits of it. It has learnt for instance, to use the phrase "Inferiority Complex" to describe what Christians used to call Modesty and gentlemen good manners. But if you stop somebody who has just used the phrase "Inferiority Complex," and ask him whether there is such a thing as "Superiority Complex," he will gape and gobble and gurgle unmeaning sounds and his legs will give way beneath him. His inferiority complex, anyhow, will be instantly and appallingly apparent. For he has never thought about the phrase he uses; he has only seen it in the newspapers. The new phrase is not in the newspapers; and he has never heard of it. But the much older and much more profound Psychology of the Christian Religion was founded on the very ancient discovery that a superiority complex was the beginning of all evil. He will also talk to you about the Œdipus Complex; the story of the heathen who murdered his father and did other odd things thought likely to brighten the lives of all "Bright Young Things." But if you ask this great apostle of science to look at the word Science where it is embedded in the word "Conscience," and think about it, you will find that he has never noticed that it is there. These new complexes are not very complex. Compared with the subtlety of the old spiritual ideas, their simplicity is babyish.

But the point here is this; that these young psychologists are backward even as babies. They have not learnt the alphabet. They have not realized even the rudiments of the study of which they talk so much. In every way, of course, we live in a period when people know the last word about everything without knowing the first word about it. They are all like people set to decode a cypher without having ever learnt to read or write. Scores of people will talk to you about the wonderful work of Einstein, not one of whom could tell you what were the primary principles of Newton. An infinite procession of idiots will discuss the Dawes Plan who have never read The Declaration of Independence. But in the case of Psychology, this is particularly true and particularly disastrous. Our fathers did not talk about psychology; they talked about a knowledge of Human Nature. But they had it; and we have not. They knew by instinct all that we ignore by the help of information. For it is exactly the first facts about human nature that are now being ignored by humanity.

For instance, if there is one obvious and outstanding truth of psychology it is what might be called the law of contrast. A lady who wishes to look striking in a black velvet dress does not stand against a black velvet curtain; a man painting a red figure of Mephistopheles does not paint him standing in front of a red-brick villa; and fireworks are not exhibited against a background of fire but against a background of darkness. One would have thought that that principle of the human mind was plain and obvious enough for anybody to observe it. Yet the whole of modern pleasure-seeking is missing all that it seeks because nobody will observe it. If people are to appreciate a pleasure it must be what children call a treat. It must stand out against the background of something else that is not quite so bright as itself. Otherwise we might as well try to paint in white on a whitewashed wall. I have seen no sign of this Age of Psychology having appreciated this elementary psychological fact. Mr. Aldous Huxley remarked, in a brilliant article the other day, that those who are now pursuing pleasure are not only fleeing from

boredom, but are actually suffering from it. It is no longer a
question of A Good Time Coming; for The Good Times have
gone with the arrival of A Good Time All the Time. Mr. Huxley is no romanticist or sentimentalist, or what some call "Mediævalist"; he is, if ever there was one, a realist. But he confessed
that he sought out the rude and secluded villages where there
are still what our fathers called Feasts. That is, there are still
festive celebrations of particular dates and events, which people
feel as exceptions and enjoy as exceptions. But men cannot even
enjoy riot when the riot is the rule. The world of which I speak
has come, by this time, to boasting of being lawless; but there is
no fun in it, because lawlessness is the law. I happen to be a person who has no tendency at all to tedium; I can truly say that
I have hardly ever been bored in my life. I have often amused
myself by thinking how amusing it might be to be in a howling
wilderness or on a desert island. The only glimpse I ever got in
my life of the hell of unbearable monotony, of something I felt
I would rather die than endure, was in some of those films describing the fast and fashionable life of New York. Then for one
instant I understood what is meant by the agony of being satisfied, or as we used to say, sated.

Another and analogous example is the psychological fact that
a man can only concentrate on one thing at a time. He cannot
get all that is to be got out of listening to a poem while he is also
solving a crossword puzzle. Some will advise him to lay aside the
puzzle, others to hurl away the poem; most of us would probably say it depends on whose poem. But anyhow, all of us might
be expected to see that fact easily and plainly enough. To judge
by the fashionable facts of the hour, none of us can see it at all.
Friends ask each other to dinner for a quiet little chat, in restaurants where they have to howl at each other through the
noise of a brass band; and cannot utter the lightest jest or the
most delicate compliment without making certain that it is
louder than the big drum. They will not listen to the music
and they cannot listen to the conversation. If these people are

pleasure-seekers they are certainly the prize idiots of all human history in their manner of seeking it. For an idiot surely deserves a prize for idiocy when he manages to destroy two pleasures by one action; and kill two singing-birds with one stone.

Now the fashionable world around us is full of such idiocy. It may be said that youth was always thoughtless. The Age of Psychology is the first in which a visitor from outside might suppose it to be brainless. In the old days the village squire went hunting and enjoyed the hunt. He did not have the village organist to carry the church organ behind him on horseback all the way, that the squire might listen to the tune of "Onward Christian Soldiers," at the same time as he was crying "Tally ho!" Common sense, that extinct branch of psychology, told him that he was not likely to enjoy both emotions to the full at the same moment. Hector drove his chariot and enjoyed the chariot-race, and doubtless regarded himself as a very fine fellow and worthy of being commemorated by Homer. But Hector did not expect Homer to run behind his chariot all the time with a large lyre, reciting the "Iliad" lest a single moment of literary appreciation should be lost. Human reason, to which the men of antiquity attached a strange importance, illuminated his mind with two truths; first, that driving horses to win a race is not the best moment for enjoying a recitation; and second, that the poet running behind might be rather too much out of breath to recite well. But inconsistencies and inconveniences quite as ludicrous as that throng around us in the contemporary hustle and hunt for pleasure. I conclude, therefore, that whatever else the hustlers know about, it is not the thing that they talk about; and that their chief mark is a quite unprecedented ignorance of psychology.

There are a great many other ways of stating the weakness; there are a great many other and more serious problems in which it is displayed. I had thought of concluding on some of these graver cases of confusion and lack of logic; on the chaos and contradiction that marriage and divorce and free love have made between them; on the perpetual chatter about private enterprise side by side with the ever increasing disappearance of private property and private independence; upon the bottomless and bewildering nonsense of the new suggestions for a faith without a creed. But all these are only graver manifestations of the weakness of the man who goes to a noisy tavern for a quiet dinner, or takes a friend to whom he cannot talk to a concert to which he cannot listen.

ON MISUNDERSTANDING

A NEWSPAPER comment on something I recently wrote has given me a momentary illusion of having really got hold of what is the matter with modernity. For that serpent is as slippery as an eel, that demon is as elusive as an elf. But for the moment I thought I had him—or at least a perfect specimen of him. I wrote recently to the effect that music at meals interferes with conversation. And certain people at once began to discuss whether music at meals interferes with digestion. And in that one detail I seemed to have caught the very devil himself by the tail.

Those who read my article know that I never even mentioned digestion. I never even thought of it. It never crosses my mind while I am eating meals. It certainly never crosses my mind when I am listening to music. Least of all did it ever cross my mind while I was writing that particular article. And the idea that it should cross anybody's mind, not to say occupy anybody's mind, in connexion with the other controversy seems to me a compendium of all the dullness, baseness, vulgarity, and fear that make up so much of the practical philosophy of this enlightened age. What I complained of was not that music interfered with animal assimilation, but that it interfered with human speech, with the talk of taverns like the Tabard or the Mermaid, with the talk of Dr. Johnson or Charles Lamb, with the *Noctes Ambrosianæ* or the Four Men of Sussex; with all the ancient Christian custom of men arguing each other's heads off and shouting each other down for the glory of reason and the truth. Those great talkers no more thought about their digestion at dinner than the heroes of the Iliad or the Song of Roland felt their own pulses and took their own temperatures in the thick of the battle. It is true that I did not confine myself to complaining of meals being spoilt by music. I also complained of music being spoilt by meals. I was so impertinent as to suggest that if we want to listen to good music we should listen to it, and honour it with our undivided attention. A fine musician might surely resent a man treating fine music as a mere background to his lunch. But a fine musician might well murder a man who treated fine music as an aid to his digestion.

But what interests me is this swift, unconscious substitution of the subject of digestion, which I had never mentioned, for the subject of human intercourse, which I had. It has hidden in it somewhere a sort of secret of our social and spiritual abnormality. It is a sort of silent signal of all that has gone wrong with our brains and tempers and memories and hearts—and also, doubtless, digestions. It is so significant that it is worth while to attempt to resolve it into the elements that make it the monstrous and ominous thing it is. Before this evil and elusive creature escapes me once more, I will attempt to dissect it and make a sort of diagram of its deformities.

First, there is that stink of stale and sham science which is one of the curses of our times. The stupidest or the wickedest action is supposed to become reasonable or respectable, not by having found a reason in scientific fact, but merely by having found any sort of excuse in scientific language. This highly grotesque and rather gross topic is supposed to take on a sort of solemnity because it is physiological. Some people even talk about proteids, vitamins—but let us draw a veil over the whole horrid scene. It is enough to note that one element in the hideous compound is a love of talking about the body as a scientific thing—that is, talking about it as if it were a serious thing.

Next, there is a morbidity and a monstrous solitude. Each man is alone with his digestion as with a familiar demon. He is not to allow either the wine or the music to melt his soul into any sociable spirit of the company. Wine is bad for his digestion and music is good for his digestion. He therefore abstains from the one and absorbs the other in the same inhuman isolation. Diogenes retired into a tub and St. Jerome into a cave; but this hermit uses his own inside as his cavern—every man is his own cask, and it is not even a wine-cask.

Third, there is materialism or the very muddiest sort of atheism. It has the obscure assumption that everything begins with the digestion, and not with the divine reason; that we must always start at the material end if we wish to work from the origins of things. In their hapless topsy-turvy philosophy, digestion is the creator and divinity of the creature. They have at the back of their minds, in short, the idea that there is really nothing at the back of their minds except the brute thing called the body. To them, therefore, there is nothing comic or incongruous about saying that a violin solo should be a servant of the body or of the brute; for there is no other god for it to serve.

There also hides in the heart of this philosopher the thing we call hypochondria and a paralysing panic. I have said that it serves the body; but many men in many ages have served their bodies. I doubt if any men in any ages were ever so much afraid of their bodies. We might represent in some symbolic drama a man running down the street pursued by his own body. It is inadequate to say of this sort of thing that it is atheism; it would be nearer the truth to say it is devil-worship. But they are not even the red devils of passion and enjoyment. They are really only the blue devils of fear.

Then there is what there always is in such philosophy, the setting of the cart to draw the horse. They do not see that digestion exists for health, and health exists for life, and life exists for the love of music or beautiful things. They reverse the process and say that the love of music is good for the process of digestion. What the process of digestion is ultimately good for they have really no idea. I think it was a great mediæval philosopher who said that all evil comes from enjoying what we ought to use and using what we ought to enjoy. A great many modern philosophers never do anything else. Thus they will sacrifice what they admit to be happiness to what they claim to be progress; though it could have no rational meaning except progress to greater happiness. Or they will subordinate goodness to efficiency; though the very name of good implies an end, and the very name of efficiency implies only a means to an end. Progress and efficiency by their very titles are only tools. Goodness and happiness by their very titles are a fruition; the fruits that are to be produced by the tools. Yet how often the fruits are treated as fancies of sentimentalism and only the tools as facts of sense. It is as if a starving man were to give away the turnip in order to eat the spade; or as if men said that there need not be any fish, so long as there were plenty of fishing-rods. There is all that queer inversion of values in talking about music as an aid not only to dinner, but even to the digestion of dinner.

There is more generally a flat, unlifted, unlaughing spirit, that can accept this topsy-turvydom without even seeing that it is topsy-turvy. It does not even rise high enough to be cynical. It does not utter its materialistic maxim even as a pessimist's paradox. It does not see the joke of saying that the Passion Music can assist a gentleman to absorb a veal cutlet, or that a Mass of Palestrina might counteract the effects of toasted cheese. What is said on this subject is said quite seriously. That seriousness is perhaps the most frivolous thing in the whole of this frivolous society. It is a spirit that cannot even rouse itself enough to laugh.

In short, it is the magic of that one trivial phrase, about music and digestion, that it calls up suddenly in the mind the image of a certain sort of man, sitting at a table in a grand restaurant, and wearing a serious and somewhat sullen expression. He is manifestly a man of considerable wealth; and beyond that he can only be described by a series of negatives. He has no traditions, and therefore knows nothing of the great traditional talking that has enriched our literature with the nights and feasts of the gods. He has no real friends, and therefore his interests are turned inwards, but more to the state of his body than of his soul. He has no religion, and therefore it comes natural to him to think that everything springs from a material source. He has no philosophy, and therefore does not know the difference between the means and the end. And, above all, there is buried deep in him a profound and stubborn repugnance to the trouble of following anybody else's argument; so that if somebody elaborately explains to him that it is often a mistake to combine two pleasures, because pleasures, like pains, can act as counter-irritants to each other, he only receives the vague impression that somebody is saying that music is bad for his digestion.

FALSE THEORY AND THE THEATRE

A THEATRICAL manager recently insisted on introducing Chinese labour into the theatrical profession. He insisted on having real Chinamen to take the parts of Chinese servants; and some actors seem to have resented it—as I think, very reasonably. A distinguished actress, who is clever enough to know better, defended it on the ground that nothing must interfere with the perfection of a work of art. I dispute the moral thesis in any case; and Nero would no doubt have urged it in defence of having real deaths in the amphitheatre. I do not admit in any case that the artist can be entirely indifferent to hunger and unemployment, any more than to lions or boiling oil. But, as a matter of fact, there is no need to raise the moral question, because the case is equally strong in relation to the artistic question. I do not think that a Chinese character being represented by a Chinese actor is the finishing touch to the perfection of a work of art. I think it is the last and lowest phase of the vulgarity that is called realism. It is in the same style and taste as the triumphs on which, I believe, some actor-managers have prided themselves: the triumphs of having real silver for goblets or real jewels for crowns. That is not the spirit of a perfect artist, but rather of a purse-proud parvenu. The perfect artist would be he who could put on a crown of gilt wire or tinsel and makes us feel he was a king.

Moreover, if the principle is to be extended from properties to persons, it is not easy to see where the principle can stop. If we are to insist on real Asiatics to act "Chu Chin Chow," why not insist on real Venetians to act "The Merchant of Venice"? We did experiment recently and I believe very successfully, in having the Jew acted by a real Jew. But I hardly think we should like to make it a rule that nobody must be allowed to act Shylock unless he can prove his racial right to call upon his father Abraham. Must the characters of Macbeth and Macduff only be represented by men with names like Macpherson and Macnab? Must the Prince of Denmark always be in private life a Dane? Must we import a crowd of Greeks before we are allowed to act "Troilus and Cressida," or a mob of real Egyptians to form the background of "Antony and Cleopatra"? Will it be necessary to kidnap an African gentleman out of Africa, by the methods of the slave trade, and force him into acting Othello? It was rather foolishly suggested at one time that our allies in Japan might be offended at the fantastic satire of "The Mikado." As a matter of fact, the satire of "The Mikado" is not at all directed against Japanese things, but exclusively against English things. But I certainly think there might be some little ill-feeling in Japan if gangs of Japanese coolies were shipped across two continents merely in order to act in it. If once this singular rule be recognized, a dramatist will certainly be rather shy of introducing Zulus or Red Indians into his dramas, owing to the difficulty in securing appropriate dramatic talent. He will hesitate before making his hero an Eskimo. He will abandon his intention of seeking his heroine in the Sandwich Islands. If he were to insist on introducing real cannibals, it seems possible that they might insist on introducing real cannibalism. This would be quite in the spirit of Nero and all the art critics of the Roman realism of the amphitheatre. But surely it would be putting almost too perfect a finishing touch to the perfection of a work of art. That kind of finishing touch is a little too finishing.

The irony grew more intense when the newspapers that had insisted on Chinamen because they could not help being Chinamen began to praise them with admiration and astonishment because they looked Chinese. This opens up a speculation so complex and contradictory that I do not propose to follow it, for I am interested here not in the particular incident but in the general idea. It will be a sufficient statement of the fundamental fact of all the arts if I say simply that I do not believe in the resemblance. I do not believe that a Chinaman does look like a Chinaman. That is, I do not believe that any Chinaman will necessarily look like *the* Chinaman—the Chinaman in the imagination of the artist and the interest of the crowd. We all know the fable of the man who imitated a pig, and his rival who was hooted by the crowd because he could only produce what was (in fact) the squeak of a real pig. The crowd was perfectly right. The crowd was a crowd of very penetrating and philosophical art critics. They had come there not to hear an ordinary pig, which they could hear by poking in any ordinary pig-sty. They had come to hear how the voice of the pig affects the immortal mind and spirit of man; what sort of satire he would make of it; what sort of fun he can get out of it; what sort of exaggeration he feels to be an exaggeration of its essence, and not of its accidents. In other words, they had come to hear a squeak, but the sort of squeak which expresses what a man thinks of a pig—not the vastly inferior squeak which only expresses what a pig thinks of a man. I have myself a poetical enthusiasm for pigs, and the paradise of my fancy is one where the pigs have wings. But it is only men, especially wise men, who discuss whether pigs can fly; we have no particular proof that pigs ever discuss it. Therefore the actor who imitated the quadruped may well have put into his squeak something of the pathetic cry of one longing for the wings of the dove. The quadruped himself might express no such sentiment; he might appear, and generally does appear, singularly unconscious of his own lack of feathers. But the same principle is true of things more dignified than the most dignified porker, though clad in the most superb plumage. If a vision of a stately Arab has risen in the imagination of an author who is an artist, he will be wise if he confides it to an actor who is also an artist. He will be much wiser to confide it to an actor than to an Arab. The actor, being a fellow-countryman and a fellow-artist, may bring out what the author thinks the Arab stands for; whereas the real Arab might be a particular individual who at that particular moment refused to stand for anything of the sort, or for anything at all. The principle is a general one; and I mean no disrespect to China in the porcine parallel, or in the figurative association of pigs and pig-tails.

But, as a matter of fact, the argument is especially apt in the case of China. For I fear that China is chiefly interesting to most of us as the other end of the world. It is valued as something far-off, and therefore fantastical, like a kingdom in the clouds of sunrise. It is not the very real virtues of the Chinese tradition—its stoicism, its sense of honour, its ancient peasant cults—that most people want to put into a play. It is the ordinary romantic feeling about something remote and extravagant, like the Martians or the Man in the Moon. It is perfectly reasonable to have that romantic feeling in moderation, like other amusements. But it is not reasonable to expect the remote person to feel remote from himself, or the man at the other end of the world not to feel it as this end. We must not ask the outlandish Oriental to feel outlandish, or a Chinaman to be astonished at being Chinese. If, therefore, the literary artist has the legitimate literary purpose of expressing the mysterious and alien atmosphere which China implies to him, he will probably do it much better with the aid of an actor who is not Chinese. Of course, I am not criticizing the particular details of the particular performance, of which I know little or nothing. I do not know the circumstances; and under the circumstances, for all I know, the experiment may have been very necessary or very successful. I merely protest against a theory of dramatic truth, urged in defence of the dramatic experiment, which seems to me calculated to falsify the whole art of the drama. It is founded on exactly the same fallacy as that of the infant in Stevenson's nursery rhyme, who thought that the Japanese children must suffer from homesickness through being always abroad in Japan.

This brings us very near to an old and rather threadbare theatrical controversy, about whether staging should be simple or elaborate. I do not mean to begin that argument all over again. What is really wanted is not so much the simple stage-manager as the simple spectator. In a very real sense, what is wanted is the simple critic, who would be in truth the most subtle critic. The healthy human instincts in these things are at least as much spoiled by sophistication in the stalls as by elaboration on the stage. A really simple mind would enjoy a simple scene—and also a gorgeous scene. A popular instinct, to be found in all folk-lore, would know well enough when the one or the other was appropriate. But what is involved here is not the whole of that sophistication, but only one particular sophistry, and against that sophistry we may well pause to protest. It is the critical fallacy of cutting off a real donkey's head to put it on Bottom the Weaver; when the head is symbolical, and in that case more appropriate to the critic than to the actor.

THE SHOP OF GHOSTS

NEARLY all the best and most precious things in the universe you can get for a halfpenny. I make an exception, of course, of the sun, the moon, the earth, people, stars, thunderstorms, and such trifles. You can get them for nothing. But the general principle will be at once apparent. In the street behind me, for instance, you can now get a ride on an electric tram for a halfpenny. To be on an electric tram is to be on a flying castle in a fairy tale. You can get quite a large number of brightly coloured sweets for a halfpenny.

But if you want to see what a vast and bewildering array of valuable things you can get at a halfpenny each you should do as I was doing last night. I was gluing my nose against the glass of a very small and dimly lit toy shop in one of the greyest and leanest of the streets of Battersea. But dim as was that square of light, it was filled (as a child once said to me) with all the colours God ever made. Those toys of the poor were like the children who buy them; they were all dirty; but they were all bright. For my part, I think brightness more important than cleanliness; since the first is of the soul, and the second of the body. You must excuse me; I am a democrat; I know I am out of fashion in the modern world.

As I looked at that palace of pigmy wonders, at small green omnibuses, at small blue elephants, at small black dolls, and small red Noah's arks, I must have fallen into some sort of un-natural trance. That lit shop-window became like the brilliantly lit stage when one is watching some highly coloured comedy. I forgot the grey houses and the grimy people behind me as one forgets the dark galleries and the dim crowds at a theatre. It seemed as if the little objects behind the glass were small, not be-cause they were toys, but because they were objects far away. The green omnibus was really a green omnibus, a green Bays-water omnibus, passing across some huge desert on its ordinary way to Bayswater. The blue elephant was no longer blue with paint; he was blue with distance. The black doll was really a negro relieved against passionate tropic foliage in the land where every weed is flaming and only man is black. The red Noah's ark was really the enormous ship of earthly salvation riding on the rain-swollen sea, red in the first morning of hope.

Every one, I suppose, knows such stunning instants of abstraction, such brilliant blanks in the mind. In such moments one can see the face of one's own best friend as an unmeaning pattern of spectacles or moustaches. They are commonly marked by the two signs of the slowness of their growth and the suddenness of their termination. The return to real thinking is often as abrupt as bumping into a man. Very often indeed (in my case) it is bumping into a man. But in any case the awakening is always emphatic and, generally speaking, it is always complete. Now, in this case, I did come back with a shock of sanity to the consciousness that I was, after all, only staring into a dingy little toy-shop; but in some strange way the mental cure did not seem to be final. There was still in my mind an unmanageable something that told me that I had strayed into some odd atmosphere, or that I had already done some odd thing. I felt as if I had worked a miracle or committed a sin. It was as if I had at any rate, stepped across some border in the soul.

To shake off this dangerous and dreamy sense I went into the shop and tried to buy wooden soldiers. The man in the shop was very old and broken, with confused white hair covering his head and half his face, hair so startlingly white that it looked almost artificial. Yet though he was senile and even sick, there was nothing of suffering in his eyes; he looked rather as if he were gradually falling asleep in a not unkindly decay. He gave me the wooden soldiers, but when I put down the money he did not at first seem to see it; then he blinked at it feebly, and then he pushed it feebly away.

"No, no," he said vaguely. "I never have. I never have. We are rather old-fashioned here."

"Not taking money," I replied, "seems to me more like an uncommonly new fashion than an old one."

"I never have," said the old man, blinking and blowing his nose; "I've always given presents. I'm too old to stop."

"Good heavens!" I said. "What can you mean? Why, you might be Father Christmas."

"I am Father Christmas," he said apologetically, and blew his nose again.

The lamps could not have been lighted yet in the street outside. At any rate, I could see nothing against the darkness but the shining shop-window. There were no sounds of steps or voices in the street; I might have strayed into some new and sunless world. But something had cut the chords of common sense, and I could not feel even surprise except sleepily. Something made me say, "You look ill, Father Christmas."

"I am dying," he said.

I did not speak, and it was he who spoke again.

"All the new people have left my shop. I cannot understand it. They seem to object to me on such curious and inconsistent sort of grounds, these scientific men, and these innovators. They say that I give people superstitions and make them too visionary; they say I give people sausages and make them too coarse. They say my heavenly parts are too heavenly; they say my earthly parts are too earthly; I don't know what they want, I'm sure. How can heavenly things be too heavenly, or earthly things too earthly? How can one be too good, or too jolly? I don't understand. But I understand one thing well enough. These modern people are living and I am dead."

"You may be dead," I replied. "You ought to know. But as for what they are doing—do not call it living."

.   .   .   .   .

A silence fell suddenly between us which I somehow expected to be unbroken. But it had not fallen for more than a few seconds when, in the utter stillness, I distinctly heard a very rapid step coming nearer and nearer along the street. The next moment a figure flung itself into the shop and stood framed in the doorway. He wore a large white hat tilted back as if in impatience; he had tight black old-fashioned pantaloons, a gaudy old-fashioned stock and waistcoat, and an old fantastic coat. He had large, wide-open, luminous eyes like those of an arresting actor; he had a pale, nervous face, and a fringe of beard. He took in the shop and the old man in a look that seemed literally a flash and uttered the exclamation of a man utterly staggered.

"Good lord!" he cried out; "it can't be you! It isn't you! I came to ask where your grave was."

"I'm not dead yet, Mr. Dickens," said the old gentleman, with a feeble smile; "but I'm dying," he hastened to add reassuringly.

"But, dash it all, you were dying in my time," said Mr. Charles Dickens with animation; "and you don't look a day older."

"I've felt like this for a long time," said Father Christmas.

Mr. Dickens turned his back and put his head out of the door into the darkness.

"Dick," he roared at the top of his voice; "he's still alive."

. . . . .

Another shadow darkened the doorway, and a much larger and more full-blooded gentleman in an enormous periwig came in, fanning his flushed face with a military hat of the cut of Queen Anne. He carried his head well back like a soldier, and his hot face had even a look of arrogance, which was suddenly contradicted by his eyes, which were literally as humble as a dog's. His sword made a great clatter, as if the shop were too small for it.

"Indeed," said Sir Richard Steele, " 'tis a most prodigious matter, for the man was dying when I wrote about Sir Roger de Coverley and his Christmas Day."

My senses were growing dimmer and the room darker. It seemed to be filled with newcomers.

"It hath ever been understood," said a burly man, who carried his head humorously and obstinately a little on one side—I think he was Ben Jonson—"It hath ever been understood, consule Jacobo, under our King James and her late Majesty, that such good and hearty customs were fallen sick, and like to pass from the world. This grey beard most surely was no lustier when I knew him than now."

And I also thought I heard a green-clad man, like Robin Hood, say in some mixed Norman French, "But I saw the man dying."

"I have felt like this a long time," said Father Christmas, in his feeble way again.

Mr. Charles Dickens suddenly leant across to him.

"Since when?" he asked. "Since you were born?"

"Yes," said the old man, and sank shaking into a chair. "I have been always dying."

Mr. Dickens took off his hat with a flourish like a man calling a mob to rise.

"I understand it now," he cried, "you will never die."

THE NIGHTMARE

A SUNSET of copper and gold had just broken down and gone to pieces in the west, and grey colours were crawling over everything in earth and heaven; also a wind was growing, a wind that laid a cold finger upon flesh and spirit. The bushes at the back of my garden began to whisper like conspirators; and then to wave like wild hands in signal. I was trying to read by the last light that died on the lawn a long poem of the decadent period, a poem about the old gods of Babylon and Egypt, about their blazing and obscene temples, their cruel and colossal faces.

"Or didst thou love the God of Flies who plagued the Hebrews
      and was splashed
 With wine unto the waist, or Pasht who had green beryls for
      her eyes?"

I read this poem because I had to review it for the *Daily News;* still it was genuine poetry of its kind. It really gave out an atmosphere, a fragrant and suffocating smoke that seemed truly to come from the Bondage of Egypt or the Burden of Tyre. There is not much in common (thank God) between my garden with the grey-green English sky-line beyond it, and these mad visions of painted palaces, huge, headless idols and mon-

strous solitudes of red or golden sand. Nevertheless (as I confessed to myself) I can fancy in such a stormy twilight some
such smell of death and fear. The ruined sunset really looks like
one of their ruined temples: a shattered heap of gold and green
marble. A black flapping thing detaches itself from one of the
sombre trees and flutters to another. I know not if it is owl or
flittermouse; I could fancy it was a black cherub, an infernal
cherub of darkness, not with the wings of a bird and the head of
a baby, but with the head of a goblin and the wings of a bat. I
think, if there were light enough, I could sit here and write some
very creditable creepy tale, about how I went up the crooked
road beyond the church and met Something—say a dog, a dog
with one eye. Then I should meet a horse, perhaps, a horse without a rider; the horse also would have one eye. Then the inhuman silence would be broken; I should meet a man (need I
say, a one-eyed man?) who would ask me the way to my own
house. Or perhaps tell me that it was burnt to the ground. I think
I could tell a very cosy little tale along some such lines. Or I
might dream of climbing for ever the tall dark trees above me.
They are so tall that I feel as if I should find at their tops the
nests of the angels; but in this mood they would be dark and
dreadful angels; angels of death.

Only, you see, this mood is all bosh. I do not believe in it in
the least. That one-eyed universe, with its one-eyed men and
beasts, was only created with one universal wink. At the top of
the tragic trees I should not find the Angel's Nest. I should only
find the Mare's Nest; the dreamy and divine nest is not there. In
the Mare's Nest I shall discover that dim, enormous opalescent
egg from which is hatched the Nightmare. For there is nothing
so delightful as a nightmare—when you know it is a nightmare.

That is the essential. That is the stern condition laid upon all
artists touching this luxury of fear. The terror must be fundamentally frivolous. Sanity may play with insanity; but insanity
must not be allowed to play with sanity. Let such poets as the

one I was reading in the garden, by all means, be free to imagine what outrageous deities and violent landscapes they like. By all means let them wander freely amid their opium pinnacles and perspectives. But these huge gods, these high cities, are toys; they must never for an instant be allowed to be anything else. Man, a gigantic child, must play with Babylon and Nineveh, with Isis and with Ashtaroth. By all means let him dream of the Bondage of Egypt, so long as he is free from it. By all means, let him take up the Burden of Tyre, so long as he can take it lightly. But the old gods must be his dolls, not his idols. His central sanctities, his true possessions, should be Christian and simple. And just as a child would cherish most a wooden horse or a sword that is a mere cross of wood, so man, the great child, must cherish most the old plain things of poetry and piety; that horse of wood that was the epic end of Ilium, or that cross of wood that redeemed and conquered the world.

. . . . . .

In one of Stevenson's letters there is a characteristically humorous remark about the appalling impression produced on him in childhood by the beasts with many eyes in the Book of Revelations: "If that was heaven, what in the name of Davy Jones was hell like?" Now in sober truth there is a magnificent idea in these monsters of the Apocalypse. It is, I suppose, the idea that beings really more beautiful or more universal than we are might appear to us frightful and even confused. Especially they might seem to have senses at once more multiplex and more staring; an idea very imaginatively seized in the multitude of eyes. I like those monsters beneath the throne very much. But I like them beneath the throne. It is when one of them goes wandering in deserts and finds a throne for himself that evil faiths begin, and there is (literally) the devil to pay—to pay in dancing girls or human sacrifice. As long as those misshapen elemental powers are around the throne, remember that the thing that they worship is the likeness of the appearance of a man.

That is, I fancy, the true doctrine on the subject of Tales of

Terror and such things, which unless a man of letters do well and truly believe, without doubt he will end by blowing his brains out or by writing badly. Man, the central pillar of the world, must be upright and straight; around him all the trees and beasts and elements and devils may crook and curl like smoke if they choose. All really imaginative literature is only the contrast between the weird curves of Nature and the straightness of the soul. Man may behold what ugliness he likes if he is sure that he will not worship it; but there are some so weak that they will worship a thing only because it is ugly. These must be chained to the beautiful. It is not always wrong even to go, like Dante, to the brink of the lowest promontory and look down at hell. It is when you look up at hell that a serious miscalculation has probably been made.

. . . . . .

Therefore I see no wrong in riding with the Nightmare to-night; she whinnies to me from the rocking tree-tops and the roaring wind; I will catch her and ride her through the awful air. Woods and weeds are alike tugging at the roots in the rising tempest, as if all wished to fly with us over the moon, like that wild amorous cow whose child was the Moon-Calf. We will rise to that mad infinite where there is neither up nor down, the high topsy-turveydom of the heavens. I will answer the call of chaos and old night. I will ride on the Nightmare; but she shall not ride on me.

THE COLDNESS OF CHLOE

WE hear much of the human error which accepts what is sham as what is real. But it is worth while to remember that with unfamiliar things we often mistake what is real for what is sham. It is true that a very young man may think the wig of an actress is her hair. But it is equally true that a child yet younger may call the hair of a negro his wig. Just because the woolly savage is remote and barbaric he seems to be unnaturally neat and tidy. Everyone must have noticed the same thing in the fixed and almost offensive color of all unfamiliar things, tropic birds and tropic blossoms. Tropic birds look like staring toys out of a toy-shop. Tropic flowers simply look like artificial flowers, like things cut out of wax. This is a deep matter, and, I think, not unconnected with divinity; but anyhow it is the truth that when we see things for the first time we feel instantly that they are fictive creations; we feel the finger of God. It is only when we are thoroughly used to them and our five wits are wearied, that we see them as wild and objectless; like the shapeless tree-tops or the shifting cloud. It is the design in Nature that strikes us first; the sense of the crosses and confusions in that design only comes afterwards through experience and an almost eerie monotony. If a man saw the stars abruptly by accident he would think them as festive and as artificial as a firework. We talk of the folly of painting the lily; but if we saw the lily without warning we should think that it was painted. We talk of the devil not being so black as he is painted; but that very phrase is a testimony to the kinship between what is called vivid and what is called artificial. If the modern sage had only one glimpse of grass and sky, he would say that grass was not as green as it was painted; that sky was not as blue as it was painted. If one could see the whole universe suddenly, it would look like a bright-colored toy, just as the South American hornbill looks like a bright-colored toy. And so they are—both of them, I mean.

But it was not with this aspect of the startling air of artifice about all strange objects that I meant to deal. I mean merely, as a guide to history, that we should not be surprised if things wrought in fashions remote from ours seem artificial; we should convince ourselves that nine times out of ten these things are nakedly and almost indecently honest. You will hear men talk of the frosted classicism of Corneille or of the powdered pomposities of the eighteenth century, but all these phrases are very superficial. There never was an artificial epoch. There never was an age of reason. Men were always men and women women: and their two generous appetites always were the expression of passion and the telling of truth. We can see something stiff and quaint in their mode of expression, just as our descendants will see something stiff and quaint in our coarsest slum sketch or our most naked pathological play. But men have never talked about anything but important things; and the next force in femininity which we have to consider can be considered best perhaps in some dusty old volume of verses by a person of quality.

The eighteenth century is spoken of as the period of artificiality, in externals at least; but, indeed, there may be two words about that. In modern speech one uses artificiality as meaning indefinitely a sort of deceit; and the eighteenth century was far too artificial to deceive. It cultivated that completest art that does not conceal the art. Its fashions and costumes positively revealed nature by avowing artifice; as in that obvious instance of a barbering that frosted every head with the same silver. It would be fantastic to call this a quaint humility that concealed youth; but, at least, it was not one with the evil pride that conceals old age. Under the eighteenth century fashion people did not so much all pretend to be young, as all agree to be old. The same applies to the most odd and unnatural of their fashions; they were freakish, but they were not false. A lady may or may not be as red as she is painted, but plainly she was not so black as she was patched.

But I only introduce the reader into this atmosphere of the older and franker fictions that he may be induced to have patience for a moment with a certain element which is very common in the decoration and literature of that age and of the two centuries preceding it. It is necessary to mention it in such a connection because it is exactly one of those things that look as superficial as powder, and are really as rooted as hair.

In all the old flowery and pastoral love-songs, those of the seventeenth and eighteenth centuries especially, you will find a perpetual reproach against woman in the matter of her coldness; ceaseless and stale similes that compare her eyes to northern stars, her heart to ice, or her bosom to snow. Now most of us have always supposed these old and itinerant phrases to be a mere pattern of dead words, a thing like a cold wall-paper. Yet I think those old cavalier poets who wrote about the coldness of Chloe had hold of a psychological truth missed in nearly all the realistic novels of today. Our psychological romancers perpetually represent wives as striking terror into their husbands by rolling on the floor, gnashing their teeth, throwing about the furniture or poisoning the coffee; all this upon some strange fixed theory that women are what they call emotional. But in truth the old and frigid form is much nearer to the vital fact. Most men if they spoke with any sincerity would agree that the most terrible quality in women, whether in friendship, courtship or marriage, was not so much being emotional as being unemotional.

There is an awful armor of ice which may be the legitimate protection of a more delicate organism; but whatever be the psychological explanation there can surely be no question of the fact. The instinctive cry of the female in anger is the *noli me tangere*. I take this as the most obvious and at the same time the least hackneyed instance of a fundamental quality in the female tradition, which has tended in our time to be almost immeasurably misunderstood, both by the cant of moralists and the cant of immoralists. The proper name for the thing is modesty; but as we live in an age of prejudice and must not call things by their right names, we will yield to a more modern nomenclature and call it dignity. Whatever else it is, it is the thing which a thousand poets and a million lovers have called the coldness of Chloe. It is akin to the classical, and is at least the opposite of the grotesque. And since we are talking here chiefly in types and symbols, perhaps as good an embodiment as any of the idea may be found in the mere fact of a woman wearing a skirt. It is highly typical of the rabid plagiarism which now passes every-

where for emancipation, that a little while ago it was common
for an "advanced" woman to claim the right to wear trousers; a
right about as grotesque as the right to wear a false nose.
Whether female liberty is much advanced by the act of wearing
a skirt on each leg I do not know; perhaps Turkish women
might offer some information on the point. But if the western
woman walks about (as it were) trailing the curtains of the
harem with her, it is quite certain that the woven mansion is
meant for a perambulating palace, not for a perambulating
prison. It is quite certain that the skirt means female dignity, not
female submission; it can be proved by the simplest of all tests.
No ruler would deliberately dress up in the recognized fetters
of a slave; no judge would appear covered with broad arrows.
But when men wish to be safely impressive, as judges, priests or
kings, they do wear skirts, the long, trailing robes of female dignity. The whole world is under petticoat government; for even
men wear petticoats when they wish to govern.

A ROMANCE OF THE MARSHES

In books as a whole marshes are described as desolate and
colourless, great fields of clay or sedge, vast horizons of drab or
grey. But this, like many other literary associations, is a piece of
poetical injustice. Monotony has nothing to do with a place;
monotony, either in its sensation or its infliction, is simply the
quality of a person. There are no dreary sights; there are only
dreary sightseers. It is a matter of taste, that is of personality,
whether marshes are monotonous; but it is a matter of fact and
science that they are not monochrome. The tops of high mountains (I am told) are all white; the depths of primeval caverns
(I am also told) are all dark. The sea will be grey or blue for
weeks together; and the desert, I have been led to believe, is the
colour of sand. The North Pole (if we found it) would be white

with cracks of blue; and Endless Space (if we went there) would, I suppose, be black with white spots. If any of these were counted of a monotonous colour I could well understand it; but on the contrary, they are always spoken of as if they had the gorgeous and chaotic colours of a cosmic kaleidoscope. Now exactly where you can find colours like those of a tulip garden or a stained-glass window, is in those sunken and sodden lands which are always called dreary. Of course the great tulip gardens did arise in Holland; which is simply one immense marsh. There is nothing in Europe so truly tropical as marshes. Also, now I come to think of it, there are few places so agreeably marshy as tropics. At any rate swamp and fenlands in England are always especially rich in gay grasses or gorgeous fungoids; and seem sometimes as glorious as a transformation scene; but also as unsubstantial. In these splendid scenes it is always very easy to put your foot through the scenery. You may sink up to your armpits; but you will sink up to your armpits in flowers. I do not deny that I myself am of a sort that sinks—except in the matter of spirits. I saw in the west counties recently a swampy field of great richness and promise. If I had stepped on it I have no doubt at all that I should have vanished; that æons hence the complete fossil of a fat Fleet Street journalist would be found in that compressed clay. I only claim that it would be found in some attitude of energy, or even of joy. But the last point is the most important of all; for as I imagined myself sinking up to the neck in what looked like a solid green field, I suddenly remembered that this very thing must have happened to certain interesting pirates quite a thousand years ago.

For, as it happened, the flat fenland in which I so nearly sunk was the fenland round the Island of Athelney, which is now an island in the fields and no longer in the waters. But on the abrupt hillock a stone still stands to say that this was that embattled islet in the Parrett where King Alfred held his last fort against the foreign invaders, in that war that nearly washed us as far from civilisation as the Solomon Islands. Here he defended the island called Athelney as he afterwards did his best to defend the island called England. For the hero always defends an island, a thing beleaguered and surrounded, like the Troy of Hector. And the highest and largest humanitarian can only rise to defending the tiny island called the earth.

One approaches the island of Athelney along a low long road like an interminable white string stretched across the flats, and lined with those dwarfish trees that are elvish in their very dulness. At one point of the journey (I cannot conceive why) one is arrested by a toll gate at which one has to pay threepence. Perhaps it is a distorted tradition of those dark ages. Perhaps Alfred, with the superior science of comparative civilisation, had calculated the economics of Denmark down to a halfpenny. Perhaps a Dane sometimes came with twopence, sometimes even with twopence-halfpenny, after the sack of many cities even with twopence three farthings; but never with threepence. Whether or no it was a permanent barrier to the barbarians it was only a temporary barrier to me. I discovered three large and complete coppers in various parts of my person, and I passed on along that strangely monotonous and strangely fascinating path. It is not merely fanciful to feel that the place expresses itself appropriately as the place where the great Christian King hid himself from the heathen. Though a marshland is always open it is still curiously secret. Fens, like deserts, are large things very apt to be mislaid. These flats feared to be overlooked in a double sense; the small trees crouched and the whole plain seemed lying on its face, as men do when shells burst. The little path ran fearlessly forward; but it seemed to run on all fours. Everything in that strange countryside seemed to be lying low, as if to avoid the incessant and rattling rain of the Danish arrows. There were indeed hills of no inconsiderable height quite within call; but those pools and flats of the old Parrett seemed to separate themselves like a central and secret sea; and in the midst of them stood up the rock of Athelney as isolate as it was to Alfred. And all across this recumbent and almost crawling country there ran the glory of the low wet lands; grass lustrous and living like the plumage of some universal bird; the flowers as gorgeous as bonfires and the weeds more beautiful than the flowers. One stooped to stroke the grass, as if the earth were all one kind beast that could feel.

Why does no decent person write an historical novel about Alfred and his fort in Athelney, in the marshes of the Parrett? Not a very historical novel. Not about his Truth-telling (please) or his founding the British Empire, or the British Navy, or the Navy League, or whichever it was he founded. Not about the Treaty of Wedmore and whether it ought (as an eminent historian says) to be called the Pact of Chippenham. But an aboriginal romance for boys about the bare, bald, beatific fact that a great hero held his fort in an island in a river. An island is fine enough, in all conscience or piratic unconscientiousness, but an island in a river sounds like the beginning of the greatest adventure story on earth. "Robinson Crusoe" is really a great tale, but think of Robinson Crusoe's feelings if he could have actually seen England and Spain from his inaccessible isle! "Treasure Island" is a spirt of genius: but what treasure could an island contain to compare with Alfred? And then consider the further elements of juvenile romance in an island that was more of an island than it looked. Athelney was masked with marshes; many a heavy harnessed Viking may have started bounding across a meadow only to find himself submerged in a sea. I feel the full fictitious splendour spreading round me; I see glimpses of a great romance that will never be written. I see a sudden shaft quivering in one of the short trees. I see a red-haired man wading madly among the tall gold flowers of the marsh, leaping onward and lurching lower. I see another shaft stand quivering in his throat. I cannot see any more, because, as I have delicately suggested, I am a heavy man. This mysterious marshland does not sustain me, and I sink into its depths with a bubbling groan.

ON KEEPING YOUR HAIR ON

In these essays I appear in the disgusting character of one advising a pause for thought; advising not only the young to think what they are doing, but also the old to think what they are denouncing. And as doing things and denouncing things are both quite easy, as compared with thinking about them, we are confronted from the first with a general and healthy human preference for talking rather than thinking. A special difficulty arises out of the nature of talk, especially modern English talk. Nothing is more misleading than the things that are always connected in language, though they are not connected in logic. There are certain combinations of words, with which we are so familiar that we think they are congruous, when they are really incongruous. We see it most clearly in that excellent and very English form of humour we call Nonsense. We instinctively connect the Cat and the Fiddle; though many of us could distinguish a difference between being soothed at twilight by the melody of violins and by the melody of cats. Yet the words seem somehow akin; perhaps there is something in the coincidence that connects cats and cat-gut. Many Victorians like myself vaguely feel that a Walrus is the same sort of animal as a Carpenter; though a logician like Lewis Carroll could duly tell us that they are not only different characters, but different categories. They are not really near enough even to be contradictory, or mutually exclusive. Absolutely in the abstract, I suppose, a walrus might be a carpenter, as a beaver may be a builder; though it may be more difficult to imagine a carpenter (by a mere act of will) becoming a walrus. Yet in that happy borderland of the English fancy, I imagine and I hope that the Walrus and the Carpenter will always walk hand in hand. Hamlet achieved the same sort of wild wedding of words when he said that (given a suitable condition of the wind) he knew a hawk from a hand-saw. And the wise commentator will eagerly note that it was for talking nonsense like this that he was sent to England. For Hamlet was a singularly English sort of Dane; and the wise man truly said, " 'Twill not be noticed in him there; there the men are as mad as he."

No Englishman who loves his country will have any profane wish that his countrymen should leave off talking nonsense. But while they have added a new note to literature in the nonsense of Lear and Lewis Carroll, they may well be warned against too complete and serene a confidence in nonsense, as the only way of settling their social and political problems. And one effect of this exaggeration is that any number of things are lumped together that do not really or reasonably go together, any more than cats and fiddles, or hawks and hand-saws, or the walrus and the practice of carpentry. These incongruous things are strung together, always in the form of phrases and often in the form of fashions. They are to be accepted in a lump or rejected in a lump. The young generally swallow them whole and the old generally spew them out entire. And the trouble is that, if you and I attempt to explain that the things are not at all like each other, and ought not to be lumped together, we have the appearance of being pedantic—or of being moderate, which is worse. We seem to be drawing a fine distinction if we venture to doubt, as a matter of practical falconry, that the hawk and the hand-saw are birds of a feather. We seem to be debating a fine shade, if we question whether a fiddle can be used as a mouse-trap or a cat is an ornament to a concert. And even in the world of Wonderland, if we say there are some features by which a Carpenter can be distinguished at sight from a Walrus, we are only asked scornfully what the difference can be 'twixt Tweedledum and Tweedledee.

I will take one small example, which has become a large and rather sprawling example. It used to be said that all politics were discussed at the barber's; and in our time all ethics and philosophy have a tendency to revolve round the hairdressers. There is a curious tendency to talk about everybody's hair, as the external emblem of everybody's head and heart. The parting of the hair is treated as the parting of the ways; as the mysterious final choice between good and evil; as if the hairdresser was already training the hair into haloes or into horns. The first discussion about modern fashions, and their alleged relation to modern faults, was made to turn almost entirely on a taste in *coiffure*. It is as if the day of judgment were indeed a demonstration that the hairs of our head are all numbered. On some heads there are not so many as there were; and by some fashions it would seem that the task of omniscience was considerably lightened. Some Moslems do indeed believe that the angel will lift them to heaven by the one lock left on a shaven head; and some modes of modernity may yet give a similar meaning to the phrase that Beauty draws us by a single hair. But even the poet who used that phrase might have been surprised at the importance of the hairy test, like that of the hand of Esau. And even a modern man of science might be sceptical about whether the whole problem of human love and hate can be explained by capillary attraction.

Now if I were to take this one case of hair, I should certainly be accused of splitting hairs. I should make certain distinctions which seem very obvious to me, but which would seem very fussy and fastidious compared with the sweeping generalizations on one side and the other. "Let us distinguish," said the envious foreigners; "let us distinguish," are words which may still linger among the last readers of Matthew Arnold; and in this matter I appear in the character of an envious foreigner. When the fashion first came in for women to cut their hair shorter, there were but two loud outcries, triumphant or tragic, from the old-fashioned or the new-fangled. The Victorian veteran would say nothing except: "There they go, bobbing and shingling and breaking down the barriers of right and wrong, blowing the very basis of society to destruction, because they cannot be content to look as beautiful as their grandmothers." And the new generation, pursuing the new fashion, could apparently say nothing except: "Yes, here we go bobbing and shingling and so by these simple methods bringing in a brighter and broader hope for the future of humanity; since it is only by our own bold effort and adventurous courage that we have avoided being our own grandmothers." Neither of these two outbursts impresses me very much; because one seems to be classing things together merely because they are fashionable, and the other merely because they are not familiar. If I am really to take hair as a social symbol, the first thing that strikes me is that the symbol called Bobbing is very nearly the opposite of the symbol called Shingling. Bobbing means letting the hair flow freely, to about the length to which a great part of humanity, during a great part of history, has thought it convenient to let it flow or fall. Bobbing in itself is a very normal and even traditional thing. It has not been done in many cases by women; but it might have been, without disturbing the general scheme of decoration or dignity. It does not seem incongruous in a picture of Joan of Arc, of which all the rest is in a strictly and even severely mediæval spirit. It is very common in mediæval pictures, especially in those later mediæval pictures which merge with the Renaissance; a great majority of men's portraits show precisely that square-cut cap of hair. Despite the historical legend about short-haired Roundheads and long-haired Cavaliers, the same was really true of the early seventeenth century. Some dandies doubtless wore very long curls and some lunatics cropped their heads to show they were not dandies; but most sensible men of both parties wore something that would now be called a long bob. The great Lord Strafford bobbed his hair. Oliver Cromwell bobbed his hair. In the time of Charles the First all sorts of people wore their hair moderately short. In the time of Charles the Second they began to wear other people's hair immoderately long. But this particular interpretation of moderate length made sufficiently numerous appearances in all periods of history, on Greek vases, in Gothic illuminations, in paintings from Perugino to Van Dyck and from Van Dyck to Reynolds, to make the general conception familiar in the case of men and not really startling in the case of women. But shingling is quite a different sort of notion. Shingling is shortening and often almost shaving, which would have been thought rather odd in many other societies besides our own. In any time, it would have been thought a queer thing for women. In any time except our time, it would have been thought a queer thing for men. For it is simply the snobbish imitation of a particular sort of cheap "hair-cut" which has become the convention for men (God knows why) within the last few years. It is the sort of hair-cut that is meant to go with a billy-cock hat; and we may hope will go with it—never to return. In its complete and logical form, when there is really a close shave and a masculine parting, it is appropriately branded with the base and snobbish title of an Eton Crop. That name alone would be enough to show how much there is in such a movement of liberty or enlargement of the mind. When ladies go about boasting that they have a Borstal Crop, I will believe in them as real revolutionists.

But the point is that a thing like the Eton Crop would have seemed eccentric in any civilization, and according to eternal principles. If a woman had appeared in any antique or mediæval city with half her head shaved, people would have thought it was some sort of extraordinary penance. They might have gone on their knees before the saintly humility that could accept such a disfigurement. They might have recoiled in horror, wondering for what nameless sin the wrath of the gods had blasted her with such a sign. I shudder to imagine what they would have thought if the lady had added to the shaven head, as some ladies have been known to do, the ghastly lopsidedness of a single eyeglass. But that horrid emblem does illustrate what is really involved. A single eye-glass is not a question of prejudice or unfamiliarity. It would be equally hideous in the other epochs; it is equally hideous in the other sex. There is not, and never was, any reason in earth or heaven or hell for a woman wearing it, except that some men are silly enough to do so—for a short time, under the terrible patience of heaven. It is against all possible permanent principles of the balance and dignity of the human form. To be monocled is literally to be one-eyed. And the French proverb is indeed true; for if that one-eyed man is king, it must be among the blind.

Now, I have taken that trivial test of the treatment of hair, since it is so frequently made to figure in discussion, as an example of what I mean by discriminating according to permanent principles, instead of blindly accepting or blindly rejecting according to fashion or reaction. It is just possible that, after beginning with the condition of the hair, some daring thinker may go on to consider the condition of the head. He may examine what are called new ideas, and inquire whether they are true ideas; not whether they are as new as they were, in a world where they are bound to grow old. He may ask what Confucius or Aristotle would think about Bolshevism, not merely what Sir William Joynson-Hicks says about Bolshevism; just as I have speculated on what a Greek or a Florentine would think about Bobbing, and not merely what our own aged aunt living in Cheltenham does happen to say about Bobbing. He would inquire whether the progressives themselves know what is the goal of the Path of Progress, not whether their gloomier relatives regard it as the Road to Ruin; just as I would hint (in the delicate matter of hair) that we need some saner principle than a perpetual idea of progression; which must end either with the Bearded Woman or with the Bald Woman.

A number of modern notions, about Divorce and Democracy and Free Love and Free Thought and things of various kinds, are in fact notions that have no more to do with each other than the tusks of a walrus have to do with the tools of a carpenter, and less than the long hair of a poet has to do with the short hair of a prize-fighter. As I have introduced the matter here with the parable of hair-dressing, I may conclude by noting that this inconsistency in innovation appears the instant we examine any of the innovations in feminine fashion. We all know that there are sombre social critics ready to compare the Modern Girl, at the very mildest, to Jezebel; and we all know that Jezebel painted her face and tired her head and looked out of the window. The critics would willingly credit the modern Jezebel with jumping through the window (indulging in window-crashing as a variation of gate-crashing), and certainly they would assure us that she will imitate the ancient Jezebel by going to the dogs. That the case is rather more complex than that, might be symbolically indicated even in the two acts of adornment. The Victorian Woman tired her head and refused to paint her face; the Modern Woman paints her face, but refuses to tire her head. But I am interested in her head in a different sense; and my real fear is that, in a sense quite different, it does tire her head to think. If I have paused in passing to play with the tangles of Neaera's hair, I think the tangle is inside as well as outside her head.

ON AIDS TO GOLF

AMONG those remarkable "Sayings of the Day" that are quoted in the daily Press, I remember a sentence that is quite significant. Sandwiched in between two other epigrams, between Sir Humphrey Pumpernickel's paradox, "The British Empire must look to Britons for its defence" and the equally arresting *bon mot* of the Dean of Ditchbury, "True religion includes the desire for truth"—interposed, I say, in the same setting between some such jewels as these, I find a remark that really seems to me to be a text for the philosopher. I have forgotten who said it; but he was somebody of a social importance equal to that of the great men I have named. And what he said was this, or in almost these words: "The Charleston may really be of great practical use in teaching a man to be a good golfer."

Now that is really interesting; for it raises so many deep questions. First of all, would it be just as good if we said, "Golf may really be of great practical use in teaching us to dance the

Charleston"? If not, why not? If so, have we established any
principle by which we can distinguish between the primary and
secondary aim? Why is one game good enough to be an end,
and the other only good enough to be a means to an end? Many
men may regard golf as an end. Some may regard it as a sad
end; or even as connected with coming to a bad end. Such was
the opinion of the Scottish minister; presumably the only Scottish minister who did not play golf. Unless, indeed, it was of
himself that he was speaking in hollow tones of remorse, when
he said of the man who plays golf, "He neglects his business; he
forsakes his wife; he forgets his God." Some have held that these
three things are arranged in their order of importance in the
mind of a Scottish Puritan. But I think this is unfair; and that the
minister was only leading up to a literary effect of climax. Anyhow, God is an end, but Golf is not an end. It is just as unphil-
osophical for a man to dance with a girl in order to play golf
as it is immoral for a man to desert a wife in order to play golf.
Girls are more than golf-clubs in any rationally arranged hierarchy of the creatures of God. And dancing is at least as good
as playing ball in any such system of relative values. It seems to
me, that, of the two, the reverse order is the more reasonable. It
really is, I think, more sensible to play golf to perfect one's dancing than to dance to perfect one's golf. Dancing has much more
approximate claim to be considered an end in itself than hitting
a little ball about with a long stick. Dancing can be beautiful;
and beauty can be an absolute; it can certainly be a joy in itself.
I do not say that I think most of the modern dancing I see is
likely to be a diabolic distraction from the beatific vision; but
that is a matter of particular taste and passing fashion. But certainly a man and a woman dancing might be something symbolical, spiritual, almost sacramental; certainly satisfying and
complete. An artist could arrange a man and a girl in such a
manner as to make a statuary group that could stand in marble
and be immortal. But I am not sure whether the artist, in arranging a man and a golf-club, could satisfy his fastidious taste with

any lines that would be at once light and final; living and yet eternally at rest. I can imagine him trying the golf-club at a good many different angles, before he got anything like a flowing melody in stone. The golf-club would give him no assistance anyhow; it could not arrange itself; while the girl might fall quite naturally into the perfect pose. Pure and absolute beauty is attainable by dancing, if not always attained by dancers. It seems clear that it ought to take precedence of what is solely a physical exercise, in any consideration of the means and the end. The ball-room where the Charleston is danced should stand at the end of the links and not at the beginning. The hero who hopes to hole out in one should be sustained by the vision of the more purely æsthetic sport. His long driving should be directed towards his late dancing. This is a normal and comprehensible order of interests. But it would certainly be most unseemly if he were suddenly to leave off dancing because he thought he had sufficiently reduced his handicap. It would be the reverse of a graceful group, in the spirit of perfect sculpture, if he were suddenly to break away from the girl and do a bolt for the door, from the feeling that he was now suddenly summoned to the higher duties of golf. He would be lacking in *finesse*, and in instinctive psychological sympathy, were he even to explain at length to the young lady that he was only dancing with her for the good of his golf. It would be almost better to rush madly away without any explanation at all; to leap wildly through the window and vanish in the direction of the links. But I am sure that arranging the ideas in this order reveals its insufficiency even in the practical manifestations of private life. It is more natural, even by the normal human habit, to treat the dance as pure enjoyment and the sport as having a little more of the character of the day's work. The very fact that the dance has generally come in the evening and the hunt in the daytime illustrates this instinct about it. The dance is in a double sense the end; it is something more like a termination and it is also something more like a goal or a prize.

I take this text because there is nothing about which men are now in such a muddle as about means and ends. Most of them have quite forgotten that there are such things. They not only put the cart before the horse, but they really believe that a cart is a mechanism constructed specially to draw horses. They not only empty out the baby with the bath, but they believe that a baby is a sort of secondary part of the bath-fittings made only to fit the bath. In all the current controversies people begin at the wrong end as readily as the right end; never stopping to consider which is really the end. A little while ago an intellectual weekly started an argument among the intellectuals about whether Man has improved the earth he lives on; whether nature as a whole was better for the presence of Man. Nobody seemed to notice that this is assuming that the end of Man is to grow more grass or improve the breed of rattlesnakes, apart from any theory about the origin or object of these things. A man may serve God and be good to mankind for that reason; or a man may serve mankind and be good to other things to preserve the standard of mankind; but it is very hard to prove exactly how far he is bound to make the jungle thicker or encourage very tall giraffes. Here again the common sense of mankind, even working unconsciously, has always stated the matter the other way round. All sane men have assumed that, while a man may be right to feel benevolently towards the jungle, he is also right to treat it as something that may be put to his use, and something which he may refuse to assist in definitely for its own sake at his own expense. A man should be kind to a giraffe; he should if necessary feed it; he may very properly stroke it or pat it on the head, even if he has to procure a ladder for these good offices. He is perfectly right to pat a giraffe; there is no objection to his patting a palm-tree. But he is not bound to regard a man as something created for the good of a palm-tree. Nor is he bound to answer the question, with any burden on his conscience: "If there were no men, would there be more palm-trees?" I only give this as one example out of many, that have caught my eye lately, of the fact that even thoughtful people seem to have forgotten how to think.

There are a great many other examples of putting the cart before the horse or the means before the end. One very common form of the blunder is to make modern conditions an absolute end and then try to fit human necessities to that end, as if they were only a means. Thus people say, "Home life is not suited to the business life of today." Which is as if they said, "Heads are not suited to the sort of hats now in fashion." Then they might go round cutting off people's heads to meet the shortage or shrinkage of hats; and calling it the Hat Problem. They have already done this if not with heads, at least with heads of hair. And if some of us ventured to say that we thought that Eve's golden garment or St. Paul's "crown of glory" refer to a rather more elementary and eternal thing than the particular shape of hat to be seen in the shops for a month or so, we are rebuked as romantic and reactionary and very much behind the times. But this is an error. We are not especially behind the times. What we are is behind the scenes. And having been behind the scenes for a reasonable period, we know pretty well how often and how rapidly the scene-shifters shift the scenes. But anyhow we do not believe in rebuilding the whole theatre to fit one piece of pasteboard marked Drop-Scene Between Acts IV and V; still less in rebuilding the whole world to suit the fashion of the theatre. We have adopted the habit of distinguishing the means from the ends.

THE ELF OF JAPAN

THERE are things in this world of which I can say seriously that I love them but I do not like them. The point is not merely verbal, but psychologically quite valid. Cats are the first things that occur to me as examples of the principle. Cats are so beautiful that a creature from another star might fall in love with them, and so incalculable that he might kill them. Some of my friends take quite a high moral line about cats. Some, like Mr. Titterton, I think, admire a cat for its moral independence and readiness to scratch anybody "if he does not behave himself." Others, like Mr. Belloc, regard the cat as cruel and secret, a fit friend for witches; one who will devour everything, except, indeed, poisoned food, "so utterly lacking is it in Christian simplicity and humility." For my part, I have neither of these feelings. I admire cats as I admire catkins; those little fluffy things that hang on trees. They are both pretty and both furry, and both declare the glory of God. And this abstract exultation in all living things is truly to be called Love; for it is a higher feeling than mere affectional convenience; it is a vision. It is heroic, and even saintly, in this: that it asks for nothing in return. I love all the cats in the street at St. Francis of Assisi loved all the birds in the wood or all the fishes in the sea; not so much, of course, but then I am not a saint. But he did not wish to bridle a bird and ride on its back, as one bridles and rides on a horse. He did not wish to put a collar round a fish's neck, marked with the name "Francis," and the address "Assisi"—as one does with a dog. He did not wish them to belong to him or himself to belong to them; in fact, it would be a very awkward experience to belong to a lot of fishes. But a man does belong to his dog, in another but an equally real sense with that in which the dog belongs to him. The two bonds of obedience and responsibility vary very much with the dogs and the men; but they are both bonds. In other words, a man does not merely love a dog; as he might (in a mystical moment) love any sparrow that perched on his window-sill or any rabbit that ran across his path. A man likes a dog; and that is a serious matter.

To me, unfortunately perhaps (for I speak merely of individual taste), a cat is a wild animal. A cat is Nature personified. Like Nature, it is so mysterious that one cannot quite repose even in its beauty. But like Nature again, it is so beautiful that one cannot believe that it is really cruel. Perhaps it isn't; and there again it is like Nature. Men of old time worshipped cats as they worshipped crocodiles; and those magnificent old mystics knew what they were about. The moment in which one really loves cats is the same as that in which one (moderately and within reason) loves crocodiles. It is that divine instant when a man feels himself—no, not absorbed into the unity of all things (a loathsome fancy)—but delighting in the difference of all things. At the moment when a man really knows he is a man he will feel, however faintly, a kind of fairy-tale pleasure in the fact that a crocodile is a crocodile. All the more will he exult in the things that are more evidently beautiful than crocodiles, such as flowers and birds and cats—which are more beautiful than either. But it does not follow that he will wish to pick all the flowers or to cage all the birds or to own all the cats.

No one who still believes in democracy and the rights of man will admit that any division between men and men can be anything but a fanciful analogy to the division between men and animals. But in the sphere of such fanciful analogy there are even human beings whom I feel to be like cats in this respect: that I can love them without liking them. I feel it about certain quaint and alien societies, especially about the Japanese. The exquisite old Japanese draughtsmanship (of which we shall see no more, now Japan has gone in for Progress and Imperialism) had a quality that was infinitely attractive and intangible. Japanese pictures were really rather like pictures made by cats. They were full of feathery softness and of sudden and spirited scratches. If any one will wander in some gallery fortunate enough to have a fine collection of those slight water-colour sketches on rice paper which come from the remote East, he will observe many elements in them which a fanciful person might consider feline. There is, for instance, that odd enjoyment of the tops of trees; those airy traceries of forks and fading twigs, up to which certainly no artist, but only a cat could climb. There is that elvish love of the full moon, as large and lucid as a

Chinese lantern, hung in these tenuous branches. That moon is so large and luminous that one can imagine a hundred cats howling under it. Then there is the exhaustive treatment of the anatomy of birds and fish; subjects in which cats are said to be interested. Then there is the slanting cat-like eye of all these Eastern gods and men—but this is getting altogether too coincident. We shall have another racial theory in no time (beginning "Are the Japs Cats?"), and though I shall not believe in my theory, somebody else might. There are people among my esteemed correspondents who might believe anything. It is enough for me to say here that in this small respect Japs affect me like cats. I mean that I love them. I love their quaint and native poetry, their instinct of easy civilisation, their unique unreplaceable art, the testimony they bear to the bustling, irrepressible activities of nature and man. If I were a real mystic looking down on them from a real mountain, I am sure I should love them more even than the strong-winged and unwearied birds or the fruitful, ever-multiplying fish. But, as for liking them, as one likes a dog—that is quite another matter. That would mean trusting them.

In the old English and Scotch ballads the fairies are regarded very much in the way that I feel inclined to regard Japs and cats. They are not specially spoken of as evil; they are enjoyed as witching and wonderful; but they are not trusted as good. You do not say the wrong words or give the wrong gifts to them; and there is a curious silence about what would happen to you if you did. Now to me, Japan, the Japan of Art, was always a fairyland. What trees as gay as flowers and peaks as white as wedding cakes; what lanterns as large as houses and houses as frail as lanterns! . . . but . . . but . . . the missionary explained (I read in the paper) that the assertion and denial about the Japanese use of torture was a mere matter of verbal translation. "The Japanese would not call twisting the thumbs back *'torture.'*"

WOMAN

A CORRESPONDENT has written me an able and interesting letter in the matter of some allusions of mine to the subject of communal kitchens. He defends communal kitchens very lucidly from the standpoint of the calculating collectivist; but, like many of his school, he cannot apparently grasp that there is another test of the whole matter, with which such calculation has nothing at all to do. He knows it would be cheaper if a number of us ate at the same time, so as to use the same table. So it would. It would also be cheaper if a number of us slept at different times, so as to use the same pair of trousers. But the question is not how cheap are we buying a thing, but what are we buying? It is cheap to own a slave. And it is cheaper still to be a slave.

My correspondent also says that the habit of dining out in restaurants, etc., is growing. So, I believe, is the habit of committing suicide. I do not desire to connect the two facts together. It seems fairly clear that a man could not dine at a restaurant because he had just committed suicide; and it would be extreme, perhaps, to suggest that he commits suicide because he has just dined at a restaurant. But the two cases when put side by side, are enough to indicate the falsity and poltroonery of this eternal modern argument from what is in fashion. The question for brave men is not whether a certain thing is increasing; the question is whether we are increasing it. I dine very often in restaurants because the nature of my trade makes it convenient: but if I thought that by dining in restaurants I was working for the creation of communal meals, I would never enter a restaurant again; I would carry bread and cheese in my pocket or eat chocolate out of automatic machines. For the personal element in some things is sacred. I heard Mr. Will Crooks put it perfectly the other day: "The most sacred thing is to be able to shut your own door."

My correspondent says, "Would not our women be spared the drudgery of cooking and all its attendant worries, leaving them free for higher culture?" The first thing that occurs to me to say about this is very simple, and is, I imagine, a part of all our experience. If my correspondent can find any way of preventing women from worrying, he will indeed be a remarkable man. I think the matter is a much deeper one. First of all, my correspondent overlooks a distinction which is elementary in our human nature. Theoretically, I suppose, every one would like to be freed from worries. But nobody in the world would always like to be freed from worrying occupations. I should very much like (as far as my feelings at the moment go) to be free from the consuming nuisance of writing this article. But it does not follow that I should like to be free from the consuming nuisance of being a journalist. Because we are worried about a thing, it does not follow that we are not interested in it. The truth is the other way. If we are not interested, why on earth should we be worried? Women are worried about housekeeping, but those that are most interested are the most worried. Women are still more worried about their husbands and their children. And I suppose if we strangled the children and poleaxed the husbands it would leave women free for higher culture. That is, it would leave them free to begin to worry about that. For women would worry about higher culture as much as they worry about everything else.

I believe this way of talking about women and their higher culture is almost entirely a growth of the classes which (unlike the journalistic class to which I belong) have always a reasonable amount of money. One odd thing I specially notice. Those who write like this seem entirely to forget the existence of the working and wage-earning classes. They say eternally, like my correspondent, that the ordinary woman is always a drudge. And what, in the name of the Nine Gods, is the ordinary man? These people seem to think that the ordinary man is a Cabinet Minister.

They are always talking about man going forth to wield power, to carve his own way, to stamp his individuality on the world, to command and to be obeyed. This may be true of a certain class. Dukes, perhaps, are not drudges; but, then, neither are Duchesses. The Ladies and Gentlemen of the Smart Set are quite free for the higher culture, which consists chiefly of motoring and Bridge. But the ordinary man who typifies and constitutes the millions that make up our civilisation is no more free for the higher culture than his wife is.

Indeed, he is not so free. Of the two sexes the woman is in the more powerful position. For the average woman is at the head of something with which she can do as she likes; the average man has to obey orders and do nothing else. He has to put one dull brick on another dull brick, and do nothing else; he has to add one dull figure to another dull figure, and do nothing else. The woman's world is a small one, perhaps, but she can alter it. The woman can tell the tradesman with whom she deals some realistic things about himself. The clerk who does this to the manager generally gets the sack, or shall we say (to avoid the vulgarism), finds himself free for higher culture. Above all, as I said in my previous article, the woman does work which is in some small degree creative and individual. She can put the flowers or the furniture in fancy arrangements of her own. I fear the bricklayer cannot put the bricks in fancy arrangements of his own, without disaster to himself and others. If the woman is only putting a patch into a carpet, she can choose the thing with regard to colour. I fear it would not do for the office boy dispatching a parcel to choose his stamps with a view to colour; to prefer the tender mauve of the sixpenny to the crude scarlet of the penny stamp. A woman cooking may not always cook artistically; still she can cook artistically. She can introduce a personal and imperceptible alteration into the composition of a soup. The clerk is not encouraged to introduce a personal and imperceptible alteration into the figures in a ledger.

The trouble is that the real question I raised is not discussed.

It is argued as a problem in pennies, not as a problem in people. It is not the proposals of these reformers that I feel to be false so much as their temper and their arguments. I am not nearly so certain that communal kitchens are wrong as I am that the defenders of communal kitchens are wrong. Of course, for one thing, there is a vast difference between the communal kitchens of which I spoke and the communal meal (*monstrum horrendum, informe*) which the darker and wilder mind of my correspondent diabolically calls up. But in both the trouble is that their defenders will not defend them humanly as human institutions. They will not interest themselves in the staring psychological fact that there are some things that a man or a woman, as the case may be, wishes to do for himself or herself. He or she must do it inventively, creatively, artistically, individually—in a word, badly. Choosing your wife (say) is one of these things. Is choosing your husband's dinner one of these things? That is the whole question: it is never asked.

And then the higher culture. I know that culture. I would not set any man free for it if I could help it. The effect of it on the rich men who are free for it is so horrible that it is worse than any of the other amusements of the millionaire—worse than gambling, worse even than philanthropy. It means thinking the smallest poet in Belgium greater than the greatest poet of England. It means losing every democratic sympathy. It means being unable to talk to a navvy about sport, or about beer, or about the Bible, or about the Derby, or about patriotism, or about anything whatever that he, the navvy, wants to talk about. It means taking literature seriously, a very amateurish thing to do. It means pardoning indecency only when it is gloomy indecency. Its disciples will call a spade a spade: but only when it is a grave-digger's spade. The higher culture is sad, cheap, impudent, unkind, without honesty and without ease. In short, it is "high." That abominable word (also applied to game) admirably describes it.

No; if you were setting women free for something else, I

might be more melted. If you can assure me, privately and gravely, that you are setting women free to dance on the mountains like Mænads, or to worship some monstrous goddess, I will make a note of your request. If you are quite sure that the ladies in Brixton, the moment they give up cooking, will beat great gongs and blow horns to Mumbo-Jumbo, then I will agree that the occupation is at least human and is more or less entertaining. Women have been set free to be Bacchantes; they have been set free to be Virgin Martyrs; they have been set free to be Witches. Do not ask them now to sink so low as the higher culture.

I have my own little notions of the possible emancipation of women; but I suppose I should not be taken very seriously if I propounded them. I should favour anything that would increase the present enormous authority of women and their creative action in their own homes. The average woman, as I have said, is a despot; the average man is a serf. I am for any scheme that any one can suggest that will make the average woman more of a despot. So far from wishing her to get her cooked meals from outside, I should like her to cook more wildly and at her own will than she does. So far from getting always the same meals from the same place, let her invent, if she likes, a new dish every day of her life. Let woman be more of a maker, not less. We are right to talk about "Woman": only blackguards talk about women. Yet all men talk about men, and that is the whole difference. Men represent the deliberative and democratic element in life. Woman represents the despotic.

ON THE NEW PRUDERY

I HAVE discovered that the New Prudery is much narrower and more prudish than the Old Prudery; even of the most dingy and dismal latter days of Puritanism. The discovery interests me not a little, for I always thought I had a pure and perfect and spotless hatred of the ordinary sort of Puritanism. But the pure Puritan is not so grim and negative and repressive as the pure Progressive. The New Prudery does not come out of stale sects or old shabby chapels: it comes out of all the new clubs, new leagues, new guilds of art and culture, new summer schools of science and philanthropy. It is altogether a thing of the Future; or at least of the Futurists, who think they will dominate the Future. It is even notably a thing of the young, and, what is far more extraordinary, of the young who would call themselves the free. And the Ten Commandments of the Christian, or even the Ten Hundred Commandments of the Puritan, are themselves like perfect freedom compared with the terrorism and rigidity of its new Taboos.

I will give a practical case to prove the sober truth of what I say. A certain lady, who happened to be looking after the child of a younger lady, discovered the infant to be showing a dark and morbid interest in the story of Joan of Arc. The younger lady belonged to this school which prides itself upon being young; not at all in the sense in which the poet speaks of drinking ale in the country of the young, but rather in that curious country of the young where nobody is allowed to drink ale, but either cold water or cocktails—sometimes winding up with arsenic. In short, she had all the most progressive ideas, and she, the lady who was the mother, informed the other lady, who was acting *in loco parentis*, that the following rules must be strictly observed in the teaching, or for that matter, the playtime, of her child. (1) The child must never read fairy-tales or be allowed to hear about fairies. (2) The child must never hear of the very existence of fighting in any form. (3) The child must be strictly guarded from the shameful rumour that there is such a thing as religion or religious beliefs. I will leave the lady confronted with the problem of narrating, under these limitations, the historical story of St. Joan of Arc. The child must not hear of the childhood of St. Joan, when she played round the tree of the fairies; the child must not hear of the life of St. Joan, which I fear was largely occupied with fighting; the child must not hear of the death of St. Joan, which was a result of the fighting and raises the very indelicate question of faith; or what St. Joan was fighting about and what she was dying for. I should like to see the expurgated or bowdlerized life of the fifteenth-century heroine.

Now it is nonsense to say that this sort of thing is liberal or emancipated; it is nonsense to pretend that it is not much more narrow and obscurantist than the blackest pessimism of the worst days of Puritanism. I am not comparing it with my own religion: I am comparing it with the religion I dislike most; and I say it is quite certain that the Puritanism I dislike most was a wild burst of freedom, and a paradise of pleasures and liberties, compared with this sort of thing. I do not like the Scottish Sabbath, or the old dark shuttered houses, or the long days passed in reading dull divinity or in doing nothing. But they were better fun than this; they were a great deal more free than this. For instance, it is not a plea for Puritanism, it is a part of the proverbial protest against Puritanism, to say that people were only allowed to read the Bible, especially on Sundays. But the Bible is an Arabian Nights of romantic and passionate stories compared with the limitations laid down by this enlightened person. The Bible is an *Encyclopaedia Britannica* of varied topics and multitudinous human interests compared with the amount of knowledge that can be conveyed under those new conditions. Nobody could read the Bible without gaining a glorious mass of information about fighting, about faith, about religions true and false, about mystical or magical or mysterious beings such as hover round man in all the legends and literature of the world. The little boys who grew up in the dark Calvinistic houses of our great-grandfathers did, in actual fact, grow up with their heads full of a noble noise of conflict and crisis; valiant and vigorous action described in the grandest English that our national history has known; the noise of the captains and the shouting; the chariots of Israel and the horsemen thereof; and he that drew a bow at a venture and smote the king between the joints of the harness; and he whose driving was known from afar off, for he drove furiously. That, under all its other disadvantages, is what I call being educated; certainly it is being much better educated than a miserable little prig who must not be told that Joan of Arc carried a battle-banner, but must be assured that she only carried an umbrella.

So far to limit war literature is simply to limit literature, and the Bible alone would be a better training than a silly scrupulosity that should remain ignorant of the war-horse whose neck was clothed with thunder, or that wild quarry that laughed at the shaking of the spear. It is odd, however, to remember that in those dark Puritan homes of which I have spoken, another exception was proverbially made, and children, even on Sundays, were allowed to read *The Pilgrim's Progress*. That is, they were allowed to read what may be a fairy-tale: what is certainly a fighting tale and what has actually, according to countless testimonies, been no bad substitute for other nursery novels or romances. Anyhow, a child with a free soul might find something in it of a fighting spirit; and never forget the instant when Apollyon straddled over the whole breadth of the way; or the dying Greatheart gave up his sword and all the trumpets sounded for him on the other side. I would rather be a dingy, dusty, bewildered, benighted seventeenth-century Calvinistic tinker than never have heard in this vale of tears any distant note of that trumpet.

The intellectual interest of this bit of bigotry lies in this: that the new philosophies and new religions and new social systems cannot draw up their own plans for emancipating mankind without still further enslaving mankind. They cannot carry out even what they regard as the most ordinary reforms without instantly imposing the most extraordinary restrictions. We are to live under a sort of martial law lest we should hear of anything martial. All our children are to be watched by the grimmest of all governesses lest they should be told, even by accident, of a fairy or a fight with robbers. Everybody is to be drilled with an antimilitarist discipline which is quite as stiff and strict as a militarist discipline. All the nursery stories are to be subject to a Censor, who shall object if they are too pretty, as the very dullest sort of Victorian or philistine Censor would object if they were too ugly. A new Mrs. Grundy shall arise, who will blush not at natural facts, but only at preternatural fancies. A new Paul Pry will be sent to sneak about our houses, or look through our keyholes, to find out whether (in some den of infamy) a child is being taught to admire courage. Whatever we may think of the relative claims of the two religions, one fact is now logically self-evident: that the new religion, every bit as much as the old religion, will be a persecuting religion. It will be, by its very nature, a thing fighting for its life against the normal forces of human nature; every bit as much as has been alleged of any system of asceticism or self-denial in the past. It is indeed a case in which extremes meet; though, in truth, extremes often meet because they are much less extreme than people suppose. The modern Pacifist is really very like the ancient Puritan; the man who now has a horror of all theology is very like the man who then had a horror of all things except theology. And the proof is in this practical case. The old Calvinist, like the new Communist, really did forbid children to read stories about fairies. The old Puritan, like the new peace-man, really would forbid boys to read a penny dreadful about pirates. This new idealist is not even new, in the manner of the babe unborn. He is our own Puritan great-grandfather dreadfully risen from the dead.

STRIKES AND THE SPIRIT OF WONDER

THERE is a story which pleases me so much that I feel sure I have repeated it in print, about an alleged and perhaps legendary lady secretary of Madam Blavatsky or Mrs. Besant, who was so much delighted with a new sofa or ottoman that she sat on it by preference when resting or reading her correspondence. At last it moved slightly, and she found it was a mahatma covered with his Eastern robe and rigid in prayer, or some more impersonal ecstasy. That a lady secretary should have a seat any gentleman will approve; that a mahatma should be sat on no Christian will deny; nevertheless, there is another possible moral to the fable which is a reproach rather to the sitter than the seat. It might be put, as in a sort of vision or allegory, by imagining that all our furniture really was made thus of living limbs instead of dead sticks. Suppose the legs of the table were literally legs—the legs of slaves standing still. Suppose the arms of an armchair really were arms—the arms of a patient domestic permanently held out, like those of an old nurse waiting for a baby. It would be calculated to make the luxurious occupant of the easy chair feel rather like a baby; which might do him good. Suppose every sofa were like that of Mrs. Besant's secretary—simply made of a man. They need not be made merely of Theosophists or Buddhists—God forbid. Many of us would greatly prefer to trust ourselves to a Moslem or Turk. This might, with strict accuracy, be called sitting on an Ottoman. I have even read, I think, of some oriental potentate who rejoiced in a name sounding like "sofa." It might even be hinted that some of them might be Christians, but there is no reason, of course, why all of them should not be praying. To sit on a man while he was praying would doubtless require some confidence. It would also give a more literal version of the possession of a prie-dieu chair. It would be easy to expand the extravagance into a vision of a whole house alive, an architecture of arms and legs, a temple of temples of the spirit. The four walls might be made of men like the squares in military formation. There is even, perhaps, a shadow of the fantasy in the popular phrases that compare the roof to the human head, that name the chimney-pot hat after the chimney, or lightly allude to all modern masculine head-dresses as "tiles." But the only value of the vision, as of most visions—even the most topsy-turvy ones—is a moral value. It figures forth, in emblem enigma, the truth that we do treat merely as furniture a number of people who are, at the very least, live stock. And the proof of it is that when they move we are startled like the secretary sitting on the praying man; but perhaps it is we who should begin to pray.

In the current criticisms of the Strikes there is a particular tone, which affects me not as a matter of politics, but rather of philosophy, or even of poetry. It is, indeed, the servile spirit expressed, if not in its poetry, at least in its rhetoric. But it is a spirit I can honestly claim to have hated and done my best to hammer long before I ever heard of the Servile State, long before I ever dreamed of applying this test to Strikes, or indeed of applying it to any political question. I felt it originally touching things at once elemental and everyday—things like grass or daylight, like stones or daisies. But in the light of it at least, I always rebelled against the trend or tone of which I speak. It may roughly be described as the spirit of taking things for granted. But, indeed, oddly enough, the very form of this phrase rather misses its own meaning. The spirit, I mean, strictly speaking, does not take things for granted. It takes them as if they had not been granted. It takes them as if it held them by something more autocratic than a right; by a cold and unconscious occupation, as stiff as a privilege and as baseless as a caprice. As a fact, things generally are granted ultimately by God, but often immediately by men. But this type of man is so unconscious of what he has been given that he is almost unconscious of what he has got; not realizing things as gifts, he hardly realizes them as goods. About the natural things, with which I began, this oblivion has only inward and spiritual, and not outward and political, effects. If we forget the sun the sun will not forget us, or, rather, he will not remember us to revenge himself by "striking" at us with a sunstroke. The stars will not go on strike or extinguish the illumination of the universe as the electricians would extinguish the illumination of the city. And so, while we repeat that there is a special providence in a falling star, we can ignore it in a fixed star. But when we at once ignore and assume thousands of thinking, brooding, free, lonely and capricious human creatures, they will remind us that we can no more order souls than we can order stars. This primary duty of doubt and wonder has nothing to do with the rights or wrongs of special industrial quarrels. The workmen might be quite wrong to go on strike, and we should still be much more wrong in never expecting them to go on strike. Ultimately, it is a mystical but most necessary mood of astonishment at everything outside one's own soul —even one's own body. It may even involve a wild vision in which one's own boots on one's own feet seem to be things distant and unfamiliar. And if this sounds a shade fantastic, it is far less fantastic than the opposite extreme—the state of the man who feels as if he owned not only his own feet, but hundreds of other human feet like a huge centipede, or as if he were a universal octopus, and all rails, tubes and tramlines were his own tentacles, the nerves of his own body, or the circulation of his own blood. That is a much worse nightmare, and at this moment a much commoner one.

Tennyson struck a true note of the nineteenth century when he talked about "the fairy tales of science and the long result of time." The Victorians had a very real and even childlike wonder at things like the steam-engine or the telephone, considered as toys. Unfortunately the long result of time, on the fairy tales of science, has been to extend the science and lessen the fairy tale, that is, the sense of the fairy tale. Take for example the current case of the Tubes. Suppose that at an age of innocence you had met a strange man who had promised to drive you by the force of the lightning through the bowels of the earth. Suppose he had offered, in a friendly way, to throw you from one end of London to the other, not only like a thunderbolt, but by the same force as a thunderbolt. Or if we picture it as pneumatic and not an electric railway; suppose he gaily promised to blow you through a pea-shooter to the other side of London Bridge. Suppose he indicated all these fascinating opportunities by pointing to a hole in the ground and telling you he would take you there in a sort of flying or falling room. I hope you would have agreed that there was a special providence in a falling room. But whether or no you could call it providential, you would agree to call it special. You would at least think that the strange man was a very strange man. You would perhaps call him a very strange and special liar, if he merely undertook to do it. You might even call him a magician, if he did do it. But the point is this, that you would not call him a Bolshevik merely because he did not do it. You would think it a wonderful thing that it should be done at all; passing in that swift car through those secret caverns, you would feel yourself whirled away like Cinderella carried off in the coach that had once been a pumpkin. But though such things happened in every fairy tale, they were not expected in any fairy tale. Nobody turned on the fairies and complained that they were not working because they were not always working wonders. The Press in those parts did not break into big headlines of "Pumpkins held up; no Transformation Scenes," or "Wands Won't Work; Famine of Coaches." They did not announce with horror a "Strike of Fairy Godmothers." They did not draw panic-stricken pictures of mobs of fairy god-mothers, meeting in parks and squares, merely because the ma-jority of pumpkins still continued to be pumpkins. Now I do not argue that we ought to treat every tube-girl as our fairy godmother; she might resent the familiarity, especially the sug-gestion of anything so near to a grandmother. But I do suggest that we should, by a return to earlier sentiments, realize that the tube servants are doing something for us that we could not do for ourselves; something that is no part of our natural capacities, or even of our natural rights. It is not inevitable, or in the nature of things, that when we have walked as we can or want to, some-body else should carry us further in a cart, even for hire: or that when we have wandered up a road and come to a river, a total stranger should take us over in a boat, even if we bribe him to do so. If we would look at things in this plain white daylight of wonder, that shines on all the roads of the fairy tales, we come to see at last the simplest truth about the Strikes, which is utterly missed in all contemporary comments on them. It is merely the fact that Strikers are not *doing* something: they are doing nothing. If you mean that they should be *made* to do something, say so, and establish slavery. But do not be muddled by the mere word "strike" into mixing it up with breaking a window or hitting a policeman on the nose. Do not be stunned by a metaphor; there are no metaphors in fairy tales.

THE INSANE NECESSITY

THE common conception among the dregs of Darwinian culture is that men have slowly worked their way out of inequality into a state of comparative equality. The truth is, I fancy, almost exactly the opposite. All men have normally and naturally begun with the idea of equality; they have only abandoned it late and reluctantly, and always for some material reason of detail. They have never naturally felt that one class of men was superior to another; they have always been driven to assume it through certain practical limitations of space and time.

For example, there is one element which must always tend to oligarchy—or rather to despotism; I mean the element of hurry. If the house has caught fire a man must ring up the fire engines; a committee cannot ring them up. If a camp is surprised by night somebody must give the order to fire; there is no time to vote it. It is solely a question of the physical limitations of time and space; not at all of any mental limitations in the mass of men commanded. If all the people in the house were men of destiny it would still be better that they should not all talk into the telephone at once; nay, it would be better that the silliest man of all should speak uninterrupted. If an army actually consisted of nothing but Hannibals and Napoleons, it would still be better in the case of a surprise that they should not all give orders together. Nay, it would be better if the stupidest of them all gave the orders. Thus, we see that merely military subordination, so far from resting on the inequality of men, actually rests on the equality of men. Discipline does not involve the Carlylean notion that somebody is always right when everybody is wrong, and that we must discover and crown that somebody. On the contrary, discipline means that in certain frightfully rapid circumstances, one can trust anybody so long as he is not everybody. The military spirit does not mean (as Carlyle fancied) obeying the strongest and wisest man. On the contrary, the military spirit means, if anything, obeying the weakest and stupidest man, obeying him merely because he is a man and not a thousand men. Submission to a weak man is discipline. Submission to a strong man is only servility.

Now it can be easily shown that the thing we call aristocracy in Europe is not in its origin and spirit an aristocracy at all. It is not a system of spiritual degrees and distinctions like, for example, the caste system of India, or even like the old Greek distinction between free-men and slaves. It is simply the remains of a military organization, framed partly to sustain the sinking Roman Empire, partly to break and avenge the awful onslaught of Islam. The word Duke simply means Colonel, just as the word Emperor simply means Commander-in-Chief. The whole story is told in the single title of Counts of the Holy Roman Empire, which merely means officers in the European army against the contemporary Yellow Peril. Now in an army nobody ever dreams of supposing that difference of rank represents a difference of moral reality. Nobody ever says about a regiment, "Your Major is very humorous and energetic; your Colonel, of course, must be even more humorous and yet more energetic." No one ever says, in reporting a mess-room conversation, "Lieutenant Jones was very witty, but was naturally inferior to Captain Smith." The essence of an army is the idea of official inequality, founded on unofficial equality. The Colonel is not obeyed because he is the best man, but because he is the Colonel. Such was probably the spirit of the system of dukes and counts when it first arose out of the military spirit and military necessities of Rome. With the decline of those necessities it has gradually ceased to have meaning as a military organization, and become honeycombed with unclean plutocracy. Even now it is not a spiritual aristocracy—it is not so bad as all that. It is simply an army without an enemy—billeted upon the people.

Man, therefore, has a specialist as well as comrade-like aspect; and the case of militarism is not the only case of such specialist submission. The tinker and tailor, as well as the soldier and sailor, require a certain rigidity of rapidity of action: at least, if the tinker is not organized that is largely why he does not tink on any large scale. The tinker and tailor often represent the two nomadic races in Europe: the Gipsy and the Jew; but the Jew alone has influence because he alone accepts some sort of discipline. Man, we say, has two sides, the specialist side where he must have subordination, and the social side where he must have equality. There is a truth in the saying that ten tailors go to make a man; but we must remember also that ten Poets Laureate or ten Astronomers Royal go to make a man, too. Ten million tradesmen go to make Man himself; but humanity consists of tradesmen when they are not talking shop. Now the peculiar peril of our time, which I call for argument's sake Imperialism or Cæsarism, is the complete eclipse of comradeship and equality by specialism and domination.

There are only two kinds of social structure conceivable—personal govenment and impersonal government. If my anarchic friends will not have rules—they will have rulers. Preferring personal government, with its tact and flexibility, is called Royalism. Preferring impersonal government, with its dogmas and definitions, is called Republicanism. Objecting broadmindedly both to kings and creeds is called Bosh; at least, I know no more philosophic word for it. You can be guided by the shrewdness or presence of mind of one ruler, or by the equality and ascertained justice of one rule; but you must have one or the other, or you are not a nation, but a nasty mess. Now men in their aspect of equality and debate adore the idea of rules; they develop and complicate them greatly to excess. A man finds far more regulations and definitions in his club, where there are rules, than in his home, where there is a ruler. A deliberative assembly, the House of Commons, for instance, carries this mummery to the point of a methodical madness. The whole system is stiff with rigid unreason; like the Royal Court in Lewis Carroll. You would think the Speaker would speak; therefore he is mostly silent. You would think a man would take off his hat to stop and put it on to go away; therefore he takes off his hat to walk out and puts it on to stop in. Names are forbidden, and a man must call his own father "my right honorable friend the member for West Birmingham." These are, perhaps, fantasies of decay: but fundamentally they answer a masculine appetite. Men feel that rules, even if irrational, are universal; men feel that law is equal, even when it is not equitable. There is a wild fairness in the thing—as there is in tossing up.

Again, it is gravely unfortunate that when critics do attack such cases as the Commons it is always on the points (perhaps the few points) where the Commons are right. They denounce the House as the Talking-Shop, and complain that it wastes time in wordy mazes. Now this is just one respect in which the Commons are actually like the Common People. If they love leisure and long debate, it is because all men love it; that they really represent England. There the Parliament does approach to the virile virtues of the pothouse.

The real truth is that adumbrated in the introductory section, when we spoke of the sense of home and property, as now we speak of the sense of counsel and community. All men do naturally love the idea of leisure, laughter, loud and equal argument; but there stands a specter in our hall. We are conscious of the towering modern challenge that is called specialism or cut-throat competition—Business. Business will have nothing to do with leisure: business will have no truck with comradeship; business will pretend to no patience with all the legal fictions and fantastic handicaps by which comradeship protects its egalitarian ideal. The modern millionaire, when engaged in the agreeable and typical task of sacking his own father, will certainly not refer to him as the right honorable clerk from the Laburnum Road, Brixton. Therefore there has arisen in modern life a literary fashion devoting itself to the romance of business, to great demigods of greed and to fairyland of finance. This popular philosophy is utterly despotic and anti-democratic; this fashion is the flower of that Cæsarism against which I am concerned to protest. The ideal millionaire is strong in the possession of a brain of steel. The fact that the real millionaire is rather more often strong in the possession of a head of wood, does not alter the spirit and trend of the idolatry. The essential argument is "Specialists must be despots; men must be specialists. You cannot have equality in a soap factory; so you cannot have it anywhere. You cannot have comradeship in a wheat corner; so you cannot have it at all. We must have commercial civilization; therefore we must destroy democracy." I know that plutocrats have seldom sufficient fancy to soar to such examples as soap or wheat. They generally confine themselves, with fine freshness of mind, to a comparison between the state and a ship. One anti-democratic writer remarked that he would not like to sail in a vessel in which the cabin-boy had an equal vote with the captain. It might easily be urged in answer that many a ship (the *Victoria*, for instance) was sunk because an admiral gave an order which a cabin-boy could see was wrong. But this is a debating reply; the essential fallacy is both deeper and simpler. The elementary fact is that we were all born in a state; we were not all born on a ship; like some of our great British bankers. A ship still remains a specialist experiment, like a diving-bell or a flying ship: in such peculiar perils the need for promptitude constitutes the need for autocracy. But we live and die in the vessel of the state; and if we cannot find freedom, camaraderie and the popular element in the state, we cannot find it at all.

And the modern doctrine of commercial despotism means that we shall not find it at all. Our specialist trades in their highly civilized state cannot (it says) be run without the whole brutal business of bossing and sacking, "too old at forty" and all the rest of the filth. And they must be run, and therefore we call on Cæsar. Nobody but the Superman could descend to do such dirty work.

Now (to reiterate my title) this is what is wrong. This is the huge modern heresy of altering the human soul to fit its conditions, instead of altering human conditions to fit the human soul. If soap-boiling is really inconsistent with brotherhood, so much the worse for soap-boiling, not for brotherhood. If civilization really cannot get on with democracy, so much the worse for civilization, not for democracy. Certainly, it would be far better to go back to village communes, if they really are communes. Certainly, it would be better to do without soap rather than to do without society. Certainly, we would sacrifice all our wires, wheels, systems, specialties, physical science and frenzied finance for one half-hour of happiness such as has often come to us with comrades in a common tavern. I do not say the sacrifice will be necessary; I only say it will be easy.

WANTED, AN UNPRACTICAL MAN

THERE is a popular philosophical joke intended to typify the endless and useless arguments of philosophers; I mean the joke about which came first, the chicken or the egg? I am not sure that properly understood, it is so futile an inquiry after all. I am not concerned here to enter on those deep metaphysical and theological differences of which the chicken and egg debate is a frivolous, but a very felicitous, type. The evolutionary materialists are appropriately enough represented in the vision of all things coming from an egg, a dim and monstrous oval germ that had laid itself by accident. That other supernatural school of thought (to which I personally adhere) would be not unworthily typified in the fancy that this round world of ours is but an egg brooded upon by a sacred unbegotten bird; the mystic dove of the prophets. But it is to much humbler functions that I here call the awful power of such a distinction. Whether or no the living bird is at the beginning of our mental chain, it is absolutely necessary that it should be at the end of our mental chain. The bird is the thing to be aimed at—not with a gun, but a life-bestowing wand. What is essential to our right thinking is this: that the egg and the bird must not be thought of as equal cosmic occurrences recurring alternatively forever. They must not become a mere egg and bird pattern, like the egg and dart pattern. One is a means and the other an end; they are in different mental worlds. Leaving the complications of the human breakfast-table out of account, in an elemental sense, the egg only exists to produce the chicken. But the chicken does not exist only in order to produce another egg. He may also exist to amuse himself, to praise God, and even to suggest ideas to a French dramatist. Being a conscious life, he is, or may be, valuable in himself. Now our modern politics are full of a noisy forgetfulness; forgetfulness that the production of this happy and conscious life is after all the aim of all complexities and compromises. We talk of nothing but useful men and working institutions; that is, we only think of the chickens as things that will lay more eggs. Instead of seeking to breed our ideal bird, the eagle of Zeus or the Swan of Avon, or whatever we happen to want, we talk entirely in terms of the process and the embryo. The process itself, divorced from its divine object, becomes doubtful and even morbid; poison enters the embryo of everything; and our politics are rotten eggs.

Idealism is only considering everything in its practical essence. Idealism only means that we should consider a poker in reference to poking before we discuss its suitability for wife-beating; that we should ask if an egg is good enough for prac-

tical poultry-rearing before we decide that the egg is bad enough
for practical politics. But I know that this primary pursuit of
the theory (which is but pursuit of the aim) exposes one to the
cheap charge of fiddling while Rome is burning. A school, of
which Lord Rosebery is representative, has endeavored to substitute for the moral or social ideals which have hitherto been the
motives of politics a general coherency or completeness in the
social system which has gained the nickname of "efficiency."
I am not very certain of the secret doctrine of this sect in the
matter. But, as far as I can make out, "efficiency" means that we
ought to discover everything about a machine except what it is
for. There has arisen in our time a most singular fancy: the fancy
that when things go very wrong we need a practical man. It
would be far truer to say, that when things go very wrong we
need an unpractical man. Certainly, at least, we need a theorist.
A practical man means a man accustomed to mere daily practice, to the way things commonly work. When things will not
work, you must have the thinker, the man who has some doctrine
about why they work at all. It is wrong to fiddle while Rome is
burning; but it is quite right to study the theory of hydraulics
while Rome is burning.

It is then necessary to drop one's daily agnosticism and attempt *rerum cognoscere causas*. If your aëroplane has a slight
indisposition, a handy man may mend it. But, if it is seriously
ill, it is all the more likely that some absent-minded old professor with wild white hair will have to be dragged out of a
college or a laboratory to analyze the evil. The more complicated the smash, the whiter-haired and more absent-minded will
be the theorist who is needed to deal with it; and in some extreme
cases, no one but the man (probably insane) who invented your
flying-ship could possibly say what was the matter with it.

"Efficiency," of course, is futile for the same reason that strong
men, will-power and the superman are futile. That is, it is futile
because it only deals with actions after they have been performed. It has no philosophy for incidents before they happen;

therefore it has no power of choice. An act can only be successful or unsuccessful when it is over; if it is to begin, it must be, in the abstract, right or wrong. There is no such thing as backing a winner; for he cannot be a winner when he is backed. There is no such thing as fighting on the winning side; one fights to find out which is the winning side. If any operation has occurred, that operation was efficient. If a man is murdered, the murder was efficient. A tropical sun is as efficient in making people lazy as a Lancashire foreman bully in making them energetic. Maeterlinck is as efficient in filling a man with strange spiritual tremors as Messrs. Crosse and Blackwell are in filling a man with jam. But it all depends on what you want to be filled with. Lord Rosebery, being a modern skeptic, probably prefers the spiritual tremors. I, being an orthodox Christian, prefer the jam. But both are efficient when they have been effected; and inefficient until they are effected. A man who thinks much about success must be the drowsiest sentimentalist; for he must be always looking back. If he only likes victory he must always come late for the battle. For the man of action there is nothing but idealism.

This definite ideal is a far more urgent and practical matter in our existing English trouble than any immediate plans or proposals. For the present chaos is due to a sort of general oblivion of all that men were originally aiming at. No man demands what he desires; each man demands what he fancies he can get. Soon people forget what the man really wanted first; and after a successful and vigorous political life, he forgets it himself. The whole is an extravagant riot of second bests, a pandemonium of *pis-aller*. Now this sort of pliability does not merely prevent any heroic consistency; it also prevents any really practical compromise. One can only find the middle distance between two points if the two points will stand still. We may make an arrangement between two litigants who cannot both get what they want; but not if they will not even tell us what they want. The keeper of a restaurant would much prefer that each customer should give his order smartly, though it were for stewed ibis or boiled elephant, rather than that each customer should sit holding his head in his hands, plunged in arithmetical calculations about how much food there can be on the premises. Most of us have suffered from a certain sort of ladies who, by their perverse unselfishness, give more trouble than the selfish; who almost clamor for the unpopular dish and scramble for the worst seat. Most of us have known parties or expeditions full of this seething fuss of self-effacement. From much meaner motives than those of such admirable women, our practical politicians keep things in the same confusion through the same doubt about their real demands. There is nothing that so much prevents a settlement as a tangle of small surrenders. We are bewildered on every side by politicians who are in favor of secular education, but think it hopeless to work for it; who desire total prohibition, but are certain they should not demand it; who regret compulsory education, but resignedly continue it; or who want peasant proprietorship and therefore vote for something else. It is this dazed and floundering opportunism that gets in the way of everything. If our statesmen were visionaries something practical might be done. If we asked for something in the abstract we might get something in the concrete. As it is, it is not only impossible to get what one wants, but it is impossible to get any part of it, because nobody can mark it out plainly like a map. That clear and even hard quality that there was in the old bargaining has wholly vanished. We forget that the word "compromise" contains, among other things, the rigid and ringing word "promise." Moderation is not vague; it is as definite as perfection. The middle point is as fixed as the extreme point.

If I am made to walk the plank by a pirate, it is vain for me to offer, as a common-sense compromise, to walk along the plank for a reasonable distance. It is exactly about the reasonable distance that the pirate and I differ. There is an exquisite mathematical split second at which the plank tips up. My common-sense ends just before that instant; the pirate's common-sense begins just beyond it. But the point itself is as hard as any geometrical diagram; as abstract as any theological dogma.

THE SECRET SOCIETY OF MANKIND

WITH that fantastic love of paradox which gives pain to so many critics, I once suggested that there may be some truth in the notion of the brotherhood of men. This was naturally a subject for severe criticism from the modern or modernist standpoint; and I remember that the cleverest refutation of it occurred in a book which was called "We Moderns." It was written by a Mr. Edward Moore, and very well written too; indeed the author did himself some injustice in insisting on his own modernity; for he was not so very modern after all, but really quite lucid and coherent. But I will venture to take his remark as a text here because it concerns a matter on which most moderns darken council in a highly incoherent manner. It concerns the nature of the unity of men; which I did certainly state in its more defiant form as the equality of man. And I said that this norm or meeting-place of mankind can be found in the two extremes of the comic and the tragic. I said that no individual tragedy could be so tragic as having to die; and all men have equally to die. I said that nothing can be funnier than having two legs; and all men can join equally in the joke.

The critic in question was terribly severe on this remark. I believe that the words of his condemnation ran as follows: "Well, in this passage, there is an error so plain, it is almost inconceivable that a responsible thinker could have put it forward even in jest. For it is clear that the tragic and comic elements of which Mr. Chesterton speaks make not only mankind, but *all life*, equal. Everything that lives must die; and therefore it is, in Mr. Chesterton's sense, tragic. Everything that lives has shape; and therefore it is, in Mr. Chesterton's sense, comic.

His premises lead to the equality not of mankind, but of all that lives; whether it be leviathan or butterfly, oak or violet, worm or eagle. . . . Would that he had said this! Then we who affirm inequality would be the first to echo him." I do not feel it hard to show that where Mr. Moore thinks equality wrong is exactly where it is right; and I will begin with mortality; premising that the same is true (for those who believe it) of immortality. Both are absolutes: a man cannot be somewhat mortal; nor can he be rather immortal.

To begin with, it must be understood that having an equality in being black or white is not even the same as being equally black or white. It is generally fair to take a familiar illustration; and I will take the ordinary expression about being all in the same boat. Mr. Moore and I and all men are not only all in the same boat, but have a very real equality implied in that fact. Nevertheless, since there is a word "inner" as well as a word "in," there is a sense in which some of us might be more in the boat than others. My fellow passengers might have stowed me at the bottom of the boat and sat on top of me, moved by a natural distaste for my sitting on top of them. I have noticed that I am often thus packed in a preliminary fashion into the back seats or basic parts of cabs, cars, or boats; there being evidently a feeling that I am the stuff of which the foundations of an edifice are made rather than its toppling minarets or tapering spires. Meanwhile Mr. Moore might be surveying the world from the masthead, if there were one, or leaning out over the prow with the forward gestures of a leader of men, or even sitting by preference on the edge of the boat with his feet paddling in the water, to indicate the utmost possible aristocratic detachment from us and our concerns. Nevertheless, in the large and ultimate matters which are the whole meaning of the phrase "all in the same boat," we should be all equally in the same boat. We should be all equally dependent upon the reassuring fact that a boat can float. If it did not float but sink, each one of us would have lost his one and only boat at the same decisive time and in the same disconcerting manner. If the King of the Cannibal Islands, upon whose principal island we might suffer the inconvenience of being wrecked, were to exclaim in a loud voice, "I will eat every single man who has arrived by that identical boat and no other," we should all be eaten, and we should all be equally eaten. For being eaten, considered as a tragedy, is not a matter of degree.

Now there is a fault in every analogy; but the fault in my analogy is not a fault in my argument; it is the chief fault in Mr. Moore's argument. It may be said that even in a shipwreck men are not equal, for some of us might be so strong that we could swim to the shore, or some of us might be so tough that the island king would repent of his rash vow after the first bite. But it is precisely here that I have again, as delicately as possible, to draw the reader's attention to the modest and little-known institution called death. We are all in a boat which will certainly drown us all, and drown us equally, the strongest with the weakest; we sail to the land of an ogre, *edax rerum*, who devours all without distinction. And the meaning in the phrase about being all in the same boat is, not that there are no degrees among the people in the boat, but that all those degrees are nothing compared with the stupendous fact that the boat goes home or goes down. And it is when I come to the particular criticism on my remarks about "the fact of having to die" that I feel most confident that I was right and that Mr. Moore is wrong.

It will be noted that I spoke of the fact of having to die, not of the fact of dying. The brotherhood of men, being a spiritual thing, is not concerned merely with the truth that all men will die, but with the truth that all men know it. It is true, as Mr. Moore says, that everything will die, "whether it be leviathan or butterfly, oak or violet, worm or eagle"; but exactly what, at the very start, we do not know is whether they know it. Can Mr. Moore draw forth leviathan with a hook, and extract his hopes and fears about the heavenly harpooner? Can he worm its philosophy out of a worm, or get the caterpillar to talk about the faint possibility of a butterfly? The caterpillar on the leaf may repeat to Blake his mother's grief; but it does not repeat to anybody its own grief about its own mother. Can he know whether oaks confront their fate with hearts of oak, as the phrase is used in a sailor's song? He cannot; and this is the whole point about human brotherhood, the point the vegetarians cannot see. This is why a harpooner is not an assassin; this is why eating whale's blubber, though not attractive to the fancy, is not repulsive to the conscience. We do not know what a whale thinks of death; still less what the other whales think of his being killed and eaten. He may be a pessimistic whale, and be perpetually wishing that this too, too solid blubber would melt, thaw and resolve itself into a dew. He may be a fanatical whale, and feel frantically certain of passing instantly into a polar paradise of whales, ruled by the sacred whale who swallowed Jonah. But we can elicit no sign or gesture from him suggestive of such reflections; and the working common sense of the thing is that no creatures outside man seem to have any sense of death at all. Mr. Moore has therefore chosen a strangely unlucky point upon which to challenge the true egalitarian doctrine. Almost the most arresting and even startling stamp of the solidarity and sameness of mankind is precisely this fact, not only of death, but of the shadow of death. We do know of any man whatever what we do not know of any other thing whatever, that his death is what we call a tragedy. From the fact that it is a tragedy flow all the forms and tests by which we say it is a murder or an execution, a martyrdom or a suicide. They all depend on an echo or vibration, not only in the soul of man, but in the souls of all men.

Oddly enough, Mr. Moore has made exactly the same mistake about the comic as about the tragic. It is true, I think, that almost everything which has a shape is humorous; but it is not true that everything which has a shape has a sense of humour. The whale may be laughable, but it is not the whale who laughs; the image indeed is almost alarming. And the instant the question is raised, we collide with another colossal fact, dwarfing all human differentiations; the fact that man is the only creature who does laugh. In the presence of this prodigious fact, the fact that men laugh in different degrees, and at different things, shrivels not merely into insignificance but into invisibility. It is true that I have often felt the physical universe is something like a firework display: the most practical of all practical jokes. But if the cosmos is meant for a joke, men seem to be the only cosmic conspirators who have been let into the joke. There could be no fraternity like our freemasonry in that secret pleasure. It is true that there are no limits to this jesting faculty, that it is not confined to common human jests; but it is confined to human jesters. Mr. Moore may burst out laughing when he beholds the morning star, or be thrown into convulsions of amusement by the effect of moonrise seen through a mist. He may, to quote his own catalogue, see all the fun of an eagle or an oak tree. We may come upon him in some quiet dell rolling about in uproarious mirth, at the sight of a violet. But we shall not find the violet in a state of uproarious mirth at Mr. Moore. He may laugh at the worm; but the worm will not turn and laugh at him. For that comfort he must come to his fellow-sinners: I shall always be ready to oblige.

The truth involved here has had many names; that man is the image of God; that he is the microcosm; that he is the measure of all things. He is the microcosm in the sense that he is the mirror, the only crystal we know in which the fantasy and fear in things are, in the double and real sense, things of reflection. In the presence of this mysterious monopoly the differences of men are like dust. That is what the equality of men means to me; and that is the only intelligible thing it ever meant to anybody. The common things of men infinitely outclass all classes. For a man to disagree with this it is necessary that he should understand it; Mr. Moore may really disagree with it; but the ordinary modern anti-egalitarian does not understand it, or apparently anything else. If a man says he had some transcendental dogma of his own, as Mr. Moore may possibly have, which mixes man with nature or claims to see other values in men, I shall say no more than that my religion is different from his, and I am uncommonly glad of it. But if he simply says that men cannot be equal because some of them are clever and some of them are stupid—why then I shall merely agree (not without tears) that some of them are very stupid.

THE SENTIMENTALISM OF DIVORCE

DIVORCE is a thing which the newspapers now not only advertise, but advocate, almost as if it were a pleasure in itself. It may be, indeed, that all the flowers and festivities will now be transferred from the fashionable wedding to the fashionable divorce. A superb iced and frosted divorce-cake will be provided for the feast, and in military circles will be cut with the co-respondent's sword. A dazzling display of divorce presents will be laid out for the inspection of the company, watched by a detective dressed as an ordinary divorce guest. Perhaps the old divorce breakfast will be revived; anyhow, toasts will be drunk, the guests will assemble on the doorstep to see the husband and wife go off in opposite directions; and all will go merry as a divorce-court bell. All this, though to some it might seem a little fanciful, would really be far less fantastic than the sort of things that are really said on the subject. I am not going to discuss the depth and substance of that subject. I myself hold a mystical view of marriage; but I am not going to debate it here. But merely in the interests of light and logic I would protest against the way in which it is frequently debated. The process cannot rationally be called a debate at all. It is a sort of chorus of sentimentalists in the sensational newspapers, perpetually intoning some such formula as this: "We respect marriage, we reverence marriage, holy, sacred, ineffably exquisite and ideal marriage. True marriage is love, and when love alters, marriage alters, and when love stops or begins again, marriage does the same; wonderful, beautiful, beatific marriage."

Now, with all reasonable sympathy with everything sentimental, I may remark that all that talk is tosh. Marriage is an institution like any other, set up deliberately to have certain functions and limitations; it is an institution like private property, or conscription, or the legal liberties of the subject. To talk as if it were made or melted with certain changing moods is a mere waste of words. The object of private property is that as many citizens as possible should have a certain dignity and pleasure in being masters of material things. But suppose a dog-stealer were to say that as soon as a man was bored with his dog it ceased to be his dog, and he ceased to be responsible for it. Suppose he were to say that by merely coveting the dog, he could immediately morally possess the dog. The answer would be that the only way to make men responsible for dogs was to make the relation a legal one, apart from the likes and dislikes of the moment. Suppose a burglar were to say: "Private property I venerate, private property I revere; but I am convinced that Mr. Brown does not truly value his silver Apostle spoons as such sacred objects should be valued; they have therefore ceased to be his property; in reality they have already become my property, for I appreciate their precious character as nobody else can do." Suppose a murderer were to say: "What can be more amiable and admirable than human life lived with a due sense of its priceless opportunity! But I regret to observe that Mr. Robinson has lately been looking decidedly tired and melancholy; life accepted in this depressing and demoralizing spirit can no longer truly be called life; it is rather my own exuberant and perhaps exaggerated joy of life which I must gratify by cutting his throat with a carving-knife."

It is obvious that these philosophers would fail to understand what we mean by a rule, quite apart from the problem of its exceptions. They would fail to grasp what we mean by an institution, whether it be the institution of law, of property, or of marriage. A reasonable person will certainly reply to the burglar: "You will hardly soothe us by merely poetical praises of property; because your case would be much more convincing if you denied, as the Communists do, that property ought to exist at all. There may be, there certainly are, gross abuses in private property; but, so long as it is an institution at all, it cannot alter merely with moods and emotions. A farm cannot simply float away from a farmer, in proportion as his interest in it grows fainter than it was. A house cannot shift away by inches from a householder, by certain fine shades of feeling that he happens to have about it. A dog cannot drift away like a dream, and begin to belong to somebody else who happens just then to be dreaming of him. And neither can the serious social relation of husband and wife, of mother and father, or even of man and woman, be resolved in all its relations by passions and reactions of sentiment." This question is quite apart from the question of whether there are exceptions to the rule of loyalty, or what they are. The primary point is that there is an institution to which to be loyal. If the new sentimentalists mean what they say, when they say they venerate that institution, they must not suggest that an institution can be actually identical with an emotion. And that is what their rhetoric does suggest, so far as it can be said to suggest anything.

These writers are always explaining to us why they believe in divorce. I think I can easily understand why they believe in divorce. What I do not understand is why they believe in marriage. Just as the philosophical burglar would be more philosophical if he were a Bolshevist, so this sort of divorce advocate would be more philosophical if he were a free-lover. For his arguments never seem to touch on marriage as an institution, or anything more than an individual experience. The real explanation of this strange indifference to the institutional idea is, I fancy, something not only deeper, but wider; something affecting all the institutions of the modern world. The truth is that

these sociologists are not at all interested in promoting the sort
of social life that marriage does promote. The sort of society
of which marriage has always been the strongest pillar is what is
sometimes called the distributive society; the society in which
most of the citizens have a tolerable share of property, especially
property in hand. Everywhere, all over the world, the farm goes
with the family and the family with the farm. Unless the whole
domestic group hold together with a sort of loyalty or local
patriotism, unless the inheritance of property is logical and legitimate, unless the family quarrels are kept out of the courts of
officialism, the tradition of family ownership cannot be handed
on unimpaired. On the other hand, the Servile State, which is
the opposite of the distributive state, has always been rather
embarrassed by the institution of marriage. It is an old story that
the negro slavery of "Uncle Tom's Cabin" did its worst work
in the breaking-up of families. But, curiously enough, the same
story is told from both sides. For the apologists of the Slave
States, or, at least, of the Southern States, make the same admission even in their own defence. If they denied breaking up the
slave family, it was because they denied that there was any slave
family to break up.

Free love is the direct enemy of freedom. It is the most obvious of all the bribes that can be offered by slavery. In servile
societies a vast amount of sexual laxity can go on in practice,
and even in theory, save when now and then some cranky specu-
lator or crazy squire has a fad for some special breed of slaves
like a breed of cattle. And even that lunacy would not last
long; for lunatics are the minority among slave-owners. Slavery
has a much more sane and a much more subtle appeal to human
nature than that. It is much more likely that, after a few such
fads and freaks, the new Servile State would settle down into the
sleepy resignation of the old Servile State; the old pagan repose
in slavery, as it was before Christianity came to trouble and
perplex the world with ideals of liberty and chivalry. One of
the conveniences of that pagan world is that, below a certain

level of society, nobody really need bother about pedigree or paternity at all. A new world began when slaves began to stand on their dignity as virgin martyrs. Christendom is the civilization that such martyrs made; and slavery is its returning enemy. But of all the bribes that the old pagan slavery can offer, this luxury and laxity is the strongest; nor do I deny that the influences desiring the degradation of human dignity have here chosen their instrument well.